Praise for R

Reasoning with God

Reclaiming Shari'ah in the Modern Age

Khaled Abou El Fadl

ROWMAN & LITTLEFIELD
Lanham • Boulder • New York • London

Published by Rowman & Littlefield
A wholly owned subsidiary of The Rowman & Littlefield Publishing Group, Inc.
4501 Forbes Boulevard, Suite 200, Lanham, Maryland 20706
www.rowman.com

Unit A, Whitacre Mews, 26-34 Stannery Street, London SE11 4AB, United Kingdom

Cover image: The beautiful cover art is the masterpiece of Mr. Koichi Fuad Honda, acclaimed Arabic calligrapher and a Japanese convert to Islam. Titled *The Blue Desert*, it contains within its design the entire chapter of the Qur'an known as Surat Luqman, which is known to represent the universal wisdom and morality that should unite human beings in virtue.

British Library Cataloguing in Publication Information Available

Library of Congress Cataloging-in-Publication Data

The hardback edition of this book was previously cataloged by the Library of Congress as follows:

Abou El Fadl, Khaled, 1963–
Reasoning with God : reclaiming Shari'ah in the modern age / Khaled Abou El Fadl.
pages cm.
Includes bibliographical references and index.
1. Islam—Customs and practices. 2. Islam—Rituals. I. Title.
BP174.A245 2014
297.1'4—dc23
2014027855

ISBN 978-0-7425-5233-3 (pbk. : alk. paper)
ISBN 978-0-7425-5232-6 (cloth : alk. paper)
ISBN 978-1-4422-3844-2 (electronic)

♾ ™ The paper used in this publication meets the minimum requirements of American National Standard for Information Sciences Permanence of Paper for Printed Library Materials, ANSI/NISO Z39.48-1992.

Printed in the United States of America

The Floating Word

The floating word

Has a waterfall spine and dexterous
Sky-scrying eyes which know

The swank, sweet caritas of rose and
Its physical temptation

And the glitch of language scudding
The rabbit's hair

Returned from the saturnine
Swim of revision, amber-lit

Like the exegesis of the sea.

Blue

A blue collected from the sky

floats like a starfish in a green

plastic pail of sea taken home by a

child to a summer's night

in Omaha. Or someplace else equally

named and distant. Harboring the sweet

complacency of time cornered

and undone. A studied blue slowly

eroding in space, captive by the

simplest taking like the fisherman's

catch in the old sea, a net rising

out of that eternity into this one.

—Laura Coyne

This book is dedicated to ʿAfaf Ahmed El-Nimr, my Mama
(May 2, 1930–December 28, 2011), whose wisdom and beauty needed
the exegesis of oceans to expound, and who taught me to corner time and
reason with the heavens. You believed in and waited for this book,
but you were always ahead of the times!

Contents

Author's Note

This was a daunting book to write not only because it is inspired by a sense of urgency and perhaps a foreboding seriousness, but more so because it is intended to be a painfully personal book. I wrote this book as a Muslim who is also an academic scholar and not as an academic scholar who happens to be Muslim. And in so doing, I abandoned any pretense of speaking from the proverbial academic tower where I could contently analyze the world from a safe distance behind the veneer of objectivity. As a Muslim, I am deeply affected by everything that impacts Islam and Muslims, and I am also deeply affected by the way that Islam and Muslims impact the world. As a Muslim, I find the beliefs, doctrines, and conceptions of the Islamic faith intellectually and spiritually fulfilling and indeed thrilling; but also as a Muslim I feel a deep sense of frustration and alienation as to the way I interact with the world and the way the world interacts with me. On the one hand, I feel that the sense of spiritual and intellectual fulfillment that I find in my Islamic faith is widely shared by many of my coreligionists. Yet so much of the spiritual teachings of Islam and so many of its intellectual traditions have become fossilized or buried under layers of forgetfulness. While generalizing and stereotyping a people or faith tells us much more about the intolerance of those doing the stereotyping, it would be delusional to deny that, thanks to the behavior of many of my coreligionists, the sense of spiritual and intellectual gratification that I, and many others, find in Islam has become incomprehensible and inaccessible to many non-Muslims.[1] While I personally, as well as so many others, find the Islamic faith to be a source of boundless wisdom and tranquility, it is difficult to deny that this same faith has become a source of anxiety and apprehension for many in the world today. On the one hand, I feel that my faith, and indeed many Muslims, are misunderstood and repulsively mistreated by those who are ignorant or prejudiced toward Islam. On the other hand, I find it difficult to escape the conclusion that many Muslims have become shamefully unjust and iniquitous toward others, each other, and themselves.

Having spent my entire life a humble student of Islamic theology and law, I fully sympathize when Muslims complain that non-Muslims are ill informed and ignorant about Islam. This without a doubt is true. But at the same time, the truth is that so many Muslims themselves are woefully misinformed about their own tradition. I, like so many other Muslims, supplicate to God at least five times a day, pleading that we be guided to the upright path of virtue, but this pious plea does not negate the fact that something has gone awfully wrong with the actual path chosen and pursued by many Muslims. Fundamentally, I think it is fair to say that the sense of frustration and alienation that I feel as a Muslim is shared by many of my coreligionists throughout the world, and it is also fair to say that the primary source of these feelings is that we, as Muslims, live submerged in a profound set of contradictions.

Among these contradictions, the mere existence of which speaks volumes, is the fact that it is a basic and foundational article of faith for every Muslim that Islam is the religion of peace, compassion, and mercy. Accordingly, Islam manifests itself by bringing peace, compassion, and mercy to humanity at large. Yet one must frankly admit that in the minds of most non-Muslim inhabitants of this earth, these are not the values that are normally associated with the Islamic faith. These paradoxes, which are an all-too-persistent part of the lived experiences of most contemporary religious and also nonreligious Muslims, could have many causes and reasons. Is the root cause of these contradictions and paradoxes a lack of education or a simple lack of knowledge of the "true" and "real" facts? Is the contested image and meaning of Islam the result of profound misunderstandings and widespread ignorance? Is this predicament the unavoidable outcome of the legacy of historical conflicts between the world of Islam and the abode of Christendom and the West? Is this predicament a logical result of the identity crisis that has befallen all Muslim countries in the postcolonial age? But at another level, to what extent is this predicament the product of religious bigotry and the result of the malignings and fabrications of Islamophobia? Is a major worldwide conspiracy to defame Islam a part of an international public relations campaign that is being waged against Muslims and Islam? Or, at least from the perspective of a believing Muslim, have many Muslims failed their religion in a serious and basic way?

In many ways, writing about one's religious faith is too personal a task; it necessarily means baring what is in one's heart and soul on paper for all to see, scrutinize, question, and if they so desire, doubt. Nothing could render a person more vulnerable than to stand without the screen of objectivity and the pretense of detachment and to share with a faceless public the cumulative results of numerous intimate moments that go into constituting one's faith and convictions about God, beauty, and humanity. What constitutes a person's faith are countless and innumerable minute moments of perception, insight, repose, and ecstasy that pervade every aspect of one's life. How could it be possible to convey to readers, who might not be privy to similar experiences, these numerous instants when one's faith becomes the nexus between life and beauty? In these instants, faith becomes the vehicle according to which metaphysical truths are felt and internalized—this faith becomes as if the bridge crossing from the physical to the supernal and sublime—from the mundane to the comprehension of beauty and the divine. Attempting to communicate and share these experiences is the province of fools, saints, or prophets, and therefore, I will attempt no such thing.

The aims of this book are far more modest. This book is an attempt to make a contribution to a theology of human moral progress within the Islamic tradition, and in doing so I hope to reassert the power of the Islamic message. It is an effort to reclaim the core of Islam, the Shari'ah (the path to goodness and ethics), which in Islam is the living fountain and source of all goodness. This book starts out with an explanation as to why I wrote it, in which I distinguish the book from my earlier publications and make explicit my belief in moral trajectories that are embedded in and emanate from the heart of Shari'ah and that should be pursued through the epistemological paradigms of Shari'ah. Before beginning the discourse of the book in earnest, I include a brief introduction as to the meaning of Shari'ah. Although I strove to define Shari'ah where relevant throughout the book, in response to many helpful comments I decided to provide a straightforward short chapter setting out the meaning, terminology, conceptions, and categories so as to act as a reference aid to readers who might not have a background in Shari'ah studies. The book then is divided into three main sections; each part can stand on its own as a comprehensive and systematic study. In the first part, I critically analyze symptoms of the ailments that currently plague Muslims. I identify and describe an array of serious problems and challenges, some of which have become as if endemic afflictions eating away at the moral fabric of contemporary Muslims. Some of these problems undermine the very core of the Islamic message and stand as serious obstacles to the moral progress of Muslims. In the second part of the book, I focus on the roots and causes of the problems identified in the first part. The primary objective in this part is to explain the main historical and sociopolitical contributors to the rise of Islamic modalities of thinking that in my view have depleted the moral potential of the Islamic tradition. In this second part, I focus on the Salafi and Wahhabi movements and other puritanical and extremist orientations, and I also address the role that these orientations played in perpetuating grave moral failures that have seriously threatened, and continue to threaten, to undermine the ethical structure of Islam. This part includes original research about the historical development of the Wahhabi movement and its system of thought that have not been published previously. The third part of the book explores possible venues for revitalizing the humanistic and ethical trajectory of the Islamic message and especially the Shari'ah. I argue that it is imperative for those who understand Islam to be a message geared toward the discovery of goodness and beauty to reorient the trajectory of Shari'ah in the modern age. The problem is not only in the avowed objectives and stated purposes of puritanical and extremist orientations but also in the methodology that such orientations utilize in approaching and attempting to comprehend the role of the divine in Islam. Any attempt at reclaiming the ethical role of Islam must focus on the method pursuant to which God's relationship to creation is explored and through which the divine will and purpose is analyzed and understood. Importantly, I address the ways that Muslims and non-Muslims can play a critical role in constructing a contributory and cooperative framework through which Islam and other religions could promote a common goodness and beauty in human life.

Throughout this work, I cite and discuss many anecdotal personal experiences that I encountered while teaching, lecturing, and working in the Islamic field. These personal encounters are typical of the experiences of most people who have worked in the Islamic field for a long time. The decision to discuss these personal experiences was not an easy one because this type of narrative does force a writer into a more vulnerable position, but it also invests the author in his text in a unique and personal way. Personal narratives create the type of bond that tends to dilute the boundaries between the text and author, and while often they create a more vigorous story, such narratives are also more threatening to their author. Nevertheless, I used personal narratives because the crisis that confronts Muslims today cannot be understood only intellectually, but must be felt at an emotional level as well. As I argue in this book, empathy is often critical for attaining a genuine understanding of the plight of a people, especially if one hopes to be able to play a constructive role toward such a plight. In addition, I think that the challenges that confront Muslims today raise issues that implicate the well-being of humanity and not just Muslims. Therefore, it was important to attempt to write a work that is not addressed to other specialists in the field, and personal anecdotes often help to make a text more accessible and more reader friendly.

I do realize that some of what I argue in this book will strike some readers as controversial and at times provocative. I do not seek controversy or provocation, but I do feel that honesty in discourse and thought is inseparable from the duty to bear witness for God. As I argue throughout this book, each age has its language and symbolisms—each age has its epistemological universes that become as undeniable as our shifting consciousness and as our evolving ideas of justice, mercy, and compassion. If the voice of the divine falls silent before the contingencies and nuances of each age, it is we human beings who bear responsibility for this silence because we have an affirmative obligation to speak and reason with the Divine. It is impossible for the Divine to fall silent and the path from God to lay barren and deserted until it is haunted by nothing but the ghosts of bygone people in bygone ages.

Because this book has the benefit of being allowed to emerge, grow, and mutate over a near decade, it has developed so many relationships with so many people who added and contributed to it in so many ways. During the course of writing this book, my friendships with so many people were tested time and time again. Sadly, a number of former friends, for reasons that are between them and God, disappeared from my life, while others embraced me and the project wholeheartedly. I say this for one particular reason. During the course of writing this book, I developed a close friendship and comradeship with 'Ali Jum'a, the former mufti of Egypt, who kindly hosted me for three months in his private residence in Fayoum as I researched and wrote, aided by his insightful questions and remarks. Sadly, we parted ways over his support of the military coup in Egypt against a democratically elected government. The same can be said about Shaykh Ahmad al-Tayyib, the current shaykh and rector of Azhar. In the course of writing this book, I was honored by his encouragement and support. In this book, I wrote about the historic Azhar document that equated Shari'ah to natural law principles and that proclaimed that liberty, egalitarianism, and justice are fundamental and core principles of Shari'ah. I believe that this historic achievement that the Shaykh of Azhar spearheaded was nothing short of thrilling, but this historic moment was followed by a historic failure when Shaykh Ahmad al-Tayyib decided to support the military coup against an elected civilian government. Perhaps what the two honorable shaykhs ended up doing is indicative of the extent to which we need to reclaim and restate our Islamic tradition so that it can no longer harbor despots and tyrants and conveniently be used to rubber-stamp political opportunism and unprincipled and unjust functional interests. The path of Shari'ah, to and from God, is righteous only if it protects the rights and dignities of human beings.

Preface

This book is not an attempt to explain or communicate my Islamic faith. However, I do write from an internal perspective to the Islamic faith. I write as someone who cares about the current Muslim condition and the future of Muslims and Islam. This book is not some self-flagellating record of my struggles and disappointments with the Islamic faith. It is, however, an attempt to come to terms with the moral trajectory of the Islamic tradition in the contemporary age. In theological terms, this book is an effort to discharge the moral obligation that I shoulder as an intellectual and as a Muslim to bear witness for God for the sake of justice and to justice for the sake of God.[1] This book is but an attempt to reason with the divine about all that is divine, including humanity, justice, love, and beauty. *Reasoning with God* is a search for the path to God and from God to all that divinity incorporates and encapsulates, including goodness, well-being, and virtue. In a word, this book is about the Shari'ah as the law of the Creator and the laws of creation, from their primordial and immutable essence to their contingent and temporal manifestations.

Through this book, I invite the reader to become a participant in a debate that has been ongoing for more than fourteen hundred years about the definition and role of the second-largest religion in our world. While aspects of this debate have become intensified in the past few decades, the process of definition and renewal and redefinition, as is the case in all systems of belief, has been ongoing for centuries. Today, the formative debate in Islam is not about the basic theological framework or the most fundamental ritualistic practices of the Islamic faith. Rather, the inventive dynamics of the faith have been about the import, impact, and effect of Islamic norms in relation to new historical contexts and emerging conceptions and meanings. For instance, since the Qur'an (the holy book of Islam) was revealed, for centuries Muslims have memorized and recited the same words and verses about compassion, mercy, and love. The words have not changed. But what did mercy, compassion, or love mean fourteen hundred years ago, and what do they mean today? It is the numerous contingencies that mediate and qualify language and meaning which constantly shift and mutate. However, it is not just language that develops, but knowledge, perception, comprehension, and interpretations of reality that shift as well. Consider the implications of the fact that fourteen hundred years ago, it was not readily possible for a Muslim to own a personal copy of the complete Qur'an—owning such a copy was an expensive proposition. Today, it is not an exaggeration to say that every Muslim home owns a nicely printed copy of the Qur'an. Similarly, fourteen hundred years ago, literacy was uncommon; today, many people can easily read the Qur'an, leave alone accessing it on television or radio, by CD or DVDs, through the Internet, or even on the latest technologies such as iTunes. In addition, fourteen hundred years ago, for a variety of reasons, most Muslims could not easily access books containing collections of reports and statements attributed to the Prophet Muhammad. Today, it is quite easy for Muslims to buy and read books of traditions for themselves—whether they can make proper sense of them is another matter altogether. Moreover, thousands of original sources, which by their very nature are historically contingent and contextual and which for centuries were accessible only to particular classes or segments of the population, are now electronically available at the simple press of a button. These irrepressible developments mean that language is in a constant creative dynamic with numerous contingencies, including the nature of human consciousness, comprehension, expression, and even the articulation of selfhood. It is fundamental to my faith as a Muslim to understand that although God is eternal, immutable, and unalterable, at the same time, creation (or nature), selfhood, and epistemology are not set in time and space. Creation, selfhood, and epistemology are constantly defining and redefining one another.

Without overstating theoretical abstractions, my point here simply is: even if the basic dogma and rituals of Islam remain unaltered for centuries, whether consciously or unconsciously, Muslims are forced to constantly restate, rearticulate, and rephrase their religious tradition. And the debates attempting to come to terms with the various conceptions, meanings, and implications of the system of beliefs and convictions generally identified as Islam will never come to an end. In essence, consecutive generations of Muslims have had to struggle with what Islam means to them and, as importantly, with what Islam means to the world in which they live. Generations of communities of shared meanings or epistemologies had to wrestle with fundamental normative questions such as what does God want from us and for us, and what follows from the belief in a loving, merciful, and compassionate God?

Generations of Muslims wrestled with these questions, and the generations of the twenty-first century and beyond will be no different. In the same way that the debates of the past acted in very vital ways to shape the debates of the present, the debates of today will act to shape those of the future. While it is important to understand the debates of each period on their own contextual and historical terms, it is equally important to understand the points of nexus and continuity as well as the trajectory of the lived and living discourses. Every theology, ideology, or system of thought has its staticists—those who reject the very idea of change, growth, or reconstruction. Extreme staticists will even refuse to admit or acknowledge the role or function of contingency and context, and if they acknowledge the possibility or existence of discourse or show any interest in it, they desperately reach for the conclusions or results of this discourse. For these staticists, the most important aspect of a historical debate is its outcome and conclusion. If purported conclusions of past debates are revisited at all, at the most it will be to make concessions for pressing exigencies and not to take account of constantly evolving contingencies. Ironically, staticists do not end up preventing change—instead of debate, they foster conflict, and instead of discourse, they inspire strife. The product of staticism is not necessarily stagnation because history is irrepressible and change takes place anyway. But instead of conscientious, principled, socially rationalized, and consensus-based development, staticism will often cause reactive defiance, alienation, and uprootedness, all of which result in forces of change that are anarchical and chaotic.

In this work, I do not invite the reader to partake in all or most of the debates that have taken place in Islamic history and not even in the numerous contemporary debates about identity, modernity, and tradition that are taking place all around the Muslim world. All I hope to do is to contribute even in some small ways to these transformative debates. I remain most concerned with, and will therefore focus on, a set of debates that have taken place roughly in the past century concerning what may be called puritan, literalist, or extremist orientations within Islam—orientations that have perpetuated what I describe as traditions of cruelty and ugliness. I remain most concerned about these orientations not only because I believe that they are alien to the heart and soul of Islam but because they are such an oddity. These orientations are in some regards staticist but in other regards profoundly radical. They are the by-product of a very particular process or even moment in history, and yet their interpretive outlooks are staunchly ahistorical, and their determinations are stubbornly dismissive of space and time contingencies. Yet, at the same time, in so many regards these movements are thoroughly modern—they enthusiastically embrace empiricism and most often rarify the idea of technological progress. Moreover, although these movements originated in and were molded by very specific cultural experiences and outlooks, over so many issues they are contemptuous toward the normative force of sociological dynamics and culture. In so many ways, these puritanical movements are uncompromisingly idealistic. Paradoxically, however, their positions and stances on so many moral and ethical issues can best be described as pragmatic and functionalist. Ultimately, in some regards, they do have precedents in Islamic history in the form of now long extinct groups such as the Khawarij, the Hashawiyya, or the infamous Assassins (Hashishiyyun), but as discussed later, in so many other ways, they are alarmingly unprecedented in Islamic history.[2] One need not look beyond the holy cities of contemporary Islam to witness the (at times) truly bewildering paradoxes of puritanism and the ways that this brand of Islam could forever alter the fate of Muslims. While puritans claim to reject every innovation and to be the strict guardians of devout authenticity, one cannot fail to notice the sad irony that it is these same puritans who have turned Mecca and Medina into virtual beacons of modern cosmopolitanism and consumerism.[3] The same irony can be somberly noted in the fact the puritanical Salafi Nour Party of Egypt supported a military coup in Egypt that overthrew the Muslim Brotherhood

and forged a secular constitution, but at the same time, the same party adamantly supports the compulsory veiling of women.

The most prominent of these puritanical orientations is Wahhabi or Saudi
Islam, which came to the attention of the West mostly after the tragic events
of 9/11. But, as discussed later, many Muslims have been in serious conflict
with this orientation at least since the 1800s. Although the Wahhabi movement is perhaps the most known and also at a global level the most influential, it far from being the only puritanical movement. Before 9/11, I had
written a few books that sounded the alarm and warned against the spread of
puritanical orientations, especially Wahhabism. But back then, the public
mood was very different, and the interest of the reading public in Islamic
topics was also much more modest. In the years that followed the terrorist
attacks, in classes, meetings, lectures, and interviews with the media, the
most frequently asked questions were: Does Islam sanction terrorism? Are
Osama Bin Laden's religious convictions representative of what Muslims in
general believe? If Bin Laden represents an extremist version of Islam, what
does a moderate version of the religion look like? How does the Islam of Bin
Laden, the Taliban, and the Saudis differ from the Islam of Muslim moderates? What are the main theological and legal points of departure between the
fanatic and more moderate versions of Islam?

Although the demand for information on Islam grew dramatically after
the terrorist attacks and after the invasions of Afghanistan and Iraq, the
quality of available information did not improve. One of the most frustrating
things was to observe the sudden emergence of many pontificating self-
declared experts rendering extremely poorly informed analyses of the theology, law, and history of Islam. Many of these so-called experts acted as if the
tensions between extremists and moderates started on 9/11 or were bound to
continue only as long as Bin Laden existed. Many others offered highly
essentialized explanations that were either highly apologetic and defensive or
belligerent and accusatory without taking account of the complicated nature
of the challenge confronting contemporary Muslims. Many pundits spewed
out advice, assurances, or warnings without adequately appreciating the awe-
some destructive powers of terrorists, religious fanatics, political absolutists,
cultural imperialists, and conceited and aggrieved world leaders bearing the
swords of righteousness. On the one hand, many seemed eager to declare that
the West and Islam are locked in a fateful battle, ignoring that neither Islam
nor the West are simple and unitary constructs. On the other hand, many
others seemed eager to wave away 9/11 as an aberration or some marginal
and insignificant incident that was not indicative of anything that is particularly pressing. Even at the personal level, it was a frustrating experience that
in speaking to the media, I often found that the media itself was eager to fit
whatever I said into an essentialized and exciting narrative in which the
forces of evil were clashing with the forces of good, and therefore provide a
form of entertainment, not analysis. But the issues and problems implicated
in this discourse are too serious for these casual and essentialized engagements. The subject deserved a book-length analytical treatment, and so I
wrote *The Great Theft*,[4] in which I tried to systematically differentiate between two opposite poles on the spectrum of contemporary Islamic thought.
On one end, there is the theology and law of what I called moderate Islam

and on the other, the puritanical schools of thought and movements. While I argued that most Muslims fall somewhere between these two ends, the overwhelming majority of Muslims, and necessarily mainstream Islam itself, are clearly at the moderate end of the spectrum. As I explained in *The Great Theft*, moderation and resisting the intemperance and agitations of extremism and zealotry is a central normative value affirmed by any catechism of Islamic theology or ethics. Even the most fanatic Muslim group, such as Bin Laden and his followers, will readily profess the centrality of this theological tenet. Apparently, the ability of human beings to derail and undermine the most lofty values and principles is limitless.

But it is not only Muslims who could be adept at subverting and corrupting their own values. Even a decade after the tragedy of 9/11, when more than ever human beings needed to recall their codependence and their unity of fate, there remains a virtual cacophony of mutually intolerant and dismissively opinionated voices willing to tear the human community apart. At a time when wisdom dictates that human beings steadfastly hold on to humane and humanistic principles—to the very basics learned after the trauma of centuries of mindless religious wars, ethnic exterminations, and ideologically driven cleansings—hordes of cacuminal voices are heard every day calling for "new standards" for the "new age" of asymmetrical warfare. The "new standards" is usually a catchphrase for diluting or loosening the restrictions of humanitarian law and human rights law so that people may kill, abuse, and torture each other more effectively. The dilution of human standards, or put differently, the standards of what human beings may lawfully do to each other, is hardly surprising in an age when so many people have allowed themselves to become the willing audience in a spectacle of hyperbolic performances of horror shows where threats and fears are peddled like commercial commodities. To paraphrase the lamentation of the Athenian general Cleon in the Peloponnesian War, it is as if 9/11 had ignited a world culture in which people had become "slaves to the pleasures of the ear," hearing only what affirmed the biases of their egos and the prejudices of their anxieties.[5] Particularly in the West, but also in the rest of the world and at times in the Muslim world itself, what became a part of the pleasures of the ear was a form of Islam-bashing that questioned the worthiness and role of the Islamic religion, as if Islam were a newly born fad or cult phenomenon that has yet to prove its contributions to humanity. Of course, there is nothing new about either Islam-bashing or any other form of religion bashing, but in this past decade, the line separating critical analysis aimed at the deconstruction of religion, as opposed to bigotry and prejudice, appeared to all but vanish. Most disconcertingly, a decade after 9/11 in the West, a persistent flow of what can be described only as a distinctively religiously bigoted and even racist discourse continued unabated. This discourse, which has been appropriately described as Islamophobic, has taken the form of a torrent of publications claiming to expose "the hidden truth" about the evil of Islam or the massive international conspiracy by something labeled "the Islamist" that aims to control and convert the world.[6] Not much different is a genre of literature that appeared with increasing frequency after 9/11, consisting of writings by what has been appropriately described as the self-deprecating testimonials of native informants. This variety of Islamophobia was propagated by self-hating, self-flagellating Muslims purporting to be experts on Islamic history, theology, and law who for the betterment of humanity have decided to bare all and reveal the dirty secrets of their ugly religion.[7] In the particularly incredulous variety of this literature, authors purport to write as Muslims struggling with their faith because their religion is both deeply troubling and troubled. At the conclusion of an obsequiously oblique discourse, the struggling Muslims end up declaring that they remain followers of the faith if only to help their wretched and dejected coreligionists to rise above the misery that is Islam. Of course, in light of all the professed errors of Islam, the decision of the authors of these books to remain Muslim appears incoherent or simply irrational. In a more honest variety of this literature, the authors claim to have been, once upon a time, devout Muslims who have finally managed to confront the horridness of their faith and turned away from Islam.

Obviously, it is not Islamophobic to critically analyze Islamic history, theology, or law or ultimately to reject the belief system espoused by Islam. As discussed later, Islamophobia, as prejudice or the performance of bigotry, is when a great canvas holding numerous complexities and subtleties, whether historically, legally, or theologically, is used to present a largely invented and artificial caricature of whatever is designated as Islamic or Muslim. The caricatured portrayals of the Islamic faith or religion in general is something of an old human sport—albeit as reckless, irresponsible, and reprehensible as it may be—that is solemnly documented in both the Qur'an and the Bible. However, Islamophobia, like other forms of prejudice and bigotry, invariably leads to a morally reductive attitude in which the value and worthiness of human beings are diminished or discounted because of presumed flaws attributable to inherent characteristics such as people's religion, ethnicity, race, gender, or culture. Such reductive attitudes, as history has shown time and again, become part of a process in which, usually in response to an anxiety of being under threat from others, it becomes far less morally objectionable to trample over the rights of the feared "other" and to ignore the suffering of the victims of bigotry. Islamophobia invariably leads to a reductive moral attitude in which it becomes both easier to exterminate Muslims and also to come to fear extermination by Muslims. In short, fear leads to hate, and hate is the root of most evil.

As discussed later, the flood of Islamophobic literature is disconcerting because it seems to reflect a significant cultural phenomenon. It is not an exaggeration to say that since 9/11, Islamophobic books have been coming out at the rate of a book a week, if not more. Add to this the anti-Islamic frenzy that plagues the electronic media and airwaves in the United States (leave alone the Western world in general), and we are forced to acknowledge that there is sufficient reason to be gravely concerned. What is rather dumbfounding is that this hate industry, which has published book after book referencing one another and all saying exactly the same thing with slight variations on the theme, can continue to find a profitable market. Assuming that this hate industry is not artificially financed by some political interest or another, the existence of a robust market for this kind of hate discourse for over a decade, especially in light of the history of confrontations between Muslims in the Middle East region and Latin Christendom, should have been troubling for intellectuals in the United States.[8] Instead, intellectuals have continued to focus on more traditional themes of racialization, ethnicity, and subjugation as if religious bigotry has not had a direct impact on the dynamics of power in the United States and the rest of the world.[9] As discussed later in this book, intellectuals have grown too comfortable with the achievements of the European Enlightenment and complacent with the beliefs that religious intolerance, violence, and wars are things of the past, and that religiously motivated violence or subjugation can be committed only by "others" against the West but not by the West against the other.

At certain points, one feared that the West was retreating back to the mentality of the Holy Roman Empire and Christendom, locked in battle with the Abode of Islam, with crusades becoming the legitimate means to lofty and higher causes, such as combating the evildoers or the Axis of Evil.[10] As I argue later in this book, the rise of Islamophobia and the paradigm of the clash of civilizations is a major moral regression that, if not resisted, will have a profound, regrettable impact on all of humanity.[11] But the impact for Muslims, for reasons addressed later, is bound to be particularly devastating. Since the age of colonialism, Western attitudes toward Islam have left pronounced and possibly permanent effects on Muslim culture, law, and theology. However, the anti-Islamic attitudes of the colonial age tended to be less vulgar and also more scholarly than most of the material venting anger and hate that dominates the market today.[12]

The main reason that a civilizational regression in the form of legalized and legitimated religious bigotry will have a monumental impact on Islam is that Muslims are currently living through a truly transformative historical moment in which Muslims and non-Muslims are, consciously or not, participating in constructing the role and function of the Islamic faith for the foreseeable future. One way or another, the way that Muslims and non-Muslims relate to the universal tradition of Islam, however constructed, will play a key role in determining the type of world our children will live in. After spending a lifetime studying especially the monumental intellectual heritage of Islamic jurisprudence and law, I have come to realize that at least for a thousand years, Islam has been, and is likely to continue to be, in one shape or another a major component in most political, economic, sociological, and moral issues that have confronted human beings. It is not only that all human beings are defining the role of Islam, but that Islam in turn affects all of our lives in material and lasting ways. The terrorist attacks and the invasions of Afghanistan and Iraq have only served to underscore the extent to which our fates as human beings are inextricably connected. Since I spent most of my life studying this one aspect of the human legacy, I could not avoid the sense of moral obligation and ethical duty to try and play, to the extent possible, an active and positive role in having some impact on the direction that Muslim and non-Muslim interactions are going to take in the future. Nevertheless, it also became clear that much of the nature of these interactions will depend on the ability of all parties concerned to put their respective houses in good moral order. I recognize that as human beings, our ability to work together in order to improve the way we treat and deal with one another is hinged on the willingness of the various sides to take part in an interactive dynamic to, so to speak, keep their own moral houses in order and to honestly and self-critically engage themselves about their own personal failures rather than to be preoccupied with the shortcomings and failures of others. Being a Muslim, I could not help but shoulder the duty of introspective and self-critical evaluation of the Muslim contribution to the modern world. If I were Christian or Jewish, I would have been bound to do the same with these respective traditions. I think that the follower of a faith or any system of thought has a moral obligation to defend and guard it, but this obligation is not met by justifying and minimizing its errors and injustices. Rather, the obligation is met by being honest and principled in confronting the past failures and future challenges confronting one's faith. This same approach was confirmed by the teachings of the Prophet Muhammad, who explained that the best way to support a fellow Muslim who is acting unjustly is to stand up for him, not against him, by restraining and preventing him from committing further injustice. This is the spirit that informed the writing of this book. The way that I sought to help my fellow Muslims and to contribute to the world I live in is by speaking out against what I believe are injustices and wrongful behavior committed in the name of Islam by my coreligionists. But the point of this book is not simply to find blame or identify and explain a major moral failure inflicting many modern-day Muslims. The objective of this book is to analyze what has gone wrong but also to explore the path for reclaiming Islam's moral and ethical fabric. I do argue that many contemporary Muslim activists have failed the ideals of Islam and deviated from its ethical teachings. Moreover, I argue that Muslims shoulder a heavy normative burden—a burden made necessary by the universal moral objectives of the Islamic message. Muslims, I argue, must not only reclaim Islam but must strive to enable the Islamic tradition to reach its moral and ethical potential. I argue that the Shari'ah, properly understood, is an essential and irreplaceable part of revitalizing and reengaging the humanitarian civilizing role of the Islamic message. The challenge, in my view, is not for Muslims to return back and reclaim some idealized moment in history, but it is for Muslims to engage the ethical tradition of their faith, especially the Shari'ah, in a dynamic process of moral progress.

Although this book deals with the theology of moral progress in Islam, this issue is of central importance to non-Muslims as well. Moral progress is untenable unless accomplished in the context of a dynamic interaction with those who are not Muslim. Other than being observers, it follows that non-Muslims are involved in this process in at least two ways. First, non-Muslims, simply by affirming or supporting particular moral values and not others, engage Muslims in a creative negotiative dynamic that in many indirect and, at times, direct ways helps shape the moral values of humanity, including those of Muslims. Second, obviously, we live in a world where it is impossible to avoid interacting not only with the "other" but with every kind of other. Non-Muslims are directly influenced by Muslim life whether this life takes place in countries that are predominantly non-Muslim or otherwise. But beyond this, I argue that the moral objective of godliness, as opposed to godlessness, is impossible to achieve on this earth without a partnership of equals working toward a collective enterprise of goodness among all communities of faith—Muslim and non-Muslim.

One final word about the writing of this book: I think this has been a difficult book to write because it is a book premised on hope. Despite the many critical and at times unpleasant topics discussed in the pages that follow, I wrote this book while believing that the golden age of Islam and humanity is yet to come. What inspired the book is my fundamental belief in divinity and humanity and that the way to each is through the other. Furthermore, I believe that divinity and justice are fused and interlocked one with the other. Being committed to the one mandates a commitment to the other, and bearing witness for one necessarily means bearing witness for the other.[13]

With varying degrees of involvement and intensity, I have been working on this book since 2003, and in these eleven years, history has delivered so many disappointments and very few pleasant surprises. As in all turbulent times, human beings continue to compete to commit extreme acts of ugliness and, at times, it looks like having faith in this species is a nasty delusion. 9/11 was shockingly immoral and ugly to the point of uniting practically all human beings against its evil. The outrage committed on that day provided the world with a sense of moral clarity and a sense of shared moral destiny. That fateful day delivered so much ugliness and evil, but there was also the opportunity and hope for healing, rejuvenation, and rebirth. This book was started in pursuit of that hope. Sadly, after 9/11, layers of ugliness were leveled on one another as the slaughter in New York was preceded by the slaughter in Bosnia and was succeeded by orgies of bloodletting in Afghanistan, Iraq, Pakistan, Lebanon, Gaza, and Yemen as well as other places; and the bloodbath continues to this day. On the positive side of things, the tyrants of Libya, Tunisia, Egypt, and Yemen were finally overthrown. But our joys were short lived as instead of democracy, the influence of Saudi Arabian puritanism and despotism has grown and spread to new unprecedented heights. The Saudi government fully recuperated from the public relations disaster of 9/11; regained its chummy relations with the United States and Europe; and aborted any democratic revolutionary potential that might have arisen in Egypt, Yemen, Bahrain, and Syria. Syria has descended into a civil war as the once promising revolution was turned into a proxy war between Iran and Saudi Arabia. Again, with ample Saudi and UAE generosity, the homicidal insanity between Sunnis and Shi'is continues in Iraq; the praetorian dictatorship has been restored to its time-honored position in Egypt; and the world turned a blind eye as countless atrocities were perpetrated against a civilian population in Bahrain. The Palestinians continue to be imprisoned by a virtual apartheid regime in the West Bank and Gaza,[14] and the United States continues to kill Muslims at will in drone attacks that no one dares call a form of terrorism.[15] Add to all this heartache that the self-appointed guardians of the two holy cities continue to destroy Islamic historical sites that are more than a thousand years old to build fancy hotels and shopping malls. They have already destroyed more than 90 percent of the historical sites in Mecca and Medina, and where the home of the Prophet's wife Khadija once stood now stands a convenient and fashionable public toilet. There are current plans to raze the Prophet's gravesite and also to destroy the burial sites of his two closest companions, Umar and Abu Bakr. A lavish expansion project will award Western companies lucrative building contracts to construct luxury

hotels, shopping centers, and restaurants in two cities that have been transformed through the piety of the Saudi government into temples where the
idolatry of self-gratification, hedonistic luxury, and material indulgences
have wiped the godliness out of the two holy cities. [16]

Considering this abysmal track record, how is hope possible? Hope is like
faith, and hope in humanity is like faith in humanity. Hope and faith are not
built on what is but rather on the possibilities of what could be. I believe that
even if human beings cannot overcome ugliness in the world, they simply
cannot afford to stop having hope and faith in the possibility of beauty.
Moreover, within the folds of every tragedy there are countless superficially
concealed acts of heroic beauty and the potential for forgiveness, restoration,
reformation, and progress. For example, for all the tragedies and atrocities
one would be remiss to fail to notice the astounding heroism of so many men,
women, and even children who bravely risked their lives and sustained grave
injury in pursuit of justice and freedom. If nothing else, because of the
sacrifices made by so many heroes, we owe them the promise of hope. As
long as people might be willing to forgo the logic of retaliation, there is
always the hope that instead of avenging the ungodly past, people could
focus on reclaiming the path to the future.

Acknowledgments

I worked on this book for well over a decade, and in the course of such a long period of time my indebtedness only grew as my memory regretfully diminished. I am grateful to so many, but I beg the forgiveness of those who I will offend because of my forgetfulness and strained memory.

I am fortunate to be surrounded by so many amazingly supportive colleagues at the UCLA School of Law, who contribute to my scholarship in so many immeasurable ways. I especially wish to acknowledge the UCLA law library's staff, particularly Linda Karr O'Connor and Myra Sanders, who make my work so much easier.

Over the years I enjoyed the privilege of working with a number of competent research assistants including Zachary Taylor, Jordan Jeffery, Jacob Chodash, Jawid Habib, Kristina Benson, Mark Williams, Ryan Riegg, and Rabea Chaudhry. I am also grateful for the support and assistance of Ufuk Topkara and Sherif Abdelkarim. I owe a special debt of gratitude to a young woman with an incredible work ethic, intellect, and spirit. Holly Robins, who I am confident is going to become a scholar and an academic of considerable distinction, has been selfless and exemplary in her assistance.

My former students Said Fares Hassan, Ayman Shabana, and Amir Boozari have helped in more ways than they realize. I remain in their debt. I also thank Nader Hashemi and Emran Qureshi for reading earlier drafts of this book and for their numerous insights, but most of all for their friendship. I also thank my colleagues Stephen Gaudbaum, Asli Bali, and Asma Sayeed for their unwavering support and friendship.

The Shaykh of Azhar Ahmad al-Tayyib and the former Mufti of Egypt 'Ali Jum'a generously hosted me in Egypt, and facilitated access to numerous sources. I appreciate their hospitality and the time invested in conversation. The Mufti 'Ali Jum'a and his young gifted advisor and assistant, Ebrahim Negm, provided the space and means for a much needed isolation and seclusion so that I could write. I only wish that this expression of true and heartfelt gratitude were not burdened, weighed down, and drowning in so much Egyptian blood.

I owe so much to the inspiring spirit and consummate intellect of my former student Dana Lee. Her gentle but hauntingly cogent remarks often forced me to complain, rethink, and then rewrite. Despite my protests, she knows I am forever grateful.

My special thanks to the poet Laura Coyne for her breathtakingly beautiful writing, and for granting me permission to use her poems. I am also grateful to artist and calligrapher Koichi Fuad Honda for permission to use his art on the book cover. No words can express my appreciation for my editors at Rowman & Littlefield, Jeremy Langford and Sarah Stanton, who believed in this book and patiently waited a whole decade for me to deliver on what I promised. This book owes its very existence to them, and their insights and suggestions throughout this entire period have sustained and maintained this project.

Finally, I thank my long-enduring family who through the never-ending storm of restless ideas, waves of arguments, and the magically multiplying papers and books manage to locate me, anchor me, and keep me going. I owe everything to my sons Cherif and Mido (Medhat) Abou El Fadl; my siblings Eanas and Tarek, and my father Medhat, all who play a critical role in infusing me with the will power to go on.

But once again in my life, it is two women who had a majestic impact on my work. My mother continued to believe in this work until the very last moments of her life. Sadly, she passed away before she could see the book come to fruition. The other woman, my wife Grace Song, picked me up, dusted me off, and got me back on my way every time. She read numerous drafts, managed countless crises, and reset the course more times than any of us can remember. Not only a partner and companion in marriage, Grace is the living expert on a system of thought she nurtured into existence. If there were a way to isolate only the majestic and beautiful in this book, and weed all that is inept, pigheaded, and uninspired, Grace would definitely be the coauthor of this book.

An Introduction to Shari'ah

The purpose of this chapter is to provide a basic and straightforward introduction to the rather amorphous system that we call Islamic law. This book is
about reasoning with God about God's law in the Islamic context, and so,
throughout, there are repeated references to Shari'ah and Islamic law without
these terms being synonymous or interchangeable. In the course of the arguments made in this book, I propose different ways in which the role and
nature of Islamic law ought to be understood, and I have done my best
wherever necessary to offer the reader functional reminders of the meaning
of the various Arabic terms associated with the Islamic legal experience.
Ultimately, however, for a variety of reasons, I decided to start out the book
with what might be described as the indispensable guide to basic Islamic law.
The brief introduction below is intended to help provide readers without any
background in the Islamic legal system with a quick crash course in the
subject. This will much better enable readers to follow the arguments made
in this book. At the same time, Shari'ah law has been the subject of so many
mischaracterizations and stereotyping that it has become necessary to simply
get the facts straight. Many discourses on the subject remain captive to either
hallucinatory mythology often spurred on by xenophobia or bigotry or to
stale apologetics that grow out of misguided false pride or, quite often, condescending tolerance. But even to serious students of Islamic law, this introduction can serve as quick review of basic concepts and categories of Shari'ah and Islamic law. I should note, however, that while this brief synopsis
of the Islamic legal system helps serve as an important orientation to the rest
of the book, it is intended to stand alone and can be omitted without interrupting the flow of narrative. As a scholastic and faith-based engagement
with the meaning and consequences of Shari'ah, this book really begins with
the following chapter. The book is akin to a journey through Islamic theology, law, and history—it is a journey through the Muslim past and present—
and so this prologue is not the journey, but it could very well be the provisions needed for a meaningful trip.

WHAT IS SHARI'AH?

Although, both in Western and native discourses, it is common to use Shari'ah (also commonly spelled *Shari'a* or *Shari'at*) interchangeably with Islamic law, Shari'ah is a much broader term. Shari'ah is a rather fungible term in that it can mean different things depending on the context. So, for instance, *al-Shari'ah al-Yahudiyya* means Jewish law, *Shari'at Musa* means the laws of Moses, and *Shari'at al-Masih* means the way of Jesus or the path of Jesus. *Shari'at Muhammad*, depending on the usage, could mean the Sunna or tradition of Muhammad or Muhammad's way of life, but the expression would not be used to refer to Islamic jurisprudence or law.

In the linguistic practices of Islamic theologians, ethicists, and jurists in the Islamic tradition, the broad meaning of Shari'ah is the way or path to well-being or goodness, the life source for well-being and thriving existence, the fountain or source of nourishment, and the natural and innate ways and order created by God. In the legal context, Shari'ah is God's eternal and immutable law—the way of truth, virtue, and justice. In essence, Shari'ah is the ideal law in an objective and noncontingent sense, as it ought to be in the divine's realm. As such, Shari'a is often used to refer to the universal, innate, and natural laws of goodness. Islamic law, or what is called *al-ahkam al-Shar'iyya* or *ahkam al-Shari'ah*, refers to the cumulative body of legal determinations and system of jurisprudential thought of numerous interpretive communities and schools of thought, all of which search the divine will and its relation to the public good. The stated objective of Islamic law is to achieve human well-being (*tahqiq masalih al-'ibad*). Islamic law is thus the fallible and imperfect attempt by Muslims over centuries to understand and implement the divine norms, to explore right and wrong, and to achieve human welfare.

WHAT IS ISLAMIC LAW?

The Islamic legal system consists of legal institutions, determinations, and practices that span a period of over fourteen hundred years, arising from a wide variety of cultural and geographic contexts that are as diverse as Arabia, Egypt, Persia, Bukhara, Turkey, Iberia, Nigeria, Mauritania, Mali, Indonesia, India, and China. Importantly, what is called Islamic law is not contained in a single or few books. Islamic law is found in an enormous corpus of volumes that document the rulings, opinions, and discourses of jurists over the span of many centuries. Despite the contextual and historical contingencies that constitute the complex reality of Islamic law, rather paradoxically, the Islamic legal legacy has been the subject of widespread and stubbornly persistent stereotypes and oversimplifications, and its legacy is highly contested and grossly understudied at the same time. Whether espoused by Muslim or non-Muslim scholars, highly simplified assumptions about Islamic law, such as the belief that Islamic legal doctrine stopped developing in the fourth/tenth century, the purported sacredness and immutability of the legal system, or the phenomenon of so-called Qadi justice (essentially, a type of law that is individualistic, unpredictable, and irrational),[1] are to a large extent products of turbulent political histories that contested and transformed Islamic law (or what is commonly referred to as Shari'ah) into a cultural and ideological symbol. Currently, our knowledge of the institutions, mechanisms, and microdynamics, discourses, and determinations of Islamic law in various places and times is very limited. At the very minimum, however, it is clear that Islamic law is a shorthand expression for an amorphous and formless body of legal rulings, judgments, and opinions that have been collected over the course of many centuries. On any point of law, one will find many conflicting opinions about what the law of God requires or mandates. The Islamic legal tradition is expressed in works that deal with jurisprudential theory and legal maxims, legal opinions (*fatawa*), adjudications in actual cases, and encyclopedic volumes that note down the positive rulings of law (*ahkam*). How does this substantial body of jurisprudence relate to divinity or to God's law? This question brings us to a crucial distinction that is central to the very logic of Islamic law. What is customarily referred to as Islamic law is actually separated into two distinct categories: Shari'ah and *fiqh*. However, before dealing with the distinction between Shari'ah and *fiqh*, we need to explain the difference between Islamic and Muslim law.

THE DIFFERENCE BETWEEN ISLAMIC LAW AND MUSLIM LAW

Much of the secondary literature tends to either lump the two, especially when dealing with the premodern era, or assume a dogmatic and artificial distinction that is fundamentalistic in nature. Not all legal systems or rules followed by Muslims are part of the Islamic legal tradition, but at the same time, the boundaries of Islamic law are far more contested and negotiable than any fundamentalist or essentialist approach may be willing to admit. Part of what makes this issue particularly challenging is that inescapably it involves judgments as to legitimacy and authenticity with regard to what is Islamic and what is not necessarily so. But more critically, the differentiation cannot be intelligibly addressed unless one takes full account of the epistemology and philosophy of Islamic jurisprudence or the rules of normativity, obligation, and authority and the processes of inclusion and exclusion in Islamic legal practice and history. Although Islamic law grew out of the normative teachings of the Prophet Muhammad and his disciples, the first generations of Muslim jurists borrowed and integrated legal practices from several sources including Persia, Mesopotamia, Egypt and other Roman provinces, Yemen and Arabia, and Jewish law. But at the same time, many existing and actual customary or executive administrative practices prevalent in premodern Muslim societies and polities were not integrated or recognized as being part of or even consistent with Islamic law or Islamic normative values. Classical Muslim jurists often denounced a particular set of customary practices, such as the tribal laws disinheriting women, or executive administrative practices, such as tax farming or excessive taxes known as *mukus*, as inconsistent with Islamic legal principles. Although such legal practices at times constituted part of the universe of rules actually implemented and followed in certain Muslim societies, these practices, even if begrudgingly tolerated as functional necessities, were never endowed with

Islamic legitimacy and thus were not integrated normatively into the Islamic legal tradition.

Distinguishing Islamic from Muslim law has only become more elusive and challenging in postcolonial modern-day Muslim societies. Most contemporary Muslim countries adopted either the French-based civil law system or some version of the British common law system and limited the application of Islamic law to personal law matters, particularly in the fields of inheritance and family law. In addition, in response to domestic political pressure, several Muslim countries in the 1970s and 1980s attempted to Islamize their legal systems by amending commercial or criminal laws in order to make them more consistent with purported Islamic legal doctrine. The fact remains, however, that the nature of the connection or relationship of any of these purportedly Islamically based or Islamized laws to the Islamic legal tradition remains debatable. As discussed further below, even in the field of personal law, where the supremacy of Shari'ah law was supposedly never seriously challenged, leave alone the various highly politicized efforts at legal Islamization, Islamic legal doctrine was grafted onto what structurally and institutionally, as well as epistemologically, were legal systems borrowed and transplanted from the West. Practically in every Muslim country, the complex institutional structures and the processes of the Islamic legal system, especially in the nineteenth century, were systematically dismantled and replaced not just by Western legal systems but, more importantly, by the legal cultures of a number of Western colonial powers. Assertions of disembodied Islamic determinations or rules in the modern age—without the contextual legal processes, institutions, and epistemology and in the absence of the legal cultures that generated these determinations in the first place—meant that the relationship between contemporary manifestations of Islamic law and the classical legal tradition remained, to say the least, debatable.

THE SOURCES OF ISLAMIC LAW

It is important to distinguish the formal sources of law in the Islamic legal tradition from what is often called the practical sources of law. Formal sources of law are an ideological construct—they are the ultimate foundations invoked by jurists and judges as the basis of legal legitimacy and authority. The practical sources, however, are the actual premises and processes utilized in legal practice in the process of producing positive rules and commandments. In theory, the foundations of all law in Islamic jurisprudence are the following: the Qur'an, the Sunna (the tradition of the Prophet Muhammad and his companions), *qiyas* (analogical or deductive reasoning), and *ijma'* (consensus or the overall agreement of Muslim jurists). In contrast to mainstream Sunni Islam, Shi'i jurisprudence as well as a minority of Sunni jurists in the particular classical orientations recognize reason (instead of *qiyas*) as a foundational source of law. These four are legitimating sources, but the practical sources of law include an array of conceptual tools that greatly expand the venues of the legal determination. For instance, practical sources include presumptions of continuity (*istishab*) and the imperative of following precedents (*taqlid*), legal rationalizations for breaking with prece-

dent and *de novo* determinations (*ijtihad*), application of customary practices
(*'urf* and *'ada*), judgments in equity, equitable relief, and necessity (*istislah,
haja, darura*, etc.), and in some cases the pursuit or the protection of public
interests or public policies (*masalih mursala* and *sadd al-dhara'i' wa al-
mafasid*). These and other practical jurisprudential sources were not employed as legal tropes in a lawless application of so-called *qadi* justice. In
fact, sophisticated conceptual frameworks were developed to regulate the
application of the various jurisprudential tools employed in the process of
legal determination. Not only were these conceptual frameworks intended to
distinguish legitimate and authoritative uses of legal tools, but collectively,
they were designed to bolster accountability, predictability, and the principle
of rule of law.

Being the ultimate sources of legitimacy, the formal sources of law do not
play solely a symbolic role in Islamic jurisprudence. Many legal debates and
determinations originated or were derived directly from the textual narrative
of the Qur'an and Sunna. Nevertheless, it would be erroneous to assume, as
many fundamentalists tend to do, that Islamic law is a literalist explication or
enunciation of the text of the Qur'an and Sunna. Only very limited portions
of the Qur'an can be said to contain specific positive legal commandments or
prohibitions. Much of the Qur'anic discourse, however, does have compelling normative connotations that were extensively explored and debated in
the classical juristic tradition. Muslim scholars developed an extensive literature on Qur'anic exegesis and legal hermeneutics as well as a body of work
(known as *ahkam al-Qur'an*) exploring the ethical and legal implications of
the Qur'anic discourse. Moreover, there is a classical tradition of disputations
and debates on what is known as the "occasions of revelation" (*asbab al-
nuzul*), which deal with the context or circumstances that surrounded the
revelation of particular Qur'anic verses or chapters and on the critical issue
of abrogation (*naskh*), or which Qur'anic prescriptions and commandments,
if any, were nullified or voided during the time of the Prophet.

Similar issues relating to historical context, abrogation, and hermeneutics
are dealt with in the juristic treatment of the legacy of the Prophet and his
companions and disciples. However, in contrast to the juristic discourses on
the Qur'an, there are extensive classical debates on the historicity or authenticity of the *hadith* (oral traditions attributed to the Prophet) and the Sunna
(historical narratives typically about the Prophet but also his companions).
While Muslim jurists agreed that the authenticity of the Qur'an, as God's
revealed word, is beyond any doubt, classical jurists recognized that many of
the traditions attributed to the Prophet were apocryphal. In this context, however, Muslim jurists did not just focus on whether a particular report was
authentic or a fabrication but on the extent or degree of reliability and the
attendant legal consequences. Importantly, Muslim jurists distinguished between the reliability and normativity of traditions. Even if a tradition proved
to be authentic, this did not necessarily mean that it is normatively binding,
because most jurists differentiated between the Prophet's sacred and temporal roles. The Prophet was understood as having performed a variety of roles
in his lifetime, including that of the bearer and conveyer of the divine message, a moral and ethical sage and instructor, a political leader, a military
commander and soldier, an arbitrator and judge, a husband and father, and a

regular human being and member of society. Not everything the Prophet said or did in these various capacities and roles created normative obligations on Muslims. The Prophet did not always act as a lawmaker or legislator, and part of the challenge for Muslim jurists was to ascertain when his statements and actions were intended to create a legal obligation or duty (*taklif*) and when they were not meant to have any normative weight. In some cases, Muslims are affirmatively prohibited from imitating the Prophet's conduct because it is believed that in certain situations the Prophet acted in his capacity as God's messenger, a status that cannot be claimed by other human beings. Other than the normative implications of the Prophet's sacred and temporal roles, a great deal of juristic disputation focused on the practices and opinions of the Prophet's family (*ahl al-bayt*), including his wives, and his companions and disciples (*sahaba*). But while Sunni jurists tended to emphasize and exhibit deference to the four Caliphs who governed the nascent Islamic state after the death of the Prophet (known in the Sunni tradition as al-Rashidun, or the rightly guided), Shi'i jurists heavily relied on the teachings of the infallible imams, all of whom were the descendants of 'Ali, the fourth Caliph and the Prophet's cousin, and his wife, Fatima, the Prophet's daughter.

It is fair to say that the Qur'an and Sunna are the two primary and formal sources of legitimacy in Islamic law. Quite aside from the question of whether most of Islamic law is derived from these two sources, the Qur'an and Sunna play the foundational role in the processes of constructing legal legitimacy. This, however, begs the question as to why instrumentalities of jurisprudence such as analogy or reason and consensus are typically listed among the four formal sources of Islamic law. The response, in part, is that the utilization of the concepts of *qiyas* (or *'aql*) and *ijma'*, not just as instrumentalities of law but as legitimating and foundational origins of law, was a necessary legal fiction. The emergence of this legal fiction in the first couple of centuries after the death of the Prophet took place after contentious and, at times, tumultuous jurisprudential debates. Ultimately, these concepts were intended to steer a middle course between unfettered and unrestrained borrowing of local customary laws and practices into Islamic law and, on the other extreme, the tendency toward literalism and overreliance on textualism as the basis of legitimacy in the process of legal development.

As legal instrumentalities, both the predominantly Sunni concept of *qiyas* and Shi'i *'aql* utilize deductive reasoning to identify the critical issue in one legal ruling and then extend the same ruling to a new case. Jurists used carefully defined analytical skills in deducing the operative cause or *ratio legis* (the element that triggers the law into action, *'illa* in Arabic) of a particular textual law or determination. Confronted by an unprecedented or novel case, often for which there is no law on point, the jurist would extend the ruling in a previous case (*asl*) to the new case (*far'*), but only if both cases shared the same operative cause.[2] The derivation of the operative cause of a ruling (*istikhraj 'illat al-hukm*) was important not only because it had become the method by which the law was extended to cover new cases but also because it became one of the primary instruments for legal systemization and also change. If the operative cause changes or no longer exists, the law, in turn, must change. The Islamic legal maxim *al-'illa tadur ma' al-*

ma'lul wujudan wa 'adaman became substantially the same as the Latin maxim providing that the law is changed if the reason of the law is changed (*mutata legis ratione mutatur et lex*). In interpretation as well as adjudication, this helped generate a more systematic legal institution; it meant that cases involving substantially the same issues were decided similarly. This practice, in turn, led to the development of the presumption that precedent ought to be followed unless there is sufficient cause for exception or change (*istishab*), which could be for changed circumstances, equity, or a number of other legal justifications.

In a similar fashion, the concept of *ijma'* (consensus) was utilized to create a more systematic and accountable legal system. The basic idea behind the doctrine of *ijma'* was that the agreement of jurists on a particular point of law or that well-established legal doctrine ought to be binding. Nevertheless, beyond this fundamental idea, which was often invoked in an effort to consolidate and stabilize the legal system, there were numerous juristic debates as to a range of issues, such as whose consensus counts or matters, whether consensus is time bound, for instance, by generation or another time contingency, whether the doctrine of consensus has a regional dimension and how, and last but not least, how to go about ascertaining that a consensus exists. As readily recognized by classical jurists, however, the claim of consensus was often polemically invoked by judges and jurists in the course of arguing that a particular issue was well settled in law when indeed it was not or, alternatively, to resist pressure in favor of legal change.

There are a number of other legal instrumentalities that allowed Muslim jurists a degree of flexibility in reaching determinations consistent with equity, avoidance of hardship, or granting special relief. Among such instrumentalities was the method of *istislah*, by which a jurist would follow a certain precedent that was not directly on point, instead of another precedent that was directly on point, for purposes of achieving equity. Another was *istihsan*, by which a jurist would break with the established precedents on a legal matter in the interest of reaching a more just or fairer result. But the exercise of equitable preference was not a matter of a simple exercise of discretion. Rather, the jurists developed a set of limiting criteria that were intended to make the process of exercising a preference more systematic and accountable.[3]

THE NATURE AND PURPOSE OF ISLAMIC LAW

One of the first political crises to confront the nascent Muslim empire forced Muslim jurists to deal with the nature, scope, and limits of divine authority and human agency. The political crisis arose out of the death of the Prophet and the ensuing struggle over whether and also to what extent one can inherit the Prophet's juridical authority. Ultimately, the political conflict over succession had a formative and lasting impact on the juristic discourse on the implications of divine authority and the role of human beings as the bearers and executors of this authority, as well as on the closely related issues of objectivity and subjectivity in law. As an essential point of departure, it is important to underscore that in jurisprudential theory, the ultimate point of

Shari'ah is to serve the well-being or achieve the welfare of people (*tahqiq masalih al-'ibad*).[4] The word *Shari'ah*, which many have very often errone-ously equated with Islamic law, means the "way of God" and the pathway of goodness, and the objective of Shari'ah is not necessarily the compliance with the commands of God for their own sake. Such compliance is a means to an end—the serving of the physical and spiritual welfare and well-being of people. Muslim jurists reasoned that if law will be made to serve the well-being of people while at the same time avoiding the pitfalls of the tyranny of human whim or unfettered reason, divine guidance or direction is necessary and indispensable. Significantly, in Islamic legal theory, God communicates God's way (the Shari'ah) through what is known as the *dalil* (pl. *adilla*). The dalil means the indicator, mark, guide, or evidence, and in Islamic legal theory, it is a fundamental building block of the search for the divine will and guidance. As a sign of God's mercy and compassion, God created or enunci-ated numerous indicators serving as guidance to human goodness, well-being (*al-hasan wa al-ma'ruf*), and ultimately, the divine will. Moreover, God ordained that human beings exert a persistent effort in investigating the di-vine indicators, or the evidence of God's Will (*badhl al-juhd fi talab al-dalil*), so that the objectives of Shari'ah may be fulfilled. Not surprisingly, the nature of the dalil became one of the formidable and formative debates of early Islamic jurisprudence. The most obvious type of indicator is an authori-tative text (sing. *nass Shar'i* or pl. *al-nusus al-Shar'iyya*), such as the Qur'an, but Muslim jurists also recognized that God's wisdom is manifested through a vast matrix of indicators found in God's physical and metaphysical crea-tion. Hence, other than texts, God's signs or indicators could manifest them-selves through reason and rationality (*'aql* and *ra'y*), intuitions (*fitra*), and human custom and practice (*'urf* and *'ada*).[5] Especially in early Islam, which of these could legitimately be counted as avenues to God's Will and to what extent were hotly debated issues. Especially with the increasing consolida-tion of the legal system after the tenth century, both Sunni and Shi'i jurists argued that most indicators are divided into rational proofs (*dalil 'aqli*) and textual proofs (*dalil nassi*). As to rational proofs, jurisprudential theory fur-ther differentiated between pure reason and practical or applied reason. Foundational legal principles and legal presumptions, such as the presump-tion of innocence or the presumption of permissibility (*al-bara'a al-asliyya*) and the presumption of continuity (*istishab al-hal*), are derived from pure reason. Interpretive tools, such as *qiyas* and *istihsan*, and hermeneutic cate-gories are all instances of applied or practical reason.

Some Western scholars such as Joseph Schacht claimed that the first generations of Muslim jurists initially were not very interested in the text (*nass*) and were much more prone to use custom and reason (*ra'y*).[6] Never-theless, this view has been adequately refuted, and there remains little doubt about the centrality of the text from the very inception of Islamic legal history.[7] It is true that in the first two centuries of Islam, one clearly observes a much greater reliance on custom, practice, and unsystematic reasoning and that both the juristic schools of Medina and Kufa incorporated what they perceived to be the established practice of local Muslims, but both schools also struggled with the role of the text, its authenticity, and its meaning. The critical issue in early Islamic jurisprudence was not the struggle over what role the text ought to play, but more substantially, it was over the methodologies by which the legal system could differentiate between determinations based on whim or a state of lawlessness (*hukm al-hawa*) and determinations based on legitimate indicators of the divine will (*hukm al-Shar'*).

In Islamic jurisprudence, the diversity and complexity of the divine indicators are considered part of the functionality and suitability of Islamic law for all times and places. The fact that the indicators are not typically precise, deterministic, or unidimensional allows jurists to read the indicators in light of the demands of time and place. So, for example, it is often noted that one of the founding fathers of Islamic jurisprudence, al-Shafi'i (d. 204/820)[8] had one set of legal opinions that he thought properly applied in Iraq but changed his positions and rulings when he moved to Egypt to account for the changed circumstances and social differences between the two regions.[9] The same idea is embodied by the Islamic legal maxim: "It may not be denied that laws will change with the change of circumstances" (*la yunkar taghayyur al-ahkam bi taghayyur al-zaman wa al-ahwal*).[10]

One of the most important aspects of the epistemological paradigm on which Islamic jurisprudence was built was the presumption that on most matters the divine will is unattainable, and even if attainable, no person or institution has the authority to claim certitude in realizing this Will. This is why the classical jurists rarely spoke in terms of legal certainties (*yaqin* and *qat'*). Rather, as is apparent in the linguistic practices of the classical juristic culture, Muslim jurists for the most part spoke in terms of probabilities or in terms of the preponderance of evidence and belief (*ghalabat al-zann*). As the influential classical jurist al-Juwayni (d. 478/1085) stated: "The most a *mujtahid* would claim was a preponderance of belief (*ghalabat al-zann*) and the balancing of the evidence. However, certainty was never claimed by any of them (the early jurists). . . . If we were charged with finding [the truth] we would not have been forgiven for failing to find it."[11] Muslim jurists emphasized that only God possesses perfect knowledge—human knowledge in legal matters is tentative or even speculative; it must rely on the weighing of competing factors and the assertion of judgment based on an assessment of the balance of evidence on any given matter. So, for example, Muslim jurists developed a rigorous field of analytical jurisprudence known as *tarjih*,[12] which dealt with the methodological principles according to which jurists would investigate, assign relative weight, and balance conflicting evidence in order to reach a preponderance of belief about potentially correct determinations.[13]

Contemporary fundamentalist and essentialistic orientations imagine Islamic law to be highly deterministic and casuistic, but this is in sharp contrast to the epistemology and institutions of the Islamic legal tradition that supported the existence of multiple equally orthodox and authoritative legal schools of thought, all of which are valid representations of the divine will. Indeed, the Islamic legal tradition was founded on a markedly pluralistic, discursive, and exploratory ethos that came to be at the very heart of its distinctive character. Thus, one of the foundational ideas of Islamic jurisprudence, variously attributed to the eponyms of the Hanafi and Shafi'i schools of law, Abu Hanifa (d. 150/767) and al-Shafi'i, asserted: "We believe that our opinions are correct but we are always cognizant of the fact that our opinions may be wrong. We also believe that the opinions of our opponents are wrong but we are always cognizant of the fact that they may be correct."[14] This, however, was much more than a pietistic declaration of humility or fair-mindedness. Muslim jurists believed that as long as a jurist exerted due diligence and was not negligent in searching the indicators and investigating the pertinent evidence, the resulting determination had an equal claim to legitimacy and authenticity. In fact, Malik bin Anas (d. 179/795), eponym of the Maliki school of thought, argued that different jurists have developed various juristic methods and determinations in different parts of the Muslim world and that it would be wrong to try to streamline or force the various methods into one.[15] Moreover, Malik bin Anas resisted the efforts of the Abbasid Caliph al-Mansur (d. 158/775) to impose the legal rulings of Malik as the uniform law of the land, arguing that no one, including the state, has the authority to sanctify one school of thought as the true law of God while all others are denounced as corruptions or heresies. Similar efforts by the Abbasid Caliph Harun al-Rashid (d. 193/809) and other rulers to have the state become the sole representative of God's Will were defeated as well. According to classical legal reasoning, no one jurist, institution, or juristic tradition may have an exclusive claim over the divine truth, and hence, the state does not have the authority to recognize the orthodoxy of one school of thought to the exclusion of all others.[16]

One of the clearest expressions of the philosophical foundations of this position was that made by the Shafi'i jurist al-Juwayni in writing: "It is as if God has said to human beings, 'My command to My servants is in accordance with the preponderance of their beliefs. So whoever preponderantly believes that they are obligated to do something, acting upon it becomes My command.'"[17] Al-Juwayni goes on to explain that God's command to human beings is to diligently search the indicators and weigh the evidence, and God's law is suspended until a human being forms a preponderance of belief about the law. At the point that a preponderance of belief is reached, God's law becomes in accordance with the preponderance of belief formed by that particular individual. In short, therefore, if a person honestly and sincerely believes that such-and-such is the law of God, then, as to that person, "that" is in fact God's law.[18] Nevertheless, this philosophy did not mean that Muslim jurists accepted legal relativism or even indeterminism in Shari'ah. As noted above, Shari'ah was considered to be the immutable, unchangeable, and objectively perfect divine truth. Human understanding of Shari'ah, however, was subjective, partial, and subject to error and change. While Shari'ah is divine, *fiqh* (the human understanding of Shari'ah) was recognized to be only potentially so, and it is the distinction between Shari'ah and *fiqh* that fueled and legitimated the practice of legal pluralism in Islamic history.

THE DIFFERENCE BETWEEN SHARI'AH AND FIQH

The conceptual distinction between Shari'ah and *fiqh* was the result of recognizing the limitations of human agency and also a reflection of the Islamic dogma that perfection belongs only to God. While Shari'ah was seen as an abstract ideal, every human effort at understanding or implementing this ideal was considered necessarily imperfect. In theory, Muslim jurists agreed that even if a jurist's determination is ultimately wrong, God will not hold such a jurist liable as long as he exerted due diligence in searching for the right answer. Beyond this, Muslim jurists debated whether in the final analysis, on every point of law there is a single correct position but this position is known only to God, and it is only in the Hereafter that this truth will be revealed. Much of this debate tended to revolve around a number of traditions attributed to the Prophet. For instance, the Prophet is reported to have said: "Every *mujtahid* (jurist who pursues the right response to a problem) is correct" or "Every *mujtahid* will be [justly] rewarded."[19] According to one group of legal theorists, those who are ultimately proved to be wrong will still be rewarded for their due diligence, but those who prove to be right will receive a greater reward. The alternative point of view, however, argued that on all matters of *fiqh* there is no single truth to be revealed by God in the Hereafter. All positions held sincerely and reached after due diligence are in God's eyes correct. God rewards people in direct proportion to the exhaustiveness, diligence, and sincerity of their search for the divine will—sincerity of conviction, the search, and the process are in themselves the ultimate moral values. It is not that there is no objective truth—rather, according to this view, the truth adheres to the search.

This classical debate had an impact on the development of various doctrines and institutions in Islamic jurisprudence, the most important of which was negotiating the dynamics between Shari'ah and *fiqh*. In the Islamic legal tradition, there is only one Shari'ah (*Shari'at Allah*), but there are a number of competing schools of thought of *fiqh* (*madhahib fiqhiyya*). Even the most ardent of the process-oriented jurists did not go as far as claiming that there are no objective and ultimate values to Shari'ah. Process-oriented jurists contended that the search for the divine will is the ultimate moral value, but only as to matters open to a *fiqh* inquiry. At the same time, although all jurists embraced the theological dogma that God's perfection cannot be reproduced or attained by human beings, this did not mean that they considered every aspect of Shari'ah to be entirely unattainable or inaccessible until the Hereafter. Some have suggested that Shari'ah contains the foundational or constitutional principles and norms of the legal system. So, for instance, Shari'ah imposes a duty (*taklif*) on Muslims to enjoin goodness and resist wrongfulness. There is little doubt that this duty is a part of Shari'ah, but what it actually means and how or who should implement it is part of *fiqh*. Nevertheless, the exact boundaries between Shari'ah and *fiqh* were often contested and negotiable, and whether there is overlap between the two categories turned out to be challenging and at times ambiguous. Muslim jurists often made the rather circular argument that issues that are considered open to the disputations of *fiqh* are those on which jurists may reasonably disagree (*al-umur al-khilafiyya*). Other popular definitions included the argument that any position, doctrine, or determination that is commonly recognized to be a necessary part of the Islamic religion is a part of Shari'ah (*ma'lum min al-din bi al-darura*), but this argument had proved to be both underexclusive and overexclusive. Moreover, like arguments that have sought to define Shari'ah as whatever Muslims have reached a consensus on (*al-mujma' 'alayh*), these definitions tended to confuse between empirical and normative claims. Be-

hind most of the jurisprudential conceptions of Shariʿah was the basic idea
that what cumulative generations of Muslims reasonably identified as fundamental to the Islamic religion (for instance, the five pillars of the Islamic
faith) ought to be part of the unassailable Shariʿah. As some have contended,
this approach might have been important to the field of theology, but in law
Shariʿah could not be limited to inherited or popular ideas. Rather, Shariʿah
comprises the foundational or constitutional normative values that constitute
the grundnorms of the Islamic legal system. For instance, the notion that the
divine will cannot be represented by a single system of *fiqh*, and the celebration of diversity are among those foundational grundnorms. In many regards,
one could say that Shariʿah is the unwritten constitutional law of the Islamic
common-law system, but because of the particular historical practices of the
schools of *fiqh*, such a reconceptualization would need to be developed analytically. For instance, it is firmly established in the Islamic legal tradition
that Shariʿah seeks to protect and promote five fundamental values: (1) life;
(2) intellect; (3) reputation or dignity; (4) lineage or family; and (5) property.
Furthermore, Muslim jurists overwhelmingly held that there are three basic
levels of attainment or fulfillment of such values: the necessities, needs, and
luxuries. Under Shariʿah law, legal imperatives increase in proportion to the
level demand for the attainment of each value. Thus, when it comes to life,
for example, the legal duty to secure a person's survival is a priori to the
obligation of guaranteeing human beings any basic needs that are above and
beyond what is necessary for survival. Nevertheless, alongside these broad
fundamental principles, historically, Muslim jurists developed specific positive commandments that were said to be necessary for the protection of the
values mentioned above, such as, for instance, the laws punishing slander,
which were said to be necessary for the protection of reputation or dignity, or
the laws punishing fornication, which were said to be necessary for the
protection of lineage and family. I will discuss the *hudud* penalties later, but
for now it is important to emphasize that many of the positive legal determinations purportedly serving the five values were often declared to be a part of
Shariʿah, and not just *fiqh*, or were left in a rather ambiguous and contested
status between Shariʿah and *fiqh*. Claiming that a positive legal commandment is not a byproduct of *fiqh* but is essentially part of Shariʿah effectively
endowed such a commandment with immunity and immutability. The boundaries between Shariʿah and *fiqh* were negotiated in a variety of highly
contextually contingent ways in the course of Islamic history, but the dynamics and processes of this history remain grossly understudied.

As noted above, the genesis of the schools of *fiqh* was in the localized
regional practices and adjudications of Kufa, Basra, Damascus, Mecca, Medina, Fustat, and other urban centers. But as early as the eighth century,
alongside the state courts run by appointed judges and administrators, already there emerged the widespread phenomenon of privately funded and
endowed centers of legal learning and schools of *fiqh*, usually organized
around the persona of a gifted law teacher. There is a long-established tradition in Islamic history of the state trying to entice or coerce particularly well-
respected and reputable jurists into serving in the state-run judiciary. However, while every founder of a personal school of thought was a *faqih* (jurist),
not every *faqih* agreed to serve as a judge (*qadi*), and not every *qadi* was a

reputable *faqih*. The tension and resistance of legal scholars (*fuqaha'*) to the temptations of power and to the allure of accepting a judicial post (*qada'*) was an ongoing theme of temptation, valor, bravery, and suffering through- out premodern Islamic history. Indeed, within the first three centuries of Islamic legal history, there is a proliferation of schools of *fiqh* and intense competition between the various schools for mass support and for private endowments funding the scholarship of teachers and students. The still-ex- tant Sunni schools are those of: Abu Hanifa (eponym of the Hanafi school), Malik bin Anas (eponym of the Maliki school), Ibn Idris al-Shafi'i (eponym of the Shafi'i school), and Ahmad bin Hanbal (d. 241/855, eponym of the Hanbali school). There are three major Shi'i schools of law: the Ja'faris (named after Ja'far al-Sadiq, d. 148/765), the Zaydis (named after Zayd bin 'Ali, d. 122/739), and the Isma'ilis, with their own unique legal heritage. Other than the Sunnis and Shi'is, there is the legal tradition of the Ibadi school, which descended from the sect of the Khawarij. There are also many extinct schools, such as these of Ibn Abi Layla (d. 148/765), Sufyan al- Thawri (d. 161/777), Ibn Jarir al-Tabari (d. 310/923), 'Abd Allah Ibn Shu- bruma (d. 145/761), al-Layth bin Sa'd (d. 175/791), Sharik al-Nakha'i (d. 187/803), al-Awza'i (d. 158/773), Ibrahim Abu Thawr (d. 240/854), Dawud bin 'Ali bin Khalaf (d. 270/884) (the Zahiris), and many more.

Even in a single school, such as that of Abu Hanifa, there could be several distinctive trends or orientations, such as the positions of Zufar (d. 775), Abu Yusuf (d. 182/798), and al-Shaybani (d. 189/804). Purportedly, by the end of the tenth century, no fewer than one hundred schools of *fiqh* had emerged in the highly competitive legal market, but for a wide variety of reasons most of these schools ultimately failed to survive. Fortunately, however, many of the diverse positions and competing views expounded by extinct schools of thought were documented in huge legal encyclopedias often written by com- petitors, and in some cases, the actual texts of extinct schools have reached us. The most striking characteristic about the legal schools that dominated the practice of law for more than three centuries after the death of the Prophet is their remarkable diversity, and in fact, one would be hard pressed to find any significant legal issue about which juristic disputations and discourses have not generated a large number of divergent opinions and conflicting determinations. At this formative stage, through discursive methods of teach- ing and disputation, the *madhahib* were going through a process of jelling in which not only did they develop their internal mechanisms, particular lin- guistic practices, and systems of discourse, but they also competed for re- sources. The dilemma was that for a variety of theological and political reasons, jurists who associated themselves too closely with the state tended to discredit themselves in the long run, and in the process they ultimately helped to sound their own death knell. Jurists who were more adept in nego- tiating their role so as to avoid the perception of complete subservience to the state, and with it the inevitable loss of stature and credibility, and at the same time, in managing to avoid the ire and brutality of the state, which could invariably make the life of such a school quite challenging, had better chances of survival. In this formative period, each school had to compete to attract the best legal minds and the most promising students to its ranks, and had to be blessed with enthusiastic supporters who enjoyed the charisma and skill to convince affluent families that their children were best educated in this or that particular *madhhab*, or that a generous philanthropic endowment would be a pious way of doing good in this life and the Hereafter. The competition of the *madhahib* or schools of law was not a short-lived phenomenon. The contingencies of history are many, and there are *madhahib* that thrived in Andalusia or Egypt, for instance, but were overcome by another *madhhab* and eventually vanished, and there are *madhahib* that looked like they were on the verge of extinction only to make a triumphant comeback centuries later.

During the age of proliferation, one does notice the incredibly broad expanse of space which came under the legitimate jurisdiction of *fiqh*. Put differently, there did not seem to be many issues in Shari'ah that were off limits for the inquiries of *fiqh*. Rather, the grand, abstract type of questions that were raised when attempting to expound a systematic demarcation of Shari'ah and *fiqh* were handled within the classical *madhahib* through the microtechnicalities of the practice of law. Rather than struggle with the larger abstract conceptual questions, the Shari'ah-*fiqh* balance was negotiated through the microdynamics of legal practice. The broad philosophical issue of theorizing an analytically sound differentiation between the respective provinces of each seems to be a particularly pressing question for Muslim constitutional lawyers in the contemporary age, especially with the challenge of authoritarian religious movements trying to rule in God's name.

Initially, what differentiated one school of law (*madhhab*) from another were methodological disagreements and not necessarily the actual determinations. With the increasing consolidation and institutionalization of schools of thought, each school developed its own distinctive cumulative interpretive culture, structural precedents, and even particular linguistic practices. Importantly, the founders of the schools of *fiqh* and the early jurists in general did not intend to generate binding legal precepts. Rather, acting more like law professors and legal scholars, they produced legal opinions and analysis, which became part of the available common law to be adopted by state-appointed judges in light of regional customary practices. Legal scholars from the different schools of thought were often far more interested in hypotheticals that illustrated their analytical models and methodologies than in passing judgments on actual disputes. This is why *fiqh* studies did not speak in terms of positive legal duties or prohibitions but analyzed legal issues in terms of five values: (1) neutral or permissible (*mubah/halal*); (2) obligatory (*fard/wajib*); (3) forbidden (*muharram*); (4) recommended (*mandub/mustahab*); and (5) reprehensible or disfavored (*makruh*). Frequently, jurists spoke in probabilistic terms, such as saying "what is more correct in our opinion," referring to the prevailing view within the jurist's school of thought (*al-murajja'a 'indana*). The critical point is that the masters of *fiqh* understood that they were not making binding law but issuing opinions of persuasive authority. The difference between *fiqh* and positive law was akin to the distinction between *fatwa* and *hukm*. A *hukm* is a binding and enforceable legal determination, but a *fatwa* (*responsa*) is a legal opinion on a particular dispute, problem, or novel issue, which, by definition, enjoys only persuasive authority. Both *fiqh* and *fatawa* (sing. *fatwa*) become binding law only if adopted as such by a person as a matter of conscience or if adopted as enforceable law by a legitimate authority such as a judge. In other words, *fiqh* and *fatawa* are normative legal proposals that are contingent on essential enabling acts or triggers: the conscientious acceptance of its mandatory authority by a Muslim practitioner or an official adoption by a proper authority. Failure to appreciate this fundamental point about the construction and structure of the legal views expressed in *fiqh* works has led to a great deal of ill-informed and misguided scholarship about Islamic law.

In theory, judges were willing to obey regulatory or administrative laws as long as they did not conflict with Shari'ah principles, but even then the most prominent jurists often resisted judicial appointments because of the fear that they would have to enforce unlawful executive orders. Islamic history is replete with anecdotal stories of legal scholars who refused to accept a judicial appointment unless they had assurances that the ruler and his agents would not interfere with their judgments or unless the judiciary was given its own police force empowered to ensure compliance with judicial determinations. After the Umayyad dynasty (49/661–132/749) and especially after the so-called Mihna (218/833–234/848), which was an Abbasid aborted inquisition against, among other things, the authority of jurists, it became increasingly common to appoint jurists from the emerging schools of law. Unless the case involved a pure administrative or regulatory law problem, which tended to come under the separate jurisdiction of executive *diwans* (*diwan al-mulk*, *diwan al-hukm*, or *diwan al-mu'amalat*, all of which connoted different administrative councils or ministries), typically judges would decide cases on the basis of the precedents of what can be called the regional or local *madhhab* or the regionally established practices and precedents of each *madhhab*. By the end of the tenth century, as more schools of *fiqh* became extinct, thriving schools became increasingly institutionalized and organized as legal guilds with complex processes of training and certification. In turn, only properly trained and certified members of the established legal guilds would be appointed to the judiciary, but there is ample evidence to suggest that after the tenth century, instead of localized or region-specific variations on the *madhhab*, legal schools of thought developed recognized majority and minority positions—majority positions reflected the formal stand of the *madhhab* on recognized legal problems (*al-mu'tamad fi al-madhhab*), and minority positions represented the dissenting opinions that emerged within the schools. Junior judges, in particular, were expected to implement the positions representative of the school, but justices of higher rank, such as the chief justice (*qadi al-quda'*), and respected senior professors had considerably more freedom in adopting minority views or advocating for a change in the law.

One of the most entrenched myths about Islamic law is that the legal system has ceased to develop or change since the tenth or eleventh centuries because, fearing diversity and fragmentation, the so-called doors of *ijtihad* were declared to be forever closed. According to this claim, Muslim jurists were expected to imitate their predecessors (practice of *taqlid*) without undertaking legal innovations (*ijtihad*). This myth seems to have emerged in the nineteenth century as a simplistic explanation of the purported stagnation of the Islamic legal system and as justification for the legal reforms of the time, which in reality amounted to little more than the importation of Euro-

pean legal systems. More importantly, this myth persisted among contemporary scholars because of the paucity of studies on the microdynamics of
Islamic law and because of the failure to properly understand some of the
basic historical realities about the development of the Islamic legal system.

By the eleventh century, the major legal schools had organized into institutionalized and structured guilds. Not only had the processes of legal training and certification become well established, but various genres of legal
literature and their different functions had become well defined. Significantly, the threshold for establishing new legal schools or guilds was much
higher after older schools had the opportunity to become more socially and
economically rooted. Instead of the uphill battle of founding a new *madhhab*,
it was much more feasible for even the most talented jurists to join an already
established school of law and rise in the ranks through regular channels.
Taqlid was not the instrument of legal stagnation; it was an important functional instrument of the rule of law. In general, *taqlid* stabilized the law by
requiring continuity in legal application and by creating a legal presumption
in favor of precedents unless a heightened burden of evidence was met in
justifying legal change. In principle, judges of the first instance were expected to follow the same rule of law from case to case, and students and
junior scholars of the law were required to first apply the existing methodology and determination of the *madhhab* to which they belonged. Higher-ranked
judges and scholars enjoying greater qualifications and stature were able to
initiate *de novo* legal determinations (*ijtihad*). Indeed, many of the most
important developments in Islamic law were accomplished by jurists centuries after the supposed doors of *ijtihad* were closed.

The essential point about the Islamic legal tradition, and especially the
role of *fiqh*, is that the juristic method and the linguistic practices of cumulative communities of legal interpretation became not only the mechanism for
legitimacy and authority but also the actual source of law. As a community of
guilded specialists with an elaborate system of insignia and rituals, in most
cases structured around a system resembling the Inns of Court in England,
the jurists played a critical role in upholding the rule of law and in mediating
between the masses and rulers. However, the primacy of the juristic method
and the organized guilds representing the various schools of law, contrary to
some stereotypical claims, did not mean that the application of Islamic law
became completely streamlined or simply mechanical and formulaic. Within
a single *madhhab* it was common for various juristic temperaments and
philosophical orientations to exist because the established schools of law
became the common platforms where conservative or activist jurists had to
pursue their legal agendas or objectives. Within a single established school of
thought there could be conservative, traditionalist, rationalist, or equity-
oriented trends, but each of these orientations had to negotiate its particular
approach within the demands of the juristic method of the *madhhab*. Far
from being formulaic or mechanical, some late jurists such as Fakhr al-Din
al-Razi (d. 606/1210), Sayf al-Din al-Amidi (d. 631/1233), Taj al-Din al-
Subki (d. 756/1370), and Ibn 'Aqil (d. 513/1119) achieved unprecedented
advancements in the use of systematic and analytical reasoning in Islamic
jurisprudence. In the case of a Shafi'i jurist such as al-Subki and a Hanbali
jurist such as Ibn 'Aqil, it is fair to say that methodologically, they became

the embodiment of the Latin maxim *ratio est radius divini luminis* (reason is a ray of divine light). Some jurists such as the Hanafi Ibn 'Abidin (d. 1252/ 1836) and the Maliki al-Shatibi (d. 790/1388) systematically integrated custom as a source of law in novel and original ways.[20] In addition, jurists from various Islamic schools of thought continued to employ concepts such as *istihsan* and *istislah* (the exercise of juristic preference in favor of a precedent not directly on point instead of a preference that is on point because of equity, in the former, and public interest, in the latter) as legitimate sources of law.[21] But these were not instruments allowing the exercise of unfettered juristic discretion. Rather, jurists developed a set of limiting criteria intended to make the process of exercising legal preferences more systematic and accountable to the juristic method.[22] Fundamentally, whether a particular legal orientation emphasized the use of the text, reason, custom, equity, or public interest, these tools had to be justified, channeled, negotiated, and limited by the juristic method.[23] The point is not just that the juristic method became the prevalent mechanism for negotiating the tools and instruments of legal analysis, but even more, the juristic method became Islamic law itself; it became the mechanism for negotiating not just the relationship between Shari'ah and *fiqh*, but the relationship between the realm of God and that of humans and, ultimately, between the sacred and the profane.

THE SACRED AND PROFANE IN ISLAMIC LAW

The relationship between the sacred and profane was negotiated in Islamic law through the ongoing historical dynamics demarcating the boundaries between Shari'ah and *fiqh*. But beyond this, there were several other conceptual categories and functional mechanisms through which sacred and temporal spaces were negotiated in Islamic law. Among these categories was the conceptual differentiation between *'ibadat* (laws dealing with matters of ritual) and *mu'amalat* (laws pertaining to human dealings and intercourses).[24] In theory, all Islamic laws are divided into one of these two categories: *'ibadat* are laws that regulate the relationship between God and humans, and *mu'amalat* are laws that regulate the relationship of humans with one another. As to issues falling under the category of *'ibadat*, there is a legal presumption in favor of literalism and for the rejection of any innovations or novel practices. However, in the case of *mu'amalat*, the opposite presumption applies; innovations or creative determinations are favored (*al-asl fi al-'ibadat al-'ittiba' wa al-asl fi al-mu'amalat al-'ibtida'*). The rationale behind this categorical division is that when it comes to space occupied exclusively by how people worship the divine, there is a presumption against deference to human reason, material interests, and discretion. Conversely, in space occupied by what the jurists used to describe as the pragmatics of social interaction, there is a presumption in favor of the rational faculties and practical experiences of human beings. Underscoring the difference between *'ibadat* and *mu'amalat* was the fact that not only were the two identified as distinct and separate fields and specialties of law, but it was also quite possible to specialize and become an authority in one field but not the other (*fiqh al-'ibadat* or *fiqh al-mu'amalat*).

Beyond this clean categorical division, negotiating the extent to which a particular human act or conduct, whether it be public or private, primarily involved *'ibadat* or *mu'amalat* was not a simple and unequivocal issue. For instance, there were lengthy debates as to whether the prohibition of *zina* (fornication or adultery) or consumption of alcoholic substances falls under the category of *'ibadat* or *mu'amalat* or alternatively some mixture of both categories. Nevertheless, as in the case of the debates regarding the parameters of Shari'ah and *fiqh*, although in principle there was a philosophical recognition that the spaces occupied by the sacred and profane require different treatments, in reality, it is the juristic method that played the defining role in determining the function of text, precedent, and rational innovation in the treatment of legal questions. Ultimately, it was not the legal presumptions attaching to either category but the institutional and methodological processes of each legal school of thought that most influenced the way issues were analyzed and determined.

It is in the historical practice of schools of thought, and especially on questions of procedure, jurisdiction, conflict of laws, and the compulsory powers of courts, that one finds the most pronounced negotiations of the space and balance between the sacred and profane. For instance, throughout Islamic history, courts rarely took jurisdiction of matters involving *'ibadat* such as performance of prayers. In a rather large genre of literature dealing with the laws of adjudication (*ahkam al-qada'*), administrative and executive laws (*ahkam al-hisba* and *al-siyasa al-Shar'iyya*), and the functions of the *muhtasib*, who in classical practice were usually market inspectors, Muslim jurists differentiated between judicial and executive functions. Related and overlapping discussions are also found in treatises dealing with the private and public normative obligation to enjoin the good and resist what is wrong (*al-amr bi al-ma'ruf wa al-nahy 'an al-munkar*). In this literature and in the actual historical practice, courts did not take jurisdiction of a matter unless there was an actual or real conflict. Courts had the duty to issue *ahkam* (judgments) and not *fatawa* (responses). At the same time, the authority and discretion of the executive to dispense summary justice or deal out summary penalties was restricted. Among other limitations, in any particular case, if either the law or the facts were disputed, the matter had to be referred to the judiciary. Only the judiciary had the legitimate power to interpret the law and establish the facts in any dispute. Interestingly, although varying according to time and place, it was not unusual for litigants to appoint a *wakil* (agent or lawyer) to argue on their behalf in civil cases, and it was common for litigants to solicit and obtain a *fatwa* in support from respected jurists, and judges considered such conflicting *responsa* as advisory or persuasive authority. Furthermore, contrary to the unfounded generalizations that plague the field, again depending on time and place, very often there was an appellate process and sophisticated procedural rules regulating the circumstances under which a higher court may overrule a lower court within the same jurisdiction or fail to recognize the judgment of another Islamic court from a different jurisdiction.

Perhaps as a practical result of the epistemology of plural orthodoxy, in Islamic jurisprudence, a court's judgment or finding was not equated with or considered the same as God's judgment. At a normative level, a court's judgment could not right a wrong or wrong a right, and it could not negate or replace the duties and responsibilities imposed by an individual's conscience. Jurists argued that individuals do have an obligation to obey court decisions as a matter of law and order, but judicial determinations do not reflect or mirror God's judgment. A classic example would be of a litigant who, for instance, follows the Hanafi school of thought and is forced to submit to the jurisdiction of a Shafi'i court. The Hanafi litigant would have to obey the judgment of the court not because it is correct, but because a duly constituted court possesses legitimate positive authority (*sultat al-ilzam*). Not surprisingly, the proper balance between the duty of obedience to the public order and the duty to follow one's conscience, or school of thought, has been the subject of considerable jurisprudential debates. It was argued that at times it becomes incumbent to disobey a lawful judgment or command even if this might mean having to suffer negative repercussions. Typically, this involved situations where a person conscientiously believes that harm or injury would be done to innocent parties or scenarios implicating personal virtue or honor, such as marital status. In the classical juristic tradition, there are situations where the state, acting through a judge, could rightfully punish disobedience to its commands, and yet an individual would have an obligation to disobey the state's commands. In the Hereafter, God would reward such an individual for his sincerity and at the same time possibly reward the judge for his effort.

Because of the reality of pluralist legal orthodoxy, in Islamic jurisprudence it is entirely conceivable even where Shari'ah is the law of the land that an individual legitimately would feel torn between his duties toward the public order and God. The legitimacy of the state and even the law were not absolute—both state and law performed a functional but necessary role. Beyond the fact that the state could not act as a proxy for God, legal determinations could not void the necessary role of personal beliefs or individual conscience because they did not replace the sovereignty of divine judgments.

A product of the institutions of legal pluralism was the rather fascinating but little understood practice of multiple territorially overlapping legal jurisdictions. There were many historical examples of governments establishing as many as four court judicial jurisdictions, each following a different *madhhab*, with a challengingly complex set of conflict-of-laws rules regulating subject matter and *in personam* jurisdiction. Normally, however, the predominant *madhhab* affiliation of the population of a region would play a determinative role on the *madhhab* followed by a court. Furthermore, frequently there was a senior or chief judge settling issues of adjudicatory law within each *madhhab*. In addition, a common practice was to appoint a supreme chief judge who enjoyed ultimate appellate authority, as far as the positive law was concerned, over all the judicial jurisdictions. Although the research in this field is poorly developed, there is considerable evidence that the supreme chief judge, although personally belonging to a particular *madhhab*, in his official function sought to resolve conflict among the jurisdictions through synchronistic or conciliatory methodology known as *al-tawfiq bayn al-madhahib* (resolving and balancing between the differences among the schools of legal thought), which was a well-developed jurisprudential field and specialty.

THE RIGHTS OF GOD AND THE RIGHTS OF HUMANS

Perhaps the clearest articulation in Islamic jurisprudence of the distinctive spaces occupied by the sacred and profane is the categorical differentiation between the rights of God (*huquq Allah*) and rights of humans (*huquq al-'ibad*). Muslim jurists agreed that humans cannot benefit or harm God, and so, unlike the rights owed to human beings, the rights of God do not involve any actual interests of God. Depending on the context, the word *huquq* (sing. *haqq*) referred to the province, jurisdiction, boundaries, or limits of God (*hudud Allah*). Interestingly, *huquq al-'ibad* did not refer to public or common rights but to the material interests and benefits belonging to each human being as an individual. The rights of God do not need a protector or vindicator because God is fully capable of redressing any transgressions committed against His boundaries or commands. But unlike God, human beings do need an agent empowered to defend them and redress any transgressions committed against their person or properties. Therefore, the state is not simply empowered but obligated to enforce the rights and obligations owed to people and may not legitimately ignore them or wave away. The state was precluded from enforcing the rights of God because the state was not God's representative and God had reserved these rights to his exclusive jurisdiction and province.

Muslim jurists clearly recognized the exceptionality and exclusivity of the sacred space and even jealously guarded it from the encroachments of the profane. Ironically, however, it is in dealing with the issue of God's clear boundaries and limits that the jurists most famously collapsed the sacred and profane into a single space, at least in theory if not in application. In what is known as the *hudud* penalties, Muslim jurists asserted that there is a category of divinely ordained punishments that apply to violations committed against a class of mixed rights (*huquq mukhtalita*), which are shared by God and human beings. As a category, mixed rights involve issues where the material interests or well-being of people are involved but at the same time, there is a discernable divine will staking a specific claim for the divine over these issues. In the case of the divinely ordained *hudud* penalties, for reasons not necessarily known to human beings, God purportedly not only explicitly determined the punishable act and the exact penalty but also the exact process by which the crime is proved and the penalty is carried out. Although not all the *hudud* crimes were mentioned in the text of the Qur'an, a general juristic consensus was said to exist as to the divine origin of the penalties. In the classical tradition, fornication or adultery (*zina*), robbery (*sariqa*), consumption of alcohol, defamation (*qadhf*), and apostasy (*ridda*) were the violations most commonly included within the *hudud*. The real paradox of the *hudud* is that while in contemporary Islam they are often imagined to be the harbinger and flagship of Islamic law, in the classical tradition the *hudud* penalties were rarely applied precisely because of the space occupied by the divine in defining and redressing the crime. On the one hand, by categorizing a crime under the *hudud*, the definition of the crime and the appropriate penalty became sanctified and immutable. But on the other hand, by placing it within the category of *hudud*, the jurists effectively endowed the penalty with a largely symbolic role because the technical requirements and administrative costs of enforcing these sacred penalties were largely prohibitive. As with all matters involving the rights of God, as far as the state is concerned, it is imperative to tread cautiously lest in trying to uphold the bounds of God, whether through ignorance, arrogance, or incompetence, the state itself ends up committing an infraction against the divine. The Prophet Muhammad's injunction, which was adapted into a legal maxim, commanded that any doubt must serve to suspend the application of the *hudud*. In addition to the presumption of innocence in application as to all criminal accusations, Muslim jurists often cited the injunction above in greatly circumscribing the application of the *hudud* penalties through a variety of doctrinal and procedural hurdles. In general, repentance, forgiveness, and doubt acted to prevent the application of the *hudud*. In dealing with the rights of God, it was always better to forgive than to punish; repentance of the defendant acted to suspend the *hudud*, and all doubt had to be construed in favor of vindicating the accused.

As far as the classical jurists were concerned, the *hudud*, like all matters implicating the rights of God, were better left to divine vindication in the Hereafter. In most cases, instead of pursuing a *hudud* penalty, the state proved a lesser included crime under a less demanding burden of proof and applied lesser penalties, normally involving imprisonment, some form of corporal punishment, banishment, or a fine. Lesser penalties for non-*hudud* crimes, or lesser included crimes, fell into two categories: *qisas* (talion) or *ta'zir* (penalties prescribed by the state for offenses against public interest). *Qisas* was treated as a private recourse and right, where pardon or forgiveness was always preferable, but *ta'zir* were thoroughly profane punitive measures left to the authority and jurisdiction of the state applied to protect the public through deterrence. Classical Muslim jurists enunciated various principles regulating and restricting the powers of the state over *ta'zir* punishments, such as the precept that no crime is committed unless there is prior notice and the ban against *ex post facto* findings of guilt. Muslim jurists stressed that summary executive punishments are impermissible in all cases involving contested questions of fact or law and that all such cases must be referred to the judiciary. Moreover, many classical jurists placed a limit on the number of lashes that could be imposed on a defendant, typically with the cap ranging from thirty to a hundred lashes, depending on the nature of the criminal offense and the record of the offender. Fundamentally, however, while *hudud* punishments were greatly circumscribed, throughout Islamic history what and how *ta'zir* punishments were applied greatly varied from one time and place to another.

By circumscribing the enforcement of the rights of divine, the classical jurists of Islam constrained the power of the state to act as God's avenger. However, doctrinally the rights of God, as a concept, played an important normative and ethical role in the Shari'ah dynamics taking place within Muslim societies. The rights of God symbolically represented the moral boundaries of appropriate social mores and values in the public space. This does not mean, as some contemporary reformists have claimed, that the rights of God are equivalent to or substantially the same as public interests or space. Normatively, the Shari'ah is expected to pervade the private and public spaces by appealing to the private consciences of individuals and to soci-

eties as collectivities. But there is one way this could happen, and that is
through voluntary compliance. For the most part, Islamic jurisprudence invoked the compulsory powers of the state in order to enforce obligations or
rights owed to people—not to God. Functionally, Islamic law was thought of
not as a means for empowering the state to act on God's behalf but as setting
limits to the powers of the state through the imposition of the rule of law.
Therefore, the greater legacy of the Islamic tradition deals with questions
involving *mu'amalat* or social intercourses and dealings or the resolution of
conflicts arising from competing claims and interests. Questions of social
etiquette or proper public manners were not treated in books of jurisprudence
but were relegated to the status of moralistic pamphlets (*kutub al-raqa'iq*)
written often by religious preachers or sometimes by qualified jurists for the
consumption of the laity.

MODERNITY AND THE DETERIORATION OF ISLAMIC LAW

With the advent of the age of colonialism, the Islamic legal system was
consistently replaced by legal systems imported from Western colonial
states. The factors contributing to the deterioration and replacement of Islamic law are numerous, but primary among those factors was the pressure
exerted by foreign powers for a system of concessions and special jurisdictions that served the economic and political interests of the colonizers and a
parasitical native elite that derived and maintained its privileged status from
the financial, military, and cultural institutions of colonial powers. Frequently, colonial powers and their dependent native elites found that their economic and commercial interests were not well served by the pluralism and localized indeterminacy of the Islamic legal system. In response, some colonial
powers such as Great Britain created hybrid legal institutions such as the
Mixed Courts of Egypt and the Anglo-Muhammadan courts of India. Of
greater significance, however, was the fact that colonial powers and their
native ruling elites found that the organized legal guilds and the system of
religious endowments (*awqaf*) that supported these guilds leveraged a considerable amount of power that was often used to resist the hegemonic powers of the modern state. Throughout the Muslim world, this led to a protracted process by which colonial powers or, in the postcolonial age, local
nationalistic governments consistently undermined the autonomy of and
eventually completely controlled the traditional legal guilds and the network
of religious endowments, not only depriving them of any meaningful political role but also deconstructing their very legitimacy in Muslim societies.

Perhaps more destructive to the Islamic legal system was the fact that the
institutional replacement of Islamic law was accompanied by a process of
cultural transformation that led to the deconstruction of the very epistemological foundations of Islamic jurisprudence. Colonial powers not only exerted considerable pressures toward greater legal uniformity and determinism, but in what has been described as a process of cultural invasion, both
the ruling elites and intelligentsia of various Muslim societies turned mostly
to Western and, to a much lesser extent, Eastern Europe for inspiration and
guidance in all fields of the arts and sciences. Increasingly, educational insti-

tutions and systems in the Muslim world were fashioned or remodeled along the lines of the educational systems of the major colonial powers. From the beginning of the nineteenth century onward and to this very day, an academic degree from Western schools became a cultural symbol of prestige and privilege. In the legal field, a Western education became a powerful venue for upward professional mobility and social status, and this led to a marked deterioration in the position and authority of classical Muslim jurists as well as in the role of the centuries-old schools of Shari'ah law all over the Muslim world.

The cultural impact of colonialism on Muslim societies was and continues to be immeasurable. In the nineteenth century, the Western-educated intelligentsia played a critical role in the birth of the reform movement that sought to modernize Islamic law. In response to the transplantation of European codes of law into the Muslim world, especially in the 1850s and 1860s, Muslim legal experts, most often trained in Western institutions, sought to reform Islamic law by making it more deterministic, uniform, and predictable. In most cases, this amounted to a process of codification, the most famous of which was the Ottoman Mejelle (also known as *Majallat al-Ahkam al-'Adliyya*) completed in 1877. But these efforts at reform meant challenging the epistemological foundations of the Islamic legal system and a radical reinvention of Islamic law from a common law–like system to a system tailored after the civil law, especially the Napoleonic Code of 1804. Very frequently, legal reformers unwittingly transformed Islamic law from a system of common laws united by shared communities of legal sources, methodological and analytical tools, technical linguistic practices, and a coherent system of authoritativeness and legitimacy to something that, other than being a compilation of deterministic commands, held little coherence and was strangely at odds with the system of law that had existed for well over a thousand years.

Perhaps among the cultural and intellectual transformations that contributed a great deal to the retreat of Islamic law in the contemporary age was the birth of the myth of "the closing of the doors" of *ijtihad* in the nineteenth century. It appears that this myth was invented by Orientalist scholars, many of whom were enlisted in the service of imperial colonial powers, and who, as part of carrying the "White Man's Burden" of civilizing backwards native cultures, sought to convince the native intelligentsia that Islamic law had ceased developing around a thousand years ago. According to the myth of closing the doors of *ijtihad* in the fourth/tenth century, Muslim jurists decided that all the questions of the divine law have been now and forever answered, and therefore, legal innovations or original determinations are not necessary and are no longer permitted. According to the myth, ever since the doors were closed, Muslim lawyers have practiced blind imitation or *taqlid*. This unsupported historical claim was frequently exploited in the context of justifying the replacement of Islamic law with transplanted Western law and also in restricting the jurisdiction of Shari'ah courts to the fields of family and personal law. Although Orientalist scholars might have invented and exploited this myth, the fact remains that Muslim intellectuals from all over the Muslim world accepted this fiction as a settled historical fact and constructed reform agendas and stratagems on the assumption that the reopening of the proverbial doors of *ijtihad* was a talismanic solution to all the challenges and woes of Islamic law in the modern age.

Both the reform movements emphasizing codification or the practice of *ijtihad* were symptomatic of a more ingrained and obstinate cultural problem. Islamic schools that used to provide training for the judges, lawyers, and law professors no longer attracted the best and brightest students because job opportunities, higher levels of pay, and professional respect and prestige had all migrated to the non-Shari'ah European-style schools of law. Throughout the second half of the nineteenth century and the first half of the twentieth century, Islamic courts and law were abolished and replaced by transplanted Western legal systems. The lasting impact of these developments was that successive generations of Muslim lawyers were very poorly trained in Islamic law and thus became increasingly alienated and distant from their own native legal tradition. In most parts of the Muslim world, lawyers by virtue of their training gained technical competence in the legal systems of their former colonizers as they grew more disassociated and distant from their own Islamic legal heritage. In short, the process that unfolded all over the Muslim world meant that the most gifted and competent legal minds found Islamic law to be marginal to their professional activity, and those who did attend the few Islamic law schools that remained in the Muslim world, in most cases, were not gifted or talented legal minds. But even worse, having become state owned and very often state controlled institutions, the surviving Islamic schools of law no longer offered legal curricula that provided adequate training for lawyers. Therefore, in most Muslim countries, training in Shari'ah does not qualify the student to join the lawyers' guild or bar, appear in court, or undertake any of the functions typically reserved for professional lawyers.

The 1970s and 1980s witnessed a highly politicized attempt at reasserting and reviving the role of Islamic law in Muslim societies. The reasons for this revival were many, but they included a long list of economic, political, and cultural grievances, all of which were made more acute by mass frustrations with the authoritarianism, ineffectiveness, and corruption of many of the governments ruling Muslim societies in the postcolonial age. Much of the populist revivalism was met with severe state repression, which usually followed short-lived periods of governmental accommodation or begrudging tolerance. The impact of the confrontations and political violence between dictatorial governments and Islamic movements was the further radicalization of those who suffered the ire of the state and survived. Such radicalization led to the articulation of visions of Islamic law that were severely distorted by siege mentalities that, inspired by their own sufferings, challenged the legitimacy of ethical principles and the practicality of insisting on lawful means. Not surprisingly, radicalized movements had no patience, use, or even opportunity to engage the layered discourses of the Islamic jurisprudential tradition.

Alongside the repression, a number of governments in the Muslim world attempted to bolster their legitimacy by engaging in highly symbolic gestures of perceived Islamicity, such as amending state constitutions to add a provision declaring that Shari'ah is the source of all legislation, or by purportedly Islamizing particular provisions in their criminal and commercial codes. Substantively, however, the state-led Islamization initiatives were of very little consequence because they were readily understood to be publicity ploys pursued for their symbolic value and not for any normative commitment in favor of the regeneration of the Islamic legal system. These so-called Islamization campaigns were undertaken to mitigate the political effects of repressing Islamic movements and to persuade the masses that the state was no less committed to Islamic law than its foes. But even in rare cases where governments were genuinely committed to Islamization or when Islamists did in fact succeed to one extent or another in coming to power, the results were still pitiful. The problem remained a product of dual impediments. On the one hand, those who were skilled and gifted lawyers were not rooted in or in command of the Islamic jurisprudential system, and on the other hand, those who qualified as *fuqaha'* in the modern age no longer received the training that would qualify them as lawyers in any real sense. The irony is that the mythology of closing the doors of *ijtihad* and the popularized belief that reform requires a reopening of the gates was used to make Islamic law more accessible to activists who enjoyed no specialized competence either in Islamic law or in legal reasoning and practice in general. Reopening the proverbial doors became the means for licensing a chaotic condition where numerous participants under the slogan of practicing *ijtihad* claimed to be authoritative experts of Islamic law. So, for instance, many of the leaders of Islamic movements were by training engineers or computer scientists, and many of the most popular and influential voices of reform were never trained in law, leave alone Islamic law. Predictably, as the twentieth century came to a close and the twenty-first century began, the field of Islamic law suffered a crippling crisis of authority as Muslims struggled to rediscover the rules and criteria for defining the authoritative in modern Islamic law. The fact remains, however, that as a legal tradition Islamic law continues to carry considerable normative weight for millions of Muslims around the world and also continues to influence, to one degree or another, the legal systems of a number of countries. The crisis of authority plaguing Islamic law today does not affect its relevance or importance. But it does mean that Islamic law does not have the effective means for regulating the reasonableness of the determinations generated on its behalf or attributed to it. In the contemporary age, many voices speak in the name of Islamic law, and the problem is that some of these voices are quite unreasonable.

Part I

The Islamic Dream and the Chaos of the Modern Condition

Chapter One

Genesis: Negotiating the Muslim and the Islamic

GROWING UP WITH THE ISLAMIC DREAM

Every morning, I woke up to the melodic sounds of the Qur'an blazing from the radio. The first thing my mother would do each morning was turn on the radio to the Qur'an station broadcasting from Cairo. The tranquil sounds of Qur'anic recitation would restore us to a state of serene consciousness. After the ablutions and morning prayers, laboriously, my siblings and I would get dressed and prepare for school. My mother would prepare for her daily struggle of trying to convince us to eat breakfast. Unfailingly, she would declare to her recalcitrant audience, "Your poor bodies need the fuel! This is the most important meal in the day, and you'll even do better in school!" On those days that I would quietly take the sandwich from her extended hand, she would burst out in euphoric supplications: "May God bless you, and bring you happiness like the happiness you've brought me! May God strengthen and aid you, and not waste your efforts and labor! May God accept and bless your *jihad*, *ya Rabb*!"[1] This, however, paled in comparison to the prayers we would get if we made my mother truly happy—accepting from her what we endearingly referred to as the "super jihad sandwich"— sliced pita bread with a generous portion of honey in the middle. My mother would remind us persistently that no less an authority than God had vouched for the curative effects of that sickly sweet substance, and indeed, in the chapter titled "The Bees," the Qur'an states that from the bellies of bees comes a drink of various hues, which contains a cure and medicine for human beings.[2] Without exception, each morning my mother would prepare the "super jihad sandwich," while being fully aware that the chances were that the honey would not find its way from the bellies of bees to our rebellious and seditious bellies. We were all believers in the powers of my mother's prayers, and the minute we would accept her offering of the "super jihad sandwich," she would break out in passionate supplications: "Ya Allah, ya

3

Allah,[3] protect them from all disease! Make them successful in every step! Allow them to enjoy the fruits of their jihad on this earth and in the Here-after! Bless them with Your love and the love of all that You've created, and instill the Qur'an in their hearts and minds—may they always be guided by Your word!" But chomping on the "super jihad sandwich" needed a brave palate, and on most mornings our bravery betrayed us.

The reason we called the disproportionate combination of pita bread and honey the "super jihad sandwich" was not because of its propensity to induce violence. Of course, my mother was not nurturing us on the idea of religious violence or holy war, and she would have been horrified if she had known that in the West the word *jihad* has become a code word for holy war. Many friends and family members proudly carried the first name "Jihad," and they most definitely were not walking declarations of war against infidels! Jihad, for my mother, as it does for most Muslims, means perseverance, endurance, and exertion toward excellence. And as far as the "super jihad sandwiches" were concerned, the name simply reflected my mother's belief that eating this sandwich transformed one into a virtual energy machine, prepared to strive and struggle without rest or pause. At least, that was her belief, and I never verified whether this belief had a basis in science.

Our stubbornness over the breakfast issue was not the only challenge of these blissful mornings in Kuwait. After resolving, in one way or another, the issue of breakfast, we piled into my father's car to be driven to our schools. My mother, who was a social worker in the state mental health hospital, always departing after we did, carpooled to her work. My father, a lawyer, was a partner in a successful law firm of six or seven lawyers. His sole partner in the firm was a frivolous and incompetent Kuwaiti lawyer who spent all of his time trading on the stock market and flying to Cyprus to court a pretty blonde woman who was the age of his daughter. Eventually, while visiting Egypt, this pretty blonde was believed to have murdered this Kuwaiti partner, but no one could prove it, and she got away with it—got away with it at least in this earthly life. Although the Kuwaiti partner hardly brought in any business to the law firm and rarely did any legal work, by law, he owned a majority interest in the legal practice.[4] For reasons that are still not clear to me, my father was obsessed with the idea of arriving at his work early in the morning, so that when the Kuwaiti partner, as usual, strolled in late, he would find my father pillared behind his desk. My father's obsession meant that we all had to be dropped off early—at least an hour—before the start of school. I hated the frantic morning rush to jump into the car and the nonleisurely drive—this beat-your-partner-to-work thing was my father's personal jihad, and we had to respect it, of course while reserving our right to whine and complain about it to our hearts' content.

The drive to school was typically an anxiety-filled ordeal. As soon as we started driving, my father was in the habit of surfing radio stations for inter-national news. At least for the six years that I remember, there was never pleasant news. Every single morning, the news was practically a litany of tragedies and then more tragedies. Invariably, a newscaster speaking in a solemn voice that sounded detached and even monotone would announce: today, in the Iran-Iraq War, a number of people were killed; in Lebanon, there has been another Israeli air raid or bombardment and a number of people were injured or killed; in Syria, a number of people were killed in clashes between the government and the Muslim Brotherhood; in Egypt, there have been more arrests and also more killed in clashes between government forces and extremist Islamic groups; there has been a new car-bomb explosion in Lebanon; there has been renewed violence in Sudan, Yemen, and the western territories of Morocco; and there has been renewed violence in the Palestinian occupied territories and further house demolitions by the Israeli army.

I usually reacted to the daily list of tragedies by suffering a comatose state of sleepiness. The morning Qur'anic recitation always brought me to a state of tranquil alertness, but the news brought about a sleepy stupor. The feeling of sorrow over all the pain and agony created this lethargic feeling of heaviness and sleepiness, but we did not feel at risk or in danger of being harmed. Living in the small Emirate of Kuwait, we felt insulated and safe—of course, these events all took place before the Iraqi invasion of Kuwait. Every once in a while, we would hear rumors of a possible invasion of Kuwait by Saddam Hussein, but it was difficult to take these rumors seriously. After invading Iran, Saddam had his bloody hands rather full with his homicidal efforts to choke the living daylights out of the Persians, the Shi'is, and the Kurds in his own country. In Kuwait, the prevailing image of Saddam was certainly homicidal but also comic. Iraqi television broadcasts easily reached Kuwait City, and on occasion, curious viewers would check out the unrelenting but simple-minded propaganda coming out of Iraq. Time after time, Iraqi television showed Saddam barging in unannounced on homes, going into the kitchen, and tasting the food being cooked. Saddam did this to prove that his people had plenty to eat, and I guess also to assess his people's gourmet abilities. Perhaps the endless jokes repeated in Kuwait about Saddam, his potbelly, and his insane inspections of private kitchens betrayed a sense of concealed fear and anxiety about the unstable leader to the north. But sometimes it is tempting to hold on to the pretense of safety lest the sense of fear brings forth the demons at the threshold.

The false sense of security that we enjoyed in Kuwait did not temper the sheer sense of sorrow that we felt listening to the news every morning. After a daily dosage of destruction and violence, a person might become numb and stop reacting, but the surreptitious impact on one's sense of beauty and hope was pestilential and baneful. All the death and destruction gnaws away at one's sensibilities, as if digging a deep hole in one's soul that becomes filled with a relentless and unwavering sense of sorrow. Upon hearing of a tragedy, in response the Prophet Muhammad would supplicate: "There is no power or strength, save in God." And throughout the drive, I would pensively mumble the same supplication, while wondering whether, when I grew up and as the driver of my own car, I would exercise my sovereign right to control the radio dial if the news remained so grim. It was difficult to come to terms with the fact of growing up in an area of the world that suffered from so many crushing disappointments and from so much visible pain, but I sincerely believed that things were bound to get better. Perhaps it was wishful thinking, but I believed that Islam would guide the way to a bright and glorious future. Islam was the solution—when Islam was reclaimed and Muslims became true to Islam, most of our problems would end, and Muslims would reclaim their past glories.

There was nothing violent or sociopathic about this belief. Perhaps this belief was naïve, but it was hardly criminal. Furthermore, there was nothing remotely anti-Western about this conviction. The restoration of Muslims to their rightful place in history was not to be accomplished at the expense of the West. There was no necessary correlation between a golden age for Islam and the infliction of harm or misery on the West. Moreover, there was nothing necessarily antidemocratic about the dream of an Islamic golden age. A very large number of Muslims believe not only that Islam mandates a democratic system of governance but even more, that the Prophet was among the founding fathers of constitutionalism and democracy. The point was not to think of Islam as an antidote to the West or its democracy but to think of Islam as an antidote to corruption, injustice, despotism, apathy, blind tribalism, and nationalism.

Like many in my position, I had no idea how Islam would become the vehicle for fulfilling so many social and political dreams. I simply had the solid conviction that in the same way that true piety led the early Muslims to establish a sparkling civilization, so would true piety do the same in the modern age. It was commonly said that in the modern age, Muslims have tried every ideology and system—socialism, pan-Arabism, nationalism, and capitalism—that all had failed, and it was due time that we gave Islam a chance.

My father, who would continue to fiddle indefatigably with the radio dial, placed all his trust in democracy. He had lived for about a year in Buffalo, New York, and always remembered his time in the United States fondly. I am not sure if his unwavering and stolid belief in democracy as a cure-all was somehow connected to this US visit, but he persistently argued that democracy was the key to solving all of the problems of the Middle East. To my father, it was not so much the idea of individual liberty that made democracy so appealing, but the idea of accountability and accessibility. Democracies made governments accessible and accountable to their citizens, and therefore, there existed a greater opportunity to expose and resist political and economic corruption. According to my father, compared to all other political systems, democracies offered the best possibility of justice, and it was the lack of justice that was at the heart of all our problems in the Middle East. Importantly, my father's commitment to democracy did not in any way mean that he distrusted or did not believe in the so-called Islamic solution. For my father, and for many of his generation, democracy was the Islamic solution. There was no contradiction between the demands of democracy and the just order that Islam sought to establish and promote in the world. Despotism, my father believed, was fundamentally at odds with democracy but also at odds with Islam.

Unlike my father, and rather typical of my generation, I was not opposed to democracy, but for me Islam—not democracy—was the objective and end all. I, and so many of my generation, believed that the priority was to rekindle the so-called Islamic order, and the rest would follow. We presumed that the Islamic order would inevitably lead to justice, fairness, and even democracy. But to our minds, the priority was to reclaim an order modeled after what the Prophet achieved more than fourteen hundred years ago in the city of Medina. In hindsight, the difference between my father and me was that he believed in a democratic solution, but I believed in an Islamic dream.

THE NIGHTMARE OF 9/11 AND ITS AFTERMATH

Although the Islamic dream could not induce me to eat my mother's "super jihad sandwiches," it was a great comfort to me in the anxiety-filled morning drives to school. If my father made a nervous remark about the bleakness of our future, in exasperation he followed it with: "There is no strength or power save in God." I would repeat the supplication but then sleepily retract a side of my cheeks into a knowing snicker, and I would say nothing else. God willing, I would confidently think to myself, the day will come when everything will be fine—it was only a matter of time.

Of course, things never got to be fine, and to this day, listening to the news still produces the same sense of anxiety and trauma that I felt then. I, however, do not have my father's fortitude, and I try to avoid listening to the news whenever possible. But how can one avoid the virtual deluge of bad news? How can one avoid confronting the reality that from the 1970s and 1980s to the 2000s, the political and economic condition of the Middle East and a good part of the Muslim world have steadily gone from bad to worse? Even if one religiously avoids listening to any media broadcasts, the trage-dies of terrorism, violence, and suffering chase after each person and force themselves on the conscience of every human being. On the miserable day of September 11, 2001, just how overwhelmingly dire the realities of the Mus-lim world had become was heavily underscored. Like most Americans, I clearly remember what I was doing when I first heard about the terrorist attacks, and naturally, I was not listening to the news. For several days before the tragic events, I suffered from the most ominously suffocating sense that something miserable was about to happen. In fact, one week before the terrorist attacks, I wrote an op-ed in the *Los Angeles Times* sharing with readers this foreboding sense that something exceptionally violent was about to happen. When it did happen, I was in bed, under the blankets, hiding from the world. "Khaled, Khaled! Get up! After you hear this, I don't think you will want to go back to sleep," was what my wife said after running into the room flooded with Southern California's bright sunlight. If her trembling and choking voice was not enough, her face said it all. The first words out of my mouth after watching the horrific scene of the second plane going into the second World Trade Center tower were, "Well, there is no power or strength save in God." The second semicoherent thought in my mind was, "Please, please God—let it not be Muslims! Let it not be Muslims who did this!"

My wife was right—it was time to wake up. In fact, after 9/11 and its equally tragic aftermath, for a Muslim who cares deeply about Islam, who understands the series of tragedies and failures that led to this horror, and who appreciates the extent of offense and defilement perpetuated against humanity and Islam, it would not be possible to sleep ever again. A tragedy like 9/11 could not happen without many of those who could have preempted it being in a state of virtual slumber. 9/11 was the culmination of a series of compounded mistakes, injustices, and grievances that continued to spiral out of control while those who could have interceded to avert the disaster remained in a state of self-induced oblivion. The morning I saw the Twin Towers crumble, I remembered the car rides to school and remembered how in my youth I used to escape the gloom by ingesting the Islamic dream. The truth is that many of us romanced the Islamic dream while we restlessly slept, only to wake up to a living nightmare. The nightmare is one in which criminal sociopaths pretend to be the guardians and ministers of the Islamic faith; one in which extremists assume the role of the spokesmen for the religion of moderation; one in which unspeakable acts of shameless ugliness are perpetuated on God's behalf and in His name; one in which the religion of compassion and mercy has become associated in people's minds with cruelty and oppression; and one in which many Muslims no longer recall the ethical norms that ought to guide their relationship to God and humanity. Even more, it is a living nightmare in which apologetics passes for rigorous thought, in which the gift of intellect and human reason is declared to be the gateway to the devil, in which the very idea of beauty and representations of beauty, such as music, are condemned as frivolous and corrupting, and perhaps most important of all, in which, in some parts of the Muslim world, in direct proportion to a person's rhetoric and ignorance, the greater is his religious authority. We have reached the point that in parts of the Muslim world, the more profound a person's ignorance about Islamic theology and law, the more expansive his bombastic demagoguery, and even the more "Islamically authentic" his wardrobe and outward appearance, the better the chances are that he will be recognized as a great leader and expert in Islam.

The Islamic dream of a world full of justice, the love of learning, mercy, compassion, moderation, tolerance, and balance seemed to be at opposite ends with our lived reality. In Islamic belief and theology, Muslims are supposed to set the moral example for the world; they are supposed to bear witness with equanimity and justice to God's primordial law in the universe; and they are supposed to be humanity's refuge away from ignorance and self-idolatry and toward embodying and manifesting the truth of divinity. As explained later, theologically, Islam is supposed to be the religion that calls to the moderate path and is supposed to espouse moderation as a moral and ethical value. I was taught in schools of theology and law that the position of being God's witnesses and the moral example to humanity was not an honorific status that God conferred upon Muslims, and not some kind of moral entitlement. According to the Qur'an, Muslims have to strive, work hard, and prove themselves worthy of the divine trust. The Qur'an even warns Muslims that if they should fail in performing their moral duties, not only will God abandon them, but even more, God will replace them with another group of people who will be more fit for the challenge and more up to the task.[5] Dreaming was simply not enough; nor was resting on their laurels, and constantly invoking and romanticizing the so-called Golden Age of bygone days. If Muslims are to fulfill their moral duties on this earth, they have to strive and engage in an indefatigable living jihad to become the moral exemplars for humanity. As explained later, this is an ideal that all Muslims are expected to work hard to try to fulfill, but they may never permit themselves the arrogance of believing that they have attained and perfected the desired moral status. Only God can adjudge the results of human efforts, but Muslims must temper their striving and jihad with the humble realization of their own fallible limitations.

WAKING UP TO THE TRUTH

In a state of complete wakefulness and conscientiousness, it is inescapable that a Muslim would realize how far from this ideal we have come. I do not deny that Muslims have suffered much injustice and violence in the modern world. Furthermore, I cannot ignore the fact that oppressive forces such as colonialism and imperialism have wreaked havoc with so many Muslim countries and Muslim lives. In my view, it is beyond dispute that many Muslims around the world have every reason to feel angry and resentful about the callous and deceitful treatment they have received from the West. And it ought not be denied that there is a long litany of grievances against the West and the now defunct Eastern bloc for invading, occupying, and dominating many Muslim countries. Such a litany of shameful offenses ranges from Napoleon's bombardment of al-Azhar Mosque in Cairo and the trampling of his horses over the Qur'ans in al-Azhar[6] to the manipulations of T. E. Lawrence, the deceitful Sykes-Picot Agreement, and the West's installation of and support for oppressive puppet regimes in Saudi Arabia and elsewhere,[7] and to the expulsion and dispossession of Palestinians and the shocking opportunism of arming both sides of the Iran-Iraq conflict,[8] leave alone the tendency since the 1980s, when in doubt, to send off cruise missiles and bomb one Muslim country or another. Now, added to this litany of grievances are the invasions of Iraq and Afghanistan and the slaughter and abusive degradations that ensued in each country; the human rights abuses against Muslims from a number of countries, including torture and degrading treatment, indefinite detentions, extrajudicial killings and arrests, and abductions; and the unconscionable war crimes committed in places like Lebanon, Jenin in the West Bank, and, more recently, Gaza.[9] For a Muslim who seeks to regain consciousness and undertake a critical reevaluation of the Muslim condition in the modern age, his or her problems are only compounded by the fact that there are severely anti-Islamic and Islamophobic works flooding the book market. The unfortunate reality is that the authors of these hate-filled treatises are anxious to jump on and exploit any revealed dirty laundry on Islam and Muslims. Nothing makes these authors happier than to know that Muslims are confronted with serious problems. Some Islam-haters, while pretending to be fair-minded and objective critics, go so far as to openly celebrate the fact that some former Muslims have abandoned the Islamic faith for Christianity or some other religion. For example, an anti-Muslim propagandist like Daniel Pipes will proudly post on his website narratives of people who allegedly discovered that Islam is a false religion or any piece of writing that questions the authenticity of the Qur'an or anything Islamic, like the very existence of Muhammad, the Prophet of Islam. While propagandists such as this pretend to encourage Muslims to reform and progress, in practice they impugn the motives of any Muslim reformer who sees any merit in the Islamic tradition whatsoever. They even go as far as claiming that any scholar who confesses his or her loyalties to the Islamic tradition is, by definition, a militant or extremist. In short, the only Muslims these Islamophobes seem to like are self-hating Muslims who are ashamed of everything related to their religion.[10] At the same time, most of these propagandists sanctimoniously, hypocritically, and, I might add, condescendingly lecture Muslims on the necessity of critically reexamining themselves and their religion. However, such authors do not exhibit the same critical abilities when dealing with their own traditions, religions, or political interests. In short, these writers are unlikely to turn their critical abilities to a reexamination of the justness of Israeli policies toward the Palestinians or to evaluating the role of Christian doctrine in promoting violence and fanaticism. While conveniently overlooking their own moral shortcomings and historical failures, such writers are happy to focus on what they believe are Muslim ailments.[11]

The important point here is to realize that this highly politicized atmosphere seriously challenges all Muslim efforts at achieving what I have called the condition of wakefulness and conscientiousness. In fact, it is fair to say that one of the primary reasons that many Muslims stubbornly insist on espousing the utopian Islamic dream is as a defensive reaction to the perceived hostility and hypocrisy of non-Muslims when dealing with Islam. The apologetic movement in Islam is fed and nurtured every day by the hate and bigotry that stares Muslims in the face all the time. This is a very serious problem, and I will have more to say about it later in the book, but for now it is important to note that it is foolish and dangerous to allow one's relationship to one's own faith to be defined by one's antipathy toward others, even if those others are bigoted Islam-haters.

There is no doubt that the hostility that confronts even progressive and moderate Muslims and the suspicion with which they are often regarded is demoralizing. Often non-Muslims fail to appreciate the extent to which the intense hostility of some Westerners frustrates many Muslims to the point that they lose faith in the morality of universal human principles. This is especially relevant to Muslims who try to build bridges between the Muslim world and the West and those who believe in universal principles that unite all of humanity. Obviously, for Muslims who believe in tolerance and in partaking in a universal humanism, hate threatens to frustrate them and render their good-faith efforts futile. Extremists, however, are always happy to reciprocate hate with hate, but this is not an option in the case of Muslims who care about their own moral integrity and the integrity of the world in which they live.

The Qur'an itself warns Muslims not to allow their anger over the injustice of others to lead them into committing injustice.[12] In my view, it is a profound injustice for a Muslim to remain oblivious, as if asleep, when his or her religion and tradition are being hijacked and corrupted. In part, this is a question of love and loyalty: if Islam is supposed to be a universal moral message to humanity but this very same message has become associated in the minds of many human beings with violence and ugliness, what are the obligations and duties of a Muslim toward his religion? I believe that if a Muslim loves his religion and is loyal to it, his first and foremost obligation becomes to save and reclaim his faith. Allowing the defilement and corruption of the religion to go unchallenged because of the fear of playing into the hands of bigots is, in my view, a betrayal of the faith. This is not just a question of priorities but also a matter of integrity and truthfulness with oneself and one's God. Bigots will be bigots regardless of whether or not one puts so-called dirty laundry before them. The real issue is the veracity and honesty of one's testimony before God and not the scoring of points in a political game. Not surprisingly, the Qur'an instructs the believers to bear witness to the truth even if such truth is embarrassing, inconvenient, or detrimental to one's material interests or the material interests of loved ones.[13]

The Qur'an is a book full of moral and ethical teachings. The Qur'an is not a book of law, history, mythology, or theology. The Qur'an describes itself as a reminder—a book that consistently reminds people of the truth and values that should be innately known to them. It is a text of moral and ethical instruction that consistently ties moral awareness and consciousness to the knowledge of the One and Only God. In engaging the text of the Qur'an, one often feels as if reconnecting to something primordial, sensible, and beautiful within oneself. This engagement is as if embarking on a journey into a partnership of discovery where one relocates the ethical and moral sensibilities that have been obfuscated by the trials and challenges of life. My own ever-developing memories of engagement with the divine text involve sublime pauses—moments in which I felt entirely reconciled with what I have always known and what I should know. One of these powerful moments that occurred while studying the Qur'an related to this issue of bearing witness in truth. I could say that this moment was truly transformative and is probably responsible for my writing this book. I remember reading about a man named Tu'ma bin Abayraq who reportedly stole a war shield because he was anxious to join in battle in defense of Muslims, but he was poor. After stealing the shield, he hid it in the store of a Jewish merchant. Within a short span of time, the shield was discovered to be with the Jewish merchant, who then led the investigators to Tu'ma, the thief. When questioned, Tu'ma accused the Jewish merchant himself of stealing the shield, but the evidence was against Tu'ma. It looked like Tu'ma was going to be convicted and the Jewish merchant exonerated. Finding himself under accusation, Tu'ma rushed to the Prophet and demanded that the Prophet help defend him and argue on his behalf against the Jewish merchant. It is important to reiterate the context at this point. Muslims were in a state of war; eager to join the battle, a Muslim stole the shield, a Jew and a Muslim stood accused, and the Prophet was being asked to defend the Muslim. In response, the Qur'anic revelation was decisive and unequivocal. The Qur'an responded, "We have sent to you the Book containing the truth, so that you will judge among the people as God has shown you, and do not be an advocate for the deceivers. . . . And he who commits a mistake or iniquity and then ascribes it to one who is innocent is guilty of calumny and brazen sin."[14] The Qur'an vindicated the Jewish merchant, condemned Tu'ma, and clearly commanded the Prophet to stand by justice and not defend deceivers, even if the culprit is Muslim.[15] Studying this incident, I was struck by the Qur'an's insistence on justice, its rejection of chauvinistic tribalism, and its rejection of political functionalism and opportunism. Even the state of war and the Muslim's patriotic motivations could not be used to sacrifice an outsider (a Jew in this case) because doing so would be a brazen sin. It seemed that the desire to shield Muslims from honest criticism would not be an excuse acceptable to God. Furthermore, the Qur'anic logic seemed to stand in sharp contrast to the logic of necessity used by terrorists to commit horrendous acts of violence. I will return to this central ethical issue later in the book.

There is a tradition attributed to the Prophet that states, in effect, that if Muslims hold steadfastly to the Qur'an, they will never go astray.[16] For Muslims, it is an article of faith that if they properly understand the Qur'an and manage their lives according to its teachings, they will fulfill their moral obligations and achieve a just existence for themselves and humanity. The problem, however, is that the Qur'an, as beautiful and sublime as it is, is first and foremost an educational text, and like all such texts, its moral achievements are contingent on the moral readiness of its students. As discussed later, the Qur'an presumes that its reader has a degree of moral sense, without which the effectiveness of its message becomes limited. In the same way that a book of philosophy cannot teach its reader good common sense, a book of ethics, such as the Qur'an, cannot teach its reader to become endowed with a basic sense of morality. Intuitive moral readiness or basic ethical awareness, like common sense, is not learned from a book but is the product of psychological predispositions shaped by upbringing, culture, personal experience, and at times sheer determination. The Qur'an employs the moral sense that already exists in readers and then refines and develops it, allowing it to reach new heights of moral awareness. In order for this process of refinement and development to work, the student of the Qur'an must be capable of engaging in a conscientious process of reflection and self-critical analysis. This, however, requires humility. An arrogant reader or a reader convinced of his own moral superiority will learn very little from the Qur'an because for such a reader, all the moral lessons of the Qur'an become filtered through a self-righteous prism that is not challenged or reformed by the text. Rather, for such a reader, the text becomes merely a means to affirm his predispositions and predilections. The text becomes an instrument to rubber-stamp the arrogant reader's biases, prejudices, and ultimately, ignorance. This is why, of all the virtues affirmed by the Qur'an and in the teachings of the Prophet, humility is always emphasized as central. Muslims are repeatedly instructed not to presume that they know God's Will with absolute certainty and are also reminded that there are matters or subjects that fall solely within God's discretion and domain.[17] These divine dominions are particular subjects such as the knowledge of *ghayb* (the metaphysical unseen), the time of the final day, and the knowledge of salvation. Ultimately, God, and only God, knows who deserves to be the recipient of God's mercy and who will attain salvation in the Hereafter.[18] It is considered fundamental in Islamic theology that God extends His mercy to whomever God wishes and that a human being cannot arrogantly presume either that he is exclusively deserving of this mercy or that others are not entitled to receive it. In the Qur'anic discourse, it is considered the height of arrogance to appoint oneself as the executor over God's mercy, pretending to decide who should be the recipient of such mercy and under what conditions. The same applies to salvation; it is God's exclusive business to determine who is saved and who is damned in the Hereafter.[19] Muslims are advised to abide by God's commands in hope of attaining salvation, but it is not up to human beings to decide who deserves to be saved. This basic humility that governs the relationship of a Muslim with God is affirmed at least five times a day when a Muslim prostrates before God in prayer and supplicates: "Praise be to God the Highest!" The point repeatedly acknowledged in prayers is the necessity of restraining and subordinating the human ego before the divine dominion and will.

There is an anecdotal tradition that nicely illustrates this important theological point. It is reported that during the Prophet's lifetime, a group of Jews, Christians, and Muslims met in the market rest house in Medina. Eventually, the group got into a heated debate about who would be saved in the Hereafter and who was entitled to enter heaven. Not surprisingly, the followers of each religious faith started listing their own merits and virtues and insisted that they, to the exclusion of others, were entitled to be the recipients of God's grace. On this occasion, the Qur'an responded with a resolute principle: "It [Salvation] is neither dependent on your [Muslims'] wishes nor the wishes of the People of the Book [Jews and Christians], but whosoever does ill will be punished for it, and will find no protector or friend apart from God. But he who performs good deeds, whether man or woman, and he is a believer will surely enter Paradise, and none will be deprived their just reward." [20] Interestingly, after this revelation it is reported that Jews and Christians would tease Muslims by saying, according to the Qur'an, "You and we are equals." [21]

The Qur'an describes the message of Islam as "Good news to those who do good," and the role of the Prophet Muhammad "as a mercy to humankind." [22] These proclamations are not just empirical claims about the historical role of the Islamic message. For the most part, these are aspirational normative statements about the moral message of Islam. Accordingly, it is not only that the followers of Muhammad should aspire to be a mercy to all of humanity, but Islam itself is an affirmation of the moral desert of all those who are virtuous or who act ethically, whether Muslim or non-Muslim. I do not believe, however, that the Qur'an is asserting that there is no moral difference between Muslims and the followers of other religions or that the Qur'an intends to affirm the moral equivalence of Muslims and non-Muslims in the eyes of God. Rather, the Qur'an aims to remind human beings of their proper moral boundaries. Salvation and heaven are God's business and no one else's. Moral worth or ethical value, especially as far as human judgment is concerned, is something other than salvation, perhaps overlapping with salvation in some respect but not defining it.

Moral worth or ethical value is not a label or title with which one can adorn oneself. It is a meritorious quality to be achieved or earned through the goodness of one's deeds. In Islamic thought, the temporal world, and where human judgment is concerned, ethical value and virtue are not contingent on being a Muslim, but they are contingent on one's conduct or behavior. Human beings are empowered to judge or, in theological terms, testify for or against themselves and the deeds of others, but not their intentions. Therefore, in Islamic thought it is indisputable that a non-Muslim who acts ethically is more praiseworthy than a Muslim who acts unethically. Indeed, as discussed later, ethical and virtuous conduct are the very essence of Islam, and therefore, one could plausibly say that a non-Muslim who acts ethically is also being more Islamic than a Muslim who fails to act ethically.[23] This means that the non-Muslim is acting in a fashion that is more consistent with the spirit and purposes of Islam than a Muslim who contravenes and perhaps undermines the ethics of his or her own faith. This is why, for instance, one of the supplications repeated in the Qur'an is: "God, do not let us be the reason that the unbelievers are led astray,"[24] meaning, "God do not let us, Muslims, be the very reason that people are repulsed away from the faith, and do not let us raise such animosity and hate in the hearts of others to the point of being the reason that they engage in wrongdoing."[25]

In the same way that moral worth and ethical value are not simply labels to be worn, salvation cannot be presumed or taken for granted. No doubt Muslims do believe that becoming or being Muslim is innate and intuitive to all human beings and that being Muslim is morally virtuous. But it does not necessarily follow that only a Muslim can be morally virtuous, and most certainly, it does not follow that all those who claim to be Muslim have succeeded in achieving moral virtue. Importantly, a Muslim of true moral virtue would not take God or any of God's creation for granted and would not presume to be entitled to salvation. For example, many Muslims learn the traditions about the ten disciples (companions) of the Prophet who were purportedly assured salvation by God. Yet neither the Prophet nor his companions, including the ten disciples, would rest on these assurances, and they refused to relax the rigor by which they worshipped and performed good deeds.[26] Piety and humility mandate that a Muslim remain cognizant that salvation is God's exclusive providence.

Because of the centrality of these concepts in Islamic theology, I will revisit them later in the book. For now, it is worth underscoring that Muslims are expected to approach the divine text with great humility and with full awareness of God's sublime dominion and their own limitations as human beings. This theological and moral refrain highlights the risks and also detrimental effects of an Islamic dream, or any religiously based dream, that is conceived in a state of blissful unconsciousness or in a state of insufficient engagement with sociopolitical and historical realities as well as social ethics. Any theology or theory can quickly falter on a bed of uncomfortable and challenging facts. Moreover, we are all too familiar with the Marxist rhetoric about religion being the opiate of the masses. There is no doubt that not just religion but any fervently held system of belief or ideology can have a delirious and numbing effect on the readiness of its adherents to acknowledge and deal with uncomfortable realities that challenge this system of belief. In fact, in the same way that any idealistically held system of belief can inspire and motivate its adherents to greater levels of accomplishment and fulfillment, it can also serve to mask serious problems instead of changing them.

For instance, I cannot recall the number of times that I have heard it repeated in mosques and Islamic centers that one cannot evaluate Islam by what Muslims do in its name. In these contexts, it is often said that Islam is perfect, but Muslims, not Islam, have problems. This claim assumes that ideas can exist outside the minds that hold them. In my view, Islam as conceived in the mind of God is neither perfect nor imperfect; it is beyond human evaluation because I accept it simply as the truth. It is a metaphysical and transcendental truth that is not subject to any earthly contingencies. This truth is not dependent for its existence on anything that human beings might or might not do, and it is not in any way affected by whether people believe it or not. The Qur'an emphasizes that God and the truth are not affected one way or the other by the number of believers or disbelievers in the world and that when it comes to matters where human agency has no role to play, reality is not contingent on human conduct or behavior.[27]

As a Muslim, I accept it as an "is," and I believe "it is" because "it is." Be that as it may, other than its metaphysical existence, Islam has a physical earthly existence as well, and in that realm, there is no escaping the challenge of human agency and the fact of human-based contingencies. For instance, in the physical world, a component of what we identify as a part of Islam are the reports and traditions attributed by generations of Muslims to the Prophet. The role of human agency in the transmission, preservation, and interpretation of such reports cannot be denied, and to the extent that human activity is fallible and imperfect, it is inescapable that the reality of human limitations and constraints will leave an imprint on these reports. What is likely to result from this is a disparity between Islam as it exists in the mind of God in the metaphysical world and Islam as it exists in the physical here and now. This, however, brings us full circle to the necessity of honest analytical and conscientious engagements when researching and discoursing on Islam and the divine will. On this earth, we will never know with a level of absolute certainty Islam as it exists in the mind of God in the metaphysical world. Nevertheless, using the Qur'an as a moral guide, Muslims with great humility must continue to critically and honestly strive toward a greater moral realization of divinity while fully acknowledging and dealing with human limitations and contingencies. If, however, as many Muslims do in the modern age, one declares Islam to be perfect and uses this conviction as an excuse to avoid dealing with the problems that confront the Islamic faith, then it is difficult to escape the conclusion that the Islamic ideal has become an escapist mechanism exploited by people to avoid having to live up to their responsibilities before God.

Moreover, although the idea of Islam as the perfect religion has had a stronghold over the Muslim imagination, it does strike me as a rather arrogant assertion. Islam, as submission to God, could be a perfect act, and as a Muslim, I accept that God could and does conceive of the prerequisites and conditions for submission in a perfect way. This, however, does not mean that Muslims have submitted perfectly or that they perfectly understand the prerequisites and conditions of submission. There is certainly a perfect metaphysical reality in God's mind, but this does not mean that there could be a perfect realization of God's mind by the human mind. It is entirely plausible for a Muslim to believe that God's revelation is perfect, but it is also arrogant for a Muslim to believe that he or she has perfectly realized the revelation. In my experience, increasingly the statement regarding the completeness and perfection of Islam is not made as an expression of personal devotion and aspiration but has become an important part of the displays of public affectation that ultimately facilitate a dynamic of moral escapism. All too often in the modern age, one finds apologists who appeal to this point to avoid dealing with their own failures, limitations, or frustrations. But human limitations and frustrations are part of the human condition, and it is misguided to expect that human beings can elevate themselves to divinity in the process of taking charge of the agency delegated to them by God. The human condition, with all its frailties and subjectivities, or what may be called human contingencies, cannot be treated as an inconvenient aberration or deviance to be dealt with contemptuously. Rather, the premises on which abstract theological and legal thought is constructed must assume the existence of these human contingencies and develop ways of becoming empowered and enriched by the robust diversity that is born out of these contingencies.

An Islamic tradition attributed to the Prophet asserts that the angels of God are distressed by what distresses humankind.[28] This tradition, like the parable of the angels prostrating before human beings at the conception of creation,[29] underscores the centrality of the human factor with all its contingencies, limitations, and weaknesses in the process of unfolding the divine will in the temporal world. The point is that human contingencies are not there to be overcome in the process of comprehending and achieving divinity—human contingencies cannot be overcome. An objectified human being who mechanically absorbs and implements the divine will without in any way processing the divine is an impossibility. This issue is of central importance, and so I will return to it later, but at this point, it is important to emphasize that digesting, processing, and effectuating the imperatives of God through the subjectivities of human consciousness is not only inevitable but purposeful. Therefore, while human contingencies cannot be overcome, it is part of the divine imperative or command that human beings engage in and struggle through a perpetual jihad to transcend their limitations and weaknesses. To submerge oneself in a struggle to transcend one's human limitations is axiomatic in Islamic theology, but to assume that one's will has come to embody the divine is blasphemous.

In a well-known Islamic proverb, it is stated: "Whoever comes to know herself will come to know her God,"[30] meaning it is only through a persistent struggle (inner jihad) to interrogate, examine, and discipline the self that one will come to know this self, and knowledge of oneself will reveal to a person the ego and its real gods or masters. Put differently, self-critical examination is key to discovering one's idols and false gods. Notably, this tradition, like many others, readily recognizes the contingency of subjectivity and the need to wrestle with this subjectivity as axiomatic in the relationship of a human being to God. God is apprehended to varying extents through confronting and disciplining the ego, but importantly, God is accessed only through human subjectivities.

Recognizing that God as well as the divine will is mediated only through human agency was a core assumption of classical Islamic theology and law. As discussed later, the epistemology and methodologies of dealing with authority, developed in the formative periods of Islamic theology and law, focused on ways of striking a balance between the need to struggle and discipline the self, on the one hand, and the need not to objectify human authority and also not to endow it with the immutability of the divine on the other. Ultimately, in the contemporary age, the balance has tended to swing sharply between two extremes—on one side, the extreme of erasing all boundaries between God and those who speak for God, and on the other extreme, the complete collapse of authoritativeness and objectivism in the dynamics of Islamic law and theology.

Chapter Two

Awakening: Reasonableness and Islam

THE PLIGHT OF MODERN MUSLIMS

There is an American cliché that states: "The devil is in the details." This cliché is aptly applicable to the Islamic dream, which was held and promoted by so many throughout the 1970s and 1980s and which continues to play a powerful role in the contemporary Islamic world. The Islamic dream as an ideal and even utopian vision of the quality of life that is possible was often pursued at the expense of paying attention to the quality of life that in fact exists. The plight of modern Islam was not born overnight, and it took decades of numerous ambiguities to produce such an ugly reality. The constant employment of the rhetoric of what I called the Islamic dream to gloss over and conveniently ignore many ethical ambiguities was bound to produce a situation where one can accurately say that the Islamic faith has been hijacked and badly abused. In that sense, 9/11 and its aftermath were the tragic outcome of an enormous number of microlevel failures in a wide variety of situations, places, and contexts. I will discuss this matter in greater detail later, but events such as the Salman Rushdie affair or the blowing up of the Buddhist historical landmarks in Afghanistan are demonstrative of this protracted process of microlevel failures.

For whatever it's worth, my own experiences growing up in Egypt and Kuwait—wrestling with the Islamic dream while at the same time searching for a definitive sense of identity—were rather illustrative of this point. Of course, mine was a less notorious and less drastic dynamic than that of some of my coreligionists who have ended up with greater frustrations and also more devastating consequences, but in some critical respects, my experiences were representative of the plight of so many young Muslims searching for identity and rootedness in the age of modernity.

The morning drive of which I spoke previously used to deliver me to my day school, a secular school placed under the governance of the Kuwaiti Ministry of Education. The day school was out at 2:30 in the afternoon, but there was a second school to which I would walk in the evening every day after attending the day school. After my mother picked up my siblings and me, she would drive us home. At home, I would rest or study until 5 p.m., and then I would promptly leave for a mosque in the vicinity of our neighborhood. For three and a half hours, from 5:30 p.m. until 9 p.m., my activity in the mosque was divided between prayer and attending classes on Islamic theology and law, after which I would return home, study until midnight, and sleep, only to wake up around 4:30 a.m. in time for morning prayers. Over a period of six years, for purposes of self-discipline, I rarely permitted myself to sleep more than six hours a night at most. Before dawn, I would wake up, get dressed in a white traditional robe, and leave to perform the *Fajr* prayers (first prayers of the day performed at dawn) at the mosque. During the academic year, after performing *Fajr*, I would return home to sleep until woken up at 6:30 a.m. by the sound of the Qur'anic recitation coming from my mother's radio. During the summer break, which I always spent in Egypt, there would be a class on Qur'anic exegesis shortly after the *Fajr* prayers. The schedule of study during the summers in Egypt was more rigorous and intensive than the one in Kuwait during the normal academic year. In Egypt, after the early morning class on Qur'anic exegesis, I attended a class in hadith (the traditions and reports attributed to the Prophet) at noon. This was followed by a class on the Arabic language and eloquence at 1:30 p.m. Other classes on Islamic jurisprudence, theology, history, and logic would follow from 5 p.m., and depending on the class and teacher, sometimes from 4 p.m. until as late as 10 p.m. These classes, which were taught by different jurists for either a nominal fee or for free, were called the *halaqas* (the circles of learning). The classes were not taught under the supervision of the Ministry of Education, or Religious Affairs, or any other ministry. Often the instructors were retired teachers from the state-controlled Azhar University or teachers who had been fired or resigned because of their political opinions, or unorthodox views, or being perceived as troublemakers in general. There were a number of teachers who were on the active faculty of al-Azhar, and in addition to their normal course load they taught one of the night-session classes. Some of the teachers, especially in Kuwait, were officially employed as *imams* in mosques (people who led the daily prayers and gave the sermon on Fridays). The most important characteristic of these teachers was that for one reason or another they were free to teach whatever they wished without having to abide by the state-made guidelines or curricula that were in force in all of the state-owned seminaries. This freedom allowed the teachers to delve into the Islamic intellectual tradition without having to abide by the politically motivated curricula set by the various governmental ministries. This loose network of teachers and students were known as the Usulis because of the nature and methodology of study in which they engaged. [1] Methodologically, instead of focusing on committing the positive commandments of Islamic law to memory, as other schools might do, the Usulis focused on the rational interpretive principles that guided legal determinations. The emphasis on comprehension and analysis instead of memorization is one of the main distinguishing features differentiating the way Islamic law is taught in Usuli circles of learning versus the puritanical and nonrationalist orientations, such as, for instance, Wahhabi circles. In this educational process, the primary emphasis was placed on research, knowledge of the sources, and the analytical skills of the jurist, and as such, the focus of this training was on Islamic jurisprudence and not necessarily the rules that constitute Islamic law. Our teachers would always remind us of the symbolic picture drawn by the Qur'an for the truly ignorant. In the Qur'an, those who memorize or preserve information but are unable or unwilling, through comprehension, to channel this information into genuine knowledge, are compared to donkeys carrying books.[2] Our teachers always warned: "Do not be like donkeys carrying books! Do not be mere receptacles for information without acquiring knowledge."

The style of teaching was often based on what we described as the disputative method—at American law schools this same style is known as the Socratic method. Instead of lecturing, the teacher would pose a query, and the students would struggle with the response. Each time the students would be close to resolving the disputed matter, the teacher would pose another question that would throw the students back into the throes of puzzlement. After being satisfied that his students had exerted and exhausted themselves while trying to solve the problem raised by the teacher, mercilessly the teacher would only add to our plight by informing us of the five or six or ten different solutions proffered by various jurists at different times and in several contexts. In this educational context, the correct answer was the best question, and asking the right question was the earmark of true knowledge. Each year, in the month of August, and at times in January, most teachers conducted their oral examinations, and those who passed were granted what is called an *ijaza* (a license which served as an attestation by the teacher that the student in question had completed a specific course of study and was entitled to respect and deference on the topic that he or she had mastered). The most marvelous thing about this system was that it was entirely voluntary and existed away from the corrupting and oppressive influence of the state. To work, it required an exceptional level of commitment and dedication because there were no officially sponsored incentives, rewards, or privileges. Those who engaged in this course of study did so because they loved knowledge and cherished God's law. A positive attestation by a teacher would open the door to more advanced circles of learning, and there were virtually no limits to how high a student could reach in this course of study. Regardless of how much a student learned, there was always a higher level of learning, and regardless of how knowledgeable, there was always a greater and more accomplished master. After the privilege of studying in this system for more than six years, I spent another five years studying Islamic law under the guidance of a singular master in the field, a Muslim jurist who teaches at Princeton University.

It is important not to confuse the *halaqa* system, which I attended, with the *madrasa* system, which I did not. In recent years in the West, there have been a lot of ill-informed discussions on the Muslim system of education known as the *madrasa*. The Western interest in the *madrasa* system was due to the fact that Bin Laden's al-Qaeda seems to have recruited extremists from *madrasas* in Afghanistan and Yemen. However, in the same way that not all *halaqa* classes utilized a rationalist method of learning, not all *madrasa* schools produced extremists. The *madrasa* is mostly a rural practice, while the *halaqa* system is primarily an urban phenomenon. *Madrasas* are usually attended by poor students and are normally staffed by teachers who are not very accomplished or prominent. Unlike the *halaqas*, the *madrasas* do depend nearly exclusively on rote memory, but instruction in the *madrasa* does not reach very advanced levels of learning. Nevertheless, whether the *madrasa* system generates extremists or moderates depends on the particular ideological orientations that prevail in certain regions of the Islamic world, meaning there is nothing inherent to the *madrasa* or *halaqa* systems that orient them either toward extremism or moderation.

Thinking back, I often reflect on why I attended these night classes and became a part of the *halaqa* system, spending so many hours in pursuit of an education that ultimately does not lead to a particular career. By the time I was growing up in the Middle East, attending the secular school system ended with earning a diploma and with qualifying to attend college. As dealt with later, in the postcolonial era, Islamic law had lost its central place in society, and the value of a religious education had sharply decreased. Although formal religious schooling was available, this system was not considered prestigious or respectable, and graduating from one of the religious schools did not qualify a student to attend one of the best colleges. Moreover, most of those who acquired a formal religious education or attended an Islamic law school ended up unemployed or as imams leading prayer in mosques. The quality of education in Islamic law schools, which were heavily regulated by the government, had deteriorated to an abysmal condition, and acquiring such a formal religious education necessarily meant a lack of upward mobility as to respectable career options. My parents insisted on all their children attending the best secular schools, achieving the best grades, and going to the best colleges. Secular schools had become a necessary reality of life, but I think that for my parents, like many in the Muslim world, their hearts remained attached to the religious tradition. In the secular schools, the quality of instruction in the Arabic language and the Qur'an was abysmal—students graduating from the secular schools were practically illiterate both in Arabic and in the Qur'an. Hoping to remedy this deficiency, my parents initially enlisted my siblings and me in classes that supplemented the amount of Arabic and Qur'an we learned in school. However, proceeding on with the *halaqas* as a systematic course of instruction and receiving concentrated learning in the various sciences of Islamic jurisprudence was not something my parents forced on us. These *halaqas* were attended out of choice and out of love. After receiving a basic education in the Qur'an, Arabic grammar, and the traditions of the Prophet, any further instruction was strictly voluntary. My mother, in particular, instilled in me the love of knowledge and helped me overcome the fear of texts. She was the one to make me feel that those who handle, carry, and read books are, as she would put it, "people who honor their past, work for the present, and respect their future." My mother was also the one who initially used to help me study and prepare for the *halaqas*, but after a year or so, the material we learned became too advanced for her, and I was on my own except for the occasional assistance I received from my father. Despite my parents' best efforts, initially I drifted toward the fundamentalist circles of instruction, but this is another story to be told some other time. Thankfully, after a period of time, my parents managed to kick some sense into me, and I abandoned the fundamentalist circles for the Usuli *halaqas*.

After completing the various cycles of learning, other than God's blessings, a student earned nothing more than self-respect, the possibility of social deference in religious matters, and a fair chance at earning the informal title *shaykh*. This title meant something very different from the oil-rich, licentious, lustful, and power-crazed "Sheikh" known to the West. *Shaykh* connoted a person of religious learning, piety, and wisdom, and in the context addressed here, earning the title depended on the authoritativeness and respect that exuded from an individual after reaching a certain level of progress in the cycles of learning. In short, if people became persuaded that a particular student had become a truly learned person, it would be the laypeople who deferred to the student's opinions and who also conferred on him the title of *shaykh*. If, on the other hand, the student failed to convince people of his competence, such a student would deserve neither deference nor title. The title *shaykh* was earned by popular approbation and social respect, but the informality of the system was also its power. It was also possible to earn the title *shaykh* by official recognition and designation. By studying full time at al-Azhar or any other state-controlled seminary, a person could earn a governmentally issued title of *shaykh*. But paradoxically, many of those officially designated as *shaykhs* turned out to be individuals of little religious learning and also little wisdom, and most importantly, of little legitimacy. It is important to remember that the informal *halaqa* system arose as a challenge to the official clergy system controlled and certified by state institutions. In the case of the *halaqas* I attended, it was rather ironic that although the possibility of social deference and the title of *shaykh* were among the very few rewards of this informal method of education, during the course of instruction it was drilled into us that we should not desire either of these benefits. To desire or crave these benefits or to seek them out in any way was considered arrogant as well as contrary to a true and genuine commitment to knowledge. As a matter of principle, the true reward that we sought was God's pleasure and the satisfaction of knowing that we really know practically nothing at all.

The long years of instruction and training in the *halaqa* system did not endow us with the right to represent God or to pontificate about the dictates of Islamic law. Rather, these years of training only gave us the tools to research and investigate Islamic law according to systematic analytic methods of inquiry. What I learned is that Islamic jurisprudence is a vast and boundless field of knowledge that yields insight only to the truly humble. Islamic jurisprudence is represented literally by thousands of texts containing the opinions and determinations of thousands of intellects accumulated and documented through the course of several centuries. To be able to benefit from this wealth of approaches and opinions preserved in these numerous texts requires not only the mastery of the technical language of the jurists but also an equanimity and humility of character that enables a reader to remain sensitive to the nuanced dynamics taking place in the text.

Indicative of the political oppression that prevails in many Muslim countries and for reasons that remain unclear to me, the Egyptian government severely clamped down on the circles of learning to which I belonged. Tragically, several of the students I studied with either were chased out of the country or perished in unlawful detention centers that function as slaughterhouses for the most dedicated and courageous members of society. The government seemed intent on dismantling this significant institution of civil society and also determined to suppress and dominate any autonomous expression of religious learning.

Very recently, while visiting Egypt as the guest of Shaykh al-Azhar (rector of Azhar University) Ahmad al-Tayyib and the Grand Mufti of Egypt, 'Ali Jum'a, I was informed that the system of circles of learning, to one extent or another, has been reconstituted in Egypt. Be that as it may, the basic dynamic between the Egyptian government and the bearers of the Islamic dream, whether intellectuals, scholars, or activists, remains unchanged to this day. In Egypt, as in many other Muslim countries, this dynamic is fraught with anxiety, fear, injustice, and oppression, where any freedom enjoyed can be as easily denied as it was extended. Autocratic Arab governments fear every manifestation of Islamicity, and even religiosity, that is not controlled and directed by the state. Therefore, if these governments give people the freedom to construct religious meaning outside the umbrella of the state, this freedom is in a precarious position at best, and when this freedom is exercised, it takes place in an inherently oppressive political environment. Especially after 9/11 and the declared war on terror, political oppression and human rights abuses in countries such as Egypt have grown steadily worse, but even in the early 1980s the situation was already quite abysmal.

The suffocating oppressiveness of this situation made the opportunity to seek an education in the United States a great blessing, for which I remain grateful to this day. As in the case of many other Muslims, there is no denying the virtuous position of the United States as the land of moral salvation and freedom. The harsh reality is that the possibilities of moral development are severely constrained in many Muslim countries because of the vicious autocratic governments that remain nestled in power in those nations. This is one of the primary reasons why for many Muslims the real hope for an effective and powerful Islamic enlightenment was the West. The West, and especially the United States, offered a tangible hope for the emergence of Islamic institutions that could lead the way to an intellectual and ethical rebirth in the Muslim world. Because of the freedom that the West offered, many Muslim reformers hoped that a conscientious and critical reappraisal of the Islamic experience in the modern age could commence in the West and that this process, in turn, would help inaugurate something akin to the Enlightenment in the Muslim world. Many believed that the emergence of such an honest Islamist discourse in the West would, in turn, filter back to the Muslim world, perhaps helping to challenge the authoritarian systems that depleted the intellectual energy of many Muslim societies in the first place.

Armed with this purposeful vision, like so many Muslim intellectuals in the twentieth century, I came to the United States hoping to achieve what was impossible to accomplish in my country of origin. The first American Muslim community with which I became acquainted was in California. Interestingly enough, inspired by the Islamic dream, this community had embarked on an ambitious program according to which the leadership of the community had set up a youth-group program, a Muslim mortuary, an Islamic magazine, television and radio programs, a chain of state-accredited schools, a publishing house, a bookstore, a library project, and even a lobbying organization of sorts. More importantly, the rhetoric in this organization was extremely ambitious. The leaders of the community not only saw themselves at the cutting edge of progressive Islamic thinking but went even further, consistently claiming that their organization, with its many branches and subsidiaries, was the hope of Islam itself. The leadership consistently emphasized to its constituency that the Islamic dream was possible and that this particular community, more than any other, was the vehicle to this dream. In youth-group meetings and retreats, it was consistently drilled into the youths that by virtue of belonging to this community, they were qualified to be the leaders of the future and indeed that the whole fate of Islam depended on them. A crucial component to the catechism of this community was the idea that the members and leaders of the community were all firm champions of democracy. In the rhetoric often repeated in the community, the Qur'an was often described, oddly enough, as the constitutional document of the Islamic state, and democracy was proclaimed as the one and only true Islamic political system. There were constant reminders about the Prophet's city-state during the Islamic Golden Age and endless subtle and not-so-subtle references to the parallels between this community and the Prophet's experience.

With an exaggerated sense of self-importance and an unrealistic view of its own potential as a movement, many within the organization conceived of themselves as the preordained saviors of this religion. Living on a steady dosage of lofty and flowery language about the centrality of the *umma* (collective Muslim nation), brotherhood, unity, justice, mercy, the rights of women, pluralism, freedom, and the importance of knowledge and thinking, it is not that surprising that many of those associated with the organization came to believe that all of the principles and ideals would inevitably pour into a manifest destiny of sorts.

Inspired by the vestiges of the Islamic dream, I embraced this community with considerable zeal, and I became involved with many of its institutions. It took many years to discover that behind the screen of the Islamic dream there existed a serious void. In terms of vision, ethical and social awareness, and the display of critical values such as tolerance and open-mindedness, this organization ranks as one of the very best in the United States, if not in the West in general. To this day, I have a great deal of respect for the elite leadership of this community that has managed to withstand onslaughts by political and religious fanatics of every ilk and that has been able to resist both Wahhabis and Islamophobes with equal vigor. Unfortunately, however, as in the case of the overwhelming majority of Muslim institutions in the West, behind the rhetoric regularly deployed by the leadership there were serious endemic problems that were oddly symptomatic of many of the challenges that confront contemporary Muslims in general. Many of these problems had to do with the pressing tensions between a community united by faith, ideology, and a system of belief as opposed to a community defined by cultural, economic, and ethnic characteristics. The community that I embraced suffered tensions emblematic of the difficulties that plague so many Muslim social units. These tensions relate to the difficult balance between institutional identity, on the one hand, and accessibility and communal participation, on the other; in addition is the balance between pragmatic activism and normatively principled positions—positions that reflect a dynamic sense of realism pitted against the need to maintain a coherent and integral sense of Islamic identity. Most important of all is the age-old challenge of balancing out charismatic euphoria about one's mission and purpose in an ideologically motivated organization with the absolute need for analytical self-criticism and what may be called a humble sense of self-skepticism.

In so many cases, the American-Muslim dreamland concealed very serious problems and at times even perversions that combined the worst of American society and the worst of the societies of origin of the immigrants who typically define the institutional edifice of these Islamic organizations. The leadership of my adopted American-Muslim community made a conscious effort to avoid bearing the cultural baggage of their countries of origin, but the community had its own share of problems. The leadership of this community had remained unchanged for over thirty years, and while there was plenty of talk about pluralism, democracy, and freedom of expression, the leaders had a difficult time working with Islamic perspectives at odds with their own. Not only access to the podium but even the distribution of fliers and literature was strictly controlled. Because the distribution of literature had to be preapproved by the administration, this led to a peculiar situation where fliers advertising businesses and commercial interests were permitted but fliers expressing religious, political, or social views were not. On a few occasions the leadership even resorted to the local police and courts to exclude dissenters or to physically remove opponents from the premises.

Eventually, I outgrew my association with this California-based organization, although I remained emotionally attached to it. Despite the best efforts of this progressive-thinking community, many of the disappointments I encountered and many of the organization's failures were a function of, and often mirrored, more endemic problems that plague Islamic movements and societies around the world. For instance, this community boasted a number of schools that were supposed to provide both a firm grounding in the Islamic religion and a competitive secular education in the curriculum followed by any accredited private school in the state. Enormous financial resources were poured into constructing and running these schools. However, after enrolling my son in one of these schools, I realized that in so many ways the institution was reminiscent of Arabic schools in Kuwait and Egypt. Obviously, the curriculum was different, but the mentalities that informed the worldview, epistemology, and general approach to education and learning were disappointingly similar. The school's staff was constituted from an odd mixture of professionalism and nepotism in the same way that religious doctrine was chaotically commingled with culture and mythology. Furthermore, very much like the schools back home, there was an indecisive and confusing admixture of teaching methodologies that relied on rote memorization on the one hand and analytical approaches on the other. Institutionally, the schools were committed to encouraging critical freethinking, but most of the teachers happened to be immigrants who distrusted and feared critical analysis and very often loathed dissent. Ironically, the one saving grace of these model American-Muslim schools was supposed to be their competence in the field of religious learning, but it was in this particular field of instruction that the teachers were woefully unqualified and the schools especially weak.

The California organization also invested resources in a regularly published magazine and a publishing house that were supposed to meet competitive professional criteria—the magazine proudly adopted the subtitle "America's Source on Islam." But like all other Muslim media in the West, the magazine and publishing house never managed to enter or engage the discourses of the mainstream. The publishing house had no clear mission other than to print the occasional book by one of the founding godfathers of the organization, and the standards employed in publishing decisions remained a complete mystery. Like most Muslim presses in the world, the marketing and distribution capabilities of the press were extremely modest. Furthermore, there were frequent invocations of language about the "highest academic standards," "forward and challenging thinking," and "originality," but as is the case with so many other Muslim presses around the world, Muslims seemed to be speaking to other Muslims with no one listening and saying nothing particularly new. Since the advent of modernity, Muslim presses have been forced to struggle with the need for the affirmation of tradition and identity on the one hand and the unavoidable pressures imposed by progress and the need for novelty on the other—with the comfort brought about by what is familiar and constant and the impulse and thrill of discovery and change. The magazine published by this California organization found itself in the unenviable position of having to reinforce catechisms instead of promoting debate or investigation, and in a pattern typical of so many Muslim publications, it quickly became irrelevant to the interests and concerns of its readership.

The Islamic dream—the near eschatological belief in a manifest objective and a promised destiny—kept me writing in this magazine for many years. Concerns about the closed circle in which we seemed to function and the low threshold for quality of discourse and debate were persistently and artificially numbed by the belief in the loftiness of the ultimate objectives. As in the case of many intellectuals and activists who believe in the moral force of Islam as a normative system of belief and as a civilizational legacy, there is an ever-so-powerful urge to assume that whatever the shortcomings and failures, in due course they would all blow over and what would remain would be the lofty Islamic results. In the pursuit of dreams, people do endure the worst nightmares. But Islam is a moral vision of goodness and beauty, and any nightmare voluntarily assumed and endured, by definition, cannot be part of the religion or the means to fulfilling its vision. Especially with the spread of the Wahhabi creed and rise of what I have described as a culture of ugliness in contemporary Islam, it became clear that the Islamic dream was at risk of becoming a delusion, that Muslims cannot afford but to confront the reality with all its harshness and its alienating hostility, and that in order to do so, honesty in discourse, analytical rationality, and ethically sound methodologies would be the necessary building blocks for any worthwhile Islamic project.

Whether in Muslim or non-Muslim countries, the reality of modern Islam is beset with a pathology of contradictions that are powerfully demonstrative of the fact that a serious void exists between the lived experience of Muslims and contemporary Islamic theological, ethical, and legal thought. Confronting these contradictions and treating them requires an honesty and openness in discourse that is woefully absent in the contemporary Islamic context. As discussed later, there is a devastating schizophrenia that plagues the modern Islamic condition and that tends to abort many of the sincere efforts undertaken by generations of Islamic activists struggling to reconcile their tradition with modernity.

The basic sentiment that draws so many to the Islamic dream—to the commitment to serve, to enduring hardships and making sacrifices—is piety, or what is known in Islamic terminology as *taqwa*. *Taqwa* deeply influences a person's conscience, emotions, convictions, and thoughts. It is the expression of a person's relationship to God, but because it has natural and inevitable external and social manifestations and because it is often articulated by and through religious injunctions and commands, it will often also have a powerful effect on a person's relationship to other human beings. In Islamic contexts, *taqwa*, or the displays and effects of piety, will often serve to communicate allegiance, inclusion, belonging, or commitment, and its manifestations will espouse various emotions ranging from trust to repulsion. *Taqwa*, or piety, however, in all its permutations and forms, is full of possible affectations. Therefore, the well-known premodern theologian Ibn Taymiyya (d. 728/1328) had once noted that piety could be a perfect cover for serious moral failures because by invoking one's relationship to God as the basis for demanding trust from people, one is invoking the inaccessible and what could also become the unaccountable. In Ibn Taymiyya's wonderful expression, cowardliness and piety are both based on "abstention and refrain."[3] The point is that piety, to the extent that it nullifies or replaces critical thought or conscientiousness, could induce a state of intellectual or moral stupor. Piety could be the road to rational and ethical obliviousness, or worse, to moral hypocrisy. The Islamic tradition is replete with anecdotal narratives that commend piety as a genuine and true love, trust, or fear of God, but it is also replete with warnings against the dishonesty and hypocrisy that could follow from public displays of piety. One of the stories from the classical Islamic tradition that I learned in my first years as a student of Islamic theology and law recounts that the companion of the Prophet and the second Caliph, Umar Ibn al-Khattab (d. 23/644), was considering doing business with a certain person and wanted to inquire about the person's character through a friend. Umar asked his friend if he knew this potential business partner, and Umar's friend resolutely answered in the positive. Umar, however, inquired, "So you do know him—have you done business with him?" The friend answered, "No." Umar continued, "Have you traveled and lived with him?" The friend responded, "No." Umar persisted: "So do you say you know him because of the fact that you see him pray in the mosque and you see him sit reciting the Qur'an?" The friend said: "Yes, this is true." Umar then commented, "Then you don't really know him!"[4]

This was one of the anecdotal reports that I memorized as a child but could not absorb until life experiences animated it with meaning. Looking back at it, I don't believe Umar intended to say that the appearance of piety makes a person in any way suspect. I believe that Umar's point was that if a person possesses true religiosity (*din*), it would not be limited to his performances in a mosque but would permeate to every aspect of his life, including doing business. In a sense, what I believe Umar was saying is that praying and reciting Qur'an in a mosque is not enough to know the true religious character of a person. If the potential business partner achieved a true understanding of religiosity, this would be clearly reflected in every aspect of his character and life, including traveling and doing business. Religiosity cannot be segmented or compartmentalized. Religiosity permeates and pervades every aspect of a person's being, and as such, if piety does not promote and further a person's intellect, ethical being, and conscience, it is defective and wanting in very basic and fundamental ways. This is exactly why in numerous Prophetic traditions it is repeatedly stressed that Islam is inseparable from ethics, or that the very essence of Islam is an ethical character and that the most faithful and pious Muslim is one who enjoys the most ethical character or whose conduct is the most ethical.[5] I will return to Islam's relationship to morality and ethics later on because of its centrality to this book.

In a powerful and profound declaration, the Qur'an enunciates what ought to become the central reality of every faithful Muslim. It instructs Muslims to proclaim that their "prayers, service, life, and death are all in the cause of God, the Lord of all the worlds."[6] For Muslims, their very existence, conduct, and service are supposed to represent an intimate engagement with the divine, and even death is a part of experiencing the immutable presence and eternal reality of God. Understanding the full import of this imperative and meeting the profound responsibility it creates on each individual Muslim is a monumental challenge. The challenge is not met simply by the performance of ritual. Although this is a point often overlooked in the contemporary context, it must be emphasized that at the heart of the Islamic faith is an ethical universe that must be traveled and reexplored by every Muslim. In describing the heart and core of his revelation, the Prophet Muhammad explained that the reason he was sent to humanity was to enable human beings to realize the perfection of their ethical character.[7] This basic point is emphasized in numerous historical testimonies rendered by people who encountered the Prophet and who consistently described him as a man of the highest moral character who was also a sage in the teachings of morality and ethics. For instance, Aktham bin Sayfi, one of the contemporaries of the Prophet who lived in non-Muslim Mecca, sent out to Medina two of his spies with instructions to find out what Muhammad's teachings were all about. After spending some time in Medina, the spies reported back that what they heard Muhammad persistently emphasize was justice and goodness (*al-ʿadl wa al-ihsan*). After reviewing his spies' report, he summarized the findings to his non-Muslim compatriots by saying, "My people, it seems from everything that I have heard that what this man [the Prophet] teaches is ethical character (*makarim al-akhlaq*), and what he discourages is what we know to be reprehensible in character (*malaʾim al-sifa*)."[8] The Prophet himself is reported to have said that those who wish to follow his example by being the most like him as well as those who are the most beloved to him and those who are the highest in God's grace in the afterlife are those who have the highest moral and ethical character.[9]

The ethical nature of the Prophet's teachings is what ultimately attracted the Arabs of Mecca and led to their adoption of Islam en masse.[10] The tradition of the Prophet is full of instances in which his conduct exemplified the type of humanistic behavior that appealed to the innate sensibilities of the many who believed in him and dedicated their lives to the Islamic message. For example, at the time that a state of war raged between the Muslims in Medina and the non-Muslims of Mecca, Mecca suffered a serious economic recession that primarily affected the poor of Mecca. Despite the presence of hostilities between Muslims and non-Muslims, the Prophet sent five hundred dinars, by the standards of the age a huge sum, to be distributed among the non-Muslim poor in Mecca.[11] This was done although a few years earlier, Muslims in Mecca suffered severe persecution, including a total economic boycott that led to starvation and the depletion of the resources of many, including that of the Prophet's wife, Khadija. In addition, Muslims lost their properties and wealth when they fled persecution from Mecca to Medina. It was also reported that at one point, due to the cost of war and the limited resources of Medina, the Prophet considered limiting welfare payments dispensed by the public treasury to needy Muslims, to the exclusion of non-Muslims. Suffering serious economic pressures, several Muslim officials in Medina thought that priority should be given to needy Muslims over non-Muslims. The Qur'anic revelation, however, came to decisively rebuke this Islamocentric approach. The Qur'an reminded Muslims that if God had willed, all people would have become Muslims—guidance is in the hands of God, and no one can claim moral authority over another.[12] After receiving this Qur'anic reminder, the Prophet decreed that needy Muslims and non-Muslims in Medina were equally entitled to public benefits dispensed by the state treasury.[13]

A different genre of traditions or reports emphasizes the Prophet's role in recognizing the fundamental worth of human beings regardless of their faith. In this genre, it is emphasized that human beings by their very nature are entitled to dignity and honor (*ikram al-insan fitrata Allah al-lati fatara al-nass 'alayha*).[14] Therefore, the Prophet instructed his disciples to stand up out of respect as the funeral procession of a Jewish woman passed them.[15] In another narrative, on hearing of the death of Najashi, the Abyssinian king who offered sanctuary to a group of Muslims who fled persecution in Mecca, the Prophet instructed his companions to pray for the soul of Najashi. Reportedly, when some Muslims protested praying for the soul of a non-Muslim, Qur'anic revelation affirmed the position of the Prophet.[16] Notably, in these and many other traditions, the anecdotal narrative that offers the ethical point—offers it to be reflected on and comprehended—is delivered through a dialectic between God and the Prophet, or the symbol and medium of divine authority, such as a text, and the Muslim community. I argue later that the anecdotal or illustrative ethical teaching establishes not a deterministic point but a learning process. Like the initial medium or mechanics that delivered the illustrative point, the process established is dialectical, open ended, and progressive with layers of meaning that could be uncovered through analytical reflection and lived experience. In many cases, not just the progressive process of comprehension and exploration but the basic ethical point itself is not learnable unless the reader or audience actively participates in the dynamics of ethical investigation. Consider, for instance, a report that every student of Islamic theology learns by heart, which asserts that some of the early Muslims gave in to their emotional pain and anger by cursing some of the polytheists who fought against them in the battle of Uhud—a battle in which Muslims were defeated. According to a number of traditions, God instructed the Prophet and his companions to refrain from doing so in this context, commenting: "You have no power over their fates or salvation" (*laysa lak min al-amr shay'a*).[17] One can take a very narrow approach and conclude that the Qur'an forbids Muslims from cursing their opponents even during times of open hostilities. I would argue, however, that doing so is equivalent to aborting entirely the ethical teachings embedded in this and similar traditions. In order to unpack the ethical lesson of these traditions, it is necessary to take a paradigmatic approach in which the reader or interpreter of text participates in the process of ethical instruction and learning by analytically investigating the normative dynamics and trajectory of these discourses.[18]

One of the passages of the Qur'an that I have always thought to be a very powerful assertion of ethical principle but which has received precious little attention from classical or modern scholars speaks of wrongfulness of opportunistic ethical standards, or what may be called status-based morality. The Qur'an states: "And there are some People of the Book [Jews, Christians, Sabians, etc.] who if you entrust them with a treasure will return it to you. There are some, however, who if you entrust them with a single dinar will not return it unless you persist in pursuing them [demanding repayment]; that is because they believe that it is not sinful to usurp the rights of Arabs. Indeed, they lie about God and they know it."[19] In this passage, the Qur'an is addressing a particular historical reality, and that is the arrogant and supremacist attitude of some toward Arab tribes. As in the case of racism and other forms of bigotry, rights to which people were entitled vacillated with their status, whether ethnic or otherwise, and this kind of moral selectivism is described as a falsification of the divine will.

Within its time and context, the ethical principle need not have been realizable, or even cognizable at the time it was upheld either by the Prophet Muhammad or any of the earlier Abrahamic prophets. Often the morality or ethical principle upheld by the Prophet and the Qur'an exceeded the prevailing understanding of the age in that what was taught or advocated was in conflict with the widespread political and social practices of his time. On the one hand, the principle established is deterministic in that a clear normative injunction is established. On the other, the principle is nondeterministic because it sets a normative potential in motion that is realizable in different ways and extents within varying time and space contingencies. For instance, one of the traditions often mentioned in Islamic sources states that a man, identified as al-Husayn al-Ansari, from the clan of Banu Salim bin 'Awf, one of the clans of Medina that adopted Islam, had young two daughters who remained Christian. Al-Husayn tried to persuade his daughters to convert to the new faith and thus join the rest of the family and clan, but to no avail. Fed up, al-Husayn wished to force his daughters to convert to Islam, and he urged the Prophet to give him permission to do so, but the Prophet refused. Many classical sources cite this incident as the occasion upon which the Qur'anic injunction that there be no compulsion in religion was revealed.[20] Although the moral import of this tradition and also the Qur'anic injunction supporting the Prophet's position were understandable to the early generations of Muslims, this did not preclude many Muslim jurists from holding that the penalty for apostasy should be death. In addition, the Qur'anic injunction and Prophetic traditions do not mean that in various phases, places, and times people were not coerced into converting to Islam. What type of impact the anticoercion injunction or the prohibition of duress had in Islamic history can only be understood in terms of a dialectical dynamic of various degrees of exploration and realization. Whether or to what extent an ethical principle was realized is not the critical point at this stage of the argument. What is important to establish is that principles mattered, and mattered a great deal. Any principle will necessarily entail a contextual relationship in which there is tension and struggle and the possibility of development and progress.

Of great relevance to our day and age, for instance, are the Islamic traditions rejecting unprincipled and opportunistic approaches to warfare and political affairs. The Prophet forbade the taking of hostages in or out of war despite the fact that the prevalent practice among nations at the time was that the taking of hostages was considered a necessary instrument of international affairs and a necessary step in concluding peace treaties. Even if the enemy executed Muslim hostages, the Prophet taught, Muslims could not hold or dispatch hostages in retaliation.[21] After the death of the Prophet, when it came to the world of politics and functional practicalities, ethical standards such as the prohibition against the taking of hostages posed innumerable challenges to Muslims that were negotiated in a variety of ways. Therefore, for instance, in a well-known historical incident, the Caliph al-Mansur (r. 136–158/754–775) wanted to retaliate against a non-Muslim force that had grabbed and murdered Muslim hostages by engaging in the same conduct. Abu Hanifa (d. 150/767), the founder of one of the main schools of legal thought, strongly protested the Caliph's plan, arguing that succumbing to the ethical standards of the enemy would inevitably lead to the destruction of Islam. For Abu Hanifa's continuing opposition, the Caliph arrested and then exiled him for a period of time, but ultimately, the Caliph was forced to relent.[22] Abu Hanifa's principled position found support in various precedents in Islamic history that rejected the logic of pure political pragmatism. So, for instance, the Prophet refused to authorize a preemptive strike against the people of Sheba in Yemen although some of his companions argued, accurately as it turned out, that these people were biding their time to commence hostilities against Muslims after the Prophet died.[23] Similarly, the companions of the Prophet for ethical reasons refused to renege on the treaty status of Khurasan as *'ard sulh* (territory that entered into Islam without armed conflict) by changing the territory's legal category despite the clear economic and political benefits that would have ensued from doing so.[24] The position of the companions, taken well after the Prophet had passed away, was rooted in the living memory of the Prophet and his teachings that persistently attested to the superiority and prevalence of principle over more opportunistic or pragmatic stands. This rather foundational and fundamental point is underscored in numerous Prophetic traditions. Rather classic examples of this genre of traditions recount that on several occasions tribes or influential individuals offered to convert to Islam only if the Prophet would support or take their side against a feuding opponent. Typically, influential leaders would state their willingness to convert on the condition that, right or wrong, Muslims would take their side either in a particular dispute with a specific party or, more broadly, against all present or future opponents. The Prophet, supported by constant Qur'anic refrains, refused to do so regardless of the precariousness of his own political situation or the practical benefits to be reaped from doing so.[25]

These reported incidents and narratives emphasize the intensity of tension between political functionality and ethical and religious principle. When religion moves from the sphere of ritual to a full engagement with life—when it is no longer confined to the mosque, church, or synagogue and becomes the repository for the normative principles that people reference in navigating through life—the risk is that each will be seriously compromised in the name of the other: religion in the name of life and life in the name of religion. Each can be exploited to undo and deform the other.

The critical centrality of the tension and balance between principle and functionality to every aspect of Muslim life today cannot be overestimated. This tension and often dilemma is confronted and resolved in one way or another by every believing Muslim, community, movement, organization, and country, but it gains special urgency because of the fact that in so many scenarios around the Muslim world, despotic leaders use religion to deny their constituencies the rational faculties by which these constituencies could evaluate the corruptions created in their lives. No less devastating is the fact that so many Muslim leaders use the functional necessities of life to corrupt religious doctrine beyond recognition. This devastating functionalism is used to justify a vast array of things, including terrorism, despotism and political apathy, political docility and the indignities of servitude, oppressive labor laws, the persecution of women, racist and ethnocentric citizenship and employment policies, and an unabashed classism in many Muslim societies. Functionalism and pragmatism override principle in seemingly imperceptible ways in the most subtle and unassuming fashion in microlevel dynamics encountered by Muslims everywhere.

I have noticed that in so many activist-run Muslim organizations in the West, the wealthy who are able to donate substantial sums of money to support an institution are treated with an honor and pride notably missing for the poor. Not only is this observable in the way people are addressed, but in many Islamic centers in North America and Europe, it extends to granting some individuals special parking privileges and even, during Friday services, designating a special entrance for the VIPs while "the commoners" are instructed to enter from the rear of the center. At pricey events organized for the purposes of publicity or fund-raising, those with modest means become "invisible" while the wealthy are able to gain entry to a privileged communal status that is often by definition exclusionary. Classism is a very common human weakness, and Muslims are not immune to it, and from a purely functional perspective, one can hardly find fault with any of these policies—the wealthy need to feel that they enjoy a special stature for obvious fund-raising purposes. But it is not the existence of class privilege in Islamic institutions that I find troubling, but the near absence of a serious discourse on the morality and ethics of such policies in light of the Islamic tradition. From a certain perspective, the example given above hardly seems significant—there are far more important cases of economic oppression and suffering that seem more compelling than any possibly bruised feelings that might result from VIP status. But the commonality of this example is what makes it significant. Ethical conscientiousness, like piety, cannot be segmented or bifurcated or applied only to some issues but not others.

Like many other Muslims, I learned that during the nascent stages of the Islamic message, the Prophet would often meet with a crowd of largely poor individuals in the market in Mecca, instructing them on the new faith of Islam. There was a constituency of wealthy Meccans interested in Islam, but they had one problem—they were not willing to be seen meeting with the Prophet and mixing with the poor folks he attracted. The rich constituency explained to the Prophet that they would like to meet with him, but they worried that foreign tribes visiting Mecca for trade would see them in the company of the poor, and this, they contended, might affect their business interests, leave alone their reputation and image. Their request was straightforward enough—they asked that the Prophet kindly designate a special time and place for them so that they could meet with him. It is important to note that they did not ask the Prophet to stop meeting with the poor, but reasonably enough, that he would designate a special meeting time for the rich. Anxious that Islam would gain acceptance among all the classes in Mecca, the Prophet was tempted and considered agreeing, but at this time, a Qur'anic revelation came down strictly forbidding him from doing so. [26]

This tradition is about the boundaries that must inevitably be drawn between functional need or practical justifications and ethical principle. If religion does not contribute such boundaries to life, it seems to me that it contributes nothing. But this is exactly what eludes many honorable Muslim organizations finding themselves in difficult or trying circumstances: if there is religion, not everything can be up for sale—affectations of piety notwithstanding, genuine piety and true religiosity are precisely about drawing such moral boundaries when confronting the many practical demands of politics and life. The issue is not whether a specific policy as opposed to another is more or less Islamic; the issue is the necessity of moral reflection and ethical thinking and the pivotal importance of an ongoing, sustained discourse on the normative import of the Islamic tradition. Without a moral and ethical compass, both piety and law could become not just misguided but false. I will return to the concept of Islamic ethics and its relationship to piety and law, but for now, it is important to stress that when speaking of ethics, I do not refer just to the proper standards for a human being's relationship with God but to social intercourses and the interactive dynamics that take place between human beings (what in Islamic terminology is known as *mu'amalat*). It is equally important to stress that there have been orientations throughout Islamic history, especially the puritanical creeds in contemporary Islam, that have tended to treat ethics, morality, and the very idea of goodness of character (*husn al-khuluq*) as if it is a function of how a person deals with God and as if it has very little to do with how a Muslim interacts with society. Moreover, typically, these orientations deal with goodness of character in a highly formalistic fashion, dealing with morality and ethics as if limited and quantified by specific deeds or misdeeds. Methodologically, these orientations treat religio-historical narratives and the texts that contain them not as anecdotal, demonstrative examples that require investigation, exploration, and development but as exhaustive and all-inclusive listings of good Islamic conduct. As discussed later, these puritanical, mechanistic, and formalistic approaches to morality and ethics practically wreaked havoc with contemporary assertions of Islamic law. At this point, the least that can be said in response to these approaches is that the concept of *akhlaq*, or ethics in Islam, cannot be understood except in terms of its normative impact on social functions or of how human beings deal with other beings and creation in general.

This does not address either absolutism or relativism in Islamic ethics, and it does not inform the discussion on the ontology or deontology in Islamic ethics.[27] My point is more basic: ethics in Islam cannot be understood as a purely vertical relationship between God and human beings. It must be understood also in terms of the horizontal relationship between beings and creation. The puritanical approach is at odds with so much of the Islamic tradition, which is replete with Prophetic narratives that evaluate ethical character in terms of how a Muslim deals with and impacts his or her surroundings. One such tradition simply states: "Those who wish to attain Salvation should, to the last day of their lives, believe in God and the Hereafter, and should do unto people as they would want done unto them."[28] In other traditions, in response to questions from believers, the Prophet explains that ethical character means to treat people well or to be giving and kind and to greet people amicably.[29]

ISLAM AS A COMPLETE WAY OF LIFE AND THE REALITY OF REALIZATION

The contradictions plaguing a large number of Muslims in the modern age are not limited to political or social practices but also extend to their very relationship with Islam. It is oft repeated that Islam is not just a religious faith in the Western sense of religion. Islam is a way of life; it offers a total and holistic approach to all the problems that could confront human beings. Many activists readily repeat the dogma that the Qur'an and Sunna offer a complete way of life that, if faithfully followed, will lead to the realization of a just society and life—like that which the Prophet established in Medina. In the contemporary Muslim world, these claims are very widespread and are even often treated as basic articles of faith. Later, I will discuss the role and impact of this dogma, but there is a basic point to be noted here.

Muslims believe that the Qur'an is the literal word of God as transmitted by the angel Gabriel to the Prophet Muhammad. When it comes to the Qur'an, the Prophet Muhammad did nothing more than communicate word for word God's revelation, and Muslims preserved the text and transmitted it in its original form and language to subsequent generations. Importantly, Muslims believe that God warranted and promised to guard the text of the Qur'an from any possible alterations, revisions, deletions, or redactions, and therefore, while Muslims may disagree about the meaning and import of the revelation, there is a broad consensus among Muslims on the integrity of the text. The Muslim belief in the integrity of the text of the Qur'an is well supported historically, but the meaning and context of the text is a far more complicated matter. At times the Qur'an addresses itself to the Prophet, specifically, but on other occasions the Qur'an speaks to all Muslims or to humanity at large. In different contexts, the Qur'an will address Jews or Christians or polytheists. There is a historical dynamic that contextualizes each of these occasions and that gives it further meaning and significance. While there is a broad consensus among Muslims on the integrity of the text of the Qur'an and also on the Qur'an's authoritativeness as God's revealed and divine word, the historical context of the text is far more debated and contested. Despite the Qur'an's unique and singular status as the literal word of God, most Muslims consider the Sunna of the Prophet as the second-most authoritative source of Islam. The Sunna is the orally transmitted record of what the Prophet said or did during his lifetime as well as various reports about the Prophet's companions. Traditions purporting to quote the Prophet verbatim on any matter are known as hadith. The Sunna, however, is a broader term; it refers to the hadith as well as narratives purporting to de-scribe the conduct of the Prophet and his companions in a variety of settings and contexts. The Sunna is represented by an amorphous body of literature containing hundreds of reports about the Prophet and his companions during the various stages of early Islamic history. Although the Qur'an and Sunna are considered the two primary sources of Islamic theology and law, there are material differences between these two sources. Unlike the Qur'an, the Sun-na is not represented by a single agreed-upon text. For Sunni Muslims, the Sunna is scattered in at least six primary texts (Bukhari, Muslim, Nisa'i, Tirmidhi, Ibn Maja, and Abu Dawud), and many other secondary texts (e.g., Ibn Hayyan, Ibn Khuzayma, *Musannaf* 'Abd al-Razzaq, Ibn Abi Shayba, and the *Musnad* of Ahmad Ibn Abi Hanbal). Shi'i Muslims usually utilize addi-tional sources for the Sunna of the Prophet and his family (*ahl al-bayt*) (e.g., the Nahj al-Balagha, Wasa'il, and al-Kafi). Unlike the Qur'an, the Sunna was not recorded and written during the Prophet's lifetime. The Sunna was not systematically collected and documented for at least two centuries after the death of the Prophet. Although some documentation movements commenced in the first century of Islam, the main efforts at systematic collection and documentation did not start until the third century of the Islamic era (ninth century of the Christian era). The late documentation of the Sunna meant that many of the reports attributed to the Prophet are apocryphal or at least are of dubious historical authenticity. In fact, one of the most complex disciplines in Islamic jurisprudence is one that attempts to differentiate between authen-tic and inauthentic traditions. Furthermore, reports attributed to the Prophet are not simply adjudged authentic or fabricated—such reports are thought of as having various degrees of authenticity, depending on the extent to which a researcher is confident that the Prophet actually performed a certain act or actually made a particular statement. Therefore, according to Muslim schol-ars, traditions could range from the highest to the lowest level of authenticity. Although Muslim scholars have tended to believe that they could ascertain whether the Prophet actually authored a particular tradition, the authorship of traditions is historically complicated. Many traditions are the end product of a cumulative development that took place through a protracted historical process, and therefore, these traditions often give expression to sociopolitical dynamics that occurred many years after the death of the Prophet.[30]

Aside from the issue of authenticity, there are several other ways that the Sunna is different from the Qur'an. The style and language of the Sunna is very distinct and different—while the Qur'an is poetical, melodic, and lyrical, the Sunna is not. Furthermore, the range of topics and issues addressed by the Sunna are much more sweeping than in the Qur'an. The Qur'an is primarily concerned with ethics and morality; the Sunna, however, contains everything ranging from enunciations of moral principles, to detailed prescriptions on various matters of personal and social conduct, to mythology and historical narratives. Not all of the Sunna can easily translate into a set of normative applications, and therefore, Muslim jurists argued that parts of the Sunna are intended as legislative and binding, while other parts are simply descriptive and, for the most part, not binding. Most importantly, the huge body of literature that embodies the Sunna is complex and generally inaccessible to the layperson. In order to systematically and comprehensively analyze what the Sunna, as a whole, has to say on a particular topic or a specific issue requires a considerable amount of technical knowledge and training. In part, this is due to the fact that the Sunna literature reflects a rather wide array of conflicting and competing ideological orientations and outlooks that exist in tension with each other. Selective, nonmethodical, and nonsystematic approaches to the Sunna produce determinations that are extremely imbalanced and that are highly skewed in favor of one particular ideological orientation or another. Yet, such nonmethodical, imbalanced, and opportunistic treatments of the Sunna of the Prophet are commonplace in the contemporary Muslim world.[31] I hasten to add that nonmethodical and opportunistic approaches to the Sunna that assume the pretense of objectivity are one thing, but methodical and critical selectivity that openly and honestly wrestles with its own subjective limitations is quite another. Because of the methodical and analytical challenges posed by the Sunna, a number of contemporary Muslim reformers have called for the rejection of this body of literature in its entirety. I strongly disagree with this approach for many reasons, among them that not only is this approach dismissive of the moral and legal authority of the Prophet as an educator and guide, but it also tends to ignore the role of history and contingency in the production of meaning. Other than the methodological problems, approaches that are dismissive of the Sunna are very often oblivious to the fact that many of the basic rituals of Islam were derived from the Sunna traditions. Furthermore, the Sunna helps in contextualizing the Qur'anic revelation and also in understanding the historical dynamics that framed and shaped the Islamic message. Therefore, it is not possible to simply ignore this formidable oral tradition or focus exclusively on the Qur'an without doing serious damage to the structure of the Islamic religion as a whole.

There is no question that the Qur'an and Sunna occupy a highly authoritative position in the Islamic faith and that they are boundless and illimitable sources for thinking about ethics, morality, law, and wisdom. But as sources of guidance, they are also multilayered and multifaceted, and when the Qur'an and Sunna are considered together, they tell a complex story. They could be a source of profound intellectual and moral guidance and empowerment. But if approached with the wrong intellectual and moral commitments or with the wrong ethical paradigms, or even if approached from within a hedonistic and noncommittal moral framework, they could contribute to a process of ethical and intellectual stagnation, if not deterioration and putrefaction. For instance, the Sunna contains a large number of traditions that could be very empowering to women, but it also contains a large number of traditions that are demeaning and deprecating toward women. To engage the Sunna on this subject, analyze it systematically, interpret it consistently with the Qur'an, and read it in such a fashion that would promote, and not undermine, the ethical objectives of Islam calls for a well-informed and sagaciously balanced intellectual and moral outlook.

Despite the complex set of issues raised by these source materials and their interpretations, many Muslims tend to treat the Qur'an and Sunna as a panacea to all the challenges that could confront them in life. Indeed, as already noted, the Qur'an and Sunna could inspire creative solutions to most problems, but this is a far cry from assuming that they can automatically and unthinkingly yield solutions to life's challenges. However, among many Muslims around the world, it has become as if it were accepted dogma that the Qur'an and Sunna provide for a complete way of life and accordingly contain an antidote to every social and political ailment that confronts Muslims. In this paradigm, one often encounters a simplistic attitude that assumes that the Qur'an and Sunna are books full of formulas and that the only thing missing in the equation is the will and determination to apply the correct formula to the appropriate problem. But to say that the Qur'an and Sunna provide a complete way of life could have two possible meanings. It could mean that these sources constitute the starting point inspiring a way of life. Alternatively, it could mean that these sources encompass the particulars of a complete way of life. In the first sense, the Qur'an and Sunna provide open possibilities for fulfillment by serving as a means for moral empowerment. In the latter sense, the Qur'an and Sunna provide a limited set of possibilities by detailing what constitutes a complete and full life. In the first, these sources provide moral possibilities, while in the second, these sources enunciate a totalitarian vision of life. These two visions are at odds with one another—one offers the possibility of an open life, while the other provides for a tightly closed and highly restrictive way of life. Each of these visions has profound implications for the possibilities of democracy—the open vision might be reconcilable with democracy, but the closed vision is more conducive to the creation of a totalitarian social and political structure.

The assertion that Islam is a complete way of life plays a central role in sustaining and promoting the Islamic dream. Yet as often as this assertion is repeated in lectures, sermons, and books, the sense in which it is used is rarely, if ever, specified. But this type of ambiguity has its seriously detrimental effects on the clarity and very coherence of Islamic thought and discourses. More fundamentally, it is impossible to assess the meaning or plausibility of such ambitious claims unless there is a systematic effort to engage in the study and critical analysis of the Islamic tradition. Nevertheless, perhaps the most troubling reality of modern Islam is the enormous gap between how broad and ambitious are the claims made on Islam's behalf and the actual willingness to seriously engage the Islamic tradition. Ideally, one would expect that there would be at least a proportional relationship between the state of knowledge on Islam and the claims made on Islam's behalf. In reality, however, it is fair to say that what exists on the ground is an inverse proportionality—the most ambitious and aggressive claims are usually made by the least knowledgeable about the Islamic theological or legal tradition. The most arrogant in claiming to know the divine will are typically the least learned and also the least intellectually developed. This observation is hardly surprising—the more ignorant a person, the easier it is for such a person to claim knowledge. However, what is surprising in this regard are the prevalent paradigms and practices in modern Islam, and how these practices dangerously overlap with activist fantasies about the Islamic dream.

A few years ago I was invited to teach Islamic law at an Islamic camp attended by youth and their parents. Among the activities of this camp was to charge groups of young women with the task of cooking dinner and creating a pleasant environment for the whole camp. One of these groups decided that it would be pleasant to turn on soft Hawaiian music as dinner was being served. I am not sure why they picked Hawaiian music in particular, but before implementing their plan, they decided to make sure that turning on this music was not an infraction or sin. Since I was the only person in the camp trained and specialized in Islamic law, they figured that it would make sense to ask me. My response to their query was that playing Hawaiian music might only be a sin because it is utterly boring, but other than that, there was no problem with serving dinner to the elevator melodies of this music. The first sign that something went wrong was when the music was turned on and then abruptly interrupted, and we finished our meal in silence. At about 10 p.m. of that evening, a messenger came to my uncomfortable bunk bed and informed me that my presence was requested at the mess hall. Arriving there, I found the camp organizers, the camp teachers, and some of the parents. They had been meeting for about two hours to discuss my Hawaiian music *fatwa* (nonbinding legal opinion), and their deliberations gravitated toward discussing my other "crimes and misdemeanors." Other than the issue of music, the main charge against me was that I taught Islamic law in a strange and un-Islamic way by encouraging rational thought and inquiry. The group informed me that: first, all forms of music are strictly prohibited in Islam, and I must promptly apologize for my offensive *fatwa*; and second, I must immediately alter the way I taught Islamic law. If I was unable or unwilling to comply, I must leave the camp immediately.

By profession, my accusers were medical doctors, engineers, computer scientists, and a few businessmen, and what interested me the most in this encounter was that not one of these accusers had attended a single class of Islamic law in their lives. They were hardly in a position to know whether my methods of teaching Islamic law were traditional and orthodox or unique and unorthodox. Moreover, on the issue of music, they were completely unwilling and uninterested in being educated in the various juristic debates about the legality of music in Islam. Most of all, they were resolute in refusing to listen to any argument based on common sense or on the psychology, anthropology, or sociology of human existence and practices. Through near mystical means, they had determined that they were privy to the divine will and consequently knew with absolute certainty that God does not like music. As it was, I ended up spending the night in the camp and left the next day. To unpack, analyze, and do full justice to this one representative incident would require a book-length treatment.[32] If the basic frame of reference that the camp accusers invoked was Islamic, and to the extent that this frame of reference derives its legitimacy from the divine will, then why were they not interested in the juristic discourses on the subject of music? The *raison d'être* and primary function of the juristic tradition consisted of investigations of the divine will, and this is the intellectual tradition where one finds the evidence for and against music discussed at length.[33] But at a more fundamental level, even more frequently than reading and writing, music has existed in every society as a basic form of human expression. Music plays a crucial and undeniable role in the psychological constitution of human beings and in the social and political institutions of every human society. It is a core component of the matrix of intuitive pleasures that defines beauty and aesthetics in human life. In Islamic discourses, it is often repeated that Islam is the religion of intuitive senses (*din al-fitra*). If music is intuitive to human beings, in the minds of the camp accusers, what becomes of this basic Islamic dogma? How could the religion of intuitive sense deny a basic component of human intuition? At the height of the Islamic civilization, Muslims produced a prodigious musical heritage that made distinctive and traceable contributions to the classical music tradition in the West. For the camp accusers, how did this sociohistorical fact enter into their purported analysis? More fundamentally, did the camp accusers consider the full import and implications of an Islam without aesthetics? Alternatively, considering the ethnic background of the camp accusers, to what extent was their position culturally determined—for instance, would they have reacted in the same fashion if the young women played Pakistani music instead of Hawaiian?

The position that the camp accusers took is consistent with the determinations of the Wahhabi creed, which, as discussed later, tends to be hostile to all forms of human aesthetics. The near pathological hostility espoused by the Wahhabis toward music and aesthetics in general has had a profoundly traumatic impact on Afghani society during the reign of the Taliban and on some provinces of Pakistan. But aside from these limited and extreme examples, the incremental and cumulative effect of the Wahhabi creed on Muslim societies in general has been quite extensive. The extent of this influence is evident in the fact, for instance, that even in 2010 the newly appointed Shaykh al-Azhar (dean or head of the Azhar Seminary), Ahmad al-Tayyib, was still fielding questions about the lawfulness of music in Islam. Although throughout history music had been a staple of every known Muslim culture, and although in today's world all genres of non-Western and Western music are readily available in every single Muslim country, Shaykh al-Azhar still had to refute numerous contemporary puritanical scholars by assuring Muslims that music is entirely lawful in Islam.[34]

I already mentioned growing up listening to the serenely melodic sounds of Qur'anic recitation. Throughout the 1950s, 1960s, and 1970s, the most popular professional readers of the Qur'an were largely Egyptians who were trained in the Azhar University in what may be called the traditional method of recitation—a tradition developed from the Ottoman heritage. Following specific and well-established rules, the recitation was performed according to scales that induced an overwhelming sense of pleasurable tranquility and deep serenity. Despite the popularity of Egyptian reciters, until recent times the most notable characteristic of traditional Qur'anic recitations was their remarkable diversity and richness. The melodic style by which the Qur'an was recited varied greatly from Turkey to Morocco to Malaysia to Bosnia, with each style being distinctively imprinted by the native style of the local culture. The followers of the Wahhabi creed, however, consider the traditional methods of recitation unlawful because of their use of tonality and harmony and because of their diversity. With the spread of the Wahhabi creed and the emergence of mostly Saudi professional readers, the 1980s and especially the 1990s witnessed a major shift in the music of Qur'anic recitation. Although technically correct, what can be called the new Wahhabi style is of an entirely different tonality and produces a very different emotive sensation. The style is sharp, atonal, often dissonant, and nasal. The Wahhabi style of recitation is energetic and even fiery, but also anxiety inducing. Curiously, it is as if this tense recitation manages to overcome the tranquil literary style of the Qur'an and to convey to listeners a nervous and unsettled energy. As is typical of Wahhabi claims, the proponents of this new style proclaim it to be more authentically Islamic and condemn traditional methods as deviant corruptions. The Wahhabis pretend as if there is some way that modern Muslims can retrieve the sound of Qur'anic recitation at the Prophet's time, and they claim to be somehow privy to how the Prophet's companions performed public readings of the Qur'an. Furthermore, the Wahhabis contend that their style makes the recitation of the Qur'an sound less musical and more literal. But not being interested in musical theory, the Wahhabis do not realize that music can exist without tonality or harmony.[35] The fact that the Wahhabi style is less tonal and harmonious does not mean it is any less musical. Unfortunately, in a phenomenon that deserves to be studied by sociologists and anthropologists, in recent years I noticed that the recordings of Saudi reciters of the Qur'an have become very widespread in many parts of the Muslim world and have even squeezed out centuries-old local styles of Qur'anic recitation. That the very nasal and atonal Wahhabi style of reciting the Qur'an has become so widespread could be a disconcerting indication of the influence of Wahhabism on contemporary Muslim cultures. Returning to my Islamic camp example, the camp accusers' dogmatic position on music was but an expression of a larger dynamic taking place in contemporary Islam. The camp accusers were acting pursuant to a vision of what constitutes true Islamicity, yet this vision was impressionistic and reactive at best. As is the case with a large number of Islamic activists, their vision was based on a set of reactionisms—anti-aestheticism, anti-intellectualism, and antitraditionalism—but it was not founded on any positive and coherent understanding rooted in Islam and its interpretive traditions.

Wahhabism has succeeded in injecting the Muslim world with a frightening hostility to all forms of spiritual aestheticism that could contribute elements of individualized beauty to Islamic practices. The Wahhabi influence has had a streamlining effect on Islam, where the richness of cultural diversity and variations is always branded as a corrupt innovation. Among the cultural practices detested by Wahhabis is a beautiful Egyptian and Turkish practice known as circles of *dhikr*. In these circles, men or women congregate in a mosque and melodically chant the name of God, "Allah," as well as other supplications repeatedly, again and again, as they swing from side to side—left and right. The repeated pronouncement of God's name or supplications and the redundant physical movement induce a state of ecstasy that could at times approach spiritual enlightenment. Partly because of its connections to Sufism, the practice has been declared by the Wahhabis to be a corrupt innovation in religion. In traveling in South Asia, I was struck by the richness of the indigenious culture of Sufi dance and music in countries such as Indonesia and Malaysia. According to local historians in the region, Islam spread in those nations largely through the music and poetry of homegrown Sufism. No less striking, however, was the hostile vehemence by which Wahhabi-influenced groups sought to eradicate what they considered to be the corruptions of Sufi music and poetry. Practically every single Muslim organization I visited in South Asia was engulfed in a dispute with locally styled puritans over the lawfulness of music.

One of the contradictions of Wahhabism is that despite their conservatism, Wahhabis have practically unfettered access to media venues in the Middle East, especially through the satellite channels. A few years ago, I watched one of the fairly typical religious programs on one of the satellite channels—this one rather arrogantly titled *Before You Are Held Accountable (in the Hereafter)*. The program visited and filmed several of the *dhikr* circles in Cairo mosques only to declare all of them heretical because the devout chants repeated by the people in the sublimation circles were melodic. The program also interviewed a senior scholar from Azhar University who politely disagreed with the program's conclusion, explaining that melody in and of itself is not forbidden by God. The program, however, closed by commenting that the senior scholar is a practitioner of sheer sophistry because any self-respecting Muslim knows with absolute certainty that God forbade all melodies—whether religious or not. One of the practices of the *dhikr* that the program cited as clear proof of heresy was the fact that these sublimation circles were frequented by men and women and that the chants were performed in the mixed company of genders. The program demanded to know: How dare the participants in the *dhikr* sublimate God in the mixed company of men and women? This, according to the program, was clearly heretical. The irony was that the puritan program was anchored by a woman who, although wearing the *hijab*, also wore very heavy makeup and also freely mixed with men in the process of interviewing them. Yet, as is typical of the opportunism of puritan orientations, the obvious contradiction of a woman mixing with men while interviewing them and condemning the mixing of genders while supplicating to God went entirely unnoticed. The further irony is that while this satellite station carries religious programs that preach such puritanical determinations, in the subsequent minute the station will broadcast Western-style Arabic music videos that not only play rock-and-roll-style beats but also feature dances that immodestly reveal their fair share of exposed human flesh—incidentally, in mixed company.

Perhaps programs like this have had a broader impact even than people thought possible. In recent years, three main centers, al-Husayn, Nafisah, and Zaynab mosques, where these mixed-sex *dhikr* circles took place in Cairo, started enforcing segregation policies requiring women to enter only from designated entrances and to stay within secluded areas in the mosque. I can only explain these new policies in reference to the expanding influence of puritanism on contemporary Muslim cultures. I had grown up observing men and women freely congregating in these mosques, and as late as 2010, less prominent but centuries-old mosques in Cairo remained unsegregated. My efforts at finding the party actually responsible for the newly established policy of segregation were not successful.[36] While I am reasonably confident that the pretentious program discussed above had no direct bearing on the adoption of these policies, it is also indisputable that puritanical orientations have utilized the electronic, digital, and broadcast media with great effectiveness to reach Muslims in and outside the Muslim world.

A year after the episodes of *Before You Are Held Accountable* aired, its anchor, Basma, an attractive Egyptian woman married to a wealthy Saudi businessman, discovered that her talents are better suited to another cause. Without much in terms of a transition or explanation, the anchorwoman took off the hijab, adorned herself in the latest Western fashions, and decided to interview film stars about their professional and private lives. In her newly launched show, she no longer speaks of God, Islam, Sufism, or mixing of the sexes but instead focuses on exploring the titillating and often raunchy gossip about the newest and hottest stars. At the time of this writing, this anchorwoman's program continues to air, and she continues to steadfastly insist that there has never been any contradiction between her earlier career and her current show. Strangely enough, considering the current prevailing practices in many Muslim countries, she may actually have a point. These kinds of contradictions have become an earmark of the deep fissures that puritanical Islam leaves on the tapestry of Muslim cultures. A striking fact of many parts of the Muslim world today is the odd influx of Islamic televangelist-type satellite stations as well as the swarm of stations dedicated to music videos or programming focused on dancing and singing. The overwhelming majority of the televangelist satellite stations are puritanical Wahhabi in orientation, while a small minority is of the puritanical Shi'i variety. Entertainment satellite stations broadcast a steady stream of both imported or locally produced programming that is strongly sexually suggestive or explicit and, at times, even licentious. The oddity of the sharp contrast between the two extremes of puritanical versus sexploitative programming is only compounded by the fact that owners and financers of both channels are the very same individuals. Typically, the puritanical/Wahhabi channels, even of the slightly enlightened variety such as the well-known Iqra' channel, and also the most sexually provocative channels, such as Melody Music or Rotana, are owned by very influential Saudi investors who have extensive track records in profit-making ventures as well as Islamic activism.[37] This seeming incongruity, as will be seen later, is in keeping with the puritanical, regimented practice of compartmentalization and segmentation of the spaces for religiosity, aesthetics, and rationality in modern life. Puritanical Islam is not so concerned with the moral quality of life as it is with orthopraxy or formalistic correctness in religious performance within the space dedicated to religion in society, but at the same time, it has made an odd bedfellow of functionalism, especially as it relates to business and material wealth.

THE MODERN CHALLENGE OF ISLAMICITY

The most problematic aspect of much modern Islamic activism has been the indulgent liberties that participants, acting on behalf of a presumed Islamicity, are willing to take with pronouncing the laws of God. The outcome of these indulgent liberties is a chaotic, confusing, and often opportunistic array of manifestations all claiming to be genuinely Islamic. Examples of this turbulent condition in modern Islam are numerous, and they clearly point to a reality that has reached the proportions of a crisis of legitimacy and identity. Elsewhere, I have written about the vacuum of religious authority that plagues contemporary Muslims and tried to analyze the dynamics of this vacuum in terms of the tension between the authoritative and authoritarian in modern Islam. I also argued that contemporary Muslims have become as if orphaned by modernity because of the disintegration of traditional institutions of learning and authority and because of the unchecked deconstruction of Islamic epistemology in the postcolonial age.[38] Empowered by its significant financial resources and aided by a simplistic but very potent system of symbolisms, puritanical Islam has been able to step into the vacuum of legitimacy and authority with great effectiveness. In dealing with and speaking for Islamic law, however, puritanism lowers the bar of competence to the point of completely diluting the standards of discourse. It is not just that the quality of Islamic discourse is greatly compromised, but as the standards for authoritativeness are broken down, the result is a predictable state of chaos. In the Middle East, the chaotic state of the discourse on religion and Islamic law is often referred to as *fawda al-fatawa*, which literally means the chaos of conflicting and contradictory Islamic determinations.[39] More specifically, the phrase refers to the messy and confusing phenomenon of numerous venues on cyberspace and satellite television stations, all claiming the authority and competence to speak for Islam and God's law.

What in my opinion is truly startling, and what deserves a great deal of further study, is the extent to which puritanism has eroded the sociocultural mores that measured reasonableness and balance in Islamic discourses. I will return to the issue of reasonableness in Islamic discourse later in the book, but for now, I want to illustrate what chaos in the Islamic discourse at the micro level actually means. Although most of the examples discussed below are anecdotal and personal, they are indicative of the widespread dynamics that take place among Muslims in both Muslim and non-Muslim countries. The way that Islamic law is made to speak and sound today by the purported bearers of the divine will very often pushes the bounds of absurdity.

I cannot recall the number of times in working with Islamic organizations that I have had lectures, seminars, or classes cancelled after self-appointed and self-declared experts on the divine will decided that either the material communicated or the style of communication was Islamically unacceptable. In a Muslim Youth of North America (MYNA) conference held in the 1980s, I taught a class on the maxims of Islamic jurisprudence, and not having been previously exposed to this fascinating field of inquiry, the students were enthralled. The following day, on my next scheduled class, I walked into an empty classroom, and a young, bashful girl was sent to inform me that my class was cancelled. Instead of attending the class, my students were instructed to go attend the performance of an Islamic rap—a takeoff on the song "Losing My Religion," except that the rapper in MYNA had found his religion instead of losing it. Later on, a sagacious looking senior gentleman told me that my disputative method of instruction was un-Islamic, dangerous, and unprecedented in the world of Islam.

At times, these speculative and whimsical determinations concerning the proper Islamic bounds reach proportions that are sadly comical. In another one of the Islamic camps to which I was invited, I taught a morning class on Islamic legal ethics. Students responded enthusiastically to the class largely because of the lack of educational opportunities to learn about the subject. Hoping to benefit from the opportunity, the students requested an additional meeting time to take place during their scheduled recreational hour, and I obliged. The camp organizer, a wealthy businessman who fancied himself a profound Islamic thinker, reciprocated the students' enthusiasm by storming into the classroom, indulging in a yelling fit, dismissing the studious students, and expelling their teacher. Why? The learned organizer had read a report attributed to the Prophet in which the Prophet advised Muslims to seek balance in their lives by dividing their daily hours fairly between praying, studying, working, and recreation. The learned organizer was offended because his campers were studying during the recreational hour, and this, in his view, was a mortal sin.

In an incident reflecting the same dynamics of casual and offhanded legalistic determinations, in an Islamic center in Texas, the board of directors, which consisted largely of computer science students, decided that it was a requirement that the person who leads the Friday services be married. According to the board members, the justification behind this ruling was that a true Muslim scholar ought to be married. And since a true scholar needs to be married, they argued, it follows that someone who leads the Friday services needs to be married as well. This so-called determination was nothing short of comical. It is certainly true that the Prophet had encouraged young Muslim men to seek stability in marriage, but this was a far cry from imposing a marriage-based disqualifier on Friday prayer leaders. To the great displeasure of the board members, I started listing the number of scholars in Islamic history who never married—a list that included someone whom they respected greatly, such as the well-known classical jurist Ibn Taymiyya (d. 728/1328). My efforts in this regard were rewarded not only by being expelled from the premises but also by earning the title of Grand Satan among certain members of the community.

Admittedly, these examples are pedantic and even embarrassingly so. In light of the challenges that confront modern Muslims, it would seem that inventing this minutia and then zealously defending its existence is a pedantic self-indulgence that committed Muslims can ill afford. Some prominent commentators have already written about the tendency of the Islamic movement, at least since the 1970s, to assert its religiosity on a plane of trivialities. In this context, various scholars have discussed the odd paradox between this contemporary tendency and the Prophetic traditions condemning *al-tanatu' fi al-din*, or the tendency of some religious practitioners to lose themselves and also negate the essence of faith in a pedantic and formalistic pursuit of technical minutiae.[40]

The dynamics in these Muslim organizations have always reminded me of the anecdotal story about the killing of flies in early Islam. In the year 61/ 680, in a very traumatic incident in Islamic history, Husayn bin 'Ali, the Prophet's beloved grandson, was killed in the Battle of Karbala. Like most Muslims of the age, Ibn 'Umar, a companion of the Prophet and one of the earliest jurists of Islam, felt a deep sense of sorrow over this loss and over the crisis that this killing triggered in the Muslim nation. In the midst of this state of mourning, a man requested to see Ibn 'Umar on what the man claimed was a very important matter. Interrupting his state of mourning, Ibn 'Umar kindly granted the man a meeting. The important question the man asked Ibn 'Umar was whether a pilgrim, while in a state of ritual purity, is permitted to kill flies. Not surprisingly, Ibn 'Umar was offended, and annoyed, he retorted: "The Prophet's grandson has been killed right in your midst, and you ask about the killing of flies!"[41] Considering the circumstances, Ibn 'Umar had every right to be upset about the man's lack of sensitivity for ethical proportionality. It is likely, however, that the man's preoccupation with the killing of flies was a form of escapism that enabled him to avoid dealing with the moral challenge set before his eyes. This is exactly the point behind much of the nonsensical minutiae confronted in many contemporary Islamic contexts.

Losing oneself in minutiae reflects a disoriented and confused sense of moral priorities. There are numerous manifestations of this confusion that are exhibited in popular Muslim culture in innumerable contexts and at innumerable occasions. In one of these occasions, I recall hearing a popular Egyptian preacher, 'Umar 'Abd al-Kafi, recount a story of what he considered to be an example of great piety and valor. According to 'Abd al-Kafi, there was a sultan who sought to punish a great Muslim scholar for expressing views that the sultan did not deem acceptable. The sultan threw the great scholar to a hungry lion so that he would be devoured. The great scholar, however, confronted the lion with remarkable calm as he continued to stare intently at the lion's mouth. At this point, the sultan decided to end the spectacle and called off the lion. The sultan brought the scholar before him and asked, "By God, tell me what you were thinking of as the hungry lion approached you—but I want you to swear to tell me the whole truth." After promising to speak frankly, the scholar responded, "As the lion approached me, the only thing on my mind was whether the saliva of the lion's mouth was pure or not." 'Abd al-Kafi reiterated to the bedazzled crowd that such should be one's piety and complete absorption with God's law. I, on the other hand, could not help but be less impressed and rather question 'Abd al-Kafi's sense of priorities. It seemed to me that the moral of the story ought to be that Muslims should find ways of restraining rulers and preventing them from throwing their people to the lions. Moreover, it seems that it would have been much more meaningful if, as the scholar was confronting the imminent possibility of his violent demise, he was absorbed in thinking about the beauty of meeting God and the ugliness of the kind of power that was being applied to force him to meet his maker. In many ways, it seems to come down to what a person thinks is the most important under the circumstances.

The contemporary religious discourse in many parts of the Muslim world suffers from a self-inflicted and self-imposed marginality and also from a lack of sensibility in setting priorities, something that tends to give it an air of unreasonableness. As elaborated upon later, classical Muslim jurists tried to develop methodological tools that would promote the rationality and reasonableness of legal determinations made in the name of Shari'ah law. It is important to bear in mind that as legal systems age and become encumbered by the cumulative weight of traditions, determinations, and formalism, they tend to lose creative energy to the habits of legalism. With the passage of time, as legal systems process the administration of justice and the resolution of conflict in increasingly legalistic, or structured and formalistic ways, legal systems run an ever-rising risk of becoming disjointed and detached from their sociopolitical constituencies. However, as they become more responsive to their own technocratic cultures and norms, they also run the risk of ceasing to be seen as rational or reasonable within their pertinent contexts. The point is that this is already a powerful sociological momentum that plagues any developed legal system, and it is a process that has had a most definite impact on Islamic law. But when one factors in the effects of puritanical thought with its dedication to literalism and its rejection of historicism and aestheticism, the results push the bounds of sanity.

Consider, for instance, the rather infamous *fatwa* issued in 2007 by Shaykh 'Izzat 'Atiyya, the dean of hadith studies at Azhar University, regarding the breast-feeding of male colleagues at the workplace. According to Islamic legal precedents, breast-feeding establishes a degree of maternal relation even if a woman nurses a child who is not biologically hers. The *fatwa* dealt with the problem of unsegregated workplaces by suggesting that women breast-feed their coworkers. According to the *fatwa*, this would allow women to commingle with male colleagues whom they breast-fed and also would allow these women to take off their veil and expose their hair in the presence of the same workers. Predictably, this *fatwa* caused an uproar all over the Muslim world, and several Azhari shaykhs denounced it. The Egyptian Minister of Religious Affairs Mahmoud Zaqzouq described it as "contrary to logic and human nature," and ultimately, Shaykh 'Atiyya was forced to retract his *fatwa*.[42] One would be tempted to ignore this *fatwa* as a gross aberration or outlier if it were not part of a trend in contemporary Islamic discourse that is dismissive and at times indignant of social contexts and contingencies. Before this *fatwa* was issued, Saudi jurists had already paved the path by invoking a long-forgotten precedent in contending that women are obligated to breast-feed their husbands if their husbands so desire.[43] Moreover, as noted earlier, puritanical Wahhabi Muslims mandate that the sexes be segregated and ban women from working in any place in which the sexes commingle. Shaykh 'Atiyya accepted the Wahhabi position as valid and therefore assumes that women should be banned from working in places that are not segregated. However, unlike many Saudi families, few families in Egypt can afford to be single-income households. For most families in Egypt, women's employment is a financial necessity, and so Shaykh 'Atiyya sought to find a technical, legalistic solution without much thought to its moral impact, social acceptability, or contextual reasonableness. The most shockingly striking aspect about this *fatwa* is its complete disregard for social and moral norms, and its insensitivity toward culturally based senses of propriety and ethical priorities based on the lived experiences of people. In this particular case, the author of the *fatwa* was forced to retract because he feared losing his job. In other contexts, the results could be devastatingly tragic and, quite literally, inhumane.

For many years, Wahhabi jurists in Saudi Arabia have insisted that laws aimed at banning child marriages are un-Islamic. The logic of these jurists is straightforward enough—any girl who reaches puberty is no longer a child, and therefore, marriages to a twelve- or thirteen-year-old girl cannot be made illegal. Every single year, Saudi newspapers are full of stories of about children who die during giving birth, or girls who are raped by a husband several decades their elder, or girls who run away and are found and killed on their wedding nights.[44] Nevertheless, Wahhabi jurists resist attempts at reform because according to puritanical legal methodologies, the social experiences and the lived tragedies have little bearing on informing or reordering the ethical priorities of the legal system.

An ethical and moral sense of priorities is what differentiates between reasonableness and absurdity in the way that any normative system impacts human affairs. Any normative system, whether legal, religious, or otherwise, asserts its pertinence or relevance to human societies by the way that it negotiates competing demands or priorities. Moreover, a normative system must make sense within its particular context or it is at risk of being seen not only as unreasonable but irrational. Recently, while visiting Philadelphia I attended a major fund-raising event that sought to raise money for the purposes of educating the American public about Islam. The organizers brought in some of the most illustrious and charismatic lecturers to impress on the audience the absolute necessity of teaching our non-Muslim neighbors about our faith as Muslims. To my surprise, the organizing foundation planned to spend the raised funds on purchasing billboards carrying a straightforward message: "Know Islam!" And on calling the telephone number conveniently provided on the billboard, if the caller were a woman, she would be sent a Qur'an and a scarf (hijab), and if a male, he would be sent a Qur'an and a skullcap (*taqiyya*). I objected to the organizers' bizarre sense of priorities in sending callers clothing when the purpose was to teach non-Muslims the essence of the religion of Islam. I argued that articles of clothing are, at best, at the periphery of the faith, but my protests were dismissed as both ignorant and impious. Far from being an odd incident or outlier, this event reminded me of when some Muslim organizations came to the aid of the beleaguered people of Bosnia-Herzegovina with an urgent shipment of Qur'ans and hijabs.[45]

Any sound legal education teaches students methodologies for evaluating and weighing competing demands, rights, and priorities, and in doing so, it at least equips its students with the tools of rationality. But ultimately, no system of legal education can teach its students reasonableness or, in the final analysis, to be rational. Any legal education—for that matter, any analytical and normative education—is only as good as its students. If an educational system cannot attract students with the appropriate sense of motivation, perception, probity, and equanimity, it will not evolve, and it will not keep up with progress.[46] If a system of education is nonexistent or as if nonexistent, the tools for dealing with ever-changing contexts and constantly renegotiated contingencies of time and space become equally lacking. Some of the most basic distinctions necessary for the survival of any normative system—such

as the differences between substance and form, constitutional and conse-
quential, absolute and contingent, or basic and peripheral—become confused
and incoherent. Any moral order or epistemological system cannot exist
without an internal order of priorities, and when the means for preserving and
transmitting the cumulative learned wisdom of communities of meaning to
new generations become seriously compromised, the resulting confusion or
chaos is hardly surprising.

As students of Islamic jurisprudence, we expended a great deal of effort
and time studying methods for evaluating and balancing between competing
rights (*huquq*) that belong to human beings and God. In this context, we read
a considerable amount about the objectives of Shari'ah law (*al-maqasid al-
Shar'iyya*), the purposes behind various laws (*hikmat al-ahkam*), and the
operative causes or issues that make particular laws applicable to specific
situations (*'ilal al-ahkam*). The classical tradition of Islamic law generated a
prodigious body of literature on legal priorities and the art of juridical prioritization (*al-tarjih wa al-muwazana* and *fiqh al-awlawiyyat*). Although the
expression *fiqh al-awlawiyyat* (the jurisprudence of priorities) is a modern
one, the idea of prioritization is hardly new. All students of the classical
tradition are expected to be grounded in resolving conflicting legal obligations (what are known as *halat al-muzahama*) by employing the principle of
prioritization and by thinking in terms of a system of antecedents, conditions,
and preconditions (*al-awwal fa awwal*).

What, then, accounts for the awkward realities discussed above? There
are two realities that are beyond dispute: one, most of those who speak for
Islamic law today have never received any systematic training in the methodologies of legal analysis and thought; and two, for a variety of reasons, the
quality of educational institutions that train practitioners in Islamic jurisprudence has deteriorated to unprecedented levels in the modern age. But in all
cases, no amount of religious or legal education can replace the need for
moral and ethical purpose, or teach the context-contingent art of reasonableness. But this is exactly where contemporary puritanism has had its most
devastating impact and how the most profound corruptions of Islam take
place.

REASONABLENESS, SOCIALIZATION, AND
CONTEMPORARY ISLAMIC LAW

The chaotic condition of Islamic law in contemporary times has very little to
do with the nature or processes of Islamic jurisprudence itself, but it does
have a great deal to do with the function or role that Islamic law has come to
play in the modern age. Islamic law has come to play a very symbolic and
politicized role—it has become a platform where ideologues score points
instead of serving more professional functions of law, such as the administration of justice or the resolution of conflicts. Elsewhere, I have argued that
this and other distortions in the role played by Islamic law in the postcolonial
era have contributed to the production of what I described as a culture of
ugliness.[47] But in fundamental respects, what plagues many assertions of
Islamic law in the contemporary world are not only their apparent cruelty,

harshness, or ugliness but their unreasonableness. The lack of reasonableness, however, is a necessary constituent part of ugliness, meaning that before generating socially traumatizing results that could be described as ugly, a legal system will produce determinations that are wildly at odds with the social contexts of that same legal system. The unreasonableness of the determinations made under the auspices of a particular legal system is a necessary step toward the generation of results that could be described as ugly. I think that it is fair to say that while every legal result that could be described as ugly will also be unreasonable, it is not necessarily the case that every unreasonable legal result will be ugly. Unreasonableness is a step toward the production of ugliness, but reasonableness and beauty are two distinct concepts.

Like all aesthetical and qualitative values, or indeed virtues, the concepts of ugliness and unreasonableness raise challenging theoretical issues relating to subjectivity, contextuality, necessity, proportionality, and ultimately, judgment. Nevertheless, not only is it impossible for the practitioners of a legal system to avoid such issues, but even more, unless Islamic law is to become obsolete, avoiding these types of issues is undesirable. Many contemporary Muslims assume that the very nature of Islamic law, especially its dependence on textual sources and divine revelation, precludes the possibility of value judgments and that such judgments are necessarily whimsical and, therefore, illegitimate. To an extent, this orientation, often encountered among secular and nonsecular Muslims, is a by-product of a false dichotomy that pits revelation against reason and that presumes that objective determinations follow from one but not the other. I call this a false dichotomy, in part, because regardless of the method, whether reason based or revelation based, ultimate judgments cannot be avoided. Furthermore, ultimate judgments by their nature are neither subjective nor objective—this in large measure depends on how one defines elusive concepts such as subjectivity or objectivity. In my view, in all cases, the real issue is whether the processes of constructing meaning, reaching determinations, and implementing judgments fulfill the criteria or meet the standards of ethical rationalism or fail to do so. I will return to ethical rationalism and its relation to reasonableness later in the book.

Because of the overpowering role of culture and socialization in the invention, reproduction, and reformulation of meaning, historical context plays a pivotal role in determining tastes, emotions, worthiness of character, and even what a society considers reasonable and rational. The construction of consciousness and knowledge is a prime function of socialization and also of any epistemological system. Epistemology is core to hermeneutics, phenomenology, and deontology, but epistemology is contextually contingent, and any theology or legal theory that fails to take sufficient account of this fact does so at its own peril. Theological and legal normativities can engage and influence and help direct processes of socialization and acculturation, but if a religious or legal system attempts to assert hegemonic influence over these processes, inevitably this will lead to a range of irreconcilable tensions and corruptions. By definition, any normative system ceases to be so if it loses legitimacy. And it loses legitimacy if it is no longer persuasive and is unable to ensure the consent and deference of those who are supposed to be loyal to that system. But if a system does not rest on a consensual foundation, its very character becomes coercive and not normative—a normative system that depends solely on the power of coercion is a contradiction in terms. Yet inevitably, whatever a system lacks in reasonableness and rationality it will be compelled to make up through coercion. As the demands made on behalf of a normative system are perceived by its target audience as unreasonable and irrational, such a system will be pressured into an increased reliance on coerciveness and compulsion in order to obtain compliance. Legitimate and persuasive systems of law do not have to resort to apologetics or artificial sociopolitical narratives in order to preserve themselves and do not regularly rely on systematic and widespread coercion to establish their normative vision of what ought or ought not to be. Legal or normative systems rely primarily on reasoned, voluntary compliance for their existence and sustenance. To ensure compliance, punitive or coercive methods can be resorted to only as exceptional measures to reinforce the very principle of the rule of law. Every time coercive methods are employed by the legal system, the law, as a normative concept, has already failed its purpose because the primary power of the law is not force or the threat of the use of force but its ability to persuade most of the people to follow its commands most of the time. If a normative system comes to be seen by its followers as mostly irrational or unreasonable, the risk is that such a system will increase its coerciveness to defend its survival. But in doing so there is the very real danger that the system will become locked into an irreversible cycle of increased coercion reciprocated by further losses of legitimacy. Importantly, part of the inescapable reality of this deterioration is the inability of those vested in defending a particular normative system to confront and deal with the reality of the system's delegitimation. We observe that systems caught in this cycle increasingly come to embrace fictitious and delusional readings of social realities that in turn proliferate with contorted and highly imaginative apologetic narratives praising the worthiness of the system and exaggerating its persuasiveness among its followers. As to outsiders or those who are a nontarget audience to the system, the proliferation of artificial and apologetic narratives defending a system that is seen as irrational or unreasonable only increases the marginality and insularity of such a system in a comparative context.

Understanding the critical roles played by contingencies, reasonableness, persuasion, coercion, and legal narratives that represent and defend perceptions of reality sets a necessary foundation for understanding the challenges confronting Islamic law today. Perhaps the most serious threat to the role of Islamic law in the contemporary age is not the production of cultures of ugliness but the absence of reasonableness in many of the determinations made by practitioners in the name of Shari'ah. Both issues—the production of ugliness and the lack of reasonableness—are interconnected with the problem of functional distortions in the role of Shari'ah law in modern Muslim societies. However, while the production of a culture of ugliness is an outgrowth of particular puritanical orientations that aggressively continue to assert themselves in present-day Islam, especially when it comes to issues pertaining to human rights, the problem of reasonableness raises more fundamental and profound questions about the temporal and historical role of

Shari'ah law in Muslim societies. Reasonableness is quintessentially about the way that a legal system and its practitioners relate to space and time. Reasonableness is the most subjective, contextual, and historically contingent of all the challenges that confronts the Islamic legal system in the modern age, but it also has the greatest impact on the potential for the formation of normative human rights commitments from within the Islamic jurisprudential tradition. Reasonableness, or the lack of it, plays the role of both cause and effect in relation to a legal system's functional distortions. The more distorted the functions of a legal system, the more unreasonable are its determinations, and at the same time, the more unreasonable the determinations associated with a particular legal system, the increasingly distorted its functions become. What I mean by reasonableness is the effort and ability to negotiate legal determinations within the framework of accepted cultural norms and socially recognized conceptions of justice. Unreasonable determinations are issued without regard either to their profound and turbulent social and cultural impact or to the internal cohesiveness and systematic application of a system of law. Reasonableness is the outcome of a negotiative act that balances between the integrity of the legal system—its coherence, consistency, and reliability—and the need for sociopolitical legitimacy and validity. The more excessively symbolic and politicized a legal system, the less culturally and socially situated its role, the more the legal system's integrity is compromised, and as a result, the more this legal system suffers functional distortions. Likewise, the less culturally and socially situated a legal system, the lesser the incentives and the less driven its practitioners are to pursue reasonable determinations. Reasonableness, however, is not simply a question of the extent to which a legal system is responsive to its relevant social or cultural contexts. To be reasonable, specific legal determinations do have to make sense within particular contexts. But the reasonableness of a legal system, as a whole, is a much broader issue that depends on the way a legal system continues to negotiate its functions within space and time. Ultimately, this negotiative process entails striking constantly shifting and changing balances between the imperatives of authoritativeness, integrity, and coherence of a legal system in light of evolving epistemologies and subjective understandings of temporality and sacredness.

Perhaps it is not all that surprising that those who are most likely to be at odds with speaking of Islamic law in terms of reasonableness are Muslim puritans and Western Orientalists. Both parties tend to believe in a conception of Islamic law that has very little to do with its lived historical experiences and its microdiscourses and details; both tend to think of Islamic law and theology as indistinguishable fields of inquiry; and both erroneously believe that Islam does not differentiate between the sacred and the profane—in Islam they are one and the same. What is surprising and also disappointing, however, is that normally prestigious academic presses in the West continue to bestow an air of respectability on treatises that propagate these largely fictitious constructs of Islamic law. One such recent publication, for instance, contends that when it comes to Islam, space and time are united in the law. Space in Islam, so the argument goes, is imbued with religious law and so with eternal time.[48] Per this Orientalist view, like its puritanical counterpart, the idea of the reasonable would be problematic because the very thought of historical evolution or progression is believed to be problematic in Islam. The notion of reasonableness has no place in Islam because Islamic law responds only to the sacred and not to social contexts and because the only relevant history is the sacred history of its sacred foundations.[49] I would readily concede that if these puritanical or Orientalist conceptions were accurate, it would make little sense to utilize a construct such as reasonableness even when addressing contemporaneous assertions of Islamic law, and for that matter, it would make little sense to speak of any potential dynamics between Islamic law and international human rights. Nevertheless, one of the main problems with these generalized claims is that they are founded on doctrinal presuppositions that invariably deemphasize the role of human agency in Islamic eschatology. I will return to the issue of human agency in the chapters that follow, but for now it is worth noting that these arguments—whether made by Muslim puritans or Western Orientalists, who speak of the "religious law in Islam" as if, depending on one's perspective, it is endowed with or burdened by immutable, universal, and transcendental conceptions of time and space—are too dogmatically committed to bother with the particulars or details. When analyzing legal systems, however, the details are everything—very often the law is only as important as its exceptions. And failing to pay sufficient attention to the details very often means that we are dealing with some aspect of Islamic historical mythology, theological catechisms, or narratives of piety but not Islamic law. Considering the state of current scholarship, it is painfully obvious that the story of Islamic law is yet to be properly understood, leave alone told. In all cases, however, it is no less clear that this story always turns out to be far more complex than Muslim puritans or Western Orientalists understand it to be.[50]

As I have already noted, reasonableness as a concept provides us with an important tool for analyzing the dynamics of Islamic law and international human rights. The concept of reasonable is not without precedent in the Islamic legal tradition—classical Muslim jurists frequently argued that appropriate standards of judgment must be founded on knowledge of what counts as the norm or average human conduct in a particular time and place.[51] Moreover, reasonableness was arguably already inherent to the concepts of public interest (*maslaha*) and custom (*'urf*) in the Islamic legal tradition. More importantly, as argued later, reasonableness entails a set of necessary values that are critical to appraising the authoritativeness of any legal system, and these values have a substantial pedigree in the Islamic legal tradition. Of course, there is a substantial philosophical and legal tradition that debates the role of reason and rationality (*'aql*) in Islamic jurisprudence. I argue later that the pertinent category for the function of law is not so much rationality or reason but reasonableness. Indeed, reorienting our reading of Islamic legal sources, and especially the debates on the role of *'aql*, as contestations about the role of reasonableness in the legal system would allow us to better understand the historical role and dynamics of the Islamic legal system.[52]

Reasonableness assumes a sense of rationality without being wedded to a specific logical path—something is reasonable when it seems to make sense and when it appears to be fair for the great majority of people existing within a specific context.[53] Naturally, what is reasonable to a people varies with time, place, and culture, but at every historical stage in human development there emerges a universal or internationally dominant way of perceiving fairness, the good, and the sensible. The more human beings share the same epistemological venues and assumptions or the same ways of knowing and sharing knowledge, the more they will be prone to having a shared sense of reasonableness. The necessary values of reasonableness are three: (1) proportionality (*tanasub*) between means and ends; (2) balance (*tawazun*) between all valid interests and roles; and (3) measuredness (*talazum*), in which the processes of law are systematized and rendered both accessible and accountable. Proportionality assumes a level of rationality in the way the law goes about achieving its objects; balance assumes a level of fairness in weight and consideration given by the legal system to the competing rights and interests; and measuredness assumes that the legal decision tailors the decision to the specific claims and demands of the particular problem in question so as to preserve the principle of reciprocity. If the legal system places the burden of obligations and duties on a particular party or parties who cannot expect reciprocal commitments from others—if the court overextends itself by validating or imposing power dynamics that undermine relational reciprocity or by making reciprocity in legal dealings lacking—one can say that the law is not properly measured because it either fails to contribute to or actually undermines the very mechanism for upholding the rule of law in society.[54] Those who are familiar with the Islamic legal tradition will recognize that the values of proportionality, balance, and measure are well represented in the Islamic discourses on *tanasub*, *tawazun*, and *iltizam*. If a legal determination or decision is disproportionate to the problem dealt with or is too one-sided, unfair, or biased or is seen as whimsical, chaotic, or idiosyncratic, it is hardly surprising that such a determination or decision would be seen as unreasonable. At a larger scale, if a legal system repeatedly appears to generate determinations that are disproportionate, imbalanced, and unmeasured, it would be fitting to describe the nature or function of this legal system as lacking reasonableness.

I will revisit this issue, and later on I will argue that normatively speaking, the concept of reasonableness is core to leading a reflective life in which one generates proportional, balanced, and measured responses to unfolding challenges and past mistakes. For now, however, to get a better sense of the challenges that confront Islamic law in the modern age, I will discuss a few illustrative examples of what I mean by manifestations of Islamic law that appear to lack reasonableness. In the examples that follow, the necessary values or components of reasonableness are woefully lacking: there is no proportionality between the purported end of the legal determination and the means that are supposed to achieve that end; there is an imbalance or inequity in the way the competing interests, roles, and rights are considered and weighed; and there is a lack of measuredness because the determination appears to ignore sociohistorical contexts as if the logic and processes of the law are beyond accountability or accessibility. Because of the lack of this quintessential element of reasonableness, such legal determinations, to say the least, appear odd, draconian, and intolerant, and very often they treat a major portion of their intended Muslim audience dismissively and offensively. The net effect of such determinations is that they make the Islamic legal system as a whole appear unreasonable, absurdly chaotic, and even outright ridiculous.

MUSINGS ON THE ABSURD

On November 14, 2007, in Qatif, Saudi Arabia, a court applying Islamic law issued a judgment that received widespread media attention as well as near universal condemnation from nongovernmental human rights organizations in both the non-Muslim and Muslim world. Although there has been some ambiguity about some details in the case, what took place is as follows: a nineteen-year-old woman, referred to only as the Qatif girl, met a man in his car in order to retrieve old photographs, purportedly used in a blackmail scheme. A group of Saudi men found the Qatif girl arguing with her black-mailing acquaintance in a car, and so they assaulted the couple. The woman ended up being abducted and raped by seven men fourteen times, and the male acquaintance was reportedly sexually assaulted by three of the offenders as well. Initially, in October 2007, a three-judge panel sentenced four of the offenders to between one and five years in prison and between eighty and one thousand lashes. But the woman and also the male acquaintance were sentenced to ninety lashes each for improper intermingling, or *ikhtilat*. The female rape victim and her lawyer, a well-known human rights activist, were vocal in protesting the sentences handed down against the rapists, which they considered too lenient. The female rape victim also complained about being mistreated by the judges in being spoken to and interrogated by the court in an offensive manner. The Qatif girl also complained that both her lawyer and her husband were excluded from substantial portions of the proceedings. According to Human Rights Watch, the offenders were convicted of kidnapping because the prosecutors could not prove rape, and the court reportedly ignored a mobile phone video in which the offenders recorded the sexual assault.[55] The storm of protests started only after the judgment was reviewed by Saudi Arabia's highest court; the same court on remand increased the convicts' sentences to between two and nine years in prison, but it also increased the rape victim's punishment to two hundred lashes and added six months of imprisonment to the sentence. The court reportedly informed the woman that her sentence was increased because she attempted to discredit and also influence the judiciary by complaining to the media. The court also took punitive measures against the lawyer, who also had spoken to the media, by banning him from the case and by confiscating his license to practice law pending further disciplinary proceedings. Understandably angered by the court's actions, the woman's lawyer reportedly described the proceedings as unjust, and referring to the court's application of Islamic law, he commented: "This is jungle Shari'ah!"[56] In December of the same year, after Human Rights Watch and other human rights organizations called on King 'Abdullah of Saudi Arabia to void the verdict immediately and drop all charges against the rape victim, the Saudi king did in fact "pardon" the "Qatif girl."[57]

My main interest here is not to prove that the Qatif court's actions violate Islamic law, although most certainly many Muslims seemed to think so. The case raises a large number of technical points, but this is not the place for a full exposition on the rather oddly cruel and vindictive legal choices of the Qatif court. The Qatif court could have handled this case in a number of ways that would not have been as unsparingly beastly. The court decided that rape was not proven because it chose to apply the strict evidentiary standards required to prove an offense of *zina* (adultery or fornication) to a case of sexual assault. Charges of adultery or fornication are very difficult to prove, and unproven allegations could result in the accusers' being punished for the crime of slander. Applying the same evidentiary rules and standards to sexual assault charges as those applied to fornication and adultery would mean that it would be practically impossible to prove sexual assaults unless they take place in public or the defendant freely confesses to committing the crime. It would have been feasible, and more jurisprudentially logical, for the court to treat this as a case of *hiraba*, where the testimony of the victim and physical evidence would have been sufficient for proving the offense and which could have resulted in possible death sentences for those convicted. Moreover, punishing a victim of sexual assault for the purported offense of mixing with the opposite sex is without foundation in the classical jurisprudential tradition of Islam. But even if one assumes a very conservative society in which a man and woman sitting in a car have committed punishable offenses, the court makes the immoral decision to punish the victim of a violent sexual crime—a decision that has serious public policy as well as moral consequences in deterring the victims of sexual assault from coming forward. It is difficult to imagine that the court is so heedless to the point of not knowing that the victims of this type of crime already experience an intolerable amount of shame and social ostracism. Nonetheless, the Saudi legal system is not alone in subjecting victims of sexual assault to criminal punishments. Of equal notoriety are a number of cases decided under Pakistani and Afghani rape laws that, as in Saudi Arabia, instead of *hiraba*, applied the evidentiary requirements of *zina* to sexual assault cases and that ended up imprisoning and/or flogging victims of sexual assault.[58] In each of these cases, courts claim to be performing if not what is Islamically compelling, then at least what is authentically Islamic. Effectively, even when these courts are making creative choices or exercising discretion, they attempt to guard against charges of injustice or unreasonableness by relying on "the Islamic"—regardless of how that "Islamic" is constructed. The assumption that underlies these adjudications is that the determinations of Islamic law are above or immune from charges such as unfairness, injustice, irrationality, or unreasonableness.

This brings me to one of the most troubling and portentous issues raised by the Qatif court, in particular, and by these type of cases in general, and that is the doctrine of what is known in Islamic jurisprudence as discretionary punishment (*ta'zir*) and its function in the contemporary age. Many of the courts' determinations are not based on any particular precedents from Islamic jurisprudence but on discretionary punitive measures applied to non-*hudud* offenses, which are subject only to public policy considerations (*al-siyasa al-Shar'iyya*) and to general Islamic legal principles (*al-mabadi' al-'amma* or *al-awwaliyya*). As in the Qatif case, although the women involved were unable to prove that they were forced into *zina*, the very accusation of sexual assault involves admitting to have been involved in sexual activity. Alternatively, an unproven accusation of sexual assault will necessarily mean that a person, who must be presumed innocent, has been slandered. Because the women involved could not prove the element of compulsion—that they were forced into sexual activity—either they have slandered an innocent person of assaulting them or they have made an admission against their own interest in that they engaged in sexual activity of some sort. As in the Qatif case, very often in such cases contemporary judges will invoke the doctrine of discretionary punishments, or *ta'zir*, to punish the purported victim not for the offense of *zina* but for some other related offense. However, aside from the obvious problems of blaming and silencing the victims, the very way that the classical doctrine of discretionary punishments is utilized opens the door to so many unreasonable applications of Islamic law in the contemporary age.

The classical juristic discourses on *ta'zir* tended to focus on two main issues: first, whether there are maximum punitive limits, for instance, as to the number of lashes, the duration of imprisonment, the type and amount of fines that could be imposed, or whether the death sentence could be imposed at all, and second, what standards regulate the proportionality of the punishment inflicted to the nature of the crime committed. Importantly, these juristic debates were not just about the technical restrictions or regulations applicable to criminal penalties but even more so about the fundamental issue of legality. Even those jurists who contended that there are no set limits to discretionary punishments did not intend that the government may do whatever it wishes. Rather, the point was that other than a specific set of crimes that are dealt with explicitly by Shari'ah texts (i.e., *hudud* crimes), all other criminal activity is left to the secular or profane lawmaking authority of the state. *Ta'zir* is applicable to all crimes that were not reserved as areas of special interest by the divine legislature and therefore accrued back to the authority of the state. Nevertheless, even if left to the authority of the state, these discretionary punishments were still subject to the principles regulating the administration of justice (*ahkam al-qada'*) in Shari'ah. And so, for instance, *ta'zir* penalties could not be applied in violation of jurisprudential principles or in contradiction to the maxims of Islamic law, such as that no punishment may be meted without notice of illegality; that what God made permissible cannot be made forbidden; that the state always carries the burden of proof; or that no person may be held guilty without sufficient process.[59] It is notable that the classical juristic discourses exhibited a great deal of concern about potential abuses of power, and so in response, most jurists argued for restrictive parameters in the application of *ta'zir* punishments.[60] In all cases, classical jurists appeared to agree that simply by labeling a punitive action as *ta'zir* does not mean that the state is acting within its legitimate powers, and I think one can add it does not mean that the legal system is acting reasonably either.

As mentioned above, reasonableness must be defined within the confines of space and time, and therefore, it is not surprising that premodern jurists tended to cite various and often contradictory legal precedents and then proceed to analyze their validity or applicability. One such precedent, for instance, claimed that the judge Abu Yusuf (d. 182/798) protested to the Caliph Harun al-Rashid that the common *ta'zir* penalty in his day and age of two hundred to three hundred lashings, depending on the crime, was unreasonably excessive.[61] Other precedents tended to focus on the element of deterrence, arguing that while hardened criminals may not be deterred by a hundred lashings, common or honorable folks may be thoroughly deterred by no more than three thrashings. Still other precedents dictated that *ta'zir* beatings are appropriate only for repeat offenders or for those who will not be deterred by a warning or fine. Reflecting what must have been socially and culturally contingent standards, other precedents emphasized that *ta'zir* beatings may not break the skin or cause bleeding; otherwise, the punishments are to be considered torturous and cruel. In these and many other precedents, which cite numerous factors and elements to be weighed in considering the legality of *ta'zir* punishments, it is quite clear that Muslim jurists struggled to produce sensible determinations—for the determinations to make sense within the inner logic of the legal system and to make sense to the people who had to live and abide by this law. In essence, they utilized their technical legal skills to reach legal determinations that did not appear whimsical, haphazard, ridiculous, or absurd within the societies and legal systems in which they functioned or, put differently, within their pertinent audience and constituency.[62] This, however, is in sharp contrast to the logic that one sees in action in many contemporary applications of Islamic law, the Qatif girl case being a painfully demonstrative example.

In the Saudi criminal system, the Qatif girl case is not the exception but apparently the rule. Saudi criminal courts, in addition to prison sentences that could be as long as ten or fifteen years, regularly sentence convicts to anywhere from a thousand to three thousand lashes and at times even more. In recent years, Saudi courts have sentenced defendants to hundreds of lashes in cases that did not involve violent crimes.[63] For instance, a case that took place in 2008 that garnered a great deal of media attention involved an Egyptian doctor who was sentenced to twenty-five hundred lashes and ten years in prison because he was accused of wrongfully prescribing pain medicine to a Saudi princess who allegedly became addicted to these prescription drugs. The facts of the case were highly contested, but arguably, the most the doctor could have been guilty of was medical malpractice. Because of the large number of Egyptian doctors working in Saudi Arabia, the case was reported very widely in Egypt, and initially, the reaction of Egyptian society was absolute shock at what appeared to be a uniquely cruel and vindictive sentence. It was soon discovered, however, that there were a large number of cases involving non-Saudi doctors who were sentenced to hundreds of lashings and several years of prison for the commission of medical malpractice. Interestingly, for a period of time, one could not tune into an Egyptian television channel or read an Egyptian journalistic publication without encountering an expression of outrage at the injustice and cruelty of these adjudications. These public discourses, however, came to an abrupt and sudden stop, and it was rumored that in response to pressure from the Saudi government, the Egyptian government instituted a ban on reporting or discussing these cases.[64]

It does appear to me that whether considered from the perspective of Islamic or non-Islamic values, regardless of the offense committed, the administration of thousands of lashings does indeed constitute torture. In Saudi Arabia, normally, the full number of lashings is not carried out all at one time—the punishment is usually administered in installments of 100 or 150 lashes a week, and in some cases, the beatings are administered daily. Nevertheless, the apportionment of hundreds of lashes over daily or weekly installments does not alter the essentially cruel and torturous nature of these punishments. It is fair to say that these punishments and the prolonged and drawn-out nature by which they are inflicted are strikingly excessive and rather shocking to the conscience. Not surprisingly, these Saudi punishments have been described as gross violations of international human rights law, and indeed it would not be difficult to prove that they are clearly at odds with a number of international law instruments and standards.[65] However, at this point in my argument, I do not want to focus on the ways in which the Saudi government is in breach of its international human rights obligations. My point is far less concrete or tangible but perhaps more intuitive, emotive, and fundamental, and that is: punishments such as those applied by Saudi Arabia are palpably unreasonable, and they contribute to the building up of the image of Islamic law as an unreasonable legal system—something that is an outlier to the normal course of human development—at odds with the progression of collective human consciousness. These punishments would strike most human beings as ugly because they appear to be grossly unreasonable. The reason they so appear, I would argue, is that these penalties are disproportionate, unfair or imbalanced, and excessive.

One obvious objection—and an objection I often encounter while at speaking engagements—is how it could be possible to speak of reasonability or its opposite in the absence of a clearly defined frame of reference. If there is a socially or empirically verifiable or legally definable frame of reference, reasonableness could be a coherent concept; otherwise, the concept is too elusive to be useful. In this context, the point usually made is that reasonableness, like the notion of offensiveness or beauty, is a judgment. Typically, the objection made does not deny the need for judgments, but the objection is that without a clear and accepted frame of reference such judgments become easy vehicles for values that are relative and subjective. Therefore, judgment becomes nothing more than preference, and these preferences become the guise for perpetuating what has been described as false universals.

I will deal with the issue of the frame of reference in Shari'ah and the concept of false universals later in this book. I do note, however, that just because there is such a thing as false universals, it does not follow that all universals are false. Indeed, it is the existence of universals that empowers us to speak of goodness, beauty, and the rights of human beings or universal rights. Without universals, the very ideas of humanity and humaneness would become incoherent. I do not take lightly the criticisms made against claims of universal truths, especially when such claims are made by the mighty and powerful. Nor do I ignore the fact that throughout human history it is the wealthy and powerful who have tended to exploit moral standards and manipulate perceptions of goodness to advance their own interests at the expense of the disempowered and weak. In fact, I believe that any morally conscientious person must be deeply troubled by the ways that dominant power shapes and skews our perceptions of morality and beauty.

In one of my typically noncharismatic but passionate lectures about the unreasonableness of Saudi criminal penalties, I remember a Qatari fellow who, with some measure of restrained frustration, confronted me with the outraged exclamation: "Why is it that people like you never manage to mention the offensively unreasonable treatment of people such as Kahlah al-Marri?" Probably confirming his suspicions about people like me, I gave him a thoroughly clueless look. I am sure he interpreted my puzzled look as vindication of his belief that an American Muslim like myself who has spent a lifetime critiquing his own tradition in search of liberal values only takes heed of wrongdoing if committed by fellow Muslims but is otherwise oblivious to the sins of the West. Of course, he was wrong. I knew quite a bit about the case of al-Marri, and I might add, numerous other cases like it. 'Ali Saleh Khalah al-Marri is a Qatari citizen who came to the United States with his wife and children to study computer programming only to be seized by the US government in December 2001 and held as a material witness. In 2003, President Bush, by presidential order, changed his designation to an enemy combatant and ordered him to be held indefinitely without charges or trial. As of the date of my lecture in February 2009, al-Marri continued to be detained indefinitely in a military facility. After it became clear that the reason for my puzzlement was that I failed to see the relevance of al-Marri's case to my arguments about unreasonable constructions of Islamic law in the modern age, the Qatari gentleman who had made the remark took a magazine out of his backpack, rummaged to a particular page, and pointing to a specific paragraph exclaimed: "Look! Some people would strongly take issue with your assessment of reasonableness!" What he was alluding to was that al-Marri was kept in complete isolation with severe restrictions on his activity for months at a time, and the combination of his isolation and uncertainty as to whether he would ever stand trial or be released had caused very serious deteriorations in al-Marri's mental health. Al-Marri was quoted as protesting the unreasonable and cruel way he had been treated and describing his condition as a slow death.

Al-Marri's is not an isolated case, and my interlocutor had a point. Indeed, one of the common criticisms of my work on the place of tolerance and on the challenge of democracy in Islam was the accusation that whether consciously or not, it appeased hegemonic power.[66] In one of its versions, this type of criticism sees liberal Islam as fundamentally a response to the hegemony of the West. Instead of choosing to resist, the advocates of liberal Islam struggle to shape Islam to accommodate and appease the West.[67] In another and perhaps more valid version, this argument is not so much about the nature of so-called liberal Islam but about power and its inextricable relation to criticism—to what is criticized and who is criticized. Not only does power often define the object of our gaze, or what we gaze at and how we gaze at it, but also whether we admit what we see. Power is corrupting not just because it limits the angle of the human gaze but also because of its ability to convince so many people to falsify their testimony about what they have seen. As valid and compelling as this objection might be, it is not so much about the objectivity of standards or references but what could be called the disproportionality of criticism—the skewed perspective from which one gazes at suffering and the inevitable imbalance that afflicts any expression of outrage.

The disproportionality of criticism objection is sufficiently widespread among so many Muslims to the point that it has become a serious emotional barrier against self-introspection and reform. Objections to the hypocrisy of human rights discourses and the double standards that plague the practice of human rights is arguably one of the most serious cultural impediments preventing the enthusiastic adoption of international human rights standards in the Muslim world. Historically, the hypocrisy of many Western countries in dealing with Palestinian rights has constructed a formidable emotional barrier against international human rights advocacy in the Arab world. But this emotional barrier has only grown more complicated in the wake of the war on terror, especially in light of the servitude of many Western legal experts and intellectuals in defending or otherwise minimizing the many human rights violations committed against Muslims in the course of this war. One, however, must be careful with this kind of argument because, first, it has been a favorite theme for both scholars and Islamophobic idealogues who have filled thousands of pages talking about the roots of Muslim rage, the wrath of Islam, or similar odious subjects.[68] Furthermore, many more have seized on the theme to argue that there is a fundamental difference between the Islamic and Western civilizations and that because of the huge disparity in their respective value systems, they will tend to clash or, at least, persist in an uneasy and friction-filled coexistence. But perhaps there is something else that should be learned here other than grievances, offenses, and reciprocal hate or anger. Many historians believe that the very idea of the West as a sociopolitical entity, with its own sense of shared value and destiny and a common cultural frame of reference, was formed largely as a defensive reaction to the threat posed by the Islamic civilization.[69] But the Islamic civilization itself had incorporated and co-opted the civilizational outproduct of the Persians, Greeks, Romans, and Turks, among others. The European Enlightenment, in turn, borrowed heavily from the Islamic civilization, including Persian and Judeo-Arab intellectuals.[70] The history of the Muslim world since colonialism and in the postcolonial age demonstrates that the cultural impact of the West on the Muslims' world is irreversible. As the recent events of the so-called Arab Spring show, certain intellectual paradigms such as civil society, democracy, public versus private space, public versus individual rights, and secular versus religious state have become an entrenched part of the modern Muslim consciousness. Whatever the particulars of the historical injustices and other grievances, the fate of Muslims depends on how they relate to and construct or reconstruct these paradigms. But even more, as shown by the rise of the Christian right and the spread of religious intolerance in Europe and the United States, the West itself is in a constant dynamic process of definition and redefinition vis-à-vis the same paradigms. The point is that while technology, economic systems, communications, and power dynamics define the amount and kind of space in which human beings dwell, no one—and no civilization—can exist outside its historical context or outside the space defining people's epistemological awareness. Civilizational purists see the world in terms of cultures that are separate and apart and believe that at most, civilizations can engage in dialogue and polite exchanges, but that somehow, cultures manage to preserve an authenticity and integrity that persists for centuries. According to purists, it is because they can exist as holistic units that civilizations can engage in conflicts or ex-changes.

I don't know if the idea of civilizational identities is historically defen-sible. But I do know that after reading Arnold Toynbee at a young age, I found the word *civilization* effortlessly seeping into my terminology. In the 1980s, every time I used this word, my political science and history profes-sors would immediately retort: What does civilization mean? What does the West mean, what does Islam mean? Back then, speaking of civilization and their conflicts was not popular—what was popular was all talk about the virtues of pluralism and multiculturalism. Eventually, I have come to realize that perhaps Toynbee had a point and there is indeed such a thing as civiliza-tional cultures. But more importantly, arguments about civilizations are a risky business because they often conceal a thinly veiled racism or religious bigotry. Furthermore, often the described characteristics of a purported civil-ization have far more to do with ideological constructs and inventions than actual or real history. After taking account of racist and bigoted motives that often inspire claims of civilizational purity and after weighing the extent to which the purported characteristics of a civilization is a construct motivated by ideology and not history, what remains? I am not entirely sure, but what-ever remains is more likely than not a product of an accrued cross-cultural product of cumulative civilizations than a pristine, purebred heritage. Human beings borrow, transplant, and adapt from one another. As the moral vision-ary Shaykh Tantawi Jawhari (d. 1358/1940) of the early twentieth century pointed out, throughout the history of human interactions, each nation and every society has been in the position of a student in relation to every other nation and society. The reality, however, is that some nations, as if bad students, learn only what is superficial, distorted, twisted, or harmful from others, while some nations, as if good students, learn what is useful, benefi-cial, authentic, and good.[71] I agree with Jawhari that nations are constantly learning from one another, but I also think whether people have the intellec-tual integrity or even the depth and expanse of knowledge to admit the extent to which they learn from one another and owe each other is something else.

Chapter Three

Crisis: Making Sense of Shari'ah Today

In 2012, Ahmad Atif Ahmad published his masterful study titled *The Fatigue of the Shari'a*, which analyzed a medieval Muslim debate that explored a critical theological and philosophical question: What happens if an age comes when divine norms are no longer available to guide Muslims? The debate known in Islamic literature as *al-qawl fi futur al-Shari'ah* (literally, the issue of the fatigue or disintegration of Shari'ah) often was founded on a pessimistic reading of history—Muslim jurists imagined that a time would come when qualified specialists in Shari'ah would become extinct and Muslims would no longer have access to divine guidance in all types of matters affecting their lives.[1] Ahmad Atif Ahmad reveals a premodern discourse of impressive complexity and richness about the nature of divine guidance and competing perspectives about the ability of human beings to do without such guidance. In all cases, Muslim jurists did not imagine a time when God would lose interest in creation and turn away from human beings. Rather, they imagined a time when human beings, for a variety of reasons, would fail to make proper use of the availability of divine guidance. Most often the imagined scenario would be a time when the skilled interpreters of divine norms and guidance would become extinct. As the author of the aforementioned book aptly notes, the task of deciding whether we are currently in such an age is better left to those who are in the business of prophesizing. As a moral and intellectual matter, to the extent that this thesis relies on the end-of-times-type logic, it can never be a justification for apathy or nihilism. As a Muslim working within the Islamic tradition, the fatigue of Shari'ah, in the sense that the interpretive tradition of Islam ceased to be clearly relevant, is an entirely different question than the death of Shari'ah. The Shari'ah in the sense of divine guidance will never die—this is something I adhere to as a

63

matter of faith. What are practical and actual implications of Shari'ah in our age and times is an entirely different question. Indeed, as a Muslim I believe that alleviating the fatigue of Shari'ah is a religious obligation that engages the spirit, conscience, and intellect in every sense.

I approach the fatigue of Shari'ah discourses as a moral warning and not as some fatalistic reading of human progress. The hypothetical posed was: What happens if qualified interpreters of divine guidance become extinct? What Ahmad Atif Ahmad argues in his book only begs the question: What constitutes a qualified interpreter in each age? What are the necessary qualifications of such an interpreter within the framework of the contemporary epistemological and phenomenological knowledge and consciousness? Scholars as disparate and different as Ibn Taymiyya and Ibn Rushd at a minimum agreed on one thing: what is ascribed to the divine cannot be irrational, unreasonable, or absurd. A number of philosophical and juristic principles coalesce to negate the possibility that divine guidance could lead to irrational, absurd, or unreasonable results.[2] To even pretend that we can start to evaluate the qualifications of the interpreters we would need to have an understanding of the nature of this divine guidance. In my opinion, it goes without saying that knowledge of the scriptures (both Qur'an and Sunna of the Prophet) is an absolute must, but this is hardly enough. But even more, mastering the methods of scriptural hermeneutics, the rules of Arabic grammar, and the other traditional requirements such as the application of casuistic deductive reasoning to reach a determination through legal analogy is all necessary but hardly sufficient to meet the challenge. I will have to return to this subject later in the book, but I think it is reasonable to say that if the nature of divine guidance must address, engage, and persuade our rational faculties, then one must be rationally equipped or qualified to authoritatively interpret this divine guidance. At a minimum, engaging the divine guidance must withstand rigorous rational analysis *according to the standards of rigor defined in each day and age*. If the standards of intellectual rigor do not shift according to the dictates of the day and age, the real risk is that the divine guidance would no longer remain persuasive to rational people within a particular age.

There is plenty of evidence that Islamic law or the interpretations of the Shari'ah have already lost much of their persuasive power in the contemporary age. I believe that if Muslims were asked about the importance of normative divine guidance in navigating their own personal lives, most devout Muslims would agree that divine guidance is important. However, if asked if Islamic law should be implemented as the law of the land, most Muslims would not wish to be governed by Islamic law.[3] Some Muslims go as far as contending that they do not believe in Shari'ah itself. In my view, I do not know what remains of Islam if Shari'ah, as opposed to Islamic law, is excluded or ignored because Shari'ah is the kernel of divine guidance in Islam. I will have to return to this critical issue later, but for now, let us continue with the question of how those who have taken on the task of interpreting the divine guidance in the lived life of Muslims have handled the task. So many assertions of Islamic law in the contemporary age are politicized and also pedantic. These pedantic and politicized readings of divine guidance are fairly strong indicators that those doing the interpretive act are hardly qualified for the task because the end results of their efforts are determinations that are unreasonable, or ones that the rational mind cannot accept. At the very least, politicized and pedantic determinations give the distinct impression that the determinations reached are opportunistic or at a minimum involve a discreet conflict of interest. The persistence of politicized and pedantic practices and the resulting appearance of unreasonableness or lack of rationality have deeply affected the ambiguous status of Islamic law in the world today. In principle, most Muslims recognize the normative importance of divine guidance in their lives, but they, to say the least, are ambiguously conflicted about the concrete implications of this guidance. Part of the reason that the position of Islamists in contemporary Muslim societies is so contested is that there is a fundamental distrust as to the integrity and reasonability of their interpretive activities. But even more, the real dilemma is that there is no degree of agreement as to who the Islamists are or what the referential criteria are that could help identify an Islamist as opposed to a Muslim. In earlier books, I dealt with the vacuum of religious authority in Islam and the absence of systematic and rational criteria for defining the authoritative in Islamic legal discourses.[4] But if one is to sum up the current condition, one could confidently say that, at a minimum, the scriptural foundation of the divine guidance is solidly recognized and established in Islam. But beyond this fact, the ambiguities are numerous. Who should interpret this guidance, and through what process? What are the requisite qualifications and levels of competence and the actual lived experience that the interpreters should enjoy? What are the interpreters' historical assumptions about the role of divine guidance in relation to Shari'ah? What are some of the basic ethical outlooks regarding the purpose and objective of human law in relation to divine guidance? And are the interpreters even necessary at all, or is there some other process by which we can access the divine guidance? All of this is highly contested among modern Muslim societies. As detailed later, add to this the fact that colonialism had thoroughly uprooted and replaced the collective historical memory of the institutions of Islamic law.[5] Isn't it rather telling and also sadly ironic that a good portion of the archival records that could be used in scholarly reconstructions of the lived Islamic legal tradition is now housed in a number of prestigious Western academic venues and not in Muslim libraries?

Any Muslim intellectual who has lived through the period from the rise of nationalism and the Islamic resurgence of the 1970s, the Islamization projects of the 1980s, and the explosion of Wahhabism on the scene all over the Muslim world from the 1970s to the end of the twentieth century would have witnessed numerous religious and cultural movements and transformations. Remarkably, however, throughout these decades and into the twenty-first century, one invariable development has been the steady growth and seemingly unstoppable rise in politicized and pedantic manifestations of Islamic law.

Examples of the production of pedantic and politicized determinations attributed to Islamic law in our contemporary age are too numerous to recount. Through the age of colonialism, Islamic law went from the common law of the land, negotiating real conflicts and disputes, to an ideological symbol of a lost history and identity. As colonialism came to an end, there

emerged a so-called reformist movement that was quintessentially synchrenistic in nature, which tried to rethink and revise Islamic law largely along
civil-law terms.[6] Whatever one may say about this synchrenistic movement,
there is no doubt that it was led by a highly educated class of intellectuals
who were possessed of viable civilizational vision and project. Visionaries
such as Muhammad 'Abduh, Muhammad Iqbal, Khayr al-Din al-Tunisi,
'Abd al-Rahman al-Kawakibi, Tantawi Jawhari, and many others understood
that reclaiming the heritage of Shari'ah could not simply be achieved by
issuing new legal opinions or *fatawa*, but that it required a reconceptualization and reconstruction of the very nature of the obligation binding human
beings to the divine. But, as discussed later, with the spread of puritanism in
the 1960s and 1970s, what occurred was a fundamental and drastic deterioration in the quality of Islamic thought, and especially in the conceptualized
and imagined space for Shari'ah. In a span of a little more than a century,
Islamic law went from constituting the common law of the land to a pedantic
practice of minutiae and to acts of intellectual escapism. As will be seen
later, much of this boiled down to one's attitude toward history. History is
the critical repository of memory and identity. More importantly, history is
the record of the ways by which memory and identity are challenged, defied,
and contested, and it is also the record of the ways in which memory and
identity are negotiated, reconstructed, and at times even reinvented. Puritans
simplified and stereotyped history to the point of effacing its processes and
dynamics. For puritans, remembering the positive commandments of Shari'ah was far more important than studying and analyzing how the inherited
memory of Shari'ah was renegotiated and reformed numerous times throughout history. But a memory and identity that fail to wrestle with the vagaries,
indeterminacies, and sheer messiness of history are invariably poorly rooted
and shallow. Puritans escaped history by forming their identity along the
lines of the positivist rules of law. However, the rules of law, without the
historically anchored institutions of culture and without the historically embedded process of negotiation and reconstruction, become little more than a
superficial and despotic assertion of a deluge of minutiae. The set of rules
and commands that are dogmatically proclaimed to be God's law become a
despotic way of escaping any serious analytical engagement with intellectual
problems of the age. This act of escapism locks the participants into a continuing regression further into minutiae and pedantry as the legal system as a
whole increasingly finds itself marginalized and becoming increasingly irrelevant.

   Delving into the distractions of minutiae is an act of moral and ideological escapism that plays a necessary role in sustaining and promoting the
utopian mythology of many Islamic movements. This submersion into endless minutiae and formalism allows the activist to feel empowered by the
sense of having conscripted all social space within a society into the service
of this ultimate goal but without having to articulate or prove the merits of
this utopian vision. But unlike the killing-flies incident mentioned earlier, the
minutiae dealt with in the contemporary context does not relate to technical
acts of sacred ritualism. The participants in the contemporary context are not
satisfied simply with orthopraxy and ritualistic practice. Rather, what is
sought and constantly exhibited is a desire to engage in the pretense of

serving the Islamic cause. The pretense is maintained by undertaking largely ornate acts that are ostentatious in nature and that are designed to promote the affectation of intellectual service to Islam. What distinguishes these acts of intellectual affectation from actual critical thought is that they arise from an immediate short-term context, rely on an emotional wishful appeal, are made unaccountable to others, and are not applied with any level of rigor, consistency, or constancy. These acts of intellectual affectation do not seek to critically analyze a particular reality and then attempt to deduce possible solutions to identifiable problems. Whatever the frame of reference, it is interested in evidence only to the extent that this evidence selectively supports a foregone conclusion—but the evidence, like the conclusion, serves a purely functional purpose that only lasts as long as its immediate instigator exists. In short, intellectual affectations are always opportunistic and never principled. Acts of intellectual affectation are escapist because while serving a functional purpose, they leave the dream or cause intact—placed well beyond the reach of any critical evaluation. This tendency toward false affectations is especially present in the Salafi/Wahhabi brand of Islam, which emphasizes public displays of religiosity at the expense of private conscience and personal virtue. The kind of practices described below are so numerous and frequent to the point that I can say with complete confidence that every Muslim who has feared the rise of the Islamists or the implementation of Shari'ah in the wake of the Arab Spring has his or her own memory bank of examples of false affectations to draw upon. In Egypt in particular, at the very height of the demonstrations, when so many were getting killed or maimed, Egypt was flooded with *fatawa* (sing. *fatwa*) either by Saudi jurists or their Wahhabi Egyptian counterparts, adamantly declaring that it is contrary to God's will to rebel even against a tyrant or unjust ruler. Accordingly, the *fatawa* declared that all those who joined the rebels in Tahrir were sinners if not worse.[7] Of course, many jurists and Islamic groups, such as the Muslim Brotherhood, did fully participate in the revolution, but the ones most willing to continue enduring the despotism and the unspeakable conditions of social and economic injustice prevailing in Egypt were the puritan/ Wahhabi groups. However, once Hosni Mubarak was overthrown and many groups started to compete for leverage and position, the puritanical groups were among the most aggressive in demanding their share of political gains. One can hardly fault the puritans for wanting to participate in shaping the identity and future of their country. The problem, however, is that the same groups who issued the *fatawa* condemning the revolution followed the same casual, off-handed, and self-gratifying methodology in ignoring the earlier position and adopting a new one. There was no effort spent in accounting for the shift in position from prohibition to the acceptance of the legitimacy of the revolutionaries or, at least, the legitimacy of what the revolutionaries accomplished. But failing to maintain a transparent, rigorous, and principled explanation for their determinations leaves one with the unsettling feeling that once again the practitioners of Shari'ah fail to respect their subject matter, their audience, or even the integrity of their own professional competence in issuing determinations worthy of being attributed to the divine.

Muhammad Morsi, effectively the candidate of the Muslim Brotherhood, eventually won the presidential elections in 2012. In order to defeat Ahmad

Shafiq, the candidate backed by the army and the clientele of Mubarak's corrupt regime, the Muslim Brotherhood had to rely on the electoral support of the puritanical groups. Shortly after the elections, many media reports started emerging about vigilante behavior perpetrated by members of puritan groups, harassing women for not covering their hair or men for not wearing a beard or interrogating men and women for being in each other's company in public. This vigilante behavior was widely condemned even by Morsi, the newly elected president, but it did underscore the fact that for many puritans, Shari'ah is anchored in a cosmetic sense of priorities. Egypt is plagued with very serious problems, including poverty, poor health care, abysmal educational systems, corruption, and many other crises. Puritans, however, give the distinct impression that Shari'ah is obsessed with dominating the social and personal space occupied by women but otherwise is disengaged from the real-life concerns of human beings.

What is the most striking is that the use of pietistic affectations instead of reasoned analysis in the practice of Shari'ah has become a widespread phenomenon not just limited to puritanical groups. Shari'ah has become a symbolic construct that is leveraged by an untold number of actors for a variety of purposes that consistently cast Shari'ah in the role of the "unreasonable." Sometimes the usage of Shari'ah is so blatantly absurd that it borders on the offensive. One of my personal favorites involves a Muslim leader who informed President Clinton that according to Islamic law, no one would be allowed to discuss his affair with Monica Lewinsky because four witnesses to the sexual act, which is required to prove fornication and adultery, had not been satisfied. I have no idea what President Clinton thought, if anything, of this so-called Shari'ah-based fantasy on a theme of political morality. But in my view, this kind of off-handed and distorted opining on Shari'ah cannot but contribute to undermining the legitimacy of the concept of Shari'ah itself. I do not know if this leader believed that Shari'ah's antipathy to sexual slander applied to ethically shield a public official from the type of scrutiny directed at President Clinton's misconduct. I also do not know if effectively this leader was arguing that American Muslims should refrain from supporting any measures that meddled into Clinton's sexual life or if the argument is that from an Islamic perspective, it is unethical to fail to respect the president's private life. In all cases, any attempt at deriving moral lessons from Shari'ah's four-witness rule and then applying the morally derived judgment to the context of an American president accused of sexual misconduct in the White House is by definition unreasonable unless it addresses numerous factors related to the specifics and particularity of the American historical and political context. At a minimum, democracies rely on a reasonable distinction between speech involving public versus private individuals. The distinction is critical for the protection of freedom of speech in a democracy, especially when one deals with elected individuals who are supposed to represent the will of the elected. Citing a purported Shari'ah rule is not a self-sufficient analytical argument, and it is deeply problematic to use its rules formalistically as a trump card in order to score largely symbolic points.

Citing a Shari'ah-based rule without rising to the challenge of understanding the objective, implications, and context of the rule means that Shari'ah will continue to be employed not as a serious interpretive tradition that derives its legitimacy from its rational and persuasive engagement with its historical contexts, but as a sacred trope deployed in purely opportunistic ways.

In the course of my career as a Muslim jurist, I have encountered more examples of shameless manipulations of Shari'ah than I can possibly recall. My experiences are hardly unique, however, and I am confident that any active Muslim would have his or her own share of uncomfortable experiences. Here, I am reminded of many situations in which those claiming to be authorities exhibit a painful lack of basic competence in extracting reasonable readings of Shari'ah within a communal context. I recall a Lebanese imam in California, a college dropout, who adorned himself with all the insignia of piety. Although his sole training consisted of a crash course in Shari'ah studies in Saudi Arabia, his skill in performing the affectations of piety had turned him into an authority on all matters concerning Shari'ah. This same fellow was up for board elections in his community. The imam declared that since Islam is a democratic religion, he would not allow anyone to lead the Friday services other than, of course, himself, unless a clear majority of the worshippers submitted a petition requesting that someone else be allowed to lead the services. To his chagrin, the most serious challenger to his spot was the woman that started the petition, who noticed that the Lebanese imam had turned the Friday pulpit into a platform for endless campaigning for the best man on the job—himself, of course. When the woman challenging him in the elections demanded that she be able to do her own campaigning by giving a public lecture, he conveniently responded with a *fatwa*. The *fatwa* proclaimed that since women may not lead the Friday services, his female challenger may not give a speech in favor of her candidacy! I presume this meant that although the female challenger had a right to compete in the board elections, she did not have a right to speak to the community!

Other examples involving the bizarre also demonstrate the crucial importance of common sense and reasonableness in understanding and implementing Islamic teachings. Not too long ago, I recall hearing an imam in Cairo bragging during the Friday services about the fact that on the very same day his wife died, he rushed to marry another woman. His point was not that he disliked his deceased wife, or that he was in love with his new wife. He sought to demonstrate his piety and willingness to obey the injunctions of Shari'ah as he understood it. In this context, he quoted a tradition attributed to the Prophet, counseling and encouraging men to marry. In this tradition, the Prophet is quoted as saying that God is pleased with those who will not spend the night except with their wife sleeping next to them. The imam argued that this tradition made it clear for him that, when his wife died, he could not let the night fall without a new wife sleeping next to him. Of course, this imam was not interested in engaging in a discussion about the context or authenticity of this report, and he was also not interested in discussing other moral values that need to be balanced and weighed against his singular focus on a speedy marriage.[8]

In a different incident that I think deserves to be categorized under the bizarre, I was introduced to an imam who generated a great affectation of profound piety when he would patiently wait until a woman had departed her seat and then proceed to fan the chair before anyone else was allowed to sit on it. The reason he engaged in this strange ritual was to ensure that the body heat of the departed woman had properly dissipated from the chair, lest a man sit in her place and be sexually aroused by the remnants of her warmth. There was an actual historical precedent to the imam's odd behavior. Centuries ago, it was reported that Abu Hanifa (d. 150/767), the founder of the Hanafi school of legal thought, had advised men not to sit where a woman was sitting until the remnants of the woman's body heat dissipated from the seat.[9] But because of the imam's poor training in the Islamic legal heritage, what he did not know was that the point of Abu Hanifa's advice was not the avoidance of sexual arousal. In Abu Hanifa's time and place, it was considered ill mannered to steal someone's seat shortly after they left it. Especially with women, the polite thing to do after a person had departed a seat was to wait for a period of time before taking the person's place, lest that person return only to find his or her seat occupied. In addition, sitting in someone's place immediately was considered a sign of lack of humility. Thus, Abu Hanifa was saying, in effect: "Be polite and wait a while before taking a woman's seat!" Notably, in contrast to the imam's behavior, instead of constituting conduct demeaning to women, Abu Hanifa sought to emphasize that in dealing with women, there is no exception to the rules of proper etiquette. Rather tellingly, a historically contingent and socially responsive precedent is transformed in the modern context into an ostentatious display of piety, and instead of being a message emphasizing respect toward women, in contemporary dynamics it is mutated into something demeaning toward women.

Another bizarre instance involved a group of three board members in the United States who sought to disqualify a woman from any public activity because, they claimed, although wearing the hijab, she was still too beautiful and, therefore, this would prevent the board members from being truly pious by challenging their ability to lower their gaze. Moreover, they argued, under no circumstances could she be elected to the board of directors of their center because they would not be able to concentrate on doing their jobs. This situation always reminded me of a historical incident in which a Caliph was deeply in love with a slave girl, so he had her murdered because as long as she lived he could not concentrate on running the nation. The notable classical jurist Ibn al-Jawzi (d. 597/1200) offered the best and most fitting analysis of this incident; he called the Caliph insane and those who obeyed him morally bankrupt.[10] The decision of the board members seems to me to be blatantly unreasonable because it gives weight only to the rights and interests of the men without regard to women. This kind of one-sided male chauvinism is typical of puritanical Islam, but the problem is that in this day and age, the type of exclusion advocated by this group effectively follows the logic of the insane Caliph mentioned above. The Caliph murdered the slave girl, but this group logic amounts to killing the souls of the excluded women.

The impact of pietistic affectations, because of their stark opportunism and their complete disregard for any principled and rational approach to Shari'ah, has been to close off avenues for critical thought and abort any possibilities for discourse. In every sense, they cheapen Islamic thought to the point that any attempt to engage in a discourse seems to be an exercise in frivolity. The dynamics of affectation and the challenge of aborted discourses are particularly aggravated when it comes to matters related to women.

Whether one is dealing with the subject of the hijab of women or the physical location of women in a mosque or Islamic center, these matters elicit such ostentatious acts of affectation that it becomes practically impossible to have a rational discussion based on the study of the evidence. In a considerable number of Islamic centers in the United States as well as mosques in the Middle East, women are placed behind curtains, in back rooms, or in separate buildings altogether in order to separate them from men. The impact of puritanical movements has been especially devastating. Growing up in the Egypt of the 1960s and 1970s, I recall that men and women interacted freely in prominent mosques such as that of al-Imam Husayn and al-Sayyida Zaynab. Whole families would meet together in mosques to socialize or to attend religious instruction. Sections designated for women were practically unknown, and it was not at all uncommon to find women praying behind men in an open space. Incidentally, for all of the puritanical zeal of the Saudi Wahhabis, they were unable to change the centuries-old practice in the mosques of Mecca and Medina, where women are not limited to a secluded area away from the public view. Although Saudi Arabia has tried to segregate men and women in these two main mosques, they have not been successful thus far. Outside of Mecca and Medina, however, the puritans have been remarkably successful. Although I am not sure when the practice of segregation was put into place, as of my last visit to Egypt in 2011, in mosques such as Masjid al-Husayn in Cairo, women were indeed secluded and cordoned off into closed sections. When I had an opportunity to discuss this development with the Shaykh al-Azhar, Ahmad al-Tayyib, and the Mufti of Egypt, 'Ali Jum'a, both somberly explained that this was not the official policy of the Egyptian Ministry of Religious Endowments but was put into effect by local puritanical activists at their own initiatives. I should note that I did notice that in centuries-old mosques that remained under the control of Sufi communities, mosques remained unsegregated. Curiously, while we do have reports attributed to the Prophet explicitly stating that women should not be prohibited from accessing mosques, and while there are cumulative reports about widespread and regular attendance of mosques at the time of the Prophet, it is remarkable how persistently men have sought to exclude or limit the access of women to places of worship. My point, however, is not to prove the Islamicity of desegregation versus segregation. I will deal with the methodology of Shari'ah interpretation later on in the book. My point is that issues of gender, sexuality, seduction, sacred space, and Shari'ah cannot be treated with the casual affectations that have come to shape so many of the dynamics relating to Islamicity, native customs, and social identities. As discussed later, citing a report or verse as self-sufficient elucidation of Shari'ah is forcing Shari'ah into a dogmatic position that is by definition unreasonable. The whole issue of *fitna* (seduction), whether by men or women, must be evaluated in light of contemporary systems of knowledge and human expectations. At a minimum, it is not possible to continue speaking of *fitna* as if social relations and gender roles have not been dramatically impacted by contemporary systems of communication and information. The failure to speak honestly and transparently about issues related to the historically constructed archetype of *fitna*, which essentially embodies all the seductions of femininity and frustrations of men, and the roles this construct plays in different societies makes the whole subject matter susceptible to pretenses and affectations of piety that play out in a highly symbolic but also dishonest fashion. The symbolic construct of *fitna*, which is taken out of its multilayered historical context in the Islamic tradition, and the way it is used to censor any serious interrogations of the contemporary understandings of gender roles has had a profound effect in producing some of the worst social pathologies in contemporary Muslim societies. This concept is conveniently cited in every exclusion of women from the public sphere—from the seclusion of women in Cairo mosques, mentioned above, to the Saudi prohibition against women driving. At the same time, emphasis on *fitna* does not necessarily produce a chaste or modest society. If anything, one observes that the obsessive focus on *fitna* discourses, especially by the puritanical vanguard, has only produced deep social pathologies and contradictions. So, for instance, the real paradox is that while Saudi Arabia has one of the most conservative and restrictive cultures, the reality is that powerful and wealthy Saudis who are close to the ruling family own many of the satellite channels, such as the famous MBC, which produces the most sexually provocative programming. While Gulf and especially Saudi money support and promote most of the puritanical schools, groups, and television channels, they are also the same sources that support the most provocative singing and dancing shows that are often modeled verbatim on American shows such as *Star Search* or *American Idol*. Moreover, in the same countries that one finds that the hijab is imposed by the government, such as Saudi Arabia and Iran, one also finds a widespread preoccupation with Western fashion. In several countries, I have noticed the clear tendency of young women to don the hijab but combine it with various ways of expressing their sexual individuality. For me, the irony comes full circle when I notice that the famous Saudi Shaykh Saleh, one of the pioneers in developing satellite stations that have pushed the boundaries of what is deemed sexually acceptable for broadcast in the Arab world, eventually decided to give himself a religious program in which he would sit for an hour-long episode (about thirty episodes in total) during which he opined about Islam and Shariʻah and, of course, warned against the evils of *fitna* and the importance of segregation!

On all issues related to gender roles, seclusion, and *fitna*, pietistic affectations have reached quite irrational proportions. Throughout the Muslim world, one observes that men compete to prove their religiosity or Islamic legitimacy by exhibiting their willingness to support positions that are essentially restrictive toward women. This, of course, can be understood at many different levels—in part, it is a reaction to political defeatism and to the male ego when it feels disempowered or dominated. In part, this is also a reaction to the aggressiveness of some native feminists who revere everything Western and arrogantly dismiss anything associated with Eastern cultures. Whatever the reasons, all matters related to gender have become subject to a level of hypersensitivity that has become a formidable obstacle to any rational discussion on the topic. Discussing the evidence as to the Islamicity of practices related to gender or their reasonableness has become taboo. Wherever one travels around the Muslim world, discussing whether women are Islamically required to cover their hair outside of prayer is treated as heresy. For instance, in one of the many reports that exist on the subject, the jurist

Khamis al-Rustaqi argues that rules of modesty, in particular, are heavily affected by the prevalent social standards and practices, which vary from time to time and place to place. He illustrates this point by claiming that in Medina, slave girls were not in the habit of covering their faces or hair, while in Oman, slave girls were expected to cover both. Al-Rustaqi argues that both practices are legitimately Islamic.[11] In twenty years of lecturing on Islamic law around the world, I have not once managed to successfully elicit a discussion on this text and others like it in an Islamic center or conference. This is not surprising because the pattern and practice of affectation has been for a group of men to enunciate the proper limits for the public appearance and public involvement of women and then close the matter to discussion.

The practice of affectation has become a widespread international phenomenon as evidenced by the fact that the issue of hijab is not taboo just among many American Muslims but also in Muslim countries around the world. The practice of hijab is often performed as a sociopolitical act symbolizing one's Islamic identity. In recent decades, Islamic movements have placed a very heavy emphasis on enforcing the hijab, in one way or another. In countries like Iran and Saudi Arabia, the state itself mandates that women not appear in public without their hair, arms, and legs fully covered. In the case of Islamic movements that are not in power, such movements tend to heavily focus on persuading women to wear the hijab. However, quite often this advocacy becomes a way of focusing on form over substance. Very often, Islamic movements will not give nearly as much attention to the moral and religious education of women as they give to the practice of the hijab. One often encounters the attitude that in many Muslim contexts, primacy is given to the formalistic act of wearing the hijab, even at the expense of the ethical and moral well-being of women.

This formalism is characteristic of the policies in Iran, Saudi Arabia, and the Taliban's Afghanistan compelling women to wear the hijab regardless of their personal choice. This at times reverberates in extreme and odd ways. It is not unusual to find that women shortly after converting to Islam are being pressured, often by other women, to wear the hijab. A convert to Islam faces the challenge of having to learn the faith, study the Qur'an, and perfect the practice of the five pillars, such as the five prayers, fasting Ramadan, and performing the pilgrimage to Mecca. Nevertheless, the wearing of the hijab is often treated as a central tenet of the Islamic religion and often placed ahead as a priority over studying the Qur'an or learning prayer. A large number of female converts, days after conversion, wear the hijab so that their outer appearance perpetuates the symbol of Islamicity. Frequently, however, their insides—their consciousness, comprehension, intellect, and moral sense—have not sufficiently developed or Islamized. This emphasis on performance and external symbolism at times reflects an unfortunate set of priorities. For example, I recall meeting women who converted to Islam but refused to wear the hijab. On several occasions, imams, with a confused sense of moral order, coldly informed these women that their conversion was invalid until they wore the hijab. Theologically, this claim, to say the least, is extremely problematic.

A more sagacious and, in my view, a more Islamically supportable approach to the issue of external symbolism versus substance is illustrated in a story reported about Hasan al-Banna (assassinated 1368/1949), the founder of the Muslim Brotherhood in Egypt. Reportedly, al-Banna found that one of his new disciples had grown a beard. Al-Banna asked the student why he had done so, and the student responded that he was following the example of the Prophet by implementing the rules of modesty for men. Al-Banna advised the student to shave off the beard because in Egyptian society at the time, by wearing the beard, the disciple in effect was setting himself up as a symbol of authentic and genuine Islamicity. Al-Banna was concerned that the disciple's moral and religious development was not proportional to the symbolic image he was portraying, and therefore, as a matter of honesty and integrity, it was not appropriate for this particular disciple to wear a beard.

The same odd sense of moral priorities is often observed in the conduct of governments that claim to be Islamic. I recall reading, for instance, that during the American war against Afghanistan, the Saudi government asked the White House to suspend the bombardment of Taliban positions during the month of Ramadan. The Saudi government claimed that the suspension of bombardment would be a heart-warming gesture toward Muslims.[12] In a more extreme example of placing form before substance and appearances before meaning, in 1998, the Ministry of Intelligence in Iran reportedly planned to have the reformer and the now Nobel laureate Shirin Ebadi assassinated. However, Dorri Najaf Abadi, a high-ranking official in the ministry, ordered that her assassination be suspended until after Ramadan so that Ebadi would have the opportunity to finish fasting the month.[13] In both of these examples, the gestures completely missed the point. Either the bombing of Afghanistan is moral or immoral—likewise, murdering Shirin Ebadi is either right or wrong. The wrongfulness of the offenses is not at all mitigated by allowing the purported victims to peacefully complete the ritual of fasting during Ramadan. Similarly, the moral culpability of the offender is not reduced by undertaking these formalistic displays of false piety. Most alarming, however, is the perception and expectation, presumably held by the Saudi, Iranian, and American officials, that such displays of formalism are convincing and effective in winning the hearts of Muslims. This perception could be entirely illusory, and it is possible that these governments are delusional about what matters or does not matter to the Muslim public. Nevertheless, there are many indicators that the arguably illusory attitudes of governments are not superimposed on Muslim societies without being based in any reality whatsoever. Even if illusory, these perceptions are still rooted in social processes that spawn these misperceptions in the first place. There is considerable circumstantial evidence indicating that especially in the past decades, Islamic practice has become increasingly focused on symbolic formalism at the expense of developing the ethical and intellectual thrust of the Islamic tradition. Later, I will further analyze this circumstantial evidence, but a painfully obvious symptom of the problem of formalism is the paucity of Muslim intellectual contributions to the modern age.

It is a sadly manifest reality that Muslims have not contributed in significant ways to the intellectual discourses of the modern age. This fact was painfully documented in the now decade old but still pressingly pertinent report issued by the United Nations on the state of intellectual acquisition among developing countries. Muslim countries, and especially Arab countries, ranked at the bottom of the Third World in scientific and intellectual accomplishments. Rather tellingly, the rate of book production and consumption was among the lowest in the world. Although 5 percent of the world population, Arab countries did not account for more than 1.1 percent of book production in the world. All the Arabic-speaking countries combined produced less literary and intellectual activity than the least accomplished European nation, Spain.[14]

Considering the significant number of Muslims and the universal impact of the Islamic faith, the absence of Muslim contributions to the major intellectual orientations of the world is troubling. Comparatively speaking, the theological and philosophical movements in Judaism and Christianity are far more vibrant than their Islamic counterparts. This is in sharp contrast to the theological and philosophical contributions of Muslims in the premodern age. Later, I will focus on analyzing the roots and import of this condition, but it is important to note that the paucity of intellectual contributions and the practice of affectations spring from a single sociological reality. Both the lack of intellectual contributions and the practice of affectations are symptomatic of the ambiguous position of the interpretive heritage of the Islamic past. In contemporary Islam, the interpretive past is not seriously engaged in a dialectical dynamic designed to identify trajectories, orientations, directions, and necessary points for reconstruction and revision. Rather, this heritage is leveraged for purely functional, short-term, and ideological purposes in a highly politicized process. In quite an abrasive and even vulgar fashion, this heritage is utilized to service power politics, which include problems of identity, gender, and class. This can be achieved only with a considerable amount of twisting, bending, writhing, and abusing of this heritage to get it to service the roles that it is ill fitted to play. Throughout this process, however, the interpretive efforts of the past are not engaged with a level of seriousness or rigor that would allow for intellectual contributions that could be considered extensions of these past efforts. But affectations of the type described above are not interested in preserving the integrity of the interpretive tradition. Such affectations are primarily concerned with communicating impressions—the impression of Islamicity. In this sense, these affectations are performances first and foremost of propaganda in a context where the symbolism of Islamicity is far more important than the substance. Because the interactions that take place in various Islamic movements are primarily concerned with communicating impressions, this in turn contributes to the air of frivolity and lack of seriousness in dealing with Islam and its tradition.[15]

MUSLIMS IN THE WEST AS A MICROCOSM

It is commonplace for mosques all over the United States to designate a closed-off area for women, usually in the back, at an upper level, or in a separate building altogether. This turns out to be very restrictive because prayers are led by men, and lectures are usually delivered in segregated halls by men as well. Sections designated for women are usually small, crowded, and noisy and leave women feeling marginalized and excluded. A few years ago, I was lecturing in one such Islamic center where women are placed in a separate section behind a curtain. On hearing that some women complained that they were unable to hear my lecture and could not be involved in the discussions, I insisted that women who wished to do so should be allowed to sit in the front rows, out of the women's section, so that they would have the opportunity to interact as intellectual equals. As usual, after a minilecture about the rights of women and Shari'ah, most men begrudgingly respected my wishes and dropped their opposition. Usually, my wishes would be respected but I would never be invited again. However, on this particular occasion, a professional-looking middle-aged man launched into a boisterous opposition, insisting that women are *fitna* and that it is intolerable to allow women to emerge from behind the curtains and interact freely. It was not too long before it became apparent that the man's knowledge of the Shari'ah tradition was modest at best, which made me curious if he was engaged in a profession that brought him into limited contact with women. To my utter bewilderment, it turned out that the man was a gynecologist and that many of the women in the community were his patients. I am not a psychologist and cannot explain the inner conflicts of this fellow, but the community that tolerated such an odd paradoxical condition fascinated me. Other than the gynecologist who spoke of the *fitna* of women, this was a community mostly of professionals with comfortable homes and incomes. After spending time at the Islamic center where women were placed behind curtains in fear of *fitna*, they all returned to their homes packed with satellite dishes and computers with access to the web. Most definitely, if sexual seduction was what the community was worried about, the interaction between men and women in the Islamic center was the least of their worries.

But as I noted above, the discourses of *fitna* in the contemporary age have gone well beyond any real socially supported concern about empirical consequences to a largely symbolic construct of a presumed authenticity. One of the very common practices in the United States that is also justified under the doctrine of *fitna* is to have separate entrances for men and women at Islamic centers. I was reminded of the odd impact of the *fitna* doctrine when my mother and I visited an Islamic center in Connecticut during off hours. The center was empty, but my seventy-year-old mother and I needed to perform our prayers. As we were removing our shoes, a man whom I assumed was the imam of the place came rushing toward us to protest that both of us came in from the same entrance. Speaking firmly, the fellow explained that there are clearly designated doors for men and women and asked that we exit and reenter in a proper fashion. My mother, who had a gentle but strong soul, looked up, straight at him, and asked the only logical question: Why? He responded without a pause, "Sister, the separate doors are there to guard against *fitna*!" My mother looked sternly at him: "Son," she said, "if an old woman with her son coming in from the men's entrance to an empty mosque causes *fitna*, then all the men of your community better stay in your homes!"

My mother was reacting to the irrationality of the situation—but for this fellow, whether he believed in the empirical possibility of *fitna* or not was immaterial. My mother reacted on the basis of the Shari'ah principles that she learned: All rulings must be closely measured to their cause or purpose, and if the law no longer serves the cause, the law is invalid; the bearer of wrong bears the burden (i.e., since it is the men who are being unreasonably seduced, then they should be the ones to bear the restriction); no person should be made to suffer for the wrongdoing of the other; the measure of correctness is decided according to predominant habits and customs of people, and so on. But the imam was reacting at a very different level—he was using *fitna* as political and cultural dogma or as a symbolic trope for several things, including Islamic cultural distinctiveness, the stability and security offered by predictable gender roles that leave men firmly in control, and the desire for cultural autonomy as well as the willingness to be a dissenter to predominant Westernized standards. The problem, however, is that regardless of whether one agrees with his unspoken motivations or not, the use of Shari'ah in this fashion employs the whole juristic tradition for purposes unrelated to its own nature or purposes. This politicized usage of Shari'ah places the tradition into an unreasonable role because it is forced to represent nonevaluative and nondeliberative functions. As discussed later, the forefathers of Shari'ah used to say that 90 percent of Shari'ah is *tarjih* (the product of evaluating, deliberating, weighing, and balancing before reaching a determination).[16] Dogma and symbolic constructs are useful in sustaining basic religious beliefs, theological precepts, and ideologies, but Shari'ah cannot perform its functions if it is reduced to a dogma. The vast majority of Shari'ah, as an ethical and legal system, is deliberative—anchored in a methodology for balancing and weighing rights and duties and adjudicating conflicts. The problem is that puritanical Islam uses Shari'ah as if it is dogma or ideology, with the predictable result that it often ends up appearing unreasonable and the possibilities for reasoned debate are foreclosed.

In the first half of 2003, I testified in court as an expert witness in a Florida case that I thought was very troubling but also sadly representative. At first, the facts of the case seemed simple enough. A husband and wife converted to Islam and had been Muslim for a few months. According to the story told by the couple, the wife sought to learn her Islamic duties and obligations, especially as to the matter of the veil. The wife spoke to the local imam and did some research on the Internet, after which she decided that it was her Islamic duty to wear a full veil that not only covered her hair but also covered her face and all of her body, including her hands and feet. With her face now hidden behind a veil, the woman decided that she needed a driver's license and demanded that the state of Florida issue her a license either without a picture or with a picture of her wearing her face veil. The state of Florida refused to do so, arguing that especially after 9/11, the state had a compelling interest in having all drivers take a full-face photograph. The state explained that it was a security risk to have drivers behind the wheel with their faces concealed by a veil and with no way of verifying their identity through a photograph. The woman responded that Islamic law requires her to cover her face, that Islamic law mandates that she does so regardless of any social or security consequences, and that the state should find a way to accommodate her conscientious beliefs.

When the state of Florida asked me to testify in this case against a fellow Muslim, it was a difficult decision. Islam commands me to empathize with my Muslim sisters and brothers, and as much as I disagreed with her particular interpretation of Islamic law, in principle I had to respect her position. Moreover, as usual, Muslim organizations in the United States stood firmly with the woman and her husband and were already accusing the state of Florida of discrimination and the persecution of Muslims, and were raising funds to support her lawsuit. To say the least, if I assisted the state of Florida on this matter, this would not endear me to the various Muslim organizations supporting the couple and might even be a very unpopular position with the Muslim community at large. However, in my view, the support of those in the Muslim community who defended the woman's right to drive with her face covered seemed to be knee-jerk and poorly thought out.

The more I studied this case, the more I was troubled by the woman's position. She seemed to entirely discount any public safety ramifications to her position. According to her, Islamic law imposes the duty to veil on women without regard for any social or political implications that might result. Therefore, her right to engage in activity while veiled was absolute and unconditional. Of course, this position has profound implications for the place of Muslims in non-Muslim societies as well as clear implications as to any participatory or collaborative role Muslims might be expected to play. In this woman's view, Shari'ah seemed incapable of considering and weighing any interests other than its own, and it cared little for any claimed public good. From the evidence available in the case, it seemed that this woman was able to reach her conclusions regarding Shari'ah with an absolute level of certitude after she and her husband had been Muslims for a relatively short period of time and after conducting the most superficial of research using only the Internet. The local imam that seemed to have guided the couple through their process of religious discovery was a computer scientist by training but appeared to have decided that instead of practicing his trade, it was more lucrative for him to make regular trips to Saudi Arabia, where he could raise money for "the Islamic cause" in the United States.

The most puzzling part of all of this was that the wife's interpretations of Shari'ah were not supported by the legal tradition itself. First, the hijab or *niqab* (*niqab* as opposed to *hijab* is the practice of covering the face; *hijab* is covering the hair and neck but not the face) are not absolute and unconditional religious duties. Even assuming that either the hijab or *niqab* is a religious duty, this duty is not among the pillars of the faith, and it would not be allowed to trump all other competing or countervailing considerations. Islamic legal practice was well acquainted with the need to balance between competing interests, and it did not admit this type of dogmatic and uncompromising application. In fact, this is exactly the reason that, with the exception of Saudi Arabia, in all Muslim countries that I have studied, women who obtained driver's licenses were required to take photographs clearly showing the face. Even Saudi Arabia, when it came to the issuance of passports, required women wearing the *niqab* to take a photograph showing their face. Second, whether Muslims lived in a Muslim or non-Muslim society, they were required to carefully consider the interests of society at large. It was simply not true that Islamic law, as the woman claimed, was not concerned with the well-being of society and the public interest.[17] Third, in deciding on the proper course of conduct, Shari'ah mandated that the image of Islam itself should be taken into account and given serious weight. If a particular behavior would alienate or threaten the non-Muslim neighbors of a Muslim and as a result damage the image of Islam, Muslims were required to take this factor into serious consideration and carefully weigh it as an important moral demand. Like most legal systems, duties not all being equal, Islamic law incorporates a system of priorities—a Muslim cannot sacrifice a first-rate interest in order to comply with a third- or fourth-rate command. This is an exhaustive field of jurisprudence known as *fiqh al-awlawiyyat*, and all the explanations offered by the woman and her husband did not exhibit even an awareness of the existence of this field of inquiry, leave alone an understanding of its centrality to Islamic legal practice. Fourth, whether the *niqab* is an Islamic practice at all is hotly debated in the juristic tradition of Islam, and the proponents of this practice are but a small minority in the Islamic legal tradition. Because this practice is the subject of intense disagreement and debate, it does not enjoy the type of sanctity and significance that might exist regarding issues that most Muslims agree on.

In short, the way that this woman practiced Shari'ah struck me as superficial and seriously flawed. If the Islamic legal tradition did not mandate this woman's position and if she had not even considered the evidence for and against, what was the basis of her insistence that Shari'ah is uncompromising in the demands that it places on her? But this puzzling case only got more troubling as I started learning more about the particulars of the life that this woman and her husband led together. It turned out that the husband, after converting to Islam, committed violent felonies of which he was convicted. Among other things, he had assaulted his wife and child with an iron, causing them serious injury. Most troubling, the husband and wife had physically abused a child in their foster care and, significantly, tried to use the *niqab* as an excuse to evade responsibility. The couple claimed to a doctor that Islam demanded that the foster child be covered head to toe and therefore, they could not permit him to examine the child. It turned out that they were attempting to conceal the child's broken arm, and they were both convicted of this crime as well. In other words, there was ample evidence that there was an ulterior motive in seeking the anonymity that the *niqab* offered, and it might even be said that the facts of this particular case exemplified the legitimacy of the state's security concerns.

Perhaps anyone following the facts of this case would not have been surprised by these revelations of criminal conduct. Perhaps there were enough indications that something was off and quite odd about the conduct of the couple from the very beginning. But this was hardly the issue. The real issue was why did this couple find a ready and willing wide support base in the Muslim community? In all likelihood, most members of the community never found out about the criminal record of the couple, but considering the objective indicators that Shari'ah law was being misapplied in this case, why were so many people eager to support the couple in their claims without further investigation or study? Clearly, Muslim organizations that supported and raised funds for this case were reacting in a knee-jerk fashion to the invocation of Islamic symbolism and affectation. Appearing to engage in pietistic conduct and under the pretense of Islamicity was enough to tap into a chorus of symbolism and more symbolism. There was a virtual rush to prove one's Islamic loyalties and character by supporting the act that appeared Islamic, regardless of the substantive considerations involved and without paying much attention to the details and particulars involved in the case.

But there is even a more serious problem amplified by the rush to support the misguided couple, and that is the lack of substantive standards for a genuine engagement with Shari'ah. In other words, if it looks like Islamic law, then it is Islamic law. This has to do with the prevailing evaluative standards that exist for assessing the competence of the discourse or conduct claiming to be Islamic. Put simply, if, for instance, the leaders of the Muslim community are not sensitized to the central importance of evaluating and weighing priorities in assessing the demands of Islamic law, it is not surprising that for them, only the most absolute and dogmatic assertions of Islamic law would be treated as the most representative and compelling. The support that this couple was able to garner in the Islamic community is itself evidence of the deprecation and general deterioration in the standards applied to Islamic law today.

I did in fact testify against the Florida couple, and in the end, they lost the case. In a well-known tradition, the Prophet taught that the best way for a Muslim brother to stand by his brother is to advise and attempt to restrain him when he is about to fall into error. The tribal-like rush to lend support to a Muslim brother whether in justice or not, in my view, clearly contravenes the teachings of the Qur'an. Therefore, when many of my Muslim brethren asked why I felt compelled to involve myself in this case and testify against a fellow Muslim, the only truthful response was: because I was convinced that it was my Islamic duty to do so—I had a duty to speak the truth as I understood it to be and to try to prevent my fellow Muslims from falling into what I was convinced was a grave error.

This case raised several issues of crucial significance—it brought to focus matters related to the tension between individual freedoms and the demands for public safety, the place and identity of Muslim minorities and the nature of their relationship to the non-Muslim countries in which they live, and the very integrity of the process by which Islamicity is constructed and defined. But the even harder question is to what extent a case like this is instructive or representative of larger dynamics taking place in the Muslim world at large—as opposed to being a parochial problem related to the exceptional circumstances of Muslims living in Western societies. Muslims living in the West do confront a unique set of challenges as minorities living in societies that not only poorly understand their religion and traditions but also that are at times hostile to them. Confronting broad-based misunderstandings and suspicions in the non-Muslim societies, Muslim minorities do not only have to contend with anxieties due to discrimination and at times persecution, but also the fear of dilution, disintegration, and absorption into the larger societies in which they live. Most often, the challenges with which Muslim minorities are forced to contend are not primarily limited to assimilation or the ability of Muslim minorities to adapt to living in non-Muslim societies. Adaptation and assimilation pose weighty problems, but in pluralist societies it is possible to acclimate to the demands of civic society without losing the distinctiveness of one's value system. Furthermore, contrary to what some have claimed, historically speaking, Muslim minorities have demonstrated remarkable flexibility and creativity in adapting to challenging conditions confronting them in non-Muslim nations.[18] The source of the greatest anxiety to Muslim minorities in the West is the possibility of the complete obliteration that comes from a gradual process of attrition and loss of Islamic commitment. In other words, what often causes Muslims in the West the greatest apprehension is that with the passing of time, eventually, there will exist generations that are only nominally Muslim or only Muslim by name, without much understanding or regard for the religious law. Understandably, this results in an anxious but tenacious adherence to behavioral patterns that are seen as earmarks of Islamicity and the exhibition of symbols that affirm a sense of Islamic identity. In this sense, the experiences of Muslim minorities in the West are exceptional because the risk of loss of Islamic identity and commitment is real, especially in the absence of legitimate and powerful institutions that guard and nurture the processes that can energize and rejuvenate Islamic efforts at self-definition.

Nevertheless, it is important to note the ways that the experiences of Muslim minorities actually mirror dynamics that more broadly take place in the Muslim world. The same anxiety about the future of Islam and Muslims in the world and the same compulsion to tenaciously adhere to symbolic acts that affirm Islamicity exists in the Muslim world at large. Perhaps Muslim minorities in the West exhibit a more exaggerated and intense version of the processes that take place in the Muslim world. Especially after the trauma of foreign domination during the age of colonialism and the advent of modernity, there is a prevailing sense of anxiety about Western intellectual and cultural invasions to the world of Islam. While Muslim minorities undergo the anxieties of living in the midst of an overwhelming non-Muslim-dominated reality, Muslim majorities undergo the same anxieties confronting a Western-dominated world. Muslim minorities have to contend with the fact that they live in a context that is replete with temptations that compete for the loyalty and commitment of young Muslims. But in the highly penetrated societies of the Muslim world—societies that have been exposed to a myriad of Western influences from nationalism, racism, socialism, capitalism, communism, and feminism to secularism—the orientations competing for the loyalty of Muslims are no less overwhelming. Moreover, as discussed later, when it comes to Shari'ah discourses and the reproduction of legal determinations, Muslims in the West remain under the heavy influence of the Wahhabi orientation.[19] The processes for determining Islamic legal obligations that we observed in the Florida case are not unusual or exceptional in the modern Islamic context. The specific conclusions reached by the Florida couple as to what God demands of them and why are not the point—as noted earlier, only a minority of Muslims wear the *niqab*. The point is the casual and even callous way that Shari'ah law determinations are made and then supported simply because such determinations invoke the appearance of Islamicity. As discussed later, due to certain historical developments, this process has become commonplace in the contemporary Muslim world.

Partly because of the moral bonds that join the two worlds, there are numerous influences from the Muslim world on Muslims living in the West. But even more than this, because of the financial and intellectual dependence of Islamic organizations in the West on support from certain Muslim countries such as Saudi Arabia and the fact that the leadership of these organizations continues to be formed largely of immigrants, we often find that the dynamics taking place in most Muslim communities in the West mirror those in particular parts of the Islamic world. The dynamics of Muslim communities in the West are often like a microcosm of what takes place in the Muslim world. However, the dynamics prevalent among Muslim minorities in the West are more intensified and focused. They are as if representations of problems prevalent in the Muslim world but according to dynamics that are more dramatic and pronounced.

There are many ways in which patterns of conduct and norms and values observed in the Muslim world are reproduced and continued in the Muslim communities in the West. The most problematic and endemic transplants from the Muslim world to Muslims in the West is the transfer of culturally based habits of political and social apathy, oligarchic institutional structures, and the failure to build independent and indigenously funded institutions. Compared to their considerable numbers and wealth, the political and social involvement and impact of Muslim minorities in the United States and Europe remains very limited. Muslim minorities have made rather modest contributions to framing the issues that most affect their lives and have added little to nonparochial and general political or social causes. In many ways, Muslim minorities in the West have become consumers of civil and political rights, but they have not been able to become affirmative contributors to the regime of rights that they enjoy. This sociological reality is part of the toilsome burden of the legacy of despotism plaguing Muslim minorities settled in the West. In despotic societies, the average citizen learns from experience that it is always much safer to remain politically and socially inactive, and apathy in this context becomes a value necessary for survival. The immigrant community in particular is affected by this apathy, and instead of mobilizing and seeking to shape policy that directly impacts their interests, the attention of these communities is often diverted into battles over identity politics.

Among the transplanted cultural habits is what might be called authoritarian mind-sets that inevitably lead to oligarchic institutional structures. By authoritarian mind-sets, I mean intellectual orientations that seek determinacy on most policy matters and that feel threatened and, therefore, are intolerant of differences of opinions. I do not mean necessarily a desire to control or dominate others, but an attitude that eschews disagreements and that considers diversity as threatening and dangerous to both identity and unity. In this context, claims of unity and autonomous identity are cited as the primary excuses for delegitimating and disregarding disagreements and a diversity of views. This process of enforcing uniformity denies Islamic thought in the West its richness and dynamism and creates a redundant homogeneity in much of the intellectual production of Muslim minorities. This is easily observable by a casual reading of the writings found in Muslim journals published in the West. One is hard pressed to find any serious debate or dynamic discourse in these publications—as if the only relevant criterion used by these journals is to attempt repeatedly to tell Muslims what they already know. In the many Muslim publications produced in the West, there is a virtual intellectual stagnation where if you read a few issues of a published journal, you have effectively read all the issues of the same journal for a coming decade. The same can easily be said about lectures delivered in many Islamic centers in the West. The stagnation, repetitiveness, and dullness of these lectures have reached unbearable proportions.

Another aspect of the legacy carried by Muslims in the West is what might be called economic or financial apathy. Muslim institutions in the West continue to be largely dependent on financial contributions originating from Muslim countries, especially the Persian Gulf region. The primary problem is the failure of Muslim minorities to maintain independent financial institutions that are funded through native sources and that are responsive to the unique concerns and problems of Muslims in the West. I am not speaking here of building mosques, places of worship, or centers of social interaction and cultural activities. Although to a large extent these institutions do rely on foreign funding as well, this is not the main concern. Considering the number of Muslims living in the West and the considerable financial resources that they possess, one finds remarkably few politically and socially effective organizations as well as a near absence of serious educational institutions.

Whether in terms of think tanks, thought institutes, universities, seminaries, libraries, or even dedicated academic chairs, the contribution of Muslims in the West is abysmal. The few institutions that do exist are entirely dependent on foreign money and, therefore, dependent on the vagaries of politics. Some of the few institutional examples, such as the Open University and the Institute for Islamic Thought in the United States, experienced near-fatal problems when Saudi Arabia decided to stop funding them. Especially, the Institute for Islamic Thought in Maryland seemed to have collapsed because of the drying up of Saudi funding and harassment by the US government. [20] There is the modestly successful example of Al-Furqan Institute in London, which is supported by the Saudi ex-minister of petroleum, Zaki Yamani, that has sponsored and produced several valuable studies. [21] There is also the widely successful Institute of Ismaili Studies in London, one of the few genuinely intellectually meritorious and impressive endeavors. [22] The Zaytuna Institute in California thus far has not moved beyond regurgitating traditional knowledge, but it is too early to make any fair assessment of its direction and potential. [23]

Aside from the few possible exceptions, the broad cultural phenomenon of which I speak is manifest to anyone who has had experience working with Muslim organizations. It is extremely difficult to get wealthy Muslims living in the West to donate money for anything that has to do with the production of thought. Part of the problem is the prevalence of authoritarian paradigms, observed in the fact that one of the biggest barriers to generating Muslim funding to institutions of thought is that most potential donors are extremely reluctant to contribute if they cannot control the thought that is produced from the recipient of their largesse. Muslims in the West fund mosques and Islamic centers because it is safer to do so. The fear that is expressed time and again by potential donors is: What if we do not like the ideas that are produced by the institution or chair that we helped to fund? This is in itself a continuation of the paradigm of political safety and determinacy. It is always safer not to invest resources in any concern that might be unpredictable or that might threaten unity by generating a diversity of ideas. This leads to another phenomenon that deserves to be studied. Assume, for example, that the donor is a medical doctor or wealthy businessman. By donating to a mosque or center, by virtue of being the source of funding, such a person virtually guarantees that he will become the authoritative voice of Islam in the center or mosque he has funded. In effect, such a doctor or businessman becomes the definer of orthodoxy and the one who sets the boundaries for legitimate differences within the community. This has created a situation in which the source of funding, whether an individual who has access to foreign donors or a rich member of the community, becomes the de facto individual who draws the boundaries for legitimate discourse within the community. What this has meant is that, in the absence of institutions of higher learning, those who are the least educated in Islamic theology and law become the ones who define the legitimate boundaries of Islamic theology and law. Whether in an Islamic camp or center, it is the medical doctor or the businessman who has never had the time or energy to seriously study the richness of the Islamic tradition who becomes the one who defines what is a legitimate opinion within Islam and what exceeds the boundaries of Islam. In my personal experience, this has resulted in the odd situation where people with long years of study in Islamic theology and law are excluded and marginalized by people who believe that the boundaries of Islam are identical to what they personally are familiar with—which means, in most cases, what they learned from their parents and what they casually picked up from different experiences in the Muslim community. It is not an exaggeration to say that the more a person knows about the richness and diversity of the Islamic tradition, the less central the person becomes to the dynamics of the mosque or Islamic center, and, in fact, what has been created is a strong social disincentive to any serious effort to study the Islamic intellectual tradition.

In the American context, one of the often-repeated jokes about wealthy Muslims is that Allah has given them money, and with the money God gave them, came the sacred right to a tax deduction. This often heard sarcastic levity mocks the impression that the wealthy seem to think that deductions are part of the divine law of Shari'ah and that without the deductions substantial donations would quickly dry up. Of course, this is highly exaggerated, but what more accurately describes the situation is that there is a prevalent financial apathy. Coming from countries in which the state funds most religious and intellectual activity, immigrant Muslims have a hard time adapting to the liberal secular state that expects its citizens to back up their social and political demands with a willingness to pay. It should be noted, however, that when it comes to institutions of thought and learning, the miserliness of wealthy Muslims in the West is fundamentally at odds with the history of educational institutions in Islam. Premodern Muslims had created a vast network of religious endowments (*awqaf*) that funded the libraries, universities, academic chairs, and student fellowships. There was a rich and complex array of privately funded institutions that supported the numerous intellectual and scientific efforts within the Islamic civilization and which guarded the autonomy of these learning institutions from the state.[24] These cultural norms were sufficiently strong to the point that some scholars argued that each student of knowledge has a right to funding, and if the wealthy members of society fail to provide for such a student, they should be forced to do so. A fellowship covering the educational and living expenses was something that a student had a right to expect would be readily available in a Muslim society, and wealthy Muslims should provide the finances, whether voluntarily or not.[25] With the dawn of modernity, however, most of the religious endowments were nationalized and became state-owned property. In 1809, the military leader of Egypt, Muhammad 'Ali, started this tragic process by, for the first time in history, imposing taxes on the religious endowments. In 1812, Muhammad 'Ali took a further step by nationalizing a substantial number of religious endowments, and this became one of the early aggressive steps eventually leading to the destruction of the religious endowments and the undoing of a core part of civil society.[26] As socialist thought and practices spread in the Muslim world, the dependence on the all-intrusive and authoritarian state became complete. For Muslims living in liberal democracies, however, this dependent attitude is disastrous.

Of course, the longer that Muslim communities live in the West, the higher the possibility that they will exhibit greater autonomy and will become more effective in their indigenous contexts. But this evolutionary progress cannot simply be assumed nor thought of as inevitable. It will depend in large measure on how Muslim minorities negotiate their contexts and actively root themselves into their newfound realities. It is possible not only that Muslim minorities would resolve the tensions that plague their lives but also that they might make positive contributions benefiting the Muslim world. However, this will require the undertaking of a conscientious and corrective process of virtual self-engineering in which the most endemic problems have to be seriously treated.

At the beginning of the 1980s, at the start of my academic journey, I once asked one of my mentors, the late Dr. Hassan Hathout, where does one go to learn to think in the language of the age and to learn to be analytical, critical, and honest? Dr. Hassan Hathout was a beautiful human being—a very devout and sincere Muslim without any false affectations—who believed that certain human values such as justice, freedom, and honesty are universal and that God favors the nation that comes closer to upholding these values than others. In response to my question, after a few dramatic seconds of silence, he said, "The United States, and for countless reasons!" Dr. Hassan was absolutely correct—the United States is a virtual universe of potentials enabling a person to become whatever a person, for better or worse, wishes to be. Eventually, after a distinguished career in medicine, Dr. Hassan retired to the United States, where he launched an illustrious career as an Islamic thinker and an advocate for ecumenical understanding and religious tolerance. The idealism and optimism of this man were truly infectious. But after the ugliness of 9/11, in due course a new ugliness swept over the United States and Europe—the ugliness of religious bigotry, intolerance, and hate. In short, Islamophobia made its ugly appearance, as Islam-bashing quickly became a multimillion-dollar industry. Dr. Hassan Hathout died in 2009, right in the midst of the plague of Islamophobia, but his memorials continued to be attended by members of every faith, including Muslims, Christians, and Jews.

After the horrendous ugliness of the terrorist attacks on New York and all the bloodshed that followed in Afghanistan and Iraq, all the ugliness of Guantanamo, Abu Ghraib, and Bagram, with secret detentions, renditions, and targeted killings, and the explosion of Islamophobia and religious intolerance, I often wondered whether Dr. Hassan Hathout's faith in human values and the specialness of America's accomplishments remained intact. The sad reality is that no system, democratic or not, has an exclusive claim to monstrosities, and so many of the democracies of today were built on the foundations of the suffering and murder of indigenous populations. Yet it is the possibilities of achieving levels of justice or the potential and opportunity for justice that matters the most. I suspect that Dr. Hassan Hathout never lost his belief in the potential and promise of justice in the United States. As ugly as Islamophobia is, this anachronistic throwback to the days of religious warfares and crusades might hold the greatest promise for Muslims in the West. Perhaps as generations of American Muslims are raised, armed with the values of self-empowerment, they will react to Islamophobia by rejecting the politics of religious affectations, puritanism, and anachronisms. Perhaps as they rise to meet the ugliness of Islamophobia and puritanical Islam, American Muslims will ignite an intellectual revolution that will be the key to reclaiming the Muslim contribution to humanity.

Chapter Four

Repose: The Islamic between Harmony and Dissonance

AFFECTATION AS PUBLIC PERFORMANCE

Affectations feed on dreams and mimic the realization of dreams and, as such, are paved with the best of intentions. Upholding the pretense of Islamicity is often motivated by a sincere desire to achieve the reality of Islamicity. Nonetheless, maintaining the pretense by engaging in symbolic displays of Islamicity most often serves to distract attention away from the substantive issues and challenges that confront those who seek to fulfill the dream of Islamicity. At times, the impact of the dynamics of affectation becomes like a cultural phenomenon anchored in widespread social practices and even sociomoral attitudes. These acts of pietistic affectation, at least for those who are impressed or swayed by them, perform an important function in affirming a sense of Islamicity. Especially since the 1970s, there has been a greater tendency toward the adoption of public performances of symbolic value that affirm the sense of accomplishing greater Islamicity. In fact, it could be said that the greater the sense of frustration in achieving tangible political and · economic successes, the more there has been a tendency to compensate for the resulting sense of failure by insisting on public performances of affectation. For instance, in recent times, Islamic movements and groups have tended to do away with expressive applause in public forums, replacing it with yelling out in unison, "God is greater" (*Allahu Akbar*). Typically, after the conclusion of a lecture or some other act that would invite applause, a member of the audience will yell out "*Takbir!*" In response, the audience will call out in unison "Allahu Akbar," repeated three times. In effect, what this practice means is that regardless of the quality of the act calling for applause, the response is always the same—three uniform "Allahu Akbar" yelled out in unison. The justification behind this practice is that since non-Muslims applaud by clapping, Muslims ought to adopt an alternative way of applauding. This is an artificial construction of Islamicity because there is nothing inherently non-Muslim in clapping and nothing particularly Islamic in refusing to clap.[1] Moreover, the mechanical, emotionally noncommittal, detached, and anti-individual way in which an audience calls out "Allahu Akbar" is conducive to the performance of acts of false affectation. Despite the success of puritans in spreading this practice in many places, I think this dogmatic and self-reductionist way of presenting Islamic ethos is palpably unreasonable. In theological terms, takbir is a supplication—a solemn affirmation that regardless of the challenge confronting a person, he/she should feel empowered and encouraged by the conviction that, whatever the difficulty, God is still the greater. It is also a prayer—a call for God's aid and support in meeting the challenges confronting a believer. This collective affirmation of God's greatness does not seem to perform the same function as that performed by applause. Calling out "Allahu Akbar" instead of applauding encourages the appearance of artificial Islamicity, but it does not in any way contribute to ensuring the substantive quality of the audience's participation—the audience's ability to express satisfaction, dissatisfaction, approval, or reproach. In this paradigm, the worst speech and the best speech are greeted with the same monotonic response. One hardly needs to note the close affinity between the monotonic and the characteristics of authoritarianism.

Sometimes the public performance of affectations of piety can become so far reaching that they take intellectualized and highly rationalized forms. I think that a prime example of this would be the rather wide-reaching but strained movement seeking to Islamize knowledge. In the 1980s, a group of intellectuals of different nationalities and countries coalesced over the idea of the Islamization of knowledge as a means for defining a uniquely Islamic contribution to civilization. The movement was inspired not only by a desire to root Muslim identity into a distinctive phenomenology and thus a radical reconstruction of memory but also by a need to claim a unique Islamic resolution to the ambiguities of meaning in postmodernity.[2] Eventually, the movement marshaled its resources into the creation of an institution in the United States called the International Institute of Islamic Thought (IIIT). IIIT published a journal, sponsored symposia and conferences, and printed books in Arabic, English, and other languages. In due course, IIIT contributed many studies that were not related to the Islamization of knowledge, but it remained the main sponsor of the project. According to the Islamization of knowledge movement, there is a unique and distinctive epistemology in all the fields of scientific knowledge, including, for instance, an Islamic approach to psychology, journalism, history, economics, and even the physical sciences such as biology, chemistry, and physics. In the view of the followers of this movement, Islam as a complete way of life must necessarily provide for a unique way of understanding and approaching all fields of knowledge. Furthermore, the principles of Islamic knowledge are objectively cognizable because they are premised on Islam's message of moderation and mediation between all extremes. Accordingly, Islamic epistemology would avoid all epistemic and normative extremes—it is neither thoroughly idealistic nor starkly pragmatic, and it is neither utterly materialistic nor singularly focused on spiritualism. The supporters of this project generated a sizeable amount of literature—most of the works with titles such as "Towards the Islamization of Knowledge." Despite the number of titles published, both the meaning and import of Islamized knowledge remained extremely vague. It remained unclear, for instance, in what ways Islamized chemistry was different from non-Islamized chemistry or how so-called Islamic journalism differed from non-Islamic journalism. Reading this literature, in my opinion it is apparent that in effect, the proponents of Islamization were calling for the observance of basic ethical principles when pursuing knowledge—such as honesty and fair-mindedness in reporting journalistic information. But these ethical principles are universally valid and universally applicable and should be a part of the ethics that would guide any serious researcher or scholar. In other words, there was nothing uniquely Islamic in the so-called Islamization process—Islamization amounted to nothing more than an emphasis on moral values and the ethos of fair-handed research. It could have been possible for this project to focus on Islamic studies as a field or discipline and to attempt to set out methodological principles for researchers who are religiously committed to the Islamic faith. Moreover, the project could have focused on analyzing the problems of reclaiming native memory in postmodernity and set out a methodology for articulating alternative historical narratives not affected by colonial historiography. In other words, there are many ways that this project could have met the standards of contemporary scholarly rigor and at the same time made a valuable contribution to Islamic normativities. There are many ways that the project could have sponsored serious scholarly explorations that are grounded in the Muslim historical and intellectual experience but that are ultimately persuasive and compelling in concrete and specific ways. In my view, this could have been possible if scholars who wish to make an "Islamic" contribution stopped constructing artificial playing fields on the thin margins of human history and acknowledged that the solution to prevailing in a difficult game is not to create a different game with much lower standards—easy to win but also entirely irrelevant. The solution to meeting demanding or elevated standards for human thought is *not* to construct a fictitious world of lower standards. Possibilities and potentialities aside, the Islamization of knowledge only helped distract the attention of Muslims away from real intellectual problems that demanded real solutions.

Despite the vagueness surrounding the call to the Islamization of knowledge, the idea spread widely and quickly in the Islamic world. Many writers and lecturers repeated and promoted it, but no one was sure what it meant. In essence, the Islamization of knowledge became a rhetorical practice of upholding the pretense of Islamicity, but it was also completely devoid of any substance. The act of referring to the Islamicity of knowledge or the Islamization of knowledge became as if a pietistic performance that signaled one's Islamic commitments, but this symbolic ritual was not analytically or critically evaluated. Like the takbirs yelled out by a complacent audience, the invocation of this label became a formulaic practice—an act of affectation affirming the Islamic longings but without any concrete substance. In short, what was affirmed was the pretense of reaching out and fulfilling a part of the longing for Islamicity, but this pretense was a distraction that perhaps brought some relief to some Muslims but ultimately only helped exacerbate the problems. This pretense, in effect, substituted for and supplanted the possibility of achieving a realistic appraisal of the actual distance between the lived reality of Muslims and the ideal to which they aspire.

I cannot leave the topic of IIIT and the Islamization of knowledge without noting an irony of our times—an irony that perhaps can also serve as a cautionary tale. I was personally acquainted with quite a few of the people who started IIIT and who worked closely with it, especially in its formative stages. Like so many institutions and situations in the Muslim world today, politics and the lack of honesty and transparency in discourse ended up posing overwhelming problems. Interestingly, some of the early founders of the institute felt constrained and suffocated by the prevailing conservatism and puritanism widespread in the Muslim world. Some, like Anwar Ibrahim, former deputy prime minister of Malaysia, and Taha Jabir al-Alwani, an accomplished scholar, were liberally oriented and dreamt of the possibility of serious Islamic reform. The reason IIIT was founded in the United States was that the founders believed that they would enjoy freedom of thought and expression and that this freedom was key for making any progress. Inconsistent with its role as a serious scholarly enterprise, IIIT ran a federally funded school, Cordoba University, to train Muslim chaplains for the Defense Department. But the inconsistencies did not end there. Purportedly, IIIT received funding from the Muslim Brotherhood and from Saudi Arabia, and like many other Muslim institutions with intellectual aspirations, no clear line was drawn between activism and scholarship. A large number of people without any scholarly qualifications or achievements joined IIIT and became seriously involved in defining the role of the institution.

After 9/11, at the urging of Islamophobes, the federal government commenced an investigation of IIIT that led to searches, arrests, and the freezing of assets that all but destroyed the institution. After studying the sum total of legal proceedings that took place concerning this institute, it was very clear that what the US government ended up conducting was a witch hunt extensively rationalized and facilitated by bigots who seem to feel threatened by any form of Muslim self-empowerment in the West. At the end, no terrorism-related charges were brought or proved against the institute, but some individuals were deported for immigration law violations.[3] The shock and trauma of being the target of a witch hunt in a country that symbolized freedom and civil rights, in my opinion, contributed to the unfortunate premature death of Mona Abou El Fadl, one of the scholars of the institute and al-Alwani's wife. Al-Alwani had been very active in condemning the terrorist attacks of 9/11 and in combating Muslim extremism in the United States and elsewhere. He had established a reputation for being a rationality-based jurist and an advocate of reform in Islamic law. Al-Alwani left IIIT and the United States, ultimately settling in Cairo. I met him at his home in Cairo, and I felt saddened by the meeting because among the various individuals involved with the IIIT project, he was without a doubt the most intellectually qualified and the most knowledgeable. I should note, however, that after a few years of being defunct, as of the summer of 2012, IIIT had resumed its activity but without al-Alwani's involvement.

In many ways, IIIT's intellectual project was doomed from the start. It is impossible to pursue a serious intellectual enterprise if one begins with an irreparable conflict of interest by accepting money from venues that are thoroughly authoritarian, dogmatic, and disinterested in, if not threatened by, serious scholarly investigations. Furthermore, it has become an endemic problem throughout the Muslim world that social and political activism and scholarly objectives are often mixed and blurred in a way that makes free explorations and investigations of thought and research impossible. For purely pragmatic political reasons, IIIT did not seek out the most qualified scholars but, rather, those willing to engage in the affectations of both piety and scholarship. Instead of valuing thought that challenged and defied them, they looked for pietistic affirmations of their institution and goals. As is the case with so many Islamic organizations around the world, a scholarly performance invoking the appropriate symbolisms of piety and religiosity was valued to a far greater extent than the integrity and honesty of the substantive scholarship. Therefore, a large number of individuals who were blatantly unqualified and without much merit as researchers or scholars came to be heavily involved with IIIT. The solution to this problem, however, is critical engagement and analytical exposure. The solution is not for so-called native informants, like Irshad Manji, Ayaan Hirsi Ali, Asra Nomani, and Wafa Sultan—self-hating Muslims, or once-upon-a-time Muslims, who are willing to condemn everything Muslim while being surrounded by the enthusiastic and unfettered acclamation and adulation of non-Muslims, who also happen to not be fair-minded people themselves—to launch unknowing testimonials as to the fanaticism of all Muslim enterprises. The solution is not political persecution such as that launched by the Islamophobes and the FBI. The only moral and ethical response is to engage these kinds of flawed intellectual enterprises and to confront them with their own irrationality and unreasonableness. I cannot assess IIIT as reincarnated in 2012. I did notice that the discourse on the Islamization of knowledge seems to have died down and that the list of titles that they planned to publish in 2012 seemed to be more sophisticated than that of their predecessors. Whether they learned anything about the dangers of accepting funding from authoritarian venues that seek to control thought rather than promote it remains to be seen.

STEREOTYPED FORMS AND THE PRACTICE OF ISLAMIC LAW

The Islamization of knowledge project was to a very large extent inspired by one of the most powerful dogmas impacting the Muslim mind in the contemporary age. This dogma is summed up in the assertion often repeated that Islam is a complete and total way of life. Numerous books written on Islam in modern times repeated this assertion until it became as if an article of faith for contemporary Muslims. Significantly, however, this phrase with its current connotations of a totalistic and comprehensive way of living, believing, behaving, and everything else is a thoroughly modern invention. Its origins are actually fairly recent, going back to Islamic apologetics in response to Orientalist (especially in the colonial age) accusations that Islam is unfit for the demands of modern civilization. In response to these attacks, a number of Muslim apologists co-opted the classical Shari'ah discourses providing that divine norms or God's guidance extends to every aspect of human life. However, in its modern co-optation, the claim was clearly influenced by the age of ideologies and the modern quest for holistic comprehensive meaning. Most contemporary Muslims would have no way of retrieving the cumulative interpretive memory that accompanied premodern discourses on the perfection of divine norms. In premodern terms, this argument was fundamentally a part of Islamic theodicy, but in modern terms, it has very different far-reaching social and political connotations. Other than the rootedness, or rather the absence of roots, in the classical tradition, the dogma of Islam being a complete way of life begs the question: In what sense? One issue is whether those who make this claim imagine that Islam has a code-law book of rules that regulates every eventuality of existence or if they imagine a set of general moral precepts that are broad enough to apply to numerous potential contingencies. Another issue, and also a bigger problem, is the imaginary construct of life on which those who make the claim rely. It becomes easier and also dangerous to deal with life's challenges if the relevant facts of such a life are identified not through sociological and cultural experiences but through a religiously motivated imaginary construct. Instead of dealing with the full complexity and richness of life and dealing with the challenges on their own terms, it is possible for the religious imaginary to limit what are considered to be the relevant facts in such a way as to avoid having to deal with the challenge in the first place. In this situation, life is not experienced and studied in its full richness and adversity, but the process of living itself is conceptualized in highly stereotyped forms that have little to do with material culture or the lived experience. Consequently, challenges are not dealt with through a dynamic of systematic analysis, and legal problems are not treated from within an exhaustive jurisprudential framework. Instead, the stereotyped forms that are used to respond to challenging facts and difficult problems sustain certain fictions of performance. In effect, contemporary practitioners rely on fictions that allow them to avoid confronting the reality existing on the ground, and then responding to the constructed fictions is done through stereotypical processes and solutions.

I will illustrate this problem by discussing a number of cases that I worked on involving the use of prenuptials in marriage agreements. In these cases, women entered into marriage contracts providing that in case of divorce, the ex-wife is entitled to a division of property and alimony only to the extent provided for in Islamic law. Typically in these cases, after twenty years of marriage, during which the wife has not been employed outside her home, the husband exercises his unilateral right to divorce his wife, usually because he wants to take a new, young wife from his homeland. According to the majority view in the classical tradition, the most that the wife is entitled to is a year of financial support and the right to reside in the marital home for a three-month period. Obviously, this is an oppressive situation for wives who, after spending most of their lives serving their families, have reached a senior age and cannot find employment. Despite the oppressiveness of this result, in every case I worked on, I found myself clashing with religious leaders in courts in the United States, Canada, and England. Incidentally, in my experience, these are often the same religious leaders who persistently engage the dogma of how Islamic law had protected and guaranteed the rights of divorced women. Testifying in court as an expert witness, I would usually go into the details of the historical context that produced these laws, and explain the legal principles and maxims that would justify providing financial security to divorced women by considering the contemporary economic and social realities. I would explain that the same principles and maxims that produced the one year of support rule can now be reapplied to provide for a legal rule that is more responsive to contemporary realities. Furthermore, I would explain the views of dissenting jurists who argued that a divorcée, without financial means of support, is entitled to support until remarriage or death. But in numerous cases, husbands retain the services of local imams, or at times, internationally known Shari'ah experts. In all of these cases, I have observed how the expert testimony supporting the traditional patriarchical position would become a complete performance in the trappings of Islamicity. To produce the full effect, the man would be adorned with a beard and dressed in a robe, and after offering an introduction about how Shari'ah (Islamic law) protected the rights of all and liberated women from oppression, he would solemnly affirm the one-year of support rule, declaring it to be the judgment of the Qur'an and Sunna. On the strength of my legal citations and scholarly presentation, the women I worked with have often prevailed in court. But I did notice that simply on the power of the performance of religiosity and the affectations of piety, the stance taken by the imams on behalf of husbands becomes associated with the more genuinely Islamic. Moreover, having convinced themselves that the one year of support is the Islamically mandated ruling, they also become convinced that by definition this ruling is also more just and more responsive to the practical demands of life.

Another rather odd but telling example arose in the context of a marital dispute about spousal rights in a Muslim community in the United States. A dignified wife who had suffered verbal abuse from her husband for a long time refused to have conjugal relations with her husband. The husband, who made the dispute public by complaining to anyone who would listen, ended up obtaining a *fatwa* (nonbinding legal opinion) from a Saudi jurist stating that the wife does not have the right to abstain from her husband. The local imam agreed with the Saudi *fatwa* and added that a woman of good character would not deny her husband conjugal rights. The local imam also speculated that this matter was conclusively established and no jurist had ever expressed a different view on the matter. On being asked, not having had an opportunity to research the matter further, I responded that I was aware of at least one source, *Al-Fatawa al-Hamadiyya*, which expressed a different view. This source mentioned that several classical jurists held that if the reason for abstaining from conjugal relations is ill treatment by the husband, it is lawful do so. But I added that this issue is more appropriately resolved by *akhlaq* (ethics) than rules of law. The reactions of the imam, several of the community leaders, and of course the husband were all that the view I expressed was palpably un-Islamic. Interestingly, I met with a group consisting of twelve wives in the community and asked them whether they believed that the position of the husband, imam, and Saudi mufti were Islamically correct, and they said they did. I asked whether they thought that their position was fair and just, and they said they did. I asked whether, if their husbands insulted them on a regular basis, they would abstain from having conjugal relations with them. After some hesitation, most of them said they would abstain because they could not be intimate with someone who insults them.

Divergence between lived experiences and legal determinations and the import of this for ethics and morality is a complicated topic, and I will attempt to tackle this issue later. For now, I want to develop the idea of the stereotypical responses in Islamic legal practice. Stereotypical responses lock Islamicity within a narrow space of interpretive or constructive possibility. A stereotyped response is reactive, and to the extent that it affirms a picture of orthodoxy in order to reassert an authoritative image of Islamicity, it is a form of religious affectation. Stereotyped responses assume a narrow view of Islamicity and then seek to reproduce this view as an affirmation of orthodoxy within a specific sense of presupposed determinations. In other words, a stereotyped response is premised on a view about what is truly and authentically Islamic as opposed to what is not and also on the dogmatic exclusion of alternatives. The Islamic intellectual heritage often contains open possibilities of creative interpretation, and the Shari'ah tradition, in particular, is rich and highly diverse. There is usually a wealth of competing and frequently conflicting opinions and perspectives on any point of positive law, and so it is not at all unusual to find ten different opinions expressed by classical jurists on a particular issue. Stereotyped responses, however, significantly narrow the range of constructive possibilities by restricting creative interpretive activity by dogmatically limiting the tools of determination—tools such as text, reason, or customs.

Stereotypical responses are very prevalent in contemporary Muslim societies. They occur over a wide range of issues where popularly constructed images had formed over what genuinely represents Shari'ah. This image, however, is vigorously and often irrationally asserted at the cost of the existence of a vibrant discursive dynamic that allows for the critical regeneration and reconstitution of Islamic law. Examples of this problem are experienced daily in the Muslim world and are quite numerous. Importantly, this kind of silencing of alternatives is not something practiced by puritans alone, and it is not limited to a conservative group of clergy. Perhaps the initial legalistic determination was made by conservative clergy or puritanical groups, but often this form of cultural restrictionism and preservationism is championed by mainstream Muslims. It appears that this is done out of a desire to experience Islam as a source of stability and reaffirmation instead of dynamic change.

I will discuss an example involving a high-ranking jurist in Egypt over an issue that normally would not raise much debate. It is well known that Islamic law prohibits Muslims from consuming pork. Recently, the former Mufti of Egypt, 'Ali Jum'a, was asked if Muslims living in the West are permitted to sell pork products in their restaurants or grocery stores. Shaykh 'Ali Jum'a responded to the inquiry by arguing that it will be financially burdensome if Muslim minorities living in non-Muslim lands are forbidden to sell pork products because refraining from doing so could result in financial losses. This seemingly benign *fatwa* on a fairly technical issue of jurisprudence ignited a deluge of recriminations and condemnations. Several specialists and nonspecialists wrote in newspapers and magazines severely criticizing the *fatwa*—stating flat out that the Mufti is clearly wrong. According to the popularly held position, if God prohibited Muslims from consuming pork, it necessarily followed that they, under any circumstance, cannot sell it. Most curiously, several of the Mufti's colleagues immediately appeared on television or wrote letters to editors claiming that the Mufti was misunderstood and alleging that he, after all, did not say what he appeared to say. In reality, the issue did not deserve to be treated in such a stereotypical and dogmatic fashion because, as I am sure the Mufti knows, this very exact issue was extensively debated in the classical legal tradition, and the jurists disagreed on the correct position. Jurists from the Hanbali and Shafi'i legal schools of thought did, in fact, hold that Muslims ought not sell swine meat, whether to Muslims or non-Muslims. However, jurists from the Hanafi and Maliki schools of legal thought disagreed. Some of them held that even in Muslim countries, a Muslim may sell swine meat to non-Muslims. Others held that a Muslim can sell the meat to Christians but not to Muslims or Jews because both Judaism and Islam prohibit the consumption of pork. Still others held that if Muslims reside in non-Muslim lands, they may trade in pork products because the commercial laws of Islam had no application or jurisdiction outside the lands of Islam. In summary, the interpretive communities of the past had reached different positions on this same issue, and there was no compelling reason to consider the topic closed to debate. In other words, there is more than ample support for the Mufti's opinion, and it is indeed alarming when a jurist of his prestige and authority is forced into silence or retraction.

A similar but even greater controversy exploded when another accomplished Egyptian mufti advised a woman that if she prays in private where no one could see her other than God, she did not have to cover her hair in prayer. The public outcry and outrage against that poor jurist was severe, and once again the colleagues quickly sprung to his defense by claiming that he was misquoted and misunderstood. Of course, I don't know if this mufti was in fact misquoted or not; nevertheless, the unequivocal response that this alleged *fatwa* generated in Egypt was, in my view, unjustified. Whether a woman may, under certain circumstances, pray with her hair uncovered was a subject of considerable debate in early Islamic legal history. Some classical jurists even argued that whether the hair needed to be covered or not depended not only on privacy but on the legal status of the woman—whether she was free or not. In the contemporary age, slavery or freedom is no longer the pertinent issue—the relevant issue is the evidence that forms the basis for the legal determination. But in every case, the evidence, whichever way it might lead, cannot be studied properly in light of dogmatic and stereotypical responses.

Stereotypical responses of the kind above do not just stunt the development of Islamic law as a field of normative discourse. They often stunt the development of serious ethical evaluations, social development of standards of reasonableness, and the cultivation of shared humane values. This occurs because practitioners fall in the habit of avoiding the pain of wrestling with uncomfortable facts, and as they escape to ready-made dogma, this acts to dull the intellect and the continual development of a critical sense of moral responsibility.

Growing up in the Middle East, I have always been bothered by the abysmal condition of feral dogs and the general social hostility to the ownership of dogs. I still remember the horrible sounds of street dogs being shot by animal control at dawn in the streets of Cairo. But the reason behind social and culturally based hostility is the belief that dogs are unclean because their saliva voids the ritual purity of worshippers and because there is a tradition attributed to the Prophet that claims that angels will not enter a dwelling that houses dogs. As a result, the hostility to dog ownership at times reaches the point of cruelty. I recall reading a *fatwa* by a Saudi jurist who advised a man to stop giving his dog food and water. The man asking for the *fatwa* used to have a dog but abandoned the dog after he was told that it was sinful to own it. Finding itself in the street, the poor dog would not go away, and the man asked the Saudi jurist if he could perhaps keep the dog as an outdoor pet. The Saudi jurist was decisive in his response—he told the man that it is unlawful to keep dogs as outdoor pets, and it was also unlawful to continue feeding the dog. If the man would stop giving the dog food and water, the Saudi jurist speculated, the dog was bound to go away. *Fatawa* urging cruelty such as this one have always caused me to suffer something of a cognitive dissonance. Reportedly, the Prophet cared for animals, and in a very famous tradition, the Prophet promised Heaven to a man who saved the life of a dog dying of thirst.[4] In addition, I was always intrigued by the fact that some Muslim scholars of the classical tradition had written books in praise of the moral quality of dogs and contended that human beings should ponder the nature of dogs in order to improve their own sense of virtue.[5] I also found that in various periods of Islamic premodern history, wealthy Muslim families created endowments (*awqaf*) for the care of homeless dogs. These were in addition to endowments created for the care of women abused by their husbands or even endowments to compensate for clay pots accidentally broken by waiters or delivery boys so that these poor laborers would not have to run the risk of losing their jobs (known as *awqaf al-zabadi*). There were endowments to help impoverished owners feed their dogs and also endowments to defray the cost of medical treatments for dogs and other animals. These traditions are at odds with the callous determination of the Saudi jurist. In the premodern period there existed a humanistic orientation that extended to the caretaking of animals, including dogs.[6]

Whatever people end up attributing to the law, God must consistently remain humane and reasonable within the parameters of the shifting sociocultural standards of time and space. The Qur'an repeatedly and consistently calls on Muslims to learn from and reflect on nature, creation, and cumulative human experience. This necessarily means that in contemplating Shari'ah, or the path of God, it is incumbent that we study not just the decontextualized and dehistoricized text but also the normative import of texts in light of rational human experience. Anyone who has spent time with domesticated dogs will be immediately struck by the nature that God has created (or evolved) in these furry friends. Dogs live to please their human owners; their nature is such that they loyally accompany their owner; the height of their happiness seems to be contingent on receiving attention from the person who cares for them; and by their very nature, dogs possess a complex psychology that is well suited for human companionship. Observing how dogs react to receiving human affection is nothing short of beautiful and sublime.

What I think is particularly troubling is when, out of a range of interpretive possibilities, a jurist selects the most unreasonable. If the interpretive tradition leaves no room for negotiation, then a jurist might have to labor much harder to make sure that he/she has discharged his/her duties of due diligence before God. But the juristic interpretive tradition on dogs was markedly broader than the stereotyped treatment of the Saudi *fatwa*. For instance, a large number of classical jurists did not consider dogs impure and did not prohibit their ownership. First, there were some reports alleging that the Prophet and some companions raised dogs. Second, many jurists argued that domesticated dogs that live as members of the household are to be considered pure. Moreover, a number of jurists made the pivotal issues to be the hygiene of dogs and what they consume. If the custodians control what a dog eats and if they bathe and clean the dog, these classical jurists maintained, such a dog is pure, and dogs may be owned even if the sole purpose of ownership is companionship.[7]

The point here is not only that those who issued the *fatawa* of condemnation ignored or concealed these precedents. Rather, the point is that even when confronted with the contrary evidence, the practitioner was not willing to concede that the issue is not perhaps as conclusively resolvable as he might have thought. In reality, the practitioner had adopted a stereotyped image of what Islam is and what it stands for. Many practitioners are not well versed in the juristic tradition, and so they will rely on stereotyped understandings to articulate their sense of Islamicity. The problem is that the more stereotyped the practice, the less reasonable its determinations will be, which in turn means that in the long run, the tradition and indeed the religion will cease to be persuasive or pertinent.

A prime contributor to the politics of affectation and to stereotypical forms of Islamic legal practice is the disintegration of institutions for jurisprudential study in the modern age. Not having an organized church, this has resulted in a crisis of authenticity and legitimacy in modern Islam. There are many factors that contributed in material ways to this situation. I will discuss this problem in greater detail later in the book, but at this point, it is useful to note that prime among the factors leading to the crisis was the nationalization and co-optation by the state of the institutions for jurisprudential learning in Islam. Not surprisingly, one of the outcomes from the disintegration of the institutions of authoritative learning in Islam was to greatly facilitate and enable the process of exploiting Shari'ah as a symbol for propaganda purposes. With the existence of an ever-increasing vacuum in moral authority, the practice of affectations became much more persuasive and effective.

The virtual whirlwind of affectations and stereotyped determinations that surround Islamic law in the contemporary age has meant that at the sociopolitical level, it is condescendingly praised in order to place it on a pedestal, where as a symbol it is exalted and exploited but not engaged in any critical fashion. At the academic level, in polite company Islamic law is paid lip service by being praised for unspecified great contributions to jurisprudential thought, but it is largely ignored in the field of comparative jurisprudential studies. Of course, one side effect of this dynamic is that Islamophobes find a wealth of demonstrative examples to exploit for the purposes of demonizing and objectifying the Muslim "other."

NATURE OF AUTHORITY IN ISLAMIC LAW AND CHAOS

Barriers to entry into the field have crumbled, and Islamic law has become accessible to anyone willing to don the stereotypes and symbols of authoritativeness. This egalitarianism, however, has been coupled with a near complete deterioration in the standards for evaluating both the competence of participants and the quality of their contributions. The disintegration of the traditional institutions of Islamic learning and authority meant a descent into a condition of virtual anarchy in regard to the mechanisms of defining Islamic authenticity. It was not so much that no one could authoritatively speak for Islam but that virtually every Muslim was suddenly considered to possess the requisite qualifications to become a representative and spokesperson for the Islamic tradition and even Shari'ah law. Most of the so-called imams or leaders in Islamic centers in the United States and elsewhere either have not received any systematic instruction in Islamic theology and law or have only received a minimal amount of instruction consisting of studying some of the positive commandments of Islamic law. Especially in the last couple of decades, a large number of imams have studied for one or two years in Saudi Arabia or in Saudi-funded and Saudi-sponsored Islamic law institutes that have sprung up all over the Muslim world. In the classical period, students needed the equivalent of fifteen to twenty years of graduate study before their opinions, especially on de novo issues of law, would have been taken seriously either culturally or at a collegiate level.[8] If we use the United States for the purposes of comparison, it is well understood that graduating from a top law school and passing a state bar does not necessarily mean that a person has become an authority on American law. Now imagine if in the course of the coming century, every student who attends community college and takes a number of undergraduate courses in American law is issued a governmental certificate declaring such a person a legal authority. I wonder how long would it be before chaos would set in because no one is quite sure what expertise in American law means.

Today, to the delight of puritanical Muslims and Islamophobes alike, the phenomenon of self-declared or poorly trained experts in Islamic law has become widespread and endemic. The problem transcends the idiosyncrasies of any one context, locality, or country. Well into the eighteenth century, the range of subjects constituting the pedagogical training of a Muslim jurist were well placed within the dominant epistemological paradigms of the age. As elaborated on later, this sharply contrasts with the dominant curricula of today, which have little to do with the prevailing epistemologies of the contemporary world. Today, it is rather notable that the leaders of Islamic fundamentalist movements are typically medical doctors, engineers, or computer scientists by training. Those speaking on a range of issues offering up the so-called Islamic position range among the wealthy individual who has enough money to build a center, organize a camp, fund a mosque or activities, or purchase a satellite television channel and declare himself a shaykh or learned authority; the cyber-mufti who sits at a computer all day long inflicting *fatawa* and opining on Islamic jurisprudence and its legacy; the charismatic preacher who promises his audience a slice of heaven if they shorten their robes and grow their beards; the frustrated male chauvinist who dresses his fantasies in religious garb and then tries to force women to wear it; the failing or bored professional who is unfulfilled by a career in computer science, engineering, or medicine so he makes a career out of using Shari'ah as a means of wrongful empowerment; and the marginalized social misfit who hopes to achieve hero status and lounge in heaven by killing innocents.

THE MUSIC OF SHARI'AH, SILENCE OF TRADITION, AND DISSONANCE OF MODERNITY

Theologically, there is no single institution that is empowered to speak on God's behalf. Morally, the only compelling authority is persuasive. I will explain this further in the following chapters, but for now, it is important to establish that, in theological theory, scholars gain authority in direct proportion to their ability to persuade fellow Muslims that they legitimately represent the wishes and commands of God. In theory, the sole criterion or qualification for authoritativeness is mastering the indicators or evidence leading to the divine will or the path from and to God. The evidence of God's Will is to be found in texts, such as the Qur'an and Sunna, but it could also be found in creation, intuition, social practices, and history as well as reason. In all cases, earthly authority is created when believers, convinced that the scholar has mastered the evidence of God's path, decide to follow and defer to the scholar's determinations and judgments. This is the only basis for the moral authority of a jurist—authority of the state in imposing positive law is a different topic addressed later. If a jurist pretends to have qualifications that he does not possess and manages to fool Muslims, in the Hereafter this is a grave sin. In this case, the jurist has misrepresented his/her competence to speak on God's behalf and fraudulently induced Muslims unjustifiably to rely on his/her baseless determinations. There could be institutions of learning that vouch for the competence of a scholar, for instance, through the grant of certifications, degrees, or diplomas, but this does not alter the basic nature of the dynamic. There is no getting around the fact that a scholar is evaluated and judged by Muslims on this earth and by God in the Hereafter. From a sociological perspective, Muslims will tend to presume that someone who has received some form of certification by an institution of learning is competent to speculate on the divine will. Theoretically, however, graduating from an institution of learning does not, in and of itself, establish the authority of a scholar. Only the willingness of Muslims to defer to the judgments of a particular scholar will establish the scholar's authority. Importantly, as long as a Muslim's reliance on the purported authority of a jurist was reasonable, such a Muslim would be considered to have discharged his/her obligation toward searching for God's path.

I will illustrate this dynamic by an analogy to classical music. The way Shari'ah law works at a moral level can be analogized to the production of classical music. Classical music follows certain rules and forms. Every composer has roots in the art of a predecessor, and so the rule and forms are based on the cumulative practice of musicians over a long span of time. A composer may receive training in the highest institutions of learning, but what establishes the art of the composer is not his training. What establishes the art of a composer is the acceptance and admiration of the audience. It is certainly true that a composer who builds on the art of his predecessors will tend to be more believable and authoritative, but the relationship between the composer and listener is direct and unmediated. The listener has to accept the art of a composer for this composer to become an authoritative figure in the field. Having said this, it is important to note that it is certainly possible for a particular composer to be ahead of his time and to be appreciated as an artist long after he is dead. It is also possible for the public taste to be so poor that only the most mediocre and substandard composer is recognized as an artist, while the most masterful composer languishes in obscurity. Bach and Mahler, for instance, went through periods of relative obscurity. This is why public taste plays a very important role in defining the standards. If the public taste is in a poor condition, the public could celebrate a salon music composer at the expense of a true master, and the cumulative effect on musical standards in a particular society could be disastrous. If this situation goes unchecked, eventually the society might no longer be able to distinguish the mediocre from the majestic and real art from sensational trash.

The example from music helps us make a couple of critical points about the dynamics that take place in contemporary Islamic law. The deterioration in the quality of the production of Shari'ah law (in our example, the music) does not occur just in the absence of qualified composers or conductors but also in the absence of a considerate and mature audience. The disintegration in the institutions of learning in the Islamic world was coupled with a significant deterioration in the prevailing standards that guide what Muslims expect from these institutions. Therefore, the deterioration has been in the very public values that reflect and guide the expectations and standards surrounding the practice of Shari'ah law. So although many Muslims insist that Islamic law is a viable option in today's world, the reality is that they do not treat it as such because they do not engage it critically and analytically. In order for Islamic law to be a viable and active option in Muslim life, it must be taken seriously enough to be enabled to confront and meet real-life challenges unmitigated by convenient fictions and stereotyped responses. Here, the idea of reasonableness is of critical importance. If the composers and conductors lose sight of the fact that their music must be accepted by the audience and produce music that no longer moves the spirit of its listeners, they have done the music a great injustice. If, on the other hand, the audience reacts to music that has become dissonant and unreasonable by the affectation of insincere applause and stereotyped praise, the composers and conductors will continue to be deluded and ineffectual.

There are many historical reasons why Muslims ended up in this condition. One of the most important factors, however, was the abolition of Shari'ah law as the commonwealth law of Muslim countries. I will explain this point in the coming chapters. But beyond the abrogation of Islamic law and its institutions, the colonial experience as a whole brought Islam, its civilization, and its law under a state of virtual siege. Feeling the threat to their religion and culture, Muslim intellectuals responded with defensive apologetic discourses intended to augment the sense of pride that Muslims feel toward their own identity and tradition. The purpose of Muslim apologetics was to empower Muslims against an imminent threat, but intellectually, the apologetics fell far short. Muslim apologists treated Islamic law as a field ripe for pietistic fictions rather than a technical tradition of complex linguistic practices and sophisticated methodologies of social and textual analysis. For the most part, as far as Shari'ah is concerned, this remains the situation, and crisis, today. There are, however, two important qualifiers to this. First, many formidable legal minds, like 'Abd al-Razzaq al-Sanhuri (d. 1391/ 1971), 'Abd al-Qadir 'Awda (d. 1374/1954), and Subhi al-Mahmassani (d. 1407/1986), did try to rise to the challenge of reimagining and reforming Shari'ah law. However, they did so by relying on the legal epistemology and phenomenology of the civil law system, especially French law, which, as I argue later, was an ill-fitted model for Islamic law. In the last analysis, without intending to do so, they often ended up playing a largely apologetic role toward Shari'ah law because much of their work focused on proving that Islamic law met the challenges posed by French law. Perhaps this was inevitable because their only living memory of law and their professional training was in the French legal system, which they experienced as the hegemonic and superior, if not supreme, legal culture of the colonizer. The second exception is more significant, and indeed it might be the exception that swallowed the rule. A broad movement started in the late nineteenth and early twentieth centuries that rebelled against the centuries-old interpretive tradition that cumulatively defines Shari'ah. In a sense, inspired by a dream of an Islamic authenticity waiting to be realized, this was the ultimate deconstructive and reconstructive movement. It thought to throw away the Islamic tradition and start fresh by reengaging and reinterpreting the primary textual sources of Shari'ah (the Qur'an and Sunna). But with the institutions of learning and law being in poor condition, the original-sources school undermined the interpretive traditions of the past without offering an alternative that transcended the apologetics of the moment. The egalitarianism of the original-sources movement set the bar so low that any person with a modest degree of knowledge of the Qur'an and the traditions of the Prophet was considered sufficiently qualified to authoritatively represent the Shari'ah, even if such a person was not familiar with the precedents and discourses of the interpretive communities of the past.[9] The Islamic intellectual culture witnessed an unprecedented level of deterioration as the Islamic heritage was reduced to the least common denominator, which often amounted to engaging in crass generalizations about the nature of Islam and the nature of the non-Muslim "other."

For decades now, pietistic affectations, stereotyped performances, and apologetics have formed a makeshift vulgar but functionalist response to the very serious challenges raised about memory, identity, and the future of Muslims. Is it possible to have an identity without a memory, and is it possible to feel empowered without an identity? And in what ways is the future affected by the construction of memory and identity? Islam will remain a formidable and powerful driving force in the lives of Muslims. But these questions, which were raised with the advent of modernity, have only grown more urgent and more pressing with each passing decade. How Muslims go about answering them will decide the nature of Islam's moral force in a world that is increasingly interdependent and interconnected. Symbolic displays of power and conflicts aside, Muslims cannot ignore that quintessentially, Islam, being the path to God and from God, is about a universal message to humanity.

THE DREAM REVISITED

This has become all the more critical because of a transformative duality that is currently sweeping through the Middle East. The so-called Arab Spring has clearly shown that people of the region are not satisfied with living under despotism. In every single country where there has been a revolution, the consistent demand has been for freedom, justice, and the rejection of despotism. Thus far, the revolution has included Egypt, Tunisia, Libya, Yemen, Syria, and Bahrain, and there are the signs of serious rumblings in Morocco, Jordan, Sudan, and Saudi Arabia. In every one of these countries, the demands have been remarkably consistent and similar—the imperative of living under a system of governance in which people elect and remove their rulers and in which rulers are held accountable for their actions. Yet at the same time, in countries such as Egypt, Tunisia, Libya, and Yemen, the Islamists have gained considerable ground. Not all Islamists are the same, and indeed these revolutions might promise to be the first opportunity for Muslims to articulate a truly indigenous, authentic, and legitimate synchronization between their tradition and the cultures of their former colonizers.[10] This might be another real opportunity for Muslims to overcome the ailments of uprootedness and moral dispossession that have become the earmark of so many cultures in the modern age. In an article I wrote a few years ago titled "The Orphans of Modernity," I described the Muslim dispossession as a reactive condition in which an agonizing sense of homelessness and longing leaves many Muslims feeling alienated and disempowered.[11] The current revolutionary momentum could be an opportunity to reconcile the Muslim self to its soul and to overcome this alienation by finding a way back to Muslims' civilizational lineage. I believe that returning to an Islamic civilizational heritage is partly a historical imperative, but for the most part, it is a normative imperative. It is a normative imperative because of the moral values embodied in the Shari'ah, which, as discussed later, is a set of natural goods that are divinely ordained and mandated. I will have to return to this argument, but what becomes of the revolutions of the Middle East will in good measure depend not so much on whether Islamists rise to power but on how they understand and construe Shari'ah. Labels often only serve to obfuscate issues, not clarify them. And so whether a particular movement rising to power describes itself as Islamist or not is not nearly as important as the substantive normative values that are internalized, adhered to, and advocated. Many Muslims in the Arab world resent the label Islamist because of a misimpression that those who carry the label are more authentically Muslim or representative of Islam than others. The argument is often made that those who employ the symbolisms and affectations of piety are not necessarily any more religious than others and not any more caring about the values of the religion than others. In the same context, secularism is not a particularly helpful category for deciphering the parties and events either. I will return to the question of secularism, but I do believe that if by secularism one has the

French example in mind, then one will find only a few Muslims in the postrevolutionary era willing to identify themselves by the label of secularism. However, if one has the secularism of Poland, Romania, or Croatia in mind, I suspect that a much greater number of Muslims would happily accept the label.[12] Indeed in many ways, in the age of science, skepticism, doubt, and disbelief in mythology, epistemologically there are very few societies left untouched by the secular age.[13] Yet if religion is a belief in higher and ultimate truths about the good and these truths are unverifiable by a frame of reference higher than themselves, then all societies to one extent or another depend on the religious for their cohesiveness and survival. My point is that we should not lose sight of the fact that words such as *secularism, Islamism,* and indeed all "isms" are often heuristic devices that reference very complex and highly contested phenomena. The critical substantive issue, in my view, will not be whether secularists or Islamists rise to power but what normative ethical and moral values those who do come to rule embody and bring to Muslim life. Regardless of the heuristic devices employed, if there is an attempt to exclude Shari'ah altogether from the domain of the normative and authoritative, the resulting strife and conflict will likely exhaust or abort any real chances for the success of a democratic project. People should not be made to choose between what embodies their normative values and sense of ultimate law and their civic and political rights—ultimately, neither will thrive. As has happened in the past and will continue to occur, the military in each country will maintain the status quo by continuing to play the role of the arbitrator and negotiator between the opposite poles.

I think that the same results will follow if Shari'ah itself is used simply as a heuristic device—if a party tries to make its authority and legitimacy immune by invoking the symbol of Shari'ah. Once again, by turning Shari'ah into a heuristic device symbolizing the dominance of the divine over the temporal and the sacred over the secular, the resulting turmoil between the polarized corners of society will make the success of democracy impossible. And in the case of most Muslim countries, the resulting social turmoil between those who embrace the symbolisms and affectations of religiosity and those who resist it will result in a military dictatorship. Military regimes will do what they have been doing since the age of colonialism—they will straddle the fence between the secular and sacred while thoroughly deforming both and while reaffirming and exasperating the paradigm of the orphans of modernity. I think it is key that the orphaned status end, but this will not happen simply because Muslims pretend to have been adopted by a culture that rejects them and keeps them at arm's length—as Europe has treated Turkey, for instance.

Some years ago, in the late 1980s, I had the good fortune of enjoying a brief but warm friendship with the late French-Muslim scholar Mohammad Arkoun (d. 1431/2010). I invited Arkoun to my home in Morton, Pennsylvania, and he kindly accepted. Our friendship was fueled by our mutual admiration for the profound Islamic scholar Abu Hayyan al-Tawhidi (d. 414/1023) and our love of perfectly brewed Turkish coffee. Around that time, some Saudi jurists had reportedly issued a legal opinion (*fatwa*) accusing Arkoun of apostasy, and he was visibly troubled by this development.[14] Arkoun had generated a prodigious number of studies on a variety of topics, including the need for new methodologies of analysis in Islamic studies. In his work, Arkoun emphasizes the history of mentalities, especially what Arkoun calls the unthought and unthinkable in the history of Muslims. These unthinkables stand as stumbling blocks preventing Muslim cultures from accurately describing reality before proceeding to interpret it.[15] I argued that besides the unthought and unthinkable, we ought to focus on the forgotten in Islamic history or what was never learned in the first place. The point I was making is that before we can explain, leave alone interpret, the historical mentalities of Muslims, it is critical that we engage the Islamic experience at the level of its microdiscourses. Especially when it comes to Shari'ah, it is critical that before speaking of juridical mind-sets in Islam, we decipher the microdynamics of the legal discourse. Only then would it be possible to begin to understand, explain, and interpret the historical experience and its meanings. I completely agreed with Arkoun's celebration of comparative knowledge as key to possessing the ability to explain historical and social phenomena. But I did have reservations about the ideological bias of phenomenological studies (the study of consciousness and experience) and, as I put it back then, "the dogma of deconstructing dogma." I learned a great deal from Arkoun and greatly admired his remarkable humility and graciousness. I got the impression that Arkoun was interested in a different set of questions or, I should say, in a different way of asking a different set of questions. However, at one point, Arkoun did wonder out loud whether a scientific approach to what he called Islamology could reach the average educated Muslim and induce a paradigm shift—a new way of thinking. A response jumped out of my mouth before I could really discern it—I said: "Professor, those who do not believe in scientific approaches to Islam will always win because they are always willing to display their piety—while we begin with being out of context because we insist that piety is purely a private matter." I think my hasty response surprised Arkoun, and judging by the fact that we drove to the train station in silence, he seems to have been disappointed.

This is not the place to discuss all the ways that this meeting had left a deep impact on me. Coming early on in my career, it helped me to define the way I thought and pursued my own intellectual project, and I found myself revisiting this conversation many times. There are many reasons that the intellectual project in Europe struggled with memory and tradition, often swinging back and forth between what borders on triumphalism and exaggerated deconstructionism. But it seemed to me to be deeply flawed for a Muslim insider hoping to pursue reform to simply transplant a heuristic apparatus from the West onto a different context with a different set of worries and concerns. Before being able to interrogate their memory from deconstructive perspectives, the Western intellectuals first felt that they owned this history. It is only the sense of confidence in controlling and directing their history that allowed Western intellectuals the confidence to challenge and undo that history. Muslims stand in a very different position. Muslims have been struck by a colonially induced amnesia toward their collective memory, and whatever they have been able to rehabilitate of that memory in the postcolonial age has been heavily influenced by the fact that all power is weighed heavily in favor of the former colonizers. Put differently, all attempts at rehabilitating historical memory (as opposed to traditional mythology) has been heavily influenced by the fact that the institutions, the tools, and very often, even the funding for learning all come from the West. In these circumstances, I think that methodologies that deconstruct a purported classical version of Muslim history in favor of a purported universal reason are suspect. It seems to me that it behooves Muslims first to attempt to reclaim as much as possible of their lost collective memory before being prepared to abandon it. But one must note that even in the West, many historians have realized the dangers of the agnosticism and nihilism arising from the deconstructionist project.

Traditions and inherited collective memory are critical for the construction of meaning, and in my view, a fiction premised on hope is better than a state of unfettered doubt resulting in the loss of all meaning. Nevertheless, an academic doing objective research may claim to be thoroughly scientific, objective, and detached. As such, such an academic can claim not to be concerned with anything but the evidence and where it might lead. Whether this leads to deconstruction or reconstruction ought not matter. Because I am a by-product of the prevailing episteme of my age, I confess, I will be skeptical and I will highly doubt that objective scholarship is possible. However, as an academic, I will respect the desire and attempt at objectivity, and I will understand that if this person is a good scholar, the conclusions reached will logically depend on the methodology of research. However, a Muslim reformer should not attempt to claim complete objectivity. A reformer is often as good as his/her critical insights, and thus, a reformer does rely on the same methodological tools utilized by a social scientist with one significant exception. A reformer must be motivated by an internally held conviction about the sacred and the divine—a teleological project, if you will. In other words, a Muslim reformer must start from the deeply held conviction in the sacrosanct and spiritual in Islam and from that perspective interrogate the Muslim memory. In fact, a Muslim reformer must possess and be willing to defend a metaphysical belief about the divine will or the lack thereof. If one adheres to the belief that God does not care about God's creation and has nothing to offer in terms of guidance, in my view it is difficult to defend, but it is still a metaphysical belief. Moreover, a belief that God has deputized human beings to inherit the earth and left them to manage their affairs without guidance beyond the initial historical moment of revelation is still a metaphysical belief. I do not believe that a reformer can avoid metaphysical positions altogether. Most importantly, whatever the metaphysical belief, the reformer must be willing to make it explicit and be willing to defend it.

I will return to the issue of reason, metaphysics, and spiritualism later, but for now I want to emphasize that the issue is not that Arkoun transplanted a heuristic apparatus from the West. Rather, the issue is that one is entitled to ask what a heuristic device contributes to the betterment of the physical and metaphysical being of those who share one's commitment to the Islamic faith. As appealing as the phenomenological approaches of Jacques Derrida and Michel Foucault or the historical insights of Roger Bastide and Marc Bloch might be, unlike a social scientist, a reformer must evaluate the qualitative contribution any methodology or analytical device will make to the collective tradition that gives meaning to what a Muslim is or should be. In Fernand Braudel's masterful work on the history of the Mediterranean, he argues that there are different speeds to historical time: the geographic, the social, and the individual or event-oriented time. I often wondered what Braudel's insights meant for social scientists, jurists, and people outside the historical discipline. Technology, communications, transportation, and public health all seem to affect the speed of time. But what does this mean for the individual who exists within his/her social time? Is it unreasonable to suspect that a person living in Paris has experienced time in a way that is different from someone who exists in Afghanistan? This is of a great deal of significance to the question of the responsibility of intellectuals or scholars toward the objects of their study. If scholars presume that the society under study had moved at a slower historical pace, they will transform their subjects into mummified anachronisms. I am thinking here, for instance, of anthropologists who are obsessed with the role of oral testimony in Muslim courts. They end up describing a legal epistemology and a state of negotiated consciousness that have very little to do with the actual historical movement of that society.[16] This raises the very serious question of the obligations of the Muslim scholar who applies epistemological investigations learned and adopted from within a cultural apparatus in a society moving at a very different speed of time. I do recall remarkably consistent experiences in which friends and family commented on a loved one returning home after studying the humanities or social sciences in France or Germany that it is as if they now live in a different time zone. This is always in the context of complaining that the native intellectual, after returning home armed with numerous sophisticated insights, becomes estranged from his/her own people and loses the ability to understand or be understood by them. This underscores the extent of the burden and the tough dilemma confronting so many Muslim intellectuals as they try to stay apace with their societies while not transforming into a force that is complacent and legitimating toward preexisting structures of power and subjugation. If a Muslim scholar "intellectualizes" at a pace different in tempo from the one experienced by Muslim societies, he/she risks alienation and marginalization. But if he/she stays at the same pace without in any way challenging it, this Muslim intellectual risks becoming a legitimating and acquiescent force of the status quo.

Toward the later part of his life, Arkoun advocated a rather complex project that he called the Emerging Reason Project, which, with all its attention to fairness of process and to integrating non-Western epistemologies and historical experiences, seemed to be a collective process toward the discovery of universally applicable reason. The obvious challenge that would confront any believer is whether, like most process-oriented proposals, ultimately the truth of religion will be subverted or made subservient to a Kantian belief in the promises of reason. I think there is no way a Muslim intellectual can avoid having to wrestle with the question of whether reason is ultimately the end or only a way to an end. It is critical to understand that like secularism, reason was often used in the Muslim world to consolidate colonialism, economic exploitation, and the dismantling of traditional societies. These traditional societies were not replaced with enlightened, rational democracies but with rational tyrannies. As we weigh the place of spiritualism and rationalism, we cannot simply disregard the collective memory of Muslims who suffered despotism under the tyranny of political orders claiming to embrace scientific rationalism. After all, the Ba'ath parties of Syria and Iraq and

Nasser's regime in Egypt saw themselves as the bearers of nationalism, rationalism, and the march of science. The dictatorships of Nasser, Asad, Saddam, Ataturk, Zeinabidin bin 'Ali of Tunisia, and al Habib Bourguiba of Tunisia all raised the banners of reason, science, and progressiveness against reactionism, by which they often meant tradition and religion. Growing up in the Middle East, the only context in which I experienced the word *raj'iyya* (reactionism) was to mean the backwardness of religious institutions and beliefs. Of course, I am not arguing that the nationalistic and often antireligion regimes of the 1960s were models of the supremacy of reason and rationality. Nor am I arguing that the quasi-religious regimes of the 1970s and 1980s (Pakistan, Saudi Arabia, Iran) are bastions of spiritualism and tradition. As I argued before, these authoritarian regimes did nothing but negotiate between secular and nonsecular forces, giving supremacy only to the logic of their own self-empowerment and tyranny. What I am arguing is that when it comes to the Muslim world, no reformer can assume that we are writing on a blank slate. Muslims have very recent and viable memories of experiencing many of the flashy dogmas of the contemporary age. Moreover, I am arguing that even the Western experience with science and reason is not by any measure an unqualified success for humanity. Beyond the Muslim world, in the age of postmodernity, reason has undergone its own biting deconstructionism, and many Western thinkers have reignited interest in spiritualism and tradition. Moreover, Muslim reformers whose project seems to extend to little more than an adoption of a universal truism, such as reason or universal human rights, persistently fail to engage the interventions of Western social scientists who insist on something mysteriously religious at the foundation and heart of Western civilization such as a Protestant work ethic, Judeo-Christian values, or the Roman Catholic shepherding of natural law.[17]

My concern here is not to support one interpretation of European history against another. Memory in all cases is an onerous challenge and a grave responsibility; it is the locus of identity and power. Its place in the past, present, and future and its force are undeniable, yet it is endlessly contestable. The relationship of an intellectual to memory is, to say the least, complex—while it is simply unethical for this relationship to be guided by pragmatism, it is misguided to believe that the relationship is simply defined by empiricism. Even in law, the famous refrain used in the movies, "Just the facts, ma'am," is recognized to be a heuristic device necessary for sustaining the principle of rule of law, but fundamentally a fiction. To speak of a legal system surrendering to claims of the truth of reason, or the sanctity of process, or the immutability of doctrine is fraught with risk. When an intellectual deals with the memory of law, such an intellectual cannot be oblivious to the fact that systems of law rely on legal fictions and mythologies that are inconsistent with logic. Whatever the normative values that ought to guide the relationship between an intellectual and the memory of a people, this relationship becomes all the more sensitive and urgent when dealing with a people who are no longer in firm control of their own memory. The historical memory that continues to be taught in Muslim universities and read by Muslim intellectuals was for the most part the creation of twentieth-century British, French, German, and other European scholars.

In the wake of the revolutions in the Middle East, I was once again reminded of my conversation with Arkoun. Many determinative questions were raised by these revolutions and the memories they would construct for ages to come. These revolutions offered the opportunity to be free of many forms of tyranny, including the tyranny of dogmas of subjugation and control as well as the dogma of colonially constructed memories that served the interests of the colonial powers of the past. These revolutions also offered the opportunity to be free of unreasonable traditions from the past that no longer served a constructed social function, and they offered the possibility of getting rid of religious affectations that stunted any potential for rational thought and growth. It seems to me that reason, as a God-given tool for defending against falsity and seeking after the truth, must be utilized to search and locate memory and must be used to challenge and expose pietistic affectations. Reason must be relied on to establish reasonability and be the very nerve and pulse of Shari'ah. But reason itself is not the end—reason is a tool necessary for ensuring the integrity of the search for the divine. Reason is the instrument that enables human beings to achieve goodness and beauty, but it is an article of faith that the divine is nothing but goodness and beauty.

The revolutions that swept through the Middle East have reignited debates about a whole host of issues, including secularism, democracy, human rights, civic rights, tradition, Westernizing influences, native cultures, Shari'ah, religion, Wahhabism and Salafism, and many other issues. In countries like Egypt and Tunisia, there are heated competitions between Islamic groups and traditional religious establishments, like al-Azhar, over who gets to define Islam's role and to what effect. I don't know what role, if any, intellectuals will play in what appears to be a formative period in the history of the Muslim world. It is possible that if vacuums of authority, meaning, and memory are not filled by convincing civil participants, military establishments will once again forcibly step in to fill the void and continue to navigate many Arab countries toward further disasters. But at times like this, it is very important that all the participants be honest and transparent about their aims and objectives. Those who purport to play the role of social scientists, who are interested in an objectified truth, have every right to be recognized as such. But those who aspire to play a normative role in the formation and shaping of Islam must also be open and transparent about their commitments. In my view, a reformer functioning within the context of a religious tradition cannot claim that piety is unimportant or irrelevant, but he/she can challenge affectations or displays of piety, especially when these displays become part of the material culture of Muslim life. Of course, in no way should I be understood to challenge someone's actual piety—this is something between a person, his/her conscience, and God. But to the extent that piety is leveraged to attain deference and authority, to the extent that public performances of piety are utilized to make claims about the divine will, or the collective memory of Muslims, or any normative claim, a person claiming to be vested in Islam—as a faith and belief about God and what God wants—must scrutinize not the conviction behind the practice but the claims made on behalf of such a practice.

Many of the religious affectations of puritanical Muslims are profoundly unreasonable, especially when placed within the context of the inherited cultural memory of Muslims. I will elaborate on this in the following chapter. But part of the difficult legacy of modernity and also of the usurpation of the symbols of Islam by puritans is that much of the Western-educated intelligentsia has developed something of an epistemological block to the very idea of Muslim culture, tradition, and indeed, memory. I am not speaking of a discerning analytical and critical reception of tradition and heritage but of a pronounced aversion to the symbolic constructs of the past, including Shariʻah, caliphate, umma (the idea of collective Muslim affinity), and Sunna (the oral traditions attributed to the Prophet, his family, and companions). Very often this aversion itself defies rationality or reasonableness. For instance, in a recent dialogue on Egyptian television, Gamal al-Banna, a self-described Islamist, argued that if it were up to him, he would throw away all the books of Islamic theology, law, Sunna, and hadith into the garbage. His statements did not surprise me because I had read some of his books, including his odd multivolume work on renewing Islamic jurisprudence. I also met with the man in a small apartment, which he called his office, quite ironically packed with books of tradition that he had never opened. The library was left to him by his older late brother, Hasan al-Banna, the founder of the Muslim Brotherhood. Gamal al-Banna, in his many books as well as in the hour of debate that took place in his crowded apartment, insisted that all Muslims need or ought to rely on is the Qur'an without historical narrative. In other words, he wants the Qur'an but without any history to the text.

In a recent conference in Germany convening "Islamic reformers," one such reformer made a presentation, the gist of which was that he accepts Islam but rejects Shariʻah. I asked if he believes that God could be the source of obligation in the Islamic faith, to which he responded, "What type of obligation?" My response was: any kind of obligation, whether ethical or otherwise and whether it is an obligation to act or to believe. His response was that God is indeed the source of many obligations. The logical follow-up question to his belief in divinely ordained obligations is, how is this any different from Shariʻah? Maybe he meant to say that he is opposed to the historical Shariʻah as represented by the cumulative interpretive communities of particular ages in the past, but this is a different argument, and if it is to be made, it must be presented with full awareness of its meanings and connotations. At a lecture at the Library of Alexandria, my audience, comprised mostly of university students, seemed confounded when I explained that one of the basic principles of Islamic jurisprudence is: whatever is mandated by reason is so mandated by Shariʻah (*ma yajibu ʻaqlan yajibu sharʻan wa ma yajaba ʻaqlan wajaba sharʻan*). I solemnly warned the students that by being so ill informed about Shariʻah, they effectively abandon it to the puritans to do with it as they will. I believe that the same effect of empowering the puritans occurs when educated Muslims abandon the historical Shariʻah altogether.

I spent the summer of 2011 in the kind hospitality of both Shaykh al-Azhar Ahmad al-Tayyib and the Mufti of Egypt, ʻAli Jumʻa. What I observed in the time I spent at both of their respective institutions, al-Azhar and Dar al-Iftaʼ, was a very complicated political and cultural situation that closely approximated the complexity of the challenges confronting the Muslim world. Both institutions saw themselves as loci for national consensus and reconciliation. Both perceived themselves in dual roles as sources of author-ity for Muslims all over the world while at the same time thoroughly an-chored and involved in their specifically national context. Both institutions had been deeply and heavily impacted by Saudi money and thus by Wahhabi puritanical influence, and both were of very modest means and grossly underfunded. Both institutions had huge inept and underqualified bureaucra-cies that were ill equipped to execute the visions or ideas of the high-ranking jurists. It was very clear from numerous official and unofficial conversations I had that the Shaykh al-Azhar and the Mufti 'Ali Jum'a, in terms of their training and theological and juristic commitments, did not belong to the puritanical school but, being at the head of their institutions, could not afford a full showdown with the parties supported by the all-powerful Saudi Arabia. I observed that the leadership of both institutions seemed to be very worried about the rise of puritanical groups to power and what that would do to the religious establishment, which has for centuries tried to be the official voice of Islam, at least in Egypt. Both Imam Ahmad al-Tayyib and Shaykh 'Ali Jum'a are impressive men in their own right—both were widely read men, and both were eager to present a tolerant, nonfanatical, and enlightened form of Islam. But despite their best desires and efforts, it was very clear that both of these venerable institutions are ill equipped to meet the demands of the current challenges in Egypt and the Middle East. The reality is that they lack the resources, the organizational skills, and the social and political capital to fill the vacuum of religious authority that has become the dominant reality of the age.

Part II

The Culture of Ugliness and the Plight of Modern Islam

Chapter Five

Faulty Paradigms in Constructing the Islamic

THE RECURRENCE OF THE UGLY IN MODERN ISLAM

It is said that the Arab Spring was ignited in Tunisia when a police officer struck a poor street vendor named Buazzizi on the face. The man could not handle the feelings of degradation and humiliation, so on the following day he burned himself alive in a public street. Thus, the Tunisian Revolution is often referred to as the Buazzizi Revolution. In Egypt, one of the main reasons that led to igniting the Egyptian Revolution is a long pattern of injustices, degradations, insults, and suffering inflicted against Egyptians at the hands of the despised security forces and police. The revolutionary explosions that continue sweeping through the countries of the Middle East are a fairly powerful indication that many Arabs are simply fed up with being subjugated, degraded, abused, and humiliated. What contributed to this reality was the incredible amount of ugliness pervading the Middle East since 9/11. The constant experiences of death, mayhem, and degradation witnessed in Iraq, Afghanistan, Palestine, the Sudan, Somalia, and Yemen, among others, got to a point that millions were willing to die for a more dignified and hopeful life.

As significant and meaningful as these developments have been, they are grounds for cautious optimism. There is much in the Arab Spring that gives one hope, but there are a number of reasons for serious pause. There were a number of anticolonial and proconstitutionalism revolutions that swept through the Arab world in the early twentieth century, but, for a variety of reasons, they were ultimately aborted.[1] It is true that the earlier proconstitutional revolutions were greatly disadvantaged by the existence of colonialism and brutal foreign interventionism, but the forces aligned against the current revolutions are no less formidable. Indeed, at a cultural and epistemological level, the threat to new democratic institutions in the Middle East is far more serious. The puritanical form of Islam and its main source of funding, Saudi

Arabia, are using the democratic atmosphere to their full advantage. This does not mean that despotic restrictions or the authoritarian exclusion of the religious from politics are solutions. It only means that when all is said and done, the most recent developments are only a part of an ongoing and never-ending process of soul searching and self-definition for Muslims.

I do not believe that there is a culture in the past or a culture that can come to be that is capable of fully embodying the human potential for goodness. The process of Muslim self-definition must not be treated with the expectation that Muslims lived up to moral goals that have been fulfilled by the West. What makes this process of self-definition particularly critical is that there are no charted historical inroads to be reproduced. Furthermore, while Muslims seek moral empowerment and dignity, this does not necessarily mean that the collective goal or cultural end product should mimic any particular existing system, including that of the West. As a practicing Muslim, as a matter of conviction, not only do I believe that Islam makes a positive contribution to the human potential for goodness, but I believe that its contribution must be necessary and indispensable. This means that the fate of Muslims in the world is inextricably intertwined with the fate of goodness in the world.

Considering the current state of Muslims and their lack of contributions to intellectual thought in modernity, I am sure that some readers would take issue with the conviction that Islam is necessary for the goodness of the world. But I do not ask non-Muslims to share in this conviction—the most I can ask for is understanding and respect. However, I would argue that this must be an article of faith for all Muslims, and therefore, the issue that all Muslims must weigh and consider is: How does their understanding or interpretation of their faith contribute to goodness in the world? Affectations or stereotyped responses, discussed in past chapters, are not an adequate or reasonable answer. Because Islam is not the religion of a tribe, race, or any particular nation but is a universal faith intended for all human beings, the response given to the question of the moral quality of the contribution must have some reasonable basis in fact to withstand scrutiny. Put differently, some people who are blinded by bigotry, racism, or hate are themselves not fair-minded and, therefore, are unreasonable people. Whether hate-filled people such as this are unconvinced that the claim of a fair contribution by a Muslim is reasonable, it ought not be a reason for further introspection or concern. However, because Islam is a message that addresses all of humanity, when I ask myself whether my comprehension of Islam contributes to goodness in the world, while I cannot expect non-Muslims to share my belief because they do not accept my metaphysical assumptions, I have to expect that fair-minded and reasonable non-Muslims will respect and perhaps even appreciate my contribution as a Muslim. For instance, if Rumi or Hafiz made a claim that their interpretations of Islam make significant contributions to the goodness of humanity, all fair-minded human beings must respect, appreciate, and honor the claim even if ultimately they cannot share in the conviction. Contrast this with a situation in which it is Osama bin Laden who was making a claim about the reasonableness of his Islamic interpretation in adding goodness to the world. Perhaps it goes without saying that this relationship with others must necessarily be reciprocal, between people of faith in goodness, so that they are not excluding each other and that beyond mere tolerance, they are respecting one another. As we will see later when discussing an Islamic debate over criminal penalties, this issue tends to raise some very strong feelings and objections. But at this point, it is worth noting that the Qur'an persistently calls Muslims and non-Muslims to their senses by the expressions *ta'qilun* and *tafakkarun*—both terms refer to the use of thought or reason to seek the truth. I believe that in using these terms the Qur'an is not referring to the rigor of deductive or inductive reasoning or to propositional logic. The Qur'an is referring to a more basic and shared form of rationality and reasonability—that if people used rationality and reasonability, they would come to realize the fundamental tenets of right from wrong and good from bad.

At this point, many Muslims might wonder: Even if they accept my argument, why would there be any difficulty for believing Muslims to make reasonable arguments that would convince reasonable people that Islam has many possible contributions to goodness in the world? In part, the problem is that Muslims have not done a good job in educating non-Muslims about their faith. There are many Islamophobes who will be impossible to reach, but there are many more fair-minded and reasonable people who could have been reached. More importantly, in past publications I have called attention to what I described as a culture of ugliness in modern Islam. In my view, this culture of ugliness continues to be the single most important obstacle to articulating reasonable narratives of legitimate possibilities of Islam's contribution to human goodness. I want to be clear on this point; I am not claiming that Muslim cultures are ugly. Quite to the contrary, fair-minded people who travel through the Muslim world or learn about it are often struck by the beauty of Muslim cultures.[2] Nevertheless, the occurrence of persistent acts of ugliness, especially those justified and rationalized on Islamic grounds, act to create a near impetuous reaction to the mental image of Islam—a reaction that creates serious epistemic barriers to understanding the reasonable possibilities and actual potential of Islam as a source for human goodness. In effect, this means that Muslims have failed their religion by not rising up to its potential for goodness.

Normally, the occurrence of acts of ugliness committed by a small percentage of a very large community of believers means nothing more than there is the inevitable sociopathic minority in any religion that will abuse its system of beliefs. But if acts of ugliness keep occurring and particular religious ideas keep getting abused, this must compel the conscientious believer to reexamine whether any interpretations associated with the faith have become susceptible to exploitation. For instance, at the time of this writing, hardly a week goes by without massive bombings killing and injuring hundreds of people in Iraq. Many of the victims of the attacks are Iraqi security forces and Shi'i Muslims. There are a number of complex sociopolitical reasons for this bloodletting, and most of those reasons can be traced back to the American occupation of Iraq. But as a Muslim, I must confront myself with the unsettling question of whether any of the existing Islamic creeds contribute to the production and escalation of this ugliness. So, for example, in the case of the bombings in Iraq, one of the creedal prime suspects are sectarian convictions that demonize and stereotype the Shi'a. The same logic applies to reports of recent ugliness involving schoolgirls in Afghanistan. News reports claimed that the Taliban poisoned more than 150 girls attending school in the Takhar province.[3] The Taliban's hostility to the empowerment of women and its ties to puritanical Islamic movements are well documented. But like the bombings in Iraq, the poisoning of schoolgirls implicates a very complicated situation involving terrorism, sabotage, tribal warfare, and sectarian conflicts. The extent to which theology or Islamic law comes into play in such a horrific event I simply do not know. But as a Muslim, I am deeply concerned about the possibility of exploiting a faith that I associate with beauty in the perpetuation of acts of sheer ugliness.

In 2009, an Egyptian ship crossing the Red Sea from Saudi Arabia to Egypt sank, killing 1,400 people, including whole families and hundreds of children. There was a sense of shock and horror in reaction to the gruesome event because the sunken ship was not seaworthy, there were no lifeboats, and many people could have been saved with minimal safety precautions. No one was held accountable for the horror, and the corrupt Mubarak regime even helped the owner of the sunken ship, a friend of the regime, to escape to Europe, where he took refuge shortly after the incident.[4] This event struck me as part of the human-made cycle of ugliness plaguing Muslim countries because it was entirely preventable. The tragedy was conspicuous because of the absence, not presence, of religious dogma in coming to terms with the event. Many of the Egyptian journalists and writers energetically resisted ascribing any moral fault to any of the actors, including those responsible for the tragedy by invoking the dogma of "we are all Muslims" and "no one is qualified to judge." I strongly disagree. The religious moral conscience should not be limited to addressing situations where God is invoked to justify wrongdoing. The religious conscience should be invoked in all situations that could create a greater sanctity and understanding of the sacred nature of human life. I will return to the issue of the civic role of religion later, but an essential component of my argument is that the religious conscience must be thoroughly engaged with everything that elevates human beings from ugliness to goodness. If this was properly understood in the Egyptian context, every Muslim would have felt aggrieved by the ugliness of the injustice endured by the victims and their families, and it would have not been so easy for the memory of the tragedy to be lost.

In my opinion, the presence of ugliness is the absence of God and the presence of beauty is the presence of God. I would be remiss if I did not comment on another aspect of the Egyptian ship disaster. Long before the famous movie, I grew up reading about the *Titanic* disaster in which around 1,500 people lost their lives in 1912. I dare say that the whole world remembers and mourns the *Titanic* while the Egyptian disaster, even in Egypt, is already all but forgotten.[5] Again confronting conscience grounded in the divine, I must consider whether similar disasters in China, the Philippines, and Senegal were not equally mourned because of deeply flawed power dynamics in the world, or the effects of racism, even of the type that is internalized and self-perpetuated by nonwhites, or because other nations and cultures have created better structures and institutions capable of better guarding against the devaluing of at least the life of their own citizens. I have not adequately studied any of the relevant shipping disasters other than the

Egyptian incident, and so I am not prepared to defend any conclusions. But my point is that as a conscientious Muslim, I have an affirmative obligation to consistently interrogate the occurrence of ugliness among Muslims and augment goodness in the world. This is part of the solemn obligation to bear witness against oneself and against the extensions of the self before God.

Interrogating acts of ugliness by the religiously grounded moral conscience is often challenging because the reality of our shared world is that neat and clear-cut divisions between the religiously motivated and that which is not are often elusive. Our normative world as human beings is most often premised on memory—as deficient and illusive as it might be. The reality is that what kind of memory motivates behavior is as complex as the fields of psychology and psychiatry are vast and limitless. This is to emphasize that interrogating ugliness is an analytical and critical process and that we must proceed with caution so that the ultimate analysis is rational and reasonable. I will return to this subject when I discuss the role played by the native informant since 9/11, but fundamentally, the process of testifying against ugliness cannot itself become its own act of ugliness. So, for instance, one of the shocking and brutal practices of the army in the Egyptian Revolution was the subjecting of female detainees to virginity tests as a way of degrading and humiliating them for participating in the revolution. A devout Muslim woman who suffered this horror brought a lawsuit against the officers who violated her body, and shockingly the court failed to convict any of the officers involved.[6] Many people immediately assumed that the virginity tests were an inheritance from the patriarchy of Islamic culture. As a Muslim scholar, I know that these types of virginity examinations were not only uncommon in the classical tradition but were also frowned on by the Islamic tradition to the point that most classical jurists were opposed to their administration before entering a marriage as an undue violation and inappropriate. The scholar Khaled Fahmy pointed out, however, that virginity inspections by the military in Egypt were first introduced in 1832 to protect their soldiers from venereal disease.[7] Initially, it was conducted by a special unit of trained midwives, but after the 1952 military coup, it became an instrument of political repression and torture. As an instrument of political repression, men were often sodomized and women inspected—and in some cases, raped. On Fahmy's looking into the event further and interviewing a couple of the officers involved, one officer admitted that some of the recruits initially resisted the command to do virginity inspections on religious grounds, believing that it would be un-Islamic to violate these women. But according to the officer, recruits usually cave in after they are threatened and told that they are here to serve the army and not God.

In contrast to the above, there are tragedies and acts of ugliness that put a Muslim squarely before his/her conscience in interrogating the role of a particular Islamic creed in contributing to the immorality in the world. There are examples where the role played by unreasonable interpretations of religion are prominent and undeniable and therefore demand a strong, direct, and upright confrontation. Tolerating and even celebrating differences of opinions in interpreting God's law is one thing, but accepting the exploitation of this law to perpetuate ugliness is quite another. One cannot forget Hannah Arendt's fitting warning about the banality of evil or that all it takes for evil to prevail is for decent people to do nothing. This is all the more so when those who perpetuate evil feel righteous and self-satisfied because they are religiously or ideologically motivated. This, of course, is not far removed from the Prophet's dire warning that wrongdoing becomes the norm when ordinary people fail to condemn it.[8] A prime example of one of those acts of ugliness that demanded an overwhelming response took place in 2002 when schoolgirls burned to death in Saudi Arabia. Around the middle of March of 2002, Saudi newspapers reported an incident that took place in Mecca, the Prophet Muhammad's birthplace. The fact that this tragedy occurred in Mecca only makes it all the more painful. According to the official count, at least fourteen young girls burned to death or were asphyxiated by smoke when an accidental fire engulfed their public school. Parents who arrived at the scene described a horrific scene in which the doors of the school were locked from the outside and the Saudi religious police, known as the *mutawwa'un*, forcibly prevented girls from escaping the burning school and also barred firemen from entering the school to save the girls by beating some of the girls and several of the civil defense personnel. According to the statements of parents, firemen, and the regular police forces present at the scene, the *mutawwa'un* would not allow the girls to escape or to be saved because they were not properly covered, and the *mutawwa'un* did not want physical contact to take place between the girls and the civil defense forces. The governmental institution that is responsible for administering the *mutawwa'un* (known as the Committee for the Promotion of Virtue and the Prevention of Vice)[9] denied beating any of the girls or civil defense workers and also denied locking the gates of the school and trapping the girls inside. But witnesses told Saudi newspapers that the *mutawwa'un* yelled at the police and firemen to stay back and beat several firemen as the *mutawwa'un* commanded the girls to go back into the burning building and retrieve their veils (known as *'abaya* and *niqab* in Saudi Arabia) before they would be allowed to leave the school. Several parents told journalists that they saw at least three girls being beaten with sticks and kicked when they attempted to argue with the *mutawwa'un*. Several girls did obey the *mutawwa'un* and returned to the school in order to retrieve their veils, only to be found dead later.[10]

In a genuinely ominous incident, Shaykh Saleh al-Fawzan, one of the highest-ranking Saudi jurists, issued a legal opinion in which he claimed that not only is slavery lawful in Islam, but that it ought to be legalized in Saudi Arabia. Al-Fawzan went further in accusing Muslim scholars who condemned and outlawed slavery of being ignorant and infidels.[11] The fact is that those who have been following the development of the Wahhabi school and its impact on the modern Muslim world would have thought that al-Fawzan's position was entirely predictable. Wahhabism had started marching down a road of moral detachment and ugliness, and it was entirely foreseeable that the followers of this school would reach the extreme points that they did reach. But what made this *fatwa* particularly ominous is that it seemed to be part of a theological and moral apparatus designed to legitimate the sexual exploitation of domestic workers in Saudi Arabia.[12]

Placed in the context of many other morally offensive events, such as the reception of *The Satanic Verses* and the ensuing death sentence against Salman Rushdie, the stoning and imprisonment of rape victims in Pakistan and

Nigeria, the degradation of women by the Taliban, the destruction of the Buddha statues in Afghanistan, the sexual violation of domestic workers in Saudi Arabia, the excommunication of writers in Egypt, and the killing of civilians in terrorist attacks, this event seems to be just another chapter in a long saga of ugliness committed by Muslims. It is truly disturbing that Muslims had started the twentieth century with a clear moral stand against slavery as an institution that is profoundly at odds with Islamic theology and morality, only to begin the twenty-first century with a major religious voice calling for the reinstitution of slavery. It is not an exaggeration to say that Muslims are experiencing a regression—a condition in which even the modest achievements of the nineteenth and twentieth centuries are being gradually abolished. As I noted before, whether the so-called Arab Spring represents a fundamental rebirth that will lead to the defeat of puritanical Islam, it is simply too early to say. It suffices to say that Arab Spring notwithstanding, it continues to be the case that when one interacts with people from different parts of the world, one consistently finds that the image of Islam is not that of a humanistic or humane religion. It is deeply troubling that for many non-Muslims around the world, Islam has become the symbol for a draconian tradition that exhibits little compassion or mercy toward human beings.

What has taken place in contemporary Islam is a process of what might be called "vulgarization" through which many Muslims have become disconnected from their own tradition and have constructed a rootless and highly artificial culture that simultaneously indulges in numerous displays of apologetics and cruelty.[13] By vulgarization, I mean the reoccurrence of events that seem to shock the human conscience or that are contrary to what most people would identify as moral and beautiful. As noted previously, Islam in the modern age has become associated with violence, harshness, and cruelty, and although mercy and compassion are core values in Islamic theology, these are not the values that most people identify with Islam. Islam in the modern age has become plagued by an arid intellectual climate and a lack of critical and creative approaches, which has greatly hampered the development of a humanistic moral orientation. In my view, in order for an intellectual tradition to develop morally and vigorously confront renewed moral challenges, a rich and critical intellectual discourse is necessary. But the contemporary Islamic world has been intellectually impoverished, and so, as noted earlier, there has been virtually no influential philosophical or critical intellectual movements emerging from the Muslim world in the modern age. As I argue later, even the most puritan and literalist movements within contemporary Islam have remained largely reactive and intellectually dependent. The apologetic trend served as the necessary prelude to the vulgarization of the Islamic context. Without the apologetics, it is unlikely that Muslims would have been enticed into the state of coma that allowed the processes of vulgarization to proceed. The apologetic orientation tried to defend Islam by empowering Muslims with a sense of assuredness that their tradition is no less worthy or meritorious than that of the West, but it also lulled Muslims into a lack of critical introspection. For all its shortcomings, however, the apologetic orientation did not deny the worthiness of universal humanistic values or the validity of intuitive goodness. This development was the singular achievement of the puritanical movement in modern Islam.

THE MUSLIM RESPONSE AND WESTERN VILIFICATIONS

This saga of ugliness has forced Muslims, who are embarrassed and offended by this legacy, to adopt apologetic rhetorical arguments that do not necessarily carry much persuasive weight. We have already raised this issue earlier, but the impact of apologetics on the future role of the Islamic tradition in the modern world is of such importance that it deserves a more detailed treatment. One of the most common arguments repeated by Muslim apologists is that it is unfair to confuse the religion of Islam with the deeds of its followers. The fact that the followers commit egregious behavior in the name of the religion does not in itself mean that the religion commands or sanctions such behavior. A similar, often repeated argument is that one must distinguish Islamic religious doctrines from the cultural practices of Muslims, the implication being that it is culture and not religion that is the culprit responsible for immoral behavior. Another more subtle argument, but one that surreptitiously betrays the same feelings of discomfort and embarrassment, is simply to remind the world that only a very small percentage of the Muslim world is Arab. Although factually correct, Muslims would not have been keen about reminding the world of this fact if the behavior of Arabs or their image was honorable. It is exactly because Arabs suffer from a troubled image in today's world that many Muslims feel the need to distance Islam from Arab identity or Arab culture. This often observed practice of emphasizing the numerical inferiority of Arabs in the Muslim world indicates that some Muslims feel ashamed of the Arab affiliation and are eager to unburden Islam from its Arab baggage. In my view, this apologetic response is as if one is putting his head in the sand to avoid dealing with the real challenges that confront Muslims. Such responses are escapist because they do not confront the substantive doctrinal problems that led to the current predicament, but ultimately, they are also not persuasive.

I call these arguments unpersuasive not because they are inaccurate—in fact, all the defensive points mentioned above are logical or factually correct. I call them unpersuasive because they fail to take account of a variety of countervailing arguments and problems. For instance, they ignore the role of history in understanding the present, and they also ignore that it is not always possible to separate with surgical accuracy a system of beliefs from the social practices that have grown around it. Specifically, these arguments fail to take account of the role of human subjectivities in determining and acting on doctrine. For example, it is true that Arabs constitute about 30 percent of the sum total of Muslims in the world today. But it must be remembered that the very racial category of Arab was socially constructed and reinvented in different periods and places of the world. In certain times and places, whoever spoke Arabic eventually became an Arab or at least came to be perceived as an Arab. The very classification of an Arab was the product of a dynamic and creative sociolinguistic process. The Arabic language itself demonstrated a remarkable ability to spread to new nations and eventually Arabize them. Consider, for instance, the complaint of the bishop of Cordoba, Alvaro, in ninth- century CE Spain, where he states:

Many of my coreligionists read verses and fairy tales of the Arabs, study the works of Muhammedan philosophers and theologians not in order to refute them but to learn to express themselves properly in the Arab language more correctly and more elegantly. Who among them studied the Gospels, and Prophets and Apostles? Alas! All talented Christian young men know only the language and literature of the Arabs, read and assiduously study the Arab books. . . . If somebody speaks of Christian books they contemptuously answer that they deserve no attention whatever (*quasi vilissima contemnentes*). Woe! The Christians have forgotten their own language, and there is hardly one among a thousand to be found who can write to a friend a decent greeting letter in Latin. But there is a numberless multitude who express themselves most elegantly in Arabic, and make poetry in this language with more beauty and more art than the Arabs themselves. [14]

One notices that, at least for conquered Spain, the relation between Arab and Muslim is far more fluid. According to Alvaro, young men were eager to learn the language of the superior culture because in that age, the Arab was not considered a symbol of reactionism or barbarity. One doubts that a Muslim living back then, when dealing with non-Muslims, would have had much incentive to differentiate between Arabs and Islam. Even in countries such as Persia and India that preserved their native languages after the Islamic invasions, scholars from these areas continued to write most books on theology and law in Arabic. [15] Alvaro's statement is significant in another respect; it reminds us of the shifting fortunes of the reputation of Muslims in the world. There is no doubt that Islam and Europe have had a long and unpleasant tradition of mutual vilification and demonization, but these processes of the past were materially different from those of the present. [16] In my view, the Western attempts to vilify Islam in the past were inspired by fear and respect, and Western perceptions of Muslims were not based on any realistic understanding of Muslim sociopolitical circumstances. Most of the vilifications were nothing more than the anxieties, fears, and aspirations of Westerners projected onto the dominant force at the time without any foundation in reality. At the intellectual, commercial, and scientific levels, one finds that Westerners borrowed heavily from Muslim social and legal thought and scientific inventiveness. By contrast, today whatever bigotry exists against Muslims, and especially the phenomenon of Islamophobia sweeping through Europe and the United States, is based on the unfortunate sociopolitical realities experienced by Muslims, which the West perceives, generalizes, and exaggerates, and which then become the basis for stereotypes. Today's prejudices against Muslims are not based on fear and respect but on the worst and most cruel type of bigotry, and that is the type that is displayed against those whom the West dominates and controls. Premodern bigotry was directed at Muslims because they competed for mastery of the world and threatened the West. Today's bigotry is directed at those who are perceived to be at the bottom of the human hierarchy—people who live politically and socially in a dependent and bonded status.

THE ORIGINS OF WESTERN HATE

Hate and bigotry are often based on what social psychologists have called the binary impulse in human beings—the primitive and vulgar tendency to define the world in terms of "us versus them." This binary impulse first attempts to find an "us" and then associates that "us" with all that is good and virtuous. At the same time, the "them" becomes associated with all that is counter to the "us," and therefore, the "other" is presumed to be not good, and even evil. What disrupts and challenges this simplistic primitive paradigm is "social need." Although human societies gravitate toward this binary instinct, the need for interaction and cooperation between different societies and nations acts as a force often inducing human societies to self-define themselves in such a way that does not exclude the "other." With a sufficient amount of overlapping interests, interactions, and conscientiousness, the paradigm could shift from an "us versus them" to an "us-us" perspective.[17] In the premodern age, although there is clear evidence of a strong binary impulse pervading both the Muslim and Western worlds, considering the scientific and intellectual achievements of Muslims, the Christian and Jewish bigotry toward Muslims had to be tempered by the element of need. Both Jews and Christians could not help but be influenced by Muslim intellectual products, and this made the dynamics with Islam complex and multifaceted.[18] Even as late as the eighteenth century, when Mozart wrote his *Rondo alla Turca* (in 1783) there was a vogue for all things Turkish in Europe. Although this vogue was part of Western Orientalism and a manifestation of cultural arrogance, it was rooted in a long history of interaction and interdependence, as well as confrontation, between Europe and the Muslim world. The problem in the modern age, however, is that binary visions of Muslims go largely unchallenged by the absence of need, or the relative sufficiency of the West, and the dependency of the Muslim world. Muslim nations are underdeveloped and economically and politically dependent, and there is little that Muslim cultures can contribute to the West other than the Muslim faith. I am discounting the West's need for Arab oil as a contribution because it is a mineral extracted by Western technology, often through the use of Western technical expertise, and which benefits Western industries. More importantly, Western dependence on oil does not lead to cross-cultural or intellectual exchanges. All cultural and intellectual influences go one way, and that is from West to East. Muslim apologists often claim that Muslim cultures can contribute a vision of family values to the West and that Muslims can transfer to the West a more compassionate and merciful approach to life. Considering the perception that Muslims have become mired in a culture of cruelty, this Muslim belief is rather ironic. In my view, at this point, arguments about Muslim family values and cultures of compassion are not sufficiently and systematically theorized and developed by Muslims to be taken seriously. Such claims are presented by Muslim apologists as if they are self-evident and undeniable facts—these claims remain not very concrete, and, therefore, largely unpersuasive.

Offensive incidents such as those mentioned above greatly impact on the way that this faith is understood in the West and further feed into binary constructs vis-à-vis Islam and Muslims.[19] Put simply, such incidents of stark ugliness lead many to believe that the Islamic tradition and civilization are fundamentally at odds with the Judeo-Christian tradition and that a civilizational showdown or confrontation between Islam and the West is inevitable. From this perspective, the schoolgirls' burning incident in Mecca, as well as many other morally problematic events such as the Salman Rushdie affair, the killing of Theo van Gogh, honor killings, or forced and underage marriages, for example, are offensive only from a Western perspective. According to the proponents of the clash of civilizations paradigm, such events are natural expressions of a variant culture—the culture of Muslims and the morality of Islam.

Every Muslim researcher eventually runs into this troubling and condescending attitude toward Muslim culture and religion. In one such instance, I was testifying in a political asylum case about the disgusting practice of retaliatory rapes in some parts of Pakistan. The judge conducting the hearing was known for his publicly held fervent Christian beliefs. As I rather passionately spoke about how Islamically offensive and shocking was the practice of retaliatory rapes, the judge, who seemed intent on mimicking a state of disinterested sleep throughout the hearing, suddenly interrupted me to say, in effect, why are you going on about this? Muslims are accustomed to this type of ugliness, and so, according to the judge, it is implausible that my client is sincere about her claim of asylum. The judge went on to pontificate that as an admittedly observant Muslim, my client had no basis for complaining because when she accepted Islam, she also accepted all the ugliness that comes with it. Although I patiently refuted the judge's absurd contentions, I could not help but think that the judge's claims were as ridiculous as if I contended that his insensitivity to human suffering is a by-product of his Christian faith.

In another political asylum hearing before a different judge, I testified on behalf of another rape survivor who held strong beliefs about the role of women in Islam. My client was sexually assaulted purportedly because she defied the local customs in her village by refusing to wear the hijab. Both my client and I were deeply offended when the judge intimated that perhaps my client should have anticipated that by defying Muslim culture and religion, she was, according to the judge, "playing with fire." In denying my client refugee status, the judge went on to claim that it is important in such cases not to superimpose Western standards of safety and well-being because "different societies and religions see life differently and have different expectations." Of course, the judge misapplied American law, and he was deservedly rebuked and reversed on appeal, but the point remains.

Constructing "the other" through a binary vision is dangerous and often leads to immoral results. Among the binary constructions that are widely adopted, especially by conservatives in the United States, is the notion that any and all Islamists are extremists or militants.[20] Like all binary constructions, this claim suffers from considerable vagueness because its proponents never define what is meant by an "Islamist." In practice, one discovers that "Islamist" means whatever these proponents associate with what is at odds with their perception of their superior self. In this binary construction, the Islamist is imagined as the irrational, fanatic, and hateful Muslim, while the inventor of the construction becomes the morally superior alternative, whatever this alternative might be. Functionally, the Islamist label becomes nothing more than a cover for expressing an anti-Muslim prejudice. For instance, it is not an accident that a binary constructionist like Daniel Pipes labels as Islamist any Muslim who threatens Pipes's own sense of superiority toward Muslims or who threatens his sense of political and social priorities. Therefore, in effect, in Pipes's constructions, any Muslim who does not perceive Islam to be a fundamentally flawed and inferior religion or any Muslim who believes that Islam can make a positive contribution to the social, political, and moral sphere is promptly declared as an Islamist, and, according to Pipes, Islamists are the moral equivalents of Nazis.[21]

This, however, is not a new phenomenon. It should be recalled that colonialists always described patriots who resisted their imperialistic projects as zealots, fanatics, and militants. All natives who opposed and attempted to resist Napoleon's invasion of Egypt in 1798 were promptly designated as zealots. A distinguished democratic reformer like Khayr al-Din al-Tunisi (d. 1308/1890) was described as a militant by the invading French armies. And reformers like Muhammad 'Abduh (d. 1323/1905) and Jamal al-Din al-Afghani (d. 1314/1897) were described as militants and fanatics by the occupying British forces, yet, incredibly, some Orientalists doubted 'Abduh's religious faith and conviction because, they argued, he was too educated and rationally inclined to be a Muslim. In short, throughout the colonial and Orientalist experience, moderate and reform-minded Islamists were always held under suspicion as zealots, extremists, militants, and fanatics.

The issue is that, although perhaps not as extreme as Pipes, there are a substantial number of writers who attempt to understand the world of Islam through a binary vision that ascribes to Islam everything that is inferior. In reality, the only Muslims they are willing to tolerate are Muslims who, in relation to others, see themselves as inferior and seriously flawed. In this paradigm, in order for Muslims to earn merit and demonstrate their worthiness, they must first acknowledge their place vis-à-vis others, but that place is indeed a lowly status. Evidence of this kind of attitude can be seen in many of the anti-Islamic books published after 9/11. Rather comically, in their writing, these authors typically set up Islam-bashing Muslims as the paragon of true virtue and as the example of sincerity and honesty for all Muslims to follow, as evidenced in books such as *Why I Am Not a Muslim*. They also extol as the true heroes for Muslims those individuals who abandoned the Islamic faith and wrote to explain why they did so. Alternatively, they pose as the true heroes those individuals who have become nominally Muslim in the sense that they no longer practice or adhere to the rituals and consider Islam not as a religion but rather as a cultural or ethnic identity. On the websites of writers such as Pipes, one will find the testimonials of apostates from the Islamic faith prominently featured. Clearly, the not-so-subtle subtext here is that the only good Muslim is one who is not a Muslim, and the best kind of Islam is one that ceases to exist. The type of Muslims that they celebrate, such as Hirsi Ali, Wafa Sultan, Nonie Darwish, or Irshad Manji, always plays the role of the native informant. The paradigm of the native informant has its roots in the colonial era, when a group of natives would affirm the subservience and inferiority of the colonized and the legitimacy of the oppression and brutality of the colonizing master by providing narratives of self-incrimination and self-recrimination. The native informants would be handsomely compensated, but they rendered a valuable service by generating testimonial narratives that would be skillfully employed to empower the colonial project. Imagine the impact of the native Apache Indian who travels to an American frontier town or fort and relates the horrors and agonies of Apache life! For the colonizer, it does not matter if a thousand Apaches insisted that the sell-out has always been a habitual liar!

Power and domination need binary constructions in order to justify the violence and devastation brought on the other. So, for instance, former US Attorney General John Ashcroft purportedly said in an interview that the difference between the Muslim and Christian God is that the Muslim God demands that people die for him, while the Christian God died for human beings. When I was appointed by President George W. Bush to serve on the US Commission for International Religious Freedom, I heard an old-time member of the same commission object when President Bush asserted that Muslims and Christians worship the same God. The commissioner insisted that it is impossible that Muslims and Christians worship the same God because Jesus calls people to love, while Muhammad calls people to submission.[22] These claims by Ashcroft and the commissioner are not only essentialistic but also inaccurate. More importantly, the attitude and the basic frame of mind of Ashcroft and the commissioner are not that different from that of the judges mentioned previously. They might differ only as to the degree or extent that they are willing to go in attributing the negative and disfavored to Islam, but fundamentally, their framework is the same. To their minds, Islam and Muslims are made into the repositories of whatever they do not wish to be. But their image of Islam and Muslims has little to do with the reality of either Islam or Muslims.

THE CLASH OF CIVILIZATIONS THESIS AS AN EXPLANATION

One of the major sources for binary constructions of Islam and Muslims and for imagining Muslims as the alien other is the clash of civilizations thesis. "Can we have a liberalized Islam? . . . Conviction grows that the reconciliation is not possible. Islam really liberalized is simply a non-Christian Unitarianism. It ceases to be essential Islam." This is what Basil Mathews wrote in 1926 in a book titled: *Young Islam on Trek: A Study in the Clash of Civilizations*, essentially a travel book that celebrates the fall of the Islamic Caliphate in Turkey and argues that Arabs can never be civilized because they are Muslim and not Western.[23] The idea that Islam forms the basis of a civilization that is fundamentally at odds with Western civilization is older and broader than Basil Mathews's conception. The idea pervades Arnold Toynbee's famous study of history and is a consistent theme in Winston Churchill's bombastic historical writings. The idea of civilizational conflict is dramatically represented in the following quote by Churchill on Islam:

> How dreadful are the curses which Mohammedanism (Islam) lays on its votaries! Besides the fanatical frenzy, which is as dangerous in a man as hydrophobia in a dog, there is this fearful fatalistic apathy. The effects are apparent in

many countries. Improvident habits, slovenly systems of agriculture, sluggish methods of commerce, and insecurity of property exist wherever the followers of the Prophet rule or live. A degraded sensualism deprives this life of its grace and refinement; the next of its dignity and sanctity. The fact that in Mohammedan law every woman must belong to some man as his absolute property—either as a child, a wife, or a concubine—must delay the final extinction of slavery until the faith of Islam has ceased to be a great power among men. Thousands become the brave and loyal soldiers of the faith: all know how to die but the influence of the religion paralyses the social development of those who follow it. No stronger retrograde force exists in the world. Far from being moribund, Mohammedanism is a militant and proselytizing faith. It has already spread throughout Central Africa, raising fearless warriors at every step; and were it not that Christianity is sheltered in the strong arms of science, the science against which it had vainly struggled, the civilisation of modern Europe might fall, as fell the civilisation of ancient Rome. [24]

Churchill's quote is hardly surprising because in many ways it was typical of the cultural logic that accompanied and also inspired the growth of colonialism. The ideological apparatus that justified and lay the ground for colonialism and imperialism utilized a variety of linguistic and conceptual constructs, including the West's "civilizing mission," "the white man's burden," the "assimilation" of natives to the values of civilization, and the obligation of Western countries to guide the "cultural development" of indigenous populations, all of which also meant embracing European Christianity.

In its more contemporaneous and more politically correct form, the "clash of civilizations" thesis was first used by Bernard Lewis in an article titled "The Roots of Muslim Rage," which later was developed into a book. [25] The bottom line of Lewis's thinly historicized civilizational argument was that Muslims are full of rage because they resent the West's success. A far more generalized and sophisticated version of the thesis was presented in Samuel Huntington's article, later developed into a book, titled "The Clash of Civilizations and the Remaking of World Order." [26] In this influential article and book, Huntington argued that the new world order is marked not with the end of ideological conflicts but with the rebirth of cultural and religious conflicts. Huntington perceived the world to be divided among major distinct cultural and religious identities, and for a variety of reasons, these cultures will tend to clash. According to Huntington, one of the main cultures at odds with Western civilization is Islamic culture. Huntington's thesis became and continues to be very popular among influential Western politicians and intellectuals and is reported to have inspired neocons' policies in the Middle East, including the invasion of Iraq. [27]

Despite its relative success, I believe that this thesis provides a largely misleading paradigm for understanding the condition of Muslims in the contemporary age. Because of its serious methodological faults, the thesis is a serious hindrance to developing a genuine understanding of the contemporary Islamic realities. In the modern age, Muslims are living through a highly contested and unsettled process of self-definition. Islam, today, both as a religion and as a civilizational heritage, is undergoing a transformative moment in which there is at least the genuine hope that Islam might be able to reclaim its humanistic moral tradition. In this context, the clash of civilizations paradigm only acts to obfuscate the issues by deemphasizing the internal complexity of Islam.

For the sake of argument, I will assume that particular values and norms might be sufficiently distinctive and prevalent that they could be considered characteristic of a particular culture or set of cultures and that these cultures could represent a category that we could identify as the West. It is possible that a particular set of values running like a common thread could unite the cultures of particular countries, which then could be described as Western. When I use the expression "the West," for instance, I am thinking of European secular liberal democracies, the United States, Canada, Australia, and New Zealand. In this regard, the existence of a common language or common religion is largely immaterial. The notion of the West as a distinctive cultural entity is informed by common historical challenges that confronted a particular group of countries and which were dealt with and resolved in substantially similar fashions. Of course, the concept of a civilizational entity like the West is elusive. Although categorizing a particular country as Western is to a large extent informed by historical factors, there are also political and ideological elements to this process. Which countries are considered Western is affected by popular political conceptions that are susceptible to being influenced and reshaped. Thus, for instance, while Turkey has put a considerable amount of effort in establishing itself as a Western country, I think more people would tend to think of Israel as closer to being a member of Western civilization than Turkey. This perception, however, is both contestable and changeable and, I suspect, would also vary depending on the ideological biases of an observer.

The issues related to civilizations, their nature, and characteristics are important because they implicate the problem of authenticity. In many ways, claims about civilizational characteristics are, in essence, assertions about what is genuine and true to a people. Such claims are a powerful heuristic device that could be used to undermine the legitimacy of dissenting views or to brand certain orientations as marginal and unrepresentative. Moreover, to the extent that one might imagine civilizations to be sufficiently unique and distinctive, one might also imagine that civilizations exist in competition and even clash with each other. This paradigm of competing or clashing civilizations has serious implications for my argument about the vulgarization of contemporary Islam from what could be described as internal and external perspectives.

From an internal perspective, one could argue that what I claim to be a vulgarization of Islam is in reality nothing more than an expression of a genuine characteristic of the Islamic civilization. In fact, a Muslim critic could even assert that by speaking about the vulgarization of Islam, I am surreptitiously attempting to judge Islamic practices by standards that are not genuine and alien to Islam. Arguably, I am taking what are essentially Western civilizational standards and superimposing them on the Islamic context, as if these Western standards are objective moral universals. In effect, as the criticism goes, I am perpetuating the fallacy of Western universals.[28] According to this position, it might be entirely consistent with the moral precepts of Islamic societies to sacrifice the lives of young girls for the sake of guarding rules of public modesty. It is argued that simply because Western societies might consider a particular type of behavior offensive does not, and should not, mean that the behavior in question is objectively and universally condemnable.

Most often, this type of criticism—the criticism that one is following false universals—is leveled by Muslims against Islamists with feminist agendas. This criticism also has been utilized rather widely against Muslims calling for self-critical reevaluations of contemporary Islamic practices in light of modern human rights standards. [29] This criticism is a powerful rhetorical device because the internal perspective critique often allows the critic to position himself as the guardian of Islamic integrity and authenticity while positioning Muslim opponents as gullible and even simpleminded in failing to resist false universal paradigms. The charge of perpetuating false universals is used as a silencing tool by invoking the emotional charge of Islamic authenticity. Those who attempt to engage in an internal critique of practices within Islam that they find morally objectionable are promptly accused of being Westernizers—of caving in to the false standards that the West attempts to force on the world. Arguably, in order to avoid falling prey to the false standards perpetuated by the West, a Muslim would have to establish the values of Islam as distinct and apart from those of the West.

Criticisms from external perspectives are substantially the same, except that such criticisms are typically made by non-Muslims. Quite often, external perspective criticisms tend to be forbearing and even condescending toward Muslims and their imagined civilization. Typically, the external perspective critic eschews the idea of universally valid standards while firmly adhering to the idea of predominant and often invariable Western values. In this paradigm, the standards set by the West for itself are appropriate and fitting for the West as authentic expressions of the Western historical experience, but it is wrongful and even immoral to expect others to adopt the same standards. For instance, external critics, like the internal critics, will tend to treat my discourse on the vulgarization of modern Islam as a misguided attempt to hold Islam to standards that it is not equipped to meet. External critics claim that moral values or standards, inspired by the West, are false universals because they are unattainable and even undesirable to cultures belonging to non-Western civilizations. Accordingly, it could be argued that what I am identifying as morally repulsive behavior is so only to Westerners who adhere to a morality that is quite distinct from the morality of Muslims. As such, recent events that I have labeled as extreme acts of ugliness are arguably no more than authentic expressions of Islamic normative values. Those normative values, the argument goes, are often fundamentally at odds with Judeo-Christian values, and therefore the current turmoil in Islam ought to be seen not as part of an inner-Islamic struggle but as a confrontation between two civilizations possessing variant and competing sets of values. Nevertheless, I call the attitude of external critics condescending because of the tendency among many of them to pretend that Muslims are simply different and, therefore, cannot genuinely aspire for the kind of dignities and rights that are attractive to the Westerners. In fact, it has become rather fashionable among new Orientalist scholars to claim that Muslims not only hold different values but even have a different conception of time and space and, thus, a view of reality that is often at odds with that of the West. [30]

The internal and external perspectives raise difficult issues regarding the appropriateness of universal moral judgments and in fact implicate the very concept of a common humanity that can or should transcend cultural and civilizational divides. The issues raised in this debate are no less important than whether there is a universal human nature and shared human aspirations and expectations. It is certainly possible to produce anthropological and sociological evidence of culturally based variations that would seem to indicate that human beings do manifest a considerable amount of diversity in their lived experiences. In other words, in an attempt to deconstruct shared ethical universals, it is possible to generate evidence of considerable cultural diversity and richness among the different nations of the world. But the fact that the anthropological practices diverge from one people to another does not necessarily mean that universal values are false. For instance, assume that there is a tribe in India that engages in the practice of retaliatory rapes in order to settle political disputes; or that another tribe engages in the practice of female genital mutilation; or that in believing that wives and husbands should be bound together in death, yet another tribe murders a wife on the death of her husband. The existence of these diverse practices does not necessarily mean that ethical standards are relative and entirely contingent on circumstance. Well-established anthropological and sociological practices could result in suffering or could result in a persistently unequal power dynamic in which a particularly privileged group exploits other disempowered groups. Anthropology and sociology could document the existence of variety in the way human beings conduct themselves. But this does not necessarily mean that morality must be defined through these disciplines. From a religious perspective, the simple fact that sociology and anthropology exist does not mean that they must necessarily substitute for the role of God. In fact, it is quite possible for universal ethical claims to be based on a theory of intuition, rationality, nature, or divinity, and anthropological and sociological evidence of cultural difference could be considered as proof of deviance, not diversity.

More fundamentally, it ought to be recognized that arguments that invoke the logic of exceptionalism and difference are methodologically risky. Often, such arguments cannot be separated from the power dynamics that they camouflage and help to conceal. Put simply, those who enjoy an advantageous position within a particular context have a strong incentive to immunize themselves from judgment by others by claiming relativism or exceptionalism. For example, men who might enjoy the advantage of patriarchy have a strong incentive to resist notions of universal feminist rights by invoking cultural relativism or exceptionalism. But the fact that a particular paradigm tends to play a conservative legitimating role in relation to established power dynamics is not necessarily disqualifying. Rather, what is called for is a healthy skepticism toward any paradigm that tends to legitimate instead of challenge established power dynamics. More specifically, instead of accepting the claim of exceptionalism at face value and deferring to the supposed particularity of a culture, one ought to search for explanations that are subversive to established power dynamics. It might be that subversive explanations are ultimately not convincing or unsatisfying and therefore ought to be abandoned, but I would contend that there should be a working presumption against explanations that tend to insulate and immunize traditional power structures from critical judgment.

In this regard, I think that claims of civilizational characteristics that are purportedly of essence to a people warrant a healthy dose of skepticism. One ought to be suspicious of any approach that tends to explain, and at times even excuse, acts of extreme ugliness and vulgarity as authentic expressions of civilizational distinctiveness or particularity. Approaches that, under the guise of respecting distinctiveness or particularity, tend to note and then ignore wide-scale human suffering ought to be regarded with considerable skepticism. If widespread human suffering exists, there ought to be a presumption that such suffering is not the product of a genuine cultural expression but is simply the product of oppression. The burden of proof ought to shift to those who seek to justify or excuse the existence of human suffering to demonstrate that what is being observed is, in fact, a genuine civilizational expression that is of essence to the character of a society or people and not simply an oppressive power dynamic in which one group preys on another. I should note, however, that it will be very difficult for dictatorial societies to carry this burden of proof since in such societies only the privileged elite is empowered to have a voice. I think that human beings are entitled to disbelieve self-serving justifications of suffering made by a power elite entrenched in privilege. In fact, in the case of suffering or other behavior that strikes most human beings as ugly and offensive, there is no reason to readily believe justifications based on a supposed authenticity unless all alternative explanations have been soundly explored and rejected. In effect, this is like asserting that we should not be eager to believe the worst about a people. This is particularly important because, as explored later, alternative explanations for the presence of extreme ugliness and vulgarity in contemporary Islam are possible and, in fact, far more persuasive than any so-called civilizational explanation. In general, considering the high risk of falling into serious methodological errors of interpretation, civilizational paradigms and explanations must be treated with extreme caution.

Many have written about the historical validity of civilizational paradigms, and analyzing this rather large body of literature would require a lengthy treatment. It is worth noting, however, that to a large extent the issue of civilizations and their distinctiveness has passed from the realm of rational analysis based on historical and doctrinal evidence to the realm of dogmatic and ideological claims and counterclaims.[31] As noted earlier, I do not wish to challenge the notion that there are cultural values that become prevalent at a particular point in time, and I also do not contest the idea that, as put by Samuel Huntington and Lawrence Harrison, "culture matters."[32] But there are several methodological difficulties that ought to be considered seriously when thinking about cultural values and the role that they are purported to play. These difficulties create a high risk of what I have called methodological errors of interpretation. When speaking of civilizational paradigms, there are four main points of methodological difficulty that are especially relevant for the Islamic context. The first point pertains to what I will call "claims of lineage," the second pertains to "claims about the other," the third relates to "the enterprise of meaning," and the fourth addresses what I call "competence."

Claims of Lineage

Proponents of civilizational paradigms seem to rely on sweeping and un-founded claims about the specificity and purity of particular values. On nu-merous occasions, they attempt to identify and classify particular values as squarely Judeo-Christian and others as squarely Islamic. In their view, it is as if values have a genealogy that can be clearly and precisely ascertained and which then can be utilized in classifying what properly belongs to the West and what belongs to the Islamic "other." But claims about the origin and lineage of values, like claims about racial genealogical purity, are essentially sociohistorical constructs that are motivated by ideological considerations. Considering the numerous cultural interactions and cross-intellectual trans-missions between the Muslim world and Europe in history, it is highly un-likely that one can identify with any level of precision values that are primar-ily Judeo-Christian as opposed to Islamic.[33] Any attempt to do so will quick-ly falter on a bed of challenging and uncomfortable historical facts. Put simply, due to the legacy of multiple historical interactions between Europe and the Muslim world, the reality is that every significant so-called Western value has a measure of Muslim blood in it.[34] Put differently, because of the pervasive historical interactions between Europe and the Muslim world, there are no primary values that have a pure and unmixed Western lineage. So, for instance, researchers have already pointed out Muslim lineage to the concept of legal trusts and to the institution of inns of court that played a critical role in the development of the English common law.[35] Moreover, the idea of social contract, which is at the foundation of Western constitutional theory, was first articulated in a coherent and distinct framework by Muslim theorists writing in the sixth/twelfth century.[36] Moreover, the influence of Ibn Rushd (Averroes) (d. 595/1198) upon Moses Maimonides (d. 1204) and Thomas Aquinas (d. 1274) and his role in the rediscovery of Aristotle in Europe cannot be denied.[37] But my point here is not merely to acknowledge the many Muslim contributions to Western thought and institutions. Rather, by recognizing the mixed lineage of ideas, a simple and straightforward taxonomy of civilizations and what they are supposed to stand for becomes much more problematic. Like racial categories, one ought to recognize that civilizational categories are artificial political constructs that do not necessar-ily fit comfortably with sociohistorical realities.

Claims about the Other

Claims about the so-called pure lineage of values lead me to the second point. Often the attempt to identify one's own civilization and distinguish it from the "other" has much more to do with one's own aspirations than the reality of the "other." Put differently, descriptions of the "other," whoever the "other" may be, often tell us much more about the author of the descrip-tion than the subject of the description.[38] For instance, when Westerners attempt to describe the Islamic civilization and what it represents, there is a very real risk that the constructed image of the Islamic civilization will reflect only the aspirations and anxieties of those Westerners. Therefore, for example, if those Westerners aspire to achieve a greater degree of democracy or are anxious about their own shortcomings vis-à-vis women's rights, it is likely that they will invent an image of the Muslim "other" as the exact antithesis of their own aspirations. By constructing the other as the exact antithesis, one is then able to be more satisfied and secure about one's own cultural achievements. For instance, the colonial images of the Orient—its exoticness, mystique, and harems—had much more to do with the anxieties and fantasies of the Western colonizer than it did with the sociological reality of the Orient.

This is the familiar, but not sufficiently appreciated, problem of projection. Whether at the level of policymakers or academics, constructed images of a Muslim or Arab are not based on an intimate knowledge of either Muslims or Arabs. To truly achieve a level of intimate knowledge of a people, one needs to reach the point of actual empathy with the object of his/her study. In other words, a researcher needs to see reality as if through the eyes of Muslims and Arabs in order to genuinely understand both Muslims and Arabs. It is not possible to authentically understand a people unless one achieves a level of personalized and intimate knowledge of the particulars and specificities that define these people. But this is impossible to achieve unless a researcher manages to reach a point of empathizing with the perceptions, aspirations, and dreams of such a people. For example, if one seeks to understand the Jewish people, their history, cultural characteristics, attributes, and aspirations as a people, it is elementary that a researcher needs to scrutinize and internalize the information analyzed to the point of reaching a state of empathy. Nevertheless, when it comes to Muslims and Arabs, it is exactly this kind of empathy that many Western researchers are extremely reluctant to achieve. This reality is keenly felt by Arab and Muslim academics. Virtually every Arab or Muslim academic comes to realize that many Western researchers and policymakers construct an emotionally created and politically and ideologically motivated barrier between themselves and the Muslims and Arabs that they study. Because many of the Western researchers and policymakers have strong political preferences related to matters such as the Arab-Israeli conflict, for instance, such researchers and policymakers are reluctant to achieve the necessary level of intimacy and empathy with their subjects of study. The inevitable gap in knowledge that results from this reluctance to know their subject intimately is invariably filled by projecting onto Muslims and Arabs the anxieties and aspirations of the Western researcher or policymaker.

To bring this idea closer to mind, imagine a researcher in the Middle East who attempts to study the United States. If, as an Arab or Muslim, such a researcher studies the United States solely through the lens of his or her own experiences, it is inevitable that the United States will become transformed, in the researcher's imagination, into a highly artificial and superficial construct. In fact, it is fair to say that this is exactly the problem with much of what is written in the Middle East about the United States. Without the requisite empathy, the researcher will not be able to sufficiently internalize the knowledge of the paradigms and dynamics of the United States, and therefore, understanding will remain an elusive goal.

Empathy is a particularly elusive goal for the proponents of civilizational paradigms. This is so because seekers of civilizational paradigms do not usually undertake their project to prove that the civilization of the other has something to offer them. Rather, they are usually motivated by a desire to point out the virtues and merits of their own civilization and to affirm the distinctiveness of their own identity in relation to all others. It is hardly surprising that the constructed image of the other's civilization becomes the embodiment of everything that the seeker's does not wish to be. Although the proponent of civilizational paradigms most often will deny that he/she is engaging in a qualitative analysis of the moral worth of one civilization as opposed to another, in effect, the civilization of the other is imagined as the inferior antithesis of one's own.

Enterprises of Meaning and Competence

There is a further problem with approaches that focus on civilizational para- digms and conflicts. Values, and their meaning in culture, are not constant or stable. They are constantly shifting, evolving, and mutating in response to a variety of influences and motivators. For instance, concepts such as *shura* (government by consultation), the Caliphate, or enjoining the good and for- bidding the evil have had very different meanings and connotations from one century to another and from one culture to another in Islamic history. Even when one is considering divinely revealed values, such values acquire mean- ing only within evolving and shifting contexts. As noted earlier, interpretive communities coalesce around revealed injunctions and values and then endow them with meaning. Put differently, there is a sociohistorical enter- prise formed of various participants that partake in the generation of mean- ing. When one speaks of Islamic justice, for instance, one is really speaking of various interpretive enterprises that existed at different times in Islamic history, which gave the notion of justice in Islam a variety of imports and connotations.[39] When commentators speak of a civilizational conflict be- tween the West and Islam, there is a further creative and inventive process engaged in by the commentator himself. Since meaning is the product of cumulative enterprises that generate communities of meaning, a student of Huntington, for instance, cannot speak in terms of an Islamic notion of jus- tice or an Islamic notion of human liberty. The most that this student can do is to speak of prevailing meanings within specific communities of interpreta- tion. Therefore, a student of Huntington, for instance, would have to speak in terms of a Mu'tazili notion of justice or an Ash'ari notion of justice. This argument about meaning being the product of interpretive enterprises gener- ated by various communities has both vertical and horizontal implications. Vertically speaking, we are reminded of the point about the purity of lineage. There are a variety of historical contributors to the production of meaning, and it is quite difficult to find a value with a purely Western or Islamic pedigree. From a horizontal perspective, what is identified as a civilization is in reality a complex bundle of competing interpretations generated by a variety of communities of meaning, with some interpretations becoming more dominant than others at different times and places. This brings me to the final point, which I described as a problem of competence.

Put simply, who has the competence to describe which of the competing communities of meaning becomes the legitimate and credible representative of the values of a civilization? In this context, I am not interested in the problem of the dynamics of power and authority within a particular system of thought. Rather, my concern here takes us back to the problem of the invention and construction of the "other." It is imperative to keep in mind that when a student of Huntington, for example, claims that the Islamic civilization stands for a particular proposition, effectively, this student is endowing a certain interpretive community with the power of representation. This student is engaging in choice making by selecting what, in his mind, is the community that best represents the Islamic civilization. For example, the interpretive community to which someone like the reformer Muhammad 'Abduh belongs is fundamentally at odds with the interpretive community to which someone like Bin Laden belongs. By claiming that someone like Bin Laden better embodies the values of the Islamic civilization, Huntington's student is making a choice about representation. The Islamic civilization incorporates many different and competing orientations that range from the humanistic to the legalistic and from the rationalistic to the traditionalist. Some orientations are more democratic while others are distinctly authoritarian, and some are inclusive while others border on the xenophobic. Likewise, some orientations are more liberating toward women while others are consistently oppressive and demeaning toward women. When students of Huntington attempt to describe the Islamic civilization, they will invariably have to make choices between the various competing orientations and will have to designate some of them as representative of the Islamic civilization while others will be ignored as marginal and unrepresentative. In short, it is inescapable that the interpreter of the Islamic civilization will have to make selections and representations, and again, these choices and selective interpretations will have much more to do with the choice makers, that is, Huntington's students, than with the actual dynamics of Islamic societies.

CLASH OF CIVILIZATIONS AND THE EXPRESSION OF PREJUDICE

These various cautionary points are intended to emphasize that claims of civilizational distinctiveness and conflict are fraught with conceptual pitfalls. Claims about civilizational clashes must necessarily reduce complex social and historical dynamics into essentialized and artificially coherent categories. From a pedagogical point of view, such claims are likely to degenerate into powerful vehicles for the expression of prejudice. As such, they tend to further misunderstandings and promote conflict without contributing insights that are closer to the historical reality. Not surprisingly, writers who clearly do not like Islam or Muslims very much have seized on and exploited Huntington's thesis. Typically, in this genre of writing, Christianity, Judaism, and Western culture are jovially all bundled up in a single unitary mass, placed in one corner, and then pitted against the fantasized concept of THE ISLAM.[40] It is no wonder that when one examines the arguments of the Western proponents of the clash of civilizations, one finds that these proponents invariably ascribe most of what they perceive to be good and desirable to the West and most what of they find distasteful or objectionable to Islam or the Islamic civilization. As a means of maintaining the air of impartiality and objectivity, quite often the proponents of the clash of civilizations rather condescendingly assert that the values of the "other," as foreign and unacceptable as they might be for Westerners, ought to be respected. Despotism, oppression, and degradation, for example, might be terrible for Westerners, but they are acceptable for Muslims because, after all, Muslims themselves do not consider their social institutions as despotic, oppressive, or degrading. What for Westerners, for instance, might be considered egregious violations of human rights must be considered bearable for Muslims because Muslims have a distinctly different set of social and cultural expectations from the Judeo-Christian West.[41]

The effect of the doctrinal commitment to the paradigm of clashing civilizations often serves to obfuscate the real dynamics that are, in fact, taking place in Islam. There are significant tensions within contemporary Islam that are bound to materially impact the world today. Acts of cruelty, such as Bin Laden's terrorism, are not simply the product of an invented system of thought that could be treated as a marginal idiosyncrasy in modern Islam, but they are also not an expression of some profound authenticity. Rather, the violence of someone like Bin Laden is an integral part of the struggle between interpretative communities, or what could be called communities of meaning, over who gets to speak for Islam and how. Despite the practice of waving the banner of Islamic authenticity and legitimacy, Muslims such as the Taliban and Bin Laden are far more anti-Western than they are pro-Islamic. Their primary concern is not to explore or investigate the parameters of Islamic values or the historical experience of the Islamic civilization but to oppose the West. As such, Islam is simply the symbolic universe in which they function. Their protest is framed in Islamic terms because they are Muslim, but it is not the case that they protest because they are Muslims or because they belong to a normative imperative that might be labeled as "the Islamic civilization." As explained later, acts of extreme ugliness and cruelty did not emerge from a civilizational experience that can be described as Islamic. Such acts are the by-product of what can appropriately be described as a state of civilizational dissonance—a state of social schizophrenia in which the challenge of modernity and the alienation from the Islamic historical experience play the predominate roles.

THE BANALITY OF UGLINESS AND THE DIALECTICS OF SIN

In 2002, in a dialogue between Bernard Lewis and myself held at the National Press Club, Lewis distinguished between Islam as a religion, or a system of beliefs, and Islam as a culture—a civilization created under the aegis of Islam as a religion.[42] Lewis added that the claim that Islam is responsible for terrorists is just as incorrect as the assertion that Christianity produced the Nazis. After official proceedings concluded, a prominent journalist who has written books on the so-called Muslim rage, wrath, and all other manners of Muslim ill-temperament commented on the event by stating that she very much doubted whether Muslims possessed the cultural tools for developing a real sense of the sanctity of life. I was not sure how to react to such a pretentious statement, but a year after 9/11, it was the type of remark that one had grown accustomed to hearing in DC circles. Admittedly irritated and offended by her statement, I was struck, however, by the expression the journalist used: "cultural tools." I am not sure what she had in mind, but for me, cultural tools meant the deeply rooted inherited norms of a society as reflected in a society's language and customs. What is most notable for me was the extent to which religion had, in fact, crafted the cultural tools for expressing sanctity, sacredness, and inviolability. Indeed, the cultural tools for recognizing not just inviolability but the ugliness of violation are interwoven in the fabric of religious philology of the languages used in Muslim societies. The issue is not absence of cultural tools that would enable Muslim societies to accomplish what is moral and good, but contravening causes, such as invasions, disasters, and other forms of trauma, that force major deformations and distortions in the normative resources of a society.

I demonstrate this point by returning to the incident recounted previously, about the schoolgirls and religious police in Mecca, which ought to give all Muslims a long conscientious pause. Shortly after the incident, I received a call from an extremely distraught father who told me that he arrived at the scene of the burning school and saw his daughter behind the gate. She seemed to have already suffered from smoke inhalation and the father was convinced that she showed signs of burns as well. According to the sobbing father, the girl yelled out to him from behind the gate, and he pleaded with the religious police to open the gate doors to let her out. But in the rush to get out of the burning building, she had left behind or forgotten her black veil (*'abaya*), and the police screamed at her, ordering her to return to the burning building to retrieve her head cover. The father said that he also saw some of the regular (nonreligious) police officers wrestling with the religious police, who formed a circle around the school, in an effort to break through and save the endangered girls. He also said that other police officers stood quietly weeping. Eventually, the father watched his daughter go back into the burning school apparently to retrieve her veil, and she never came out again.

The father repeated several times that the panicked, terrified, and confused face of his daughter as she stood at the gate and before she went back into the school is what tormented him the most. He said that as the religious police refused to let the girls out of the burning school while coldly announcing to them that it is forbidden for them to appear in public with their hair and faces uncovered, the girls yelled back, "*Haram 'alikum! Haram 'alikum!*" The father himself yelled the same, as did several of the police officers who tried to break through to the girls. The father admitted that the image of his daughter screaming, "*Haram 'alikum!*" tormented him, and I admit that visualizing the scene continues to torment and deeply offend me.

This expression "*haram 'alikum*" is precisely the kind of cultural tool to which the journalist in DC and the puritans of Saudi Arabia are equally oblivious. No expression could have more perfectly summed up the feelings of the victims in this incident and indeed in every incident in which an Arabic speaker suffers the degradation of an injustice or ugliness. Literally, the expression means, "You are committing a sin!" But this hardly captures the nuance of this expression. *Haram* means something forbidden or sinful, and *'alaykum* (*'alikum* is a colloquial version of the classical word *'alaykum*) means on, upon, for, or to you. But when the two words are put together, they connote the commission of a sinful act in which the sinner voids himself of all mercy or compassion and shame. *Haram 'alaykum* is what millions of victims of crimes and cruelty screamed out at their tormentors. It is also what millions of victims of torture, sexual assault, or honor crimes screamed out in desperation as their suffering persisted. And in 2011, throughout the thousands of incidents of cruelty witnessed in different Arab societies, the same expression was uttered in reaction to every atrocity. The expression simultaneously connotes sanctity and its violation. The expression is a powerful indicator of our innate and intuitive knowledge that behavior that lacks mercy and compassion toward other living beings—behavior that exhibits a degree of depraved cruelty—is offensive to God and a sin. Notably, this innate repulsion toward what is cruel and merciless does not come out of books and does not require much theorizing. Even if the offenders and tormenters bury their conscience and harden their hearts, the victims always know. In prayer and outside of prayer, Muslims repeat numerous times each day the expression: "By the name of God, the Most Compassionate and Most Merciful." The absence of compassion and mercy is the absence of God because if God is present in any context, God's compassion and mercy must manifest. If there is no manifestation of either compassion or mercy, how could God be present?

Consider another situation in which one often hears screams of "*Haram 'alaykum.*" A woman is discovered to be pregnant out of wedlock. According to classical Islamic law, pregnancy does not prove fornication—only a freely given admission without duress or coercion or four witnesses seeing the actual act of sexual penetration can prove fornication. In Islamic law, pregnancy cannot prove fornication, leave alone adultery, because one cannot exclude the possibility that the woman was sexually assaulted or any other unusual circumstance. Nevertheless, due to patriarchic cultural practices and not religious law, if a woman is found pregnant out of wedlock, she suffers a terrible fate. In the rural areas of Egypt, Jordan, or Syria, she might become the victim of an honor killing. In Pakistan, Nigeria, and Saudi Arabia, unless she can do the impossible and prove she was raped, she either suffers corporal punishment or is jailed. Anyone who has witnessed it cannot forget the wailing screams of "*Haram 'alaykum*" of women who find themselves in these horridly reprehensible situations. But what it also points to is the extent to which Islamic culture is saturated with the realization of the intimate connection between the absence of God and cruelty, and sin and the lack of mercy. This is exactly what happened to these girls in Mecca that was so shockingly foreign to the Islamic faith. How could such profound cruelty be perpetrated in the name of the religion that anchors itself on the qualities of compassion and mercy? Certain political realities and ideological orientations have given particularly cruel elements in Muslim societies the ability to inflict much suffering, and these elements have gained the ability to speak in a loud and deafening voice. But the natural and deeply ingrained language and sounds of Muslim society, as in the expression *haram 'alaykum*, underscore the fact that these voices will remain alien and unnatural to the essential fabric of Islam. These are the cultural tools formed under, to use Bernard Lewis's expression, "the aegis of the Islamic civilization," and these tools are as if ingrained in the soil and soul of Muslims. I argue later that these norms, memorialized in the language and cultures of Muslims, are important reflections of humanity's law and of Shari'ah itself. Moreover, when people react at an innate and natural level by sanctifying and honoring something and simultaneously object or protest its violation, this is a powerful indication of reasonability. By definition, when people, drawing on their cultural tools, utter this statement of empathy, and in the very same utterance make a natural (nonlegalistic) claim that the conduct they are witnessing is an infraction against God, people are offering a claim about what is unreasonable and also what is ugly.

There are destabilizing and uprooting forces that cause Muslims to fail to exploit their cultural tools in the way they should. Among those forces are foreign invasions and occupations. But even more ominous and potentially destructive are ideologies that are artificial and alien to people's sense of reasonability, decency, or goodness. Tragic and harrowing events like the school fire incident bring people back to an innate sense of reasonability and drawing on their culturally ingrained language, and they bear witness as to what in truth they know is offensive to the inviolabilities and sanctities endorsed and sanctioned by God. As discussed later, puritanism, like forms of secularism, is an ideology that neutralizes the cultural tools of Islamic societies. Even more critically, it is an ideology that twists and corrupts Shari'ah to the point that it ends up clashing with the very cultures that it fostered over centuries of formation. So, for instance, the school fire incident represents not just a serious departure from the mechanics of Shari'ah but a complete negation and violation of the path of God, which Shari'ah is supposed to embody. This incident symbolizes not only the abysmal condition of women within certain theological orientations in modern Islam but also the gross misuse of the doctrines and traditions of Islamic law in the contemporary age. At the most basic level, even if one assumes that Islamic law does command strict adherence to rules of seclusion and veiling, the necessity of preserving human life would trump any such rule. The well-established Islamic legal maxim provides: Necessities will render the forbidden permissible (*al-darurat tubih al-mahzurat*), and the preservation of human life is considered in Islamic jurisprudence to be the most basic and fundamental necessity of all. Preservation of human life, in the order of Islamic values, is a greater priority than even the safeguarding of God's rights (*huquq Allah*).[43] But even more, the Qur'an itself clearly states that, whatever rules of seclusion might have been commanded at one time or another for women, these rules had one and only one justification, and that is the safeguarding of women from molestation or harm.[44] The death of these girls was contrary to the very raison d'etre and every possible rational basis for the laws of seclusion. One even wonders, if the preservation of the lives of these girls had any value whatsoever to the Saudi religious police, why the police did not do something as simple as unlocking the gates of the burning schools and then withdrawing all the men from the area so that the girls could escape to safety without being seen by men. If the religious police were sufficiently concerned, they could have even removed their own headgear (known as the *ghutra*) and placed it on the heads of the escaping girls, thus helping them to survive.[45] The point, however, is not the Saudi religious police's lack of creative problem solving or its abnormal obsession with the seductive power of women, or even its callous disregard for the value of human life, especially the lives of women. The point is that this event symbolizes a truly troubling level of moral degeneration in the collective life of contemporary Muslims. It is strong evidence of a phenomenon, discussed later in this book, and that is the "social death" of particular groups, such as women, in the social imagination of some influential theological orientations within contemporary Islam.

As ugly as it is, the schoolgirls tragedy was not an isolated incident but comes as part of a pattern that is symptomatic of a dangerous orientation that is anti-intuitive, anticultural, antihistorical, and antirational that wants to alter the intuitively grounded sense of morality of Muslims and replace it with a rigid textualism and literalism. The predicament that the puritanical orientation ends up forcing on all Muslims is that it justifies its acts of ugliness by citing the divine as the uncompromising and unwavering sole motivation behind its actions. Therefore, any Muslim who finds conduct committed by the puritanical creed troubling is by definition rebelling against God's orders and God himself. And such a rebel does not have a right to appeal to God through the expression "*Haram 'alaykum*" when he/she had rejected the very principle of God's will. Or at least, it becomes readily feasible for such an orientation to entirely ignore the pleas anchored in a cultural apparatus by simply accusing the bleeding hearts shocked and dismayed by the ugliness they witness of having watched too many American movies, Egyptian soap operas, or some other tool of un-Islamic propaganda.

I have not met too many Muslims in my life who are willing to believe that their innate emotive reactions are determined by the American, Egyptian, or Indian film industry for that matter. But I have met many people who are not willing to go through the discomfort of having their natural feelings challenged by puritans who quote the Qur'an and Sunna, chapter and verse, leaving the poor layperson feeling like he should enroll in Islamic kindergarten classes. Although I firmly believe that in the long term, puritanical ideology can disrupt and neutralize the cultural tools for a period of time, ultimately, what is good, natural, and reasonable will prevail. The problem, of course, is that these acts of ugliness have a very real and very heavy cost paid in human misery and suffering. Since the rise of puritanism in modern Islam there has been a steady, uninterrupted occurrence of these events of ugliness, ranging from the highly visible and infamous, such as the 9/11 suicide/mass slaughter of mostly non-Muslims, to less visible and lesser-known incidents. Puritanism has left victims not just in Arabic-speaking countries or the West but also in Pakistan, Malaysia, Indonesia, Singapore, the Philippines, Nigeria, Chad, Ethiopia, and many other places. Regardless of whether the numbers of those hurt were many or one, the morality and religious principle does not change by the counting of the number of victims. Whether the victim is one or many, the nature of the moral offense and the magnitude of its wrongfulness is the same. The Qur'an affirms this ethical standard by declaring that in God's eyes, the killing of an innocent human being is like the murdering of humanity.[46] In Islamic theology, life is a principle affirming the presence of the divine, and its unjust termination constitutes a desecration of the principle. Life is sacred as an ultimate expression of God, and destroying it is as if desecrating the script of the divine and as if committing sacrilege against the essence of existence. This does not mean that the number of human beings killed does not matter. With the murder of every single human being, existence and humanity is defiled and negated time and again. In contemporary history, events involving a small number of relatively unknown individuals do not achieve much notoriety, but this does not make them less immoral or offensive. The duty to bear witness against wrongdoing and ugliness remains the same. In Shari'ah, the duty to bear witness is a *fard 'ayn* (an individual unmitigated obligation), not a *fard kifaya* (a collective obligation that is discharged as long as someone does it), and therefore, the obligation is unwavering; it is not affected by the identity, race, religion, gender, or social status of the victim or offender. This is an essential value because in unjust societies, one often encounters the attitude that the suffering of isolated individuals or just a few people is somehow less objectionable or offensive and therefore could be overlooked. This attitude in and of itself is the very embodiment of human ugliness. This kind of functional utilitarianism is at the heart of the worst violations against human beings, such as the logic that justifies torturing a few for the good of all. As I discuss below, the principles of Shari'ah require that each good or harm be seen from the point of view or perspective of the victim and not the victimizer. If an offense ends the life of a victim, then from the perspective of this victim, all of life, and for all time, has ended as well. This precludes utilitarian logic that allows for harming the few to benefit the majority.

On December 13, 1996, 'Abd al-Karim al-Naqshabandi, a Syrian citizen, was beheaded in Saudi Arabia for allegedly practicing sorcery against his Saudi employer, Prince Salman bin Sa'ud bin 'Abd al-'Aziz, a nephew of King Fahd. The primary evidence warranting the execution of al-Naqshabandi was an amulet with Qur'anic verses inscribed on it, found in his desk drawer at work. According to al-Naqshabandi, the amulet was given to him by his mother in Syria in the belief that it would ward off envy and evil spirits. The Saudi government, however, considered the possession of the amulet, and some books on Sufism allegedly found in the defendant's home, to be grievous acts of heresy (*a'mal bid'iyya wa shirkiyya*) that warranted nothing less than death. I worked on this case very closely with Human Rights Watch in a vain attempt to save al-Naqshabandi's life. For three years, al-Naqshabandi, after his arrest and despite being tortured, continued to profess his innocence, reaffirm his Muslim faith, and state that he had never believed in or practiced witchcraft, until the very end. In fact, citing the works of premodern theologian Ibn Taymiyya, al-Naqshabandi wrote several long letters to the judge in charge of his case, arguing that no authority in Islamic law had ever held that the punishment for possession of an amulet was death, and insisted that he was a believing and practicing Muslim. He also asserted that his employer framed him, that he was never allowed to consult a lawyer after his arrest, and that the court had refused to call to testify any of the twenty-two witnesses who could have helped him prove his innocence. The Committee for the Promotion of Virtue and Prevention of Vice and the Saudi Ministry of the Interior justified the execution by charging that al-Naqshabandi "undertook the practice of works of magic and spells and the possession of a collection of polytheistic and superstitious books. . . .

In view of what magic and witchcraft produce in the way of serious damage to the individual and society with respect to religion, the soul, money, and intellect, and considering that what the defendant did has the potential of producing great harm, his acts are worthy of severe punishment so that his evil will be terminated and others will be deterred. Therefore, it was decided that he be sentenced to the discretionary punishment of death." According to the Ministry of the Interior, the death sentence was reviewed and affirmed by the Saudi Appeals Committee (*hay'at al-tamyiz*) and the Higher Judicial Council. Having worked on the case and after reviewing all evidence and legal material, I was thoroughly convinced that this man was unjustly murdered, but even if he was guilty as charged, his execution was a flagrant violation of Shari'ah and ethics. [47]

As a Muslim, I have to believe that killing an innocent person in this fashion constitutes a murder committed against humanity. The theological question that a Muslim must confront and struggle with is: Is it possible that God would bless and aid a people who desecrate the divine presence in this fashion? Can the label of Islamicity somehow alter the nature of the desecration? Put differently, just because a people label themselves "Muslim," or "Christian," or any other faith, is it conceivable that God would overlook the moral quality of their acts? Theologically speaking, the earth is one of God's dominions, and human beings, representing various collectivities, are entrusted to guard and preserve the divine presence, each in their area of responsibility. As explained later, desecration represents a fundamental breach of the covenant with God, and by its very nature it is also a breach of Shari'ah, and for a Muslim, when the breach is committed in Islam's name, it ought to be all the more offensive. It is as if someone uses the superficially technical Shari'ah to violate Shari'ah. Contrary to what some seem to believe, the invocation of the Islamic label to desecrate life and the divine presence does not shield the act from scrutiny. If anything, it ought to strengthen the vigilance of Muslims to end the violation and hold the offenders accountable. The Qur'an resolutely affirms the principle of apt responsibility for the moral character of society when it declares: "Verily, God does not change the condition of a people until they (first) change themselves."[48] Moreover, what is often described as the sixth pillar of Islam is the individual obligation to call for the good (*ma'ruf*) and advocate against what is bad (*munkar*).[49] The Qur'anic terminology of *ma'ruf* and munkar is very significant here. The Qur'an uses different terms to connote good and evil, and terms used in each context are important for understanding the ethical language of the Qur'an and Shari'ah. *Ma'ruf* means what is known to be good, and munkar is what is known to be foreign, disapproved, or bad. The terms refer to what is known to be good or bad by virtue of the law of humanity, which roughly translates into what a decent person would know or should know.[50] Both terms appeal to what is innate or natural within the human conscience in a social context. Classical jurists often point out that a rule of thumb guiding a reasonable person or helping the average socialized human being recognize *ma'ruf* or *munkar* is to treat others as a person would want to be treated. In Qur'anic usage, those who lie to themselves or deny this innate and inner recognition of what is good and desirable in contrast to what is bad and reprehensible are described as hypocrites (*munafiqun*) because they are engaged in self-deception, and in doing so, they deceive others. Importantly, what the Qur'an calls *qist* (the equitable or reasonable justice) cannot be achieved unless the grievance and remedy is considered from the point of view of the consciousness of the victim and what recourse or remedy the aggrieved party would reasonably demand.[51]

In Shari'ah, as noted above, the obligation is not just to do ethical deeds and refrain from unethical deeds; the obligation is to testify justly for God against evil, even if it is against oneself and loved ones. This is a critical foundation for our covenant with God and for inheriting the earth and continuing on God's path. Crucially, numerous Muslim jurists have long realized that this religious obligation to speak out against evil and to speak out in support of what is just and good is impossible to fulfill in unjust and oppressive societies.[52] After the Egyptian Revolution overthrew Hosni Mubarak in 2011, al-Azhar, the oldest seminary in the Muslim world, issued a historical document acknowledging this fact and that tyranny is a violation of God's natural law (Shari'ah).[53] Regardless of how often such a country invokes the Islamic label to shelter itself from criticism, in such a country it is virtually impossible to fulfill one of the most basic religious obligations in Islam.

Perhaps because of the awareness of the fact that the realization of God's grace and absolution is contingent on the willingness of people to strive to change and, at the same time, awareness of the overwhelming obstacles posed by tyranny to effectuating such a change, one finds the Islamic tradition replete with exhortations about the merit of standing up against unjust and despotic rulers. There are a large number of Prophetic reports that emphasize that the highest form of martyrdom is to suffer death while speaking a word of truth before a despotic ruler. Moreover, a significant number of jurists went as far as either refusing to punish rebels who rose up against unjust rulers or even calling on Muslims to support rebels against unjust rulers and to refuse to cooperate with tyrants.[54] Most Muslim jurists argued that at a minimum, Muslims should refrain from implementing the unlawful commands of their superiors, and especially if a superior's command meant the destruction of an innocent life, then, it was maintained, a claim of necessity is not a defense, and a Muslim must be willing to sacrifice himself rather than kill an innocent soul. Indeed, most jurists even rejected utilitarian calculations even in situations of dire necessity. While they upheld the principle of self-defense, they argued that no claim of necessity could justify sacrificing the one to save the many.[55] In fact, according to most jurists, someone like Naqshabandi would be considered a martyr because he died a victim of injustice. The same recognition of the principles of natural goodness and justice occurred in the Arab Spring revolts. Most Muslims around the world began referring to those killed resisting despotic regimes as martyrs, streets were named after them, and songs were written about their martyrdom. However, it should go without saying, the martyrdom of someone like Naqshabandi does not somehow alleviate the collective responsibility placed on Muslims for this death. The sad reality that every Islamist must honestly and bravely confront is that, like the father of the martyred schoolgirl, Naqshabandi's mother and brother had to protest the murder of Naqshabandi by reaching out to Human Rights Watch—a secular human rights organization based in the West. It is impractical, in light of the despotic government in power and the threat of serious harm, to expect that Naqshabandi's family could have sought help from a local Muslim organization. But the issue that merits serious reflection is considering that the desecration often takes place in Mecca and Medina, the most sanctified and holy of Muslim lands, it seems unconscionable that there are no nongovernmental international Muslim organizations concerned with addressing these human rights violations. In addition, it is due time that modern Muslims consider the full implications of repeated acts of desecration against the divine persistently defiling the most holy sites of the Islamic faith. If God's assistance is contingent on Muslims helping and changing themselves, despotism stands as a very serious obstacle. Warding off injustice by fulfilling the Islamic duty of enjoining the good is an essential tool for achieving moral change, but the despotism that prevails in many Muslim lands, including the holy sites, undermines the very means for achieving moral accountability and, ultimately, growth.

In the Islamic classical tradition, human life is described as having *'isma*—which means that it enjoys immutability. Conceptually, *'isma* is like a zone of immunity that surrounds the life of the individual that cannot be breached except for the most compelling reasons.[56] The expression often used and repeated by classical moral theorists as well as the ethically oriented jurists was: the human soul is immune (*al-nafs al-bashariyya ma'suma*). The idea of *'isma* did not mean only that human life should not be taken except for just cause but went much further than this. The zone of immunities surrounding human life meant that not only is human life inviolable but that, by extension, there are derivative principles necessary for the protection of human life. The basic and essential inviolability of human life meant that things necessary for the preservation and guarding of this life had to be respected and rendered inviolable as well. For instance, the presumption of innocence (*bara'at al-dhimma*) afforded to the accused in Islamic law was a necessary derivation from this zone of immunities. Furthermore, a considerable number of moral theorists and jurists strictly prohibited the practice known as *takfir*—accusing someone who holds himself out as Muslim of not really being a Muslim and producing circumstantial evidence to prove it. Therefore, many jurists refused to take part in any legal or political proceedings that sought to prove that a particular person or group is apostate or heretical. But beyond this, jurists even argued that to think ill of or suspect a fellow Muslim unjustifiably imposes on the protective zone set out around *'isma* and contended that the preventive detention of suspected rebels unduly compromises this zone. The idea of a protective zone around the *'isma* was further supported by a Prophetic tradition asserting that the soul, body, property, and honor of Muslims are sanctified and inviolable.[57]

Although *'isma* was a moral concept with profound legal and political implications, it remained insufficiently developed or realized in Islamic history. It was articulated as a moral concept that to a large extent was aspirational in nature—it set out an Islamically inspired ideal of the position that human life ought to occupy in the thought and practice not only of Muslims but of humanity in general. The point insufficiently explored or developed in Islamic history is the impact of despotism and silence on *'isma* and its implications. Affording *'isma* the honor and respect it demands would require a moral framework that celebrates the individual as the locus of sanctity and divinity. To do the concept justice, Muslims would need to develop a socio-political theory that guarantees the rights of the individual—not just the right to life but also all other necessary and corollary rights necessary for safe-guarding the full sanctity of the individual. Classical Muslim jurists recognized the protective zone of *'isma* in bits and pieces, depending on the demands of time and age. Therefore, they articulated a right to a presumption of innocence, opposed preventive detention of suspects, condemned the practice of *takfir*, and advocated against backbiting and slander as well as deducing several other humanistic doctrines and practices. Nevertheless, what remained missing was a coherent moral framework and sociopolitical theory that ensures that the individual's *'isma* is sufficiently safeguarded under all circumstances. The very idea of the *'isma* of human life, however, represented a significant moral commitment, even if insufficiently realized, that had become central to Islamic theology and belief. The reality in the modern age, however, is that far from developing the concept of *'isma* into a genuine moral fulfillment, it seems to have become another part of the neglected aspects of the Islamic tradition. Like so many aspects of the lost Islamic civilization, realizing the morality of the inviolability of souls requires a conscientiousness and ethical seriousness that is sorely missing in the contemporary age.

It seems quite reasonable to say that whether in the innate cry of *haram 'alaykum*, or in the particulars of recognizing and testifying for goodness, or in the concept of *'isma* and many other constructs I have not yet discussed, Muslims have ample cultural tools to sanctify life and uphold its sacredness. As discussed later, all these constructs and instruments are encompassed by Shari'ah, and they need to be reclaimed fully and thoroughly by contemporary Muslims, especially now that several Muslim countries have already made huge sacrifices to bring an end to tyranny. But unless Muslims reclaim these Shari'ah tools in their fight against tyranny, they risk having puritans undo every single progress achieved.

ISLAM, CRUELTY, AND MODERNITY

In the modern annals of Mecca and Medina, the Naqshabandi case was not unusual, and in fact, it was preceded by many executions that were equally whimsical and shocking. On August 11, 1995, the Saudi government executed the notable human rights activist 'Abdullah al-Hudhaif on charges of rebellion and heresy. Al-Hudhaif was active with the human rights organization the Committee for the Defense of Legitimate Rights and had distributed the organization's publications and written various tracts critical of the human rights record of the Saudi government. In May 1995, al-Hudhaif was tried and sentenced to twenty years in prison, but after the Ministry of Interior protested that his sentence was too light, he was retried and sentenced to death by a Shari'ah court. Importantly, although al-Hudhaif was an Islamic reformer, the Saudi government justified his execution on exclusively religious grounds, claiming that he had insulted Islam.[58] As has become the consistent practice of the Saudi government, criticism of the Saudi regime is equated with religious blasphemy and even apostasy.

The execution of al-Hudhaif, like the execution of Naqshabandi, could be justified under Shari'ah only if Islamic law is given the most inhumane and opportunistic interpretation.[59] Relying on the moral teachings of the Prophet, the classical jurists had argued that especially when it comes to matters relating to the preservation of life, it is always better to let a thousand guilty people go free than to wrongfully murder a single innocent person.[60] The issue is the basic attitude toward the sanctity of life. The truth is that a state can always manipulate the processes and doctrines of law in order to kill. This is all the more so when the state is despotic and it is able to invoke the authority of God without there being an earthly power capable of holding it accountable. But here, however, I am not addressing either issue related to substantive legal doctrine or the rules of procedure and evidence. I am talking about the basic moral attitude that pervades a society and that acts as a source of self-enforcing restraint. The issue is the dominant ethical paradigm within society: whether it is one that is willing to sacrifice a thousand innocent people to punish a single guilty person or whether it is oriented the other way around. Stated differently, the issue is whether the ethical framework that is embedded in the general social consciousness genuinely embodies and expresses fully the divine sanctification of human life. When the Qur'an declares that the murder of a single person constitutes the murdering of humanity, it is not just articulating a rational principle to be analyzed and explored. It is also expressing a sentiment, passion, and zeal about the worth of human beings. And the question that human beings must confront themselves with is: Is the prevailing social sentiment consistent with the expressed Qur'anic command as to the necessary ardor and zeal?

The Naqshabandi and al-Hudhaif incidents were widely condemned by human rights activists worldwide, but they were confronted with a chilling silence in Muslim countries. Despite the fact that these individuals, like many others, were killed in the name of Islam, Islamic activists did not seem to feel any particular obligation to speak out in protest, as if they had grown accustomed to the occurrence of such tragedies. Even more troubling was the silence of Islamic organizations in the West, who are able to enjoy the freedoms of thought and speech not available to those who live under authoritarian governments. In principle, these organizations do not confront impediments to their ability to carry out the Islamic duty of calling for the good and just and resisting evil and injustice. Yet the silence of the Western-based Islamic organizations was indicative of an endemic and pervasive problem.

The silence of so many Muslims before such extreme acts of ugliness begs the question of the nature of the duty toward the Islamic tradition. In the case of ugliness committed in the name of Islam, it is reasonable to expect that it is Muslims themselves who must shoulder the burden and moral duty of engaging in a corrective discourse. If Muslims who are in a position to speak are silent, this can only be understood as a concession to the only voices that can be heard. Even if one assumes that Islamic activists did not address incidents such as the execution of Naqshabandi and al-Hudhaif because these particular incidents were not sufficiently notorious, it is difficult to explain the silence in the cases of extremely visible and highly publicized acts of cruelty. For instance, in July 1987, Saudi security forces killed over four hundred and wounded well over six hundred unarmed, mostly Persian demonstrators in Mecca. Many of those killed or injured were women and children pilgrims. It is deeply troubling that this mass slaughter took place in the holiest of sites—a place of absolute sanctity, where the spilling of blood is an act nothing short of sacrilege.

What is most unsettling is that responses to atrocities have become selective and politicized. Selective outrage, or being offended at atrocities depending on the identity or affiliation of the victim, is, to use Qur'anic terminology, hypocrisy. Selective testimony is a form of perjury, and as such, it is failure to discharge the obligation of bearing witness before God. I recall, for instance, that in June 1992, because of a dispute with the Iraqi government, the Saudi government denied food and water to a number of Iraqi pilgrims detained in a camp near Medina for five days, leading to the death of at least ten of them of thirst.[61] In both this incident and in the slaughter of Iranian pilgrims, the Saudi government cited political reasons for the killings, but the very idea of sanctified places and sanctified lives precisely means that their inviolabilities and immunities are supposed to rise above politics or any other functional consideration. If lives, places, or space can be violated and defiled for the sake of gaining political advantages or because of utilitarian and functional considerations, it seems that the very idea of sanctity and inviolability means very little. Yet despite the fact that these killings involved pilgrims and took place in the most holy sanctuaries of Islam, the response of Muslim organizations and governments remained largely political. Those sympathetic to Iran or Iraq condemned the killings, and the rest remained silent. More recently, this blatantly indefensible behavior took place in response to political turmoil in Bahrain. In the context of the Arab Spring, Bahrain witnessed massive pro-democracy demonstrations protesting the despotic rule of the Al Khalifa family. The government responded with a massive crackdown against the opposition in the course of which the security forces committed a long list of human rights abuses. Furthermore, Saudi Arabia sent troops to Bahrain, where they are reported to have committed many atrocities. Bahrain is about 70 percent Shi'i and 30 percent Sunni, but the ruling family and security forces all belong to the Sunni minority. In March 2011, Yusuf al-Qaradawi, purportedly the most influential Sunni cleric alive, expressed broad support to all of the Arab revolutions and strongly condemned the atrocities committed against demonstrators. Al-Qaradawi, however, made an exception with Bahrain, where he was quite clear about supporting the Bahraini government and excusing the violations committed against the opposition. Al-Qaradawi supported his position by arguing that the Bahraini revolution was a sectarian and not a democratic uprising. The truly offensive implication in al-Qaradawi's position is that the atrocities committed against civilians that include a long list of horrendous violations are not that troubling because they are committed against Shi'i Muslims.[62] This kind of immoral and hypocritical selectivity unfortunately is not new. Saudi Arabia has had a long history of persecuting the Isma'ili Shi'a of Najran with the complicit silence of all other Muslim countries with the exception of Iran. In 2012, when the Shi'a of Najran tried to organize demonstrations, they were brutally repressed.[63]

The consistent commission of repulsive acts of ugliness by people who believe that they are acting in the name of Islam ought to give Muslims serious pause. Confronted by this reality, from the perspective of a believing Muslim, I must worry about God's covenant with the Muslim people, especially that the Qur'an is full of warnings to Muslims that if they fail to establish justice and bear witness to the truth, God owes us, Muslims, nothing and is bound to replace us with another people who are more capable of honoring God through establishing justice on this earth. [64] The covenant identified in the Qur'an and given to Muslims is not an entitlement. The Qur'an consistently emphasizes that the covenant given to Muslims is contingent and that the failure to do it justice will lead God to abandon those once entrusted with the divine covenant to their own vices and the consequences of their evil deeds. [65] According to the Qur'an, God entered into a covenantal relationship with Muslims. Per this covenant, the role of Muslims in relation to the rest of the world is to bear witness on God's behalf, to call for the good and just, and to resist what is evil and unjust. [66] Pursuant to the terms of this covenant, in order for Muslims to be in a position to bear witness for God, they must embrace and embody the divine attributes. Without embracing and embodying the divine attributes, there is no basis on which the testimony of Muslims could be premised. It is of crucial importance to note that theologically speaking, as part of their covenantal obligation, Muslims are supposed to embody the divine attributes of mercy and compassion. Muslims are supposed to set an example of mercy and compassion, which are values repeatedly emphasized in the Qur'an and in the daily Muslim prayers. Significantly, in Islamic jurisprudential theory, mercy and compassion are essential characteristics of the justice that Muslims are charged with establishing on earth. In a powerful symbolic discourse, the Qur'an sets out the fate of those who forget their covenant with God, fail to deal with each other in compassion and mercy, and fail to achieve justice. For those who forget God, not only does God forget them, but God no longer intervenes on their behalf, and they ultimately forget themselves. [67]

The Qur'an does not detail the identifying characteristics of a people who forget themselves. But there are numerous indications that in the Qur'anic outlook, such a people are considered to have lost their moral anchor and are overcome by widespread and rampant despotism. Such a people are plagued by instability, turmoil, suffering, and cruelty. In the Qur'anic outlook, a people who have forgotten themselves are plagued by conditions that could be said to be the exact opposite of justice, mercy, and compassion. The Qur'an describes the condition of such a people as one in which they become governed by corrupt and despotic rulers. Those who abandon themselves to self-forgetfulness and, as a result, whom God forgets become plagued by rulers who are tyrants and who fail to honor either the lives of people or their sanctities. [68] It is significant that in the Qur'anic discourse, despotism and tyranny are always equated with the spread of injustice and corruption, and in fact, despotism and tyranny are never correlated with a desirable or moral condition. The Qur'an elaborates on the condition of despotism by noting that tyrants have little or no regard or respect for the people they govern. Tyrants treat their people as essentially worthless, and as the oppressed eventually internalize the attitudes of their oppressors, the oppressed continue to forget their own self-worth and sense of moral value, and they willingly submit themselves to the will of tyranny. [69] The Prophet complements the

Qur'anic discourse on this point by explaining, "As you are you will be led"—in other words, "As people are, they will be led."[70] The Qur'an sums up the condition of people in a state of forgetfulness by stating that ultimately, "Thus, by the deeds they have earned, [God] will have the unjust rule the unjust."[71]

Although mercy and compassion are core concepts in Islamic theology, it is nothing short of tragic that these are not the values that most people associate with Islam in the contemporary age. Furthermore, one would be hard pressed to claim that modern Muslims have led the world in setting an example in promoting systems of justice that are premised on the core values of mercy and compassion. This could represent a serious failure in discharging the covenant that binds Muslims to God. Furthermore, observing the amount of despotism that exists in the Muslim world today, a Muslim cannot help but be concerned that indeed the unjust have come to rule the unjust. The Arab Spring has given many Arabs hope, but the challenge is formidable. As discussed here, I think that there is no question that through the tradition of Shari'ah, the cultural tools for overcoming the legacies of ugliness are available. There are many signs that while some countries have succeeded in overthrowing the tyrant ruling them, the cultural apparatus of despotism is still intact.

Social psychologists have emphasized that widespread human rights abuses take place after a process of socialization into what is described as a culture of cruelty. Observing or participating in successive incidents of brutality contributes to this process of socialization, or "internalized alterations," where the normal human sense of outrage at acts of cruelty is progressively undermined until a person becomes morally disengaged and therefore willing to participate in or tolerate acts of brutality.[72] From a sociological perspective, the commission of violently repulsive acts is often the by-product of ongoing social malignancies that fester for a long time before manifesting in publicly visible acts. Therefore, it is risky and quite foolish to wave away socially and politically pathological behavior as marginal corruptions in society. Put rather bluntly, people do not just wake up one day and decide to commit an act of terrorism or decide to kill a person for practicing witchcraft; rather, such acts are preceded by social dynamics that desensitize and deconstruct society's sense of moral virtue and ethics. Especially as far as theological constructs are concerned, the commission of and social responses to acts of cruelty typically undergo long processes of indoctrination, acculturation, and socialization that both facilitate the commission of such acts and mute or mitigate the sense of social outrage on the commission of offensive behavior.

Especially in light of the theological framework discussed previously, a probing and conscientious Muslim ought to be concerned at the evidence of the emergence of a consistent pattern and practice of abusive conduct. In Shari'ah, murder, torture, abuse, and suffering is munkar, and sanctity of life, family, home and property, mercy, kindness, and compassion are all part of *ma'ruf*. But if this is so, how does it come to be that someone of al-Qaradawi's position is not outraged by the atrocities in Bahrain? In June 2012, after a summary trial in Najran, Saudi Arabia beheaded a man, Muri' bin Isa al-'Asiri, on charges of sorcery because he possessed offending books.[73] Except from fellow Shi'is, the execution proceeded without protest from al-

Qaradawi or any other major Shari'ah authority in the Muslim world. In addition, when one finds that Islam is repeatedly and consistently being exploited to justify immoral behavior, this must be considered as a pattern of practice that ought to give Muslims cause for serious concern. This is all the more so because, in many ways, it is history that sets the future in motion. Each abusive act committed in the name of Islam becomes a historical precedent, and each precedent could carry normative weight and therefore influence the meaning of Islam in the future. Even when one is considering divinely revealed values, such values acquire meaning only within evolving and shifting contexts. Functioning within different and particularized contexts, interpretive communities coalesce around revealed injunctions and values and then endow them with meaning. Put differently, there is a sociohistorical enterprise formed of various participants that partake in the generation of meaning. The participants in these various sociohistorical enterprises are known as interpretive communities—a group of people who share common hermeneutical methodologies, linguistic skills, and epistemological values who coalesce around a particular set of texts and determine the meaning and import of these texts. The determinations of the participants in a sociohistorical enterprise become precedents that help set the meaning and practical applications of a text, even if the text is sacred, such as the Qur'an. Therefore, when we speak about the meaning of Shari'ah today, we are really talking about the product of cumulative enterprises that generated communities of interpretation through a long span of history.[74] What this means is that Muslims played an active and decisive role in the past in constructing the import and meaning of Islam and will continue to do so in the future. Muslims play the determinative role in shaping what Islam comes to represent in every age, and this places the burden of the faith squarely on their shoulders.

In my view, it is imperative for Muslim intellectuals to engage the various precedents set in the name of Islam and to negotiate the meaning of their religion. Shirking this responsibility or dealing with it in an irresponsible, apologetic fashion would be tantamount to the abandonment of Islam and a violation of the solemn obligation to promote what is good in life (or the *ma'ruf*) and reject what is wrong and unjust (or the *munkar*). As noted before, according to the Qur'an, the merit of the Muslim nation hinges on its discharging of this obligation of bearing witness, on God's behalf, to goodness and justice.[75] Naturally, testifying to the injustice committed by non-Muslims against Muslims is infinitely easier than testifying to the injustice committed by Muslims, whether it be against fellow Muslims or non-Muslims. This is why the Qur'an explicitly commands Muslims to bear witness for truth and justice, even if the testimony is against themselves or against loved ones. And, as noted above, the Qur'an specifically identifies such truthful testimony against self-interest as testimony rendered on God's behalf.[76] In my view, truthful testimony is rendered on God's behalf because silence in the face of a wrong committed in the name of Islam is a form of suborning the corruption of the religion. From this perspective, the worst injustice and the one most worthy of Muslim outrage is an injustice committed by Muslims in Islam's name because this is more deprecating to God and God's law than any supposed heresy or legal infraction. It is out of concern for the sanctity of their own religion and tradition that one would imagine that Muslims would be the most boisterous and vigilant in protesting injustices committed in Islam's name, whether against Muslims or non-Muslims. The Muslim covenant with God requires that they be among the messengers of beauty and goodness in the world. I believe that all Muslims would agree that this is not a privilege and not an election to a special class of being—it is a burdensome challenge. The covenant is not to follow the law but to embody God's law—the viceroyship of the covenant is to witness by becoming the embodiment of God's beauty, compassion, and mercy. Unfortunately, puritans think that they should dispense mercy and compassion sitting as judges rendered infallible by virtue of their power and authority. But there is a world of difference between the role of a judge empowered by legal fictions with immutability and that of a witness empowered only by his/her good character, honesty, and credibility. As I argue in the chapters that follow, in the beginning of the twenty-first century, two groups are boisterously wrestling over the fate of Islam and its legacy. Puritans seek to sit on the bench of judgment, but they are not troubled by how unreasonable or draconian their judgments appear to anyone, including the witnesses, audience, or defendants. Sitting as judges, they believe their judgments by definition are merciful by virtue of being the determinations provided by the edifice of the law. Therefore, those who find these judgments cruel or unjust are themselves defective or flawed. But secularists seem to believe that the only solution to the unreasonableness of the puritanical judges and their interpretation of the law is to ban Islam from the courtroom altogether. I think that to be forced to choose between these two options is itself draconian and that there are choices that are far more reasonable. I think that the efforts to invent an Islam without a covenant, obligation, or divine path will in the end frustrate these efforts and only perpetuate the chaos of modernity.

Chapter Six

Beyond Islamophobia

THE *JAHILIYYA* OF MODERN IGNORANCE

In Islamic dogma, it is common to refer to the period preceding the Prophet's revelation in Mecca as the *jahiliyya*. However, I do not believe *jahiliyya* is a historical category as much as it is a moral concept. Every epoch of human history has suffered its share of *jahl* and *jahiliyya*. *Jahl* means ignorance, heedlessness, the lack of awareness, and even idiocy or foolishness, but with the clear connotation of the perverse, pernicious, the dark, foreboding, and inauspicious. In Islamic eschatology, it is common to refer to a people plagued by ignorance, injustice, cruelty, and hatred as a people living in a state of *jahiliyya*. Ingratitude, selfishness, and arrogance are all thought to be characteristics of *jahiliyya* as well as the prevalence of vice and inequity in any society. The Prophet taught that blind ethnic and tribal allegiances are a part of *jahiliyya*—part of existing in a state of moral ignorance. *Jahiliyya*, however, has been as entrenched in human history as the social ailments of bigotry, racism, hatred, and oppression. *Jahiliyya* is a condition that exists to varying degrees at varying times inside of a person's heart of narcissism, self-involvement, anger, and ignorance that must be cleansed by God's light and love. [1]

But I believe that therein is the enduring and unyielding role of Islam—Islam is submission and surrender only to God. And it is resistance and rebellion against the personal *jahiliyya* of the iniquitous and uprooted soul and against social conditions and structures that compel the sufferance of ignorance and hatred and that ultimately deny human beings the fair chance to come out to the light. The theology of Islam resists the state of *jahiliyya* by calling on human beings to wage a relentless jihad in pursuit of enlightenment and against the oppressiveness of ignorance and against the social and political deformities and illnesses that spread in the absence of justice. The jihad against *jahiliyya* is a constant struggle to bring balance and peace to one's own soul and to pursue balance and peace for one's society and for humanity. In other words, it is a jihad to bring justice within and without—

for oneself and for all of humanity. This jihad is a never-ending effort at self-enlightenment as well as the pursuit of enlightenment at the communitarian and social level. In Islamic theology, a Muslim is in a state of constant resistance to the state of *jahl* and the disease of *jahiliyya*. In a sense, in struggling to submit to the Almighty, a Muslim struggles for liberation from and against falling captive to godlessness. Godliness is not just a conviction or belief; it is a practice and state of being. And this state, which is quintessentially interconnected with beauty—with the attributes of divinity such as love, mercy, justice, tranquility, humility, and peace—is in direct antipathy to *jahiliyya*, which in turn is associated with the ailments suffered in a state of godlessness such as hate, cruelty, inequity, arrogance, anxiety, and fear. This jihad should be pursued on behalf of the oppressed regardless of the oppressed's religious or ideological affiliation. So, for instance, if Muslims are persecuted by non-Muslims, then this *jahiliyya* must be resisted and eliminated. But if it is Christians who are persecuted or mistreated by Muslims, then in this case the perpetrators of the state of *jahiliyya* are the Muslim aggressors, and Muslims have an obligation to work to bring an end to the persecution.

As noted above, every time and age suffers from its share of *jahiliyya*, but what is distinctive about the moral failures of our age is not their nature or kind. Indeed, the moral failures of our age remain discouragingly similar to those of past ages. But what is different about our age is that while the moral failures remain the same, more than any other time in the past, these same failures—these *jahiliyyas*—are more inexcusable and less and less understandable. Human beings continue to suffer from ignorance, but our ability to teach, learn, and communicate is better than in any previous age. We continue to suffer from hate, bigotry, and racism, but our knowledge of human sociology, anthropology, and history—our collective experiences as human beings—make these failures less understandable, leave alone excusable, than in any other time in history. We continue to wage war and slaughter each other, but at the same time, our ability to kill and cause destruction is more lethal and dangerous than at any other time in history. But our codependence on each other as human beings and our increasingly interlinked world in addition to the unprecedented dangers posed by our weapons make our constant resort to war and violence incoherent, incomprehensible, and definitely less forgivable than in any other time in history. In every sense, we possess the methods and tools for the anesthetization of pain and the pursuit of pleasure but not for the end of suffering and the realization of happiness.

In this age, the problem is not our technical abilities or our know-how—the problem is in our will, in our sense of purpose, in our normative values, and indeed, in our very comprehension of humanness. Paradoxically, while our collective sense of the humane—our understanding of rights, denial, and suffering—has improved, and while our technical ability to protect rights or remove suffering has also been augmented, our ability to get beyond our isolation and limitations as individuals and to reach for the transcendental and perennial in what is human has deteriorated. In the modern age, our rational sense of the humane has increased but our spiritual grasp of the humane has deteriorated. Perhaps this is why so many philosophers have described the modern age as the age of anxiety, restlessness, uprootedness, or groundlessness. Indeed, the predicament of the modern age has been that while our intellectual capacities have sprung forth by leaps and bounds, our spiritual abilities, to say the least, have not. Our ability to access information about each other and to collect and organize data about our world has given us a greater sense of control and has raised our expectations as human beings, but all of this has done little to raise our sense of consciousness. We can see more of our world and farther into the universe than at any other time in history, yet our failure to decipher and perceive the truth of reality, leave alone beauty, has only grown more intense and also inexcusable.

In Islamic thought, we tend to see religion and religiosity as fundamentally antithetical to *jahiliyya* and all the ugliness that it represents. There is no doubt that throughout human history, religion has been a powerful instigator of change—in fact, religion has possessed the power of truly transformative moments in history. Not too many forces in history have had the power of religion to inspire, motivate, and inform. Moreover, many social theorists have recognized the positive and, in my view, necessary role that religion ought to play in remedying many of the ailments suffered in modernity. However, for any true believer—a believer who does not go through the affectations of belief, but a person who has felt anchored, inspired, and empowered by belief—for the believer who because of his/her religious conviction was able to reach out for godliness, for the perennial, transcendental, sublime, and beautiful—for that kind of believer, there is no alternative to fending off the *jahiliyya* of modernity or of any age, for that matter, without the empowerment and the enlightenment of faith. It is precisely for the believer whose engagement with the divine has translated into nothing but a sense of beauty, peace, balance, mercy, and love that a particular kind of *jahiliyya* is more offensive than all others.

This *jahiliyya* of which I speak is the *jahiliyya* that is instigated and perpetuated in the name of religion itself. It is when religion is usurped and turned into an instrument of hatred, bigotry, prejudice, ignorance, suffering, and ugliness. As a believer, this deeply offends me because more than ever before, I feel that humanity needs the love, mercy, and light of God. To use religion to perpetuate a state of godlessness is, to say the least, offensive. But as a Muslim, the perpetuation of *jahiliyya* in the name of Islam is more than offensive; it is an abomination—it is a complete breakdown in the logic and rationale of existence. As a Muslim, I think of this abomination as a fundamental and inherent contradiction in terms. The two cannot coexist because the illuminations of God cannot coexist with the darkness of *jahiliyya*. But I must admit that in the same way that I find the *jahiliyya* of those who hate in the name of Islam simply grotesque, I also find the very widespread and sadly trendy *jahiliyya* of Islam-hating, Islamophobia, and prejudice against Muslims to be no less disturbing.

THE IMPERATIVE OF EMPATHETIC KNOWING

Several months after 9/11, I was invited to lecture at a law school in New York, and this was the first public speaking engagement that I had accepted after the tragic events. After the trauma of 9/11, like many other Muslim intellectuals, I went through a period of feeling utterly futile and powerless and felt like withdrawing from a world that seemed increasingly chaotic and thoroughly irrational. I knew that most often, violence only begets violence, and I braced myself for the bombardments, invasions, occupations, and slaughter that inevitably would follow. Considering that the world was about to embark on a period in which the reverberations of guns would drown out all other sounds, what was the point of rational investigations and discourse? By extension, even teaching classes and engaging students in studies seemed like an act of deception. We teach students to listen and speak within a critical framework, and part of the educational process is for students to believe in the potential and promise of ideas. In all educational discourses, there is a constant tension between fear and thought—fear is reactive, but thought is reflective. In educational processes, as teachers, we ask students to believe that the best possible response in all circumstances is thought— critical and analytical reflection—and that in every possible situation, reactive responses based on fear are not productive. The serious problem, however, is that terrorism is quintessentially a crime intended to exploit the element of fear and induce an overwhelming sense of insecurity and extreme unpredictability in its victims. Importantly, historically speaking, terrorism works—in most cases, the victims of terrorism do in fact suffer a gripping sense of fear and react in a fashion that perpetuates the paradigms of political and social insecurity and chaos. If history was any indicator, 9/11 was going to herald a period of instability in which the space available for rational discourse and thought was going to be very limited. The impending sense of disaster and doom left every conscientious Muslim intellectual as if frozen in time with grief and anxiety.

Nevertheless, the consistent experience of Muslim intellectuals throughout most of the twentieth century was one of being locked in an unwavering paradigm of anxiety and grief. For Muslims in the modern age, there never seems to be a time free of an overwhelming sense of anxiety or grief and never a time to undertake a critical pursuit of knowledge. In the modern age, Muslims simply seem to move from one crisis state to another without a critical pause during which Muslims can shift paradigms from reactiveness to reflection.

Thinking that the need for rational and reflective discourse is perhaps the greatest exactly when the world seems to stand at the brink of chaos, I decided to accept the invitation to speak about making an Islamic commitment to human rights in the age of terrorism. When conditions had turned so ugly, it appeared that the need was at its most compelling for those dreamers who insist on articulating visions of goodness to be vigilantly pursued by humanity. In New York, for more than an hour, I spoke about the shameless legacy of hate and ugliness and set out what at that time I described as a competing vision of shared goodness that must be pursued by human beings. Muslims and non-Muslims, I argued, must participate in a collective enterprise of shared goodness because, I contended, the evolutionary engagement of human beings with the divine has made such a pursuit both appropriate for the age we live in and also a moral imperative. After I concluded what I thought was a nuanced and intellectually vigorous appeal, an older woman from the audience stood up to ask a question. With blazing eyes, tense posture, and a noticeably indignant facial expression, the woman asked a question that remains embedded in my memory. She first complained that since 9/11, she has not been able to feel secure in her city. The woman then stated: "Sir, I want you to know that I am scared of people that look like you—whenever I am walking and I see one of your people, I am scared. So what can you tell me to make me feel safe?"

To say the least, I was deeply disappointed. I had spent over an hour communicating as a human being to another human being and as an individual to other individuals, and regardless of what I said, this woman could only respond to me as an archetype or as a category. What I sought was an engagement at the level of ideas, but the way she engaged me was at the level of physical characteristics. Moreover, the reality that terrorism and violence forces on people is one in which people interact with each other only at the most base and primitive level, and what this woman did not know was that at that level, I was the one scared of her.

I was not scared that this woman would commit acts of violence against me, but I did fear her fear. This woman's fear stood as an insurmountable obstacle to any possibility that she would be able to get beyond my physical characteristics and join me in the realm of ideas. In addition, and more damagingly, fear is only reciprocated with fear—not understanding or empathy. For too long, non-Muslims, like this woman, and Muslims have been locked in a cycle of fear and suspicion, and if anything, the very point of my lecturing and teaching was to break away from this cycle and move toward a process that is more productive and more consistent with a state of divinity.

Sadly, looking back at the past decade, the woman in New York was a real harbinger of the bad times to come. The sheer number of people hurt and families devastated in the aftermath of 9/11 has been truly bewildering. I think back to that New York lecture in 2002, and I realize that the decade that followed could have been much worse, but it was still worse than what most hoped and prayed for. Some people believe that we are well beyond 9/11 and its aftermath, but I think that the real effect of this past decade will only be realized by historians writing a century or more from now. 9/11 did not only spark the war on terror, but also the phenomenon of contemporary Islamophobia. In my view, there is no doubt that an important part of the events leading to the buildup to the Arab revolts of 2011–2012 were connected to the post-9/11 decade. The degrading images of Abu Ghraib, Guantanamo, and others and the atrocities committed in Iraq and Gaza left an indelible mark on the Arab psyche. Few people in the West realize that the Arab revolts were in good measure an expression of the complete loss of legitimacy suffered by Arab leaders because of the perception that they were complicit or ineffective in responding to the general sense of humiliation and disempowerment; most people felt helpless to stop the constant chain of atrocities, which included pictures of naked men being sexually abused in Abu Ghraib and numerous narratives of innocent civilians killed or hurt. It appeared to many that Arabs and Muslims everywhere were being made to pay for the crimes of a sociopathological fringe group living on the margins of society. Particular images and associations, such as naked men wearing panties on their heads, the desecration of the Qur'an and human corpses, biblical quotes or symbols written on the weapons of American or British

soldiers, various reports about American involvement in defining the pedagogy of Islam in the Middle East, the incompetent and chaotic interventions
in places like Somalia, the debacle of the Goldstone Report and the images of
children and civilians horribly burned by Israeli phosphorus bombs in Gaza,
the drama of the embargo on Gaza and its daily consequences, the news
stories about CIA targeted killings or abductions, the constant flow of stories
of proxy torture conducted in Egypt, Tunisia, and Saudi Arabia as a favor to
the United States, and many other similar events that persistently stabbed at a
people's sense of dignity and safety in the world—all of these contributed in
direct and unmistakable ways to the popular explosions that ensued in 2011
and more that are yet to come. The role played by Islamophobia in adding to
the tensions and sense of grievance and to the creation of a polarized world is
yet to be fully understood.

For the purposes of reclaiming Shari'ah as a spiritual and moral inspirational force, I fear that the reactiveness, or what may be termed the mutual-
ization and normalization of hatreds between those sympathetic to Islamophobia and those sympathetic to Muslim puritans will further add to a culture
of mutual repulsion between Muslims and Christian Westerners. It should
not be forgotten that a country like Iran once offered the most exciting
intellectual possibilities for a truly original synthesis of Western constitutionalism and Islamic egalitarianism in the beginning of the twentieth century
and again in the 1950s before the Shah came to power.[2] But this promising
humanistic synthesis was aborted by first British and then American intervention. Indeed, Iraq had its own remarkable proconstitutionalist revolution
in the 1930s that was militarily aborted by the British. As importantly, the
policy of polarized politics based on mutual cultural ignorance only strengthened the hand of conservatives in Iran and the United States and has now put
us on the brink of yet another devastating and ugly war. Moreover, if due to
cultural ignorance or very myopic foreign policy advice the United States is
persuaded to support Saudi Arabia's current ongoing efforts to abort the
democratic impetus in the region, the disastrous consequences could be suffered for centuries to come. Imagine if any series of tragedies propel the
Islamophobes of Europe into power and they start their own ill-defined perpetual war on what they are fond of calling "Euroabia"—does anyone really
doubt that the result will be concentration camps and genocides that will
have repercussions throughout the world? The Islamophobes, very much like
the Muslim puritans, were not a product of happenstance and coincidence;
they were carefully funded and directed exactly like a propaganda campaign.[3] If the puritan experience in Islam is any indication, we have every
reason to fear that well-funded, planned, and directed campaigns will have a
great deal of success in reaching their goals.

As I argued in the section on Islamophobia, as a Muslim scholar, my role
in addressing Islamophobes and attempting to change their perceptions is
very limited. They need to be engaged, persuaded, shamed, and defied by
people from within their faith, political, or social communities. My role is to
engage those within my relevant community, which includes Muslims and
non-Muslim scholars and academics who are fair-minded. According to the
Qur'an, becoming trapped into a state of social hate and rancor is equated
with the corruption of the earth (*fasad fi al-ard*), while achieving social

intercourse and understanding (*ta'aruf*) are pursuits of divinity. This is an Islamic normative Shari'ah value of supreme importance; to achieve knowledge of the other is an act of divinity and beauty, but to fail to understand and fall back on anxieties and fears is ugliness and the corruption of the divine presence. Cycles of reciprocated fears lead only to a spiraling descent into a thoroughly corrupted earth—an earth without divine presence.

Having said this, it is important to distinguish between refusing to indulge the logic of fear and hate—refusing to become branded by the demented delusions of hatemongers—and the failure to take full responsibility for acts of ugliness perpetuated in the name of Islam. It is one thing to refuse to succumb to prejudice, but it is quite another to ignore extreme acts of cruelty and treat them as accidental aberrations rather than seeking to understand their roots and full implications. There is no doubt that to treat all Muslims or even Islam as a source of constant danger simply because of the actions of a criminal few is bigotry. But on the other hand, when extreme acts of cruelty occur, it is critical to inspect the contributory factors that led to such a disaster. Put simply, in the presence of such ugliness, it is imperative to clean house fully. Ultimately, this has little to do with appeasing the West or any other group of people, but it has everything to do with taking moral responsibility for the Islamic tradition and its impact in the modern age.

In this context, I hasten to add that part of the process of taking moral responsibility for the Islamic tradition is to educate non-Muslims about the Islamic faith. Doing so, however, does not mean engaging in apologetics or in a defensive discourse designed to present an artificially positive picture of the Muslim condition. Engaging in such a self-serving discourse only breeds mistrust and prevents the parties to a conversation from achieving a genuine understanding. In addition, integrity and honesty in discourse are indivisible. It is not possible to develop a duality of discourse, one that is honest and that is directed at Muslims and the other that is less honest and that is directed at non-Muslims. Speaking the truth is a unitary and single act as well as a moral attitude. To speak in two voices or more, depending on the audience, is immoral and dishonest and will invariably lead to Muslims and non-Muslims engaging each other with considerable suspicion and disbelief. As discussed earlier, to achieve genuine understanding between human beings, empathy is an imperative moral value. Apologetics or dishonest dualities in discourse seriously impair efforts at reaching a level of empathy because although engaging each other, the parties do not achieve a genuine knowledge of one another.

Naturally, advocating honesty in discourse and full moral accountability is easier said than done. The political situation after 9/11 did turn increasingly chaotic, and the increasingly polarized political atmosphere took a serious toll on the integrity of discourses post 9/11. Events of the magnitude of 9/11 presented human beings, whether Muslim or not, with an enormous challenge. Opening channels of discourse and achieving an empathetic mutual understanding was the only rational and decisively effective way to respond to and deconstruct the paradigms aggressively sought out by the Bin Ladens of the world. The invasions of Afghanistan and Iraq, the endless cycle of attacks and counterattacks in Israel and Palestine, and the many terrorist attacks around the world, as well as the seemingly countless number of writers and publishers willing to accommodate and capitalize on the most base fears, anxieties, and prejudices made any advocacy of empathetic mutual understanding appear nothing short of naïve and even silly. The trauma of 9/11 demanded transparency, integrity, and honesty in discourse, but the increasingly violent responses to this trauma only left people more vulnerable. And with the post-9/11 tragedies, this sense of vulnerability was felt in the Muslim and non-Muslim worlds. For those who search for shared grounds of commonality between Muslims and non-Muslims, they could have found more than ample shared similarities in the pervasive sense of vulnerability that was only augmented by every act of violence and counter-violence. In response, far from reaching any of the requisite levels of transparency and integrity of discourse, in both the Muslim and non-Muslims worlds there was a virtual army of opportunists who cashed in on the situation by producing a flood of alarmist literature. Most frustrating was the willingness of the public in both the Muslim and non-Muslims worlds not just to tolerate but to popularize these works and to amply reward the merchants of fear by making the production of this material a lucrative enterprise.

It is so demoralizing to observe how often in history societies enter into spirals of madness where people appear determined to run down a path of violence before there is any serious willingness to search for less blood-drenched alternatives. There is a redundant pattern of getting caught up in the escalations leading to the outbreak of violence before the memories of past traumas are invoked and public moods swing back to a search for peaceful ways of resolving and avoiding violent conflicts. The moral obligations of people, at times of escalating grievances bound to lead to violence, have been long-standing. In Islamic theology, whether one should stand by principle even if it means violence or whether nonviolence and pacifist stands are always morally superior has been a topic of extensive discussions under the general rubric of *i'tizal al-fitan* (abstaining from conflicts). In Islamic history, this debate often had sectarian overtones, but the principle or moral issue that Muslim theorists wrestled with remains as valid and pertinent as ever. For me, the compelling question is, what should people of religious faith or moral conviction do when many in the world have entered into one of these escalations toward violence? Whether the conflict is with fellow Muslims or non-Muslims, the first and a priori moral obligation is that of empathetic knowing. Other than situations involving imminent threats of attack when there is no time or opportunity to ponder, reflect, interact, and understand, any decision to use violence without first fulfilling the moral duty of empathetic knowing is necessarily immoral. It is immoral because by necessity it means that potential venues for peaceful resolution were not exhausted and one is promoting hostility, demonization, and confrontation. Those writers who claim to discover the incipient and hidden detrimental truth about a major religious tradition, like Islam, and use these supposed discoveries to justify policies premised on hate and violence offer morally bankrupt options. Major religious traditions that have existed for centuries and that have earned the commitment of millions of adherents cannot be dealt with in the arrogant and crass fashion that is frequently exhibited and that lately appears to have become increasingly accepted by writers who pretend to have discovered the violent or intolerant essence of this or that religion. The religious traditions that are rooted in human history, like Islam, Christianity, and Judaism, are integral to what defines humans as ethical beings—they have been and will remain primary participants in the moral fabric that defines the various cultures of the world. The historical and sociological, as well as legal and theological, realities of these religious traditions are too rich, diverse, and even magnanimous to be susceptible to the essentialisms that are heralded against them by some. Nevertheless, whether among Muslims or non-Muslims, there is no shortage of individuals who, with shameless effrontery, pretend that the truth of Christianity can be summed up in the Crusades and medieval Inquisitions, or Judaism in the idea of the chosen people and *Protocols of the Elders of Zion*, or Islam in the institutions of jihad and *jizya* (poll tax levied against non-Muslims). People who do so might take a nucleus or iota of truth, but they exaggerate, essentialize, and generalize it into mythical and threatening constructs. But just as problematic, these threatening and alarmist constructs present people with a damning inevitability. Assuming for the sake of argument that any of these religious traditions are as morally impoverished as these haranguers claim, the question is: What follows? For instance, I often ask those who claim that Islam spread by the edge of the sword and that it is an intolerant religion, assuming that their claims are true, what do they think should follow? Quite rightly, Muslims will not abandon their religion, and so the logic that follows from the reasoning of these haranguers is one of endless confrontation and conflict.

More importantly, those who have expended a serious amount of energy studying any of the major religious, moral, or intellectual traditions in the world would quickly realize that these traditions survive and spread because of the significant contributions they have made to humanity. Put differently, the traditions that have little to offer humanity—the traditions that primarily contributed cruelty and suffering, such as fascism, colonialism, or communism—do not persist for long. This sociohistorical reality is powerfully captured by the Qur'an when it says: "This is how God determines truth from falsehood. The froth in due time disappears, but that which is useful to human beings remains on the earth. This is how God sets forth the precepts of wisdom."[4] The froth that duly disappears is sparkling but short lived; creeds of anger or hate endure only as long as good people do not resist. But to demonize any of the major religious traditions in general, and Abrahamic traditions in particular, is not possible without an astoundingly crude and ignominious reading of history.

It is exactly history that provides the reason to speak out despite the distressing realities a decade after 9/11. In the short term, calls for empathetic mutual understanding do seem naïve, futile, and ineffective, but long term, there is no other moral alternative. Although the immediate political condition and reciprocal cycles of violence and hate act as a powerful disincentive, it remains imperative for those carrying a moral vision to transcend their immediate contexts and act on their moral obligations toward humanity and God. In my view, it is imperative that communities of faith not succumb to the temptations of hate and instead insist on a common human venture seeking moral advancement and a greater fulfillment of divinity on earth. But to do so mandates what may be described as the constituent elements of such a moral enterprise: (1) an empathetic engagement with the other; (2) transparency and honesty in discourse; and (3) self-criticism. Without these three basic elements, it would be extremely difficult to generate the trust and respect necessary for knowing the other and joining in a common enterprise. Put differently, these three constituent elements are necessary for achieving the Qur'anic ideal of *ta'aruf* (knowledge of the other and social intercourse).

The Qur'an sets out an effective moral agenda for achieving the ideal of *ta'aruf*, both among Muslims and among human beings in general. The Qur'an starts out the discourse by addressing conflict resolution between Muslims. It emphasizes the essential brotherhood between all Muslims and then urges Muslims to make peace between disputing Muslims while persevering in the way of justice. Justice mandates adherence to the dual imperatives of impartiality and equity. Addressing itself to "those who believe," the Qur'an proceeds to address what are necessary steps for the fulfillment of peaceful conflict resolution while adhering to the mandates of justice. It commands "the believers" not to mock one another and not to indulge in name-calling and slander against one another. Then the Qur'an instructs Muslims on ethical personality traits: Muslims are to refrain from dealing in suspicions instead of verified facts; they are to refrain from backbiting and speaking without knowledge about other human beings; and they are to refrain from spying and prying into the affairs of others. After setting out this ethical course of conduct, the Qur'an shifts from addressing Muslims in particular to addressing all human beings. It states: "O people, we have created you from male and female, and we have made you into nations and tribes so that you will come to know one another, and that who has greater integrity has indeed a greater degree of honor with God. Surely, God is all-knowing and most wise."[5] As importantly, the Qur'an explicates a moral and sociological principle of grave significance—it states that diversity is a principle of creation. People are different and will remain so until the end of times, and in a most intriguing statement, the Qur'an asserts that if God had willed, human beings would have ceased to be different, but they will not, and "for that God created them."[6]

The idea that diversity is a purpose of creation is intriguing but also challenging. If diversity is one of the purposes of creation, then far from being resisted or mistrusted, it must be embraced and promoted. Historically, Muslim scholars to a large extent accepted the inevitability of diversity, and this was one of the factors that influenced the practice of tolerance in the Islamic tradition. Compared to the prevailing paradigms in the premodern age, the Muslim civilization has been exceptionally tolerant of the other. In recent times, some pundits, largely motivated by religious and political bigotry, have tried to cast doubt on the historical fact of tolerance in the Islamic civilization. Suffice it to say, however, that in the premodern era, Muslim minorities were systematically annihilated in Europe and Africa while non-Muslim minorities in Muslim territories survived. Furthermore, a comparative analysis of the way premodern legal systems dealt with religious minorities reveals that Islamic law, in its premodern context, was tolerant within the context of its age. Seen in a comparative perspective, the system of *jizya* levied against religious minorities in Islamic law was not by any means exceptional, and in fact, considering the alternatives available to conquerors at the time, it was considered highly desirable by defeated nations confronting execution and enslavement. In the pre-Islamic era, Arab tribes of Mesopotamia paid a poll tax to the Persian Empire, as did the Arab tribes of Syria to the Byzantine Empire. Although the levying of a poll tax against religious or ethnic minorities was a familiar and accepted practice in the premodern age, the much more common alternative enforced by different legal traditions at different times, including the Roman, Persian, Anglo-Saxon, Frankish, canon, and Jewish legal systems, was either enslavement or slaughter. Seen in a historical perspective, the acceptance by a conquering force of a poll tax instead of enslavement or annihilation was considered a magnanimous privilege that sovereigns in Europe, Africa, and China were extremely loath to accept. Although most premodern legal systems incorporated the practice of collecting a poll tax levied against minorities, it was not the favored choice for most conquering powers because the collection of poll taxes was a sign of waning power or financial dependence—a sign that a conqueror was unable to thoroughly assert its dominance. So even as late as the nineteenth century, a Protestant theologian in a commentary on the book of Judges argues that it was "indolence and love of gain, [that] made Israel content with imposing tribute, even when strong enough to have extirpated [the Canaanites]."[7] Writing in the twelfth century, in addressing the perpetual state of conflict between Jews and the Amalekites, Maimonides explains that the Amalekites must promise to obey the universal laws of Noah and pay a tribute to Jews in order for their lives to be spared, but if they refused to pay the tax, then they must be dispatched.[8]

Most often, the collection of poll taxes was not done out of principle but out of functional necessity. However, instead of a vulgar assertion of hegemonic power, constraints on military abilities and financial dependence had the desirable effect of encouraging trade and peaceful exchanges between nations. For example, the second half of the twelfth century was a period of regular and thriving trade between Muslims and Christians in Montpellier, despite church prohibitions. Nevertheless, Muslims were not allowed to reside permanently in Montpellier, but this prohibition against permanent residence was the norm in European cities. Muslims temporarily entering the city for the purposes of trade were considered taxable objects listed in a special category next to pigs.[9] Significantly, at the time, it was the balance of military powers between Muslims and non-Muslims and the reality of mutual dependence that allowed for the emergence of a thriving trade practice. In Montpellier, this period was marked by a considerable degree of toleration between Muslims and non-Muslims, and the enforcement of poll taxes against Muslims was thought to be consistent with the prevailing ethics of tolerance. Fundamental to this conception of tolerance was the realization that considering the alternatives, the poll tax was the most humane available option when dealing with the other. In fact, historically speaking, even the practice of forcible conversions, reluctantly accepted in some situations in Christian Spain, for instance, although offensive by modern standards, was considered by conquering powers a more humane course of action. Instead of enslavement or death, the conquered would be given an opportunity to join the culture of the dominant power, albeit in a subservient state.

Although the Qur'an makes reference to the poll tax, the institution itself has no sanctity in Islamic theology or law—it is a means to an objective and not an objective in and of itself.[10] As discussed later, during a particular historical period, the institution of the poll tax could have been a part of what successfully preserved the diversity of religions, cultures, and identities, but in the modern age, this institution now serves the opposite purpose, and it is no longer morally acceptable. In the historical epoch in which it was enforced, the poll tax institution played an important role in maintaining the autonomy, rights, and freedoms of non-Muslim minorities.[11] In fact, Alfonso X (the Wise, king of León and Castile) cited the Muslim law regarding the treatment of non-Muslims as a legal precedent to follow in dealing with non-Christians.[12] It is rather telling, for example, that it was not until 1888 that the Catholic Church allowed the professing of a non-Christian faith in public in a Christian state. In the encyclical on human liberty, Pope Leo XIII dictated that Catholic states should publicly profess the one and only true religion and restrict the practice of other religions.[13]

Despite the understandable historical role played by the institution of *jizya*, a considerable number of contemporary Muslim scholars have recognized that this institution has outlived its political function as well as its moral justification. This issue, however, puts into emphasis not just the contextuality of certain moral precepts but also the imperative of moral growth. I will develop this concept at a later point, but it is important to note that the Qur'anic moral goal of human interaction and interknowledge in light of an inevitable and normatively desirable diversity is an ideal that could be realized to different extents under a variety of circumstances. Each generation is charged with striving after a greater fulfillment of the moral ideal, but it is undeniable that each historical epoch will pose its unique set of problems and challenges. The challenge in the current historical period is considerable.

The Qur'anic challenge is, in light of the enormous diversity, for human beings to get to know each other. This does not mean inventing an artificial construct of the other and then coming to know that construct. And it also does not mean that regardless of the actions of the other, their ethics and actions must be deemed acceptable and legitimate. While recognizing the legitimacy of a considerable amount of difference, the Qur'an insists on moral and ethical objectives and universal standards encapsulated in the idea of equity and justice. Furthermore, the Qur'an considers particular characteristics such as spying, backbiting, and slander to be inconsistent with the ethical precepts necessary for a just and equitable existence. The acceptance of diversity and pluralism and genuine knowledge of the other is a moral objective in and of itself, but it also serves an important functional purpose. Undertaking such a process enables human beings to discover and learn to differentiate between the universal precepts of morality on the one hand and the contingent and subjective on the other.

As I mentioned above, to pursue the Qur'anic ideal of knowing the other requires an empathetic engagement, transparency and honesty in discourse, and self-criticism. Self-criticism is necessary not only for achieving transparency and honesty in discourse but also for self-knowledge. A critical engagement with the self is fundamental to being able to critically engage the other. Without such self-critical engagement, it is inescapable that the other will become the object of numerous projections and that the other will unwittingly become the scapegoat for ambiguous frustrations and fears. Critical self-knowledge as well as honesty in confronting one's own ambiguities is necessary if one is to avoid the risk of scapegoating and projecting onto the other one's own frustrations and failures. The process of *ta'aruf* is not limited to learning about the other but learning about the self, and conscientious self-engagement is key for avoiding the all-too-familiar problem of inventing the other in an entirely self-serving way.

THE CRITICAL IMPERATIVE

A fundamental point of departure for all attempts at self-critical appraisal is the problem of what is commonly referred to as the issue of universalism versus exceptionalism. Implicated under this general rubric are a whole range of issues relating to individual and cultural autonomy, the right to self-determination, the philosophical basis of ethics, and the possibility of an objective psychology of human beings. Beyond simple tolerance of the other—in a sense, simply enduring or putting up with the other—if human beings are to join in a common enterprise seeking justice and ethical goodness, there must be a shared human morality that serves as a common bond and unifying goal. Exceptionalism, on the other hand, is very often at odds with the requisites of transparency and accountability to the other. But universalism is plagued with a political reality that cannot simply be ignored. There is an unmistakable tendency for proponents of universalism to overreach, largely by confusing ethical standards with cultural choices and preferences. It happens all too frequently that proponents of universalism objectify their own cultural preferences and claim their choices as universal moral imperatives. In this context, it is not unusual to find that the claimant of an overreaching universalism is proclaiming as a human right an act or practice that matters only to the most privileged, as well as quite often, Westernized classes. The difference is between a right to education as opposed to, for instance, a proclaimed right to dance in nightclubs. The difference could also be, for example, between the right to sustenance as opposed to the right to consumption—a proclaimed right to consume imported materials without obstacles to one's choice. Most often, an overreaching universalism goes hand in hand with a hypocritical attitude toward the other while refraining from any meaningful act of self-criticism. Naturally, most frequently this is part and parcel of a political reality in which there are severe imbalances of power. The reality is that politically dominant and often hegemonic powers are able to gaze freely on the disempowered other while that other is rarely able to return the gaze. Furthermore, while the politically powerful might demand and expect self-criticism from the disempowered, the politically powerful fails completely to engage in any meaningful self-criticism.

A rather notable example of this can be observed in the best-selling book by the well-known Orientalist Bernard Lewis, titled *What Went Wrong?*[14] In essence, Lewis deals with the question of what went wrong with Muslims in the contemporary age, and he identifies several institutional, cultural, and intellectual failures that played key roles in Muslims lagging behind the West in coping with modernity. Lewis identifies what he considers to be endemic problems that prevented Muslims from adopting a democratic political system, a culture of civil rights, and even a refined aesthetic taste in classical music.[15] Whether one agrees with Lewis's analysis or not, it is noticeable that Lewis at no point turns his gaze to the Western contribution to what went wrong with Muslims. Lewis does not even mention the historical legacies of colonialism or the role that Israel played in contributing to the problems of Muslims in the Middle East. Because Lewis is willing to critically engage Muslims but not willing to critically evaluate any possible wrongdoing by the West and Israel, this ultimately undermines the credibility of his analysis. In my view, being a non-Muslim writing about a sensitive issue where his analysis is necessarily premised on a particular set of value judgments, Lewis has a moral obligation to be particularly vigilant about turning the gaze inward rather than focusing it exclusively outward. Lewis has strong emotional attachments to Israel that are evident in much of his writing, and in fact, in his long career and extensive writing, he has never made a single critical remark toward Israel, the Jewish tradition, or the colonial legacy. At the same time, however, he strongly advocates that Muslims adopt a critical and reconstructive posture toward their own tradition. In terms of the ethics of discourse, I think that Lewis's approach is problematic.

Works like those of Bernard Lewis not only get a remarkable amount of press and high sales, but they also are translated and reach every corner of the world, including Muslim countries. A common reaction to the type of approach represented by Lewis is for writers on the other side of the ideological or political spectrum to produce works that are either very defensive toward the Islamic tradition or extremely one-sided in their criticism of the non-Muslim other. Not only is this methodologically erroneous, but as discussed later, this type of defensive reactionism has proved extremely detrimental to the Islamic tradition itself. Certainly, hypocrisy in discourse and serious power imbalances do pose a serious challenge to all discursive interactions, especially when this discourse attempts to find shared human universalisms. Furthermore, confronted by what appear as rampant hypocrisy and endemic power imbalances, self-critical approaches start looking like an indulgence or luxury that the disempowered can ill afford.

This particular attitude resonates very strongly in the Muslim world, as many publicists believe that priority should be given to uncovering Western hypocrisy or achieving a balance of powers before indulging in self-criticism. As the argument goes, self-critical engagements are appropriate, but only after Muslims achieve a level of equity of power with the non-Muslim West, in particular. Proponents of this approach believe that first Muslims must become economically, socially, and politically strong and independent, and until Muslims reach this level of autonomy, it is not constructive and is even dangerous for Muslims to orient themselves toward self-critical engagements because doing so will only undermine and dilute their sense of confidence and pride.

It is not possible to overemphasize the impact of this defensive posture on the contemporary Muslim reality, and in fact, its effect has been nothing short of devastating on the quality of Muslim criticism. The whole issue, however, rouses very strong emotions and often generates imbalanced claims about loyalty and betrayal toward Islam as a commitment and faith. Especially in the last four decades, attempts at raising what might be called the critical imperative in Islamic discourses is met with a censorious and bruising response. Here, it is important to distinguish between two types of processes and responses that have repeatedly taken place in the contemporary age. In the first, many scholars, in a rather dogmatic fashion, have emphasized the critical imperative in a broad and nonspecific way. Typically, this is done by calling for a rebirth of *ijtihad* (new thinking about old problems) or for the necessity of the so-called opening of the doors of *ijtihad*. This erroneously assumes a historical incident called "the closing of the doors of *ijtihad*" and that innovative legal thinking came to an end in the fourth/tenth century. The so-called closing of the doors of *ijtihad* is a myth perpetuated by Western Orientalist scholars; nevertheless, a large number of Muslims perpetuated and promoted this myth by claiming that the way out of the Muslim plight is to rekindle independent legal thinking in the form of *ijtihad*. This was often justified by the argument that *taqlid* (imitation or following precedent) is reprehensible and that adherence to the classical schools of thought in jurisprudence was unjustified. In the late nineteenth and early twentieth centuries, motivated by a desire to break out of the shackles of outmoded traditions and also to respond to Orientalist criticism of Islamic law, a large number of scholars emphasized the importance of *ijtihad* (innovative and creative determinations) and severely criticized the practice of *taqlid*.

In this approach, the critical imperative is highlighted indirectly and by implication, but calls for renewed *ijtihad* rarely go beyond stereotyped responses to specific challenges. Ironically, proponents of the new *ijtihad* are usually people with the most superficial familiarity with Islamic jurisprudence, and perhaps this contributes to the fact that *ijtihad* is asserted as a cure-all without any analytical basis. The hoped-for new *ijtihad* is usually justified by very broad and vague references to the doctrine of *maslaha* (public interest) in Islamic law as the key that will unlock the doors of new thinking and bring an end to intellectual stagnation. Because the proponents of this approach are usually individuals who have the most cursory familiarity with Islamic jurisprudence, they tend to rely on the language of *maslaha* as a catch-all expression to justify practically anything that a particular advocate happens to fancy at a particular moment in time. Calls for *ijtihad* in this fashion have become a means of intellectual escapism that maintains the pretense of reform and originality but that fails to critically and systematically deal with anything concrete. In contemporary practice, calls for renewed *ijtihad* have become, in effect, like saying, "We need new thinking to deal with our problems," but without actually bothering to engage in the necessary thinking about any real problem. Not surprisingly, being stereotypical and benign, these claims of *ijtihad* raise no controversies and meet little resistance.

The second response to the critical imperative has been to attempt to reengage aspects of the Islamic tradition by working through the interpretive communities of the past and reconstructing or deconstructing the inherited meanings that these communities had established. Proponents of this approach tend to focus on trying to produce a new hermeneutics or epistemology in reading Islamic texts or to focus on generating a new historiography in order to properly contextualize Islamic texts. But efforts such as these have been few and far between, and they usually generate an exaggerated hostile response—one that doubts the motives and convictions of the reformers—and very little in terms of moral or financial support. An even smaller number of reformers have attempted to investigate, reconstruct, or deconstruct the ethical visions that informed the formation of Islamic jurisprudence or Shari'ah in general. It is crucial to emphasize that as to this second group, I am not talking about those who attempt to engage Islamic law or theology in order to negate them or prove them unfit for any age or time. Those who have no commitment to Islamic law and theology might be reformers of some sort, but they are not Islamic reformers. As noted earlier, some anti-Muslim pundits had attempted to confuse this issue by trying to pose certain atheists or strict secularists as Islamic reformers. I think that it ought to be obvious that to be an Islamic reformer, one must first believe in Islam, and to play a role as a reformer of Islamic law, first one must be committed to Islamic law as a discipline and conviction.

Among those who clearly hold themselves out as committed and devout Muslims, few rise to meet the challenge of the critical imperative in any meaningful way. One of the main reasons for the relatively low number of those able or willing to do so is the abysmal quality of Islamic education in the modern world. Other than that, however, is the ostracism and near lynching reaction that confronts those scholars who attempt to undertake the second approach outlined previously. For instance, it is a near impossibility to seriously and creatively study Islamic hermeneutics, epistemology, historiography, ethics, and ontology without criticism. In order to make any serious advancements in these fields, it is imperative to study these issues within a critical framework—without criticism it is impossible to reconstruct anything meaningful. But therein lies the problem. In the modern age, Muslims have not developed a critical culture that could support analytically rigorous intellectual efforts. This is partly due, among other reasons, to the destruction of institutions of Islamic higher learning, partly due to the culture of authoritarianism and political despotism, and partly due to reactionism in confrontation with colonialism; but in my view, as discussed later, it is largely due to the impact of what I have called puritanical Islam or neo-Salafism.[16]

As I hope is clear from the discussion thus far, the critical imperative allows for the criticism of the other as long as it is preceded by the imperative of the empathetic knowing of the other and by the obligation of self-criticism. I do not intend to set out a comprehensive pedagogy of intercultural epistemic exchanges. But there are many practical difficulties to coming even close to the kind of dynamic that would allow us to move beyond a paradigm of mutual ignorance. To put it as directly as possible, intellectuals on both sides of the spectrum, Muslim and non-Muslim, including myself, often assume that a mutual discourse is possible for the betterment of all of humanity. But I do have to wonder if this is at all possible as long as the Islamic world remains overconcerned and even obsessed with what the West thinks while the West could hardly be bothered with what the whole Islamic world thinks. Anyone who has been to the Muslim world, leave alone fanatically Westernized areas such as Dubai and Beirut, will be struck by the enormity of the inequality of the cultural exchange. As I have noted before,

Muslim intellectuals are often obsessed with scholarship coming out of West and with obtaining degrees from Western academic institutions. However, there is practically no interest among Western intellectuals about what Muslim intellectuals or scholars think or write.

This situation does bring to mind George Eliot's famous novel *Daniel Deronda*, which has been praised widely for its vindication of Jews and its upright stand against anti-Semitism. I recall that at one point in the novel, Eliot writes of how the hero, Daniel Deronda, started out thinking of Jews as an antiquated sect that educated people can "dispense with studying and leave to specialists" but then matures to an awareness of the narcissism and arrogance with which Jews are treated.[17] I read this novel as a part of an undergraduate course at Yale, and I remember fully sympathizing with the hero's moral transformation and development except for the ending of the novel. Like other writers of the colonial era, Eliot seems entirely oblivious to the existence of an indigenous population in Palestine. I was reminded of this book after all these years because I read Martha Nussbaum's recent book on the new religious intolerance where she discusses some of Eliot's works. Like the situation described by Eliot, Western culture was only interested in Muslims to the extent that knowing anything about them validated their own being. In her book, Martha Nussbaum argues for an ethic of respect and sympathetic imagination in dealing with the other, and inspired by Eliot's work, Nussbaum underscores the critical importance of imagination in rising beyond self-serving and narcissistic knowledge. Most powerfully, according to Nussbaum, Eliot believed that this narcissistic lack of imagination in understanding the other is akin to the worst kind of "irreligion" because this state of arrogant ignorance allows people to deny the reality and equality of other human beings.[18]

In the early 1980s, when I read the book, the arrogance, aloofness, and narcissism with which the English people treated Jews could have applied equally to Western attitudes toward Muslims. Racially, Arabs, South Asians, and Africans, which tended to be the main ethnic groups that constituted Muslims, were all part of the subalterns who were presumed to be culturally, socially, and morally flawed and inferior in one way or another. So, for instance, even in Kuwait of the 1960s, Americans and Europeans had specially designated bathrooms and entertainment lounges in schools and certain corporations. When I attended the American School of Kuwait, teachers did not treat Arab Christians much better, and fellow American students seemed to have the hardest time remembering that slighting the Qur'an or the Prophet will not get a rise out of a schoolmate who is Arab but Christian. Interestingly, I have noticed an interesting phenomenon that, if verified, is worthy of study—Catholic churches built after the age of colonialism, which I visited in a number of Arab countries, depicted Jesus as fair skinned or white—older churches depicted Jesus as Mediterranean or African.

Coming back to my original point, if society in Eliot's time was content to ignore the Jewish thought as antiquated, pointless, and better left to specialists, there is a current trend in the West to treat everything that comes from Islam as either better accomplished by the Judeo-Christian tradition or as affirmatively evil.[19] I address the issue of Islamophobia in the next section, but there is a very common contemporary trend that deals with the

Islamic tradition as too vacuous and superficially flat to require any level of specialization. I don't know if other traditions have encountered this problem, but it has been a very prominent phenomenon for Western culture to accept the writings of people who have no specialized education, training, or even linguistic skill as experts on Shari'ah. Many laws schools in the United States offer courses on Shari'ah law, but the clear majority of these courses are not taught by specialists. As a part of this phenomenon, there have been movements to ban the Shari'ah in a number of American states, to ban minarets in Switzerland, and to ban the hijab in France without any attempt at achieving any level of sophistication about the Shari'ah. In all of these and many other activities, there is a prevailing attitude in Western society that there can hardly be anything sophisticated, complex, or rich or anything requiring specialization about Islamic law or theology. One of the consistent points that I often emphasize in my teaching, writings, and lectures is that Islamic law is a complex legal system that requires years of study and that the more you learn about that tradition, the more you realize how little you actually know. One of the themes harped on by bigots is that any claim regarding the complexity or need for specialization in the study of Islamic law is but a tactic to obfuscate the issues and shield Shari'ah from criticism.[20]

This state of determined ignorance about so much of the Islamic tradition has resulted in a rather odd practice that has not received the analytical attention it deserves. There is a proverb in Arabic that says something to the effect of, "If your home is made of glass, do not throw rocks at others," and it aptly applies to this situation. It is as if there is an epistemic block that prevents researchers on Islam from benefiting from comparative commonalities to other religious and cultural traditions. Especially when it comes to law and the Islamic legal experience, many of those writing on Islam act as if they are encountering problems that are unparalleled and unprecedented when contrasted to other traditions.

Much of what has been written on the Qur'an and its treatment of warfare falls into this ignoble category. I think that it is safe to say that anyone who has read through the Old and New Testaments would find the Qur'anic discourse on violence restrained in comparison. In an impressive new book, Philip Jenkins echoes the same kind of concerns when he wonders, with all of the plentiful attacks on the Qur'an because of its treatment of warfare, whether the Christian and Jewish authors of these attacks are really oblivious to a no less problematic discourse on violence in their own traditions. Jenkins does a critical appraisal of the biblical and Qur'anic narratives on violence and concludes that the Qur'anic approach to violence, within its historical context, is measured and restrained. Jenkins then concludes: "Islam above all stands at the center of anxious debates about how ancient religions can adapt to modernity, with the Qur'an as a potent symbol of the clash of values. So can a religion overcome what appears to be the violence and primitivism of its scriptures, without compromising its integrity? Christians and Jews are the last people who should be asking such a question of others."[21] Jenkins is referring to the problems raised by biblical texts on violence and the long and bloody legacy inspired by these texts.[22]

At times, I am truly surprised by the depth of the epistemic block that prevents even well-intentioned and usually rigorous scholars from noticing the offhanded or indifferent way by which the Islamic tradition is treated. Let me return to Martha Nussbaum for a moment. In her book, Nussbaum discusses the German play *Nathan the Wise*, written by the philosopher Gotthold Ephrain Lessing in 1770. In the play, Lessing relates a beautifully tolerant parable in which during the Crusades, the great Muslim leader Saladin asks Nathan, the main character of the play, which of the three Abrahamic religions is true. Nathan answers by conveying a long parable, the gist of which is that the three religions are like three valuable rings; only one of those rings is authentic, but we will not know which of the three valuable rings is the authentic and legitimate one until the Hereafter, when the matter can be resolved by God. Saladin learns that each bearer believes that he is wearing the true and authentic ring because each ring can cause equal good on this earth, but only in the Hereafter will the bearers of the ring find out which of the three was truly authentic, at least in God's eyes.[23] Although I do believe that Lessing was a moral visionary and that we badly need his message today, I do wonder how many non-Muslims, or Muslims for that matter, realize that the moral of the parable Nathan conveyed to Saladin would hardly have been news to the Muslim leader. The idea has a firm genesis in the Qur'anic text and commentaries on it.[24] And at the philosophical level, by the tenth century it was already well co-opted from Greek philosophy and firmly established in Muslim culture.[25]

The epistemic block to which I refer is a way of saying that, especially when it comes to Islam, there is a tendency to emphasize the faults of the other and to minimize or ignore one's own. However, there is an additional dimension to this problem that is most intricate. As noted earlier, the current balance of power is weighed heavily in favor of the West, which means that cultural influences are inordinately flowing from the West to others. As a result, a shockingly high number of Muslims suffer from the same epistemic isolation, and so not only do they take Western criticisms as unique and distinctive, but they also assume that the challenges that confront their own religious tradition have no parallels elsewhere. For instance, I am often surprised at how many Muslims, including legal specialists in Muslim countries, do not know that corporal punishment, which is often employed in the classical tradition, is not unique to Islam. So in Deuteronomy we find the well-known passage: "And it shall be, if the wicked man be worthy to be beaten, that the judge shall cause him to lie down, and to be beaten before his face, according to his fault, by a certain number. Forty lashes he may give him and not exceed."[26] According to Augustin Calmet's *Dictionary of the Bible*, there are no less than 168 offenses punishable by flogging. But other than the biblical tradition, corporal punishments were in very wide use until the early twentieth century. Especially in the West, there is a well-documented legal history of a struggle to abolish corporal punishments as cruel and torturous.[27] This comparative knowledge is important at several levels, including a legitimate appraisal of the particularity or exceptionality of Islamic prescriptions. As discussed later, this knowledge could play an important role in understanding divine normative commands and the role of historical contingency. It also plays a necessary function in assessing the dynamics of social episte-

mology and changing notions of reasonableness. It seems to me a rather
obvious point that before coming to the conclusion that any particular punitive concept or act is unique to Islamic law that such a claim be put to the test
of comparativism.

I have argued that it is critical that Muslims and non-Muslims join their
hands and hearts to resist the corruption of this earth and to promote a shared
goodness. I also argued that this is not possible without empathetic knowledge of the other accompanied by a self-critical narrative and an honest self-
confrontation leading to a better understanding of the self. It is very difficult,
if not impossible, that without self-perception and introspection any kind of
fair knowledge of the other can be achieved. But one of the truly exigent and
intractable problems is that because of the huge disparity in power and because of the Muslim dependency on the West in many different fields, many
Muslims can gaze on themselves only through the eyes of the West. For
many Muslims, they want to believe as Muslims but only relate to their
religion as Western unbelievers.

Several years ago, I was delivering a lecture at the British University at
Cairo when I read the following passage to my audience of about two hundred students and professors:

> The husband has by law power and dominion over his wife, and may keep her
> by force within the bounds of duty, and may beat her, but not in a violent or
> cruel manner; for in such case, she may have legal recourse against him.

Although my lecture was on comparative legal history, I was rather surprised
that not one person in the audience entertained the possibility that the source
could have been other than Muslim. My largely Muslim audience assumed
that this type of legal discourse must have come from a Muslim text, especially because of the refrain that the beating cannot be violent or cruel.
Delivering substantially the same lecture in Kuwait, I had the same experience. I believe that the results were very similar because of the widespread
apologetic belief that the limiting qualifier that the beating be light and not
painful is uniquely Islamic. There was a considerable degree of surprise and
at least, on one occasion, disbelief and incredulity when I explained that the
quote was from a reliable nineteenth-century English legal hornbook.[28] In
both lectures, I went on to explain that the initial position, based on ecclesias-
tical law of the wife being *sub virga viri* (under the rod of the husband) and
completely under his authority and pleasure with practically no rights, was
undone in England only with the valiant legal struggle to abolish the husband's right to discipline a disobedient wife. This legal struggle took many
years, eventually leading to the very famous and, at the time, very controversial decision of *R. v Jackson* (1891), which abolished the common-law defenses of reasonable chastisement or confinement, and thus ended a husband's right to beat or imprison his wife.[29] And, of course, just because
patriarchy was denied the legal right to chastise, confine, or beat wives, this
is no indication of what actually takes place at the societal level.

It was rather interesting that a good number of the students were surprised
that a country like England has struggled with such an issue at all, while a
few students were incredulous when told that spousal abuse remains a very

serious problem in the West. Of course, I do realize that the students of the British University at Cairo are not necessarily representative of a broad segment of society and that my observations in this context are hardly scientific. But the point is that the assumption of exceptionalism or particularism, whether adopted to support a false sense of being better than others or whether induced by a sense of inferiority and deprecation, is very dangerous. It undercuts any real effort at self-realization because of the distorted perception of the self and the other.

In the next chapter I will expand on the tension between universalism and particularism because of the centrality of the topic to any reform program. The balance between universal and relative cultural values is at the core of all debates about the possibility of humanity pursuing a shared sense of goodness. However, before moving on to this topic, I feel it is necessary to pause to discuss a special kind of evil—an evil that institutionalizes and legitimates religious bigotry and racism against Muslims in a way that effectively precludes all possibilities of taʻarruf or any sense of shared goodness. As we will see later from some of the internal debates taking place in Muslim societies, this evil threatens to aggravate discrimination against Muslims in non-Muslim countries and also discrimination against Christians and Jews in Muslim countries. I am speaking, of course, of the blight of Islamophobia in the modern age.

ISLAMOPHOBIA AND THE DANGER TO THE WORLD

I have to admit that the aftermath of 9/11 was worse than the most pessimistic expectations. The fear and anxiety felt by the West had devastating consequences for Muslims, for the West, and for Western Muslims—Muslims living in Western countries and who are thoroughly Western and Muslim at the same time. Other than the continuing slaughter in Iraq and Afghanistan, numerous human rights abuses continue to be committed against Muslims around the world, including disappearances and renditions, extrajudicial killings (murder), torture and degrading and demeaning treatment, and long-term detentions, with inadequate due process.[30] It is virtually impossible to count the number of people killed or lives ruined in the ongoing war on terrorism. Considering the number of countries involved, the lack of accountability, and the secrecy surrounding many of the abuses, it is equally impossible to get any real sense of the extent of culpability or actual guilt of the people who have been targeted since the war on terror began. But one of the most ugly consequences of the war on terror has been a type of regression back to the age of religious intolerance, with devastating consequences to humanity.[31] This regressive phenomenon has been appropriately called Islamophobia, and like all convictions founded on fear and anxiety, it leaves one with an intractable sense of despair and hopelessness.

Now, of course, Islam-hating enjoys a long and firmly established pedigree. Islam-hating is a practice rich with tradition. Starting with the early Muslim challenge to the dominance and hegemony of the Persian and Byzantine superpowers around fourteen hundred years ago, Islam has become the object of highly motivated sociocultural processes that were hate filled and hate promoting. In response to the spread of Islam, an elaborate institutional practice was born in Christian societies, which was supported by a tradition of theological and ideological dogma and ignited by a web of political and social anxieties. The function performed by this institutional practice was, at least initially, defensive and reactive—it sought to contain the threat of Islam not only by promoting cultures plagued by a sense of siege, but even more, by promoting a sense of revulsion and outrage at the Muslim heathen. The same processes that constructed the archetypal Muslim who induced fear also nurtured a mythology of a culture at the brink of suffering God's wrath and damnation because of the Muslim heathen. Leading up to the beginning of the Western Crusades, narratives of piety and antiheresy provided that without being reinforced with adequate private and public performances of outrage and disgust at the infidel (Muslim), society risked incurring God's vengeance, wrath, and even damnation. Some contemporary historians have argued that the very idea of the West—the very notion of the abode of Christendom, which was historically wedded to the institutions of Catholicism—as a unit defined by a coherent identity, cultural unity, and a basic set of shared political interests developed in direct response to the rise of the Islamic civilization.

Feeling challenged, threatened, and also defeated, the West, with its reactively formed identity, perhaps had no choice but to develop narratives of fear and self-preservation directed against Muslims and Islam. In these narratives of fear, anxiety, and obsession—narratives that stereotyped, exaggerated, and demonized the Muslim as a symbolic construct, Islam is cast into the role of the eminent and everlasting threat, and the Muslim does not just embody the image of the enemy but is made into the proverbial bogeyman—the infidel whose very existence, leave alone the infidel's successes and victories, is a horrific blasphemy and outrage against God, king, and church. In feudalistic Europe, at a time when political dissent, blasphemy, and heresy were hardly differentiated, Islam was seen as an atrocity against God and majesty, the cause of divine wrath and damnation.[32]

It took the West, led by the Catholic Church, about four centuries of incitement and sacred rage to build up the frenzy of intolerance and hate that would fire up and sustain six centuries of waves of Western invasions of Muslim lands known collectively as the Crusades. Contrary to popular belief, the Crusades did not just target the Holy Land and Jerusalem but included Andalusia and eventually Granada, Syria, Egypt, Tunisia, Morocco, and even the Eastern Orthodox Church of Constantinople. Eventually, the repeated invasions of the Crusaders were defeated, but not before leaving a trail of fear and hate that eventually culminated in the Ottoman invasions of eastern Europe. However, hardly had the Ottoman invasions been repulsed and defeated, incidentally without much help from western Europe, when a new chapter of religious bigotry and hatred had been perpetuated through the pseudoreligious culture of Western colonialism and its brainchild movement, Orientalism.

As the decolonization movement surged and nations gained the right to national liberation and self-determination, humanity seemed to be on the verge of unprecedented advancements in finally becoming united over core values, among them tolerance as a necessary and compelling moral and ethical virtue. Of course, I am not claiming that when nations and governments were busily adopting, ratifying, or affirming the United Nations charter, the Universal Declaration of Human Rights, and many international human rights treaties—among other things, banning racial discrimination, religious bigotry, and gender inequality—these governments actually meant to implement what they pledged themselves to do. The reality, especially from a Muslim point of view, is that the rise of the contemporary regime of human rights and humanitarian institutions and laws is replete with unresolved and perhaps irresolvable contradictions and paradoxical tensions. For Muslims emerging from the hypocritically enlightened and pathologically self-righteous but invariably exploitative and bloody dungeons of colonialism into a new age radiating with the glitter of principles such as the right to self-determination, national liberation, nonintervention, and the prohibition against the use of force, the world must have looked very promising but also confusing. The confusion was the by-product of the Cold War and the hypocrisies elicited by the logic of political realism and the doctrine of realpolitik; and the confusion and bitterness grew with the reality of aggressive hegemony of contemporary imperialism. But from the very inception of the age of rights, or what I call the age of promises, the confusion started with the destruction of Palestine, the dispossession of Palestinians, and the reoccupation of Jerusalem by the Crusader reminiscent historical movement of "pilgrims from the West." All of this had to cast doubt on the credibility and integrity of contemporary ethical universalisms and their inclusiveness toward Muslims. For instance, Muslims could not fail to notice the tension and irony in the fact that 1948, the year that the Universal Declaration of Human Rights was passed, was also the year the Palestinians lost their homeland and the Israelis gained theirs. Nevertheless, regardless of the challenges and contradictions that confronted Muslims in the modern age, there is no question that as human beings moved through the twentieth century and advanced toward the twenty-first, there were tangible successes in that, in principle, finally there was collective recognition of the wrongfulness and immorality of racism, ethnocentrism, bigotry, and religious and cultural intolerance, among other vices. Also, even if just in principle, a collective recognition and admission was reached that all human beings are, at a minimum, entitled to life, security, and dignity. In other words, in the postcolonial era, and especially by the end of the Cold War, it looked like after centuries of creating and suffering so much man-made misery, at least there were concrete and tangible achievements—finally, human beings had learned something worthwhile.

This is exactly why the religious bigotry of Islamophobia is so distressing—it is an indication that after all, perhaps we have learned nothing. It is distressing to think that despite the horrendous history of senseless slaughter and persecution, humans do not develop higher states of consciousness or more reflective and balanced senses of being but only grow ever more sophisticated in obfuscating the difference between reality and dreams. The currently trendy phenomenon of Islamophobia and the lucrative business of Islam-slamming ominously condemn us to recycling history through the irrational processes of reciprocated hate. But it is much more than the fear of repeating history that is at stake here.

Today is not like yesterday, and tomorrow will be more different still. Muslims are no longer the representatives of a dominant civilization and are not coparticipants in defining the norms of our lived world. No part of the Muslim world could be considered coherent units of integrated economic and political power as in the cases of Europe, Russia, China, or India, and Muslims leverage very limited actual power in their lived world. But according to the dogma of the modern world, wars of aggression and foreign occupation are no longer permitted, and unlike premodern barbarisms, people and individuals need not rely on their ability to leverage power because all human beings and all nations have rights. Indeed, the very idea of rights—the *raison d'être* of humanitarian protections and immunities—is founded on the notion of protecting the weakest elements of society—whether nationally or internationally, rights exist to protect those who are members of target groups or those who are members of groups that are in weak and insular positions and therefore unable to protect themselves. Today, the whole paradigm of world order and international law is founded on the notion that instead of the protection of force, the weak should be able to rely on the protection of principle or, alternatively, on principled protection. In other words, today's world is different than any other age because today there is authoritative legality in the world order, and in principle, there is rule of international law.

I am not so naïve as to believe that the United Nations is truly a parliament of democratic governance, that the Security Council implements international law impartially and fairly, or that most international legal obligations are applied fairly and impartially. But the gap between the reality and the ideal is what makes the contemporary condition so precarious for Muslims. There is not a single permanent member of the Security Council that is Muslim, and in this age, Muslims play a largely marginal role in governing or influencing global issues. In fact, the fate and well-being of most Muslim countries in the modern world depends on the good faith and fair-mindedness of the non-Muslim world powers toward Muslims—the opposite is not true.

Considering the distribution and structure of power in the modern age, much of the role of Muslims in today's world and much of what is done to and with Muslim nations is contingent on two critical presumptive premises: (1) The major powers that run the world today are no longer motivated by religious bias or rancor. Policy pursued by these world powers does not seek to promote or harm one set of religious beliefs over others and does not favor or disfavor a people or nation because they belong to one religious tradition or another. Put differently, the dominant powers of the world do not govern in the name of Western Christendom, and their economic and political powers are not used to leverage the supremacy of the Judeo-Christian civilization, for instance, against others. (2) The decisions and policies of the dominant operative powers in today's world are based on rational choices and shared interests and not on historical, racial, or religious bias or any other type of prejudice.

Among other things, these two presumptive premises fundamentally mean that religious wars have ended and that we live in a rationally driven world. Without the fulfillment of these two premises, the reality becomes that Muslims live in a world that they do not control and more so in a world in which they do not have much power; they also live in a world in which they are very likely to become the targets and, considering their limited power, even victims of bigoted policies. Now I think that it is rather obvious that these two premises are not perfectly fulfilled and indeed can never be perfectly fulfilled. World powers that have near hegemonic influence on today's world are not immune to the numerous subjectivities that normally affect decision making. What is important, however, is not if these two premises are fulfilled but the extent to which they are fulfilled at any given time. For example, the rule of law and world order in the modern age is premised on the assumption of the illegitimacy and wrongfulness of racially biased policies, but no one would seriously suggest that racism wittingly or unwittingly does not affect the subjectivities of policymakers. This, however, is one of the reasons that Islamophobia and Islam-hating is emblematic of the foundational failures of the modern age—policies that target or profile Muslims as a group, or that speak of the dangers of a Muslim cultural invasion of Europe, or that legitimate the denunciation and deprecation of the Islamic faith, very much like the institution and logic of apartheid, undermine the fundamental structure of legitimacy in the modern age. In this regard, there are many reasons to be very concerned.

Policies that are founded on the presumed inherent dangers of Islamic theology or law, or policymakers who effectively legitimate religious bigotry by seeking the "expert" counsel of professional Islam haters do nothing less than undermine the very logic that provides structure and authoritativeness to the order of this age. I emphasize that the problem is not the existence of discreet and surreptitious religious bigotry—the problem is the fact that this religious bigotry is rationalized and legitimated; it is cleansed of all sense of shame or fault and then stated as a normative value: the truth that needs to be uncovered. Here, the evidence on the ground, so to speak, is shocking, deeply troubling, and overwhelming. For example, since 2002, thousands of books published in the United States and Europe spewed sheer hateful venom against Islamic theology, law, and history. More troubling is the fact that many of these pseudointellectualized displays of bigotry became massive best sellers in Western countries. The writers of these hate-filled tracts were endowed with star status in the West as they consistently appeared as authoritative voices on everything Muslim in the media and were integrated into positions of authority by being given various institutional roles, either as advisors to governments, members of government, or references for specialized agencies within government. As I mentioned earlier, part of the very widespread phenomenon of religious bigotry was the opportunistic and parasitical celebration and promotion of so-called native informants—people who fit the Muslim ethnic and cultural profile claimed either that they are Muslim or used to be Muslim and above all were willing to perform the dramatic role of the archetypal Muslim who gazes in the mirror only to discover his/her hideous ugliness (contrasted, of course, to the beauty of the non-Muslim other) and then, overcome by tragic destiny, plunges into cathartic self-flagellation (or, more precisely, Islam-flagellation), which ends with the entirely predictable realization that all the ugliness in the mirror, after all, is Islam's fault. Of course, for the bigoted but paying reader's ecstatic enjoyment, the native informant climactically confesses Islam's sins and bombastically declares, lest it be damned, that Islam and, of course, Muslims too must repent! The classic and also the most indulgently obnoxious examples of this pornographically oriented exploitation of nonreligiosity, or perhaps antireligiosity, are the money-raking books of Hirsi Ali, Irshad Manji, Wafa Sultan, Nonie Darwish, and the like.

What fuels the Islam-hating industry in the West is that many sincerely believe that they are reacting rationally to a cultural, political, and militaristic threat. But it is important to remember that every social movement that has demonized a feared and hated other has constructed its hate narrative as an unpleasant but necessary defensive response to a perceived threat—whether real or imagined. The very nature of bigotry and prejudice is that they are paranoid reconstructions of reality—they grossly exaggerate a kernel of truth into an enormous lie. So, for instance, bigots do not imagine that Muslim terrorists exist, but they imagine that terrorism is the prevailing reality of Islam.

What is especially troubling about Islam-hating is that it is a powerful indication that the West, which led the world into modernity, has been unable to overcome its own historically rooted religious prejudices and bigotry. Islam-hating and Islamophobia are among the few remaining sanitized and legitimate social pathologies in the West, not because bigotry against Islam and Muslims is practiced or tolerated, but because it is affirmatively honored and even glorified as part of the analytical discipline of national security and interest.

In some regards, Islam-hating or Islamophobia is fairly unremarkable because, like all prejudices, it is rationalized from a defensive posture and it thrives in a fertile ground of misinformation and ignorance. But what is remarkable about this particular form of prejudice and bigotry is that despite its deep roots in history—although it was exploited in the past to rationalize and incite numerous acts of aggression and violence and although it continues to do so today—there is remarkable resistance in the West to acknowledging its existence or to coming to terms with the crimes committed because of it, leave alone to attempt to atone for its consequences. A person who openly advocates racism, for instance, or anti-Semitism will be seen as a pariah and an outlier to mainstream society. No mainstream publisher or media outlet will broadcast speech that is openly racist or anti-Semitic not because these social ills do not exist. They do exist! But there are social processes that shame, ostracize, and hold accountable those who blatantly indulge these pathologies. The same is not true for those Islam- or Muslim-haters. For example, intellectuals and policymakers are admirably frank about studying, admitting, and atoning for the Western legacy of anti-Semitism. Studies that document and analyze the pathology of anti-Semitism have emerged into a sophisticated critical discipline, and no serious intellectual would question whether anti-Semitism has been a recurring form of prejudice and bigotry in Western history. Logically, however, if one admits that anti-Semitism is a widespread social pathology that must be resisted and not encouraged, it would seem to follow that substantially the same position should be adopted in regard to anti-Muslim prejudice and Islamophobia. Put simply, one can hardly imagine any place or time in Europe where Jews were persecuted while Muslims were tolerated. Without exception, any time Jews were the target of persecution in Western history, this persecution included the archetypal representative of Islam of the time—whether that archetype was the Turk, Arab, Saracen, Morisco, or Mohammedan.[33] Moreover, as is well illustrated by the complex and problematic notion of a Judeo-Christian culture or civilization, the history of Jews in the West was a complex one—it ebbed and flowed and went back and forth between begrudging tolerance to outright persecution, to eventual efforts at reconciliation, and, at times, to atonement, as in the Western guilt-ridden support for the Zionist movement. But the history of Muslims in the West has consistently ranged from slaughter to begrudging tolerance, to extermination, and eventually to total and unequivocal hegemony and domination. My point is that if examined from a historical logic, the reluctance, dead silence, and quiet avoidance that confronts the Muslim victims of religious persecution in the West and that confronts researchers in the pathology of Islamophobia and Islam-hating is itself a shocking manifestation of the pathology. What is rather symptomatic of the deeply ingrained prejudice is the continual effort to justify Muslim suffering as an unfortunate but necessary cost for security or to understate and minimize the existence of actual concrete and harmful results from the existence of such a prejudice. An example of this is the insistence on the part of some that the use of torture against Muslims in Iraq, Afghanistan, and elsewhere is not linked to deeply rooted prejudices as to the ego, pride, sexuality, religiosity, and body of a Muslim man or woman. Another common tactic that is actually symptomatic of the deep entrenchment of the problem is to admit that anti-Muslim prejudice exists but to minimize it as a passing condition instead of a pathology with a stubbornly persistent history or to dilute its particularity and distinctiveness by dismissively equating it to other prejudices and biases minorities suffered and in due time defeated. The relatively muted response of the intelligentsia in the West at the widespread occurrence of civil rights violations against Muslims in the West and also in reaction to the documented humanitarian violations and war crimes inflicted on Muslims in several countries and contexts in the name of the war on terror is again a strong indication of the desensitization and suppressed consciousness of the West toward the presence and wrongfulness of anti-Muslim prejudices. Sadly, the West has managed to confront many of the demons of its own history, but its fear of Muslims and hate of Islam is one demon that has proved too powerful to confront.

The one thing that the so-called war on terror has shown is the fragility of the Western ego, which, as already explained, was inordinately shaped by its antithesis to Islam. After the terrorist attack of 2001 on the United States, it is truly remarkable how quickly so many intellectuals and policymakers were willing to abandon the arduous human labor that took human beings through two world wars and that painfully created the structure of legitimacy for the world in the twenty-first century, only to revert back to the dichotomous paradigms of the good versus evil, the forces of light against the forces of darkness, the knights of Christendom versus infidel barbarians, the clash of civilizations, and ultimately, the satanic religion that is out to haunt the world with demonic forces. The fragility of the Western ego leaves one wondering: If murderous terrorist attacks can generate such a powerfully effective and lucrative hate culture in the enlightened West, what could centuries of colonization, occupation, and brutalization produce in the Muslim world?

This, however, seems to me to be the wrong kind of question, or at least it seems to be a dangerous question. As the Qur'an consistently teaches, one injustice cannot justify another—in the same way that no amount of terrorism committed by people who affiliate themselves with the Islamic faith may possibly justify religious prejudice and bigotry, no amount of persecution or oppression may excuse or justify the harming or terrorizing of civilians in order to protest an injustice. I believe that the most rudimentary and basic moral order would recognize that if injustice is reciprocated by further injustice, we do not somehow miraculously end up with a just situation or with justice achieved. But this itself points to a quintessential affinity between all acts of terrorism—no matter the trappings, the ugliness remains the same. Whether terrorism is committed by a particular group holding a person hostage in order to win certain concessions or by an army holding a population hostage in order to force submission to its will, the moral quality of the act is the same. This, of course, is in moral theory alone; the reality is very different. In legal theory, for instance, the rich and the poor are treated according to the same standards of justice—although an ideal, it is seldom fulfilled. Nevertheless, the ideal must remain the normative yardstick, and the failures of reality must never be treated as normatively correct.

This is precisely why I find Islamophobia and Islam-hating so unsettling—it is not a concession to reality while upholding the ideal; it is a corruption of reality while deforming the ideal. Islam-hating is extreme in its ugliness because it stands everything on its head; it twists and distorts the space that Muslims are pushed into occupying in the modern age. If it is allowed to persist, then the whole Muslim experience since colonialism becomes nothing but a deceptive fantasy. Not only does this prejudice mean the failure of the ideals on which modernity was built and a regression to the exploitatively religious wars of the Crusades and countercrusades, but worst of all, it means that religion will be denied the role of the medicinal healer to the ignorance suffered in this age.

Among its endlessly circular and incoherently inconsistent long list of wrongs, Islamophobia rationalizes the continued victimization of disempowered people by dreaming up conspiracy theories in which the offenders pretend to be the victims. It claims that because Muslims are plagued by paranoid conspiracy theories, Muslims have a weak grasp of reality, but simultaneously, Islamophobes imagine every Muslim with a pulse to be a coconspirator in a massive plot for world domination. Islamophobes smugly declare that Muslims do not have cultural commitments to human rights and self-servingly announce that any commitment to human rights by a Muslim culture is not authentic and is therefore insincere. By the same logic, Shari'ah is denounced as fundamentally inconsistent with human rights, but at the same time, any jurisprudential doctrine consistent with human rights cannot be an authentic part of Shari'ah. This circular logic goes on and on: Islamophobia perpetuates violence and many abuses against Muslims by claiming that Muslims are not really victims because Muslims are inherently violent; it reaffirms its lies by accusing every challenge to its hate-filled view of Muslims of being a lie. It justifies the disproportionate and indiscriminate slaughter of Muslims as moral and just while contently claiming that Muslims lack a just war tradition. Islamophobes preach hate against Islam because by definition Islam only teaches hate. Islamophobes will gloat about how they belong to cultures that cherish the idea of liberty but as a matter of course will denounce any Muslim movement that claims the right to self-determination or that demands the right to live free of foreign occupation. Islamophobes will accuse Muslims of despotism and of being incapable of practicing democracy, but at the same time, they will seek to exclude Islamic parties from participation in democratic governance. Similarly, Islamophobes will vigilantly support the right of Christian parties or Christian organizations to be actively engaged in the political field and will defend Jewish religious parties calling for the application of Jewish law as a necessary part of the exercise of democracy. Meanwhile, they transform a bogeyman labeled "political Islam" into the embodied reincarnation of fascist ideology. Islamophobes pretend to honor the right to freedom of belief but spew nothing but venom at those who believe in Islam as their spiritual and moral system of guidance. Sadly, however, as is the case with most prejudices and biases, the problem is not the absence of reasoning or the paucity of accurate information. Most prejudices and biases persist because of the lack of moral will— the will to adopt conscientious and ethical positions toward others, especially those who because of habit or interest we have a reason to hate.

This is what makes Islamophobia particularly pernicious and dangerous. It is like anti-Semitism, racism, or other forms of bigotry founded on mythologies not subject to rational engagement or analytical persuasion. By training and education, Muslim scholars can engage those who hate in Islam's name by challenging their ignorance with theological and jurisprudential refutations. And for many years, I focused all my teaching and writing on challenging and deconstructing the beliefs and claims of Muslim bigots. But how can a Muslim scholar challenge the pathology of Islamophobia? I think this is one field where Muslims need to draw on the intellectual experiences of race theorists and also feminism—in other words, areas of specialty where the disempowered subaltern challenged dominant mythologies of power and domination and enjoyed a degree of success. I do admit, however, that Islamophobia does raise a set of concerns that are unique and especially destructive, and I do worry that the West is simply not accustomed to thinking of or resisting this kind of bigotry. Here, I am not just referring to the specific historical legacy pitting the West against Islam but to the dissimulations of Islamophobia as a plausible intellectual position. When it comes to religion, as opposed to race or ethnicity, the Western intellectual heritage has developed a doctrine of religious tolerance, which, at least in some Western countries, means that the state treats all religions equally. Although international law condemns all forms of religious bigotry and hatred, in the Western intellectual heritage the wrongfulness of this kind of bigotry is greatly modified by the principle of freedom of speech.[34] Explicit or outright racism, as that found in *The Turner Diaries*, for instance, although tolerated at the margins of legality, is rightly condemned as immoral and unethical, and so most respectable newspapers will recognize explicit racism and refuse to publish it. But religious bigotry occupies a different category altogether. Religious bigotry is still seen from within the paradigm of freedom of belief and freedom of speech. Culturally speaking, institutions and individuals will feel far more conscious and also uncomfortable in tolerating someone who hates a race or ethnicity as opposed to someone who hates a religion. This was quite apparent when the TLC television network cancelled its show *All-American Muslim* because of a very public Islamophobic campaign and that forced several advertisers to publicly withdraw their endorsements. Most telling was the complete silence of public intellectuals about the event, as if this were a problem of competing religious preferences being fought out over a show. For many well-intentioned Western intellectuals, while they are bothered by the toxic speech of Islamophobia, they do not know how to resist it without appearing to support Islam as a system of belief. They might be for tolerance, but Islamophobia remains a speech problem—it does not rise to the level of an offense or crime. Many of my colleagues and friends see Islamophobia as the ignorant speaking to the ignorant, but ultimately, there is no crime committed or person getting hurt.

This is actually the point that I have tried to reflect on and study. Islamophobia quickly appealed to people who were predisposed to hating Islam because with all the ugliness of terrorism and violence, there was much anxiety and hate that needed to be directed somewhere. From this perspective, the most that would happen because of Islamophobes is that one would either not believe or believe them and eventually tire of them as more compelling problems would come to demand his/her attention. But like all hate speech, there are real victims who get hurt in very real ways because of this bigotry. Since the explosion of this type of speech in 2002 and onward, there has been an ever-rising number of victims of hate crimes. These hate crimes have very real victims suffering irreparable damage. I do not want to get gory, but such crimes included an imam having his eyes gouged out, a mother being shot and killed in a German court, taxi drivers and shop owners being assaulted and killed, abductions and rapes of women wearing the hijab, numerous properties, including mosques, suffering arson attacks or some other damage, numerous people unfairly terminated from their jobs, and hundreds refused the right to board a plane or suffering other forms of harassment. Governments all over the Western world violated the privacy rights of thousands and investigated and arrested hundreds but won very few convictions. Add to this the number of Islamophobes like Robert Spencer, Walid Phares, or Walid Shoebat who played critical roles in getting people investigated and livelihoods destroyed or who helped place people on lists that eventually got them renditioned to countries where they were brutally tortured—and the unimaginable chilling effect that all of this has had on philanthropic activity among Muslims, which after all is only an integral part of the freedom of speech.[35]

In so many forums, when I lecture about the real human costs of the indulgences in Islamophobia, some people invariably object that they came to the lecture to hear a talk on Shari'ah, but instead they only got to hear me whine about the alleged suffering of Muslims, which they are sure is highly exaggerated anyway. This type of criticism is itself typical of racists and bigots—denying that the suffering exists is part of the dehumanization of the victim—of rendering the victim silent and mute. Denying the victim's suffering is part of the paradigm of bigotry that constructs the victim as a consummate liar—the object of bigotry lies about his/her intentions, plans, conspiracies, and suffering.

Aside from the narratives of individual suffering, I fear the complacency of democracies because of the false sense of security and the sense of moral confidence or arrogance that they permit. In our age, democracy represents the enlightened way of life, the path of goodness, and uprightness. Democracies have become a symbol of human enlightenment because they succeed in doing what other systems cannot do, and that is respecting the civic rights of their citizenry. But one of the very powerful mythologies of democracy is that just because they respect the civic rights of their citizenry, this also means that democracies respect human rights. But this does not necessarily follow, and indeed, because of the sense of enlightened moralism and cultural superiority that often pervade the external outlook of successful democracies, they righteously end up undervaluing the human rights of outsiders or noncitizens. As the histories of colonialism and imperialism demonstrate, empowered with a sense of self-righteousness and confident of their well-rooted sense of humanism, democracies will end up minimizing the import of human-rights denial that they perpetuate against perceived outsiders.

On the issue of Islamophobia, my greatest worry is that this sense of confidence and righteousness will have a lulling effect on the majority of those who could do something about the problem before it is too late. The success of Geert Wilders's Freedom Party in the Netherlands and Europe as well as the rise of right-wing anti-immigrant movements across Europe should have been quite alarming. Wilders is famous for his pathological hatred of Islam and his comparing of the Qur'an to Hitler's *Mein Kampf.*[36] The terrorist attacks in Norway in 2011 by Anders Breivik, who was heavily influenced by the writings of American Islamophobes, killed seventy-seven people, which is to say the least alarming.[37] But long before 9/11, what has been consistently ignored and marginalized in the consciousness of the West and what the West has yet to interrogate its own conscience about is the Bosnian genocide. What is often forgotten is the extent to which Serbian nationalistic ideology relied very heavily on the archetypal constructions of Islamophobia. Furthermore, apologists for the Serbian perpetrators of the genocide argued that the Serbs were protecting Europe from the wrath of Islamic fundamentalism and from the birth of Islamism in the heart of Europe.[38] One of the most shocking political admissions confirming that Europe failed to intervene to stop the ongoing genocide because of its anxieties about the possibility of a European Muslim nation was documented by President Bill Clinton. In a conversation in 1993, President Clinton noted to the French president, François Mitterrand, that he did not understand Europe's reluctance to intervene. The French president in effect responded that it is due time that Europe reclaimed its Christian heritage.[39] Beyond Europe, Islamophobic propaganda has been exploited in the commission of atrocities against Muslims in a number of countries and conflicts.[40]

If it continues unchecked, Islamophobia is likely to produce more ugliness and suffering, but will it have a deep long-term effect on Western culture? I am not sure anyone can answer this question because much depends on whether there are further terrorist attacks, military invasions, or other world events that might elicit the madness of the crowds in one direction or another. I think that thus far, Islamophobia has had a very minimal impact on academic and scholarly research on Islam in the West. Academic presses and journals continue to publish sophisticated and rich studies on Muslims and Islam. So I do admit that from the proverbial ivory tower of academia, it does appear that Islamophobes have not succeeded in altering, at least, the more nuanced and informed discourse on Islam. However, I make the following preliminary observations based on my experiences, but a more systematic study of the identified elements is needed. Since 9/11, I have noticed that both in the United States and in Europe there is a greater reliance on self-identified experts on Islam, such as Nina Shea or David Horowitz, instead of academics or scholars in the fields of antiterrorism, national security, legal proceedings involving expert testimony, congressional hearings, and conservative think tanks. I have witnessed a clear trend in these circles to rely on individuals who position themselves as experts on the Islamic threat, even if the objectivity of these individuals is seriously in doubt because of strong evangelical or pro-Israeli views. This has been accompanied by a tendency to steer away from specialists who present a complex or multilayered view of any Islamic context. At the same time, there has been an unmistakable tendency to doubt native Muslim voices that present a nondogmatic and nonstereotyped view of Islam. Even Muslim academics have found their credibility rendered suspect in public policy forums by an irrefutable presumption that they only "whitewash" the truth. This social alienation from public forums has placed many Muslim intellectuals in impossible situations. The highly charged and polarized atmosphere to which Islamophobes and puritanical Muslims contribute becomes too toxic for the survival of any rational arguments seeking to find moderated and balanced positions. Put bluntly, my experience has been that Islamophobia has only served to help the cause of extremists on every front in the Muslim and non-Muslim worlds. Islamophobia has greatly hurt the cause of the moderates in Iran and has greatly helped the cause of puritans in Egypt and Tunisia. It has also strengthened Wahhabi Islam inside of Saudi Arabia and has been exploited by Islamic conservatives in Pakistan, Ethiopia, Somalia, Mali, and Mauritania. The Internet has ended censorship, but it has also allowed discourses irresponsibly generated in one cultural context to be received in another culture without any mediating context. Therefore, Islamophobic discourses casually bantered around in the West are transmitted to English-proficient Muslim countries as the predominant voice of the West, or *the* voice of the West. Understandably, witnessing their faith maligned time and again in national and international forums, the average Muslim intellectual is tempted to avoid giving ammunition to the Islamophobes through self-critical discourses or becomes zealously protective of all Islamic symbols and unsympathetic to any critical remarks from any quarter.

Chapter Seven

God the Universal

The Prophet of Islam described the act of engaging the self, critically and honestly—the confrontation of the self with the self—as the highest form of jihad (*al-jihad al-akbar*, or the greater jihad).[1] It is quite true that it is very hard to gaze long and hard at oneself and see the inequities and faults, not as an excuse for nihilistic self-effacement and apathy but as part of an ongoing struggle to cleanse, purify, and grow with divinity or into divinity. Indeed, this is much harder than any armed war one could engage in. Living to persistently and patiently sacrifice the ego for the love of God is much harder than a simple death in the name of God. The sages of Islamic mysticism have written so much about the perils of leading a life without introspection and self-criticism and of the maladies of a soul that allows fear, anxiety, and insecurity to distract it from the greatest jihad—the jihad against the self.[2] Without introspection and self-judgment a person grows complacent with his/her ego until all sense of reasonable and just self-perception is gone. And according to the sages of Sufism and Islamic theosophy, self-knowledge and knowledge of God are inseparable.

If at the level of the individual a person who fails to be self-critical becomes so self-indulgent to the point of losing the ability, or perhaps courage, to differentiate between right and wrong, what becomes of societies that do the same? Earlier, I explained that Shari'ah does not only call for individual moral introspection but for society as a whole to be concerned with promoting moral goodness and to resist what is abhorrent and reprehensible. But it stands to reason that if society as a whole, for whatever reasons, does not encourage analytical and critical discourses and has grown accustomed to hearing old truths affirmed again and again without variation, this society will stagnate and become apathetic toward the excitement of ideas or the search for originality. In this kind of society, there will truly be, as discussed earlier, the unthought, the unthinkable, and the forgotten. The importance of this point is underscored by the tragic fate of the Arab Spring. Although in 2011 and 2012 there were revolutions across the Muslim world, I regret that the above describes the continuing fortunes of critical discourses in much of the Muslim world.

Is this too pessimistic an assessment? After all, the Arab revolutions have been a source of considerable hope, and arguably, this level of sacrifice and bravery cannot come about without the power of introspection and transformation. As I discuss later, the revolutions did in fact generate discourses, such as the Azhar document, that potentially could be culturally and intellectually transformative. However, the modern Muslim experience in the postcolonial era does strongly suggest further introspective caution.

In 1936, an Arab writer, 'Ali 'Abd Allah al-Qusaymi, started out his book: "In Egypt there is a revolution, in Syria there is a revolution, in Palestine there is a revolution, in the countries of the Maghreb there is a revolution . . . in every country and every direction there is revolution!"[3] The author poignantly describes the great upheaval sweeping through many Arab countries after the fall of the Ottoman Caliphate and the rise of Arab nationalism and also constitutionalism in what the historian Albert Hourani appropriately described as the Arab liberal age.[4] From the point of view of someone living at the time, the period must have seemed truly transformative and promising, but for a variety of reasons, as I discuss in the chapters that follow, the promise never materialized. What strikes me the most about al-Qusaymi's writings is that after the statement above, he goes on to describe the Saudi revolution in Arabia at the time while defending it as the best of all revolutions. Al-Qusaymi was one among many Muslim intellectuals who believed that the future of Islam is best served by the Wahhabi revolution in Arabia because it was seen as representing an Islamic renaissance and a return to an enlightenment of sorts. In the nineteenth century, Western Orientalists such as Louis Olivier de Corancez, J. L. Burckhardt, and Harry St. John Philby projected a romanticized image of the Wahhabis as the representatives of the true Islamic faith and the reformers ridding Islam of its superstitions and stagnant tradition. Some of these Orientalists compared the founder of Wahhabism to Martin Luther and the Wahhabis to the European Reformation.[5] It has to be more than a coincidence that a number of Western-educated Muslim intellectuals repeated the same jargon. Speaking before an English audience in 1929, Shaykh Hafiz Wahba emphasized that the Wahhabis represent nothing less than the revolution of reason against the oppression of the church and priesthood—a veritable re-creation of the Enlightenment brought about by the Protestant Reformation in Europe.[6] As explained later, I can understand the positive assessments by the Western Orientalists, who for the most part were officers in Her Majesty's Armed Forces and projected onto Wahhabis their own insecure and misguided images of how Islam *should be*—a religion of simple desert folks who know nothing about the burdens of civilization. And so these writers celebrate the Wahhabis' desert austerity and egalitarianism and the Wahhabis' hostility to individuality, art, music, literature, and philosophy. They have much praise for the wisdom of tribal chiefs, their accessibility, and their absolute authority and despotism. Most of all, they repeatedly underscore that all of these characteristics are most fitting for the natural inclinations of the Muslim mind and its culture.[7] So in short, Wahhabism is good enough for Muslims. The extent to which these writers struggle with their own projected stereotypes can be seen, for instance, in passages in which Corancez expresses outrage at the Turks, who he claims are shamelessly outwardly expressive about their homosexuality, but he is comforted by the fact that homosexuality barely exists among the Wahhabis.[8]

Far less understandable are prominent Muslim intellectuals, such as Rashid Rida, discussed in the following chapter, who minimized the import of the acts of intolerance and violence committed by the Wahhabis and defended them because of one political perspective or another. It took an incredible amount of oblivious lack of introspection and self-criticism for the momentum of the 1930s to be aborted. It took an even greater amount of complacency, apologetics, and a failure to nourish the ethical imperative of the greater jihad within generation after generation until we got to the point that once again new revolutions were needed to express people's renewed sense of frustration. There is a sense of truly tragic irony that in 1936 the liberal revolutions were threatened in a very remote and distant way by the nascent Wahhabi specter rising in the desert of Arabia. Today, the Arab revolutions calling for liberty are once again confronting the threat of Wahhabism—but as we will see, this Wahhabism is powerful, rich, and dominant, and it poses a very serious threat of aborting and neutralizing whatever progress these revolutions achieved. The only hope for overcoming the challenge of puritanism this time around is in learning to promote the personal jihad of honest self-criticism and introspection so as to open a dynamic process for engagement, catharsis, and growth. Numerous acts of cruelty and ugliness were perpetrated in the name of higher causes, human idols, and divine destinies without being Islamically challenged or impeded.

Muslim discourses involving a critical appraisal of the self, for the most part, remain captive to the postcolonial experience. These discourses are sufficiently politicized and polarized to the extent that a Muslim intellectual who takes a critical approach to the Islamic tradition often feels that he is stepping into a highly volatile minefield. It is difficult for contemporary Muslim scholars to take a critical position on a wide array of topics, including violence, women, relations with non-Muslims, the Caliphate, the idea of Muslim unity (*umma*), and a host of other issues without becoming the subject of suspicions and even accusations. In addition, it has become a rather powerful rhetorical device to contend that the West is perpetuating false universalisms and to accuse Muslim critics of being deluded into accepting these universalisms as a God-given truth. These Muslim critics, it is claimed, then project the West's truth onto the Islamic tradition, as if what the West sees as true and good must necessarily be so and therefore must be adopted by all Muslims. Not surprisingly, critics of Western universalism and the proponents of Muslim exceptionalism are often able to position themselves as the jealous guardians of an Islamic authenticity and a supposed genuineness and, in doing so, are often able to marginalize their opponents as heretical or lacking authenticity.[9] As an extension of the relativism argument, it is often argued that it is immaterial whether the West or anyone else in the world is offended or shocked by the legal and social practices of Muslims. Islam, it is argued, has its own set of standards for justice and righteousness, and it is of no consequence if those standards happen to be inconsistent with the moral sensitivities of non-Muslims. This argument was repeated often in the context of justifying and defending the Salman Rushdie affair, the destruction of the Buddha statues in Afghanistan, and the treatment of women by the Taliban, and it has also been the subject of a very recent controversy, which I will discuss later, on the application of hudud punishments in Egypt and other countries. On its face, this argument is attractive because it seems to affirm a sense of Islamic autonomy and authentic uniqueness that is arguably consistent with the notion that God is sovereign and that the divine law is not in any way contingent on the whim of human beings. In a sense, it is as if one claims it matters not if the world thinks that Muslims are acting unreasonably because Muslims only answer to God. But, of course, this is not the only possibility. One can make a reciprocity-fairness kind of argument: it matters not what the world thinks because the world does not care if Muslims think that the world is acting unreasonably. Or one can make a process-type argument: it matters not what the world thinks because there is no way of verifying what the world thinks. We only hear claims of unreasonableness made by the powerful and dominant, but the rest of the world is for all practical purposes silent. There is also the philosophical objection questioning whether reasonableness as a concept has a coherent meaning that communicates something of substance at all.

The point is that the issue of what is now commonly described as cultural relativism, exceptionalism, or particularism versus universalism is rather complex, and there are a number of nuanced ways to approach it. Often cross-cultural critiques or even value-based self-critiques are hopelessly divisive and polarized because people are talking at cross-purposes or are methodologically unclear. The tension between objective or objectified claims or standards and more subjectively relativistic contestations, especially as it relates to the Islamic context, to be done justice needs a separate book-length treatment. But I do need to deal with the issue to the extent that it helps us understand the epistemological and normative world of Islamic puritans and also to the extent necessary for setting forth an argument for reclaiming Shari'ah.

I think that any effort to deal with this issue must start by acknowledging that Islam itself, like all religions, is founded on certain universals, such as mercy, justice, compassion, and dignity.[10] The very concept of Shari'ah as the path to and from God is necessarily premised on the idea of human good, which in turn embodies what are known as rational or natural moral values that are at the heart of any set of obligations that might be warranted under the law. These rational values precede the law but are recognized by the law. In other words, the law does not create these rational values because they exist regardless of the law. I will return to this argument because of its critical importance, but for now it is important to note that the Qur'an itself consistently uses terminology that presupposes the existence of universal values and presumes such values to be recognizable by human beings universally. Much of the Qur'anic discourse on values such as justice, mercy, truth, kindness, and generosity would make little sense if one rejects the existence of universal values.[11] The Qur'an states, for instance: "And God does not desire for human beings to suffer injustice."[12] A statement such as this generates layers of meaning, but it is reasonable to conclude that the Qur'an recognizes certain ethical principles as universally applicable and pertinent. Furthermore, claims of ontological truth, whether based on reason or revelation, are not anathema to Islam.[13] From an Islamic perspective, Muslims are not forbidden, and in my opinion are even encouraged, to search for moral universals that could serve as shared and common goals with humanity at large.[14] This seems to me to be an essential characteristic of a universal religion that is addressed to humanity at large and not to an exclusive cultural or social group. The Qur'an insists that it is the bearer of a message to all humankind, and not to a particular tribe or race.[15] Moreover, the Qur'an asserts that the Prophet Muhammad, and in fact the Qur'an itself, was sent to all peoples as a blessing and mercy.[16] The Qur'an also persistently emphasizes the ethical quality of mercy as a core attribute of God and as a fundamental and basic pursuit of Islam.[17] The Qur'an informs human beings that God has decreed and mandated mercy even on himself and therefore is bound to extend it to human beings. Not only that, but the Qur'an links God's mercy to peace. Put differently, to enjoy a state of peace is to be blessed with mercy.[18] Human beings are in turn bound to pursue, establish, and spread mercy and compassion in all matters and in all interactions. Acts of mercy, the quality of mercifulness, and the enjoyment of peace are recognized, felt, and appreciated by all human beings. Thus, it stands to reason that if Islam is a universal message addressed to all human beings and if this message is founded on the principle of mercifulness, then Muslims cannot afford to claim that they are not concerned with how the rest of the world sees and evaluates their actions. A universal religion and a merciful faith must be accessible and accountable to others so that it can remain pertinent to humanity at large. A universal religion that is neither accessible nor accountable to humanity at large becomes like a private and closed club with bylaws and practices that make sense only to its members. Even worse, a merciful faith whose mercifulness is not comprehensible to others or whose logic of mercy is not understood by others becomes self-serving and ultimately arrogant.

It seems to me that responding to criticisms from interlocutors by engaging in a knee-jerk reaction of protesting false Western universals and rejecting introspective self-critical approaches plays well into the hands of a siege mentality that has pervaded much of contemporary Muslim thought. If critical approaches to the tradition will be consistently dismissed as Western influenced or as a form of "Westoxification" (a derogatory expression used to describe self-hating Muslims who are in awe of everything Western to the point that they seem to be intoxicated on the West), it is difficult to imagine how Muslims will be able to emerge out of what might be described as a state of intellectual dissonance and into a more constructive engagement with modernity. By intellectual dissonance, I mean a state of social and cultural schizophrenia in which Muslims experience simultaneously the challenge of modernity, a severe alienation and evasiveness toward the Islamic intellectual experience, and at the same time a symbolic identification and an idealization of that experience. There are a number of scholars who have argued that most modern Muslim societies are characterized by a cultural schizophrenia in which there are profound distortions in the self-consciousness clearly exhibited in irreconcilable and inconsistent social and intellectual practices.[19]

What is meant by this is that there is an enormous gap between what Muslim societies declare to be unassailable and sacrosanct and their actual lived experiences. For instance, as a matter of social practice and the lived experience, one finds that in Muslim societies, what is considered desirable and prestigious is symbolically associated with the West. Socially, for example, holding an academic degree from a Western university, being well acquainted with dons of Western literature such as Shakespeare or Bernard Shaw, listening to the latest in Western music, wearing the latest Western fashions, enjoying the latest Western consumer labels in all things—ranging from fancy pen labels to sunglasses, to cell phones—and craving the latest Western products, from furniture to electronics, to cars are all considered signs of social prestige and status. Fields like medicine or engineering are taught in English at Muslim universities. In addition, fields like law, history, sociology, and anthropology in Muslim universities are imitations of Western categories and concepts. Even in a subject like Islamic studies, it is a sign of prestige and status for a professor in this field to study in the West or to master the translated works of Orientalist scholars.

This last point is not well known or understood and deserves to be addressed in some detail. One would assume that a field like Islamic studies is sufficiently close to the national feelings of Muslims that it would be permeated with concepts and categories produced by native Muslim scholarship. Surprisingly, however, the disciplines of Islamic history and law are thoroughly dominated by concepts and categories shaped by Western scholarship produced mostly in the first half of the twentieth century. There are many illustrative examples of this, but I will focus on some of the most influential ideas generated by Western scholarship which are uncritically accepted by Muslim academics and intellectuals. At the beginning of the twentieth century, Orientalists relying on some rhetorical jargon and idiomatic expressions found in Muslim texts—jargon and expressions which they grossly misunderstood—claimed that Islamic law stopped developing in the fourth/tenth century after Muslims "closed the doors of *ijtihad*." According to these Orientalists, after the doors of *ijtihad* were closed, for a thousand years, Muslim jurists limited themselves to repeating and regurgitating the ideas produced in the first four hundred. All along, however, Orientalist scholars claimed, Islamic jurisprudence was always theoretical and not practical—a product of speculative juristic thought that was applied as a legal system only in very limited ways and during very short historical periods. Therefore, Orientalist scholars contended, Islamic law was never a living legal system but was always like a museum piece—rarified and sanctified but entirely irrelevant to the lived experiences of Muslims.

These Orientalist claims from beginning to end are no better than mythology. They do not comport with the historical realities of Islamic law because not only were the doors of *ijtihad* never closed, but more fundamentally, there were no doors that could be closed, and no one had the authority to close these proverbial doors.[20] Islamic law continued to develop at least until the tenth/sixteenth century, and in fact, some of the most important and intellectually rigorous scholars and doctrines of Islamic jurisprudence came to be as late as the ninth/fifteenth century. Furthermore, Islamic law was implemented by the judiciaries of various dynasties and empires throughout

Islamic history, but it was supplemented by administrative and regulatory rules issued by the different governments in power at different times. Nevertheless, despite the fact that the Orientalist approach on this matter is not supported by the historical record, Muslim academics and intellectuals throughout the twentieth century and to this day continue to repeat the dogma about closing the doors of *ijtihad* and even theorize about how to solve this fictitious problem. Furthermore, the average Muslim academic and intellectual uncritically accepts the idea that Islamic law remained a theoretical construct for most of its existence. Ironically, the Orientalist paradigm regarding Islamic law played an essential role in the spread of Salafi thought, which idealized the first fifty years of Islam and treated the balance of Islamic legal history as a marginal irrelevancy. This in good measure was due to the fact that Muslims did not produce an alternative literary discourse deconstructing the Orientalist paradigms. It is very telling that the challenge to the ideas of closing the doors of *ijtihad* and the impracticality of Islamic law came only recently from scholars living in the West—not the Muslim world.

Orientalist scholars dealt with history in a rather peculiar fashion. Typical of European historiographical practice of the early twentieth century, Orientalist scholars focused on macrohistories of the Muslim world in which they described the history of Islam in general and broad outlines. Orientalist scholars treated the Muslim world as a set, unitary category and produced universal histories of Islam in which the Middle East was placed at the center of the Islamic experience. Interestingly enough, Muslim historiography in the premodern period, especially post seventh/thirteenth century, produced a very substantial amount of regional and biographical histories as well as histories of nongovernmental institutions, such as particular schools of jurisprudence, and histories of sectarian groups. Although Orientalist scholars played an important role in editing and printing some of these works, most of the histories they wrote attempted to outline the general progress of Islam while capturing, so to speak, the true spirit of Islam. Orientalist scholars projected an image of what they considered to be the true and real Islam. They tended to see the genuine Islam to have lasted a very short period of time—roughly fifty years. According to the Orientalists, the Caliphate became corrupted with the start of the Umayyad dynasty, the first dynasty of Islam, and completely disintegrated around the fourth/tenth century, after the peak of the Abbasid empire, the second dynasty of Islam.

From this basic framework, several conclusions unfolded. Orientalists made five major points that they consistently repeated and emphasized: First, the history of Islam was one of frustrated expectations. After a relatively short period of great success, Islamic institutions and indeed Islam itself continued to disintegrate as it went from bad to worse. The Islamic legacy was portrayed as unitary and singular, and it is a progressive story of failure. Second, Muslim jurists and scholars went from dreamers to political quietists. According to Orientalist scholars, Muslims articulated a theory of government that was highly idealistic and impractical. However, as Muslim institutions failed, Muslims migrated from political idealism to cynical pragmatism. Increasingly, Muslim jurists accepted the de facto state of affairs, adopted political quietism, and became conservative legitimists of the status quo. Third, although Orientalists insisted that Islamic law was speculative and theoretical, inconsistently they contended that Muslims were not theoretically oriented. Unlike Christians, Muslims did not emphasize theology or correct belief systems, but correct practice. Therefore, Orientalist scholars maintained that in Islam there is no orthodoxy but only orthopraxy. Fourth, since Orientalists saw Muslims as a unitary and singular entity, they maintained that Islam divided the world into two abodes—the abode of Islam and the abode of infidels or war. According to Orientalists, Muslims held a bipolar view of the world pursuant to which they divided the earth into two abodes, and they also believed that the abode of Islam was in a perpetual state of war with the abode of infidels. Fifth, largely due to this understanding, Orientalists ignored the sizeable number of Muslim minorities throughout history. In fact, Orientalists argued that Muslims were accustomed to being in power and control, and therefore, Muslims were oblivious toward minorities living in non-Muslim lands. In essence, Orientalists treated Muslim minorities as marginal to the Muslim reality—as unrepresentative of the true Islam—and projected this belief onto Muslims themselves. Therefore, according to Orientalists, although Muslim minorities made up 30 percent of the Muslim population of the world, since these minorities were not a part of the abode of Islam, they were insignificant in terms of defining the Islamic reality.

These five Orientalist positions, although based on a kernel of truth, for the most part are historical fictions. The realities of Muslims were far more complex than the Orientalist scholars of the nineteenth and twentieth centuries made them out to be. In fact, these five positions owe their existence to the projections of Western scholars struggling to come to terms with their own anxieties about Islam far more than being based on lived Muslim experiences. On every single one of the five issues, the Islamic historical reality turned out to be far more complex and rich than portrayed in Orientalist scholarship.[21] For instance, premodern Muslims did not hold a bipolar view of the world but did believe in a general broad-based spiritual unity of all Muslims. Premodern Muslims discussed many different types of abodes, depending on the particular objective being considered, whether territorial, theological, jurisdictional, or legal. But in all cases, it is a gross oversimplification to claim that in Islam, the world is divided into the abode of Islam and the abode of infidels or war.[22] Such a claim is simply not supported by the textual discussions or debates found in the classical sources. Similarly, premodern Muslim scholars were neither quietists nor activists. Their attitudes toward power were far more diverse and complex than any of the constructions formulated by Orientalist scholars.[23]

Regardless of the arguments for and against the Orientalist positions outlined above, the remarkable fact is that among academics and intellectuals in the Muslim world, these ideas became widely held and repeated.[24] Most Muslim academics and intellectuals uncritically repeat the dogma about closing the doors of *ijtihad*, orthopraxy, quietism, and the two abodes of Islam without substantial revision. Furthermore, Muslims accept the notion that the Islamic legacy is one in which Islam peaked in its first fifty years and that the history of Islam is one of frustrated idealism, corrupted dreams, and unfortunate compromises. It is nothing short of amazing that in the postcolonial age, the paradigms of Muslim academics and intellectuals regarding their own history continue to be based on the contributions of Orientalist scholars of the first half of the twentieth century. Muslim academics and intellectuals have not substantially developed, revised, or reconsidered the inherited wisdom of Orientalist scholarship. It is not that the Orientalist positions are not challenged and deconstructed at all—they are. But whatever intellectual challenges are posed to the Orientalist positions, they invariably come from the West and filter back to the Muslim world. In good part, this is due to the prestige factor. For the educated and academic segments of society, as noted earlier, prestige and status continues to be defined by reference to the West. The academics and intellectuals who gain the most official and institutional respect and those who reach the highest status are those who attained an advanced degree in the West and those who in their writings or lectures are able to reference the works of Western authors. One of the very telling indications is the lofty and envied status achieved by those who study in Western educational institutions in the Muslim world, such as the American University of Cairo or the American University of Beirut.

As I argued earlier, Muslims suffer from a state of amnesia regarding their precolonial history, and what they do know or react to comes very often from Western constructions of Islam. Growing up in the Middle East and later on lecturing and teaching in many parts of the Muslim world, I became increasingly struck by the fact that wherever I went, I found that Muslims' knowledge of their history is limited to the Prophet and four Caliphs that ruled after his death. Otherwise, their knowledge of Islamic history did not extend beyond a few selective anecdotal stories of glamour or glory. Beyond that, the intelligentsia regurgitated the inherited mind-sets of Orientalist scholars and even based their own agendas of reform on these inherited wisdoms. It continues to confound me when I hear educated Muslims lecture and write at length about the tragedy of the closing of the doors of *ijtihad* and the compelling need to reopen these doors once again. It is similarly confounding when I hear the Muslim intelligentsia repeat the dogma about the abode of Islam and the abode of war or infidels. These categories of thought could not have come from research in the Islamic textual tradition because such a research would have quickly challenged these long-held ideas. Considering the dynamics of higher education in the Muslim world, it is near certain that these ideas came from secondary and not primary sources—more specifically, secondary sources written by Orientalists and their Muslim students. Other than the amnesia regarding most of the precolonial history, what facilitates the unthinking borrowing from the West is the absence of honest self-criticism and introspection—in short, the frustration of the critical imperative in modern Islam.

Despite the widespread dependence of the Muslim world on all things Western, there is a severe reluctance to come to terms with the full implications and consequences of this dependence. In fact, the extent of this dependence and its pervasiveness is rarely admitted, and often, Western ideas are co-opted and declared as genuinely Islamic while obfuscating their Western lineage. For example, Sayyid Qutb's influential and famous work *Milestones on the Road* offered a description of the genuine Islamic society and the true Islamic faith; but in reality, Qutb's book did nothing more than attempt to add an Islamic veneer to a thoroughly fascist ideological construct. Qutb was heavily influenced by the German philosopher Carl Schmitt, and although Qutb does not once mention Schmitt in his works, many of Qutb's ideas, constructs, and phrases are clearly adapted from the works of Schmitt. Of course, what helped disseminate Qutb's ideas and establish his reputation as a genuine Islamist was the fact that he died a martyr—executed by ex-president Nasser in Egypt in 1966.

The recent events in France regarding the planned ban on wearing the veil in public institutions served to underscore the pervasive impact of the West on Muslim efforts to search for and articulate a genuine Islamic authenticity. As mentioned earlier, the status and position of the hijab, or veil, is a contested issue that has acquired clear political and sociological overtones in modern Islam. Furthermore, considering the evidentiary basis in Islamic jurisprudence for veiling, the practice deserves to be critically reevaluated and restudied.[25] Puritans and Wahhabis, however, have been strongly opposed to any such effort and have expended a considerable amount of resources in spreading their own particular style and form of veiling around the Muslim world. French plans to ban all religious symbols in public institutions raised a storm of controversy in the Muslim world, as many Muslims considered the proposed laws to be motivated by a clear anti-Muslim animus. Perhaps most importantly, as a direct response to the French plans, a large number of Muslim scholars and activists rushed to emphasize that the veil is a fundamental Islamic obligation. An influential jurist like Yusuf al-Qaradawi, in an interview on Al Jazeera channel, eagerly stressed that it is beyond dispute that the veil is an absolute Islamic obligation and that all Muslim scholars have reached consensus on this point. Meanwhile, however, the Grand Mufti of Egypt, Shaykh Tantawi, disagreeing with al-Qaradawi, expressed his view that the veil is not the sole and exclusive issue worthy of consideration when deciding how to react to the French proposed laws. Tantawi argued that the duty of the veil has to be weighed against more compelling factors such as the necessity of educating Muslim women, and, therefore, how French Muslims should appropriately react to the proposed French legislation warrants further consideration and reflection. Tantawi was met with an uproar of protests expressing outrage at what was perceived as an attempt to appease the French government at the expense of a sacrosanct Islamic religious duty. But as is rather typical of many Muslim dynamics in the contemporary age, in this process, what was deemed to be genuinely and authentically Islamic was defined largely in reaction to political dynamics originating with the West. In an effort to resist the perceived intolerance and belligerence of a Western country, many around the Muslim world emphasized and elevated the status of the practice of veiling into a major and fundamental religious obligation, and in order to present a united front against France, many Muslims declared the law of veiling to be beyond discussion or debate. In my view, this way of dealing with Islamic doctrine has been devastating for the tradition. Whether the veil is an Islamic obligation or not, Islamic law should not be defined in such a reactive and uncritical fashion. It would have been much more appropriate to criticize France's secularism as fanatic and extreme but without transforming Islamic law into an appendage to international politics.

The Muslim search for originality and authenticity is challenged by the ambiguous positions of both the Islamic tradition and the West. What appears Islamic could be Western, and what is thought of and treated as Western could be firmly anchored in the Islamic tradition. But in order to engage a process of discernment and differentiation, it is necessary to undertake an introspective and self-critical discourse. The absence of such a discourse has resulted in extreme ideological and social inconsistencies and disconnects—what writers referred to as cultural schizophrenia. Put bluntly, in this state, the Islamic heritage is sanctified and rarified in theory but marginalized and ignored in practice. On the other hand, the impact of the West is minimized and understated in theory, but in practice, the West's impact is all engrossing and nearly hegemonic. Specifically in relation to Islam, there is a powerful intellectual dissonance in which Islam occupies inconsistent positions and plays irreconcilable roles and in which Islam is simultaneously embraced and discarded.

There are many manifestations of this intellectual dissonance in regard to Islam. For example, consider the fact that the original nature of Islamic law is based on indeterminacy. Islamic law is represented by many living and extinct schools of jurisprudence that disagree on numerous points of law, and that produced on any particular legal matter as many as ten different opinions.[26] Islamic law has a fluid character, where it takes shape through an incremental and cumulative process of growth based on building on precedent and analogy. In that sense, classical Islamic law is similar in character to the classical common law system, which was represented by legal guilds producing competing doctrines of law. Nevertheless, throughout the twentieth century, Muslim lawyers had superimposed the paradigms, criteria, and processes of the civil law system on Islamic law.

In the age of modernity, most Muslim nations experienced the wholesale borrowing and transplanting of civil law systems, particularly the French civil and criminal codes.[27] In effect, instead of the dialectical and indeterminate methodology of traditional Islamic jurisprudence, Muslim nations opted for a more centralized, determinative, and often code-based system of law.[28] These developments only contributed to the power of the state, which had become extremely intrusive and which was now capable of a level of centralization that was inconceivable just two centuries ago. The civil law is code based and is a highly determinative system of law founded on holistic and systematic theories of jurisprudence that can accommodate different schools of thought only to a limited extent. In addition, the civil law system does not rely on precedents for its development to the same extent as in the common law system.

Practically every effort at reforming Islamic law in the modern age has completely ignored its common law character and has projected onto it the logic of the civil law system. Muslim modernists, who attempted to reform Islamic jurisprudence, were heavily influenced by the civil law system and thus sought to resist the indeterminate fluidity of Islamic law and increase its unitary and centralized character. This was due to nothing more than the fact that most Muslim modernists, who also tended to be lawyers, were trained in the civil law system. Muslim activists who did not have legal training at all did not treat Islamic law as a legal system. Being very poorly informed about the processes and mechanics of Islamic law, they treated it as an ideology—not law. On the other hand, those trained in law were usually trained in the civil law system, and when they approached Islamic law, they did so as if Shari'ah was a civil law system of law. Consequently, between ideology and the civil law, in the modern age, it is not an exaggeration to say that Islamic law, as it existed and was practiced in the classical age, does not exist.

Other indicators of intellectual dissonance produce equally incoherent results. As discussed earlier, Muslims often make the rhetorical claim that Islamic law is perfect—that contained within Islamic law is the salvation of the Muslim nation. Nevertheless, although not aware of its source, most Muslims accept the claim that Islamic law was ignored for most of its historical existence—that Islamic law was not the product of a dynamic and dialectical historical practice but was the result of abstractions and idealistic theorizing made by jurists over a span of about three hundred years after the death of the Prophet. This begs the logical question: If the Islamic law was the product of idealized abstractions produced more than a thousand years ago, in what sense is it perfect? What does perfection mean in this situation? If one accepts the claims of Orientalists and contends that Islamic law was never implemented and that it was the product of idealistic theory, then how could it be claimed that the Islamic law is fit for every day and age? A similar objection can be made regarding the idea that Islam reached its peak in the first century of its existence and that the balance of Islam's historical existence were manifestations of corruption and decay. Muslims often defensively cite the grandeur of the Islamic civilization as evidence of Islam's and Muslim's contributions to humanity. But one cannot have it both ways—one cannot claim that over thirteen hundred years of Islamic history was un-Islamic, in the sense that it represented a corruption of the ideal, and then claim the grandeur of the Islamic civilization as evidence of the greatness of Islam. Either Islamic history is to be embraced or rejected, but it cannot be embraced and rejected depending on the ideological point one aims to score at a particular moment in time.

These inconsistencies do not simply point to certain gaps in logic but also to powerful ambiguities in Muslim societies regarding the place and identity of Islam in the modern age. These ambiguities exist because while Islamic law and history play very influential symbolic roles in defining the Muslim identity, nevertheless, the nature, character, and content of Islamic law and history are disputed and ill defined in the modern age. Even more, in the contemporary intellectual confusion, what is considered to be genuinely Islamic, or a Western construction injected into the Muslim psychology, or, as discussed later, a modern Muslim construction superimposed on the Islamic tradition are all interwoven and intermixed, and only a critical and introspective discourse could start disentangling the issues and making this complex matrix of ideas coherent.

This precisely is what makes the issue of universalism and exceptionalism so pressing and also very tricky. Those who eschew universalisms most often aspire to keep with the West what belongs to the West. However, it is imperative to realize that while mired in this state of intellectual dissonance, there is the very real risk that in our defensive effort to expunge the moral universals of the West, Muslims will also end up dismissing the moral universals of Islam itself. For instance, when contemporary Muslim scholars rise to emphasize the numerous moral and humanistic aspects of the Islamic tradition and they are accused by their fellow Muslims of seeking to appease the West, the real danger is that in this highly polarized and politicized climate, much of what is authentically Islamic and genuinely beautiful will be lost or forgotten for a long period to come. This, in turn, points to a basic and very serious fallacy, and that is, as discussed earlier, the tendency, usually exhibited by religious fundamentalists and ideological purists, to presume that moral values have a pure lineage that can be precisely identified as Western or non-Western. Whether Muslims or not, purists tend to classify particular values as squarely Judeo-Christian, while others are Islamic. As noted earlier, values do not have a genealogy that can be clearly and precisely ascertained, which then can be utilized in classifying what properly belongs to the West and what belongs to Islam. But the important point is not merely to acknowledge the Muslim contribution to Western thought. Rather, by recognizing the mixed lineage of ideas, a simple and straightforward taxonomy of moral values and civilizations and what civilizations are supposed to stand for or represent becomes much more problematic. Like racial or ethnic categories, one ought to recognize that civilizational categories are artificial political constructs that do not necessarily fit comfortably with sociohistorical realities and that many moral values do not carry a manufacturer's label or an owner's tag.

THE UNIVERSALITY OF UGLINESS AND BEAUTY

People do not need to agree on a universal definition of ugliness for ugliness to be universally recognizable. In the same way that justice and mercy are recognized as qualities of beauty, suffering can always be recognized as a quality of ugliness. In some situations, suffering might be justified, as when a person suffers disagreeable medicine in order to treat a disease or when a criminal suffers punishment for his crimes, but suffering remains in all cases ugly. Although suffering is accepted at times in order to achieve a particular objective, such as justice or health, it remains in all cases and in all times ugly. Because suffering is inherently ugly, it must be accepted reluctantly and only to the extent absolutely necessary to achieve a particular legitimate moral objective. Muslim scholars recognized this basic idea in a legal maxim, which is simply stated: in all cases, hardship must be alleviated. Recognizing the inherent ugliness of all suffering is an important moral attitude because, at a minimum, it is realized that the burden of justification is always on those causing the suffering to either adequately and convincingly justify it or promptly remove or alleviate it. The inherent ugliness of suffering could serve as a core universal value uniting all human beings and could provide the basis for a collective pursuit of goodness. If suffering is inherently ugly, it follows that mercy and compassion are universally good. The essence of mercy and compassion is to remove or alleviate all unjustified physical or spiritual suffering and to maximize the objective conditions that contribute to the end of suffering.

It is of crucial importance to realize that from an Islamic point of view, embracing the values of mercy and compassion as central to a universal concept of goodness is morally, theologically, and legally imperative. If the Qur'anic discourse on mercy and human diversity is going to be taken seriously, Muslims have no alternative but to embrace the universal and to study and explore the meaning of human diversity as a manifestation of divine mercy. This is not alien to Muslims. There is a maxim attributed by some to the Prophet that was memorized, preserved, and repeated by premodern Muslims over the course of many centuries, which states: "The disagreements of the scholars are a source of mercy for my nation." Clearly, the maxim refers to the diversity of opinions and determinations among Muslims as a mercy that should be embraced and celebrated, not distrusted and resisted. The Qur'an, however, makes the wisdom of this maxim applicable not just to Muslims but to humanity at large. I do not believe that Muslims are discharging their moral duty toward their own religion if they fail to pursue and strive to fulfill the ethical visions of the Qur'an.

As Muslims, as a part of our covenantal relationship of vicegerency with God, we have been charged with the duty of striving to safeguard the well-being and dignity of human beings, and we have also been charged with the obligation of achieving justice. But dignity and justice need compassion and mercy. Knowing the other, which as discussed is an Islamic norm, requires empathy, and empathy itself is but a function of compassion and mercy. Fundamentally, Muslims are charged with the obligation to teach mercy, but in the same way that one cannot learn to speak before learning to listen, one cannot teach unless one is also willing to learn. To take the ethic of mercy seriously, we must first learn to care, and this is why it does matter what humanity at large thinks of our interpretations and applications of the divine mandate. If humans cannot understand our version of mercy, from a theological point of view, claiming cultural exceptionalism or relativism avails us nothing. This is especially so if we, as Muslims, are engaging the rest of humanity in a collective enterprise to establish goodness and well-being on this earth. Considering the enormous diversity of human beings, we have no choice but to take each contribution to a vision of goodness seriously and to ask which of the proffered visions comes closer to attempting to fulfill the divine charge. But we cannot lose sight of the fact that, as human beings, the charge and ultimate responsibility are ours. This means that in acting on the duties of vicegerency on this earth, we must take the imperative of engaging in a collective enterprise of goodness seriously, and in doing so, we must be willing to persuade and be persuaded as to what is necessary for a moral and virtuous existence on this earth. The Qur'anic revelation powerfully captures this moral imperative in its statement: "To each of you We have given a law and a pattern and way of life. If God would have pleased, He surely could have made you into a single nation and people, but God wished to try and test you according to what He has given each you. So excel all together in good deeds. To God you will return in the end, and God will tell you about that which you were at variance."[29] Incidentally, this is the gist of the lesson mentioned earlier about religions as valuable rings that so impressed Saladin!

It is reasonable to conclude that God will most certainly vindicate God's rights in the Hereafter in the fashion that God deems most fitting, but on this earth, our primary moral responsibility is the vindication of the rights of human beings. To be able to excel and strive all together in good deeds, the integrity, safety, security, and well-being of people must be guaranteed. The guarantee of a system of rights is of central importance in order to protect the human potential—the capacity to recognize and pursue the good. Important-ly, rights cannot be contingent on achieving the right results—if rights are conditioned on people reaching particular results, they become meaningless. The point is for rights to safeguard the ability of the individual to do good without regard to how this ability is actually utilized. As such, a system of rights is a commitment to human beings that is founded on conviction and trust. A system of rights is premised on a good-faith belief in human potential and capacity for goodness. Like the presumption of innocence or the Proph-et's instruction to let the guilty go free if it prevents the innocent from being unjustly convicted, a system of rights as a matter of faith and commitment is premised on a resolute belief in the potential of human beings to achieve goodness.[30] The idea of a human right is interwoven in the very fact of having been given life. Human beings are given life by God in good faith because of their potential to do good, and in becoming alive they acquire a set of rights related to their potential for goodness. Whether they are likely to fulfill or do in fact fulfill this potential for goodness is entirely irrelevant—the rights acquired at creation can never be voided, and society must be constructed on the premise of maximizing the opportunity for this potential to be realized.

Yet no rights can be built on suffering. Suffering and hardship severely undermine the capacity of individuals and collectivities to pursue the good because, as serious distractions, they diminish the ability of people to reflect, think, learn, and work toward the fulfillment of their potential. Often, those who suffer can do no more than persevere and endure their hardship without having the stability or energy that would enable them to look beyond their plight. It is therefore rather elementary that the basic premise of any system of rights is that human beings should not needlessly and unjustly suffer. People create and possess a political or legal right, first, in order to protect themselves from unjustified suffering, and second, to pursue and establish conditions or create a status in which they establish an added buffer against unjustified suffering. Acts of mercy and compassion implicitly recognize that people have a moral right to create a zone of safety guarding against the risks of unjustified suffering. And it is this zone of safety that provides the space for moral growth and the fulfillment of the potential for the good.

The search for universal human rights that are consistent with the impera-tives of mercy and compassion, far from being anathema to Islam, is a commitment that must be made by Muslims as a fundamental part of fulfill-ing the obligations of their vicegerency and covenant with God. God, it should be realized, has already made such a commitment when God invested so much of the God-self in each and every person. This is why, as noted earlier, the Qur'an asserts that if anyone kills a fellow human being unjustly, it is as if he/she has murdered all of humanity—it is as if the killer has murdered the divine sanctity and defiled the very meaning of divinity.[31] The Qur'an does not differentiate between the sanctity of a Muslim or non-Mus-lim. Although some premodern jurists did discriminate between Muslim and non-Muslim, especially in matters pertaining to criminal liability and compensation for torts, these opinions should be considered erroneous and inconsistent with the ethical objectives of the Qur'an. As explained earlier, the Qur'an enunciated ethical objectives to be vigilantly pursued by Muslims, and in many cases the historical efforts of Muslims fell short or missed the path leading to these objectives altogether. It is important to build on and perfect the efforts of past Muslim generations, but it is also necessary to acknowledge honestly and bravely those situations when the efforts of past generations failed or even undermined the Qur'anic ethical objectives.

The Qur'an repeatedly asserts that no human being can limit the divine mercy in any way or even regulate who is entitled to it. The Qur'an expresses indignation against human beings who attempt to restrict or constrain the divine mercy according to their whims and prejudices.[32] I take this to mean that non-Muslims as well as Muslims could be the recipients and the givers of divine mercy. It is within God's exclusive purview to decide who is entitled to the divine mercy and under what conditions. There is no doubt that human beings are tempted to meddle in the divine sovereignty by arrogantly trying to regulate and apportion out the divine mercy. Although a usurpation of divine sovereignty, attempting to possess the mercy of the divine and portion it out for self-serving purposes yields an intoxicating but also corrupting sense of power. It is empowering for human beings to position themselves as the bearers of the divine will and to marshal such a power in the service of their mundane prejudices. As empowering as it may be, this act of usurpation denies the divine its integrity and superimposes the mundane subjectivities on the divine. Instead of the mundane being enriched by being rooted in divinity and by the pursuit of divinity, the mundane is allowed to impoverish the divine. The difference between the two conditions is that in the first, people pursue the divine but never assume that they have acquired it, while in the second, they arrogantly assume that they have acquired the divine but no longer pursue it. This is why, in my view, the Qur'an expects human beings to learn from the divine mercy and to seek after it but gravely warns human beings against pretending or assuming that they have become the possessors of this mercy.

If all human beings could be the recipients and givers of divine mercy, then it is imperative that instead of competition, people come together to learn from each other and join together in the pursuit of mercy. Put bluntly, Muslims could teach non-Muslims something about the nature and conditions of mercy. At the same time, non-Muslims could teach Muslims the same. Since mercy is exclusively apportioned by God and since the recipients of mercy could be Muslim or non-Muslim, there is no moral alternative but for human beings to join together in an educational collective enterprise in which they teach, learn, and pursue the goodness of mercy. The measure of moral virtue on this earth is who is able to come closer to divinity through mercy, compassion, and justice, and not who carries the correct religious or irreligious label. The measure in the Hereafter is a different matter, but it is a matter that is in the purview of God's exclusive jurisdiction.

UNIVERSAL MERCY AND EXTREME ACTS OF UGLINESS

I must confess that from the perspective of a believing Muslim, it is utterly confounding when Islam is used to justify extreme acts of ugliness. As explained earlier, all persistent conditions of suffering, injustice, bigotry, hate, and ignorance are considered *jahiliyya*, which is anathema to Islam. Aside from the persistent emphasis on mercy and compassion as core concepts, the Qur'an repeatedly rejects any association between religion and hardship to human beings. In the Qur'anic discourse, God did not send this religion to human beings to cause hardship, and the Qur'an even insists that the Islamic message should not be used to justify the imposition of unjust suffering on people.[33] The problem is not that there is any Muslim who believes that Islam should be used to make people suffer. Rather, the problem is that there is a large enough number of Muslims who have become desensitized to human suffering. Like a military man who uses military training and regulations to professionalize his attitude toward human suffering and to become freed of the burden of sympathy, there is a large number of Muslims who have come to rely on the technical regulations of law to reach a similar dissociative state. In a sense, at many different levels, there has been a militarization of Islam. Individuals, however, who use the law to buffer themselves from the need to feel or make conscientious judgments have a most superficial knowledge of Islamic jurisprudence because they only focus on the positive commandments of the law while ignoring its ethical motivations and also ignore the processes and procedures that seek to establish equity and alleviate human hardship and suffering.

In legal theory, there is a distrust of suffering as a measure or standard of judgment because of its subjectivity. The concern is that people have different levels of tolerance and endurance, and what is considered unbearable suffering by some could be entirely acceptable to others. Therefore, the worry is that if law is to respond to or seek to accommodate subjective narratives of suffering, the law will become standardless and lose its authoritativeness. In the common law system, the problem is solved by adopting the standard of the reasonable person—if the subjective feelings of a purported victim are not reasonable, the law does not accommodate those feelings. In Islamic law, the standard used is that of the average person—whether the law recognizes the suffering of a person depends on the standard set according to the average person. The bottom line is that different legal systems will adopt different conceptual tools to ensure that the subjectivities of human beings do not render the law standardless and ineffective. But technical issues aside, all legal systems struggle with striking the balance between the demands of equity, which require that the subjectivities of people be accommodated, and the demands of legal order, which require that objective and inflexible but reliable and predictable standards be adopted. This is a far cry, however, from ethical dissociation, in which people simply do not care about suffering. The challenge of struggling with standards that balance between legal order and equity is not an excuse to stop caring about human suffering and to cite the integrity of the legal order as a justification for ethical obliviousness.

The essential tension is between the role of a Muslim as a practitioner of ethics and as a practitioner of law. It is disastrous if the adherents of a religion come to fancy themselves as would-be lawyers. Many of the chaotic circumstances discussed earlier in the book are a by-product of this same exact phenomenon—Islam has become afflicted with many followers who ache to become self-declared lawyers before first becoming humble and decent worshippers. I realize that this claim is, to say the least, controversial and deserves some elaboration. Law and lawyers deal with rules, and these rules are solely concerned with equity, mercy, and substantive justice. The rules of law are equally concerned, if not primarily concerned, with the integrity of the legal system itself. In legal practice, the ultimate justice might be the justice of process and procedure—reliability, predictability, and detachment are primary concerns for a legal system. For instance, the Prophet, in a famous narration, explained that although his legal judgment resolving a particular dispute between two litigants could resolve the matter as far as law and order are concerned, moral accountability before God remained a separate issue. The Prophet's legal judgment might have allowed one of the litigants to prevail as a matter of legal process, but moral and ethical accountability remain something else. Simply because, as a procedural matter, one of the litigants prevailed over the other, the mundane judgment did not resolve the moral issue before God. A person could win his case before a judge and still be a loser before God.

Islamic law itself repeatedly differentiated between the ruling of a judge and sinfulness before God. For example, a spouse could have a legal right to divorce his wife or her husband, and this right could be exercised effectively and conclusively. Nevertheless, whether or not the divorce is just, fair, and equitable is something for God to judge in the Hereafter. In another example, a person could enter into an entirely legal and effective contract, yet in the Hereafter, the contract could be considered unfair and immoral. In an additional example, assume that a man seeks to marry a woman, consequently pays the dowry, and writes a contract before two witnesses. However, secretly the man desires to marry the woman not to build a family but to abuse and degrade her because he holds a grudge against her father. The marriage could be legally valid and effective, but before God, the man committed a grave sin for which he will be held liable in the Hereafter. Islamic law is replete with situations in which the judgment of the legal order does not necessarily mirror or correlate with the judgment of ethics and God. Similarly, there are many situations in which a legal ruling does not mirror or correlate with the results mandated by mercy and compassion. Islamic law contains tools that allow a judge to take note of exceptional circumstances by suspending the formalities of law in order to achieve equity, but the application of these tools is a technical matter that requires a high level of legal expertise and knowledge. Legal tools aside, however, the divine mercy and compassion that people ought to seek are not necessarily represented in the judgment of law. For instance, in an action for debt, a judge might be obligated to give judgment in favor of a rich man against a poor man. However, divine mercy and compassion would urge the rich man to forgive the debt. On many occasions, the Qur'an enunciates a legal right but then goes on to urge people to do the merciful and compassionate thing by, for instance, forgiving the right.

Because of the pervasive influence of the puritan orientation discussed later, there has been a clear tendency in modern Islam not just to limit ethics, mercy, and even beauty to the boundaries of law, but for the average Muslim to become a pretender in law—to assume the pretense of competence in law. Instead of struggling with subjective ethical and moral evaluations and wrestling with the pangs of personal conscience, the average Muslim projects the burden of morality onto the law. Because law or legal practice replaces ethical inquiries and moral judgments, a powerful incentive is created for the average Muslim to assume the role of a legal practitioner. Since law becomes the only available means for expressing values, the practice of religiosity becomes a legalistic and technical endeavor, and in effect, the community of believers becomes indistinguishable from a community of lawyers—in reality, bad and poorly qualified lawyers. The tragedy is that this is done without competence in law, and therefore, the determinations that emerge seem odd and pedantic. It is not that a large number of Muslims rise to master the discipline of law—rather, the law is molded and shaped to mirror the practices of lay Muslims. The end result has been an inevitable degradation of the quality of legal practice and Islamic law and a degradation of the quality of ethical practice as well. Islamic law has become the proverbial scapegoat through which the challenge of moral and ethical judgments is avoided. In the difficult sociopolitical circumstances that plague Muslims, there is an escape to the technicalities of law, except that those piloting the escape possess no real competence over the intricacies of law.

In my view, as Muslims, in the same way that when confronted by extreme acts of ugliness our citing exceptionalism and pretending that there are no universal human standards will avail us nothing, citing the technicalities of law as a means of avoiding the problem will also avail us nothing. The problem is much more fundamental and far more basic. The fundamental issue is: Confronted by extreme acts of ugliness, what are the obligations of each Muslim? In my view, confronted by such extreme acts of ugliness, there is no alternative for a Muslim who is interested in reclaiming the moral authority of Islam but to confront the quintessential questions of: Is this Islam? Can this be Islam? And should this be Islam? It is simply too easy to shift responsibility for extreme acts of ugliness to Western imperialism and colonialism, to engage in the morally evasive strategy of complaining about false universals, and to blame everything and everyone else but refuse a confrontation with one's own conscience. With every major human tragedy committed in the name of Islam, I think that it is imperative for every Muslim to put aside, for a while, the various intellectual methods by which responsibility is projected, transferred, diluted, and distributed, and to engage in a conscientious pause. In this pause, a Muslim ought to critically evaluate the prevailing systems of belief within Islam and reflect on the ways that these systems of belief might have contributed to, legitimated, or in any way facilitated the tragedy. In my view, this is the only way for a Muslim to honor human life, dignify God's creation, and uphold the integrity of the Islamic religion.

If one engages in this conscientious and self-reflective pause, I believe that Muslims would realize that a supremacist and puritanical orientation in contemporary Islam shoulders the primary responsibility for the vast majority of extreme acts of ugliness that are witnessed today in the Islamic world. In my view, Muslims must come to terms with and reclaim their religion from a supremacist puritanism that has been born of a siege mentality—a mentality that this supremacist puritanical orientation continues to perpetuate as the primary mode of responding to the challenge of modernity. Importantly, this orientation is dismissive of all moral norms or ethical values, regardless of the identity of their origins or foundations. In this orientation, the prime and nearly singular concern is power and its symbols. Somehow, all other values, traditions, and normativities are made subservient. As argued later, this orientation, which I will call Puritanical-Salafism, was and remains uninterested in critical historical inquiry. It responded to the challenge of modernity by escaping to the secure haven of the text, but it treated rational moral insight as fundamentally corrupting of the purity of the Islamic message. As a result, it ultimately ended up undermining the integrity and viability of the Islamic text and, in the process, arrested and stunted the development of Islamic normative ethical thinking.

Chapter Eight

What *Really* Went Wrong

POSTCOLONIALISM AND THE RISE OF MODERN APOLOGETICS

In the age of postcolonialism, Muslims have become largely preoccupied with the attempt to remedy a collective feeling of powerlessness and a persistent and frustrating sense of political defeat, often by engaging in highly sensationalistic acts of power symbolism. Political interests have come to dominate public discourses to the point that moral and ethical investigations and thinking have become marginalized. Islamic ethical philosophy has not experienced major transformational advances since the seventeenth century. In my view, Mulla Sadra (d. 1050/1640) was the last true master of Islamic ethical theory of the caliber of the great sages of the past, such as Ibn Sina (d. 428/1037), Ibn Rushd (d. 595/1198), Ibn Baja (d. 533/1139), Ibn 'Aqil (d. 513/1119), and Abu Nasr al-Farabi (d. 339/950). Of course, there have been a number of gifted intellectuals since the seventeenth century who have made insightful and important contributions, but they are of a markedly different quality and impact.[1] At least since the eighteenth century, the normative imperatives and intellectual subtleties of the Islamic moral tradition have been not treated with the analytic and critical rigor that the Islamic tradition rightly deserves but are rendered subservient to political expedience and symbolic displays of power. Elsewhere, I have described this contemporary doctrinal dynamic as the predominance of the theology of power in modern Islam, and it is this theology that is a direct contributor to the emergence of highly radicalized Islamic groups, and also to the desensitization and transference by which Muslims are forced to confront extreme acts of ugliness.[2] Far from being authentic expressions of inherited Islamic paradigms or a natural outgrowth of the classical tradition, these groups and their impulsive and reactive modes of thinking are a by-product of colonialism and modernity. These highly dissonant and defensive modes of thinking are dissociated from the Islamic civilizational experience with all its richness and diversity, and they invariably end up reducing Islam to a single dynamic—the dynamic of power. They tend to define Islam as an ideology of nationalistic defiance to the "other"—a rather vulgar form of obstructionism to the hegemony of the Western world.[3] Therefore, instead of Islam being a moral vision given to humanity, it becomes constructed into a nationalistic cause that is often the antithesis of the West. In this sense, in the world constructed by puritan modes of thinking and their groups, there is no Islam; there is only opposition to the West. This type of Islam that the puritan orientations offer is akin to a perpetual state of emergency, where expedience trumps principle and illegitimate means are consistently justified by invoking higher ends. In essence, what prevails is an aggravated siege mentality that suspends the moral principles of the religion in pursuit of the vindications of political power and the symbolic displays of defiance to Western domination.[4] In this siege mentality, there is no room for analytical or critical thought, and there is no room for seriously engaging the Islamic intellectual heritage. There is only room for bombastic dogma and for a stark functionalism that ultimately impoverishes the Islamic heritage.

One of the most salient characteristics of the puritan orientation is a rabidly aggressive form of patriarchy that responds to feelings of political and social defeatism by engaging in symbolic displays of power that are systematically degrading to women. In my view, for example, the girls who died in Mecca were the direct victims of the sense of frustration and disempowerment felt by puritan men over the humiliations experienced in Afghanistan and Palestine. Furthermore, I believe that the absurd position of a prominent Saudi Arabian jurist proclaiming the lawfulness of slavery in Islam, which is a determination that effectively legitimates the trafficking in and sexual exploitation of so-called domestic workers in the Gulf region, and especially Saudi Arabia, was a direct response to the American invasion of Iraq.[5] Of course, this is one of those associations that are virtually impossible to prove empirically, but in my experience in studying puritan orientations in modern Islam, one finds that women are not targeted and degraded simply because of textual commitments or determinations.[6] Rather, there is a certain undeniable vehemence and angst in the treatment of women, as if the more women are made to suffer, the more the political future of Islam is made secure. Puritan orientations do not hesitate to treat all theological arguments aimed at honoring women by augmenting their autonomy and social mobility as if they are a part of the Western conspiracy designed to destroy Islam. This is also manifested in the puritans' tendency to look at Muslim women as a consistent source of danger and vulnerability for Islam and to go so far as to brand women as the main source of social corruption and evil. This is often expressed in terms of describing women as the worst *fitna* (source of enticement and social discord) and claiming that women will constitute the vast majority of the residents of hellfire and that most men in hell will be there because of women.[7] Furthermore, among the consistent practices of Muslim puritans is to collect, publish, and disperse traditions attributed to the Prophet or the companions that are demeaning to women. Such collections then act as a foundation for issuing determinations deprecating to women by consistently casting them in the role of the perpetual seductress or in the function of beings created for men's fulfillment. Muhammad bin 'Abd al-Wahhab (d. 1206/1792), the founder of the Wahhabi movement, himself set the precedent by collecting a group of these women-deprecating traditions and listing them under the subheading "Living with women."[8]

Of course, demeaning attitudes toward women were not invented or exclusively adopted only by modern puritan orientations. Patriarchy has a long and inglorious history in Islam as well as other religions. But it is important to understand the uniqueness and distinctiveness of the current puritan challenge in this specific historical juncture of Islamic history. What makes the puritan challenge today particularly compelling and singularly threatening to the humanistic tradition in Islam is the deconstruction of the institutions of religious authority in the age of modernity. Historically, these institutions played the primary role in undermining and marginalizing the supremacist and puritanical movements of the past. In addition, given the primacy of apologetic intellectual orientations within contemporary Islam, not only does it not bode well for the ability of Muslims to overcome these supremacist and puritanical movements, but even more, such apologetics are the main undercurrent feeding into such movements. Of course, the institutions of traditional or classical learning—the institutions that, as explained before, used to produce the *fuqaha'* (jurists)—have their own heavy share of patriarchy. But the existence of a complex interpretive tradition and institutionalized mechanisms for negotiating the Shari'ah made these classical institutions far more susceptible to development and open to progress. This is why despite the entrenched patriarchy there is a respectable historically rooted tradition of women scholasticism that emerged from within the classical juristic institutions.[9]

Puritanical orientations have played a role and exercised an influence not commensurate with the numerical size of their groups. Percentage-wise, their numbers are marginal in modern Islam, but their influence has been pervasive. In a sense, the puritanical orientations are like the proverbial tip of the iceberg or the narrow height of a pyramid. More important than the numbers that constitute their ranks are the intellectual and spiritual trends they represent. They are a culmination of a long historical process—the most extreme expression that resounds with deafening impact in a long, ongoing soliloquy. The puritan trend is able to speak in a very loud voice that silences all else. But its strength is due to weaknesses that have long eaten away at the integrity of the Islamic structure. Currently, the puritan trend represents the single most important challenge to Muslims, but the danger it poses is not due to its own inherent strength. Various factors coalesced to propel puritanism into the prominent role it has come to play.

In order to adequately explain the puritan trend and its role, it is necessary to address the undercurrents that contributed to its formation and power, most notably the apologetic and Salafi fundamentalist orientations. To avoid confusion and to maintain the integrity of the narrative, it will be necessary that we revisit some of the issues already raised in the book, except that this time we focus on the connections to puritanism. Some of the problems and issues discussed earlier in the book laid the groundwork, enabling the puritan trend to take hold and anchor itself in the modern Muslim reality. The narrative must start with the apologists because they created the climate most conducive to the spread of the puritan trend. The irony is that the apologists did not share with the puritans their purpose or cause, and many of the arguments of the two orientations were clearly at odds with each other. Nevertheless, it is highly doubtful that without the apologetic orientation the puritans would have been able to impose themselves as a serious force in contemporary Islam.

The apologetic orientation consisted of an effort by a large number of commentators to defend and salvage the Islamic system of belief and tradition from the onslaught of Orientalism, Westernization, and modernity by simultaneously emphasizing both the compatibility and also the supremacy of Islam. Apologists responded to the intellectual challenges of modernity by adopting pietistic fictions about the Islamic tradition that eschewed any critical evaluation of Islamic doctrines. The main methodological tactic of the apologists was to celebrate Islam as a perfect holistic totality. In the wake of the crumbling of the Ottoman Empire and the fall of the Caliphate in the early twentieth century, the apologists believed that Islam confronted an overwhelming and devastating danger. During the colonial era, Orientalist scholars had unfettered and free access to premodern Islamic texts, which they edited, printed, and interpreted, and also took great liberties with transferring the manuscripts to their home academic institutions in the West. To a very large extent, this is why every prestigious academic institution in the West, from the University of Leiden to Oxford and Cambridge to Harvard and Princeton has sizeable Islamic manuscript collections. In addition, colonial powers gave a free hand to Christian missionary movements that consistently portrayed Islam as despotic, oppressive of women, and backwards. Most importantly, an intelligentsia, ostensibly Muslim, emerged that was thoroughly Westernized and secular and that was eager to reform Muslim societies by distancing them from their Muslim heritage. The rabid pro-Westernism and anti-Islamism of Kemal Ataturk (d. 1357/1938) in secularizing Turkey became a living symbol of the dangers confronting Muslim societies. Ataturk's brand of secularism had its admirers in many parts of the Muslim world. Most notably, and also most poignantly, staunch secularistic and nationalistic ideologies tended to be very dominant among the military forces of the respective Muslim countries. During the colonial era and the early postcolonial period, the armed forces of most Muslim countries had been organized, trained, and supplied by colonial powers and were by and large indoctrinated in a thoroughly secular creed. The ideologies and cultural roots of the militaries of Muslim countries and the ways that they had been shaped and reshaped by the colonial era is a subject still in need of considerable research. But as can be seen from the militaries of countries such as Algeria, Syria, Iraq, Egypt, Mauritania, Senegal, and the Sudan, the new class of military officers trained under colonial administrations were not rooted in nativist Islamic cultures, and very often, even their command of a native language, as opposed to the language of the colonizer, was very poor. This helps explain the quick rise of secular nationalistic military regimes to power in most Muslim countries in the postcolonial era.

Facing what felt like an orchestrated Western onslaught against Islam, apologists responded by trying to persuade Muslims of the completeness and perfection of their religion and fought to retain the loyalty of Muslims to their faith. In addition, apologists also responded to the European tendency in the late nineteenth and twentieth centuries to emphasize enlightened rationalism at the expense of religion. Apologists took it as an article of faith that even if Europe needed to secularize in order to advance, in the case of Islam it was possible for Muslims to modernize while holding steadfast to their religious traditions. According to the apologists, nothing in the Islamic tradition needed to change in order for Muslims to catch up with European modernism. But the essential point emphasized by the apologists is that in a world of civilizational competition, the West has nothing that favors it over Islam.

A common heuristic device of apologetics was to argue that any meritorious or worthwhile modern institutions were first invented and realized by Muslims. Therefore, according to the apologists, Islam liberated women, created a democracy, endorsed pluralism, protected human rights, and guaranteed social security long before these institutions ever existed in the West. Nonetheless, these concepts were not asserted out of critical understanding or genuine ideological commitment but primarily as a means of resisting the deconstructive effects of modernity, affirming self-worth, and attaining a measure of emotional empowerment. Although apologetics initially arose as a response to a particular historical challenge, the impact of this orientation far exceeded the context in which it arose. Once Islamist intellectuals utilized the paradigms of apologetics, it became very difficult to alter the terms of the discourse. Apologetics are easy to generate and superficially satisfying. Often in this type of literature, an author in a single book would address all problems, ranging from the liberation of women to democracy, to economics, to law and any other topic that was deemed necessary to prove the superiority of Islam to all other possible competition. In many ways, the practice of apologetics proved to be like an addictive drug—it induced a pleasant state of oblivion and artificial self-confidence, but the problems remained unchanged. The practice gave easy, simplistic, and holistic responses to every challenge, but it also immunized its audience against critical thought. The habit-forming sociology of apologetics is quite remarkable. In one of my recent visits to al-Azhar, I had an opportunity to review some of the inquiries the venerable institution receives from non-Muslim countries around the world. There is a special department set up to respond to educational questions (not to be confused with Dar al-Ifta', or the official body that issues *fatawa*) that has a significant body of literature that it sends out to interested parties. I was rather amazed and disappointed to find that the material being sent out by the department literally could have been copied from the pages of apologetics books. The arguments proffered by the apologists of the 1930s and 1940s were still in use more than fifty years later.

I think that it is beyond dispute that Muslim apologists were sincere, well intentioned, and eager to defend Islam against domestic- and foreign-inspired skepticism and also against aggressive missionary and evangelical campaigns. The main effect of apologetics, however, was to contribute to a sense of intellectual self-sufficiency that often descended into moral arrogance. To the extent that apologetics were habit forming, they produced a culture that eschewed self-critical and introspective insight and embraced the projection of blame and a fantasy-like level of confidence and arrogance. Effectively, apologists got into the habit of paying homage to the presumed superiority of the Islamic tradition but marginalized the Islamic intellectual heritage in everyday life. While apologists revered Islam in the abstract, they failed to engage the Islamic tradition as a dynamic and viable living tradition. To a large extent, apologists turned Islam into an untouchable but also entirely ineffective prize simply to be admired and showcased as a symbol but not to be critically engaged or dealt with.[10]

The real irony is that apologists ended up reproducing the legacy of Orientalism—a legacy of which they were very critical. Orientalists dealt with the Islamic tradition as a static and, perhaps, even mummified heritage that is represented by a set of self-contained intellectual paradigms and that is incapable of adapting to the demands of modernity without becoming thoroughly deconstructed and collapsing onto itself. In essence, Orientalists, who worked in the service of colonialism, paid nothing more than lip service to Islam but otherwise negated the practical value of Islamic culture. The most typical strategy was for Orientalists to insist that the Islamic tradition, while generally decent, lacked essential features necessary for rational modernization. As such, it is not so much that Orientalists deprecated Islam as a religion; rather, they cast serious doubts on the ability of what might be called "active" or "dynamic" Islam to deal with rational modernity.[11] Ironically, Muslim apologists ended up with the same basic construct. They paid lip service to the Islamic tradition by, among other things, insisting that not only was Islam compatible with modernity but in fact had already achieved "rational modernization" fourteen hundred years ago. Effectively, apologists treated the Islamic tradition as if it were fossilized at the time of the Prophet and the rightly guided companions and thus rendered this tradition nondynamic and unliving. But if Islam figured out all the major answers to the challenges of modernity at the time of the Prophet and his companions, there was no incentive to engage in any further thinking or analysis about the Islamic tradition or to engage Islam creatively and innovatively, save for the most marginal issues. It is no coincidence that puritans took this apologetic point to its logical extreme and constructed a discourse that is markedly hostile to innovations or creative thinking (referred to as *bid'a*, sing., and *bida'*, pl.).

Not only was the practice of apologetics detrimental in dealing with the challenges of modernity, but it also significantly contributed to the sense of intellectual dissonance felt in many parts of the Muslim world. The problems posed by the apologetic response to modernity were only aggravated by the fact that Islam was, and continues to this day, to live through a major paradigm shift the likes of which it has not experienced in the past. Under a different set of historical circumstances, the apologetic orientation could have had a marginal impact, and like other past apologetic orientations, it could have served a limited rhetorical purpose without affecting the intellectual progress of Muslims. However, what made the apologetic orientation particularly impactful was the profound vacuum in religious authority in modern Islam, where it no longer became clear who speaks for the religion and how. As I mentioned earlier, traditionally, the institutions of Islamic law have been decentralized, and Islamic epistemology tolerated and even celebrated differences of opinions and a variety of schools of thought. Classical Islam developed semiautonomous institutions of law and theology that trained and qualified jurists, who then provided a class of individuals who authoritatively spoke for, and most often disagreed about, the divine law.

And, as mentioned earlier, the institutions of religion and law were supported by a complex system of private endowments, which enabled Muslim scholars to generate a remarkably rich intellectual tradition. The guardians of Islamic authority were the *fuqaha'*, whose legitimacy to a large extent rested on their semi-independence from the political system, which was already fairly decentralized, and on their dual function of representing the interests of the state to the laity and the interests of the laity to the state.[12] Of course, this drastically changed as the traditional institutions that once sustained the juristic discourse have all but vanished in the modern age. After colonialism formally dismantled the traditional institutions of civil society, Muslims witnessed the emergence of highly centralized and despotic, often corrupt governments that nationalized the institutions of religious learning and brought the religious endowments fully under state control. Effectively, this process led to bringing the mediating role of jurists in Muslim societies to an end. The fact that nearly all charitable religious endowments became state-controlled entities and that Muslim jurists in most Muslim nations became salaried state employees delegitimated the traditional clergy and effectively transformed them into what may be called "court priests."[13] Perhaps a sign of this unprecedented weakness was that after the revolutions of the Arab Spring in countries such as Egypt and Tunisia, the official religious institutions were among those most worried about the rise of Islamists to power. The fear among institutions such as al-Azhar was and remains that Islamists would have absolutely no functional need even for the minimal role these institutions had come to play in the postcolonial era.

The disintegration of the mediating role of jurists and the extinction of their influence meant that the normative categories and moral foundations that once mapped out Islamic law and theology have disintegrated, leaving an unsettling epistemological vacuum. Popular and charismatic activists like Hasan al-Banna (assassinated in 1368/1949) and fundamentalist organizations such as the Muslim Brotherhood attempted to fill this vacuum and continue to do so. At times, in addition to fundamentalist movements, in the first half of the twentieth century, politically active Sufi orders vied to fill the gap in religious authority. However, in most cases these activist movements, whether fundamentalist or Sufi, were violently suppressed by the Westernized secular governments in power in most Muslim countries. The end result of these developments was that in the twentieth century, the paradigm for authoritativeness in religion had shifted in a disruptively drastic fashion. Apologetic discourses became dominant because there were no other influential alternatives. Over the course of roughly twelve hundred years of history, apologetics, which primarily consisted of refutations and polemics directed at Christian theology, was on the sidelines of the Islamic civilization—earning the cheap cheers of street preachers, and the dignified scoff of the most serious scholars. In the new paradigm shift, apologetics moved to the center of Islamic discourses and became the unfortunate preoccupation of the majority of Muslim scholars.

In this highly unstable condition, perhaps it was understandable and even inevitable that, increasingly, activists tried to artificially limit the amount of diversity and variation in the doctrines of Shari'ah. As noted earlier, a part of the problem was that Muslim modernists, who attempted to reform Islamic jurisprudence, were heavily influenced by the civil law system and thus sought to resist the indeterminate fluidity of Islamic law and increase its unitary and centralized character. But even beyond that, while ostensibly condemning it, perhaps Muslims found it useful to co-opt and exploit the idea that the doors of *ijtihad* were closed in the fourth/tenth century. While various activists and modernists continued to claim that it is imperative to reopen the doors and exercise new *ijtihad*, when it came to the reality on the ground, the doctrine of closed doors played a very useful dogmatic function. Activists and modernists were able to pretend that since purportedly there had been no development in Islamic law for the past eleven hundred years or so, then by implication this meant that Muslims had achieved consensus (*ijma'*) on most points of law for the same period of time. Practically speaking, calls for new thinking served the opposite effect of their avowed purpose. Such calls served to establish the pretense that the doctrines of Islamic law were settled and foreclosed, and the burden of proof was implicitly placed on anyone offering new thinking. Certainly, this would explain the sociological fact that the same activists and modernists who espoused an open-door policy and called for new *ijtihad* were also the people who treated differences of opinion and diversity in Islamic law with utter contempt. This would also explain the fact that despite the repeated calls for new *ijtihad* throughout the twentieth century, those like 'Ali 'Abd al-Raziq (d. 1386/ 1966) or Hasan al-'Ashmawi, who attempted to present new thought, were severely ostracized and marginalized. In short, if calls for new *ijtihad* were yet more displays of modern-day affectations intended to serve a conservative legitimist role toward the status quo, this would explain why despite those repeated calls there has been no memorable new thinking and certainly no new *ijtihad*.

The polemics on the new *ijtihad* signified another dominant reality in the modern Muslim condition—a reality that would play a critical role in the emergence of the puritanical trend. In the late nineteenth and early twentieth centuries, as a part of supporting the call for a renewed *ijtihad*, a large number of scholars severely criticized the practice of *taqlid* (imitation or following precedent). According to these scholars, in order to break out of the shackles of outmoded traditions, it was important for Muslims to recognize that *taqlid* was reprehensible and that Muslims should not be bound by the legal determinations of past generations. Moreover, the opponents of *taqlid* contended that Muslims should not be bound to follow the classical schools of jurisprudence but should feel free to pick and choose from any of the schools whatever is useful to address contemporary problems—a practice known as *talfiq*. But the opponents of *taqlid* went further and, relying on the idea that most of Muslim history has been a deviation and corruption, they contended that the interpretive communities of the past were, for the most part, irrelevant to modern Islam. In producing new thinking or *ijtihad*, they argued, Muslims should go back to the source materials of the Qur'an and Sunna and render fresh interpretations and judgments without being burdened by the past's legacy. In addition, the opponents of *taqlid* attempted to remove the barriers to original and innovative thinking by arguing that since Islam is a simple and straightforward religion, the Qur'an and Sunna should be considered accessible to all. Therefore, any Muslim should be deemed qualified to consult the Qur'an and Sunna for themselves and render an opinion on any matter pertaining to Islam. This attitude was enshrined in a motto co-opted from Islamic history: *hum rijal wa-nahnu rijal* (they were men and we are men)—an expression espousing the confident belief that in the same way the predecessors made laws appropriate for their age, the current generations competently could do the same. Of course, in principle, the idea is quite reasonable, but removing the historically embedded barriers that negotiated and mediated the original sources, such as the Qur'an and Sunna, also meant opening the Shari'ah to a wide range of engagements and engagers. The production of Shari'ah was popularized without proportional parameters of authoritativeness or indeed reasonableness.

The sociological impact of the ideology of modern *ijtihad* was quite different from its theoretical aspirations. In effect, this conceptual framework contributed further to the deconstruction of the place of the interpretive communities of the past and to exacerbating the vacuum of authority in modern Islam. Although the idea of becoming liberated from the burdens of the past has its obvious appeal, especially to modernists and reformers, the idea of going back to the Qur'an and Sunna as somehow objectified bearers of the original truth proved to be much harder than conceived. It is practically impossible to disentangle the Qur'an and Sunna from the interpretive communities of the past that preserved and perpetuated these sources, and to attempt to deal with historically embedded sources as if they have no history or context is nothing more than a flight of fantasy. Fundamentally, Muslims did not really unburden themselves of the past; instead, they deformed the past and then continued to suffer the mutilated past on their backs. With the dominance of the apologetics movement, what was retained or discarded of the past became highly political, unprincipled, and reactive. Furthermore, because of the influence of puritans on the development of Muslim contemporary thought, the anti-*taqlid* movement amounted to the destruction of the interpretive communities of the past and their replacement with the determinations of the new but intellectually inferior interpretive communities of the contemporary age. So, for instance, as early as in 1933, the prominent Azharite Maliki jurist Yusuf al-Dijawi (d. 1365/1946) noted with great concern that puritan orientations, such as the Wahhabis, were deprecating the Islamic tradition by enabling people with a very limited education in Islamic sciences to become self-proclaimed experts in Shari'ah. As we will see, poor training in the jurisprudential sciences of Shari'ah becomes one of the most often repeated complaints about Wahhabism. [14]

At this point, it deserves emphasis that the centralization and what may be described as the officialization of the practice of Islamic orthodoxy in the hand of the intrusive modern state, the resulting vacuum in religious authority, the cheapening of the Islamic intellectual heritage through apologetics, and, as a response, the rising tide of determinism and codification of Islamic law were all antecedent and perhaps necessary conditions or undercurrents that acted to propel the puritanical orientation into prominence in modern Islam. The impact of the puritanical orientation, as I described it earlier, was to militarize Islamic law, in the sense of reducing the jurisprudential tradition into an uncompromising command-and-obey structure.

Perhaps the most important side to this story was the deep penetration of Western culture into everything Muslim. Muslims had entered into a self-perpetuating cycle. Western influence contributed to the breakdown of the Islamic tradition, and the more the Islamic tradition crumbled, the greater it became susceptible to Western influence. Western cultural symbols, modes of production, and normative social values aggressively penetrated the Muslim world, seriously challenging inherited normative categories and practices and adding to a profound sense of sociocultural alienation and dissonance. But importantly, not only were the concepts of law heavily influenced by the European legal tradition, but even the ideologies of resistance employed by Muslims became laden with third-world notions of national liberation and self-determination. For instance, modern nationalistic thought exercised a greater influence on the resistance ideologies of Muslim and Arab national liberation movements than anything in the Islamic tradition. But the most fervent Arab nationalists, such as Michel Aflaq (d. 1989) and Salah al-Din al-Bitar (d. 1400/1980), were educated and heavily influenced by French ideologies of resistance. Although national liberation ideologies were distinctively nationalistic and secular, they had a profound influence on theologies of Islamic liberation. The Islamic tradition was reconstructed to fit third-world nationalistic ideologies of anticolonialism and anti-imperialism rather than the other way around.

Other than vulgar apologetics, the new interpretive community, replacing the classical legacy and primarily interested in resisting the Western cultural invasion, reinvented and reconstituted the Islamic tradition into a vehicle for displays of power symbolisms. These power symbolisms were motivated by the desire to overcome a pervasive sense of powerlessness and to express resistance to Western hegemony, as well as to provide a means of voicing national aspirations for political, social, and cultural independence. The irony, however, was that these advocates of Islamic self-determination and independence were trained only in Western scientific methods and according to Western-invented educational curriculums, and therefore, methodologically and epistemologically they were effectively a part of Western culture. Although defiant and rebellious, in every way they were the children of the West, despite the power symbolisms of resistance in which they engaged. Whether fundamentalists or puritans, in theory they advocated inventive creativity and intellectual independence and autonomy. In practice they were mostly educated as engineers, medical doctors, computer scientists, chemists, and the like. Since they claimed that the Shari'ah could be discovered by referring back to the original sources unhampered by precedent or legal technicalities, they had removed the conceptual barriers to their claim of expertise in Shari'ah law. Although they vehemently denied having any attachments or dependencies on anything but a pristine Islamic authenticity, in reality, by deconstructing the interpretive communities of the past, the puritans unwittingly rendered the very idea of Islamic authenticity problematic. And by lowering the barrier to the production of Shari'ah determinations, they compromised and diluted the force and authority of the idea. There is a rather peculiar cognitive dissonance in the claim of reopening the doors of *ijtihad* by returning to the original sources. Once that paradigm was accepted, there was no way, other than through sheer authoritarianism, for the puritans to act as gatekeepers or to control the outcome of these engagements with the so-called original sources. The irony is that the puritans of Islam unwittingly ended up greatly enhancing the secularization and Westernization of Muslim societies.

In the beginning of the twentieth century, Arnold Toynbee (d. 1975), the well-known British historian, had noted the fact that many Muslims had hoped to import Western scientific methods, especially the military sciences, while insulating themselves from the rest of Western culture. Toynbee thought that what he called "the zealots" were not going to succeed because it was not possible to adopt scientific and military products without becoming influenced by the cultural institutions that ultimately resulted in the production of the science.[15] Today, many Muslim puritans come to the West to learn the Western physical sciences while hoping to insulate themselves from the influence of Western culture by, for example, refusing to study the humanities or social sciences. In this practice, which continues to be prevalent, it is believed that it is possible to borrow the modern sciences from the West and to become advanced and industrialized while maintaining full cultural and intellectual autonomy—an autonomy that is thoroughly based on the Qur'an and Sunna. This objective, however, has proved to be much harder to achieve in practice than in theory. As they searched Islam for black-and-white, definitive answers to all their sociopolitical problems, these Muslim activists superimposed the logic of empirical precision and the determinism of Western scientific methods on the Islamic intellectual, and particularly the juristic, tradition. This is clear, for instance, in very popular slogans such as "Islam is the solution" and "The Qur'an is our constitution." If considered from a historical perspective, both of these slogans, which betray an unmistakable determinism and empiricism, are entire anachronisms.

With the deconstruction of the traditional institutions of religious authority emerged organizations such as the al-Jama'at al-Islamiyya, Hizb al-Tahrir, Shabab Muhammad, Jihad, Tanzim al-Qaeda, and the Taliban, which were influenced by the resistance paradigms of national liberation and anticolonialist ideologies but which also anchored themselves in a religious orientation that is distinctively puritan, supremacist, and thoroughly opportunistic in nature. This theology is the by-product of the emergence and eventual primacy of a synchronistic orientation that unites Wahhabism and Salafism in modern Islam. Puritan orientations, such as the Wahhabis, imagine that God's perfection and immutability are fully attainable by human beings in this lifetime. It is as if God's perfection had been deposited in the divine law, and by giving effect to this law, it is possible to create a social order that mirrors the divine truth. But by associating themselves with the Supreme Being in this fashion, puritan groups are able to claim a self-righteous perfectionism that easily slips into a pretense of supremacy. This supremacy is based on a legalism that is utterly essentializing toward the diversity and richness of life, and it is rabidly hostile to any sense of individualism and to manifestations of aesthetics. The Qur'an, for example, often counsels the believers to respond to moral challenges with what can be described as an aesthetic magnanimity. In response to various emotionally taxing situations, the Qur'anic advice is: respond with beautiful forgiveness, respond with beautiful patience, avoid hostility and enmity in a beautiful fashion, or afford divorced women a beautiful release.[16] What the Qur'an is teaching is the developing and nurturing of an ability to respond to adversities with beauty—a response that expresses moral magnanimity or that embodies an aesthetic refinement that could be described as beautiful. Nevertheless, in the puritan orientations, no moral beauty can exist outside the boundaries of the law. Since the law is perfection embodied, once the legal injunctions are obeyed, there is no space for beauty, and there is no room for aesthetical judgments that needlessly complicate the reality with which the law must deal. In other words, in the puritan paradigm, life must be essentialized and streamlined, and nuances and complications must be ignored, aesthetical variations must be removed, and diversity must be extinguished so that the supposedly perfect law is not challenged and undermined by complexities. Ultimately, this is accomplished at an unbearably high cost to the individual and to any intangibles that cannot be legislated or legally dictated, such as beauty.

The existence of this puritan orientation in Islam is hardly surprising. All religious systems have suffered at one time or another from absolutist extremism, and Islam is not an exception. Within the first century of Islam, religious extremists known as the Khawarij (literally, "the secessionists") slaughtered a large number of Muslims and non-Muslims and were even responsible for the assassination of the Prophet's cousin and companion, the Caliph 'Ali bin Abi Talib (d. 40/661). The descendants of the Khawarij exist today in Oman and Algeria, but after centuries of bloodshed, the descendants of the original Khawarij became moderates, if not pacifists. Other than the Khawarij, there were other extremists such as the Qaramites and the Assassins, whose terror was their *raison d'être* and who earned unmitigated infamy in the writings of Muslim historians, theologians, and jurists. Again, after centuries of bloodshed, these two groups learned moderation, and they continue to exist in small numbers in North Africa and Iraq, but the descendants are nothing like their forefathers. The essential lesson taught by Islamic history is that extremist groups, such as those mentioned before and others, are ejected from the mainstream of Islam; they are marginalized, and they eventually come to be treated as a heretical aberration to the Islamic message. Historically, the Muslim moderate mainstream has weathered and prevailed over many extremist and violent groups and orientations. The problem, however, as noted earlier, is that the traditional institutions of Islam that historically acted to marginalize extremist creeds no longer exist. This is what makes this period of Islamic history far more troublesome than any other, and this is also what makes modern puritan orientations far more threatening to the integrity of the morality and values of Islam than any of the previous extremist movements. Extreme acts of ugliness today represent the culmination of a process that has been in the making for the past two centuries. In the same fashion, the culmination of Salafism, Wahhabism, apologetics, and Islamic nationalisms has become a synchronism that I have called Puritanical-Salafism.

WAHHABISM: THE PURITANS OF ISLAM

I started writing about the pervasive impact of Wahhabi Islam on the contemporary Muslim consciousness in the second half of the 1990s. At the time, the only Muslim critiques of Wahhabism were written from sectarian, typically Shi'i, or Sufi perspectives. The narrative that I presented and the conclusions I drew were at that time fraught with controversy and were rarely made or heard. It is difficult to describe the range of reactions that a nonsectarian and non-Sufi criticism of Wahhabism managed to arouse at that time. To contend that Wahhabi Islam cannot be understood as some form of reform movement that sought to restore the pristine egalitarianism and pure monotheism of Islam to its former self was, to say the least, bound to be unsettling for many people. There were two reasons for this: one, any Muslim intellectuals that took on the task of criticizing Wahhabism understood very well that they were inviting nothing less than the ire of Saudi Arabia at a time when Saudi influence spanned not just the Muslim world but the majority of Islamic institutions in the West. Even more, many Western academic institutions had accepted generous grants of funding from the Saudis or their allies, and that gave the Saudis a certain amount of leverage in academia that could not simply be ignored. Two, and more importantly, there was an emotional barrier of sorts and a considerable amount of reluctance on the part of most Muslims to acknowledge and confront the extent to which the Wahhabi creed had deeply penetrated and influenced the way Muslims related to their own religious tradition. This realization would come to constitute a rude and painful awakening. September 11, 2001, constituted a watershed moment—the psychological barrier was broken, and suddenly Saudi Arabia found itself on the defensive as a virtual flood of publications, I should add of very uneven quality, appeared, pointing a finger at Wahhabi Islam as the ideology responsible for so much intolerance, brutality, and ugliness, and for the global organizations such as the Taliban, al-Qaeda, and the terrorists of the 9/11 attacks. But as the decade since 9/11 progressed, as we would see, several academic voices rose to defend the good name of the Wahhabis and the state they created. A number of policymakers in the West realized that while all those involved with al-Qaeda and the Taliban were Wahhabis, not all Wahhabis sympathized with these organizations. Much more importantly, many Western scholars and policymakers recognized that while Wahhabism is largely responsible for the bad name it gives Islam in the contemporary age, it is not an ideology that is necessarily hostile to the West. They realized that mainstream Wahhabism reserves the worst of its ire for fellow Muslims and that in the spectrum of ideologies, mainstream Wahhabism does not pose the gravest threat to the security of the West. All of this set a duality in motion: on the one hand, the near absolute immunity from criticism or exposure that the Wahhabis enjoyed before 9/11 was greatly shaken, and in only a few years, one found open discussions in the media of the Muslim world on Wahhabism and its role, which was practically unheard of just a couple of years earlier. But with the breach of immunity that Wahhabism suffered, we witnessed a very intensified effort by Saudi Arabia to regain the ideological footing it had lost. As far as Western countries were concerned, as long as the impact and effect was on intra-Muslim conflicts, such as the Iranian-Saudi conflict, they were willing to look the other way as Saudi Arabia attempted to rebuild its theological empire. And now, as mentioned before, the biggest challenge confronting the countries affected by the Arab Spring, leave alone countries such as Somalia, Senegal, or Ethiopia, is the rededication of Saudi resources so that Wahhabism can reassert its former influence in the Muslim world.

So what is Wahhabism, and does it really have the impact and import that various writings, including my own, have ascribed to it?[17] It is impossible to quantify the exact amount of influence that Wahhabism has had on modern Muslim thinking, but it is notable that Islamist groups such as the Taliban and al-Qaeda have been heavily influenced by Wahhabi thought. The desecration of Sufi shrines and the destruction of cultural heritage sites is a uniquely Wahhabi trademark. It is very telling that mausoleums and shrines that have stood unmolested for centuries across the Muslim world have been attacked and destroyed by radical groups, all espousing distinctive Wahhabi beliefs, for the first time in history. Just since the beginning of the Arab Spring, such groups have attacked Sufi and Shi'i shrines in Iraq, Egypt, Libya, Mali, Pakistan, Senegal, Somalia, Sri Lanka, India, Kashmir, Afghanistan, Bosnia-Herzegovina, Ceuta (a Spanish North African enclave), and many others. It bears emphasis that these kinds of attacks are a unique trademark of Wahhabism and that in nearly every case, the site attacked had been revered by local Muslims for centuries. In each location mentioned above, there were multiple attacks on multiple sites, where even UNESCO World Heritage sites were attacked, people were killed, and corpses were desecrated, usually by being burned. Furthermore, since 9/11, attacks throughout the Muslim world against churches and other places of worship by Wahhabi groups have seen a very large increase.

This alarming escalation in attacks against sacred places is evidence of the broad destructive ability of the Wahhabi movement. But in addition to this, particularly as to issues involving women, Wahhabis tend to espouse some of the most patriarchic and exclusionary orientations within contemporary Islam. In every single situation where Wahhabi movements have appeared in the Muslim world, there have been corollary developments where women practically disappear from public life and their sense of empowerment as well as their political and social rights are sharply eroded. Moreover, one notices in countries that have attempted to apply Islamic law as a positive set of legal commandments that such efforts at implementation have tended to be heavily influenced by Wahhabi paradigms and systems of thought. This is so even in countries that are predominately Hanafi, such as Pakistan, or predominantly Maliki, such as Nigeria. Finally, many of the theological paradigms of Wahhabism, such as anti-rationalism, the rejection of the doctrine of intercession, the hostility to mysticism, the reliance on isolated hadith (reports attributed to the Prophet) in the deduction of laws, the prohibition of music, or the emphasis on ritualism at the expense of spiritualism have become part of the pervasive system of belief adopted by a wide variety of Sunni Islamic movements. One finds that even the pedantic doctrines adopted by Wahhabis became widespread in various parts of the Muslim world, including: whether it is permissible to use prayer beads, whether one may wipe his/her neck during the ablutions before prayer, whether women may attend funeral services or visit graves, whether it is lawful for Muslims to applaud by clapping, whether it is permissible to celebrate the Prophet's birthday or to celebrate the birthdays of loved ones in general, whether it is lawful to sing or listen to music, whether it is permissible to draw or paint human or animal figures and to frame or hang paintings, whether men should shorten their garments or tunics to the ankles, whether it is permissible for a Muslim to greet a non-Muslim with *al-salamu 'alaykum*, whether it is lawful to smile at a non-Muslim, whether women's foreheads and ears must be covered by a veil, whether the voices of women are a source of sexual enticement, whether men and women may shake hands, or whether women should be segregated by a curtain in mosques. As late as the 1970s, for the most part, all of these issues and many more had become settled as localized social practices and cultures manifested and developed a very broad array of native Islamicities. However, with the spread of Wahhabism, these and many other telltale indicators of Wahhabi thought once again jumped to the forefront of the Muslim controversies over Islamicity after having been marginal and dormant for centuries. For centuries, one could observe an enormous amount of diversity and richness in the ways various Muslim cultures expressed themselves in clothing, architecture, food, art, and music. Wahhabism, however, armed with texts that arose from an austere, grave, and ascetic culture, imposes a unidimensional textual existence that is what one might call ultracultural or countercultural. Wahhabism imagines that the only justified and authentic culture is the one that the text outlines and dictates. This often amounts to imposing an existence that is perceived to be beyond culture or an affirmative eradication of culture in favor of textually constructed order.

It is truly astounding how in just the past few decades, distinctively Wahhabi positions have spread to every corner of the Islamic world and have become a part of what the average Muslim identifies as genuinely Islamic. At times it is difficult to explain, especially to those who have not lived through the period of transition in which Wahhabism seeped into every aspect of Muslim life, the extent to which the Wahhabi attempt to replace genuinely rooted cultural expressions with text-based constructions of life, which is truly an unprecedented aberration in Islamic history. Because of its puritanical, idealized, and thoroughly mythologized view of the past, the Wahhabi orientation cannot reconcile between its understanding of this idealized view of the past and the complexity and diversity of cultures. It replaces cultures with orders of laws that are not the least concerned with all matters of beauty that would help the soul flourish. As a result, Wahhabi influence has added a dimension of oppressiveness and vehemence to contemporary Muslim life that frequently borders on the morbid. In my view, if the seeming ugliness that one witnesses today was a part of Islam from its very inception, there simply would have been no way for Islam to survive and thrive as a religion for over 1,400 years. Even for the generations born in the 1940s, 1950s, and 1960s, the Islam that most Muslims grew up with was distinctively more rational and humane than the forms of puritan Islam that became widespread in the 1980s and 1990s and that remain prevalent today.

To illustrate what I mean by the imposition of systems or orders of law instead of accommodating or celebrating the varieties of cultural expression,

I will give an example taken from a very popular Wahhabi book that I have encountered being cheaply sold or distributed for free in the Arab world, the United States, Canada, Europe, Indonesia, Malaysia, and Singapore. I am fairly sure that it has been translated to even more languages and has reached every corner of the globe where Muslims exist. The sheer unreasonableness and pronounced misogyny in this brand of literature is truly bewildering.[18] The book was published and distributed by a Lebanese press, probably with Saudi backing and funding, and it is authoritatively titled: *Rules for the Lives of Muslim Women*.[19] Even after the extremely bloody Lebanese civil war and the Israeli invasion and occupation of southern Lebanon, this country rightly prided itself on a very robust and free publishing industry in which there was a culture that resisted intellectual censorship, even when attempted by the government. Recently, however, Saudi interests have invested heavily in the Lebanese publishing industry, and this has had an unfortunate impact on the kind and quality of titles that have been coming out, at least from the Sunni publishing houses of Lebanon. The author introduces his book by assuring Muslim women that they will find no culture or system of thought that will serve their well-being on this earth and in the Hereafter like the clear path of God. The author warns Muslim women against becoming seduced by the allures of Satan by abandoning God's way and following the whims and false glamour of the West. If they do so, they are bound to lose their honor and dignity and their happiness, security, and faith. The author then proceeds to reproduce a set of puritanical determinations that have become commonplace in contemporary Muslim culture. The following is a partial list of the determinations of this author in the order in which they appear in his book: according to the author, a Muslim wife may not worship God by fasting without the permission of her husband because her husband may want to have sex with her during the day (when Muslims fast, they may not engage in sexual intercourse or ejaculate); a woman may not speak with her fiancée over the telephone because she may seduce him; a woman engaged to a man may not go out with him in public because she may seduce him; a bride seated in a car with her groom and driven by a relative must make sure not to wear perfume because she may seduce the relative driver; a woman who wishes to go to the mosque to learn the Qur'an must obey her father if he forbids her from going, and the father need not express any reason for his opposition; the same applies to the husband's command; a man who marries a woman with the intention of divorcing her after having his pleasure with her but fails to inform her of his intention does not commit a sin, and the marriage is valid; a woman may not refuse her husband sex except if she is ill, and refusing a husband sex without compelling justification is a grave sin (*kabira*). On the other hand, a husband may refuse his wife sex for any reason or no reason at all; as a legal matter, the voice of a woman is not an *'awra* (a privacy that must be concealed from all except a *mahram*, the blood kin of a woman who she may not marry); nonetheless, because of its seductive powers, the voice of women should not be heard in public or in a private setting where it might cause sexual enticement; women should not mix with men in public ways or forums, even if women are wearing the hijab; even if wearing the hijab, women should not travel unless accompanied by a male *mahram*; a woman may not chew gum because it is seductive; women may not dance in front of other women in a wedding, even if there are no men around, because it might be sexually arousing to other women; women may not shorten their head hair because doing so is considered imitating men. However, women *must* remove any facial hair, such as a beard or mustache, because it is more feminine to do so and because a woman must be sexually appealing to her husband (i.e., facial hair on a woman is not sexually appealing); women should not attend funerals or gravesites or convey their condolences to foreign men so as to avoid sexual enticement; a husband may command his wife not to see or talk to her parents, but she may not do the same; a husband may prohibit his wife from keeping certain company or having certain friends, but she cannot do the same. [20]

This is just a sample from this genre of literature that floods the Muslim markets and that pretends to represent the doctrines of Shari'ah law. This kind of discourse is oblivious to culture (*'urf*), often dealing with culture, if at all, as a nuisance or a state of ignorance to be overcome. [21] However, the determinations above do not reflect the culture or lived experience of the vast majority of Muslims around the world as their cultures developed over the centuries. As noted above, these determinations, which betray a compulsive obsession with sexual allurements, are based on texts that emerged at different times of Islamic history and from a number of geographic and demographic localities and were attributed to the Prophet as a form of hadith. Yet puritans take these singular reports as if they never had a sociohistorical context and assert them as the laws of living or the rules defining what should be the proper way for living, and in doing so, they invariably clash with and attempt to negate culture. Most Muslims, not living in puritanically controlled states, would find an undeniable tension between their Islamically influenced consciousness and the very different state of consciousness that would be required to live according to the rules above. Most Muslims would find the determinations above unreasonable because they clash with their lived experiences in existing Muslim cultures and also because they would innately feel that the determinations above are at odds with ideas that they were raised with, such as that Islam vindicated the rights of women or that Islam honored and celebrated women. The disturbing fact, however, is that although many Muslims will be troubled by these determinations, many will not find the confidence or courage to be repulsed by them and reject them outright. And herein is the real success and danger of Wahhabism. Because of the circumstances described below, Wahhabism has succeeded in putting so many Muslims on the defensive, as these Muslims feel neither the sense of juristic competence nor the strength to stand up in a systematic and concerted way to the moral and sometimes physical assaults of the Wahhabis.

By the arguments above, I do not mean to intimate that cultures, as opposed to what I called orders of law, are always right or morally superior. However, cultures play a material role in defining the *ma'ruf* (social good), which, as discussed earlier, means what is perceived or recognized to be good from the prism of socialization. As noted earlier, antisocial values or behavior would be known as *munkar*, while *ma'ruf* is a socially contingent good. Cultures do not necessarily define correctness or goodness, but cultures do embody what, through the cumulative conduct of generations of people, have come to be recognized as normatively desirable. By their nature, cultures entail a level of consensus similar to certain conceptions of *ijma'* in Islamic jurisprudence. Cultures are also subject to reform and change as a particular socially based consensus crumbles and others emerge after new normative demands are negotiated and renegotiated. In contrast, orders of law are artificial constructs of life without acculturation—they are normative demands that did not withstand the test of social negotiation. Of course, as people accept orders of law and try to live according to their system of demands, an inevitable process of acculturation takes place as people are forced to renegotiate competing interests and desires within the coercive confines of the imposed order.

Similar to codes of law, orders of law provide for straightforward rules and positive commands, but unlike codified legal systems, orders of law do resolve actual or potential social problems or conflicts. The purpose of these de facto orders of law is the law itself—the laws come to embody the object and purpose because the laws are seen as inherently good. There might be apologetic justifications that claim that the orders of law serve desirable functional or practical purposes, but these justifications are secondary and marginal. They are asserted not as a result of any empirical reality from which the laws emerge. Rather, the orders of law exist first, and then the functional and practical justifications and defenses are found later.

Apologetic rhetoric does not change the quality of the empirical lived reality that people are forced to experience as they endure orders of law that cause hardship or harm. Likewise, apologetic rhetoric does not alter or improve the moral quality of acts. And no amount of apologetic rhetoric about how Islam liberated and honored women will make determinations about women such as those discussed above more ethically palatable. There is also no escaping the fact that these are ugly determinations, and this forces us to confront the existential question: Is it possible for God to will such ugliness? How can we be sure that we are not projecting onto the divine text our own weaknesses and ugliness and then using God to rubberstamp our most base desires? I have dealt with very similar determinations in my book titled *Speaking in God's Name* and attempted to prove that such determinations are not objectively mandated by Islamic sources. In fact, because of their selective treatment of the textual evidence, these determinations engage in what I called textual authoritarianism by abusing the integrity of the text. It bears emphasis that I am not claiming that there is simply no basis whatsoever for these determinations. What I am saying is that I do not believe that a fair and balanced or reasonable reading of the Qur'an, the traditions of the Prophet, and the precedents of the companions, as well as benefiting from sociological and anthropological evidence, utilizing the insights of gender studies, the employment of reason and rational analysis, and the exercise of moral and ethical philosophy would support the claimed Islamicity of these determinations. Aside from betraying a profound obsession with sexual enticement, these determinations have the clear effect of denying women their intellect and soul, and they exclude women as viable and necessary contributors to society. They turn women into a heaving bundle of sexual enticements and allures and then punish them for the sexual fantasies men have projected onto them. This, in my view, is inconsistent with the history and ethics of Islam and the nature and role of divinity.

I recall that in 2004, the BBC reported that a Muslim cleric living in Spain was sentenced to fifteen months in prison and fined for writing a book purportedly advising Muslim men on how to discipline and beat a disobedient wife. According to the BBC, the cleric wrote: "The blows should be concentrated on the hands and feet using a rod that is thin and light so that it does not leave scars or bruises on the body." In his own defense, the cleric claimed that he was simply practicing his religion and interpreting passages of the Qur'an. Issues of freedom of speech aside, the tragedy in my view is that this cleric and his book do not represent some marginal and insignificant phenomenon in modern Islam that can be simply dismissed as unrepresentative, fanatic, or extreme.[22] Yet at the same time, it is certain that most Muslims who hear of this case will immediately protest that what this cleric wrote is not the true Islam and will actively distance themselves from his position. Most certainly, the vast majority of Muslim women, at least those who are educated, would not accept that their husbands have a right to strike or discipline them. Furthermore, the personal laws of most Muslim countries consider striking a spouse sufficient grounds for divorce. Be that as it may, one cannot pretend that the cleric's position is not founded on a valid, but in my opinion incorrect, reading of the textual sources in Shari'ah.[23] The reality is that Islamic books are replete with references about how, under exceptional circumstances, a disobedient wife could be reprimanded by being beaten lightly by her husband. Typically, such works emphasize that a disobedient wife should not be beaten in a fashion that causes pain or that leaves marks or bruises and that the face should not be struck. These restrictions and qualifiers are cited as sufficient proof of the humanism and mercifulness of the law toward women.[24] Nevertheless, I think it is fair to say that modern, educated Muslims feel sufficiently uncomfortable and restless about the wife-beating positions and especially the purported Qur'anic reference to the topic.[25] I think the very fact that modern Muslims try so hard to mitigate and understate the effect of the wife-beating texts is a strong indication of the intuitive level of moral discomfort that most Muslims feel about the existence of these types of determinations. Furthermore, it is fair to say that intuitively, most Muslims feel that any laws legitimating the beating of disobedient wives are inconsistent with the morality and ethics of the Islamic message itself. Despite this intuitive discomfort, few Muslims dare challenge this type of literature because a combination of the puritan and apologetic discourses in Islam have succeeded in convincing most Muslims that these determinations are embedded in the original religious texts—namely, the Qur'an and Sunna.[26] And those who challenge these misogynist determinations, if they manage to escape being branded as heretics, quickly find themselves placed on the margins of contemporary Islamic orthodoxy.

The truth of the matter is that when this cleric in Spain argued that his discourse was mandated by nothing other than the original text and that he is powerless to change the meaning of religious texts, he was probably being sincere and honest in believing that he had no other options or choices. What I think is problematic is not the opinion of this one cleric or another but the whole dynamic that typically follows from the expression of these kinds of opinions. Shortly after the conviction of the cleric, some Western writers claimed that the Muslim cleric's views are further evidence of the enormity of the cultural gap between Western and Muslim values. Muslims in Europe and elsewhere responded by condemning the West's hypocrisy and double standards in banning the cleric's writings and in imprisoning him while pontificating endlessly about the absence of such liberal values of freedom in Muslim cultures. What usually emerges from this is that while some Muslims will claim that this kind of incident is further proof of the West's ill intent toward Islam, some Western writers will come forward to triumphantly and self-servingly ponder: "Why do these Muslims hate us!"[27] Inevitably, Islamophobes indulge their bigotries and capitalize on the situation by unleashing rabid attacks on Islam. Meanwhile, Muslim apologists rush to the defense of their faith by minimizing the import of views such as those held by the cleric and thus end up sweeping any unyielding problems under the proverbial rug. Ultimately, puritans exacerbate the adversity by taking a defiant stance insisting that whatever the West finds desirable must be undesirable for Muslims and that indeed the West is right about one thing: Islam and the West are exact opposites, and they will always clash.

This whole dynamic is stiflingly inhibitive of the development of productive thought because of its fundamentally reactive nature. But it is this reactive environment that allows puritanical thought to thrive. In my view, if instead of abandoning it to the puritans Muslims would take moral responsibility for Shari'ah, they would quickly realize that far from being mandated or inevitable under Islamic law, these misogynist determinations represent an ethical choice. The textual sources of Shari'ah provide moral directions, and it is up to Muslims to decide which course to take. For example, the Islamic tradition is full of admonitions uttered by the Prophet and the companions strictly prohibiting physical violence against women and also prohibiting the striking of wives. In some interesting historical reports, it is stated that in the cultural practice of Arabs, if a man struck a woman for any reason, this man would be ostracized and shamed for the rest of his life, and that because of this man's conduct, his lineage would be greatly shamed as well for many generations to come.[28] But, as noted earlier, the traditions and reports that challenge and deconstruct the purported Islamicity of the misogynist positions and that prove the illegality of wife beating in Islamic law are not accessible or commonly known to most Muslims.[29] Therefore, the ethical (or unethical) choices of the puritans and Wahhabis have a virtual monopoly over the field, and they are able to position their interpretations and determinations as the only real and true Islamic position. And, as noted above, this further exacerbates the role of apologetics in Islam because of the tension felt by most Muslims between their intuitive sense about the ethics of Islam and the morally inconsistent legal determinations promoted in Islam's name. Trying to mitigate tension between the inherited tradition and contemporary notions of reasonableness and goodness by emphasizing the technical limitations set on wife beating is not only morally dishonest and self-delusional, but it is also quite unnecessary. If the Wahhabis and puritans did not possess a virtual monopoly over Islamic legal discourse, the misogynist tradition in Islam could be deconstructed from its very roots without having to resort to apologetics.

The influence of Wahhabism in contemporary Islam is demonstrated not only by the ability of authors of misogynist literature to position themselves as the bearers of "the one and true Islam," but by something even more basic and much more troubling. Wahhabism managed to persuade Muslims of what may be called the tyranny of the text. According to this paradigm, the text is not a major participant in the search for God's law but it is the only participant. The rational premises of the Shari'ah and, therefore, also the reasonableness of its determinations and outcomes are contained only in the text as a fully exhausted moral potential. Hence, there is no untapped moral potential contained in the text or possibly achievable through the text because rationality and reasonableness are not enabled and empowered by the text. Rather, the text makes the role of rationality and reasonableness redundant and thus largely irrelevant. I will explain this argument further in the next section of the book, but for now it is important to emphasize that Wahhabis—for all their talk about going back to the original sources, and as many of their contemporaries in as early as the nineteenth century pointed out—espoused a fundamentally static and tyrannical paradigm. As noted earlier, they went back to the original sources not to perform dynamic and innovative *ijtihad* but to uncover what they already believed to be the one and only correct law of God. This is why on hearing that the Grand Rector of Azhar Shaykh al-Maraghi (d. 1364/1945) had affirmed that Shari'ah law must change and develop with the shifting demands of time and place, the Wahhabi apologist 'Ali 'Abd Allah al-Qusaymi (d. 1417/1996) scoffed at the very idea. Al-Qusaymi insisted that it is well known that the rules of Shari'ah are eternal and valid for every time, place, and circumstance and that it should be obvious that God's legislation, which is found in the Qur'an and Sunna, are perfect and permanent.[30] As discussed earlier, this amounts to a rejection of all contingencies in the determination of the law and, with that, the very possibility of perpetuating a viable and dynamic legal system. The Wahhabis believe that text has but a single meaning, and if not, then only a very limited range of meanings. This belief, coupled with the conviction that more than anything else the reasons for *khilaf* and *ikhtilaf* (disagreements and competing interpretations or determinations) are impiety and the insidious conniving of the devil, accounts for the Wahhabi's notorious legendary intolerance for all Muslims who did not share their understandings of Shari'ah. It became much easier for the Wahhabis to consider their Muslim opponents heretics and apostates once it was decided that such Muslims suffered from deep moral flaws instead of a difference of opinion. I will return to the subject of the intolerance of the Wahhabi sect, but the real paradox was that what attracted many in the late nineteenth and early twentieth centuries to the ideas of Wahhabism was Wahhabism's liberating rhetoric about reactivating *ijtihad* by returning to the original sources instead of relying on the legal precedents of the law guilds. Influential scholars such as Rashid Rida (d. 1354/1935), Shah Wali Allah (d. 1176/1762), Muhammad al-Shawkani (d. 1250/1834), Hafiz Wahba (d. 1387/1967), Ghulam Rasul (d. 1247/1831), and Wilayat 'Ali (d. 1269/1852) played ill-conceived roles in advocating the cause of Wahhabism, but a careful reading of their writings clearly shows that the only aspects of Wahhabism to which they were drawn was its rejection of superstitious practices and social customs that they considered antithetical to the spirit and message of Islam. Keenly aware of the challenges of colonialism and modernity, these thinkers were drawn to any movement that raised the banner of the reactivation of *ijtihad* because in their minds this would open the gateway to innovative and dynamic thinking in an age of fast-paced and sweeping industrial, technological, economic, and cultural changes in the world. Wahhabism, however, was ill equipped to play this role because of its fanatic hostility to rationalism and to what Wahhabis called *bida'*, or innovations, which doctrinally was used in a conservative and reactionary fashion to guard against change or development.[31] Retrospectively, the paradoxical inconsistencies between the way some intellectuals, such as those mentioned above, perceived the Wahhabi movement and the movement's reality as reflected by its actual practices might appear blatantly obvious. But for reasons that will become more apparent, the Wahhabis employed a dogma and rhetoric that positioned them as guardians of the faith and did it in a fashion that was difficult to penetrate or challenge. Nevertheless, many scholars living at the time of the emergence of Wahhabism did notice and warn against the Wahhabis' exaggerated proclivity toward exclusionism and did go to some pains in pointing out that the Wahhabis' claim of returning to the original sources created a very narrow orthodoxy that invariably favored Wahhabi positions and excluded all else. Indeed, one notes with some irony that compelled by their own pedagogical and methodological commitments, the Wahhabis were eventually forced to condemn their one-time supporters, such as Rashid Rida, as heretics. Below I cite a number of nineteenth- and early twentieth-century scholars who went to great lengths to condemn "the Wahhabi paradox," that of raising the banner of returning to the original sources and *ijtihad* while at the same time opposing any *ijtihad* that fell out of the narrow confines of what Wahhabis accepted as orthodox. Many of the same scholars decried the fact that the Wahhabis were particularly adept at constructing perceptions of their roles as the guardians of the faith—constructions that were difficult to penetrate or challenge. The Wahhabis succeeded in constructing cogently powerful archetypes of religious meaning by claiming a pristine relationship to revelation through the medium of the text and by treating the oral tradition (hadith and Sunna) as a textualized positivistic narrative. In reality, the Wahhabis projected backward their socialized and accultured normativities onto the tradition and then objectified this tradition so as to render their constructs unassailable. This problem has led to the spread of what amounts to a pervasive epistemic block that has been meticulously constructed by Wahhabi missionaries and their rhetoric and that has been effective in preventing contemporary Muslims from noticing the fundamental inconsistencies and lack of coherence in Wahhabi doctrines regarding *ijtihad*, on the one hand, and their hatred of *bida'*, on the other, and their doctrinal endorsement of *ijtihad* to one extent or another countered by their staunch anti-rationalism.

Beyond this, it is a true measure of the impact of Wahhabis today that within the contested circles of orthodoxy, it is virtually impossible to introduce into the discursive dynamics any form of endorsement of the use of or reliance on rationality and reasonableness in Islamic law. The proper balance to be struck between rationality and textuality has been the subject of a protracted and complex history in the Islamic civilization. Furthermore, for most of Islamic history, there has been a spirited and often vigorous debate between the textual literalists (Ahl al-Hadith and al-Akhbariyyun), on the one hand, and on the other, the other schools of thought that integrated methods for weighing the objectives or purposes of the law, the original intent of the legislator, the desired public goods or goals, and equity (Ahl al-Ra'y and al-Usuliyyun). Right now is not the place to give a full account of these schools of thought and their historical struggles. Nevertheless, it is important to note that the narrative of these struggles, at least as told by Orientalist scholars, is fairly straightforward with an identified period of ascent and descent. In this traditional scholarly narrative, reason, equity, and discretion were in very wide use in the first centuries of the Islamic civilization. Indeed, there was an active widespread movement of borrowing, co-opting, preserving, and translating the Greek philosophical texts into Arabic, and this led to the rise of the rationalist school (the Mu'tazila) and the neo-Platonist philosophers in Islam. In response to the rise of the rationalist schools of thought and to a perceived threat to orthodoxy, conservative textualist and literalist schools of thought, usually called the traditionists, emerged that opposed the use of philosophy and unfettered reason. The conflict between the rationalist camp and the traditionists became so intense and feverish that the state was forced to step in, clearly favoring the rationalists over the traditionists. In the third Islamic century, the Abbasid state imposed an inquisition (known as the Mihna) that lasted around fifteen years from 833 to 848, during which the state persecuted the traditionists and tried to force all scholars to accept the foundational principles of the Mu'tazili rationalist school of thought. Eventually, the Mihna proved to be an utter failure, and the Abbasids were forced to relent, officially ending the Inquisition, which was seen as a great victory for the traditionists.[32] Very much like the thesis alleging that the doors of *ijtihad* were closed in the fourth/tenth century and that Islamic law ceased to produce anything new, here it is alleged that Islamic rationalism was well on its way to death around the same period. If ending the inquisition did not herald the triumph of Islamic anti-rationalism, it is often argued that the Sunni Shafi'i jurist and theologian Abu Hamid al-Ghazali (d. 505/1111) finished the task off by writing such a supposedly convincing refutation of Hellenistic philosophy that for all practical purposes, the rationalist school in Islam had ceased to exist from there on. This narrative of the rise and demise of rationalism in Islam is not only accepted by most Orientalists but also by most Muslim scholars.[33]

I think this narrative that strains to prove the dominance of the Ash'ari theological school and the death of the Mu'tazila and that implies that Islamic law and theology were overtaken by a suffocating traditionalism after rationalist orientations were pushed into oblivion are simply too essentialized and linear to be useful. These narratives were developed by Orientalists to address an ideologically predispositioned question that seemed to haunt so many of them: What went wrong with Islam? The Muslim acceptance of such simplified and streamlined narratives served a useful political purpose. These narratives gave modern Muslims the comfortable illusion that all that needs to be done to revitalize the Islamic civilization is for Muslims to reopen the doors of *ijtihad* and to reclaim rationalism in modern Muslim theology and jurisprudence. But these highly generalized megahistories that tell of the extinction of the Mu'tazila and the dominance of the Ash'ariyya and the hegemony of traditionalism and the death of rationalism often falter on the hard bedrock of microfacts and microhistory. This is not the place for a full exposition on this topic, but with more nuanced and narrower scopes of inquiry, one discovers that the picture is far more complicated and must be qualified by the specification of time periods and regional variations in the world of Islam. So, for instance, rationalism could have thrived in Oman at the same time that anti-reason-based traditionalism dominated in Nishapur. In any case, the extent and breadth of the anti-rationalist impact that Wahhabism has had on the Muslim world is unprecedented and unparalleled in Islamic history. Until very recently, any respectable education in Shari'ah sciences included texts on logic, jurisprudential philosophy, and the study of disputations (*'ilm al-munazarat*). Only after Wahhabism took root did it become possible for purported jurists to rely on nothing more than the sciences of transmission and little else to gain social credibility not as simple narrators of inherited reports but as full-fledged jurists or *fuqaha*. The widespread impact of Wahhabism is not so much because of the doctrinal substance of Wahhabism—Wahhabis drew on the long history of the Hanbali Ahl al-Hadith movement in Islam, which has distinguished itself by its unwavering textualism and anti-rationalism. Ahl al-Hadith, like the early Wahhabis, considered Ash'ari theology as deviant and heretical as Mu'tazilism. Indeed, Wahhabi sources, like their Ahl al-Hadith or Akhbari predecessors, are full of diatribes against the heresies of all Muslim theological schools, including Ash'arism, and all forms of Usuli methodologies. But it is largely for political reasons that some scholars have tried to obfuscate the difference or reconcile Ahl al-Hadith and Ash'arism.[34] The near hegemonic influence of Wahhabism on modern Islam is due to the incredibly long-arm reach of Wahhabism and its enormous financial resources. Ironically, the reach and penetration of Wahhabism has been greatly facilitated by modernity and the popularizing opportunities made available by mass media and communications technology. Of all the current Islamic orientations, puritanism, with its variations on the basic themes of Wahhabism, is unmatched in its effective utilization of the venues of mass communications, including publications, electronic media, recordings, and so on. Through the deployment of these tools, the influence of Wahhabism has taken root in modern Islam to the point that, especially among many Muslim youth, when one makes reference to the dictates of reason or what can be noted and relied on as a reasonable position, the burden of proof has been stood on its head. One very often will be confronted with an objection that people cannot take notice of something known to be true by reason (the rationally known, or *al-'aqliyyat*) or of the reasonability of certain assumptions unless a text exists that affirms that such-and-such conclusion is rational or reasonable. This is akin to saying that nothing can be shown or relied on as rational or reasonable unless a text can affirm the same. In effect, Wahhabism has succeeded in divorcing reason and reasonableness from the mechanics of Shari'ah to such an extent that it shifts the burden of proof on any claim based on common sense or logic to come up with corroborating text. As specialists of Islamic jurisprudence have known and argued for centuries, this position is so extreme that, of necessity, it will produce utterly absurd legal results and make a mockery of the legal system.[35]

As mentioned above, the financial resources made available to the creators and propagators of the Wahhabi creed are unprecedented because they far exceed the resources available to any other creed in Islamic history. But part of what accounts for the spread of Wahhabi influence in the Muslim world is Saudi Arabia's unique position as the guardian of the two holy sites of Mecca and Medina. Through the regulation of orthodoxy at pilgrimage, Wahhabis have an opportunity to influence the way Islam is practiced around the world. Being the custodians of Mecca and Medina, the Wahhabis in Saudi Arabia have a monopoly on defining the acceptable rites and rituals during pilgrimage, and besides having a captive audience for a limited period of time during the annual pilgrimage, they enjoy a powerful symbolic position as the protectors of Islamic authenticity and purity in the two most holy sites.[36] Even before the discovery of oil, Wahhabis aggressively proselytized their doctrines, although, as explained below, they have not done so under their own banner or label. In fact, from their inception and to this day, Wahhabis refuse to consider themselves a creed, sect, or school of thought. They have presented and continue to present themselves as the bearers and protectors of the one and only true Islam.

MUHAMMAD BIN 'ABD AL-WAHHAB: THE FOUNDER AND HIS THOUGHT

The foundations of Wahhabi theology were set into place by the eighteenth-century evangelist Muhammad bin 'Abd al-Wahhab (d. 1206/1792). He grew up in a family of Hanbali jurists from the area of Najd, which in comparison to the Hijaz (where Mecca and Medina are located) was far less cosmopolitan and far more austere and insular. The Hijaz was at least exposed to the broad plurality of Muslim cultures and practices because of the constant flow of pilgrims and merchants from around the Muslim world. Mecca and Medina in particular had preserved a centuries-old tradition of tolerance and acceptance toward the broad array of schools, creeds, and sects that constituted Islam. Every substantial school of thought, jurisprudential or theological, including many Sufi mystical orders, maintained a permanent or, at the very least, frequent presence in Mecca. Before the commencement of the Wahhabi period, the post of the sharif (governor) of the holy sites entailed many honorific and charitable roles, but there was a persistent and uninterrupted custom of tolerating a broad array of manifestations of Islamicities. *Zandaqa* (heresy) prosecutions were practically unheard of in the Hijaz because of the very large number of *du'a* (evangelists) representing and promoting their sects and causes that flooded into the holy cities each year. Interestingly, according to some notable literary historians, Medina and Mecca became the hot spots for art, poetry, polemicists, and dissenting ideas from the time of the Umayyads onward.[37] In comparison to the dynamic culture of the Hijaz, Ibn 'Abd al-Wahhab was raised in a little, eventless, and sheltered town named Dar'iyya, located in the already austere and insular area of Najd. Even during the Ottoman era, it was difficult to determine which, if any, of the schools of legal thought was the most widespread in the Hijaz. However, there is sufficient evidence to suggest that the rather conservative Hanbali school of thought predominated in the region of Najd, and this is the school in which Ibn 'Abd al-Wahhab was raised. Ibn 'Abd al-Wahhab's father was a Hanbali judge, and a number of his brothers were certified jurists within the same school of thought. Ibn 'Abd al-Wahhab travelled outside of Najd to the eastern oasis of al-Ahsa' Najd, the Hijaz, Syria, and Iraq, but he was apparently shocked and dismayed at the many syncretistic practices, folkloric customs, and social and theological diversity that had become the mark of most Muslim cultures. To his mind, this could only have happened because people strayed from the clear, straight path God set out and followed their whims and desires instead. Equally culpable in his view were the jurists who failed to put an end to these deviations and heresies. With an unrelenting puritanical zeal, Ibn 'Abd al-Wahhab sought to rid Islam of all the corruptions that he believed had crept into the religion—such corruptions practically included anything that was inconsistent with Ibn 'Abd al-Wahhab's austere upbringing in the deserts of Najd. Nevertheless, even in his hometown in Najd, most established Hanbali jurists, including his father, strongly disagreed with his message and methods and denounced him publicly, even going as far as eventually exiling him from his own home.[38] As discussed below, the spread of Ibn 'Abd al-Wahhab's thought in the Muslim world had little to do with the thought of the founder of the movement. Much of its missionary success is due to its successful co-optation of archetypal symbolisms of Islamic authenticity and legitimacy. Ibn 'Abd al-Wahhab resisted the indeterminacy of the modern age by escaping to a strict literalism in which the text became the sole source of legitimacy—more accurately, the selectively chosen texts that the Wahhabis deemed authoritative. Part of this paradigm is a strong antipathy to any form of historicism. But perhaps it is exactly because Ibn 'Abd al-Wahhab's thought was so much a product of his own context that he and his disciples were so opposed to any form of contextualism in understanding Islam.

According to Ibn 'Abd al-Wahhab's son and disciple, only the first three centuries of Islam could be said to have been authentically Islamic to any extent at all. After these centuries, Islamic history ceased to be Islamic as the religion was overcome by heretical innovations and corruptions.[39] The dialectical and indeterminate hermeneutics of the classical jurisprudential tradition were considered corruptions of the purity of the faith and law. Wahhabis were intolerant of the long-established Islamic practice of considering a variety of schools of thought to be equally orthodox and attempted to narrow considerably the range of issues on which Muslims may legitimately disagree. Orthodoxy was narrowly defined, and Ibn 'Abd al-Wahhab himself was fond of creating long lists of beliefs and acts which he considered hypocritical and the adoption or commission of which would immediately render a Muslim an unbeliever and an infidel. In one of the demonstrative examples, Ibn 'Abd al-Wahhab used the claim that if a Muslim, for instance, asserts that the consumption of bread or meat is unlawful in Islam, then he has become an infidel because it is clear that bread and meat are lawful in Islamic law. Likewise, if a Muslim tries to prohibit something that is permitted or permit something that is forbidden, he becomes an infidel. This, according to Ibn 'Abd al-Wahhab, applies to all things that are clear in Islam, and in that category falls the overwhelming majority of issues, because God made most matters clear and only left a narrow range of issues that are ambiguous and therefore subject to disagreement. [40] According to Ibn ʻAbd al-Wahhab, Muslim jurists often disagreed without sufficient reason, needlessly complicated matters, and indulged in pure sophistry. Most of their disagreements were caused by their reliance on reason and whim instead of just obeying the text. By their many disagreements, Muslim jurists divided Islam and caused Muslims to become weak. Ibn ʻAbd al-Wahhab was relentlessly hostile to all forms of intellectualism, mysticism, such as Sufism, and any sectarianism, such as Shiʻism, within Islam, considering all of these to be corrupt innovations that had crept into the religion due to un-Islamic influences. In Ibn ʻAbd al-Wahhab's view, Islam was fundamentally at odds with the pluralism, diversity, and richness that emerged in the Islamic civilization because, in his view, the truth was easily attainable, and the only challenge was in physical submission to the truth—not in comprehension or understanding. Therefore, disagreements and discourse were symptomatic of stubbornness and argumentativeness in failing to recognize the obvious and clear truth, and failure to physically submit was proof of weakness of faith. The Wahhabi creed also considered any form of moral thought that was not entirely dependent on the text as a form of self-idolatry and treated humanistic fields of knowledge, especially philosophy, as "the sciences of the devil."[41]

In what would become a regular Wahhabi practice, Wahhabis prepared pamphlet-sized collections containing traditions, attributed to the Prophet or companions, which condemned debate, argumentativeness, excessive eloquence, or sophistry. [42] Read without a historical or intellectual context, these oral reports were exploited in a dynamic that engineered sharply demarcated lines differentiating between a true Muslim who is willing to obey and submit without questions or hesitations, and a false or hypocritical Muslim who allows the intellect to get in the way of true submission. In an often exploited pedagogical method, Wahhabis generated absolutist categorical lists in which people, acts, or ideas would be classified as authentically Islamic or false innovations. In a very recent example, a Wahhabi writer and publisher generated a multivolume compendium listing heretical and blasphemous authors and books that must be avoided by all Muslims. Other than books that are critical of the Wahhabi approach, most of the books that made it to this blacklist are those that advocate any kind of rationalism in understanding or interpreting Islam. [43] This kind of exclusionary hostility to intellectualism and to historical contingencies might explain the Wahhabis' insistence on destroying most of the invaluable historical sites in Arabia, which dated back to the time of the Prophet and companions and even to the pre-Islamic era. [44] One of the unforgettable outrages committed by the Wahhabis took place in 1924, when the Wahhabis invaded and occupied Mecca. Among other atrocities, they burned an invaluable library containing forty thousand manuscripts and historical documents, sixty thousand very rare printed texts, and many historical artifacts. The library in Mecca was considered an invaluable collection containing manuscripts and items going back to the founding years of Islam and numerous sources on early and extinct schools of thought. But it is exactly because this library contained a diversified collection that could be mined to challenge the Wahhabi narrative on Islamic history, theology, and law that it was razed and burned to the ground. [45]

Ibn 'Abd al-Wahhab had a near obsessive preoccupation with the doctrine of *shirk* (associating partners with God, as in idolatry). For him, a practicing Muslim could commit particular acts that would expose or reveal the impurity of his belief in God and Islam. Such acts, according to Ibn 'Abd al-Wahhab, betrayed a willingness to engage in *shirk* and thus would result in taking a person out of the fold of Islam. In his writings, he consistently emphasized that there was no middle of the road for a Muslim—either a Muslim was a true believer or not, and if a Muslim was not a true believer, Ibn 'Abd al-Wahhab had no qualms about declaring the Muslim to be an infidel and treating him as such.[46] In fact, acting on his idea, the Wahhabis of Ibn 'Abd al-Wahhab presumed all Muslims to be apostates and infidels until such Muslims proved otherwise.[47] The only way to rebut the presumption and escape being put to death was to swear allegiance to the Wahhabis and their creed. But other than the practice of *takfir* (accusing Muslims of heresy and of being infidels), perhaps the most stultifying and even deadly characteristic of Wahhabism was its hostility to any human practice that would excite the imagination or bolster creativity. According to the Wahhabis, only frivolous people would be fond of the arts, such as music or poetry. In fact, according to them, any act that excites the imagination or augments individual creativity constitutes a step toward *kufr* (becoming an infidel) because it is bound to lead to heretical thoughts. A primary example in Wahhabi thought is music. Of course, the lawfulness of music was a hotly contested issue in Islamic law because, historically, jurists associated music gatherings (*majalis al-'azf*) with the consumption of wine and presence of scantly clad dancing girls (*majalis al-khamr wa al-mu'anasa* or *wa al-uns*). Usually, these festive meetings would be well attended by singing slave girls (*al-qiyan*), musicians, and prostitutes (*al-ghawani*), and Muslim jurists usually warned pious people of commingling with the corrupt youth who would frequent such establishments.[48] Regardless of the archetypal association in the minds of some jurists between music and moral depravity, the reality is the composition and performance of music has existed throughout Islamic history in practically every known Muslim society. There is no period in history where music and dancing failed to be a part of the lived reality of both urban and rural Muslim societies, and so the puritanical hostility of the Wahhabis to music is exceptional in its scale and determination. But as noted above, what is also unique about the Wahhabi approach on the issue is its explicit reference to the evils of individual creativity as a general matter and its unequivocal condemnation of imaginative or artistic thinking.[49] Therefore, not only music is forbidden, but even poetry written in praise of the Prophet is reprehensible if it indulges in exaggerations and excessive imagery. Ibn 'Abd al-Wahhab's son, for instance, wrote a long treatise attacking a poet for writing a poem praising the Prophet. In this treatise, he emphasized, time and again, that poetic imagery, if not based on physical and empirical facts, is sinful because it exaggerates the truth. In addition, he emphasized that any poetry that appears to sanctify the Prophet or give him superhuman qualities is heretical. According to Ibn 'Abd al-Wahhab's son, there is no such thing as a poetic license to exaggerate or misrepresent the physical and concrete facts of life.[50]

Ibn 'Abd al-Wahhab was unrelentingly hostile toward non-Muslims as well, insisting that a Muslim should adopt none of the customs of non-

Muslims and should not befriend them either. He argued that it was entirely immaterial what a non-Muslim might think about Muslim practices, and in fact it was a sign of spiritual weakness to care about whether non-Muslims were impressed by Muslim behavior or not. Ibn 'Abd al-Wahhab argued that Muslims must show enmity and hostility to unbelievers (*mushrikun*). Pursuant to a doctrine known as *al-wala' wa al-bara'* (literally, the doctrine of loyalty and disassociation), Ibn 'Abd al-Wahhab argued that it is imperative for Muslims not to befriend, ally themselves with, or imitate non-Muslims. This enmity and hostility of Muslims toward non-Muslims must be visible and unequivocal. For example, the Wahhabis prohibited the use of labels of respect, intended to honor human beings, such as "doctor," "Mr.," or "sir." Ibn 'Abd al-Wahhab argued that such prefixes were a form of associating partners with God, and, therefore, using them is enough to make a Muslim an infidel. But, more importantly, Ibn 'Abd al-Wahhab argued, the prefixes and labels were condemnable because using them constituted an imitation of the Western unbelievers and those who imitate the unbelievers are themselves unbelievers.[51] It is important to note that among those designated as unbelievers were Muslims who, in Ibn 'Abd al-Wahhab's view, became infidels because of their beliefs or actions. Therefore, in Ibn 'Abd al-Wahhab's thought, true Muslims should distance themselves not only from Christians or Jews, for instance, but also from infidel Muslims. In the balance of things, infidel Muslims are considered worse than Christians and Jews because their heretical beliefs or actions have rendered them into apostates. But in Ibn 'Abd al-Wahhab's view, all Muslims not subscribing to his understanding of Islam were considered either hypocrites or apostates, and in either case, they would be put to death.[52] For this reason, it is not surprising that a number of Western travellers who witnessed the events in question commented that while the Wahhabis treated the Jews and Christians well, they were brutal with fellow Muslims.[53]

Effectively, Ibn 'Abd al-Wahhab espoused a self-sufficient and closed system of belief that had no reason to engage or interact with the other except from a position of dominance. Rather tellingly, Ibn 'Abd al-Wahhab's orientation does not materially differ from the approach adopted by later Muslim groups concerning the irrelevance of universal moral values to the Islamic mission. This insularism and moral isolationism, clearly manifested in the writings of Ibn 'Abd al-Wahhab, was powerfully reproduced by ideologues of subsequent Islamic movements. This was, for instance, reproduced in Sayyid Qutb's (d. 1386/1966) notion that the world, including the Muslim world, is living in *jahiliyya* (darkness and ignorance associated with the pre-Islamic era).[54] This intellectual and moral isolationism was resisted, perhaps not very successfully, by a variety of jurists in the first half of the twentieth century. For instance, many of the articles published in the Azhar journal *Nur al-Islam* in the 1930s and 1940s attempted to engage, interact, and discourse with world thought. It is clear that at that time, many Muslim scholars tried to stay informed about the latest in European thought and attempted to discuss how the latest ideas in philosophy and sociology would impact Muslim culture. This more enlightened and universal orientation was soon marginalized by the much better funded Wahhabi orientation.

As noted above, despite his hostility to non-Muslims, Ibn 'Abd al-Wahhab's primary concern and interest was not with non-Muslims but with purportedly corrupt Muslims, with which he included the Ottoman Turks. In this sense, like later puritan movements, there was a strong political and nationalistic component to Ibn 'Abd al-Wahhab's thought. He described the Turks as the moral equivalents of the Mongols who invaded Muslim territories and then converted to Islam. However, their conversion to Islam was in name only, and they remained heathens. The Ottoman Turks, according to Ibn 'Abd al-Wahhab, should be treated as the primary enemies of Islam because they have always exercised a corrupting influence on the religion. In one of his treatises, Ibn 'Abd al-Wahhab described the Ottoman Caliphate as a heretical or infidel nation (*al-dawla al-kufriyya*), and claimed that supporting or allying oneself with the Ottomans was as bad a sin as supporting or allying oneself with Christians or Jews.[55] These anti-Turkish and anti-Ottoman arguments betrayed a clear Arab nationalism and perhaps an ethnocentrism in Ibn 'Abd al-Wahhab's thought. Ibn 'Abd al-Wahhab's disciples went even further with these ideas—they allied themselves with the non-Muslim British against the Muslim Ottomans in a bloody rebellion supported and often directed by the British.[56] Nevertheless, in Wahhabi thought this was hardly surprising because they considered the Ottomans heretics, and in their thinking, there was no sin worse than heresy.

Ibn 'Abd al-Wahhab argued that Muslims who engage in acts of *shirk* must be fought and killed, and he interpreted precedents set by the first Rightly-Guided Caliph, Abu Bakr (d. 13/634), in support of the argument that although people might hold themselves out as Muslims, they could and should be killed as hypocrites. Ibn 'Abd al-Wahhab claimed that Abu Bakr fought and killed many so-called hypocrites despite the fact that they practiced the five pillars of Islam. Arguing that his followers were justified in killing their Muslim opponents, he contended that the Ottoman Turks, their allies, and all other heretical and hypocritical Muslims were in truth infidels deserving of the worst death. He was also fond of citing a precedent in which Abu Bakr reportedly burned so-called hypocrites to death and used this purported precedent to argue that his supporters are justified in torturing their opponents.[57] For many reasons, there is no doubt that the Abu Bakr precedent cited by Ibn 'Abd al-Wahhab is apocryphal, but it is clearly demonstrative of Ibn 'Abd al-Wahhab's tendency to select precedents from the Islamic tradition that support cruel and inhumane behavior. This identical phenomenon of scouring through the vast annals of the tradition in search of cruel anti-humanistic reports that have been long dead and then rehabilitating, spreading, and empowering them so that they can justify the commission of acts of ugliness was widely used by al-Qaeda and many other militant groups. In all cases, most scholars who studied the purported Abu Bakr precedent concluded that the claim that Abu Bakr accused people who upheld the five pillars of hypocrisy and fought them is without support. Furthermore, the use of fire against Muslim or non-Muslim enemies is severely condemned in classical Islamic law. Several scholars documented that the report of Abu Bakr using fire against Muslim opponents was invented by his opponents and reported by highly suspect individuals.[58] Nevertheless, Ibn 'Abd al-Wahhab ignored this considerable body of contravening literature in his effort to justify killing and torturing those he considered heretical Muslims. It is worth noting that while apologist Muslims ignored purported precedents of cruelty in the Islamic tradition, the students of Ibn 'Abd al-Wahhab embraced and legitimated these precedents. The interpretive communities of the past had already expended a considerable amount of effort challenging and deconstructing these precedents. Classical scholars would often challenge the authenticity and historical veracity of these reports, or if the historical origins of such reports were inaccessible or unknown, the classical scholars often argued that precedents of cruelty were contrary to the ethics of the Qur'an and the Prophet. But by discarding and at times demonizing the interpretive communities of the past, Ibn 'Abd al-Wahhab had unfettered access to the precedents of cruelty unencumbered by the deconstructions of past scholars. Ibn 'Abd al-Wahhab was able to reinject these precedents into the heart of Muslim theology and law and therefore reinvent Islam on the basis of a new immorality.

Not surprisingly, Ibn 'Abd al-Wahhab and his followers engaged in rhetorical tirades against prominent medieval and contemporaneous jurists whom they considered heretical. They even ordered the execution or assassination of a large number of jurists with whom they disagreed. In his writings, Ibn 'Abd al-Wahhab frequently referred to jurists as "devils" or the spawn of Satan (*shayatin* and *a'wan al-shayatin*) and therefore removed any psychological barrier to violating the memories or lives of distinguished scholars.[59] According to Ibn 'Abd al-Wahhab and his followers, the juristic tradition, save a few jurists such as Ibn Taymiyya (d. 728/1328), whom they held in high esteem, was largely corrupt, and deference to the well-established schools of jurisprudential thought or even to contemporaneous jurists was an act of heresy.[60] Among the medieval jurists that the Wahhabis explicitly condemned as *kuffar* (infidels) were prominent scholars such as Fakhr al-Din al-Razi (d. 606/1210), Abu Sa'id al-Baydawi (d. 710/1310), Abu Hayyan al-Gharnati (d. 745/1344), al-Khazin (d. 741/1341), Muhammad al-Balkhi (d. 830/1426), Shihab al-Din al-Qastalani (d. 923/1517), Abu Sa'ud al-'Imadi (d. 982/1574), and many others. The characteristic common to these jurists was that as far as textual interpretation was concerned, they were not strict literalists. In addition, some of these scholars were suspected of harboring Shi'i sympathies or had integrated rationalist methods of analysis into their interpretive approaches to Islamic texts.[61]

Considering the dismissive attitude of the Wahhabis toward Islamic history and law, the movement came under severe criticism by a considerable number of contemporaneous scholars, most notably Ibn 'Abd al-Wahhab's own brother, Sulayman, and reportedly his father as well.[62] The main criticisms leveled against Ibn 'Abd al-Wahhab and his followers were that they exhibited very little regard for Islamic history, historical monuments, the Islamic intellectual tradition, and the sanctity of Muslim life.[63] Ibn 'Abd al-Wahhab's brother, as well as other critics, claimed that Ibn 'Abd al-Wahhab himself was an ill-educated, intolerant man who was ignorantly and arrogantly dismissive of any thoughts or individuals that disagreed with him.[64] Interestingly, according to the mufti of the Hanbalis in Mecca, Ibn Humaydi (d. 1295/1878) reported that Ibn 'Abd al-Wahhab's own father was seriously disappointed in his son because Ibn 'Abd al-Wahhab was not a diligent student of Islamic jurisprudence, and although he failed to understand the material taught in class, he was arrogantly defiant toward his teachers.[65] In fact, impatient with what he perceived as pointless complexity and needless sophistry, Ibn 'Abd al-Wahhab obstinately refused to complete his jurisprudential studies and dropped out of Shari'ah school.[66] However, Ibn Humaydi reports that fearing the wrath of his father, Ibn 'Abd al-Wahhab did not dare to start preaching his puritan message until after his father's death.[67]

Sulayman, Ibn 'Abd al-Wahhab's brother and a distinguished Hanbali scholar in his own right, wrote a treatise criticizing his brother and complaining that except for the most extreme and fringe fanatical elements, his brother's views were without precedent in Islamic history. In support of his argument that Ibn 'Abd al-Wahhab's behavior was unprecedented, Sulayman contended that the respectable scholars of Islam refrained from accusing the rationalists and mystics of heresy and instead tried to debate and persuade them peacefully. Sulayman in principle did not disagree that rationalism and mysticism were erroneous approaches to Islam, but according to Sulayman, none of the distinguished scholars dared to accuse their opponents of being infidels or hypocrites. In addition, the proper ethics and manners of Muslim scholars are to engage their opponents in discussion and debate and attempt to convince and persuade, not to coerce or threaten.[68] The problem was, according to Sulayman, that Muhammad bin 'Abd al-Wahhab did not concern himself with reading or understanding the works of the juristic predecessors, and so he was poorly rooted in the Islamic tradition. But at the same time, Muhammad bin 'Abd al-Wahhab tended to treat the words of some scholars, such as the Hanbali jurist Ibn Taymiyya, as if they were divinely revealed and not to be questioned or debated. But even then, Muhammad bin 'Abd al-Wahhab was very selective with the works of Ibn Taymiyya, citing only what he liked and ignoring the rest.[69] Sulayman and other scholars noted the irony in the fact that Muhammad bin 'Abd al-Wahhab and his followers, while prohibiting *taqlid* (imitation or following the precedents of jurists), ended up affirming and even mandating it, but in a different form. The Wahhabis prohibited the practice of *taqlid* as far as it related to jurists whom they did not like but demanded that Muslims imitate the Wahhabis themselves blindly and unthinkingly. In essence, the Wahhabis selected whatever they liked from the works of certain scholars in Islamic history and then demanded that all Muslims abide by their preferences. If any Muslim dared to challenge the preferences or choices of the Wahhabis, such a Muslim would be accused of hypocrisy and heresy. But as discussed previously, the problems perceptively noted by Sulayman were, in fact, illustrative of serious methodological contradictions of the anti-*taqlid* movement in the wake of modernity.

Sulayman complained that the Wahhabi methodology was based on a profound sense of despotism, where the whole of the Islamic intellectual tradition was dismissed out of hand and Muslims were given the choice of either accepting the idiosyncratic Wahhabi interpretations of Islam or being declared *kuffar* (infidels) and then risking getting killed at the hand of Wahhabis.[70] Effectively, Sulayman argued, the Wahhabis pretend as if they alone, after seven hundred years of history, discovered the truth about Islam, and consider themselves as if infallible. Therefore, in the Wahhabi paradigm, the only actual measure of commitment to Islam is to follow and obey them. If a Muslim disagrees with them, then by definition that Muslim is a heretic. As Sulayman succinctly put it, "You [Wahhabis] make the measure of people's faith their agreement with you and the measure of their disbelief, their disagreement with you."[71] Reportedly, Sulayman once asked his brother, "How many pillars are there in Islam?" Not surprisingly, Ibn 'Abd al-Wahhab responded by stating the obvious: "Everyone knows that the pillars of Islam are five," he answered. Sulayman promptly retorted: "Brother, you have made the pillars six, not five, and the sixth pillar is that all Muslims must agree with you because whoever does not you decree that he is an infidel (*kafir*)!"[72]

According to Sulayman, declaring Muslims infidels is considered a grave sin in Islam, and even Ibn Taymiyya prohibited the practice of *takfir* (branding Muslims as infidels).[73] In order to prove his point, Sulayman concluded his treatise by quoting fifty-two traditions, attributed to the Prophet and some of the companions, on the sin of accusing a Muslim of being an unbeliever or heretic.[74] Nevertheless, the Wahhabis were not swayed by the cumulative textual evidence or by the historical precedents because, Sulayman asserted, the Wahhabis believe Islam to have been in error for at least seven hundred years. The Wahhabis did not hesitate to call past Muslim generations in every location around the Muslim world heretics and infidels, and even the inhabitants and past generations of Mecca have not escaped these accusations.[75] Sulayman contends that from a theological point of view, the Wahhabi claims are very troubling because it is impossible for all Muslims, especially the inhabitants of the Prophet's city, Mecca, to have been deluded and mistaken in understanding and practicing their religion for so long.[76]

The simplicity, decisiveness, and incorruptibility of the religious thought of Ibn 'Abd al-Wahhab made it attractive to the desert tribes, especially in the area of Najd.[77] Ultimately, however, Ibn 'Abd al-Wahhab's ideas were too radical and extreme to have widespread influence on the Arab world, leave alone the Muslim world, during his lifetime.[78] In fact, it is quite likely that Ibn 'Abd al-Wahhab's ideas would not have spread even in Arabia had it not been for the fact that in the late eighteenth century, the Al Saud family united itself with the Wahhabi movement and rebelled against Ottoman rule in Arabia.[79] Armed with religious zeal and a strong sense of Arab nationalism, the rebellion was considerable, at one point reaching as far as Damascus in the north and Oman in the south. Egyptian forces under the leadership of Muhammad Ali in 1818, however, after several failed expeditions, quashed the rebellion, and Wahhabism, like other extremist movements in Islamic history, seemed to be on its way to extinction.[80] Egyptian and Turkish forces destroyed the city of Dar'iyya, the hometown of the first Saudi kingdom, and in retaliation committed their own atrocities by massacring the city's inhabitants. After occupying Mecca and Medina for a few years, confident that the Wahhabi danger had subsided, Muhammad 'Ali withdrew his forces and returned to Egypt.[81]

The various Wahhabi rebellions in the nineteenth century were very bloody as the Wahhabis indiscriminately slaughtered large numbers of Muslims, especially those belonging to Sufi orders and the Shi'i sect. In 1802, for example, the Wahhabi forces massacred the Shi'i inhabitants of Karbala, and in 1803, 1804, and 1806 the Wahhabis executed a large number of Sunnis whom they considered heretical in Mecca and Medina.[82] There are a number of surviving texts written by contemporaneous scholars or Western travellers that describe the Wahhabi treatment of Muslims in gruesome and vivid details.[83] Typically, on conquering a territory, even Mecca and Medina, the Wahhabis would put all males of fighting age to death and sexually assault the women before taking them and the surviving children captive. Properties of the conquered Muslims were confiscated as loot, with one fifth going to their Saudi leader. On many occasions towns would be given an opportunity to convert to Islam (which meant subscribe to Wahhabi dogma) before being attacked, but very frequently, populations were given guarantees of safe conduct (*aman*) only to be betrayed—the men were quickly dispatched and women and children became captives.[84]

The reports of Wahhabi outrages shocked the Muslim conscience, and the horror only increased when the Wahhabis audaciously attacked and pillaged even the *hajj* pilgrim caravans coming from Egypt, Syria, and other places.[85] This level of brutality and extreme intolerance exhibited by the Wahhabis was very reminiscent of the highly vilified heretics of the early Khawarij, Hashshashun (Assassins), and Qaramites. In the classical legal history, the violent and indiscriminate methods employed by these groups earned them the label of bandits or highway robbers (*muharibun*), which was one of the most morally reprehensible and severely punished crimes in Islamic law. Furthermore, Mecca and Medina were, in part because of a Qur'anic narrative, not just sacred but sanctified spaces where wars and the spilling of blood and violence were forbidden. All the blood spilled in these sacred spaces by the Wahhabi forces and the looting of the treasures preserved and protected for centuries inside the Ka'ba, as well as the destruction of a countless number of historical sites going back to the Prophet, his family, and companions affronted and aggrieved Muslims around the world.[86] At a minimum, the threat posed by the Wahhabis to pilgrims led several nations to abstain from participating in the annual *hajj* on a number of occasions.[87] More fundamentally, however, many Muslims recognized that they were confronting a new type of extremism in the heartland of Islam that until then could have only represented the extreme margins of Islam.

This led several mainstream jurists writing during this time period, such as the Hanafi jurist Ibn 'Abidin (d. 1253/1837) and the Maliki jurist al-Sawi (d. 1241/1825), to condemn Wahhabis as a fanatic fringe group and label them the "modern day Khawarij of Islam."[88] The irony is that most scholars writing in the nineteenth century believed that the Wahhabis were destined to become extinct because of their fanaticism.[89] For most scholars, it was simply inconceivable that Wahhabism would become a serious orientation in Islamic theological thought.[90] Wahhabism as a theology most certainly would have been thoroughly discredited and destabilized had it not been for the return of Al Saud and the founding of the Saudi state in 1932.

Wahhabism was resuscitated once again in the early twentieth century under the leadership of 'Abd al-'Aziz bin Al Saud (aka Ibn Saud) (r. 1344–1373/1926–1953), who adopted the puritanical theology of the Wahhabis and allied himself with the tribes of Najd, thereby establishing the nascent beginnings of what would become Saudi Arabia. In 1912, Ibn Saud formed a fighting force known as the Ikhwan, which was constituted of Najdi religious zealots strongly committed to the thought of Ibn 'Abd al-Wahhab. The Ikhwan played an effective role in establishing and expanding Ibn Saud's control, but they eventually became dissatisfied with what they saw as Ibn Saud's liberalism and willingness to cooperate with non-Muslims. Increasingly, the Ikhwan crossed the British, who were Ibn Saud's main allies against the Ottoman Turks, by raiding the territories of British allies. Ibn Saud tried to prevent the Ikhwan from raiding neighboring territories under British control and also tried to restrain the Ikhwan from interfering with pilgrims coming to Mecca from outside of Arabia, whom the Ikhwan had a habit of attacking and punishing for engaging in purported un-Islamic practices. This led to the Ikhwan rebelling against the king in 1929, but with the assistance of the British, who used their airpower to massacre them, the king crushed and disbanded their forces.[91] In effect, Ibn Saud played with fire, it burned him, and he ultimately needed the British to extinguish the flames. The fact that the British came to Ibn Saud's aid by crushing the Ikhwan rebellion is hardly surprising. Since the early 1900s, Ibn Saud had received arms from the British, arranged for Najd to become a British protectorate, and had become one of the Arab rulers to regularly receive a salary from the British colonial government.[92]

King Ibn Saud's legacy with the Ikhwan is reminiscent of the dynamics between the current Saudi government and Bin Laden. The current Saudi government was also eventually bitten by the beast it raised, and it needed the United States to destroy the monster. But in the same way that the current Saudi government could not afford to turn against the system of thought that gave birth to the beast, the government of Ibn Saud, similarly, could not afford to do the same. Having destroyed the Ikhwan as an organized militant group, King Ibn Saud could not afford to distance himself from the Wahhabi creed itself. In fact, because King Ibn Saud used non-Muslims to slaughter the militant Ikhwan, he was forced to prove his Islamic legitimacy by conceding greater control to Wahhabi forces over the social and religious lives of Muslims in Saudi Arabia. Importantly, the Ikhwan were destroyed not because of their militancy against fellow Muslims but because they clashed with the British. As long as the Wahhabis limited their zealotry to Muslims, Al Saud tolerated and supported them.

In the areas that fell under their control, the Wahhabis introduced practices that considerably expanded the intrusive powers of the state by making the state into the enforcer of a narrowly defined code of behavior, which, in their view, was the only correct Islam. For instance, the Wahhabis regularly flogged the residents of their territories for listening to music, shaving their beards, wearing silk or gold (forbidden only to men, not women), smoking, playing backgammon, chess, or cards, or failing to observe strict rules of sexual segregation, and they destroyed all the shrines and most of the Muslim historical monuments found in Arabia.[93] The Wahhabis also criminalized all forms of Sufi chants and dances in Mecca and Medina and eventually in all of Saudi Arabia.[94] They also introduced the first reported precedent in Islamic history of taking roll call at prayers.[95] The Wahhabis prepared lists of the inhabitants of a city and called off the names during the five daily prayers in the mosque, and anyone absent without a sufficient excuse was flogged.[96] It

is also reported that the Wahhabis were the first to stone to death an adulte-
ress in well over a thousand years in Arabia.[97] The execution is reported to
have shocked and revolted Hijazi society, and people who observed the
incident commented on its brutality and barbarism. The Wahhabis dismissively ignored the qualifying and mitigating jurisprudence of cumulative
interpretive communities that has made this punishment largely an anachro-
nism in the Muslim world.[98] But being the caretakers of Mecca and Medina,
the Wahhabis were uniquely positioned to enforce their version of orthodoxy
on Muslim pilgrims from around the world. As an indication of the limited
popularity of the Wahhabi creed, at that stage of their development, the
uncompromisingly austere practices of the Wahhabis during pilgrimage led
to several clashes with pilgrims coming from Africa and Southeast Asia. In
1926, for example, the Wahhabi hostility to all forms of musical instruments
led to a crisis between Egypt and Saudi Arabia, when Egyptian soldiers
carrying the ceremonial palanquin to the sound of bugles during pilgrimage
were attacked, beaten, and had their musical instruments destroyed. There
was a huge public outcry in Egypt over the incident, and the Egyptian media
severely criticized the Wahhabi actions as unprecedented in Islamic history
and as inconsistent with the duties of the caretakers of Mecca and Medina.[99]
Today, the Wahhabis remain in control in Mecca and Medina, and the Egyptian customary practices at pilgrimage ended many years ago. In fact, the
practices and rituals of pilgrimage from around the Muslim world to Mecca
and Medina are strictly regulated according to austere Wahhabi standards.

The Wahhabi conquest of Arabia in the 1920s and the founding of the
Kingdom of Saudi Arabia in 1932 changed the face of Islam in profound and
drastic ways. Nevertheless, well into the 1930s, Wahhabism was thought to
be a regional phenomenon confined to Arabia and having little or no chance
of influencing more developed, educated, and urbanized Muslim societies.
Even the Hanbali school of thought, known for its literalism and restrictive-
ness, by the nineteenth century had retreated to the confines of Najd and
therefore was threatened with extinction until it was saved and disseminated
by the Saudis in the twentieth century. From the 1920s to 1950s, Wahhabism
was understood to be a particularly puritanical sect of Islam limited to the
special circumstances of Arabia, which for centuries had been neglected and
had experienced very little sustained economic and social development, but
that ultimately would have little effect on the rest of the Muslim world.[100]
Once the powerful duo of the fanatic Wahhabi dogma and the Al Saud family
was supported by the dominant colonial power in the Middle East, which at
the time was Britain, in 1924–1925 the puritanical force from Najd was able
to secure control over the Hijaz, where the Holy cities of Medina and Mecca
are located.[101] Until then, with a few notable exceptions, the Hijaz was
treated as too sanctified and sacred to be dominated and controlled by any
exclusionary sect. For centuries, the Ottomans administered the Hijaz and
oversaw the pilgrimage, but the Ottomans did not enforce their Hanafi school
of thought as the only acceptable orthodoxy. The Hijaz was governed by the
Ashraf (reported descendants of the Prophet) of Mecca and by a representative consultative council, but no single sectarian or jurisprudential school of
thought dominated.[102] In 1908, consistent with its long-established practice,
the Ottomans appointed another member of the Ashraf, Husayn bin 'Ali, as

the Grand Sharif of the Hijaz. In 1916, however, with British instigation, Sharif Husayn led the Arab revolt against the Ottomans in Arabia. Sharif Husayn served British interests in fighting against the Ottomans in return for a promise that Britain would recognize him as the "King of Arab Lands" after the conclusion of the First World War. For all practical purposes, however, the true commander of the Hashemite revolt was the colorful British agent Lawrence of Arabia. It should be noted that on September 30, 1918, the Syrian supporters of the Arab revolt pledged their allegiance to Sharif Husayn, who in the same year had been named the King of Arabs by the notables and scholars of the Hijaz. However, after the dismantling of the Ottoman Empire, it has become clear that Arabs and Muslims did not have the power of self-determination. The San Remo Conference of 1920 and the infamous Sykes-Picot Agreement, signed in 1916 by the Triple Entente of Britain, France, and Russia, had determined the fate of the Middle East by dividing the region into mandates and spheres of influence to be shared by the colonial powers.[103]

Sharif Husayn was deeply disappointed when it became obvious that Britain did not intend to keep its promises to him.[104] There are reports that before the beginning of the Arab revolt, Britain had even promised to support him if he declared himself the new Caliph of Muslims. After the abolition of the Ottoman Caliphate, Sharif Husayn made a rather desperate attempt to appoint himself the new Caliph of the Muslim world in 1924. In a relatively small ceremony near Amman (Jordan) before delegations of religious figures representing Sunni and Shi'i Muslims from Palestine, Syria, Iraq, Egypt, and other places, Sharif Husayn received allegiances, delivered a speech, and led prayer in his new capacity as the Caliph of Muslims.[105] According to the supporters of King Husayn, Muslim leaders from around the world sent him telegrams rejoicing and supporting and recognizing him as the new Caliph of Muslims.[106] Husayn, however, was thoroughly disappointed when his claim to the Caliphate did not receive the support of Britain, and indeed, he seemed crushed and demoralized by the realization that the British were far more interested in supporting Ibn Saud.[107] Adding insult to injury, in 1925, when Sharif Husayn asked to renew a diplomatic representative to London, the British government responded that whether in an official or an unofficial capacity, it would not accept such a representative.[108] It is hardly surprising that Britain did not recognize Sharif Husayn's claim to the Caliphate, leave alone the fact that colonial powers had gone to great lengths to deliberately dismantle the Ottoman Caliphate and were not about to replace it with an Arab one.[109] The prevailing political dogma in the West at the time and the dogma still prevalent today imagined that the Caliphate as an institution and as a symbol posed a threat to the security of the West. Sharif Husayn, whatever his motivations, still strove to preserve the Caliphate as an institution while Ibn Saud had no interest in keeping the institution alive, and in fact, many Wahhabi scholars challenged whether the preservation of the Caliphate is an Islamic obligation. In many ways, considering the hegemonic role of colonial powers in the region, the only indigenous movements that had a chance of success were those consistent with the interests of the dominant colonial powers at the time. The persistence of the Caliphate was not one of these consistent interests. I do not believe it was inconsequential or immaterial that as early as 1915, a gifted British officer with the interesting name Captain William Shakespear was killed in battle while assisting Wahhabi forces defeat tribal foes, the Al Rashid, only to be replaced by the resourceful John Philby.[110] With the formal abolition of the Ottoman Caliphate in 1924 and assured of British support, King Ibn Saud moved to occupy the Hijaz, and with that the Wahhabis were put in control of the heartland of Islam.[111]

Of course, it is very difficult to imagine how the Muslim world would have looked today had the Wahhabis not conquered Mecca and Medina and remained a marginal movement limited to the deserts of Najd. At the very least, so many historical archeological sites would have remained, and so much could have been learned about early Muslim societies and cultures. But beyond this, throughout Islamic history the Hijaz was held in special regard and treated as the collective legacy of all Muslims where numerous schools of thought, sects, and theological orientations were represented. In fact, the reason that the puritanical Wahhabis were so scandalized by what they perceived to be unchecked heretical innovations was that there were so many cultural expressions of religiosity and pluralistic representation of the richness of Islamic theological, legal, and cultural diversity. There is no question that most Hijazis did not support the Wahhabis and were gripped by fear at the prospect of a Wahhabi takeover.[112] In 1924, the Wahhabi Ikhwan invaded Taif, a Hijazi town close to Mecca, and they committed horrific atrocities over the course of three days.[113] The Taif massacre and the terror that gripped surrounding areas, such as Mecca, created an internal refugee problem as displaced populations fled before advancing Wahhabi forces.[114] Ibn Saud was well aware of the anxiety gripping the Hijazis and the rest of the Muslim world about the Wahhabis' reputation for fanaticism and intolerance.[115] Therefore, Ibn Saud sought to give assurances that a repeat of the Taif massacre would not reoccur and that his suzerainty over his Hijaz would not change the culture or bring an end to Hijazi practice of accommodating differences.[116] In fact, Ibn Saud even promised to guarantee religious freedom to the Shiʻis if they would give him their pledge of allegiance, a promise that went unfulfilled.[117]

With the fall of the Hijaz to Saudi control, initially, Ibn Saud assured the Muslim world that Najd did not seek to dominate the Hijaz and that the Hijaz would enjoy the right to self-determination.[118] And, as noted above, he also assured the Muslim world that he intended to respect and uphold the sectarian and jurisprudential diversity of Mecca and Medina.[119] In 1926, acting on British advice, Ibn Saud reluctantly held a conference to which he invited twenty-two Muslim countries in order to address the future of the Hijaz and assuage Muslim anxieties about the intolerant practices of the Wahhabis in the sacred cities.[120] It became clear, however, that Ibn Saud had no intention of upholding any of his promises with regard to the Hijaz. Furthermore, as has been noted in a number of memoirs of Muslim politicians who attended the 1926 conference, Ibn Saud had realized that the only real limits to his plans in Arabia were the acquiescence of the dominant colonial powers and not the consent of any of the Muslim countries. Consequently, Ibn Saud made it abundantly clear in the 1926 conference that he would not accept any Muslim interventions in the affairs of the Hijaz and that the future of the holy cities was subject to the sole sovereign discretion of his government.[121] This resulted in a tense and uncomfortable conference as a number of delegations walked out in protest. India demanded that the Hijaz be administered by a democratically elected council, and among other countries, Egypt and Iran refused to recognize Saudi sovereignty over the Hijaz and complained bitterly about the ill treatment of the pilgrims. Practically every Muslim country vigorously protested the desecration of shrines, and to Ibn Saud's considerable irritation, the attendees issued a united statement demanding that all the sites destroyed by the Wahhabis be restored—a demand to which Ibn Saud acceded but did not implement.[122] The Rector of al-Azhar at the time, Shaykh al-Zawahiri, further annoyed Ibn Saud by giving an emphatic and somewhat belligerent speech about the shared heritage of the Hijaz, the virtues of diversity and pluralism in Islam, the wickedness of *takfir*, and the abominations of desecrating the holy sites.[123] Britain, France, Holland, Switzerland, and the Soviet Union promptly recognized Ibn Saud's sovereignty over the Hijaz.[124] In 1927, Britain and Ibn Saud signed a treaty of friendship and protection known as the Treaty of Jedda, per which Britain recognized Ibn Saud's sovereignty and Ibn Saud recognized Britain's special status in relation to its Gulf emirate protectorates.[125]

At the time of the seizure of the Hijaz, the average Muslim did not necessarily have an informed understanding of Wahhabism. In the early twentieth century, Muslims were scandalized by stories of the Ikhwan's brutality, and Muslims living in territories neighboring the Wahhabis, such as southern Iraq, Yemen, and Oman, feared falling victim to the Wahhabis' infamous intolerance. But for most Muslims, Wahhabism was still a remote reality not likely to have a direct impact on the way they related to or practiced their religion. After the Hijaz became a part of the Kingdom of Saudi Arabia, just like most of the legacy of the colonial age, the hegemony of Wahhabism had become a *fait accompli* that ultimately was rationalized and then fully adopted by Muslims. However, as difficult as it might be for contemporary Muslims to imagine, the fact remains that the Wahhabis implanted themselves in a largely hostile and unsupportive environment. Within a short period of time, Wahhabis clashed with and tried to eradicate centuries of folkloric expressions, accumulated cultural nuances, and the cumulative intellectual legacies of numerous interpretive communities.[126] Certainly, the Saudi Arabian government, once it possessed the resources to do so, had done everything possible to reinvent the historical narrative so that Wahhabism would be cast in the role of the restorer of Islam to its original purity and Muslims portrayed as having recognized the essential truth of Wahhabism and enthusiastically adopting it. However, as discussed below, Wahhabism could not have spread in the Muslim world without a number of intervening factors, chief among them the active promotion of the Saudi state apparatus with all its resources.[127] The critical point often overlooked by modern historians is that Wahhabism was born in the early nineteenth century, and its supporters fought virtually nonstop in violent rebellion against all other Muslims for over a hundred years. The Al Saud family continued to struggle with a perpetual line of contenders and rebellions up to the establishment of the state in 1932 and well beyond. One can only speculate as to whether the Saudis could have been able to subdue and hold on to the Hijaz and remain in power as the absolute rulers of a unified Arabia for decades had it not been for the backing and support of Western world powers. The point is that it is rather disingenuous to presume that Wahhabism was a natural invocation of an Islamic praxis or a return to an unattested Islamic authenticity or original-ism. That Wahhabism is a breach with the historical tradition and intellectual heritage of Islam is a theme that reverberates through the many juristic texts written in refutation of Wahhabism. For example, one of the important repre-sentative texts printed in 1926, but not reprinted since, conveys a sense of the upheaval and pains of change caused by Wahhabism. Hanana, the author, expresses an utter sense of shock at the fact that what he describes as the ill-educated and uncivilized Bedouins of Najd having asserted control over the far more cultured and enlightened Hijaz. According to the author, Ibn Saud does not seem capable of expressing himself eloquently in classical Arabic or of uttering statements free of grammatical errors. Nevertheless, Hanana is bewildered at the fact that Ibn Saud and his Wahhabi jurists expect Muslims everywhere, including those from more civilized regions (*aqtar islamiyya raqiya*) such as Egypt, Damascus, and Baghdad, to defer to their (Wahhabi) understandings and interpretations. Hanana goes on to state:

> [According to the Wahhabis] it is incumbent upon Muslims all over the world to ignore the books of Islamic jurisprudence written by scholars and burn all the interpretive works produced by their sages. Instead, Muslims are expected to refer all Islamic matters to this Wahhabi bunch [*al-tughma al-Wahhabiyya*] that came from the desert and seized the Hijaz acting upon the instructions of one of the Colonial powers. This would mean that we (Muslims) are expected to dismiss all Islamic law books composed during the ages of the early cali-phate, the Umayyads, and Abbasids, and also during every epoch in which Muslims reached the height of civilization and instead should consult the Wahhabi jurists after adopting the new [Wahhabi] religion [*dinahum al-jadid*] and after abrogating all the classical schools of thought [*al-madhahib al-Isla-miyya*].[128]

The point to emphasize here is that in the early decades of the twentieth century, to the extent that Wahhabism as a creed was known, it represented a breach with the established and continued customs of Muslims in Arabia and elsewhere. It was also widely known that the various Saudi leaders or rulers of Wahhabism were regularly allied with British colonial interests against the Ottoman Caliphate.[129] This was not the result of any particular affinity to-ward the British, their values, or interests, but a preference for what in the Wahhabi creed would be a lesser of two evils. There is no doubt that Ibn Saud himself did prefer the British and espoused what appeared to him to be at times a one-sided sense of friendship and loyalty with Britain.[130] But there is also no question that for his loyalty to the British, Ibn Saud received critical strategic, political, and moral support. Indeed, for all the services rendered, King Ibn Saud remains one of the very few Arab leaders to enjoy having bestowed on him the Grand Cross of the Order of Bath, which British diplomats presented to the king in a closed ceremony in Riyadh in 1935.[131]

This, however, had little to do with the Wahhabi creed, and indeed one of the reasons for the Ikhwan's revolt against their king was their revulsion at his close relationship to the British.[132] Considering the overall legacy of Wahhabism by the time Saudi Arabia declared its independence in 1932, the

obvious and pressing question is how did the Wahhabi creed within a relatively short time manage to have such an emphatic impact on the way Muslims understood their religion, tradition, and culture? It should be recalled
that the legacy of the combined Wahhabi/Saudi coalition included not just an
alliance with colonial powers and contributing to the destruction of the Caliphate but also the annihilation of the historically influential Ashraf of Hijaz,
the raiding and disruption of *hajj* convoys, the usurpation and institution of
hegemonic control over expressions of Muslim piety in the sacred space of
Mecca and Medina, the eradication of a broad array of devotional cultures
centered around the festivities of the pilgrimage, the killing, imprisoning, or
exiling of a large number of jurists from various schools of Islamic thought,
and the banning of established and historically rooted Sufi orders and practices in the Hijaz and the rest of Arabia. Add to this record the destruction of
numerous historical texts, sites, and artifacts that had survived unharmed for
centuries, the desecration of the tombs of the Prophet and his companions,
and the purported looting of the treasures gifted by various rulers and nobles
over a long span of time to the Prophet's shrine. [133]

With its legacy of outrages, one would have expected Wahhabism to
become another part of the derisory but transient phases of the tumultuous
age of colonialism. But today nearly all of the issues and problematics that
interested and preoccupied Wahhabi theology and thought have been injected
into the Muslim mainstream and in fact have come to permeate Muslim
social interactions and debates. [134] What were at one time considered impru-
dent fixations on minutiae marginal to the faith by an intemperate group of
Bedouins now had become the center of Muslim debates. [135] How did the
Wahhabi/Saudi alliance manage to numb the memory of the dual legacy of
belligerence and marginality? Moreover, how did this alliance succeed in
erasing the memory of the rupture inflicted on Islamic history?

The response to these questions is multifaceted and nuanced because, as
explained below, Wahhabism spread all over the Muslim world by dissimu-
lating and co-opting the symbolisms and linguistic practices of a much older
and better-rooted theological orientation in Islam known as *al-salafiyya*. But
before addressing the relationship between Wahhabism and Salafism, it is
important to identify a number of significant contributing contextual factors
that helped foster the Wahhabi creed in the colonial age.

As discussed below, some jurists, like Rashid Rida (d. 1354/1935), motivated by Arab nationalism shared the Wahhabi hostility toward the Ottomans
and therefore tended to be sympathetic toward any movement that opposed
Turkish control. [136] For the most part, these jurists wishfully hoped that the
weakening of the Ottomans would mean the rebirth of an Arab Caliphate.
Many of the jurists who defended the Wahhabis did so as a means to a
tangential political end not related to the doctrines of Wahhabism. Other
scholars, especially from Najd, greatly admired the Wahhabi religious zeal
and sedulous rigor in carrying out rituals. Moreover, many Wahhabi apologists praised the movement for cleansing the Hijaz from its heresies and its
supposed licentious and unscrupulous ways. According to these writers,
Muslims in the Hijaz and the rest of Arabia had become corrupt and indulgent to the point that the uncompromising extremism and militancy of the
Wahhabis was needed to cleanse Arabia of its indiscretions. [137]

More significantly, in the early decades of the twentieth century, some Muslim intellectuals adopted the rather odd belief that Wahhabism was akin to the European Enlightenment and that as a reformation movement it would be the vehicle for an Arab rebirth.[138] On the merits, it is difficult to take this idea seriously, but it was part of the regular propaganda of the Egyptian Western-educated Wahhabi apologist Hafiz Wahba. And for the Western-educated elite, who lacked direct knowledge of the Wahhabi movement, this claim proved to be influential not so much in generating support for the movement but in persuading some important intellectuals not to oppose it.[139] Considering the genesis and roots of the idea, it gave credibility to the movement especially that, as already noted, reliable information in the nineteenth and early twentieth centuries about the actual belief-system of the Wahhabis was sparse. The origins of the idea that the Wahhabis constitute a reform movement akin to the Protestant Reformation in Europe precedes Hafiz Wahba, and it is found in the writings of a number of European travellers who wrote eyewitness accounts of unfolding events in Arabia.[140] In many of these accounts, European travellers would duly note the acts of fanaticism and intolerance committed by the Wahhabis, but they would end up with a positive assessment of the movement as returning Islam to its pristine and pure origins. So, for instance, after commenting on the austere and extremist practices of the Wahhabis, Andrew Crichton in 1834 writes: "The doctrines of Abdel Wahab . . . were not those of a new religion; though they were so represented by his enemies, and have been described as such by several European travelers. His sole guide was the Koran and the orthodox traditions; and his efforts were entirely directed to remove corruptions and abuses, and restore the faith of Islam to its original purity."[141] Several pages later the same source states:

> Some writers lament the suppression of the Wahabees, from a belief the downfall of Islam was to follow the propagation of their doctrines, and that a purer religion would be established in its stead. These regrets appear to be inspired by erroneous conceptions of the principles of this sect, which are nothing else than the gross and primitive superstitions of the Koran enforced with greater rigour. Their creed was even more sanguinary and intolerant than that which the first followers of Mohammed offered to the nations on the points of their swords. Their reform extended only to a few absurd or scandalous practices, and the more strict injunction of certain moral precepts; but they left untouched all the impious and heretical dogmas of the Moslem faith. Their chief merit consisted, not in their teaching their countrymen a more refined and rational theology, but in suppressing their infidel indifference to all religion; in improving their political condition; and in subjecting their wild passions to the restraint of law and justice.[142]

John Burckhardt, writing in the 1830s, is unequivocal in his defense of the Wahhabis, claiming that Muslims had reached a point of venerating their saints as highly as those of the Catholic Church and that the Wahhabis sought to return Islam to its purity.[143] In Burckhardt's view, Islam's "code of law" was originally promulgated for Bedouins, and Wahhabis took the faith back to these pristine origins. Accordingly, the Wahhabis actually follow the laws that other Muslims neglect or ceased to observe altogether. Burckhardt thus concludes: "To describe, therefore, the Wahhaby religion, would be to reca-pitulate the Muselman faith; and to show in what points this sect differs from the Turks, would be to give a list of all the abuses of which the latter are guilty."[144] Similarly, in a book published in 1810, the French consular Louis Olivier de Corancez states succinctly: "Mohammed [bin Abd al-Wahhab] was thus a reformer of Islam rather than the founder of a new sect; and the religion of the Wahhabis is that of the Koran in its original purity."[145]

Of course, there were many European travellers who fully appreciated the destructive power of Wahhabism. William Gifford Palgrave, whose book on central and eastern Arabia was published in 1865, gave a grim but perceptive assessment of Wahhabism and its lack of potential for inspiring civilized values. Commenting on the violence and fanaticism of the Wahhabis, he wrote of Wahhabism: "Incapable of true internal progress, hostile to com-merce, unfavourable to arts and even agriculture, and in the highest degree intolerant and aggressive, it can neither better itself nor benefit others; while the order and calm which it sometimes spreads over the lands of its conquest, are described in the oft-cited *ubi solitudinem faciunt pacem appellant* (what they turn to desert they call it peace)."[146]

Of all the Western colonial-era writers who exalted the virtues of Wah-habism, none rival Harry St. John Philby. Besides being a British intelligence officer, he also served as a close advisor to King 'Abd al-'Aziz Al Saud (aka King Ibn Saud) and wrote a number of important and influential books on Arabia, King Ibn Saud, and Wahhabism. Philby was an enigmatic character and a person of many contradictions, but in his many writings on Arabia there are some persistent and distinctive themes and characteristics. He writes in the tone of the bumptious, haughty, and self-important Englishman, patronizingly and at times even mockingly conferring his penetrating insights about Islam, Arabs, Bedouins, and at times, his fellow British colleagues and superiors. A number of studies have struggled to make sense of Philby's many contradictions and eccentricities, but what is not disputed is Philby's enthusiastic and even exuberant support of Wahhabism. In his many writ-ings, Philby heaped praise on Wahhabism as the creed that authentically represents the spirit and true nature of Islam. Invariably, he also praised his patron, King Ibn Saud, and repeatedly assured his readers of the king's loyalty and commitment to British interests. Philby brokered the special rela-tionship between Ibn Saud and British oil companies and later on with American oil companies, for which he secured hefty commissions.[147] Some historians maintain that Philby played the most pivotal role in enabling Ibn Saud to establish Saudi Arabia and consolidate the hegemonic power of the Al Saud family.[148] To prove his fidelity to King Ibn Saud, in a highly publi-cized move Philby even converted to Wahhabi Islam and lived in Riyadh until Ibn Saud's death, although he did continue to travel back and forth between Saudi Arabia and England.[149]

Interestingly, while Philby persistently praised the Wahhabis, portraying them in the role of the zealous reformers returning Islam to its pristine origins, he openly commented on their intolerance and violence. According to Philby, Wahhabis' "most remarkable characteristic" was their "uncompro-mising hatred of their Muslim neighbours. . . . The Shi'as are frankly con-demned as infidels and polytheists, but it is for the orthodox congregation of

the four Sunni churches—Turks, Egyptians, Hijazis, Syrians, Mesopota-
mians, Indians and the like—that the Wahhabis reserve the undiluted venom
of their hatred."[150] Philby consistently refers to the Wahhabis as "puritans"
and frequently acknowledges that their fanatic extremism often terrified their
subjects and posed problems to King Ibn Saud, whom Philby greatly admired. Yet with the same frankness, Philby openly admitted that he did not
find the fanaticism of the Wahhabis to be morally troubling, and indeed he
did not seem to be the least distressed by their violence. In one of the very
few occasions that Philby explained his decision to convert to Islam, after
explaining that he found Indian Islam, Sunni Iraqi Islam, and Shi'i Islam
unappealing, he wrote the following:

> So it was not till I went to Arabia that, I came into contact with what seemed to
> me undeniably a pure form of Islam, deriving exclusively from the original
> sources of its inspiration, the Quran and the Traditions of the Prophet, and
> owing nothing to subsequent theological interpolation and exegesis. The Wah-
> habi creed seemed to me, as the result of deep study, to be the ideal form of
> religion, and the fanaticism of its followers did not displease me. They had the
> merit of practicing what they believed and preached, while their religion
> seemed to be admirably suited to the needs of human life and society in their
> simplest form. It was a religion which one could accept without intellectual
> dishonesty as a guide to life and conduct, and whose ethical standards seem to
> conform better than those of other religions—Christianity for instance—to the
> basic needs of humanity.[151]

Philby goes on to note that even if the "code" of Islam might appear strict,
for him this is not troublesome because Islam refuses to countenance "bas-
tardy," and its moral order is superior to the Ten Commandments.[152] It appears callous and even rather dissolute for Philby to treat the atrocities of
Wahhabism in such a perfunctory manner. Philby was well aware that this
"strict" Wahhabi code resulted in the commission of mass atrocities and
many massacres in the towns and cities they invaded. And during the period
that Philby so ably helped King Ibn Saud spread and consolidate his power,
the *mutawwa'un* (religious enforcers) carried out hundreds of decapitations
and thousands of amputations in addition to countless numbers of beatings
and incidents of degradation.[153] Indeed, we know from historical sources that
the Wahhabis would inspire such terror and hate in the towns they invaded
that shopkeepers would be forced to close their shutters and attempt to
hide.[154] Of course, being a British subject and a close advisor to King Ibn
Saud, Philby never had to concern himself with the risk of being on the
receiving end of Wahhabi fanaticism. One cannot escape the feeling that
Philby's apologetics on behalf of Wahhabism are self-indulgent in the extreme. For his apologetics, Philby enjoyed wealth, power, and even slave
girls, gifted to him by King Ibn Saud. Although by his own admission Philby
encountered many sophisticated and nuanced Muslim cultures in India,
Egypt, Istanbul, and other places, nevertheless he persisted in the belief that
the interpretive and intellectual heritage of Islam is but a corruption of the
pristine nature of the faith and that it is the primal and simplistic but brutish
savage that best represents the true Islam.

In one of his well-known and typically frank assessments, a report presented to the British government titled *The Reconstruction of Arabia*, T. E. Lawrence cogently noted that after the First World War, British policy was driven by "the urgent need to divide Islam" and "to create a ring of client states, themselves insisting on the patronage of the British Empire."[155] To an extent, this statement cuts through the elaborate intellectualized pretenses of colonial functionaries, like Philby, and gets to the heart of the matter. I think that the colonial project itself and its indispensable tools, which involve the manufacturing of mythologies of superiority, cultural altruism, and narratives as to the inescapable burdens of shared humanity—the colonial project with its rootedness in ideologies about genuine and inherent cultural differences, as well as cultural deficiencies and weaknesses, with its half-hearted beliefs in economic altruism, dependency, and the developmental possibilities—but most of all, the colonial tools of subjugation and domination, and also the inevitable apologetics in defense of hegemony accompanied by elaborate constructions about reciprocity, cooperation, and mutual benefits—all of this comes much closer to being the real explanation for Philby's overindulgent views toward the Wahhabi fanatics. Stated differently, Philby's understanding of Wahhabi Islam had a great deal to do with his role as a colonial functionary and with what this role needed Wahhabi Islam to be.

At the same time that one must take note of the possible impact of some Orientalists in beautifying the image of the Wahhabis by drawing parallels between the movement and enlightened movements in European history, it is important to recall that many Westerners had no qualms about describing the true nature and actions of the movement. One of the dependable and honest voices was that of Dutch diplomat Daniel Van der Meulen, who travelled through Arabia and witnessed many of the events in question. Van der Meulen documented many of the fanatic abuses committed by the Wahhabis, and in a important passage he nicely summed up the intractable tragedy created by extremist movements such as Wahhabism. After describing the often unbridled violence and cruelty of the Wahhabi Ikhwan, he wrote: "If religion is used to encourage self-righteousness and feeling of superiority in primitive souls and if it then teaches the duty of holy war, the result is heroism, cruelty, narrowing of the mind and atrophy of what is humane and what is of true value, in a man and in a people."[156]

Apologetic writings by Western scholars defending Wahhabism did have an impact on the Muslim Western-educated elite in the first half of the twentieth century, which tended to see the movement as performing a necessary cleansing of the superstitious heritage of premodernity.[157] Most of the Western-educated Muslim elite, especially those who attended missionary-run schools founded during the colonial era, tended to see their native cultures as having been corrupted by superstition and irrationalism. Ironically, both the Westernized elite and Wahhabis shared the same attitude toward Islamic history—both treated this history as a narrative of degeneration, frustrated possibilities, and failure. Further, for very different reasons, both groups considered the natively spun heritage and cultures of Muslims to be deeply flawed and in need of cleansing of superstitious beliefs and practices. These commonalities could explain the relative ambivalence of the Westernized elites toward Wahhabism during its early years, before Wahhabism became a worldwide movement.

I would be remiss to leave this topic without noting that the rather dubious tradition of Western apologetics on behalf of Wahhabism persists to this very day. In the contemporary world, several Western academics continue to represent Wahhabism as a return to the pristine origins of Islam and continue to compare it to the Protestant Reformation in Europe.[158] Moreover, it has become a common practice for Muslim apologists writing in defense of Wahhabism to include lengthy quotes from old and new writings by European and American scholars exalting the role of Wahhabism.[159] The point of the practice of quoting Western scholars is to demonstrate that even the infidel non-Muslims could not but tell the truth about the virtues of Wahhabism. More significantly, such quotes are usually employed in an effort to perpetuate the perception of Wahhabism as the true form of Salafism, or conversely, of Salafiyya as being indistinguishable from Wahhabiyya. I will discuss the interrelationship between Wahhabism and Salafism below, but in essence, Wahhabism sought to cleanse all that it considered to be nontextual innovations and accretions to pristine and pure Islamic doctrines. This led to the deliberate and most often forceful eradication of cultural and social practices that the Wahhabis deemed to be un-Islamic. Wahhabi apologists often described the targeted cultural practices as founded on superstition or mythological lore, which meant that they were considered to be if not necessarily heretical, then quintessentially without any redeeming value. Obviously, however, the destruction or eradication of social institutions and practices that were deemed to be superstitious should not be confused with a prorationalist stance or with the recognition of the value of reason as a tool of cultural and social critique or reform. Although Wahhabis often described heretical cultural or social practices as superstitious, this meant that those practices were thought to be inconsistent with the literal meanings of text and not that such practices were irrational or contrary to reason. Be that as it may, Wahhabi apologists continued to utilize Western testimonials comparing their movement to the European Reformation because of the misleading impressions such testimonials gave about the attitude of Wahhabism toward reason and rationality. The practice of quoting the favorable testimony of non-Muslims on behalf of Wahhabism did play an important obfuscating role that was indeed helpful to the supporters of the movement, at least in the early years of the founding of the Saudi state. This practice continues to this very day, but I suspect that it has lost its effect or appeal; at this time and age, most Muslims have had direct experiences with Wahhabi beliefs and practices, and it is unlikely that apologetic Western testimonials continue to have near the impact that they once might have had.

WHY DID WAHHABISM SURVIVE AND SPREAD?

By employing the literal text to cleanse and sterilize the lives of Muslims from heretical contaminations, Wahhabis sought to reclaim what they believed was the true and uncorrupted Shari'ah.[160] What is truly remarkable is the extent to which the Orientalist and Wahhabi conceptions of Shari'ah coalesced in understanding and function. Both saw Shari'ah as a formalistic system of rules that are immutable and noncontingent and that are traced back to an imagined pristine period of true Islamicity. But since human societies are highly contingent and often nonformalistic, the historically negotiated solutions reached by Muslim societies in a wide spectrum of times, places, and spaces were deemed at best to be deviations from the true path of Shari'ah. Wedded to their stereotypical views of Shari'ah, both Wahhabis and their Orientalist admirers were forced to see Shari'ah as standing at the sidelines of Muslim societies and most of Islamic history. In Arabia, the Wahhabis sought to reclaim the role of Shari'ah by compelling people to abandon their deviant practices and to mold their ideas and behavior according to the immutable and noncontingent Shari'ah. This necessarily led to the founding of an absolutist and despotic state in Arabia as the state had to rely on coercion and violence to force Arabian society to mirror or mimic the uncorrupted Shari'ah.

The influence of Wahhabism today has far exceeded the once sparsely populated lands of Arabia and now plays a major role in the ways that Muslims around the world relate to and understand the nature and role of Shari'ah. At this point, it would be helpful to set out the most significant factors that enabled Wahhabism to expand beyond its modest origins in Arabia to a prevalent theological and legal paradigm affecting contemporary Muslims and non-Muslims alike. In my view, there were four main reasons for the thriving of Wahhabism in the Muslim world, which can be summarized as the following: first, by rebelling against the Ottomans, Wahhabism appealed to the emerging ideologies of Arab nationalism in the eighteenth century. By treating Muslim Ottoman rule as a foreign occupying power, Wahhabism set a powerful precedent for notions of Arab self-determination and autonomy.[161] Second, as noted before, Wahhabism advocated the return to the pristine and pure origins of Islam. Accordingly, Wahhabism rejected the cumulative weight of historical baggage and insisted on a return to the precedents of the "rightly guided" early generations (*al-salaf al-salih*). This idea was intuitively liberating for Muslim reformers since it meant the rebirth of *ijtihad*, or the return to de novo examination and determination of legal issues unencumbered by the accretions of precedents and inherited doctrines. Third, by controlling Mecca and Medina, Saudi Arabia became naturally positioned to exercise a considerable influence on Muslim culture and thinking. The holy cities of Mecca and Medina are the symbolic heart of Islam and are the sites where millions of Muslims perform pilgrimages each year. Therefore, by regulating what might be considered orthodox belief and practice while at pilgrimage, Saudi Arabia became uniquely positioned to influence greatly the belief systems of Islam itself. For instance, for purely symbolic purposes, the king of Saudi Arabia adopted the lowly title of "Custodian and Servant of the two Holy Sites." The Saudi government's unique and singular position as the custodian of the holy sites gives it a remarkable forum to influence the Islamic world. So, for instance, since the invasions of Afghanistan and Iraq, it has become a rather regular practice for high-ranking clerics in Saudi Arabia during the pilgrimage seasons to preach to a captive audience of more than two million Muslims condemning as heretics all those who criticize the policies of the Saudi government or its clerics. It has become typical for these clerics to describe Muslim reformers who speak out against Wahhabism as the "seditious sinners who are seeking to weaken Islam by airing the dirty laundry of Muslims" and to brand Muslim scholars who call for greater rights for women or who advocate democracy as inciters to evil and promiscuity and to warn Muslims around the world against listening to them. More recently, Saudi preachers have used the podiums provided by the holy sites to condemn the spread of so-called liberal ideas in the wake of the Arab Spring that might entice impious youth to rebel against true Islamic governments (i.e., Saudi Arabia but not Iran), but more dangerously, to incite an unabated level of hysteria against Shi'a Muslims and also the purported impending dangers posed by Shi'i conspiracies against the true Islam. At the same time, it has now become fairly common during the pilgrimage season for television channels around the Muslim world to carry documentaries exalting the custodianship of the Saudi government over the holy sites and praising its many purported achievements on behalf of Muslims.[162]

From the time that Ibn Saud anointed himself King of Hijaz and his claim over the region was recognized by European powers through to this very date, the Saudi government has jealously guarded its absolute sovereignty over the holy cities and has maintained an uncompromising policy of noninterference. This has taken many forms over the decades, including banning critical media venues, such as Al Jazeera, from covering the *hajj* season each year, refusing any external investigations or oversight into the accidents in which many people perish during pilgrimage each year, and ignoring all protests by Muslim countries against the destruction of historical sites, and the systematic transformation of Mecca into a central cosmopolitan commercial metropolis. Put simply, the Saudi government has been fully aware of the enduring virtual goldmine of religious influence and authority that comes with having absolute power and control over the Hijaz and has not been willing to share this moral authority with any other Muslim country. Speaking figuratively, the voices of the holy cities, with all the symbolic weight that these voices bring to bear, are heard only through the Wahhabi-Saudi establishment, and they can never be heard to say anything contrary to this establishment. All the voices that are allowed to enter to become part of the authoritative voice of the Hijaz and the voices that exist are monopolized by the same Wahhabi-Saudi establishment.

Fourth, and most importantly, the discovery and exploitation of oil provided Saudi Arabia with high liquidity. Especially post-1975, with the sharp rise in oil prices, Saudi Arabia aggressively promoted Wahhabi thought around the Muslim world. Even a cursory examination of the predominant ideas and practices would reveal the widespread influence of Wahhabi thought on the Muslim world today. Part of the reason for Saudi Arabia aggressively proselytizing its creed is related to the third element mentioned above. It would have been politically awkward for Saudi Arabia to be the custodian of the two holy sites but at the same time adopt a system of belief that is at odds with the rest of the Muslim world. To say the least, custodianship of the holy sites is a sensitive position in the Muslim world, and the Saudi exclusive claim to sovereignty over these cities remained problematic from the 1920s through the 1960s, especially because of the Wahhabis' intolerant attitude toward ritualistic practices that they deem unorthodox. In the 1950s and 1960s, Saudi Arabia was coming under considerable pressure from republican and Arab nationalist regimes who tended to consider the Saudi system archaic and reactionary. In the 1970s, Saudi Arabia finally possessed the financial means to address its legitimacy concerns. The Wahhabis either had to alter their own system of belief to make it more consistent with the convictions of other Muslims, or they had to aggressively spread their convictions to the rest of the Muslim world. The first would have required the Saudi regime to reinvent itself, but, in many ways, it was easier to attempt to reinvent the Muslim world, and that is the option they chose.

Critically, however, Wahhabism did not spread in the modern Muslim world under its own banner. Considering the marginal origins of the Wahhabi creed, this would have been quite difficult to accomplish. Wahhabism spread in the Muslim world under the banner of Salafism. It is important to note that even the term *Wahhabism* is considered derogatory to the followers of Muhammad bin 'Abd-al-Wahhab since Wahhabis prefer to see themselves as the representatives of Islamic orthodoxy. According to its adherents, Wahhabism is not a school of thought within Islam but is Islam itself, and it is the only possible Islam. Wahhabi literature will often make it a point to stress that it is only the enemies of Wahhabism that will employ this term in reference to the followers of the thought of Muhammad bin 'Abd al-Wahhab. Most often, these same narratives will emphasize that the proper expression to describe Ibn 'Abd al-Wahhab and his school is Ahl al-Sunna wa al-Jama'a, which in essence means "mainstream Muslims" or the Muslims embodying the orthodox positions of Islam. Fundamentally, the expression "Ahl al-Sunna wa al-Jama'a" is akin to asserting that they follow and adhere to the well-founded, indisputable, and incontrovertible doctrines of Islam, which is a claimed status, but tells us little about the methodological path the group has chosen to take. As to methodological path or orientation, the Wahhabis insisted that they are Salafis, and indeed, *the* Salafis. The fact that Wahhabism rejected the use of a school label taken from its eponym gave Wahhabism a rather diffuse quality and made many of its doctrines and methodologies eminently transferable. Salafism, unlike Wahhabism, was a far more credible paradigm in Islam and in many ways an ideal vehicle for Wahhabism. Therefore, in their literature, Wahhabi clerics have consistently described themselves as Salafis (adherents of Salafism) and not Wahhabis.

THE SALAFIS

Salafism is a creed founded in the late nineteenth century by Muslim reformers such as Muhammad 'Abduh (d. 1323/1905), Jamal al-Din al-Afghani (d. 1314/1897), Muhammad Rashid Rida (d. 1354/1935), Muhammad al-Shawkani (d. 1250/1834), and al-Jalal al-San'ani (d. 1225/1810). Salafism appealed to a very basic and fundamental concept in Islam—that Muslims ought to follow the precedent of the Prophet and his rightly guided companions (*al-salaf al-salih*). Methodologically, Salafism was nearly identical to Wahhabism except that Wahhabism is far less tolerant of diversity and differences of opinions. In many ways, Salafism was intuitively undeniable, partly because of its epistemological promise. The founders of Salafism maintained that on all issues, Muslims ought to return to the original textual sources of the Qur'an and the Sunna (precedent) of the Prophet. In doing so, Muslims ought to reinterpret the original sources in light of modern needs and demands without being slavishly bound to the interpretive precedents of earlier Muslim generations. As originally conceived, Salafism was not necessarily anti-intellectual, but like Wahhabism, it did tend to be uninterested in history. By emphasizing a presumed golden age in Islam, the adherents of Salafism idealized the time of the Prophet and his companions and ignored or demonized the balance of Islamic history. Furthermore, by rejecting juristic precedents and undervaluing tradition as a source of authoritativeness, Salafism adopted a form of egalitarianism that deconstructed traditional notions of established authority within Islam. According to Salafism, effectively, anyone was considered qualified to return to the original sources and speak for the divine will. By liberating Muslims from the burdens of the technocratic tradition of the jurists, Salafism contributed to a real vacuum of authority in contemporary Islam. However, unlike Wahhabism, Salafism was not hostile to the juristic tradition or the practice of various competing schools of thought. In addition, Salafism was not hostile to mysticism or Sufism. The proponents of Salafism were eager to throw off the shackles of tradition and to engage in the rethinking of Islamic solutions in light of modern demands. As far as the juristic tradition was concerned, Salafi scholars were synchronizers; they tended to engage in a practice known as *talfiq*, in which they mixed and matched various opinions from the past in order to emerge with novel approaches to problems. Importantly, for the most part, Salafism was founded by Muslim nationalists who were eager to read the values of modernism into the original sources of Islam. Hence, Salafism was not necessarily anti-Western. In fact, its founders strove to project contemporary institutions such as democracy, constitutionalism, or socialism onto the foundational texts and to justify the paradigm of the modern nation-state within Islam. In this sense, Salafism, as originally conceived, betrayed a degree of opportunism. Its proponents tended to be more interested in the end results than in maintaining the integrity or coherence of the juristic method. Salafism was marked by an anxiety to reach results that would render Islam compatible with modernity far more than a desire to critically understand either modernity or the Islamic tradition itself. For instance, the Salafis of the nineteenth and early twentieth centuries heavily emphasized the predominance of the concept of *maslaha* (public interest) in the formulation of Islamic law. Accordingly, it was consistently emphasized that whatever would fulfill the public interest ought to be deemed a part of Islamic law. [163]

Although Muhammad 'Abduh and al-Afghani are usually credited with being the founders of Salafism, and some people even attribute the creed to Ibn Taymiyya (d. 728/1328) and his student Ibn Qayyim al-Jawziyya (d. 751/1350), it was Rashid Rida who best exemplified the ideas and contradictions of Salafism and its elusive relationship with Wahhabism. Rashid Rida, a prominent Syrian reformer who trained in the Azhar seminary and lived in Egypt, was one of the most influential jurists of the early twentieth century. [164] He is today, however, demonized by Wahhabis for his rationalist and humanitarian approaches to Islam, and his jurisprudential works are banned and frequently attacked in Saudi Arabia and outside of Arabia by various puritan Salafi groups. This is quite ironic because Rida was a staunch defender of the Wahhabi movement against the criticisms of various Azhari jurists, most notably the Maliki jurist al-Dijawi (d. 1365/1946), and even a friend of King Ibn 'Abd al-'Aziz (Ibn Saud) of Saudi Arabia.[165]

Today, it is practically inconceivable that any jurist affiliated with the Azhar seminary would criticize the Wahhabis in any serious fashion. Even after the attacks of 9/11 and the role of al-Qaeda and Bin Laden, none of the Azhari scholars dared say anything critical of the Wahhabi influence in the contemporary age. As noted earlier, the Egyptian Revolution weakened the grasp of Saudi Arabia over al-Azhar, but the fact remains that no Azhari scholar supportive of the revolution has dared to challenge Wahhabi thought clearly and directly. This politically privileged position that Wahhabism enjoys, however, is very different from the prevailing climate at the Azhar seminary in the 1930s and 1940s. In the 1930s, al-Dijawi, supported by a substantial number of scholars from Azhar, severely criticized the Wahhabi theology and history. Rida stubbornly defended the Wahhabis, severely criticized al-Dijawi, accusing him of leading the campaign against Wahhabism, and was even critical of the Azhar seminary itself for being a nest of much hostility toward Wahhabis.[166] The controversy over Wahhabism had become a cause of major rifts in the Azhar and eventually led some scholars to organize meetings in an attempt to reconcile between the Wahhabi and anti-Wahhabi camps. The effort, however, failed, and the clash between the two camps continued—with the pro-Wahhabi camp led by Rida.[167] Even conceding that the founder of the creed, Ibn 'Abd al-Wahhab, was intolerant toward others and that the Wahhabis of his time engaged in fanatic behavior, Rida still insisted that the Wahhabis deserved the support of Muslims as a Salafi movement.[168] In many respects, this claim was incongruous because, contrary to the Wahhabis, Rida advocated a critical approach to the evaluation of the authenticity of Prophetic traditions (hadith) and also advocated the use of rationalist methods in the practice of Islamic law.[169] Rida consistently argued that in response to modernity, Islamic law must be interpreted in such a way that human rights and public interests are adequately respected, and he supported the study of philosophy and the practice of parliamentary democracy, both of which were anathema to the Wahhabis.[170] In addition, quite unlike the Wahhabis, Rida, who was a classically trained jurist himself, was strongly supportive of the juristic tradition and the status and role of the classically trained jurists in modern Islam.[171]

As a Salafi, Rida shared certain commonalities with the Wahhabis.[172] Rida was critical of the practices and theology of Sufi orders, particularly the doctrine of intercession and saint worship. Rida was particularly critical of the fact that in Sufi orders, a disciple surrenders his free agency to a master and is expected to follow the rules set by the master blindly. He was also critical of the superstitious beliefs of some Sufi orders and their practice of miracles. But unlike the Wahhabis, Rida did not condemn Sufis as heretics or *kuffar*.[173] Like the Wahhabis, Rida was critical of the doctrine of *taqlid* (imitation) and a strong advocate of renewed *ijtihad*, although his position was considerably more subtle and nuanced than that of the Wahhabis. For instance, among other things, Rida wrote a fascinating fictitious debate between a reformer and conservative traditionalist. In this debate, and in other articles, he acknowledges that adherence to juristic precedent is, in many cases, appropriate and even important. But he insists on the necessity of rethinking certain classical law positions in response to the new challenges confronting Muslims in the modern age. In this context, Rida also argued for the importance of Muslims mastering history and philosophy in responding to the challenges of modernity.[174] Quite clearly, Rida's approach to the juristic tradition only superficially resembled that of the Wahhabis.

The commonalities between Rida's thought and the Wahhabi creed were not sufficiently compelling to explain Rida's willingness to overlook the intolerant and frequently violent practices of the Wahhabis.[175] Nonetheless, the reason that Rida defended the Wahhabis was because of politics—Rida was an Arab nationalist who was also increasingly anti-Ottoman. It is clear from his own writings that Rida welcomed the Wahhabi rebellion against the Ottomans as an Arab revolution being waged against their Turkish masters.[176] In a sense, Rida found himself caught in a difficult position. As a Salafi, his loyalties had to be with Islam and not with a particular ethnicity.[177] As an Arab nationalist, he wanted Arabs to be reinstated to their rightful place as the leaders of the Islamic world. The reality that Rida tried hard not to see was that the leaders of the so-called Islamic Arab revolution were morally bankrupt.[178] Rida, as an Islamist, was not pleased with the Ottoman tendency to defer to custom over Islamic law and with de facto secularism over many public issues.[179] The Wahhabis raised the banner of Islamicity, and Rida confronted a challenging choice. Either he supported the Islamic banner and Arab ethnicity regardless of its ethical content, or he supported the ethics of Islam regardless of the available political options. Like many Salafis that came after him, Rida decided to support the movement that invoked the Islamic dream or symbol, even if at the expense of moral and ethical principles. Rida's insistence on defending the Wahhabis by excusing their acts of cruelty is reminiscent of the Salafis who continued to defend and excuse the Taliban and al-Qaeda despite the cumulative evidence of their cruelty.

This exemplifies a problem that came to plague Salafi thought throughout the twentieth century—its political opportunism. Salafism, which initially promised a liberal type of renaissance in the Islamic world, persistently compromised theological principle to power dynamics and political expedience. Confronted by the challenge of nationalism, Salafis, often invoking the logic of public interest and necessity, consistently transformed Islam into a politically reactive force engaged in a mundane struggle for identity and self-determination.[180] Practically in every situation, Salafis like Rida had to make a choice of whether to excuse inhumane and cruel behavior as justified by the necessities and exigencies of the time or to stand by principle and affirm the ethics of Islam regardless of the political cost. Invariably, Rida excused the autocracy and cruelty of the king of Saudi Arabia and the Wahhabis by citing the immorality of their opponents or by being singularly focused on the banner of Islamic pride raised by the Wahhabis instead of the moral substance. Adopting an attitude which would become typical in the modern Islamic reality, Rida thought that unethical as they might be, at least the Wahhabis raised the flag of Islam, and because of this dogmatic stand, Rida slipped into being an apologist for the culture of cruelty that was increasingly overtaking Muslims in the postcolonial era. As a result, Salafism became a highly diluted and unprincipled moral force, constantly restructuring and redefining itself to respond to a never-ending and constantly shifting power dynamic. In the end, no one could be entirely sure about the ethical and moral principles that Salafism represented, other than those of a stark form of functionalism that constantly shifted in response to the political demands of the day.

By the mid-twentieth century, it had become clear that Salafism had drifted into stifling apologetics. The incipient opportunism in Salafi approaches had degenerated into an intellectual carelessness and whimsicalness that had all but destroyed any efforts at systematic and rigorous analysis. By the 1960s, the initial optimistic liberalism had dissipated, and what remained of this liberal bent had become largely apologetic. Through a complex sociopolitical process, Wahhabism was able to rid itself of some of its extreme forms of intolerance and proceeded to co-opt the language and symbolisms of Salafism in the 1970s until the two had become practically indistinguishable. The word *salaf* means "predecessors" and usually refers to the period of the companions of the Prophet and his successors. The term *salafi* has a natural appeal because it connotes authenticity and legitimacy, and therefore, it is easily exploitable and abused by any movement that seeks the shroud of Islamicity. In the early twentieth century, Wahhabis referred to themselves as Salafis; however, the term did not become inextricably associated with the Wahhabi creed until the 1970s.[181]

Both Wahhabism and Salafism imagined a golden age within Islam; this entailed a belief in a near historical utopia that would be entirely retrievable and reproducible in contemporary Islam. In the same way that the Islamic dream could be retained only by turning an oblivious eye to the moral failures plaguing the contemporary reality, the same attitude marked the Salafi and Wahhabi approaches to early Islamic history. In order to retain the utopian belief in an ideal golden age, it required a considerable degree of obliviousness in regard to Islamic history. Both remained uninterested in critical historical inquiry and responded to the challenge of modernity by escaping to the secure haven of the text. And both advocated a form of egalitarianism and anti-elitism to the point that they came to consider intellectualism and rational moral insight to be inaccessible and thus corruptions to the purity of the Islamic message. These similarities between the two facilitated the Wahhabi co-optation of Salafism. Wahhabism, from its very inception, and Salafism, especially after it entered into the apologetic phase, were infested with a kind of supremacist thinking that prevails until today. The level of intellectual sophistication found in the writings of Rashid Rida, for example, became increasingly rare, and increasingly, the texts written by Salafis became often indistinguishable from those written by Wahhabis. This merging of Wahhabi and Salafi thought was not inevitable or inextricable, but it is an intellectual admixture that emerged because of a political and rhetorical process that occurred over a period of time. So as to distinguish between the reform-oriented Salafism that pervaded many places in the Muslim world in the early twentieth century from the later phenomenon of wedding Wahhabism to Salafism, I will call the latter "Puritanical-Salafism."

Puritanical-Salafism takes things to their logical extreme. The bonding of the theologies of Wahhabism and Salafism produced a contemporary orientation that is anchored in profound feelings of defeatism, alienation, and frustration but also in the intense desire to reclaim a lost authenticity and religiosity. The synchronistic product of these two theologies is one of profound alienation, not only from the institutions of power of the modern world but also from the epistemological legacies of colonialism and modernity. There is no question that Puritanical-Salafism longs for a sense of Islamic identity, which in this case means a collective consciousness based on archetypal categories and symbolism anchored in an Islamic epistemology. But the paradox is that although Puritanical-Salafism sought to be the embodiment of an authentic sense of Islamic being, as a normative movement it was disembodied from the Islamic heritage and tradition. It adopts some idealized aspects of the Islamic historical experience to project the external image of Islamicity, but its moral struggles and intellectual challenges are not rooted in Islamic sociohistorical experiences. At the same time, although Puritanical-Salafism grew out of a sense of alienation toward modernity, for the most part, the epistemological and paradigmatic tools at its disposal were those of modernity. Puritanical-Salafism reacted to the alienation felt by many uprooted native societies, but its paradigms, categories, and epistemology were thoroughly dependent on the same modernity that it strove to resist.

Neither Wahhabism nor Salafism, nor the synchronistic Puritanical-Salafism, are represented by formal institutions; these are theological orientations and not structured schools of thought. Therefore, one finds a broad range of ideological variations and tendencies within each orientation. But the consistent characteristic of Puritanical-Salafism is a supremacist idealism that compensates for feelings of defeatism, disempowerment, and alienation with a distinct sense of self-righteous arrogance vis-à-vis the nondescript "other"— whether the "others" are nonbelievers in general or misguided Muslims. This trend devalues the moral worth of not only non-Muslims alone but also those that it considers inferior or of a lesser station, such as women or heretical or misguided Muslims. Instead of simple apologetics, Puritanical-Salafism responds to the feelings of powerlessness and defeat with uncompromising and arrogant symbolic displays of power, not only against non-Muslims but more so against fellow Muslims.

Puritanical-Salafism anchors itself in the confident security of texts. Texts are considered to be the conveyers of the divine will, and this orientation prides itself on its unrecalcitrant and intractable commitment to be in an obedient relationship with the text. But far from upholding the integrity of the text, Puritanical-Salafism is abusive toward the text because, as a hermeneutic orientation, it empowers its adherents to project their sociopolitical frustrations and insecurities on the text. Elsewhere, I have described the dynamics of Puritanical-Salafism vis-à-vis the text as thoroughly despotic and authoritarian. This is often the result of ignoring the complex processes that surround the construction of texts and the no less complex dynamics that regulate the relationship between the text and its reader. Therefore, consistently, religious texts became as if whips to be exploited by a select class of readers in order to affirm reactionary power dynamics in society.[182] The adherents of Puritanical-Salafism, unlike the apologists, no longer concerned themselves with co-opting or claiming Western institutions as their own. Under the guise of reclaiming the true and real Islam, they proceeded to define Islam as the exact antithesis of the West. Apologetic attempts at proving Islam's compatibility with the West were dismissed as inherently defeatist. Puritanical-Salafis argued that colonialism had ingrained into Muslims a lack of self-pride or dignity and convinced Muslims of the inferiority of their religion. This, Puritanical-Salafis contended, has trapped Muslims into an endless and futile race to appease the West by proving Islam's worthiness. According to this model, in reality, there are only two paths in life—the path of God, or the straight path, and the path of Satan, or the crooked path. By attempting to integrate and co-opt Western ideas such as feminism, democracy, or human rights, Puritanical-Salafis argued, Muslims have fallen prey to the temptations of Satan by accepting ungodly innovations (*bida'*, sing. *bid'a*). Puritanical-Salafis believe that Islam is the only straight path in life and such a way must be pursued regardless of what others think and regardless of how it impacts the rights and well-being of others. Importantly, the straight path (*al-sirat al-mustaqim*) is firmly anchored in a system of divine laws that trump any considerations of morality or ethical normative values. God is manifested through a set of determinable legal commands that cover nearly all aspects of life, and the sole purpose of human beings is to realize the divine manifestation by dutifully and faithfully implementing the divine law. Puritanical-Salafis insist that only the mechanics and technicalities of Islamic law define morality—there are no moral considerations that can be found outside the technical law. This fairly technical and legalistic way of life is considered inherently superior to all others, and the followers of any other way are considered either infidels (*kuffar*), hypocrites (*munafiqun*), or iniquitous (*fasiqun*). Anchored in the security and assuredness of a determinable law, it becomes fairly easy to differentiate between the rightly guided and the misguided. The rightly guided obey the law; the misguided either deny, attempt to dilute, or argue about the law. Any method of thought or process that would lead to indeterminate results, such as social theory, philosophy, or any speculative thought, is part of the crooked path of Satan. According to the Puritanical-Salafis, lives that are lived outside the divine law are inherently unlawful and therefore an offense against God that must be actively fought or punished.

The impact of Puritanical-Salafism on the Islamic intellectual heritage and the humanistic and universalistic orientations within Islam has been devastating. The range and number of issues on which Puritanical-Salafism has had a powerful impact in contemporary Islam are numerous, but there are two particular issues where the impact of Puritanical-Salafism has been particularly pronounced, and the responses to these issues have become among the characteristics that distinguish Puritanical-Salafi thought from other Islamic approaches. The two issues I am referring to here are, first, whether the religious text is intended to regulate most aspects of life and, second, whether aesthetics or an innate human capacity to reflect on and realize the good and reasonable is possible. Puritanical-Salafis augment the role of the text and minimize the role of the human agent who interprets the religious text. According to Puritanical-Salafism, not only does the text regulate most aspects of human life, but also the author of the text determines the meaning of the text, while the reader's job in engaging the text is to simply understand and enforce the commands of the text without contributing anything else to that text. In the Puritanical-Salafist paradigm, subjectivities of the interpreting agent are irrelevant to the realization and implementation of the divine command, which is fully and comprehensively contained in the text. Therefore, the aesthetics and moral insights or the contingencies and experiences of the interpreting agent are considered irrelevant or inadmissible. Puritanical-Salafism seeks to anchor itself in the assured confidence of objectivity, and it is the text that is sought to embody and represent this objectivity. The problem, however, is that this assuredness is more often than not an illusion, not because objectivities do not exist. Most certainly, objective textual qualities, as well as objective values and virtues, do exist, but there is no way of channeling or processing these objectivities without grappling with human subjectivities. The objectivities of a text only achieve balance or reasonableness within the context of human contingencies. It is fair to say that Puritanical-Salafism objectifies its subjectivities. By insisting on ignoring the historical contingencies that the text sought to address in the first place and disregarding the contingencies that modulate and negotiate the agent attempting to read, comprehend, and give effect to the text, Puritanical-Salafism endows itself with the power of determinism and immutability. Interestingly, there is an exception to Puritanical-Salafism's tendency to distrust human contingencies and resist indeterminism, and that is in its admission of public interests or public harms (*al-masalih wa al mafasid al-'amma*). Puritanical-Salafism often invokes concepts of public interests or public harms in the context of gender relations, especially the purported interest in protecting society from the sexual allures of women, and also in the context of powers of the state and the prosecution of political violence. It is often asserted that public interests or harms can be the basis of legislation because the objective text (in this case, Qur'an and Sunna) recognized public interests (*masalih 'amma*) and public harms (*mafasid 'amma*) as sufficient grounds for legal determinations, provided that the recognized interest (*maslaha*) or harm (*mafsada*) are themselves recognized by the text. For example, according to this reasoning, protecting society from sexual allurements is a recognizable good because the text said so. At the same time, permitting the sources of sexual enticements or allurements is a public harm because the text recognized them as such. There is much to say about this point, but for now, one should note that the logic of public goods or harms, as understood and applied by Puritanical-Salafis in the contemporary age, has most often amounted to unabashed political opportunism. As applied time and again in Iran, Saudi Arabia, Pakistan, and Afghanistan, there has been an unmistakable affinity between the recognized public goods and harms and traditional or typical power dynamics. The concept is used not to empower the disempowered, but to legitimate the affirmation and expansion of political power. So, for instance, while the concept has been used by men to impose restrictions on women, it has never been used to alleviate the oppressiveness of poverty or to limit the discretion and reach of the modern state.

In the narratives and writings of Puritanical-Salafis, it is often claimed that in contrast to moral or ethical values and aesthetic judgments, public interests and harms are empirically verifiable and therefore not subject to the whimsical interventions of human desires and, hence, objectively determinable. Meanwhile, values like human dignity, love, mercy, and compassion are considered not subject to quantification and therefore cannot be integrated into legal determinations. There are a number of theological, philosophical, and methodological objections to the assumptions and claims of Puritanical-Salafism about empiricism and the approach to ethical values and virtues, but I will leave these arguments to the chapters that follow. But one would be remiss not to note, once again, that the way Puritanical-Salafism has translated in practice its enthusiasm for empirically verifiable goods and harms and its skepticism toward claims having to do with ethics and morality is that, especially on a wide range of political issues, Puritanical-Salafism has demonstrated a remarkable level of flexibility and pliability that frequently turns into opportunism and intransigence. The synchronistic approach of Puritanical-Salafism, which combines a trust in textual determinism with a pragmatic functionalism and empiricism and that is simultaneously dismissive toward the subjectivities of interpreting agents, while treating aesthetic and moral judgments as anathema, has had a very paradoxical impact on contemporary Muslim consciousness. On the one hand, Puritanical-Salafism is a rebellion against the sense of cultural and political defeatism resulting from the loss of identity and uprootedness that continued to persist in subaltern societies after the end of colonialism and the escalation of imperialism. But on the other hand, Puritanical-Salafism unwittingly embraced and perpetuated this sense of defeatism. By marginalizing and dismissing most of Islamic history and cultural practices as having gone astray and having become corrupt, Puritanical-Salafism ended up diminishing and even deprecating the intellectual and moral achievements of the interpretive communities of past generations. Puritanical-Salafi narratives about the Islamic tradition tend to persistently alternate between triumphalism and repudiation and abnegation—either a particular historical period, historical character, or school of thought or particular texts are conceived of as perfect prototypes of Islam's unparalleled triumphs, or in the alternative, the same are considered examples of what went wrong and of the ways Muslims failed and betrayed Islam. These purported ailments and betrayals must be repudiated and denounced by all Muslims if God is to empower Muslims to reclaim their lost glory and once again rekindle their golden age. In other words, in what is an unmistakable tendency toward reductionism, Puritanical-Salafis end up idolizing or denouncing particular concepts, characters, moments in history, or schools of thought and then struggle to relate to the Islamic tradition from the prism of a praxis based on these highly artificial polarizations. Therefore, for example, Puritanical-Salafis will glorify Ahl al-Hadith and denounce Ahl al-Ra'y or venerate the genre of literature memorializing the Sunna of the Prophet while disparaging literature dealing with *kalam* (theological disputations). Consequently, Puritanical-Salafism produces its own dichotomous narratives casting the Islamic tradition in terms of protagonists and antagonists or as villains and heroes, but then it expects that all Muslims relate to the Islamic tradition according to the same essentialized terms. The result of this process is the inevitable cheapening of the Islamic tradition into superficial parodies and caricatures that ultimately numbs or empties the tradition of its intellectual and moral potentialities. These parodies and caricatures are steadily utilized in bolstering highly idealized Islamic archetypes that certainly are capable of exciting the fervor of many of the passionate hearts that then fill the ranks of the various Puritanical-Salafi movements. However, these ideal-ized constructed archetypes are quickly marginalized, ignored, or betrayed by the majority of Muslims, and even by those who once perpetuated them, because they lack reasonability. There is an essential difference between the archetypes of Puritanical-Salafism and archetypes that inspire, excite, and induce people to unleash the untapped creative energies and moral potential-ities laden within a civilization's tradition. There are archetypes that provide the necessary confidence, intellectual steadiness, and convictional solidity so that people can feel rooted and anchored as they are empowered to bring out the moral, beautiful, and humanistic potential to be unleashed in their tradi-tions. But to marshal archetypes of perfectionism that trivialize or exclude the great majority of the civilizational historical experience and the role of historical analysis, to insist on a stultifying determinism while rejecting mo-ral inquiries, rationalism, and creative innovations (*bida'*) renders the arche-type unwieldy and unreasonable. Such an archetype is given lip-service praise and affirmation, but because of its structural flaws, it can only gener-ate unreasonable expectations and demands and will tend to invite false affectations and ostentatious interactions that in due course will only widen the gap between those who continue to herald the archetype and those who, quite often surreptitiously or even subconsciously, have repudiated or are no longer aroused by the ideal. This predicament results in an incongruous and irreconcilable situation where, for a number of sentimental and cultural rea-sons, a large number of people will continue to pay tribute to the symbols representing the archetypal ideal but are no longer inspired by this ideal to profound acts of creativity and moral value.

Puritanical-Salafism championed idealized archetypes of Islamicity that are superficial and desultory.[183] With the hegemonic spread of Puritanical-Salafism in the past four decades, this creed effectively ushered in a culture of social hypocrisy in which it became customary to pay homage to con-structed ideals about the Prophet, his family and companions, the city-state of Medina, and the Shari'ah, among other Islamic symbols, but to completely ignore the moral and ethical values embodied in these institutions and sym-bols. The irony is that with the diffusion of Puritanical-Salafism in the 1970s, while the appearances of Islamicity spread all over the Muslim world, sub-stantively, the movement trivialized the Islamic tradition with all its textured complexity and richness. Practically, for the three decades of the seventies, eighties, and nineties, only a few voices from within Sunni Islam dared challenge the dominance of Puritanical-Salafism.[184] The political and finan-cial sway of Saudi-backed institutions effectively isolated any dissenting voices speaking from within the Islamic tradition and increasingly drove critical and analytical perspectives to speak from without the tradition. In these three decades, an astounding insipidity and monotony befell Islamic discourses as creative Muslim scholars felt unrelentingly pressured to speak from nonreligious or secular epistemological foundations or risk ostracism, marginalization, or at times, violence of oil-money-funded puritanical insti-tutions. Most importantly, because of its economic and political influence, Saudi Arabia got to write and disseminate the history of modern Islam and succeeded in marginalizing all competing narratives. History as invented and constructed by the victorious Al Sauds normalized the historically peculiar notion that the land of Hijaz, traditionally the spiritual center of the Muslim world, is to be rightfully merged with the land of Najd and then become subsumed under a sovereign political entity named after the historically obscure Al Saud clan. This same history, as narrated by the victorious Al Saud and their supporters, transformed Wahhabism from the margins of extremism, schismaticism, and heterodoxy to the heartland of mainstream Islam. Remarkably, in what became the established and standard historical narrative, the theological positions of the outlandish Ibn 'Abd al-Wahhab were equated with the complex and highly textured ideas of the medieval Ibn Taymiyya and his student Ibn al-Qayyim, and the intolerant and narrow theological opinions of Ibn 'Abd al-Wahhab became representative of the one and only true Islam. Moreover, the Hanbali school of legal thought was transformed from a school that because of its literalism and lack of adaptability was on the verge of extinction at the dawn of the twentieth century to the most influential and representative school in contemporary times. Puritanical-Salafism not only monopolized the power of historical narrative and definition, but it has fueled the spread of Islamism around the globe. It has succeeded in promulgating its paradigm of Islamicity all over the Muslim world, but at the same time, it depleted the Islamic tradition of all meaningful moral content. In short, whatever Puritanical-Salafism gained on the ground, it did so at the expense of the entire Islamic heritage and its moral legacy.

In my view, one of the most revealing watershed events in contemporary Islam took place in Egypt of the late 1980s, when the Azhari jurist Shaykh Muhammad al-Ghazali (d. 1416/1996) published a book criticizing what he described as the phenomenon of "Bedouin Islam." Early historians and critics writing in the eighteenth and nineteenth centuries often referred to the movement coming out of Najd and to the teachings of Ibn 'Abd al-Wahhab's followers as Bedouin or desert Islam. But what makes this event, which involved the publication of the book and the ensuing controversy, especially worthy of attention is that not only did it demonstrate the role that Puritanical-Salafism had come to play in promoting the marked state of ambivalence which plagues current attitudes toward the Islamic intellectual heritage, but it also underscored the urgent need for methodologies that recognize the importance of reasonability and reasonableness in contemporary Islamic approaches. Decades of enduring chimerical constructs in the name of textual fealty had only succeeded in buttressing cultures of ethical banality and intellectual lethargy that all but emptied the Islamic tradition of its inspirational and creative powers. Through his long and prolific career, Shaykh al-Ghazali struggled against the ideas of benighted Islamic movements that gravitated toward the pedantic and obtuse. In al-Ghazali's estimation, such movements led to the trivialization of the normative role and moral force of Shari'ah. In many of his critical writings, al-Ghazali emphasized that contemporaneous Islamic movements used the text as a shield against reason and rationality, and in so doing they persistently forced the Shari'ah to stand for irrational or unreasonable propositions. However, for most of his career, al-Ghazali challenged extremist and militant groups while avoiding making explicit references to the precise ideological and epistemological foundations of these movements in the modern age.

Like Rashid Rida and like most of the Muslim reformers of the twentieth century, al-Ghazali described himself as a Salafi. But at the same time, al-Ghazali grew increasingly weary of the anti-rationalism and self-righteous absolutism of many extremist movements that described themselves as Salafis. Although aware of the influence of Saudi Arabia and Wahhabism, in his many writings al-Ghazali had not alluded to the growing grip of Saudi Arabia over the Azhar seminary and had not criticized Wahhabism explicitly. Al-Ghazali did often express his strong disagreement with the ideas of Sayyid Qutb, especially the ideas Qutb set forth in his book *Milestones on the Road* (*Ma'alim fi al-Tariq*), but al-Ghazali recognized that Qutb was not the main source of influence on the growing phenomenon of Puritanical-Salafism. Al-Ghazali rejected Qutb's *Milestones* because of its intolerant and exclusionist arguments and its authoritarian social and political constructs. Al-Ghazali saw Qutb's *Milestones* primarily as a misguided reaction to the despotic savagery of the Nasser regime in Egypt, a regime that eventually ended up executing Sayyid Qutb. And, in fact, Qutb's methodology did diverge from that of the Wahhabis in many critical respects, including Qutb's willingness to use reason and rationality as sound methods for interrogating and analyzing the necessary role that Islam should play in the contemporary scene.

Al-Ghazali rejected the arguments of *Milestones on the Road* because of their despotism, but he was well aware that Qutb was far from rejecting reason or rationality. In all cases, al-Ghazali believed that the ideas expressed in Qutb's *Milestones on the Road* could not account for the pervasive influence of Saudi-based theology in the Muslim world. But by the 1990s, with a few notable exceptions, mostly from the Shi'i sect, a complete wall of silence had descended on the Muslim Sunni world, and only a handful of brave souls dared to criticize the aggressive proselytizing and dissemination of Wahhabi thought throughout the Islamic world. Moreover, thanks in large measure to Saudi largesse and a well-organized incentive system, the decades of the 1980s and 1990s witnessed the curious phenomenon of Muslim scholars who were known for their liberal and rationalist approaches to Islamic theology and law writing books defending Ibn 'Abd al-Wahhab and Wahhabism— portraying Wahhabism as the movement most capable of confronting the challenges of modernity by rejecting superstition and embracing rationalism and scientific inquiry.[185] The disparity in wealth between most Muslim countries and Saudi Arabia and the hegemonic influence of oil money in the Muslim world created a virtually irresistible incentive system to see history in a light most favorable to the Wahhabis, and al-Ghazali, who throughout his life had obstinately resisted being the recipient of Saudi generosity, arrived at the conviction that it was no longer acceptable to maintain an abstinent diplomatic silence toward the hegemonic spread of Wahhabi influence.[186] Therefore, not surprisingly, instead of criticizing the Wahhabis directly, al-Ghazali wrote a book severely criticizing what he called the modern-day Ahl al-Hadith, their literalism, anti-rationalism, and anti-interpretive approaches. For al-Ghazali, the approach of many Muslims to Islamic text was very reminiscent of the pedantic literalism of the Ahl al-Hadith in the premodern period, who opposed every rationalist orientation in Islam.[187] Ahl al-Hadith is an amorphous term that refers to literalist movements in Islamic history that claimed to adhere to the traditions of the Prophet faithfully, without the corrupting influence of human interpretations or reason. Ahl al-Hadith concerned themselves with collecting, documenting, and transmitting traditions attributed to the Prophet and the companions and claimed to base their legal determinations on these traditions without the interference of human subjectivities. In the fourth/tenth century, there was a close affinity between the followers of Ahmad Ibn Hanbal (d. 241/855), the founder of the Hanbali school of thought, and the Ahl al-Hadith—although the Ahl al-Hadith claimed not to follow any of the established schools of thought and to simply be the adherents of the truth. This affinity was sufficiently close that for a period of time, the term *Ahl al-Hadith* referred to the literalist and strict constructionist Hanbali scholars.[188] By using the expression *Ahl al-Hadith*, al-Ghazali was also referring to an old historical controversy between what some called the pharmacists and doctors of Islam. According to some scholars, those who collected and transmitted traditions, Ahl al-Hadith, were like pharmacists who made and preserved the chemicals, but did not know how to diagnose a disease or prescribe the appropriate medicine. The jurists, however, were more akin to doctors who used the material supplied by the pharmacists but who also used superior knowledge and training to treat diseases.[189] Likewise, al-Ghazali believed that the literalists knew how to collect and memorize the traditions but did not know how the source material could interact with legal methodology in order to produce jurisprudence. The traditionists (the pharmacists) did not know how to apply the methods of law to the raw materials, to balance between competing and contradictory pieces of evidence, to weigh the objectives of the law against the means, to evaluate private against public interests, to analyze tensions between rules and principles, to balance between deference to precedents and demands for change, to comprehend the reason for differences of opinion, and to study the many other subtleties that go into the production of a legal judgment. According to al-Ghazali, when the traditionists transgress on jurisprudence and attempt to practice law, they end up acting as if hadith-hurlers—hurling traditions at their opponents to score cheap points. However, al-Ghazali went beyond accusing Ahl al-Hadith of corrupting Islamic law.

Al-Ghazali blamed the modern Ahl al-Hadith for perpetuating acts of fanaticism that have defiled the image of Islam in the world. He contended that the Ahl al-Hadith suffer from an isolationist and arrogant attitude that makes them uninterested in what the rest of humanity thinks about Islam or Muslims. In al-Ghazali's view, this arrogant and intolerant attitude has deprecated and impoverished Islamic thinking and denied Islam its universalism and humanism. Rather tellingly, al-Ghazali claimed that the modern Ahl al-Hadith have trapped Islam in an arid, harsh, and Bedouin-like environment in which the earmarks of a humanist civilization were clearly absent. This, of course, was an indirect reference to the Wahhabis and their legacy. In addition, al-Ghazali strongly defended the juristic tradition in Islam and decried the ambivalence and dismissiveness with which this tradition was being treated. Being aware of the confusion that had come to surround the meaning of the word *Salafism*, al-Ghazali avoided engaging in an argument about who

were the real and genuine Salafis, but he did advocate a return to the methodologies of the scholars, such as Muhammad 'Abduh and Rashid Rida, both
of whom were pioneers of the Salafi movement. In other words, al-Ghazali
tried to bring Salafi thought back to its liberal and enlightened origins as a
genuine reform movement. Implicitly, he was once again trying to differentiate and divorce Salafism from Wahhabism, claiming that the latter had
corrupted the former. Not since the 1930s had a major Muslim scholar attempted such a task. Furthermore, al-Ghazali engaged in an introspective
critical assessment of the state of Muslim thought and concluded that the
failures of Muslims were their own. Al-Ghazali insisted that the failure to
democratize, respect human rights, modernize, and defend the reputation of
Islam around the world was not the product of an anti-Islamic world conspiracy and that it was contrary to the ethics of Islam for Muslims to fault anyone
for these failures but themselves.

The reaction to al-Ghazali's book was very strong, with a large number of
Puritanical-Salafis writing to condemn him and to question his motives and
competence. Several major conferences were held in Egypt and Saudi Arabia
to criticize the book, and the Saudi paper *al-Sharq al-Awsat* published several long articles responding to al-Ghazali in 1989. Notably, perhaps as an
indication of Saudi influence and contrary to what one would expect, most of
the books written against al-Ghazali were published in Egypt and not Saudi
Arabia.[190] Many of al-Ghazali's critics made the rather implausible claim
that al-Ghazali was not well educated in Islamic law, while others accused
him of being awestruck by the West or simply of treason. It is difficult to
assess whether the virulent response to the book was indicative of any anxiety felt by the Puritanical-Salafis over losing their grip over Muslims because
of the power of al-Ghazali's arguments. In any case, the response to al-
Ghazali's book was, to say the least, intimidating to any other Muslim scholar who would dare to undertake a similarly self-critical approach. It was
simply much safer to stick to apologetics or popular political causes and to
leave the issue of Wahhabism alone. As noted earlier, apologetics and the
sheer financial power of the Saudis has made critiques of Wahhabism, written from within a non-Sufi juristic perspective, exceedingly rare. By the
1990s, the only Islamic critics of the Wahhabis were Sufis or Shi'is, but even
Sufi scholars had become heavily influenced by the Puritanical-Salafi methodology. It was not unusual to find Sufi scholars engage in the same literalist
and myopic adherence to hadith, which al-Ghazali had so strongly criticized.
Although the main issues of contention between the Sufis and Wahhabis
remained the validity of the doctrine of intercession and the legality of rever-
ing saints, the methodological problems identified by al-Ghazali were far
more widespread than even he realized. The death of the jurisprudential
method and the reliance on impressionistic hadith-hurling had become an all-
pervasive phenomenon plaguing the various orientations within Islam, including the Sufis.[191]

Muhammad al-Ghazali died shortly after suffering through the controversy that surrounded his book. After funding a phenomenal campaign against
al-Ghazali, successfully isolating him and neutralizing the impact of his
work, when al-Ghazali died the Saudi government magnanimously announced that it would accommodate his dying wish to be buried in the Hijaz.

When al-Ghazali's family accepted this generous offer, Saudi Arabia, typical of its mode of operation, effectively circulated a rumor that on his deathbed al-Ghazali realized the error of his ways, repented, and disavowed his works. Wahhabi authors have made the same claim about every Muslim jurist who challenged the legitimacy of their ideas. Although al-Ghazali's book did not receive the kind of attention and fair hearing it deserved, his book has come to symbolize a cry of protest over the fate of Salafism and its transformation into Puritanical-Salafism—a transformation that ultimately undermined much of the efforts of the Muslim reformers writing at the end of the nineteenth and beginning of the twentieth centuries. A powerful indicator of the extent of regression that had taken place in the past fifty years is the fact that many sensitive subjects that were openly debated by Muslim jurists had become taboo topics by the end of the twentieth century. For example, at the beginning of the twentieth century there was a vigorous critical juristic debate about the authenticity of traditions attributed to the Prophet, but this same introspective discourse had become inconceivable by the late twentieth century.[192] For al-Ghazali this was a particularly troubling point because in many of his works, al-Ghazali emphasized that oral traditions attributed to the Prophet and his companions must be critically scrutinized according to analytical, ethical, and rational standards. Indeed, throughout his scholarly career, al-Ghazali emphasized that the original sources of Islam must be evaluated in the light of reason, science, and history. Therefore, in the technical terminology of the field, an oral tradition attributed to the Prophet, his family, or companions had to be evaluated not only in terms of its *isnad* (the chain of transmission from one narrator to another) but also in terms of its *matn* (the substantive claim of the report has to be consistent with well-known historical facts, scientific knowledge, and rational scrutiny). This approach promised to critically engage the oral tradition of Islam and open the door for historicizing tradition as a necessary step toward a rational interrogation of the tradition. In my view, if this was performed with the requisite methodological vigilance and disciplined analytical insight by those who not only enjoyed a mastery of the tradition but also were committed and loyal to this tradition, this could have greatly contributed to the viability and relevance of the Islamic tradition in the modern age.

Al-Ghazali was the progeny of a long line of jurists such as Muhammad 'Abduh (d. 1323/1905), Mahmoud Shaltout (d. 1383/1963), Mustafa al-Maraghi (d. 1364/1945), 'Abd al-Halim Mahmoud (d. 1398/1978), Mustafa 'Abd al-Raziq (d. 1366/1947), Muhammad bin 'Abd Allah Darraz (d. 1377/1958), and others who had a mastery of and fidelity to the juristic interpretive tradition. But, as significantly, this line of jurists strove to anchor their approaches to Shari'ah in the methodological disciplines and epistemological standards of their day and age. These scholars did not treat the Shari'ah as an object in and of itself, but true to its literal meaning, they thought of Shari'ah as a normative path in an effort to attain or accomplish divine mercy. Like many of their classical predecessors, al-Ghazali and jurists such as those mentioned above treated the assertion that there can be no contradiction between reason (*'aql*) and God's law (*Shar'*) as if an article of faith or at least a foundational principle of Islamic theology and law. In classical theological and philosophical discourses, what they meant by reason is something quite specific: *'aql* was equated with formalistic or propositional logic. The way that reason was utilized in the processes of jurisprudence had far less to do with formal logic and much more to do with the reasonableness or the reasonability of legal determinations. And the achievement of reasonableness was not possible without mastering the relevant methodological disciplines and epistemologies particular to each time and place. In the approach of these jurists, scholars are considered to be interpretive agents and mediators laboring under an affirmative obligation in pursuing the divine will to make God's mercy expressed through the reasonableness of their determinations on behalf of the Shari'ah.

Reformers like al-Ghazali were determined to meet the challenge of modernity with and through the Islamic tradition. They realized that modernity poses a challenge to all traditional systems of belief, but they also held onto the confident conviction that the Islamic tradition offers the only venue for meeting this challenge without a complete loss of identity. Puritanical-Salafism, however, did not see modernity as posing any kind of challenge, but this inevitably led to the subversion of both the lived reality and tradition of Muslims. Al-Ghazali realized that by subverting the legitimacy and silencing the reformers, Puritanical-Salafism left the door open wide to a third orientation, which al-Ghazali was well aware had already been on the rise in the 1980s. This third orientation was poorly anchored in the Islamic moral and intellectual legacy and had little or no fidelity to that tradition. Authors such as Muhammad Shahrour, Gamal al-Banna, Muhammad Sa'id al-'Ashmawi, and others took the claims of Puritanical-Salafism at face value and started from where the puritans ended.[193] This new breed of reformers sought to deconstruct and do away with the Islamic intellectual tradition as too burdensome, unfit, unworkable, or without redeeming value. If Puritanical-Salafism made it impossible to adopt a critical perspective from within the Islamic tradition, the solution was to function without the tradition. If it was not possible to interrogate and revise the Islamic interpretive tradition according to rational and ethical standards, writers of the third orientation adopted a variety of strategies to minimize or ignore that tradition altogether. The most common of these strategies was to challenge the authenticity and authority of all voices representing the Islamic tradition except for the Qur'an. Accordingly, only the Qur'an, and nothing else, is relevant to defining Islamicity, and only the Qur'an possesses the authority to guide the lives of Muslims in any respect. In recent years, some commentators have labeled this movement the "Qur'anists" or al-Qur'aniyyun. I will have more to say about this Qur'an-centric reform movement in the chapters that follow, but for now, it is worth underscoring that as al-Ghazali potently foresaw and as borne out by events that followed his death, the obstinate intransigence of what al-Ghazali called the modern-day Ahl al-Hadith led to a further epistemological polarization among contemporary Muslims. And as al-Ghazali feared, the normative place of Shari'ah in Muslim societies became among the real casualties of this process of polarization.

Al-Ghazali, however, could not have foreseen that a little over a decade after his death, the wall of silence protecting Wahhabism would come crumbling down. After 2001 and the events that followed 9/11, feeling under a great deal of pressure because of the US rage over the terrorist attacks for a period of time, the Saudi government appeared to have lost control and had become powerless to stem the flood of criticisms directed at Wahhabism. For the first time in decades, in the Muslim and non-Muslim worlds, numerous voices could be heard indicting Wahhabism for inciting terrorism and fanaticism.[194]

It is worth noting that the outlooks of Bin Laden, Ayman al-Zawahiri, and many other militant orientations do belong to what I have called Puritanical-Salafism. Despite much of what has been written, the truth is that not all adherents of the Wahhabi orientation are necessarily militant or would endorse terrorism. Bin Laden, although raised in a Wahhabi environment, was not, strictly speaking, part of that creed. Wahhabism is distinctively introverted—although focused on power, it primarily asserts power over other Muslims. And as explained above, Wahhabi Islam is obsessed with orthodoxy and correct ritualistic practice, especially as it pertains to the seclusion of women. Militant puritanical groups, however, are both introverted and extroverted—they attempt to assert power against both Muslims and non-Muslims. As populist movements, they are a reaction to the disempowerment most Muslims have suffered in the modern age at the hands of harshly despotic governments and at the hands of interventionist foreign powers.

As discussed, Wahhabism greatly contributed to the emergence of Puritanical-Salafism, and so much of the criticism directed at the Saudi movement after 9/11 was well justified. Interestingly, in the first decade of the twenty-first century, Wahhabi institutions effectively responded to the crumbling of the wall of silence that has concealed the movement's role for a long time. Even more, had it not been for the revolutions of the Arab Spring and the overthrow of the regimes closely allied to Saudi Arabia in Tunisia and Egypt, I suspect that it is quite probable that, at least for a period of time, the Saudi regime could have reconstructed that wall of silence again. However, as demonstrated by the explosive proliferation of privately owned satellite radio and television channels, newspapers and magazines, and the numerous writings on the electronic media openly and unabashedly criticizing not only Wahhabism but the whole Islamist project, I strongly suspect that the sociological and cultural topography of the Muslim world has forever been changed. The changes are not just the product of the overthrow of the regimes in Tunisia, Egypt, and Libya, and the slaughter in Yemen and Bahrain, and the de facto civil war in Syria, and the division of Sudan, but these tumultuous developments, like those of the beginning of the twentieth century, reflect deep-seated normative and epistemological transformations in the Muslim world. It is not an exaggeration to conclude that the Muslim world is witnessing truly transformative moments that will affect the future trajectory of Islam and Muslims in ways that will likely be properly understood only in retrospection at least a century after the unfolding of these historic events. For now, however, it is not difficult to foresee that Muslim societies will continue to be thoroughly destabilized and traumatized by alienation and the search for identity. As already has been witnessed in several Muslim countries, the temptation of escaping the sense of turmoil and tribulation by resorting to something like Puritanical-Salafism will remain.

It is precisely because of the continued temptation and draw of Puritanical-Salafism that it is necessary to understand the actual role that this orientation has played in shaping the current challenges confronting Muslims. Ultimately, Puritanical-Salafism not only failed to deliver on its promise of Islamicity, but its failures have exacerbated the sense of rootlessness and alienation felt by many Muslims in the modern world. In other words, Puritanical-Salafism ended up exacerbating the problem that had fueled its existence in the first place. By invoking the symbols of Islamicity, puritans invoked archetypal constructs that are deeply embedded in the historical and cultural psyches of many Muslims. These archetypes created the illusory promise of tradition, of rootedness, and of being grounded in something familiar, authentic, and determinative. But beyond the symbolism and rhetoric and beyond the pietistic affectations, what Puritanical-Salafism offered was no more familiar, innate, or authentic—in other words, no less alienating—than postcolonial modernity. The reality is that beyond impressionistic and superficial claims of authentic Islamicity, the lived Islamic historical experience remained as inaccessible to Puritanical-Salafism as it was to most postcolonial Muslim societies. But the paradoxical duality of simultaneously affirming tradition and authenticity while eschewing the discipline of history as a necessary tool for the construction of authenticity lent an unmistakable lack of coherence to Salafi methodologies in general. However, Puritanical-Salafism (as opposed to Salafism in general) goes a step beyond this by raising the banner of authenticity while contemptuously dismissing the authority of tradition and the formative role of historical processes. Effectively, this meant that the construct of Islamicity that Puritanical-Salafism invited others to embrace was always erratic, idiosyncratic, anomalous, and individualistic.[195] And as evidenced by the sheer intensity of the conflicts and tensions that emerged in postrevolutionary countries such as Egypt and Tunisia, the search for any sense of clarity on the meaning of Islamicity or for common foundations on which a functional consensus can be forged between Islamicists and non-Islamists to say the least has proven to be painfully tumultuous. The exacerbation of the problems of alienation and rootlessness and the failure of Puritanical-Salafism in offering a reasonable and persuasive sense of authenticity and Islamicity led to further polarization and radicalization in Muslim societies as the venues for consensus building and the construction of reasonable solutions for civic coexistence between Islamicists and non-Islamicists became increasingly unattainable.

The paradoxes and internal inconsistencies of Puritanical-Salafism led to critical points of despondent degeneration through which particular ideological elements within Puritanical-Salafism descended into a cult of self-destructive violence. Self-destructive violence or suicide bombing as practiced by militant Puritanical-Salafis betrayed a profound sense of frustration with the world and its system of values. The act of self-annihilation and annihilation of others indulged in by the suicide bomber is as if a cathartic act that seeks to punish society and the self for its failure to realize and root itself in the dream of Islamicity. At the same time, the deluded perpetrator imagines himself playing the role of a martyr absolving society and himself from the sin of abandoning the Islamic ideal and for bringing God's wrath on society itself. The bomber perceives himself as the agent of God's wrath acting to purge his people of their deadly sins. The numerous prohibitions in the Islamic tradition against self-destruction and the destruction of others and the psychology of hopefulness long stood as firm bulwarks against such sense-less acts of violence. It is only with the rise of despair and the erosion of the authority of the classical tradition that this delusional cathartic violence became possible. Indeed, this is precisely why the spread of suicide bombings and other senseless acts of destructive defeatism that have plagued Muslim and non-Muslim countries are such a compelling testament to the bankruptcy of Puritanical-Salafism. Most certainly not every Puritanical-Salafi is prone to commit acts of senseless violence; it is indicative that every suicide bomber to date has been an adherent of Puritanical-Salafism.

I do not want to close this chapter on a despairing note. Progress often results from the reconciliation of contradictions or, put differently, from the creative resolutions that emerge from dialectical historical processes. I believe that embedded within the failures of each historical period are the seeds for a triumphant solution. In thinking about the trajectory of the future, considering the recent history of Muslims, there are certain points or considerations that ought to be elementary and undeniable. In the same way that it is futile and foolhardy to attempt to ignore the prevalent epistemological foundations of the age in which people live, it is equally misguided to try to deny a people their history and the system of values that have become the collective inheritance embedded in their consciences and intellects. Not surprisingly, there have been a considerable number of Muslim intellectuals who have tried to forge a way forward for Muslims by attempting a reconciliation between modernity and tradition.[196] The intellectual efforts worthy of study and reflection are too many to mention, but a partial list of the most noteworthy would have to include those of Tantawi al-Jawhari, Rif'at Sa'id, Malik bin Nabi, Muhammad Iqbal, Fazlur Rahman, Abdolkarim Soroush, Said Nursi, and Baqir al-Sadr. Common to these authors is a systematic attempt at understanding the unique challenges posed by modernity and the ways that the Islamic tradition can respond and, as importantly, contribute to the normative values of the contemporary age. Each of the approaches articulated by these intellectuals has much to commend them, but I will not attempt to describe their approaches in any detailed way.

I have not attempted to set out anything approaching a comprehensive project of reform, and I must confess that I am somewhat skeptical about the usefulness of grand theories for comprehensive change. Before reaching a stage in which metatheories of reform and reconstruction could be effective, a considerable amount of investigatory work needs to be accomplished in order to reclaim memory and to better understand the normative values that we need to develop and nurture in the effort to be true witnesses to God's mercy. A critical component to this project is to explain the nature and role of Shari'ah in the Islamic tradition. In the chapters that follow, I will analyze the nature of Shari'ah and the impact that various contemporary movements have had on defining the role and image of Shari'ah in the modern age. Most critically, I believe that writers like Abdullahi An-Naim who try to limit the role of Shari'ah to a purely private one are only constructing one of these axiomatic contradictions that will only do more damage and create more turmoil. More importantly, by doing this they deny Muslims a normative system that possesses a profound moral potential that, if properly understood and engaged, could become a powerful elevating moral force that could bring considerable healing, peace, and stability to the Muslim search for identity in the contemporary world. To achieve this, I must set out a detailed explanation of what Shari'ah means and what it ought to mean in the upcoming historically decisive moments that are bound to challenge Muslims.

Chapter Nine

God, Shari'ah, and Beauty

PURITANICAL-SALAFISM, THE AUTHORITARIAN SPECTER, AND SOCIAL DEATH

The problems of modernity, alienation, and identity are hardly unique to Muslims. Fundamentally, alienation and rootlessness in modernity is about the construction and anchoring of identity at a time in which globalization has made the maintenance of cultural particularity and uniqueness a real challenge. In meeting this challenge, it is reasonable to expect that each culture would draw on its own unique sense of history and cumulative normative traditions—on its evolved sense of memory and meaning and its particular epistemological history of self-perception and self-invention—in the process of negotiating its sense of identity. But the Muslim predicament is complicated and aggravated by a number of paradoxical realities related to the fact that Islam embodies a very contextually diverse historical legacy as well as a set of normative ideals and aspirations. Furthermore, although the forebearers of a once great and powerful civilization, most Muslim states today are part of the disempowered and dominated subaltern world. And, as noted earlier, colonialism and Wahhabism coalesced rather unprovidentially to disrupt and expunge Muslim memory, and at the same time, these same forces preserved and furthered notional memories and mythologies of a conflict between an imagined Islam and an imagined West.

Although I do believe that Shari'ah can help anchor and root contemporary Muslims, the role of the Shari'ah goes well-beyond functioning as a temperate instrument of preservation and restoration. The Shari'ah can serve as a catalyst for hope and moral progress, and it can play a dynamic role in treating the social ailments that afflict the collective Muslim psyche. But of course, this all depends on the meaning or kind of Shari'ah that is understood and pursued by contemporary Muslims. This has become all the more obvious since the breakout of the revolutionary fervor of the so-called Arab Spring. For all of the good intentions that drove millions of Arabs to the take to the streets in hope of toppling failed despotic regimes, the fact remains that

271

there are social ailments and deformities that will abort any effort at meaningful change unless dynamic mechanisms are utilized to root out and cleanse these maladies. At the time of this writing, the so-called Arab Spring has deteriorated into a vicious and often bloody conflict over identity and vulgar power politics. The fact that the revolutionary idealistic zeal in Bahrain, Syria, Yemen, and even Egypt[1] has increasingly been forced to succumb to sectarian zeal and religious schismatic conflicts illustrates the obstinate hold of entrenched cultural maladies that need to be eradicated from their very roots. I call these cultural maladies the bane of social death and the malediction of authoritarian specter.

Muslims bear a responsibility not just toward themselves but toward humanity and the world. This is a critical point because, as mentioned earlier, Muslims are charged with the burden of bearing witness not just for or against themselves but for or against all of humanity. It is a basic theological premise in Islam that if one fails to bear witness for God and against what is wrong and immoral (*al-munkar*), then one becomes an accomplice to this wrong. This is the basic and quintessential doctrine of *shahada* (to testify belief in God) in Islam. In the same way that nothing remains of *iman* (faith) if one does not believe in the covenantal bond with God, nothing remains of Islam as a religion if one does not accept the duty of *shahada*. Sacrosanct and venerable Islamic theological tenets such as the obligation to pursue goodness and resist wrongfulness, and also jihad (struggling for just causes) grow out of the basic covenant of *shahada*. Furthermore, the pivotal and sublime virtue of *ihsan* (to do what is more virtuous and beautiful in all circumstances), which is deontologically interlinked with the very nature of Islam, is inextricably an expression of *shahada*.

At various stages and contexts in Islamic history, the doctrine of *shahada* provided the dynamic impetus that led Muslims to explore and integrate traditions and cultures as diverse as the Greek, Persian, Roman, Indian, Chinese, Berber, Kazak, Kurdish, Turkic, Habashi or Ethiopian, Tajik, Uzbek, Malay, Javanese, and many more. Of course, as in the case of all human endeavors, many abuses and excesses were committed in the pursuit of and in the name of the ideals of *tawhid* (divine unity) and *shahada*. But at the same time, it must be recognized that this same dogma gave Muslims a sense of mission, or what can even be called a manifest destiny, that served as the catalyst for building a dynamic normative movement that produced one of the world's main civilizational experiences. In this context, Muslims established new paradigms furthering human thinking about tolerance, individual accountability, procedural and evidentiary justice, gender politics, and scientific thinking. What, at the time, Muslims offered the world was comparatively more humane, fair, just, civilized, and beautiful than what prevailed in the various cultures of the world, and this made Islam an irrepressible moral force.[2] It is important to remember that Muslim luminaries such as al-Kindi (d. 256/873), Abu Nasr al-Farabi (d. 339/950), al-Qadi 'Abd al-Jabbar (d. 415/1025), Ibn Sina (Avicenna) (d. 428/1037), Ibn 'Aqil (d. 513/1119), Ibn Baja (Avempace) (d. 533/1138), Abu Hamid al-Ghazali (d. 505/1111), Ibn Rushd (Averroes) (d. 595/1198), Ibn Tufayl (Abubacer) (d. 581/1185), Shihab al-Din al-Suhrawardi (d. 587/1191), Fakhr al-Din al-Razi (d. 606/1210), Farid al-Din 'Attar (d. 617/1220), Ibn 'Arabi (638/1240), Jalal al-Din Rumi

(d. 672/1273), Ibn Battuta (d. 770/1369), Hafiz of Shiraz (d. 791/1389), Ibn Khaldun (d. 808/1406), and many others made contributions that transcended narrow denominational contexts and that greatly enriched the collective civilizational heritage of humanity. These luminaries, as diverse and different as they are, do not represent Islamic orthodoxy, or the average Muslim scholar, nor do they symbolize the freethinking outliers to the Islamic civilization. They do represent, however, the dynamic culture and momentum of the Islamic civilization. The recurring emergence of intellectuals who have made critical paradigm-shifting interventions in the cumulative order of human norms is demonstrative of the zeitgeist of the civilizational culture from which they emerged. It takes hundreds of ordinary or above-average intellectuals before someone of the caliber of Ibn Rushd or Thomas Aquinas (d. 1274) emerges, but the normative culture of the civilization to which a truly brilliant thinker belongs must be conducive to such a momentum or trajectory.

The key point that I wish to get across is that there is considerable evidence that Islamic concepts, such as *tawhid*, *shahada*, and *ihsan* sparked many movements that coalesced into normative projects that engaged humanity at large. For instance, if one reads the early Islamic apologetics responding to existing systems of belief such as Christianity, Judaism, Hinduism, Zoroastrianism, or Stoicism, one is definitely struck by the sheer confidence and certitude found in these texts. But even more striking is the fact that this sense of certitude did not dilute the sophistication of the responses or descend into an aloof arrogance toward the other. Whether a particular apologetic effort is deemed persuasive or successful is beside the point. What is key, however, is that the civilizational culture set in motion by Islam created an impetus, or what might be called a normative velocity in which scholars felt driven to fully engage their intellectual milieu as part of engaging questions material to humanity.

The same point can be reemphasized by considering the anatomy of cultures, or the normative constitution of cultures, that led to the massive translation movement that preserved and augmented the Greek philosophical tradition, or that gave rise to numerous prestigious colleges in medieval Islam, or that led to the sprouting of grand libraries from Baghdad to Timbuktu.[3] But what is more telling are the discourses that surrounded the birth or followed from the birth of particular moralistic traditions in Islam. Consider, for instance, a tradition attributed to the Prophet Muhammad stating: "God is beautiful and loves beauty."[4] It would already have required a particular level of sophisticated moral sensibility to generate, preserve, and develop this tradition. But beyond its origins, a considerable interpretive discourse grew around this tradition in which aesthetic value was philosophically linked with ethical obligations and other normative duties. Moreover, this interpretive culture investigated the nature of creation in relation to the nature of virtue and obligation. These interpretive discourses were all part and parcel of exploring the meaning and mandates of the Shari'ah.[5] I will elaborate on the Shari'ah aspect of this, but for now, I want to emphasize two important points. First, the sophisticated interpretive explorations that developed around this tradition and many others like it would not have been possible without a richly nuanced literary culture. And considering that these discourses flourished around the third/fourth or ninth/tenth centuries, the normative trajectory or velocity of the culture that nurtured these discourses was clearly conducive to making contributions that greatly benefited and elevated humanity. Second, this tradition and others like it are still a part of the Islamic tradition, but contemporary Muslims have not attempted to accomplish anything even approximating the accomplishments of their ancestors.

I am absolutely certain that if Puritanical-Salafism had the type of influence on Islamic culture that it has today, Muslims would have not built a civilization, and they would have contributed nothing to humanity. Today, the moral and aesthetic lead has been taken by democracy, pluralism, and human rights, and the inescapable and challenging question that confronts all religious traditions is: What can they offer that could constitute moral progress in a postmodern world? Of course, this type of grand or ultimate question is beyond the aims of this book. But in the Islamic case, I have persistently argued that Islam is already an embedded and inseparable part of the epistemological and normative culture through which Muslims are compelled to confront postmodernity. But beyond this, attempts at ignoring or excluding the normative role of religion in Muslim societies will only lead to deeper ruptures and further traumatic extirpations, and without any real advantages or gains. Democracy and human rights will flourish in Muslim societies by anchoring their principles and processes in Islamic normativities and not by clashing with embedded Islamic norms. Nevertheless, the greater challenge that Muslims, as the bearers of the *shahada*, must tackle is how to add goodness or godliness to the world by making it more just, beautiful, or fair. For instance, in the contemporary age, the single most troublesome issue that confronts the paradigms of democracy and human rights is political hypocrisy, or, put differently, the most serious problem is the fact that regardless of all the rhetoric, democracy and human rights remain the exclusive privilege of particular classes, races, and nationalities. It does not seem that those who have inherited the moral leadership of the world have been able to move beyond the moral failures of racism, classism, and nationalism. In regard to democracy and human rights, can the Muslim contribution be, for instance, that Muslims are able to rise above class, race, and nationalism? My point is that in the age of democracy and human rights, it is not the case that opportunities for moral contribution and growth have been foreclosed and the sole function of all systems of thought is simply to walk in the footsteps of the forebearers. Beyond myopic relativism, it is possible, and indeed imperative, to make universal moral contributions that constitute advancement in beauty and ethics. But to do so requires critical reflection and serious ethical thinking—the difficult realization is that for Muslims to make a universal contribution mandates a move away from focusing on political struggles and functional opportunism to becoming fully engaged in ethical thought and adherence to moral principle.

The hard and morally oppressive fact is that before being in a position to contribute to the moral growth of the world, Muslims must first deal with the problem of ugliness or the deformities generated by those who claim to espouse Islamic normativities. After the many extreme acts of ugliness that have become associated with the words *Islam, Islamist,* or *Islamic,* the question is: Can Muslims return to the proverbial Islamic without falling into the fold of Puritanical-Salafism? Considering the sheer amount of suffering and contextual malformations persistently instigated by Puritanical-Salafism, will Muslims be able to marginalize this orientation and render it, like many of the extremist movements that preceded it, a historical curiosity?

The burden on Muslim intellectuals today is heavy indeed. They need to marginalize Puritanical-Salafism and establish a moral alternative despite the power of oil money and despite the poor social consciousness of the educated elite in Muslim countries. As discussed earlier, many of the intelligentsia in Muslim countries have abandoned the field and left Islamic normative discourses to Puritanical-Salafism. Muslim intellectuals who understand the transformative role of religion in constructing and undermining cultural mores and who remain committed to Islam as a normative agent in the trajectory of Muslim societies cannot afford to relinquish the field to Puritanical-Salafism. These Muslim intellectuals, however, need to reorient Islamic discourses away from a preoccupation with political power to investigating the key to moral and ethical empowerment. I understand that currently Muslims are experiencing a level of political disempowerment and oppression that is understandably traumatizing. However, the irony is that this position of political vulnerability and the reality of becoming among the most oppressed people on the earth afford Muslims unprecedented opportunities to discover the power of moral victories in the midst of political defeats. It affords Muslims a critical moral stance of bearing witness as the oppressed and not the oppressors. As Islamic theology teaches, no witness is as compelling in the eyes of the Lord as the testimony of the oppressed. Put differently, there is a world of difference between a martyr who affirms the principle of life in his death and a martyr who cheapens the value of life while dying. The difference is between a victim who affirms the value of justice while suffering injustice and a victim who perpetuates injustice as a response to injustice.

Classical Muslim jurists would often repeat that political power is necessary to safeguard the interests of religion, but they also used to warn that political power is fundamentally corrupting of the human conscience and also of the premises of justice. Political power, some jurists argued, thrusts human beings into contexts in which they are tempted to partake in the functions and authority of God—people in authority sit in judgment over others and often bend the will of others to their own. Human beings, however, are ill equipped to perform this role because humans tend to trump principle in the name of expedience and an asserted public good. But eventually, human beings will be tempted to trump public good and expedience in order to guard against personal insecurities that arise from their ambiguous relationship with authority. Because human beings do not have the equanimity and wisdom of the divine, it is inevitable that they will confuse the public good and personal gain, and thus the powerful will always imagine that whatever is good for themselves is also good for everyone else. By failing to differentiate between the cravings of the personal ego and the public good, human beings will inevitably commit injustice. According to some classical scholars, in time, power becomes as addictive as an intoxicant, and it is pursued for its own sake, despite its delusions and false promises. Those who are intoxicated and corrupted by power become imbalanced as they lose the ability to differentiate between the rights of God (*huquq Allah*), the rights of people (*huquq al-'ibad*), and their own personal interests (*al-masalih al-fardiyya* or *al-masalih shakhsiyya*). The solution, for the classical jurists, was simple enough: compel the powerful to abide by the rule of Shari'ah, and this cycle will be broken. If Muslims live according to the Shari'ah, the classical jurists argued, principle will constrain personal interests and expedience, and the balance, which is needed in order to achieve justice, will be maintained.[6]

This classical warning about the corrupting influence of power is particularly applicable to the current Muslim reality. However, in the current reality, it is not so much the presence or the actuality of realized power that is corrupting. Rather, the source of many problems is the obsessive preoccupation with power that followed the extreme sense of disempowerment experienced during the age of colonialism—in other words, what is corrupting in the modern age is not the actuality of power but the promise of power. The preoccupation with the desire to compensate for the aggravated sense of social insecurity and instability that followed the age of colonialism has generated a state of imbalance and disorientation in modern Muslim consciousness.[7] This imbalance has manifested itself in a series of events of extreme ugliness, the primary victims of which, of course, were Muslims themselves. Extreme acts of ugliness perpetrated in the name of Islam were stark manifestations of a way of thinking that has come to value a superficial sense of independence, control, security, and power, regardless of their moral antecedents or consequences. For instance, at the time of this writing, acts of cruelty and ugliness include the poisoning of schoolgirls in Afghanistan.[8]

Doctrinally, Puritanical-Salafism became the main vehicle for rationalizing and often institutionalizing such extreme ugliness in Islam. Socially, Puritanical-Salafism found fertile grounds in the culture of alienation and anxiety that seemed to prevail in the Muslim world in general and in the Arabic-speaking world specifically. The relationship between Puritanical-Salafism, colonialism, and power, or the lack thereof, is particularly visible in two distinct aspects of the modern historical experience: the moral disengagement of the perpetrators of acts of cruelty, and what might be called the social death of the victim.

Colonialism as an extreme form of external dominance and praetorian autocracies, which in the postcolonial era became the prevailing form of government in the Muslim world, had distinctive legacies that fed into the Puritanical-Salafi phenomenon and that were, in turn, sustained and legitimated by Puritanical-Salafism. Colonialism and authoritarianism as systems of dominance are destructive toward any sense of collective or individual moral agency.[9] In such systems, moral responsibility is consistently shifted to those who hold the reins of power and to those who are able to establish a hegemonic system of control. Autonomous or semiautonomous moral agents are considered dangerous from the point of view of both the holders of power and those subjugated by this power. Those living under such systems are promptly socialized into realizing that exhibiting moral agency or independence could be very costly because it is likely to lead to persecution.[10] This process is particularly effective in the modern nation-state, where governments are capable of centralizing and exercising power in ways that would have been inconceivable in the premodern era. In such a context, moral disengagement often becomes a necessary tool of survival. Moral disengagement does not refer only to a general reluctance to make moral judgments, but even more, to the diffusion of moral responsibility to anything or anyone but oneself. In this process, not only is moral responsibility diffused and diluted, but the moral imperative itself, or the very meaning of morality, is also thoroughly undermined.[11]

The other main feature of control and hegemony is the effective devaluation of the "other," however that other is defined. In order to dominate and control a people sufficiently, it often becomes necessary to cause their social death by stereotyping, dehumanizing, and reducing the dominated persons to essentialized constructs. It becomes possible to inflict suffering and commit acts of extreme ugliness toward people who have become sufficiently demonized to the extent that they become as if socially dead. But the status of the socially dead need not be limited to those who have become demonized to the point of becoming as if the embodiment of evil. In fact, it is possible to render socially dead any segment of humanity that is seen as dangerous, threatening, or simply different. Social death of a people could be the result of a process of stereotyping that transforms a people into artificial constructs and desensitizes would-be aggressors to the humanness and "realness" of the potential victims. This could be the result of hate, prejudice, bigotry, or ignorance and could be the result of the adoption of socially and morally irresponsible language toward a group of people.[12] The status of social death makes the infliction of cruelty and suffering on the bearers of this status far more palpable both to those inflicting the suffering and to bystanders as well.[13] But this status is an invented social construct, and therefore, it could be shifting, evolving, and changeable. For instance, in a society such as the one constructed by the Taliban, the status of the socially dead could include women, who are seen as the source of sexual enticement and danger and who are often spoken about in deprecating and condescending language.[14]

Various factors in the 1960s and 1970s created a culture that strongly supported the processes of moral disengagement and social death in the Middle East. Among those factors were the autocratic and often praetorian regimes in power in Middle Eastern countries that consistently demonized their opponents and denied them the most basic human rights. In addition, the experience with colonialism and the disastrous Arab-Israeli conflict contributed to the sense of external danger as well as intensified feelings of political and social insecurity. The continuing suffering of the Palestinians, the relative impotence of the Arab governments in dealing with this problem, and the repeated defeats suffered by the Arab militaries only aggravated the problem. Furthermore, largely because of the political policies of the West and the very demeaning images of Muslims portrayed in the venues of the Western media, many Muslims became convinced that to the West they are effectively socially dead.

All of this created fertile grounds that Puritanical-Salafism, as a power-focused orientation, was able to exploit. Puritanical-Salafism contributed to a process of moral disengagement by displacing moral responsibility from the individual to the text. As explained above, the Puritanical-Salafi creed eschewed notions of moral autonomy, or individualized moral judgment, by claiming to rely on the literal text. By replacing the need for moral inquiry with a strict adherence to legal rules, Puritanical-Salafism ultimately placed moral responsibility with an infallible and irreproachable theoretical construct known as the Qur'an and Sunna. In pretending that Puritanical-Salafi determinations are anchored in these immutable sources and that these determinations are themselves immutable, Puritanical-Salafis insulated and immunized their determinations from the possibility of critical engagement and denied any role to the human conscience in the construction of Islamic norms. This process of diffusion of moral responsibility meant the rationalization of moral disengagement. Such a disengagement was justified as necessary for a faithful and strict adherence to the will of God as it is found in the religious texts of Islam.

Although when social psychologists speak of the processes of moral disengagement they are usually referring to the diffusion of responsibility within a hierarchical power structure, I think that the religious text, as a source of authority, can play an analogous role.[15] Functionally, a text can play a role very similar to that played by commands received from a superior. A hierarchical power structure under a claim of authority demands the deferment of personal judgment and the implementation of the orders of a superior. But if a text commands the commitment and allegiance of its followers, especially when this text incorporates a system of rewards and punishments as a subjective matter, the text could act as the functional equivalent of a power structure that helps diffuse moral responsibility.

Ideologically, Puritanical-Salafism was perfectly equipped to invent and further the phenomenon of social death. By promoting a bipolar view of the world and adopting an uncompromising belief in good versus evil, the saved versus the damned, and those on the straight and narrow path versus everyone else, Puritanical-Salafism tended to relegate "the other" to a lowly status. In Puritanical-Salafi thought, there is an idealistic, near-perfect, constructed, and even caricatured image of the pious and righteous. This is evident in their narratives recounting the glories of the rightly guided companions of the Prophet and also in their rejection of any narratives that complicate or challenge the caricature of the Islamic golden age. Meanwhile, there is an equally caricatured image of "the other," who is considered the antithesis of the pious and righteous. These caricatured constructs play a central role in the promotion of the politics of affectation and the stereotyped responses that were discussed earlier. But the amalgamation of affectation and stereotyped responses as well as the prevalence of apologetics disabled Muslims from confronting many of the complex challenges posed by modernity and postmodernity. To react to the complexity offered by modern and postmodern technology and epistemology by an insistence on caricatured, stereotyped, prepackaged, and anecdotal responses necessarily meant the irrelevance of Islam. But this irrelevance is offensive and hurtful to Muslims—the children of a civilization that was eminently relevant and central to affairs of human beings. The feelings of injury, however, are dealt with in Puritanical-Salafi paradigms by a further vehement insistence on the constructs that caused the irrelevance of Islamic thought in the first place and by an obsessive search for scapegoats. It bears emphasis that the feelings of irrelevance and marginality to world thought painfully felt by numerous Muslims were caused in the first place by the apologetics, stereotyped responses, the pervasive reliance on politics of affectation, and prepackaged caricatures that are hurled at the complex challenges posed by modernity (or, in the language of some, postmodernity). But instead of leading to major self-critical and reconstructive efforts, the prevalent response has been to further insist on the very same problem-filled constructs. The dissonance, alienation, and frustration that result from the feelings of marginalization and irrelevance lead to the unconstructive search for venues of blame, and in the Puritanical-Salafi orientation, blame is invariably found with the nondistinct "other."

Social psychologists have demonstrated convincingly that the projection of blame and the act of scapegoating are central to the process of the construction of a culture of cruelty. For the perpetrators of cruelty, blaming others for their own failures allows for an artificial sense of control over their own lives and the lives of others. Projection diminishes the perpetrator's sense of responsibility and facilitates the process of moral disengagement while augmenting the perpetrator's sense of self-esteem. Significantly, projection and blaming the other are crucial steps in achieving the social death of a potential victim. As social psychologists have argued, it is not feasible to cause the social death of the other without idealizing the self-worth of the perpetrator and ascribing fault to a whole class of potential victims.[16]

Because Puritanical-Salafism is not interested in history or social experience, it became fairly easy for its followers to idealize themselves and deprecate or even demonize "the other." In Puritanical-Salafi thought, the deprecation of the other played a dual function, both of which became an essential part of the Puritanical-Salafi historical experience. On the one hand, demeaning the other supported an egoism that in the Puritanical-Salafi historical experience had become distinctly supremacist in nature. On the other hand, the demonizing of the other was essential to a process of scapegoating and projection of blame, which was clearly manifested in the rampant apologetics and the strong aversion to self-criticism that had become one of the earmarks of Puritanical-Salafism. But it is exactly the demonization of the other, a process that we tragically had an occasion to observe in 9/11, which was also at the heart of the phenomenon described as the social death of victims—a phenomenon that is at the heart of the construction of a culture of cruelty. In essence, the people who perished in the World Trade Centers, the girls who burned to death in the Saudi school, the pilgrims who were slaughtered in Mecca and Medina, the Syrian man executed for allegedly practicing sorcery, the women denied medical treatment and education by the Taliban, the long list of Muslims accused of being heretical or apostates, and the many other victims of Puritanical-Salafi abuses were thought of as socially dead before becoming clinically dead. It was the social death of these victims that made it possible to act with cruelty and disregard toward them and to ultimately render many of them clinically dead as well.[17]

Moral disengagement and social death are common ailments of an environment that perpetuates and justifies acts of ugliness and cruelty, but they are also the recurring ailments of abusive power. Both processes are inextricably related to an exercise of power that has become, as the classical Muslim jurists would have put it, seriously imbalanced.[18] As noted before, the classical jurists believed that the application of Shari'ah law is fundamental for the restoration of the balance and for the just exercise of power. This might very well be the case, but as the experience of modern Islam with

Puritanical-Salafism amply demonstrates, a legal system that relies on its own authoritative frame of reference in order to do away with the need for morality, history, and critical insight or that is incapable of valuing the integrity of the individual conscience and that demonizes dissent is also a legal system that is likely to be corrupted by these ailments. In many ways, history, morality, and mechanisms for self-criticism act to balance the power of a legal system so that it does not become entirely self-referential. An entirely self-referential legal system lacks the elements that can maintain a balance within it and prevent power from thoroughly consuming and corrupting the legal system itself. In a legal system, if the only measure or yardstick of righteousness is the rules and procedures of the system itself, the legal system becomes self-referential. Adhering to the processes and doctrines of that legal system becomes the only way of differentiating between right and wrong, and therefore, the system lacks an agent, such as morality or conscience, that can provide critical oversight over such a system. In effect, sole power is deposited in the mechanisms of the legal system itself without any outside restraining influence, such as morality, history, or sociology, and so it is inevitable that such a system will become self-perpetuating regardless of whether it plays any useful moral or social function. The human agents who work within such a legal system become validated, authenticated, and empowered only by the autonomous system in which they function. Effectively, the autonomous and self-perpetuating system will act to perpetuate the status and privilege of the human agents who constitute it. In other words, a legal system that claims to be autonomous from morality, society, and history becomes nothing more than a vehicle that is exploited in order to allow the human agents who work within it to continue enjoying their privileged status without oversight by any outside participants. Instead of perpetuating the autonomy of the legal system, what is ultimately perpetuated is the privileged status of the human actors who run the system and exploit it for their own benefit.

Puritanical-Salafis claimed Islamic law to be a self-referential system, and therefore, ethical, moral, philosophical, and historical insights could not act to balance out the formalism and arrogant autonomy of the legal system. By making the Shari'ah autonomous and self-referential, far from being able to act as a restraint on power in society, the Puritanical-Salafis rendered Islamic law subject to abuse by the people who claimed to represent it. The Puritanical-Salafis transformed Islamic law into an institution for the preservation of the privileged status of the men who constitute the system—for instance, the privileged status of men over women, or the position of the Puritanical-Salafi over the non-Puritanical-Salafi. Since in the Puritanical-Salafi paradigm Islamic law did not have to make sense rationally, historically, sociologically, ethically, or morally, the status of those privileged by the legal system could go undisputed and unchallenged. In reality, Puritanical-Salafis were not insulating Shari'ah from critical insights, but under the guise of guarding the integrity of Shari'ah they were protecting themselves from criticism.

I think that Islamic law will inevitably mirror the intellectual and moral state of Muslims, and so it is not the rules of Islamic jurisprudence that will lead to reclaiming Islam and empowering it to be a major moral force on the world scene. But until this point, I have been using Islamic law and Shari'ah law interchangeably as if they mean the same thing. Besides being inaccurate, it is not a helpful way to think about the Islamic jurisprudential heritage. Later, I will argue that there is a crucial distinction between Shari'ah and Islamic law and that Shari'ah can play the role of an instigator of reform but Islamic law cannot—it can only reflect or give expression to it. For now, it is of crucial significance to note that it is clear that no set of laws can repair the damage done by Puritanical-Salafism to Islam's moral and ethical fabric. Mercy and compassion, for instance, are core values in the Islamic faith, but no possible application of Islamic law can, by itself, establish a merciful and compassionate social order. The founding of such an order needs an extensive intellectual tradition that critically identifies the current points of ugliness and cruelty and engages in a rethinking of the Muslim historical experience with the express purpose of promoting these core values. But herein is the whole problem. Since the spread of Puritanical-Salafism, Muslim intellectual activities have been abysmal. In the recent past, when contemporary Muslim intellectuals have attempted a critical engagement with their tradition and a search for the moral and humanistic aspects of their intellectual heritage, invariably they have been confronted by the specter of colonialism and postcolonialism; their efforts have been evaluated purely in terms of whether it appeases or displeases the West and whether it politically and socially empowers Muslims or not, and their efforts were accepted or rejected by many Muslims accordingly. Since the age of colonialism, Muslims have become politically hyperactive—a hyperactivity that has often led to much infighting, divisiveness, and intra-Muslim persecution—but they have also remained morally lethargic. By politically hyperactive, I mean that there has been an overabundance of Muslims willing to join Islamic political movements around the world, and in the West there has been a virtual queue of young Muslims eager to earn the designation of "Muslim activist." These considerable numbers of Muslims have been eager to work with power, whether social or political, to mobilize, organize, hold conferences, camps, and lectures, and create a thousand other structures, all with the intent of working to achieve something. But there is no moral vision, no ethical principles, and no intellectual processes that provide any level of reasonable guidance to these busybody activists. They want to go somewhere and take Islam with them, but other than a few slogans of the most pedantic type, the hyperactive young and Muslim generations do not know where, exactly, they should end up. They are largely oblivious to what the possible contributions are that Muslim activism can offer the world or why the world should even value their contributions.

If Islam is to be reclaimed from colonialism, blind nationalism, political hyperactivism, and Puritanical-Salafism, this moral lethargy must be transformed. But in my view, this moral lethargy can only be transformed through an intellectual commitment and activism that honors the Islamic heritage by honestly and critically engaging it and that also honors Islam by honestly and critically confronting any extreme act of ugliness perpetrated in Islam's name. It is not an exaggeration to say that Islam is now living through its proverbial dark ages. In my view, the material issue is not whether one calls for an Islamic reformation or calls for a return to an original moral and humanistic Islamic tradition. The point is that as Muslims confront acts of extreme ugliness committed in their religion's name, they have no choice but to take a long pause and critically evaluate where things might have gone wrong. In essence, Muslims have no choice but to reengage morality in order to generate an effective social rebirth.

CLASSICAL MUSIC AND THE QUR'AN

Years ago, purely out of curiosity, I bought a group of cassettes that would change my life. Normally, whatever money I had (or even did not have) was spent on books. My whole childhood could be summed up by an endless quest for books and the never-ending chase for money that could be spent on books. For reasons that never became clear to me, this one time I managed to save some money but did not feel like buying more books and instead, on an impulse, bought a set of cassette tapes titled *Classical Music Jewels* by Gramophone. What I heard was enthralling and enrapturing—as if I had managed to find the key that made all the books fall into place with perfect synchronicity. In ways that defy description, it did not matter that all the books that I read did not lead me to a perfect conclusive result. Each book left me with innumerable questions and puzzlements, but that did not seem to matter. All these books—the ones that confirmed my beliefs and the ones that defied them—the ones that strengthened my faith and the ones that caused me to be skeptical and critical—just like a symphony or concerto, all flowed together as a whole, making up a single expression of beauty. Each book was like a group of notes that could express tension and contradiction or express harmony and melody, but in their totality they expressed a symphonic beauty. For me, it was an odd experience to find myself affected by what I heard to this extent, and still suffering from a considerable amount of legalism, I became scared. It did not seem right for a student of Islamic law to fall instantly in love with something so Western as classical music, and not only that, but to find so much meaning in it.

With the box of cassettes under my arm, I went to visit Shaykh 'Adil 'Id, one of my Islamic law teachers who spent twenty years of his life in a political prison accused of being a member of the Muslim Brotherhood organization in Egypt. With considerable alarm, I played about five minutes of, I think, a Chopin concerto and confided in my teacher the reason for my plight. It was as if the music I heard, I explained, expressed a primordial beauty left concealed only for human beings to uncover. Like the physical laws of nature, God created them, but human beings discover and harness these laws to their benefit. It was as if God had created the secret of this rhythmic beauty but left it hidden only to be found and restructured to pay homage to the very idea of beauty. Breathlessly and incoherently, I continued explaining to the graceful shaykh that as I listened to these cassettes over and over again, I started seeing the interactive back-and-forth between authors and books as if a piece of music. In fact, creation started looking the same to me—a garden like a harmonic melody and a swamp like an atonal tension—that made sense only when considered in its totality. The Qur'an as well seemed like a composition giving expression to a primordial truth, and although a single symphonic work, it was expressed in divergent tonalities and moods. Shaykh 'Id looked at me with what seemed like annoyed puzzlement. It was clear that he was not enraptured by the music I played, but he also did not seem to see the problem. Suffering his confused gaze, I finally said, "How could something that shook the foundation of my life be authored by non-Muslims?"

I think that what was most troubling to me was that this reality which had thoroughly affected the way I understand my world did not arise from and was not rooted in my own culture. Was it possible, for instance, that I could borrow a paradigm anchored in a non-Muslim foundation and use it to better understand my Muslim context? In a completely matter-of-fact way, Shaykh 'Id said, "Didn't our Prophet say, wisdom is the province of a Muslim, wherever he may find it, he follows it?" The tradition cited by the shaykh expressed a straightforward principle: wisdom is of a universal character, and so regardless of the source, if a Muslim finds what is wise, he should follow it. But what I appreciated the most about my teacher is that although he did not see the wisdom that I saw in this music, he let me follow my own path. He did not attempt to talk me out of what must have been to him a most odd obsession.

Many years later, my obsession with classical music has continued unabated, and I continue to learn an enormous amount from this majestic creation where the mundane and temporal appear to meet. The wisdom of classical music is manifold, and if I had musical talent, I could have learned so much more. What seemed to be confirmed by this music is the fact of beauty—the space in which we exist and the air that surrounds us seems to be filled with beauty that waits for those who can discover the instruments and tools to bring it out. People can disagree on whether Chopin's or Mozart's compositions are beautiful or not, but what they cannot disagree on is that these compositions are expressions of beauty. In the same way, one person may prefer a flower or not, but the essential beauty of flowers is undeniable. All compositions seem to reach toward a primordial archetype of perfection, but none fully embody it. Whether I or anyone else at one time prefers to listen to Bach or Vivaldi—Schubert or Schumann—is relative, but what is not relative is the objective reality of beauty that these composers express. In addition, taking a symphony, concerto, or sonata apart and breaking it into groups of notes, one could end up with a beautiful melody or nothing at all, but only when the parts are combined together as a totality does the balance and beauty fully appear.

The ecstatic feeling—the feeling of balance and beauty I experienced when listening to classical music—reminded me most clearly of my emotions when reading the Qur'an. The feeling is one of elevation—of aching for a greater fulfillment of beauty and for a perfection that can never be fully realized. The Qur'an is like a message that aims to ignite in its audience an aching for greater fulfillment and a fuller achievement of emotional and intellectual beauty. The Qur'an opens the door to venues of moral achievements that in their essence are conditions of beauty. A person could hear a musical composition, and not finding much nuance or many possibilities of meaning, the listener quickly tires of what he hears. Put differently, the most successful musical composition is that which ignites many possibilities for reaching new realms of beauty. Similarly, Muslims who presume the Qur'an to be a closed book—a book that takes its reader to a predetermined and preset stage of beauty but that cannot transcend that stage—deny the Qur'an its richness. It is not the compositions that sounded the prettiest that were the most impactful—rather, the most powerful compositions were those that created infinite potential for reaching the most diverse and higher plains of beauty. Similarly, the Qur'an is not powerful because it takes all its readers to the same exact level and point of beauty. It is powerful because it creates trajectories of beauty—each one reaching a different level and point—with infinite possibility for continuous growth.

There is another regard in which experiencing the beauty of classical music allowed me to gain insight into the beauty of the Qur'an. I can approach a symphony, sonata, or concerto and listen to a comprehensive part—an *allegro*, *menuetto*, or *adagio*, for instance. No doubt, I might very well hear something wholesome, seemingly comprehensive, and I might even be propelled toward further possibilities of beauty. But if I wish to understand the full nuance of a piece and achieve a fully balanced perspective, I must hear and consider the full composition from beginning to end. I simply do not know the full potential of a violin or piano concerto unless I hear all the parts and consider the message in its totality. The same logic is clearly applicable to the Qur'an. Most interpreters and scholars through history have approached the Qur'an in a piecemeal fashion. They would consider each verse or group of verses independently, or they might even focus on a full chapter at a time. Often, however, readers would not consider the Qur'an in its totality, as a comprehensive work, and would not attempt to understand the parts in light of the whole. Each part can express a tone, mood, melody, countermelody, tonality, or atonality, but a fully balanced perspective does not emerge unless the text is considered as a whole and in its totality. Only then can one truly appreciate the moral thrust of the Qur'an or start to consider the possibilities it offers or the potentialities toward beauty that it sets in motion.

Failure to understand the Qur'an as an ethical message with a strong moral thrust led to the overly legalistic and mechanical treatments that one often finds in Islamic literature. The Qur'an has often been treated as a road map that guides the reader to the straight and narrow path—a path with clear, determinable boundaries and a specific and particular destination. This situation, I think, is similar to a listener who listens to a symphony in order to discover its one and true meaning. Instead of opening up possibilities of higher aesthetic consciousness and the potential for realizing new levels of engagement with beauty, for that listener a symphony simply communicates a set of identifiable facts, the meanings of which are predetermined. Importantly, for that listener, every engagement with this same symphony should reach the same conclusions and realize the same set of facts. Not only does this approach deny the symphony its richness, but the dynamic with the work of art will necessarily become despotic and authoritarian. It is impossible for every member of the audience to reach the same conclusions about a symphony without someone assuming the power to define the only legitimate meaning and then coercing others into accepting this predetermined meaning. The Qur'an does lead to a straight path, but it is not narrow. It is a path toward the unbounded discovery and realization of beauty—of unbounded discovery and realization of divinity.

SUBMITTING TO INFINITE DIVINITY

One way of approaching this issue is to reconsider the idea of submission to God. It is well known that the word *Islam* means submission, and the basic Islamic demand is that human beings submit themselves to God and to no one else and nothing else. Human beings should struggle to defeat their weaknesses, control their urges, and gain mastery over themselves. Only by gaining mastery over the self can that self be meaningfully submitted to God. If the self is controlled or mastered by the ego, urges, fears, anxieties, desires, and whims, then attempting to submit this highly compromised self is not very meaningful—one cannot submit what he does not control in the first place.

Furthermore, according to the Qur'an, human beings are God's viceroys and agents on this earth. They possess a divinely delegated power to civilize the earth (*ta'mir al-ard*), and they are commanded not to corrupt it. Human beings are individually accountable, and no human being can carry the sins of another or be held responsible in the Hereafter for the actions of the other. Since human beings are directly accountable to God, their submission to God necessarily means that they submit to no other. Surrendering one's will or autonomy to another human being is like reneging on the relationship of agency with God. Every person, as a direct agent of God, must exercise his or her conscience and mind and be fully responsible for his or her thoughts and actions. If a person surrenders his autonomy to another, in effect, such a person is violating the terms of his agency. Such a person would be assigning his agency responsibilities to another person and defaulting on his fiduciary duties toward God.

Thus, the first obligation of a Muslim is to gain control and mastery over himself; the second obligation is ensure that he does not unlawfully surrender his will and autonomy as an agent to another; and the third obligation is to surrender fully and completely to God. However, this act of surrender cannot be grudging or based on desperation and cannot arise out of a sense that there is no alternative but to surrender. To surrender out of anxiety or fear of punishment is better than defying God, but it is a meaningless and empty submission. Submission must be anchored in feelings of longing and love. Submission is not a merely a physical act of resignation and acceptance. Rather, genuine submission must be guided by a longing and love for union with the divine. Therefore, those who submit do not find fulfillment simply in obedience but in love—a love for the very divinity from which they came.

Needless to say, the Puritanical-Salafi orientation in the process of militarizing Islam portrayed the act of submission as if it is an act of obedience by lowly soldiers to the orders of a superior officer. Furthermore, because Puritanical-Salafism imagined that submission is a process of order and obedience, it was compelled to reduce God's discourse to a set of commands. The Qur'an, in the Puritanical-Salafi imagination, became as if a military manual setting out the marching orders of the high command. The violence done to the Qur'an and Islam from this militarized orientation has been nothing short of devastating. But considering the Puritanical-Salafi preoccupation with power, it is not surprising that the sublime text of the Qur'an was transformed into a text that is primarily concerned with the dynamics of power, not beauty, and that submission to God also became an exercise in power, not love.

The Puritanical-Salafi approach to the Qur'an and to the theology of submission necessarily meant the projection onto God of egotistical human needs. Instead of our relationship with divinity becoming a path toward expanding the human consciousness into the realm of the sublime, divinity was made subservient to the mundane—instead of the temporal guiding the mundane, the mundane dominated the divine, and instead of endowing humanity with divinity, divinity became humanized. Insecure, threatened, and anxious about indeterminacy, Puritanical-Salafism projected the limitations of the physical world on God, and thus it limited the potentialities offered by divinity. The tendency toward anthropomorphism in puritan beliefs is a symptom of this problem.

To love God and be loved by God is the highest form of submission—the surrender of love is the real and true surrender. However, in order to love, as numerous classical scholars pointed out, it is important for the lover to love the truth of the beloved, meaning the lover ought to guard against projecting onto the other a construct and then falling in love with the construct instead of the truth of the beloved. Take, for example, a married couple—it is a common problem that instead of genuinely knowing one another and loving the real character and traits of the other, each spouse would construct an artificial image of the other and then fall in love with the constructed image. The least one can say about this common problem is that each person does not necessarily love the other but loves the construct invented of the other. In the case of God, as a matter of faith, Muslims assume that God has perfect and immutable knowledge, and therefore, God knows the truth about the beloved. As to the human being, the challenge is to know the truth about God without projecting himself onto God. By critical self-reflection, the worshipper can come to know himself and by knowing himself struggle not to project his own subjectivities, limitations, and anxieties on God. In seeking to love God, the challenge and real struggle is not to use God as a stepping-stone toward self-idolatry. As importantly, one's submission to God cannot be transformed into a relationship in which one uses the divine as a crutch to assert power over others. As explained earlier, the highest form of jihad is the struggle to know and cleanse oneself. This self-knowledge and critical engagement with the self is necessary for loving the truth of God, but aspiring to control others or seeking the power to dominate others is a failure of submission to God.

There is, however, an even more fundamental issue implicated here, and this is: What does it mean to submit to the divine, who is infinite? If a human being submits to another, we know what that means—the will of one is made subservient to the will of another, and submission is achieved when one person obeys the other. But when a human being submits to the omnipotent, immutable, and infinite, how is the relationship defined? It seems to me that to say the human being is to obey God is insufficient and unsatisfactory. To even say that the human being loves God by itself tells us little. In submission, the human being does not obey or love a quantifiable sum or a limited reality that can be reduced to a set of injunctions or emotions. To love God is like asserting that one loves nature, or the universe, or some unquantifiable reality like love itself. In many ways, when a human being loves God, a human being is in love with love—in love with infinite virtue and illimitable beauty. If one submits to God solely by obeying commands, unwittingly one has quantified God and rendered the divine reducible. This is so because it is as if one has made the act of submission to God fully represented by the reductionist act of obedience. Instead of being in love with God, one is in love with a distilled and limited construct called the commands of God.

Submitting to God is submitting to limitless and unbounded potentialities. Obedience to what one believes is God's will is necessary, but the will that one believes is God's cannot be made to fully represent the divine. Obedience to what a believer sincerely believes is God's will is an essential and elementary step. God is not represented by a set of commands or by a particular set of identifiable intents or determinations. God is limitless, and thus, submission to God is like submitting to the unlimited. This makes submission a commitment to unlimited potentialities of ever-greater realizations of divinity. Take, for instance, if one is in love with beauty. Submitting oneself to beauty necessarily means submitting to the various possibilities of beauty—not submitting to a single and definite expression of beauty. To bring the concept closer to mind, imagine if one is in love with classical music and this love reaches a point that a particular person wishes to submit himself to this music. Such a submission might very well mean accepting, learning, and obeying certain forms of expression of music. The lover might understand and follow music in the form of a symphony, concerto, sonata, and so on. However, music is a larger reality than the forms that express it, and it is certainly possible to discover new forms that allow for a better and more perfect understanding of music. However, to be in love with classical music means to be love with the potentialities and possibilities offered by this music, which far transcend any particular set of forms.

This understanding regarding the nature of submission in Islam is of core significance to the reclamation of the Islamic message to humanity. As explained earlier, Muslims have a covenantal relationship with God pursuant to which they are to bear witness to moral virtues such as justice, mercy, and compassion. These virtues, according to the Qur'an, are part of the goodness and beauty of God. Submission to God, in my view, necessarily means discharging the obligations of the covenant by seeking after a loving relationship with God. But God's beauty is not expressed simply in abstract terms or undirected theoretical constructs. It is crucial to appreciate that God's beauty is expressed, among other things, in terms of kindness and goodness toward human beings. The object of justice, compassion, and mercy, for instance, is not an unidentifiable abstraction—the object of these virtues is humanity. Therefore, the Prophet, for example, is reported to have said: "A true Muslim is one who refrains from offending people with his tongue or hands." One's relationship with God means the pursuit of greater levels of perfection of beauty. The beauty of submission is not in empowering oneself over people—it is in putting oneself in the service of people.

The approach explicated here presumes a process of moral growth. In my view, to be in love and submit to God necessarily means a constant, never-ending pursuit of beauty. In my view, a relationship with the divine must offer endless possibilities of moral growth, and such a relationship cannot mean stagnation in a set of determinable laws. If God is beauty, how can a relationship with God be but an exploration of beauty? I describe it as an exploration because the mundane can never perfectly realize the supernal— the mundane can only seek after the supernal and seek to become in the process more sublime.

God's path offers potentialities that are limitless, but there is a tension between the notion of a path that leads to numerous possibilities of growth and the determinable law of God. If the divine's beauty is limitless and infinite, and if human beings seek the divine but can never assume to have fully realized it, doesn't this, in effect, negate any basis for an institution of law in Islam?

Part III

Reclaiming Shari'ah in the Modern Age

Chapter Ten

Shari'ah as Reasoning with God

THE SHARI'AH PREDICAMENT

In 2005, Tariq Ramadan, a Muslim reformer and professor of Islamic studies at Oxford University, issued a well-publicized statement in which he called for a moratorium on corporal punishment, stoning, and the death penalty in all Muslim countries. Citing well-known evidence from Islamic legal history, Ramadan argued that *hudud* penalties should not be enforced because they are often misapplied, resulting in grave injustices, and are regularly exploited by Islamophobes to defame the Islamic faith. The moratorium in theory would continue as long as conditions and circumstances for their fair application did not exist. Ramadan's statement did not specify which Muslim countries committed gross injustices in the name of applying the *hudud*, but one can imagine that he had countries such as Saudi Arabia in mind.

Interestingly, as mentioned earlier, most Muslim countries do not enforce the *hudud* punishments, and so the call for a moratorium might have seemed surprising. But Ramadan had a point. Countries such as Iran, Saudi Arabia, Pakistan, Nigeria, and Afghanistan, which have attempted to apply these punishments in some form or another, have at different times and circumstances committed injustices that could only be described as thoroughly ugly. Most surprising about this incident is that Ramadan's call for a moratorium ignited a wave of criticisms and attacks by many Muslim intellectuals and institutions. Puritanical-Salafi orientations reacted with expected disdain and dismissiveness. Curiously, however, many of those who reacted negatively were well-known moderates, such as Tariq al-Bishri, Taha Jabir Alwani, and Mustafa al-Shuk'a, among others. Of this group, the critics appeared to emphasize one of two points. The first objection questioned whether it was the opportune time to raise the issue of the *hudud* penalties when they are hardly in application anywhere in the Muslim world and raising this issue would only serve to cause confusion and unnecessary divisiveness. The second main point raised by many critics was more substantive, in that they questioned the lawfulness of Ramadan's call. Al-Azhar Legal Research Commit-

tee issued a response in which they stated in part: "Whoever denies the
hudud (Islamic Penal Code) recognized as revealed and confirmed or who
demands that they be cancelled or suspended, despite final and indisputable
evidence, is to be regarded as somebody who has forsaken a recognized
element which forms the basis of the religion." According to the committee
headed by Dr. Mustafa al-Shuk'a, the *hudud* are a component of the Islamic
faith, and they cannot be the subject of debate or denial. Most of the other
critics insisted that Ramadan sought to ignore or void laws that were enacted
through authentic and explicit religious text and that doing so is simply
impermissible. Many of the same critics implicitly or explicitly accused
Ramadan of seeking to appease the West, and that in doing so he compromised the dignity of Shari'ah.[1]

This incident powerfully demonstrates not just the politics that surround
the issue of Shari'ah but the confounding level of incoherence in the discourses and the schizophrenic attitudes surrounding the subject among contemporary Muslims. Practically every single scholar who attacked Ramadan's call readily agreed that the *hudud* penalties are not correctly or legitimately applied anywhere in the Muslim world. Other than the Puritanical-
Salafis, I believe that all of Ramadan's critics would agree that Saudi Arabia
and Iran do not apply the *hudud* penalties correctly. Perhaps some of the
critics were provoked by the fact that Ramadan called for a moratorium on
hudud penalties without clearly stating where he believes this moratorium
should take effect. In other words, perhaps if Ramadan had been less diplomatic and specified that he was calling for the moratorium in Saudi Arabia,
for instance, his plea would have received greater support. The question
remains, however, as Egypt's Mufti 'Ali Jum'a pointed out, the *hudud* penalties have not been applied in a country like Egypt for over a thousand years;
so what explains the deluge of criticisms that confronted Ramadan's moratorium?

The answer has to do with text and mythology. Whether accurately or not,
most of the critics took Ramadan's call for a moratorium to mean that he is
denying the applicability of *hudud* penalties in modern times. Contemporary
Muslim thinkers have long held onto a fiction that the so-called *hudud* penalties are an irreversible part of the divine law and that the *hudud* punishments,
in theory, can be applied when the proper preconditions for their application
exist. These preconditions that are supposed to exist before the *hudud* penalties may be legitimately applied are near utopian. The preconditions consist
of a hypothetical situation where society becomes truly pious, poverty and
need disappears, perfect justice exists, and under these circumstances, the
application of the *hudud* penalties constitutes a part of an Islamic criminal
justice system that would serve its proper objectives and purposes. In other
words, a sacred mythology has to be maintained in which (1) the *hudud*
penalties are believed to be a part of the immutable and unchanging laws of
God; (2) these immutable laws cannot be applied without the proper antecedents, which consist of a system of just rule and a pious and moral society;
(3) only then will the *hudud* penalties achieve the divine objectives for which
they were decreed and will not result in injustice or unfair suffering.

Tariq Ramadan's response to his critics was essentially to deny that he
ever questioned that the *hudud* penalties are mandatory and are an essential

or necessary component of the faith (*ma'lum min al-din bi'l darura*). He only asserted that in the current social and political contexts, the conditions for the application of these punishments are not met, and so as a matter of principle, it is wrong to attempt to apply them.[2] From Ramadan's response it would appear that he and his critics began with the same premise and relied on the same argumentative logic; therefore, no real disagreement exists. All parties agreed on the validity and legitimacy of the *hudud* laws because all of the parties believe in the supremacy of an objective text that sets out a determinative law. But if this is the case, then the decision on whether the circumstances and preconditions for the application of the *hudud* have been fulfilled becomes a matter of subjective assessment of how to read the empirical situation. In other words, this controversy gives the impression that the debate over the *hudud* is a disagreement over process and procedure rather than over principle.

The irony of this contentious exchange is that the majority of those who criticized Ramadan do not believe that the proper conditions for applying the *hudud* will ever exist. Alternatively, they believe that even if the proper conditions could exist, this will not happen for many centuries to come. More importantly, most of these thinkers have made sincere concessions to the ideas of the modern nation-state, democracy, and human rights. These same thinkers have claimed that Shari'ah is entirely consistent with the contemporary notions of human rights, but they assiduously avoid having to deal with obvious inconsistencies between modern notions of human rights and the *hudud* penalties and other premodern legal institutions, such as the law of talion. So, for instance, in 2013 a Saudi court caused outrage in human rights circles when it sentenced a man who had struck and paralyzed his victim to either a fine of one million riyals or to be paralyzed himself.[3] Previously, human rights organizations condemned judgments that, under the law of talion, ordered eye gouging and the extraction of teeth. The fact is that the institutions of al-Azhar and the other thinkers who defended Islamic criminal penalties as an essential part of the Shari'ah not only have not called for or worked toward the application of Shari'ah criminal penalties in their own countries, but they have even thoroughly acclimated themselves to living under European-inspired legal systems that have been in place since colonialism. Indeed, like most contemporary Islamic institutions and thinkers, al-Azhar has not called for or attempted to apply the Shari'ah in the modern nation-state. Furthermore, although classical Islamic law penalizes the consumption of alcohol and orders the application of corporal punishment to the offense, al-Azhar and most Muslim intellectuals, such as Tariq al-Bishri, have consistently treated this issue as a matter of personal freedom, diplomatically skirting the issue whenever possible. In short, for all the fireworks that Ramadan's call for a moratorium seemed to set off, the odd paradox is that neither al-Azhar nor the other moderate thinkers who criticized this call would support the application of any of the provisions of classical Islamic criminal law under any circumstances in the foreseeable future.

The critical issue is that contemporary Muslims have a largely apologetic and contradictory relationship with the Islamic text. All of those who defended the legitimacy of the *hudud* penalties believe that at least some of the criminal laws were explicitly set out in the Qur'an and the Sunna of the

Prophet. Therefore, it is a very dangerous precedent to deny the validity of or in any way challenge laws that have a clear meaning and authenticity, because this opens the door to questioning the wisdom or relevance of the sacred text. However, they intuitively know that there have been fundamental and considerable changes in the time and circumstances in which these penalties were originally set out. They are also aware that the overwhelming majority of modern Muslims would not accept the application of the *hudud* penalties because with their modern sensibilities, such Muslims would find stoning, flogging, severing limbs, mutilation, or torture shocking and offensive. This leaves Muslims in a predicament. While they uphold the validity of what they understand to be sacred law and pay lip service to its wisdom and immutability, in practice they create impossible conditions for its application and enforcement.

This approach, which has been rather typical of contemporary Muslims, betrays an unfortunate lack of analytical and normative seriousness in dealing with Islamic texts and in thinking about the Shari'ah tradition. At the time they were decreed in their medieval context, Islamic criminal penalties were rather unremarkable. Indeed, the prevailing character of the so-called Shari'ah criminal system is that it is rooted in the Mosaic laws, or the laws of Moses, as they exist in the Pentateuch. The Shari'ah criminal system added to the Mosaic laws tradition elements borrowed from the customs of Arabia, Roman provincial laws, and some aspects of ancient Persian law. Premodern jurists assiduously tried to avoid applying the *hudud* penalties, but as discussed below, this was not because they considered the *hudud* to be inhumane or cruel.[4] Their legal policies were thoroughly embedded in the legal epistemology of their own historical evolution. The interpretive framework that they pursued was interconnected with a systematic theory about the nature of legal obligations and claims. Penal laws were synchronized with the cultural customs and practices prevalent in their respective societies, so essentially there was no friction caused by the literal meaning of the text and the moral sensibilities of people. As a result, as noted earlier, certain penalties, such as stoning, had not been applied in the Muslim world in more than a thousand years, and when the Wahhabis stoned a woman in Mecca, this was viewed with horror and outrage.[5] This, of course, begs the question: Why did God mention specific criminal penalties in the text of the Qur'an and not others? Were such penalties set out in the text because at the time of revelation they represented a reasonable way to achieve moral objectives, or are these penalties in themselves God's objectives? Were these penalties a means to an end or an end in themselves? How are Muslims to approach a text as rich and nuanced as the Qur'an in what some theorists have described as the age of cosmopolitanism? As a concept, cosmopolitanism draws attention to the fact that the epistemological sensibilities and value systems are constructed today under a historically unique and particular set of sociological and cultural conditions. Today, the sensibilities, tastes, and epistemologies are formed through a full and unavoidable engagement with the world at large. People live in full awareness of each other and in full engagement with one another, and that means that all normative perspectives cannot avoid the critical gaze of the other.[6] This does not mean that all perspectives and causes receive an equal and fair consideration or hearing, but it does mean that human consciousness is increasingly a result of cumulatively and collectively shared human experiences. Critically, these revolutionary shifts in the construction of human consciousness, self-awareness, and epistemology must have profound changes on the way that religious communities approach and interpret their inherited sacred texts.

Returning to the question raised by Tariq Ramadan's plea for the suspension of the *hudud*, we are forced to ask whether it is true that regardless of the nature of contemporary human sensibilities the Qur'anic text is strictly locked into a specific set of meanings that cannot be reinterpreted or renegotiated by its readers. Is it true that the *hudud* penalties must remain an ultimate normative goal that can only be deferred for a period of time but never abandoned? To a great extent, the responses to these questions depend on our understanding of the nature and source of normative obligations in Shari'ah and the extent to which we expect the divinely inspired text to yield determinative results that transcend human contingencies. Alternatively, our responses are a function of the extent to which we understand the interpretive process to be guided by overriding evaluative principles, such as mercifulness, compassion, or reasonableness—principles or boundaries that mediate and ultimately define the parameters of a legitimate negotiation between the human reader and the divine text.

Part of the predicament of Shari'ah discourses in the contemporary age is the considerable ambiguity that surrounds the issue of the state and its obligation to implement a set of positive commandments that embody or represent the divine will. Puritanical-Islamism has resolved this question by recognizing the state's competence to claim that certain determinable laws are in fact divine and granting the state the power to implement these laws in God's name. Among other problems, the difficulty with this approach is that paradoxically it ends up negating and undermining the very point of Shari'ah. By ignoring the pressures of contemporary cosmopolitanism and the changing epistemological subjectivities of the socialized being, this approach ends up defeating the pursuit of virtues, such as justice, equity, and fairness, as well as the imperative of reasonableness (*ta'aqqul wa al-'aqlaniyya*) in the mechanisms of Shari'ah. As I argued before, the inevitable result of approaches that reduce Shari'ah to a determinable code to be enforced by the state in God's name is the marginalization and degradation of Shari'ah's critical role as a normative agent for inspiration and moral guidance in the lives of Muslims. My argument here is not about the separation of church and state or whether religion should play a role in the public sphere. Indeed, a pivotal component of my argument is that in Muslim societies, the state's position toward Shari'ah should be akin to a modern state's duties toward the ethics of virtue. I do not believe that the modern state should remain neutral toward the existence or legitimacy of virtue ethics or the obligation to search and pursue goodness and avoid harm. But this does not mean that the state should be granted the power or discretion to decide on what constitutes the real meaning of virtue to the exclusion of competing views or interpretations of virtue. Similarly, there is a world of difference between the state enforcing a code of law as the true and real embodiment of Shari'ah and the state pursuing Shari'ah as an overarching moral system representing the principle of godliness or divinity.

I am jumping ahead of myself a bit here because the issue of the state and its relationship to Shari'ah depends in large part on how Shari'ah is conceptualized and understood in the modern age. If Shari'ah is seen as a basic value system equivalent to natural virtues, goodness, and beauty, then it is far more feasible to reconcile a commitment to Shari'ah with a commitment to nonauthoritarian systems of governance. Alternatively, if the state is able to exploit Shari'ah in order to shelter itself from civic accountability and to immunize determinations made in the name of God, then it becomes exceedingly difficult to maintain the requisite space for the self-autonomy and self-development necessary for democratic governance. But aside from the issue of the system of governance, before proceeding further, it is important to recall the conceptual framework on which all definitions of Shari'ah rely and the relationship of the concept of Shari'ah to objective values and to human subjectivities.

In this context, it is important to note that in Islamic literature the term *Shari'ah* is employed to refer not just to the way of life, or what one may call the philosophy and method of life of Muslims alone, but also to any other group of people bonded by a common set of beliefs or convictions. Therefore, Islamic sources, such as the Qur'an, will often speak of "the ways of previous generations" (*shar'* or *shari'at man sabaq* or *man qablana*), "the Jewish way of life" (*shar'* or *shari'at al-yahud*), or even "the methods of Greek logicians" (*shar' al-falasifa* or *tariqat al-falasifa*). In Islamic legal usage, typically, the expression *shari'at Allah* or *shar' Allah* refers to the broad concept of the all-inclusive and total path to and from God, which equated, by necessity, to the path leading to and resulting from social goodness (*ma'ruf*) and moral goodness (*husn* or *husna or ihsan*). *Shar' Allah* or Shari'ah does not necessarily denote a positive set of divine commands which humans must comply with, but rather denotes the ultimate good God desires for human beings. On the other hand, Islamic law, or what is called *al-ahkam al-Shar'iyya* or *ahkam al-Shari'ah*, refers to the cumulative body and system of jurisprudential thought of numerous communities and schools about the divine will and its relation to the public good. Islamic law is thus the fallible and imperfect attempt by human beings over centuries to explore right and wrong and to discern what is good for human beings. The moral and ethical foundations and principles of natural justice in Shari'ah are accessible and cognizable by human beings, but this does not necessarily lead to a determinative system of law. Although Shari'ah, as the foundation and pathway to goodness, is immutable, unchangeable, and perfect, this foundation and pathway is not perfectly cognizable or realizable by human beings. In the classical paradigms of Islamic jurisprudence, the law of the state, as opposed to the law of God, was never recognized as objectively good or morally correct. The law of the state was always contingent and contextual— it was authoritative because it is the positive law of the land and not because it is objectively correct or good. The legitimacy of the state's law was a function of the soundness or reasonableness of the state's interpretation of the rational and natural divine will. Therefore, the legitimacy of state law was invariably negotiable, contestable, and ultimately accountable to objective Shari'ah values as argued and claimed by human beings. As discussed in the first chapter, presumptively, state law was thought to be based on political expedience, public interests, and functionality. Hence, Shari'ah played a largely limiting negative role in relation to the law of the state. In principle, it would intervene only to censor or void state laws that were clearly in contravention of Shari'ah law. Classical Muslim jurists were very cognizant of the fact that Shari'ah law was, in principle, supposed to perform a negative constitutional function of defining the outer limits beyond which the law of the state cannot infringe. In fact, classical jurists very often would underscore that what distinguishes and differentiates an Islamic legal system from other legal systems is that the sultan's or prince's legal authority is constrained and limited by the law of God, while other non-Muslim legal systems were either limited by customary cultural practices without guiding principles or limitations, or granted absolute sovereignty to the crown, who was fettered only by his own discretion. In other words, in classical discourses, Muslim jurists emphasized that there were three main systems of law in their day and age.[7] The first was a system in which the law only reflected cultural habits and customary practices, without guiding rational or normative principles. The second was a system in which the crown, prince, or emperor is considered sovereign, and the only limitation on the sovereign is his own discretion. Thus, in the second system, the law is based solely on the will of the human sovereign, but the law is not made subject to rational principles of justice or to any limitations set by a higher authority, such as God or *hikma* (the pure or infallible intellect). Finally, Muslim scholars emphasized a third system of law, in which the governor or ruler acts as an agent (*wakil*) on behalf of the governed and is thus obligated to seek after their interests and well-being. Classical scholars emphasized that this agency or representative relationship need not be expressed verbally nor be reduced to writing. The nature of the relationship is implied in law and defined by Shari'ah. All classical jurists contended that if the ruler betrayed those whom he represents by violating his fiduciary duties, he is liable for the grave sin of treachery and breach of trust before God. But some classical scholars went well beyond this by contending that breach of trust could justify punishing the ruler or removing him from office, violently if necessary.[8]

The classical scholars were attempting to demonstrate that the Islamic system of law is superior to its alternatives because it contains principled limitations to power and, also, the law had to answer to higher organizing natural or rational principles that would always interrogate the legitimacy of what they called political or administrative laws (*al-ahkam al-sultaniyya*). However, at the same time, it ought to be remembered that according to the classical theory, while state law can be limited by Shari'ah principles, state law could never embody or represent Shari'ah law to any extent. As explained earlier, according to the classical constructs, only the legal determinations that have gone through the rigorous analytical process of studying all the indicators to God's will (*adilla*), both textual and rational, then those assessed according to an evaluative process, known as *tarjih*, could produce laws that are a part of the Shari'ah. In practice, what were maintained and preserved as part of the Shari'ah were the judgments of learned and esteemed judges, the responses (*fatawa*) of qualified jurists, and the treatises written by law professors. What made jurists' law a presumptive part of the Shari'ah, while executive rules of the state and rules based on customs and social practices not a part of the Shari'ah, was that both executive and custom-based law were sought to be based on expedience and not on disciplined textual and rational principles of justice. The main difference was that executive law and customary law had no normative weight beyond the temporal institutions or circumstances that justified their existence. However, juristic and judicial opinions and determinations carried normative weight for any case involving the same legal issues, operative causes, or legal principles. This is why for the many centuries of its premodern existence, Islamic law can be best understood as a common-law system in which rational and for-malistic legal principles interact with questions of epistemological contin-gency, custom, and equity to produce what can be described as a noncorpo-rate communal system of law.

As emphasized in my introduction to Shari'ah, there is a significant dif-ference between the Islamic communal systems of law applied over many centuries in Muslim polities and the symbolic construct of Shari'ah, which was employed as an archetypal signifier for the true justice, dignity, or mercy ordained by God. Therefore, it is not at all surprising to find throughout Islamic history both rebels and their opponents sincerely appealing to Sha-ri'ah as an objective and as the ultimate source of legitimacy for their respec-tive positions. Not surprisingly, a substantial philosophical and jurispruden-tial discourse emerged that explored the relationship of Shari'ah to ultimate moral values and virtues. Perhaps the most popular in Islamic history was the tendency to see Shari'ah as embodied and fully manifested by the principle of justice. Accordingly, if there is any irreconcilable difference between Shari'ah and justice, then there is a fundamental betrayal of Shari'ah and its essence. Ibn Qayyim al-Jawziyya (d. 751/1350) described the Shari'ah as the following:

> The Shari'ah is God's justice among His servants, and His mercy among His creatures. It is God's shadow on this earth. It is His wisdom, which leads to Him in the most exact way and the most exact affirmation of the truthfulness of His Prophet. It is His light, which enlightens the seekers and His guidance for the rightly guided. It is the absolute cure for all ills and the straight path which if followed will lead to righteousness. . . . It is life and nutrition, the medicine, the light, the cure and the safeguard. Every good in this life is derived from it and achieved through it, and every deficiency in existence results from its dissipation. If it had not been for the fact that some of its rules remain [in this world] this world would become corrupted and the universe would be dissipated. . . . If God would wish to destroy the world and dissolve existence, He would void whatever remains of its injunctions. For the Shari'ah which was sent to His Prophet . . . is the pillar of existence and the key to success in this world and the Hereafter. [9]

Others argued that Shari'ah embodies virtue and so there can be conflict between the norms. Many such as al-Kindi (d. 256/873) argued for a pro-found affinity between Shari'ah and *fadila*, or the virtue of achieving godli-ness within oneself. Abu Hamid al-Ghazali (d. 504/1111) argued that it is impossible for Shari'ah to diverge from the civic value of public goodness. Still others saw Shari'ah as an embodiment of genuine and true philosophical wisdom (*hikma*). Of course, there is also the very important orientation represented by Ibn Rushd that tended to see Shari'ah as a blessed revealing light, and he believed the intellect to be the same, and so, as he is reported to have said, "The light of one cannot negate the light of the other." Still, others emphasized the profound affinity between Shari'ah and *ihsan* or *husn* (the elevation of humans to a beautified state of godliness).[10] Importantly, this did not mean that any of these approaches were willing to ignore the literal command of the text whenever it conflicted with their theory of reason, virtue, goodness, or beauty. Rather, when it came to law, jurists espousing one moral view or another articulated their theory of moral objectives and purposes of Shari'ah as an evaluative standard through which the desirability of legal schools of thought or legal orientations may be assessed and modified. Many contemporary Muslims have tended to ask the wrong question, and that is whether jurists are willing to ignore the prescription of a legal text while giving their own moral vision or sense of justice priority. Of course, this approach misses the point because no self-respecting jurist in any legal system will be willing to simply flout the express legal text for his or her own private musings. The real issue was the extent to which various legal approaches were willing to devise methodological legal techniques to overcome the obstacle of an unmaneuverable explicit legal text in order to achieve the higher objectives of the legal system. To what extent the moral aspirations of the legal system had an impact on the shaping of positive Islamic law at different places and times is a very complex topic. Later, I will have an opportunity to discuss this issue in more detail, but for now, I emphasize that the concept of Shari'ah was never a simple amalgamation of positive prescriptions or rules and was not simply based on a list of textual commands claiming to be rooted with varying degrees of credibility to divine revelation. Perhaps, with the exception of the most literalist and strict constructionist school, such as the followers of Ahmad Ibn Hanbal, all legal schools understood that claiming to read texts as if one were unpacking a mathematical equation is a delusion. The irony is that even the Hanbali school produced some of the most analytical and normatively dynamic legal scholars, such as Ibn 'Aqil (d. 513/1119), al-Tufi (d. 716/1316), and Ibn Qayyim al-Jawziyya, in the history of Islamic jurisprudence, scholars who had developed rather sophisticated paradigms for evaluating the role of lawyers as opposed to that of socioreligious preachers and critics. Critically, whatever the hermeneutical approach of one school of thought or jurist, the innate relationship between the principles of natural justice and Shari'ah had been a firm and unwavering part of the Muslim consciousness from the inception of Islam and to the current age. However, to what extent this innate relationship is understood and absorbed and how this relationship is expressed diverges greatly from one historical context to another. Most importantly, any attempt at expressing or asserting this relationship was always deeply influenced by the prevalent epistemological categories and ideas of the age and day. What remains constant is the association of the Shari'ah with the notion of natural justice, right, or goodness, but depending on the era and the language of the age, the articulation of the desired goodness or right was, at one time, expressed in terms of the utopian city-state of philosopher kings, or, at another time, in terms of the maintenance of an imperial power in the age of empires, or in our contemporary age, in terms of the construction of civic societies and democratic polities. So, for instance, after the so-called Arab Spring, many Muslims took to the streets demanding more freedom, equality, greater political rights, and a democratic system of government. Furthermore, most of those who were killed trying to overthrow tyrants such as Muammar Qadhafi of Libya, Hosni Mubarak of Egypt, and Bashar al-Assad of Syria became known in popular Islamic culture as *shuhada'*, or martyrs killed while performing jihad. Moreover, at the time of the Egyptian Revolution, the rector of al-Azhar issued what became known as the Azhar Declaration of 2011, pronouncing democracy to be the political order mandated by Shari'ah.[11] In each of these cases, as in many others in the modern age, Muslims are expressing what in their perceptions of the self and its archetypes are organic and inherent relationships between the principles of justice, human dignity, or the ethical virtues at the heart of human goodness, and Shari'ah. It would be thoroughly artificial and flawed to see this as simply a by-product of Western transplants or Western influence. Rather, the rootedness of humanistic values in the Shari'ah, as a normative order, enables Muslims to remain faithful to the Islamic tradition by reclaiming its humanistic values, but the process of expressing these values is invariably done in the language of the age.

To argue that as a sociohistorical matter Shari'ah was always understood, constructed, and articulated within the prevalent epistemological parameters of the age is not in and of itself a normative argument for one interpretive framework over others. It only means that it is naïve and misleading to believe that it is possible to avoid or to ignore the epistemological parameters allowed by each cultural age. A text will invoke an extremely wide range of responses and reactions from readers who more or less share the epistemological universe of the author and readers. But when the gap between the time and context of the writing and the circumstances of the reader is ever more different or far more removed, it takes a great deal of learning and training on the part of the dedicated reader to try to master an epistemology that belonged to the author at the time of writing but is no longer accessible to the reader. However, when the author of a text is divine, we end up with a very different dynamic. According to Islamic belief, God is immutable and beyond human limitations, and so it cannot be claimed that God is subject to any epistemological constraints. However, although the divine author is not limited by an epistemological understanding, God may indeed choose to embrace a historically bounded epistemology as the one epistemology valid for all times and places. There is, of course, a serious problem with arguing that God intended to lock the epistemology of the seventh century into the immutable text of the Qur'an and then intended to hold Muslims hostage to this epistemological framework for all ages to come. Among other things, this would limit the dynamism and effectiveness of divine text because the Qur'an would be forever locked within a knowledge paradigm that is very difficult to retrieve or re-create. But even more, it would stand to reason that since the author of the text is divine, this author would have foreknowledge about the dramatic shifts and evolutions that are going to take place in human epistemologies and methods of knowledge. As Muslim theologians would have put it, because God has foreknowledge of coming changes and challenges, then God's mercy and compassion would necessitate that God would enable Muslims to have the tools and means of effectively dealing with this challenge. Furthermore, it would stand to reason that God would produce a text that is immanently negotiable and dynamic. In essence, knowing that human beings will achieve major advances in the technology of acquiring, retrieving, and storing data and that doing so will alter their state of consciousness, perceptions, comprehensions, and sensitivities, it is inconceivable that God would leave Muslims with a revelation that is not fully equipped to deal with these defining challenges at every age.

The argument about epistemological relevance is not a roundabout way of trying to abrogate or void all Qur'anic laws as historically outdated or invalid. There are many problems with arguments that assume that the Qur'an was intended to address the historical problems of the seventh century without normative implications for the centuries that follow. The problem with the historical approach as opposed to what may be called the epistemological approach is that it often assumes a material explanation for the Qur'anic text without considering the moral trajectory or objective of the text. Of course, the historical approach does not pose a methodological problem for analysts who do believe in the divinity of the Qur'an. However, for a Muslim, the historical approach poses a problem because it does not necessarily recognize the existence of unified, coherent, and infinite transcendental values to the Qur'an. As a methodology, the historical approach is very useful in that it helps explain the contextual circumstances of Qur'anic discourses, but it is unable to go beyond immediate material causes to look at the Qur'an as a transcendental project of divine guidance. Therefore, in such an approach, all Qur'anic determinations could be seen as solely the result of a particular set of historical circumstance and hence no longer of any significance for any age beyond which they were revealed. I think any methodology that relies on the logic of abrogation or invalidation is theologically problematic and intellectually dishonest. In the approach that I am advocating, the question is not whether any text is relevant to Shari'ah, such as the Qur'an, continues to be valid or relevant. I think that any and all Qur'anic determinations continue to be relevant, valid, and significant. The issue is, rather, what did the Qur'anic determination mean when it was revealed, and assuming that the Qur'an is an active and dynamic ongoing revelation, what should a historical determination mean for today? So, for instance, if we consider the *hudud* penalties that were mentioned in the text of the Qur'an, there is no indication that by choosing particular punishments, the Qur'an intended to be particularly severe or cruel. The punishments decreed were well within the range of criminal penalties imposed at the time, and indeed when compared to the various forms of corporal punishments prevalent in the medieval era, these penalties were not understood by its contemporaries as exceptional or unusual. Furthermore, especially in premodern religious legal systems, law performed important metaphorical and symbolic roles that were often far more significant than the ability of the state to enforce or apply laws. In premodern societies, most crimes or offenses were dealt with at a communal level and through a set of socially established institutions that mediated, resolved, and defused most conflicts in ways that made the punishments of the state a rarely enforced threat and also, rarely, the preferred method of resolving conflicts. I think it is fair to say that the prescription of specific penalties for a particular set of acts of misconduct was not intended to sanctify particular penalties or specific forms of punishment over all others. Rather, there were many normative reasons for these Qur'anic prescriptions, none of them having to do with the method of punishment but with the moral condemnation of certain acts of misconduct. Since the objective of the Qur'anic prescriptions is not to engage in cruelty or in punishments beyond the pale of normalcy, a contemporary Muslim who wishes to apply the *hudud* penalties will confront a number of serious difficulties. In an age of cosmopolitanism, it is impossible to apply the same penalties without communicating a message of cruelty and barbarism, which would completely undermine and corrupt the original intended message of the Qur'anic determinations. If a Muslim insists on advocating the *hudud* penalties, the only choice is to engage the consciousness of Muslims and non-Muslims and persuade them that such penalties are not barbaric or cruel. Again, putting forward a message that communicates barbarism and cruelty would be completely at odds with the objectives of the Qur'an, which emphasizes mercy, compassion, and forgiveness as core values. More critically, there is no indication from the very verses that prescribed the *hudud* penalties that cruelty or savagery is an intended Qur'anic objective. As the term *hudud* connotes, the objective of these Qur'anic prescriptions is the protection of particular moral interests, or put differently, the guarding of specific ethical boundaries.[12] Many contemporary Muslims believe that the purpose behind the *hudud* penalties is effective deterrence—the punishments are said to be so severe that it would be an effective way to deter would-be offenders. The deterrence argument, however, is made without any supporting empirical evidence. Indeed, there is much to suggest that criminal deterrence, as opposed to moral denunciation and censure, was not part of the relevant epistemological dynamic of the *hudud* Qur'anic verses. The numerous evidentiary obstacles to enforcement, such as the principle of forgiveness when in doubt, the discouragement of confessions against the self, or the prohibition against government spying or the use of circumstantial evidence in proving the commission of the crimes, are all indicators the penalties set out in the Qur'an text were not centered on the theme of deterrence.[13] Moreover, if one adopts an epistemological analytical approach, it would make little sense to make an argument about deterrence in the twenty-first century without studying contemporary knowledge fields such as criminal psychology and sociology as well as the politics of criminal enforcement. It would be unreasonable to leap from the logic of deterrence in ancient Mosaic laws or the laws of Medina in the seventh century to a claim about deterrence in the very different economic, sociological, and even biological realities of the often alienated and fragmented humanity of the twenty-first century.

There is a further consideration that cannot be ignored when thinking about the coercive and compulsory powers that the modern state may claim on God's behalf to punish offenders in the name of God. When Qur'anic prescriptions addressed the Prophet and his community of early Muslims, in the epistemology of the time and place of the revelation, law was governed by communal and consensual standards that adhered to very different rules of inclusion and exclusion than our own. This is powerfully demonstrated in the Qur'anic discourse in which God puts a rhetorical but very powerful question to people who were oppressed and subjugated on earth. The Qur'an posits a reasonable question for those who resign themselves to exploitation and subjugation; it asks them: Wasn't God's earth large enough for you to migrate elsewhere and escape your persecution?[14] Within the epistemological paradigms of our age, this question could mean something very different from what was originally intended—it might refer to spiritual, moral, and intellectual space that needs to be reclaimed by the oppressed to resist subjugation and to maintain a reasonable autonomy of conscience. The important point, however, is that physical migration, autonomy, and communal self-determination has become infinitely more challenging and complex in the age of nation-states, monitored national boundaries, and passports. Likewise, the state's ability to obtain coercive compliance to its laws through the use of force is diametrically enhanced with the current advances in transportation, communication, surveillance, monitoring, and the processing of information. The intrusive powers of the state and its near hegemonic ability to occupy the public space, if need be through brutality or manipulation, has witnessed a dramatic rise in the modern age. Not only has the state become far more powerful than at any other time in history, but more critically, the relative ability of the individuals to reserve an amount of space for the autonomous or semiautonomous exercise of consciousness has been greatly eroded by the development of regularized and systematized means of producing information. This has meant that massive corporate interests have succeeded not only in influencing, shaping, and regulating supply, but also in inventing and perpetuating demand around the globe. At the national and international levels, the reach of governing institutions and their sheer capacity to intervene, occupy, and dominate both public and private spaces has risen to unprecedented levels in human history. Therefore, for instance, as scholars have noted, the emergence of totalitarian, as opposed to authoritarian, regimes is a phenomenon that arose with modernity. Advancements in the technology of administrative repression and in the systematization and regularization of the use of violence, or the threat of violence, gave the state a hegemonic capacity to dominate and control.[15] The power dynamics of modernity pose the most formidable of all the epistemological challenges to contemporary Muslims. As explained earlier, the extent to which the Shari'ah was implemented through a legal system enabled Muslim jurists to set a barrier between the law of God and the law of the state. This was not just a matter of challenging the state's claim of being privy to and also the bearer of the divine will, but it materially altered the nature of the dynamic between the functions of law and society. Part of the modern state's arsenal of power and control is the practice of codifying laws so that ultimately it is the state that retains the power to define legal causes, material interests, and the procedural rules of the very mechanics by which grievances are raised and resolved. Codification, systematization, categorization, and regularization have been powerful forces in modernity because they create legal systems that are more predictable and more conducive to serving corporate institutions such as commercial businesses, financial institutions, security, and defense forces. As explained earlier, traditional Islamic law worked through semiautonomous legal guilds and inns of courts that resembled the common-law system in its most salient features. The Islamic legal system was commu-

nal in the sense that many of the processes for resolving conflicts and disputes relied heavily on localized customs and practices and on the mitigating
and negotiating functions played by community elders, tribal chiefs, and
semiofficial neighborhood patriarchs (such as Shaykh al-Hara, the Mukhtar,
the 'Ummda, and many other titles that developed in the numerous cultures
of the Muslim world). This network of community leaders provided an invaluable source for the judiciary in assessing the credibility of witnesses and in
reaching reasonable legal judgments that did not clash with the complex
matrix of dominant social and cultural practices. Most significantly, these
community elders usually gained respect and credibility not so much for their
wise decisions or probative judgments but for their ability to consult with
influential notables in society, to act as consensus builders, and to settle or
resolve conflicts without having to involve the state. Therefore, when in-
specting certain genres of text in the classical jurisprudential tradition, such
as texts on *ahkam al-qada'* (judicial processes) and *al-mukhasamat wa'l
munaza'at* (litigation), one notices that judges would often try to pressure
litigants to work with the community elders to amicably resolve or arbitrate
conflicts. In such texts, it is often noted that communal arbitration or conflict
resolution is more conducive to the preservation of social harmony than
formal litigation or official judicial determinations.

As explained earlier, Muslim jurists resisted codification and also the co-
optation of the legal system by the state well into the Ottoman and Safavid
periods. The real challenge is that the communal model of judicial administration that developed in the Islamic legal system, which relied on legal
pluralism and the differentiation between the law of the state and the common or communal law, required strong social institutions in which there is a
de facto balance of power between the state, judiciary, tradesmen and mer-
cantile classes, landed nobility, and most importantly, professional guilds
such as the Islamic law guilds. In fact, with the rise and fall of various
dynastic rules in Islam, it is the strong social institutions and guilds, especially the vast network of Islamic *awqaf* (endowments), that gave the Islamic
civilization its intellectual and cultural continuity.

Colonialism, with its system of economic and legal capitulations and the
creation of mixed courts, started a systematic movement toward legal codification that eventually led to the dismantling of the Islamic legal system. The
formidable challenge is that sociologically, communal legal systems take
centuries to construct, but the movement toward codification, like other drifts
toward centralization and consolidation of power, is very swift. Especially in
the modern age, even countries with a solid common-law tradition have
found themselves drawn toward statutory restatements or reprisals of legal
doctrines. In the case of Islamic law, it is not an exaggeration to assert that
reversing the movement toward codification and legal centralization and re-
storing something resembling the precolonial legal system would be extremely difficult in the modern age. But this underscores the predicament of
Shari'ah in the present age. All modern attempts at grafting some form of
Islamic law onto existing modern political systems in Pakistan, Afghanistan,
Nigeria, Pakistan, or Saudi Arabia have produced grotesque mutations that
cannot be identified as being a part of any respectable legal tradition.

But my point here is even more basic. Today, the law in democratic systems of governance, at least in theory, belongs to the people and their representatives. In addition, controlling, navigating, and changing the law is considered a critical function of the contemporary state. It is practically inevitable that any attempt at applying Islamic law in the contemporary system of nation-states will, by definition, place the state in the position of the custodian and guardian of that law. In other words, what Muslim jurists resisted for at least twelve centuries has now become the inescapable reality. Contemporary political theories presume that sovereignty belongs to the citizenry of the state, and thus, the citizenry is the source of legitimacy, which includes the legitimacy of power and law. All modern states, whether despotic or not, claim to govern in the name of their citizenry and also base their claim of authority over law on their purported status as the people's representatives. The problem is that due to the instrumentalities of the modern state, it is unavoidable that the state will become the voice of God, and in doing so, it will possess the power to shroud itself with the claim of being the enforcer of God's law. To say the least, this will constitute a radical restructuring and reconstructing of the whole epistemological framework of Islamic jurisprudence.

At this point it is useful to return to a theme mentioned earlier: what a contemporary scholar aptly titled "the fatigue of Shari'ah."[16] The classical debate focused on the ominous possibility that a time would come when the Shari'ah would cease to be relevant among Muslims. Muslim theologians debated the theological and philosophical implications of a humanity that can no longer attain divine guidance because human beings in general and Muslims in particular have turned away from God's grace. Interestingly, in the writings of the classical scholars, the most often imagined instrumentality for the occurrence of this possibility was to assume a time when all the gifted and truly qualified scholars of Shari'ah would become irrelevant or extinct. There are a number of ways of understanding the framing of this debate. It is possible that Muslim jurists imagined a time when, because of the lack of piety or proper spirituality, it would become increasingly difficult for students of Shari'ah to fully comprehend or appreciate Shari'ah commands or objectives. But it is also possible that Muslim jurists imagined that it is the believers themselves who would become so alienated from their religion that they would no longer be willing to defer to the guidance provided by Shari'ah specialists. In other words, it is possible to see this perceived danger as either a supply or demand problem—one in which the supply or production of competent jurists would become scarce or, alternatively, one in which the demand for competent jurists would dry up or become minimal. Importantly, however, the imagined predicament of Shari'ah law was not thought to be in the vanishing of the instrumentalities of Shari'ah application or enforcement. In other words, the classical scholars did not conceive of the problem as one in which the rulers would no longer implement Islamic law. This is particularly important because in the mind of most modern Islamists, the failure of the state to enforce and implement Islamic law would be seen as the very definition of failure and lack of commitment to Shari'ah. I think the problem, however, is multifaceted and far more complex. If the state adopts a single determinative interpretation of the law of God and implements it without regard to competing interpretations and constructions, the state has, in fact, caused the extinction of the Shari'ah because, in effect, the state usurped the Shari'ah and equated its own interpretations to the will and truth of God. Alternatively, if the state keeps all Shari'ah values out of the public sphere and insists that all demands and all articulations of normative values be made in strictly nonreligious and non-Shari'ah terms, this also means effectively the extinction of Shari'ah. The exclusion of Shari'ah from the public sphere extinguishes the possibility of furthering godliness in society. Contrary to the claims of some, the exclusion of Shari'ah from public discourses or as grounds for public policy does not mean that the state is value neutral.[17] If religion is excluded from the public sphere, this only means that the shared space occupied by civic institutions favors nonreligious rationales, arguments, and values—if people cannot cite their understanding of the divine will as justification for public policies, this favors normative positions that do not recognize God's authority or will. If in the public arena nonreligious justifications are favored over religious justifications, it is disingenuous to pretend that the space dedicated to the functioning of civic society is neutral toward what may be called godliness. But even more, if as a condition of engaging the public sphere citizens are required to omit God from the public discourse, by definition, the state is favoring discourses that are godless. This, in effect, becomes an endorsement by the state of godless public reasoning over godly public reasoning. According to the logic of Shari'ah, Muslims are obligated to investigate what God wants from and for them and to pursue the divine goodness not just within the realm of their own private consciences but to the extent possible, to strive to advocate and promote godliness in the norms that guide society. The theological demand to bear witness on God's behalf and to enjoin the good and resist what is not good (*al-amr bi'l ma'ruf wa'l nahy 'an al-munkar*) is core to the imperative of furthering godly social norms. For the sake of brevity, I will hereinafter refer to the obligation of striving to promote guiding social norms that reflect the values of godliness as "the imperative of godliness."

The imperative of godliness is emphasized repeatedly in the Qur'an in a narrative that calls on Muslims to be a nation of people who enjoin goodness and resist wrongfulness as a necessary function of bearing witness for God.[18] On the one hand, it is reasonable to believe that the imperative of godliness mandates that the state be involved in upholding, or rather protecting, the divine boundaries in some way or fashion. But to presume that the state has an exclusive claim to knowing what is good or bad or that it is especially qualified to understand or pursue godliness is highly problematic. In fact, as noted above, because of its exceptional ability to leverage power, the modern state is especially positioned to exploit the label of godliness for very ungodly reasons. Moreover, very often the imperative of godliness and the obligation to bear witness mandate that just people testify against power and not for it. Indeed, it would seem that more often than not, the very possession of power, especially the kind of power that is backed up by the exclusive right to use force, is fundamentally at odds with godliness. It is somewhat paradoxical that the imperative of godliness requires the modern state to respect and safeguard certain values and virtues, such as human dignity or the sanctity of life, as God-given objective truths. Yet at the same time, the same imperative makes it critical that people bear witness against the state's mis-handling or abuse of these objective truths. From an Islamic perspective, while it is important that the respect and honor of the principle of godliness be upheld, it is exceedingly dangerous that the state be permitted the pretense of being godly. Because power is inherently corrupting, it is necessary to be cognizant of the fact that the truly just or pious will stand at a distance from power, bearing witness against it. It is reasonable to expect that the state respect the principle of godliness and for just people to demand that the state act in ways that are consistent with this principle. However, it is also critical that it be understood that the modern state is inherently corrupted by power and that ultimately, godliness cannot be achieved through the power of the state. Even more, in the modern age, fields of knowledge such as political science and the sociology and psychology of power demand that there be a new epistemological paradigm shift in the way we think about the state, Shari'ah, and power. In this paradigm shift, we do not need, as Mohammad Arkoun put it, to think of the unthinkable, but we need to recall the forgotten and to reconstruct the collective interpretive tradition of Islam. It ought to be recalled that once the jurists, the traditional defenders of Shari'ah, were co-opted by power, they lost all legitimacy and credibility and, for the most part, became themselves corrupted. In fact, once co-opted by the state, the juristic class lost its influence over the hearts and minds of Muslims as they increasingly testified for power and rarely against it. The issue is not for the Shari'ah to become part of the oppressive apparatus of the state, but for the Shari'ah, as the symbol of God's normative order, to become the vehicle by which testimony is rendered for God and against power.

The modern state cannot and should not pretend to be the representative of God's law. The state is not a consecrated church that has been empowered to divine God's will, and in all cases, the compulsive power of the modern state makes its enforcement of some version of God's law inherently oppressive and tyrannical. Yet as explained earlier, there is no question that Islam obligates its followers to search for and act on divine guidance. There is an inevitable tension in the idea of an objective or determinative Shari'ah that ought to be asserted in opposition to state power but not by the state in furtherance of its power. If Shari'ah is an objective and determinative set of divine commands, then it would follow that the state, civil society at large, or perhaps individuals would be able to comprehend and assert it in equal measure. In other words, if the Shari'ah is a known set of laws—of dos and don'ts or rights and wrongs—it ought to follow that these known laws could be validly asserted by private individuals or the state without distinction. In fact, it is common among many Muslims to claim either that Shari'ah is a quantifiable and known sum that should be faithfully applied by the state or that Muslims can never quantify a well-defined and known Shari'ah and, therefore, it ought not be applied at all. I believe that both approaches are unsatisfying. When I encounter revelation that commands Muslims to rule by God's law or to act as a nation that pursues goodness and resists evil, I do not believe that the Qur'an is commanding either what is impossible or nonexis-tent.[19] If God's law did not exist, then the Qur'an would be ordering Muslims to do the impossible. Furthermore, as I argue below, the life of the Prophet Muhammad is but a testimonial and exemplar not just to Muslims as individuals but Muslims as social communities. However, social and communal obligations do not necessarily have to be state duties, and in fact, as I argue below, they must not be so.

I will need to explore the issue of subjectivity and objectivity in Shari'ah before I can set forth my argument about the role of Shari'ah in the contemporary age. For now, I need to underscore that the imperative of godliness is firmly anchored in the Islamic faith and it is fundamental to Shari'ah that divine guidance be searched on the basis of both reason and revelation (what Islamic jurisprudence calls textual and rational indicators). There is nothing like a consecrated church that can embody divinity in any sense, but, in theory, all believers have been deputized to represent godliness on earth. However, it is unreasonable to expect that the citizenry of a modern state will base its social demands and desires on a sagacious and diligent study of the rational and textual indicators of the divine will. Considering this, it is reasonable to ask who, then, is to speak for the divine will in the modern age, and how is God's law to play any meaningful role in the age of modernity? These questions are not about the institutions or instrumentalities of the political system in the modern age, but they are about the very nature of divine guidance. We must differentiate between the nature of guidance and what makes the norms of guidance obligatory. It might be that whether a norm is obligatory or not depends on my subjective belief as to whether such a belief is mandatory. However, my subjective belief about whether I am bound by such a norm tells us nothing about the nature of the norm itself. In other words, whether I consider myself bound by the norm or not does not affect the nature of that norm—the norm could be truly from God, or it could be a product of my personal delusions. This, however, does not mean that the understanding, articulation, and assertion of divine norms are free subjective contingencies. For instance, God's law is discoverable through reason and revelation, which involves the deployment of rational indicators and textual indicators per a systematic jurisprudential methodology in the hope of discovering and realizing God's directive on a particular matter. But the very meaning of rationality is epistemologically contingent because our understanding of logic, of mathematical relations, relativity, proportionality, and time and space are constantly developing. Likewise, our understandings of texts of revelation are epistemologically contingent and developing. Our comprehension of the nature of texts, or what are the symbolic functions of texts, and our understanding of philology, hermeneutics, narrative, social memory, communities of meaning, and historical transmissions and transfusions are constantly developing. Put simply, reason and text cannot be approached today the way they were approached not a thousand years ago but even a decade ago. It seems that searching for the divine reason is critically a process of reasoning with God. But in order to better explain what I mean by the expression *reasoning with God* requires that we better explore the dialectical balance between objectivities and subjectivities in Shari'ah.

SHARI'AH: BETWEEN OBJECTIVITY AND SUBJECTIVITY

There is a pronounced tension between the obligation to live by God's law and the fact that this law is manifested only through subjective interpretive determinations. Even if there is a unified realization that a particular positive command does express the divine law, there is still a vast array of possible subjective executions and applications. The very notion of submission to the limitless God offers an equally limitless range of subjective engagements with the divine. Inevitably, human beings who submit to God and through this submission reach for the sublime will end up with a wide range of subjective experiences and various realizations of divinity or godliness. If God's beauty can manifest through a limitless range of subjective engagements, on what basis can there be a determinable law in Shari'ah? If Shari'ah does not have a determinable law and if it does not offer a determinable path, then what is the point of having Shari'ah?

As explained in previous chapters, the tension in legal Islamic discourses was resolved by distinguishing between Shari'ah and *fiqh*.[20] Shari'ah, it was argued, is the divine ideal, immutable, immaculate, and flawless—*fiqh* is not. *Fiqh* was treated as the human attempt to understand and apply the divine ideal, and several schools of legal thought were considered equally orthodox and authoritative.[21] As part of the doctrinal foundations for this discourse, Muslim jurists focused on traditions attributed to the Prophet stating: "Every *mujtahid* [jurist who strives to find the correct answer] is correct," or "Every *mujtahid* will be [justly] rewarded."[22] This implied that there could be more than a single correct answer to the same exact question. For Muslim jurists, this raised the issue of the purpose or the motivation behind the search for the divine will. What is the divine purpose behind setting out indicators to the divine law and then requiring that human beings engage in a search? If the divine wants human beings to reach *the* correct understanding, then how could every interpreter or jurist be correct?

The juristic discourse focused on whether or not the Shari'ah had a determinable result or demand in all cases, and if there is such a determinable result or demand, are Muslims obligated to find it? Put differently, is there a correct legal response to all legal problems, and are Muslims charged with the legal obligation of finding that response? The overwhelming majority of Muslim jurists agreed that good-faith diligence in searching for the divine will is sufficient to protect a researcher from liability before God. As long as the researcher exercises due diligence in the search, the researcher will not be held liable nor incur a sin, regardless of the result. Beyond this, the jurists were divided into two main camps. The first school, known as the *mukhatti'a*, argued that ultimately, there is a correct answer to every legal problem. However, only God knows what the correct response is, and the truth will not be revealed until the Final Day. Human beings, for the most part, cannot conclusively know whether they have found that correct response. In this sense, every *mujtahid* is correct in trying to find the answer; however, one seeker might reach the truth while the others might mistake it. God, on the Final Day, will inform all seekers who was right and who was wrong. Correctness here means that the *mujtahid* is to be commended for putting in the effort, but it does not mean that all responses are equally valid.

The second school, known as the *musawwiba*, included prominent jurists such as al-Juwayni (d. 478/1085), Jalal al-Din al-Suyuti (d. 911/1505), Abu Hamid al-Ghazali (d. 505/1111), and Fakhr al-Din al-Razi (d. 606/1210), and it is reported that the Mu'tazila (the rationalist school of thought) were followers of this school as well.[23] The *musawwiba* argued that there is no specific and correct answer (*hukm mu'ayyan*) that God wants human beings to discover, in part, because if there were a correct answer, God would have made the evidence indicating a divine rule conclusive and clear. God cannot charge human beings with the duty to find the correct answer when there is no objective means to discovering the correctness of a textual or legal problem. If there were an objective truth to everything, God would have made such a truth ascertainable in this life. Legal truth, or correctness, in most circumstances, depends on belief and evidence, and the validity of a legal rule or act is often contingent on the rules of recognition that provide for its existence. Human beings are not charged with the obligation of finding some abstract or inaccessible legally correct result. Rather, they are charged with the duty to diligently investigate a problem and then follow the results of their own *ijtihad*. Al-Juwayni explains this point by asserting, "The most a *mujtahid* would claim is a preponderance of belief [*ghalabat al-zann*] and the balancing of the evidence. However, certainty was never claimed by any of them [the early jurists]. . . . If we were charged with finding [the truth] we would not have been forgiven for failing to find it."[24] According to al-Juwayni, what God wants or intends is for human beings to search—to live a life fully and thoroughly engaged with the divine. Al-Juwayni explains: it is as if God has said to human beings, "My command to My servants is in accordance with the preponderance of their beliefs. So whoever preponderantly believes that they are obligated to do something, acting on it becomes My command."[25] God's command to human beings is to diligently search, and God's law is suspended until a human being forms a preponderance of belief about the law. At the point that a preponderance of belief is formed, God's law becomes in accordance with the preponderance of belief formed by that particular individual. In summary, if a person honestly and sincerely believes that such and such is the law of God, then, as to that person "that" is in fact God's law.[26]

Building on this intellectual heritage, I would suggest that Shari'ah ought to stand in an Islamic polity as a symbolic construct for the divine perfection that is unreachable by human effort—a concept summed up in the Islamic tradition by the word *husn,* or "beauty." It is the epitome of justice, goodness, and beauty as conceived and retained by God. Its perfection is preserved, so to speak, in the mind of God, but anything that is channeled through human agency is necessarily marred by human imperfection. Put differently, Shari'ah as conceived by God is flawless, but as understood by human beings, Shari'ah is imperfect and contingent. Jurists ought to continue exploring the ideal of Shari'ah and ought to continue expounding their imperfect attempts at understanding God's perfection. As long as the argument constructed is normative, it is an unfulfilled potential for reaching the divine will. Significantly, any law applied is necessarily a potential unrealized. Shari'ah is not simply a bunch of *ahkam* (a set of positive rules) but is also a set of principles, a methodology, and a discursive process that searches for the divine ideals. As such, Shari'ah is a work in progress that is never complete. To put it more concretely, a juristic argument about what God commands is only potentially God's law, either because on the Final Day we will discover its correctness (the first school) or because its correctness is contingent on the sincerity of belief of the person who decides to follow it (the second school). It is important to note that the paradigm proposed above does not exclude the possibility of objectified and even universalistic moral standards. It simply shifts the responsibility for moral commitments and the outcome of such commitments to human beings. Morality could originate with God or could be learned by reflecting on the state of nature that God has created, but the attempts to fulfill such a morality and give it actual effect are human. In fact, the paradigm proposed here would require certain moral commitments from human beings that ought to be adopted as part of their discharge of their agency on God's behalf.[27] For instance, arguably, the fulfillment of this paradigm is not possible unless it is recognized that people must enjoy certain immunities that are necessarily implied by the very purpose of creation in Islam. Neither the first nor second views of Shari'ah epistemology are possible unless people are guaranteed the right to rational development. Furthermore, the right to rational development means that people ought to be entitled to minimum standards of well-being, in both the physical and intellectual sense. It is impossible to pursue rational development if one is not fed, housed, educated, and above all, safe from physical harm or persecution. In addition, people cannot pursue a reflective life unless they are guaranteed freedom of conscience, expression, and assembly with like-minded people.

Once Muslims are able to assert that morality is divine, but law and legal divisions and rules are mundane, I think that this will represent a major advancement in the attempt to justify a paradigm of godliness and beauty in Islam. More concretely, reflecting on divinity, I, as a Muslim, might be able to assert that justice and mercy are objective and universal moral values. I might even try to convince others that justice and mercy are part of the divine charge to humanity—God wants humans to be merciful and just. This represents a moral commitment that I am inviting other human beings to adopt as well. But under the paradigm proposed here, while I can claim that moral rules emanate or originate from God, a claim which people are free to accept or dispute, I cannot claim that any laws that attempt to implement or give effect to this moral commitment are divine as well. This is very much like the natural law tradition in that while we may deduce the natural principles of justice or a preemptive norm mandating human dignity, no deduction of derivative positive commandments can be the objective fulfillment of such natural principles.

DO WE NEED SHARI'AH?

Many contemporary Muslims do not believe that Shari'ah is a normative or mandated part of the Islamic religion. It is often difficult to ascertain what exactly is meant by this claim. Most Muslims who make this argument do not reject Shari'ah as a set of particularized ritualistic practices, such as praying, fasting, or paying alms, or as general moral principles. What one often discovers is that many modern Muslims, like their non-Muslim counterparts, confuse Puritanical-Salafi interpretations of Islam with Shari'ah, and so what they mean to reject is the transformation of the faith into a dogmatic set of absolute laws that governs every aspect of a human being's life. Other Muslims confuse the concept of Shari'ah with the classical interpretive tradition found in the books of *fiqh*. What contributes a great deal of confusion to the difference between Shari'ah and *fiqh* among contemporary Muslims is the confounding identity politics that are often fought over the *fiqh* interpretive tradition. The *fuqaha'* or *'ulama* act as the bearers and guardians of the *fiqh* tradition as if it is a sacred and untouchable legacy. After their co-optation by the state and their increasing irrelevance in the cultural and social lives of Muslims, they defended their position as the gatekeepers and key holders of the copious interpretive tradition of *fiqh* not as an interpretive tradition that is relevant or important to the lives of Muslims but as a sanctified, rarefied, and untouchable sacred shrine. This glorious mummified symbol, known as the *fiqh*, stands in honor of the *'ulama*'s own past intellectual glory and contemporary marginality and irrelevance. Interestingly, as the incident with Tariq Ramadan illustrates, the *'ulama* fight turf wars, jealously guarding their position as the exclusive protectors of the sacred knowledge, but have little interest and very often lack the intellectual ability to adapt this knowledge to the epistemological understandings of the contemporary age or to the moral and ethical needs of people in postmodernity. This is exactly why the contemporary *'ulama* have found it relatively easy to adapt to the modern authoritarian secular state. For the most part, the *'ulama* no longer see themselves as witnesses on behalf of God or the masses, and they bear no compulsion to testify against privilege or power. Rather, as long as the secular state allows the *'ulama* to remain the lords of their feudal sacred estate (i.e., the inherited *fiqh* tradition), and as long as the state suppresses all competitors, often in the form of Muslim intellectual reformers or mass Islamist movements such as the Muslim Brotherhood, the *'ulama* are content to make no ethical or moral demands in the name of Shari'ah on the state. As discussed earlier, this complacent relationship with the autocratic secular nation-state has contributed a great deal to the spread of Puritanical-Salafism. Although Puritanical-Salafism vulgarizes the *fiqh* tradition with its unabashedly functionalist and opportunistic utilization of the Islamic theological and legal interpretive tradition, the generosity of oil-producing countries has most often earned the *'ulama*'s complacent silence.

Caught between the mummified showcasing of Shari'ah and *fiqh* by the *'ulama* and the ugly vulgarization of the Islamic tradition by Puritanical-Salafis, it is hardly surprising that many Muslims are tempted to resolve the problem by holding on to their Islamic faith but dogmatically denouncing everything found in the classical sources, including the discourses on Shari'ah. Some Muslims go a step further by distinguishing between the Islam of the Qur'an and the historical Islam. They accept Qur'anic Islam as genuine and true but reject everything else, including the oral tradition of the Prophet, his family, and companions, the stunningly multilayered and sophisticated theological, philosophical, legal, and literary tradition of Islam. They imagine that by doing so they have rid themselves of the cumbersome burdens of the past and are free to confront the modern challenges of their world with nothing but the Qur'an's guidance and their rational faculties.

This approach, popularly known as the Qur'anist school, has an unmistakable intuitive appeal. Arguably, if Islam started out with the Qur'an alone and no other text, it would make sense to return to these pristine origins where the Qur'anic text stands alone as God's uncorrupted revelation. The idea of throwing away the interpretive communities of the past and starting afresh without the encumbrance of history is not a new idea. To an extent, a shedding of the past is necessary for any advancement or progress, and this realization has been at the heart of every Muslim reform movement that has existed in the modern age. Interestingly, many Western travellers reported that the original Wahhabi theology was to rely on the Qur'an alone to the exclusion of the traditions attributed to the Prophet.[28] Although I doubt the accuracy of these reports, the history of puritanical Islam ought to act as a reminder that what replaces tradition is not always an improvement. In fact, before indulging in unfettered deconstructionism it would be well advised to think about what will replace what has been torn down. Indeed, tradition—respect for the inherited and cumulative meanings of the past—including the retained wisdom of society represented in folklore and mythology—plays a critical role in anchoring society and mediating progress. Moreover, tradition, as it is found in the cultural habits, anthropological practices, inherited social roles and expectations, and the memorialized narratives of society, provides a necessary foundation and a much-needed rootedness for any nation as it confronts the demands for change and rebirth. Many Muslim intellectuals make the unwarranted assumption that following tradition would be fundamentally inconsistent with rationalism. However, as Hans Gadamer has argued, traditionalism and rationalism are not necessarily at odds. He states:

> It seems to me, however, that there is no such unconditional antithesis between tradition and reason. However problematical the conscious restoration of old or the creation of new traditions may be, the romantic faith in the "growth of tradition," before which all reason must remain silent, is fundamentally like the Enlightenment, and just as prejudiced. The fact is that in tradition there is always an element of freedom and of history itself. Even the most genuine and pure tradition does not persist because of the inertia of what once existed. It needs to be affirmed, embraced, cultivated. It is, essentially, preservation, and it is active in all historical change. But preservation is an act of reason, though an inconspicuous one. For this reason, only innovation and planning appear to be the result of reason. But this is an illusion. Even where life changes violently, as in ages of revolution, far more of the old is preserved in the supposed transformation of everything than anyone knows, and it combines with the new to create a new value. At any rate, preservation is as much a freely chosen action as are revolution and renewal. That is why both the Enlightenment's critique of tradition and the romantic rehabilitation of it lag behind their true historical being.[29]

Traditionalism is an attitude and a presumption toward the social and intellectual product of past generations and inherited social conventions. One can and should have a respectful deference to tradition while at the same time critically engaging and reinventing to respond to ongoing demands and imperatives.

Many Qur'anists, however, would argue that the Islamic tradition is inherently unsalvageable because it embodies an attitude that has for long rejected reason and rationalism in favor of deference to the sanctified idols of the past. I will say more about the relation of the Islamic tradition to rationalism later, but I have two main objections to arguments about the inherently irrational nature of the Islamic tradition. The first main objection is that we must differentiate between the character of a tradition and its instrumental representatives at a particular historical moment in time. There is little doubt, especially after the defeat of the short-lived enlightened reform movement at the end of the nineteenth and beginning of the twentieth century and the rise of puritanical Islamism, that the *'ulama* or *fuqaha'* have indeed turned the Islamic tradition into a sacred, untouchable altar. However, contrary to the mythology of the closing of the doors of *ijtihad*, the Islamic tradition is difficult to essentialize or stereotype. Moreover, the relationship between tradition and history is complicated and problematic. Since the invention of history as an analytic discipline it has become possible to interrogate, reconstruct, and even reinvent intellectual traditions.[30] Intellectual traditions are often as effective and powerful as their interpreters. For example, the current Muslim knowledge of their intellectual traditions is entirely a product of their colonial and postcolonial experiences. Commonly held so-called intellectual orthodoxies in contemporary Islam about so many topics, including the closing of the doors of *ijtihad*, the role of Ash'arism, and the roles of figures such as Ahmad Ibn Hanbal and al-Shafi'i, has far more to do with the way Islamic traditions were interpreted or constructed in the nineteenth and twentieth centuries than any actual culturally retained historical memory or practice. Suffice it to say that until the rise of Wahhabi-Salafism, the most sociologically prevalent form of Islam in the eighteenth and nineteenth centuries was Sufism. However, most Muslims today have become convinced that Sufism is a marginal aberration rather than the dominant form of Islamicity through many centuries of Islamic history. Islamic history includes such widely different and contrasting intellectual figures ranging from Nasr al-Din al-Tusi (d. 672/1274) and Ibn Tufayl (d. 581/1185) to Ibn al-Jawzi (d. 597/1201) and Ibn Taymiyya (d. 728/1328). My point is not to say that traditions do not have particular normative impacts that could shape the behavior of people—tradition holds the worst of what a people are and the best of what they could be. Rather, my point is that the Islamic tradition has many competing orientations and trajectories. Since the birth of historical analysis as an epistemology and since the invention of phenomenology as a discipline of meaning and intentionality, cultures have gained very powerful tools by which they rationally and purposively influence their traditions. But the painful reality today is that Western-educated Muslims know precious little about their own intellectual heritage other than what they read and accept as the gospel truth in books published by academic presses in the West. I have always been both surprised and dismayed at the perfunctory, superfluous, and often flippant way that so many in the Muslim intelligentsia approach the Islamic intellectual tradition. It is incumbent that instead of branding their tradition as irrational and dismissing it, Muslim intellectuals challenge the old guardians who have smothered and stifled this tradition and engage it to locate the rationalist and enlightened orientations and persuade fellow Muslims that their tradition embodies imperative humanistic, rationalistic, and enlightened elements that must be augmented and embraced.

The second main objection I have to the so-called Qur'anist argument has to do with the way many Muslims deal with the hadith and Sunna tradition. Many of the Qur'an-only advocates presume that it is possible to excise the Qur'an from the rest of the cumulative tradition that constitutes Islam. As the argument goes, only the Qur'an is the revealed word of God while the rest of the oral tradition attributed to the Prophet, his family, or companions is unreliable and cannot act as a source of normative determinations. Essential to this argument is an assumption that the Qur'an and Islam as a religion is distinguishable from the body of oral traditions and inherited reports that preserved the cumulative memory of the Islamic legacy. I do not take issue with the belief that the Qur'an's authenticity is of a different quality and significance than the rest of the oral tradition. There is ample evidence to suggest that for at least the first three centuries of Islam, Muslim interest in preserving and transmitting the Qur'an far exceeded Muslim interest in preserving other oral traditions such as the hadith.[31] Moreover, it is clear that the hadith and Sunna were tapestries on which many factions fought heated political, philosophical, and theological controversies. Nonetheless, any dogmatic approach to the question of authenticity of these oral traditions will not work. After all, it is oral traditions of the hadith and Sunna that detail every aspect of the Muslim faith, including the five pillars of the faith, the specifics of rituals, or numerous other aspects related to everything from paternity rights to the norms that govern marriage agreements and contracts. My point is that it is not so easy to differentiate in a systematic and consistent fashion between the historical transmissions of the Qur'an and the other traditions setting out the basics of the Islamic religion, on the one hand, and the many other hadith that reformers find troubling, on the other hand.

I completely agree with approaches that differentiate between the Qur'an as sacred revelation and the hadith and Sunna as the product of a protracted process of transference and dissemination. The problem, however, is that even the most determined Qur'anist will find that it is impossible to speak of the Islamic religion without the living cumulative tradition that sprouted and grew out from the Qur'an. So many of the narratives that contextualize the revelations of the Qur'an and that set out the broad historical experiences in Mecca and Medina and record testimonials about how the early generations of Muslims understood and practiced their faith are part of the hadith and Sunna that the Qur'anists wish to excise and abolish. But doing so will solve little, if anything, because it will leave the text of the Qur'an standing alone without its history, the circumstances that motivated it, and the challenges that inspired it, and questions relating to intentionality, purposefulness, and objective will become far more difficult to resolve.

Unfortunately, I feel that many of those who describe themselves as Muslim reformers tend to know the Qur'an and the hadith traditions only through the writings of Western Orientalists. This is why I am often surprised at the number of inaccurate statements made erroneously attributing certain rulings to the Qur'an or Sunna. Why does this matter? It matters because some of the determinations that reformers find troubling, such as that a sister inherits half of what a brother would, and other Qur'anic texts that treat women and men unequally, originate from the Qur'an and not the hadith. On the other hand, many Muslims who are eager to ignore the hadith do not realize that many of these hadith traditions contain profound moral and humanistic insights and affirm basic ethical principles that have become interwoven in the very fabric of Muslim cultures. The oral traditions of Islam require a systematic and normative-based approach of analysis that differentiates between narratives that are consistent with the Islamic message and those that are not. The reality is that the hadith and Sunna were platforms on which various competing trends and orientations, including some that were affirmatively anti-Muslim, anti-Muhammad, anti-'Ali, anti-Umar, anti-Umayyad, and so on, tried to gain legitimacy and credibility. Although Ahl al-Hadith have claimed that they devised an objective method of evaluating the authenticity of the traditions based on what is known as *'ilm al-rijal*, it is oddly anachronistic to either accept their work product or reject it. The Ahl al-Hadith's assessment of the credibility and authenticity of the various individuals involved in the transmission of a hadith report could be considered as part of the evidence in evaluating the historicity of a particular genre of report. However, the categorization of *sahih* (authentic), *da'if* (weak), *batil* (invalid), and so on cannot be considered conclusive in establishing or critiquing knowledge in the current age.

Most of the hadith and Sunna traditions that we inherited today represent what I have called in the past authorial enterprises of cumulative transmitters through cumulative ages and epochs.[32] What I mean by this is that it is virtually impossible to attribute any specific report to a particular person in history, whether the Prophet or any of the early generations of Muslims. At the same time, it is impossible to conclude that any report does not belong to one particular individual. What we can take from the oral traditions is an affirmation that particular normative or historical themes were retained in the memory of the early generations of Muslims. The more affirmations there are from various regional foundations that the Prophet or companions might have acted or not acted in a certain way, the more we can feel confident that the broad theme did in fact belong to the Prophet. For instance, we do know a great deal about how, and how often, the Prophet prayed because of the numerous sources and venues of transmission that described his prayers. However, it is the authorial enterprise of generations of transmitters and narrators that transformed the five daily prayers into a cornerstone of the Islamic tradition. Consider the many competing and conflicting reports attributed to the Prophet concerning obedience to political authority. If we consider the regional origins and the circumstances surrounding each of the reports, what we can conclude is that there is a kernel of truth in each report that might go back to the Prophet—a kernel that reflected different responses to a variety of circumstances—but none of these traditions were authored word for word by the Prophet. Instead, each report reflects competing authorial enterprises by competing ideological orientations in early Islamic history.

The mechanical and nearly mathematical methodology that Ahl al-Hadith apply to the hadith and Sunna in light of our modern epistemological knowledge about reality, meaning, fiction, archetypes, symbolism, phenomenology, and especially history is untenable. Reports contained in the books of hadith and Sunna are not there necessarily because the Prophet or a companion uttered a statement word for word, as has become documented and preserved in books. In fact, the oral reports that are commonly titled the books of hadith often construct and narrate a performance—a performance that preserves a memory of the Prophet in some form but that also documents the epistemological attitudes of early Muslim generations. Under the best of circumstances, an oral report captures a kernel of what the Prophet or one of his companions was or a hint of some event that left its impact on the consciousness of early Muslims. If we find numerous reports coming from a number of venues attesting to the same kernel of truth, then this provides further assurance that we are indeed dealing with something that goes back to the origins. But beyond the kernel, each report or set of reports invariably documents what generation after generation of Muslims thought was significant or at times critical to the tradition. Without malice or intent, generations of Muslims will embellish, elaborate, systematize, coordinate, and organize reports so that the original kernel can be made more compelling, convincing, or decisive. This in no way detracts from the significance of the hadith or Sunna as prescriptive and normative sources of knowledge. But it would mean recognizing that the hadith and Sunna are part of the Islamic tradition—a tradition that includes a variety of competing and inconsistent orientations. It would also caution substantial skepticism before attributing a particular set of words to the Prophet. Yet at the same time, this approach would strongly counsel that we mine the oral tradition for normative and ethical values that most early Muslims understood to be part of the Islamic legacy. Isolated reports attributed to a particular companion or successor would not be allowed to overrule moral and ethical values attested by the authorial enterprises of early Muslims. Much of the approach I am suggesting here has its genesis in early Islamic schools of thought that argued that positive legal prescription could be based only on *mutawatir* (successive) hadith.

My approach also has its genesis in the early Maliki approach that considered the custom and practice of the people of Medina at the time of the Prophet and companions to be more authoritatively compelling than any transmitted report attributed to the Prophet. The Maliki approach was premised on the argument that the people of Medina are collectively more likely to retain and reflect a true memory of the Prophet's teachings than any isolated report transmitted by one or a few people. Finally, another well-established approach rooted in Islamic history contended that hadith that conflicted or were inconsistent in any way with the Qur'an must be rejected as fabrications. The historian and historiographer Ibn Khaldun (d. 808/1406) protested the Ahl al-Hadith method of transmission and advocated a more sociohistorically sensitive approach. For instance, Ibn Khaldun states in part:

> When it comes to reports, if one relies only on the [method] of transmission without evaluating [these reports] in light of the principles of human conduct, the fundamentals of politics, the nature of civilization, and the conditions for social associations, and without comparing ancient sources to contemporary sources and the present to the past, he [or she] could fall into errors and mistakes and could deviate from the path of truth. Historians, [Qur'anic] interpreters and leading transmitters have often fallen into error by accepting [the authenticity of certain] reports in light of [fundamental] principles of [histori-

cal analysis] or compare the reports to each other or examine them according
to the standards of wisdom or investigate the nature of beings. Furthermore,
they did not decide on the authenticity of these reports according to the standards of reason and discernment. Consequently, they were led astray from the
truth and became lost in the wilderness of error and delusion.[33]

I recognize that the issue of the fitting methodology for hadith evaluation
requires a separate book-length study. My basic point here is that the tendency among modern Muslims is to adopt an unequivocal draconian approach—
either the method of Ahl al-Hadith is uncritically embraced or, other than the
Qur'an, the entire tradition is thrown out. The point emphasized here is that
the tradition of the early generation of Muslims, including the hadith and
Sunna, is important to retain because this oral tradition is an organic growth
from the period of revelation which resulted in the Qur'an, and it cannot be
hacked off without doing substantial damage to the religion of Islam itself.
This early tradition is rich with historical reports, mythology, folklore, and
teachings that express, embody, elucidate, and demonstrate ethical morality
and virtue that must be preserved, studied, and absorbed by the modern mind.
But the study of this rich tradition must be accomplished through the epistemological arsenal that is available to us today—not through the epistemological tools that existed more than ten centuries ago.

As I noted, Ahl al-Hadith's objectified constructionist method has been
repeatedly challenged through Islamic history.[34] But more importantly, for
most of Islamic history and until the rise of Puritanical-Salafism, the average
Muslim did not come into contact with the hadith as raw material. At the
level of law guilds, the juristic class, who interpreted and evaluated the
authority and relevance of the oral reports, mediated the hadith and its impact. At the more popular level, the so-called *qussas* and *wu'az* (folklore
performers and preachers) interpreted the hadith to the laity and made it
dramatic, relevant, and entertaining. In fact, until the rise of the Wahhabi
movement in Arabia, the Ahl al-Hadith and the Hanbali school were on the
verge of extinction. With the spread of literacy and the dissemination of
printed materials, the books of hadith could be found in every Muslim home
and could now be accessed by the most casual and unqualified reader. The
reality is that books of hadith are replete with dramatized performances that
are deeply embedded in the epistemological and phenomenological dialectics
of the first centuries of Islam. These books could be mined for a great deal of
historical, theological, ethical, and moral insights, but they cannot be approached with the kind of literalism that many Muslims afford them today.
As importantly, they cannot simply be dismissed as marginal to the Islamic
faith or as simple fabrications or inventions.

REASONING WITH GOD

Shari'ah is God's path. And certainly, it would be peculiar, to say the least, to
accept God's religion but not God's path. But most Muslims who deny
Shari'ah do not intend to reject God's path. Most intend to reject an anachronistic medieval system of laws that they believe is coequal with Shari'ah.

This understanding of Shari'ah, however, is rather dogmatic because, among other things, it does not seriously consider the numerous ways that the transcendental concept of God's path is at the core of the process of migrating to godliness, both at the level of the individual and at the level of social consciousness.

The methodological starting point for Shari'ah is that it is fundamentally linked to *huquq* (rights). *Huquq* are rights that are due to a recipient because of the existence of an obligation (*taklif*) toward that recipient. An obligation could arise toward one's God, oneself, or other human beings. The path of God mandates that the believers engage in an ongoing conscientious reflection on the obligations owed and also on the rights deserved to and from individuals and society. This point is wonderfully illustrated by Ibn Tufayl in his work *Hayy Ibn Yaqzan*, where he constructs a hypothetical in which an individual, called Ibn Yaqzan, finds himself alone on an abandoned island. In this original condition, the hypothetical Ibn Yaqzan is compelled to reflect on what rights or duties he owes himself and God. Eventually, Ibn Yaqzan travels to a neighboring island inhabited by a primitive people. Having to coexist within a social setting, Ibn Yaqzan starts reflecting on the laws needed to balance between his rights, the rights of others, and the rights of God. The matter of the rights of God, however, witnesses a diametrical paradigm shift when a prophet appears in the island informing the tribespeople of God's path. Of course, Ibn Tufayl's point is to demonstrate that as far as personal and social rights and duties are concerned, reason and revelation lead to the same results.[35] My point here is not to offer an adequate study of Ibn Tufayl's brilliant thought, but his treatment helps focus on the nexus between Shari'ah, on the one hand, and the concept of rights and obligation on the other.[36] I should note at the outset that I do not agree with Ibn Tufayl's broad position that when it comes to social laws, Shari'ah and reason inevitably and consistently accomplish overlapping functions. This, however, is a question of political philosophy, which is not the discipline that nurtured the growth of the concepts of *huquq*. Of course, my skepticism about what reason and revelation can achieve in terms of determinable and absolute results is itself a reflection of the postmodern epistemological consciousness, which in this case I believe is a good thing. In the Islamic tradition, the concept of *huquq* developed in the discipline of jurisprudence and legal epistemology, a fact that contributed to its flexibility and pragmatism as a dynamic concept during substantial periods of Islamic history.

As Ibn Tufayl argued, the human intellect may be able to reason through what agreements, concessions, and implied contracts would be necessary to make in order to promote social intercourse. If one uses the principle of reciprocity and the basic concept of equal worth, human beings could deduct what obligations are owed from one person to another and also the basic rules for the acquisition and fulfillment of rights. This rational scheme of obligations and rights are necessary to avoid conflicts and social discord. Rights toward God come from reflecting on what a person owes God and what he has a right to expect from God. The rights and obligations that one expects from himself require a deeper level of thought and a level of isolation, self-reflection, and introspection to finally to come to understand that obligations to and from God and the self have many layers of perception and depth that ultimately could lead to true enlightenment. According to Ibn Tufayl, because societies demand division of labor, revelation shortcuts the protracted process of introspection, reflection, and comprehension by directly instructing those who are unable to dedicate themselves to the process of reasoning through the requisites of a just and fair life. In other words, revelation is a shortcut to the truth that is otherwise accessible through reason.

In legal discourses, as noted in earlier chapters, Muslim jurists divided rights into more pragmatic but less philosophically coherent categories. They argued that all rights, unless otherwise reserved to God, belong to people. God's rights are reserved by direct revelation as if God defines a particular set of acts or interests as subject to divine jurisdiction. For instance, prayer and other matters of ritual are within the province of the rights of God because they are performed for God and are covered by revelation. All matters involving property, commercial, or financial rights belong to people. There is an elusive category of rights known as mixed rights (*huquq mukhtalita*) involving acts that were addressed by revelation but at the same time implicate the material interests of people. An example of mixed rights would be the *hadd* (pl. *hudud*) for theft—the right of God would be the prescribed punishment for robbery, but at the same time it involves the usurpation of property that belongs to individuals. The critical point in the juristic paradigm is that the presumption in the case of the rights of people is that such right must be implemented or protected by the state. The presumption in the case of the rights of God is nonenforcement unless specific and certain conditions are met. In juristic theory, the state acts as an agent (*wakil*) or representative (*naqib*) of the people under its jurisdiction, and so the state is under a strict obligation to enforce their rights. The state, however, is not God's representative, and moreover, God does not need human beings to guard the divine rights. The Maliki jurist Ibn al-'Arabi (d. 543/1148) states the following:

> The rights of human beings are not forgiven by God unless the human being concerned forgives them first, and the claims for such rights are not dismissed [by God] unless they are dismissed by the person concerned. . . . The rights of a Muslim cannot be abandoned except by the possessor of the right. Even the imam (ruler) does not have the right to demand [or abandon] such rights. This is because the imam is not empowered to act as the agent for a specific set of individuals over their specific rights. Rather, the imam only represents people, generally, over their general and unspecified rights.[37]

The tripartite division of rights (people's, God's, and mixed rights) in Islamic jurisprudence grew out of a dynamic involving theory and practicalities of a living and functioning legal system. But in the contemporary age, the paradigm of obligations and rights needs to be reconceptualized to take account of the power dynamics of the modern state and its institutions. Any social structure or polity is indeed premised on the idea of obligations and rights, but any democratic system needs to have a system of individual rights that are held against the state in particular. The key, however, is that any rights owed to God must be held as a matter of personal commitment and conscience. It is well established in Islamic law that coercion cannot make up for the lack of intent or faith and that God judges human beings according to their intentions, not just their actions.[38]

The intervention of the modern state in an obligation that a person owes himself or God is in most cases unwarranted and unjustified. Any obligation that an individual might owe God is not discharged unless sincerity of intent and belief exists. If the state forces me to perform any ritual, unless I have the actual intent to worship, the performance of such a ritual is invalid. Furthermore, I would contend that neither reason nor revelation would empower the state to intervene in the obligations I owe to God as an individual. What I owe God as an individual, without a social context, is strictly between God and me. I must admit that I doubt the argument offered by so many philosophers that the duties of an individual toward God can be deduced through reason alone. And I tend to agree with those who believe that revelation is necessary to instruct individuals to know what they owe God and how they must discharge their obligations. But in all cases, the state has no role to play in regulating, mediating, or otherwise enforcing these obligations.

How about obligations that an individual owes himself or herself? Can reason and revelation both establish what I owe myself as a human being? For instance, do I have a duty toward myself to eat moderately, or to exercise and stay fit, or not to smoke, or not to drink intoxicants? Assume for the moment that none of these acts have social consequences; if I as an individual lived on Ibn Tufayl's island, would I need revelation to know what is good for me or not? Furthermore, do the duties that I owe myself also constitute rights of God? Here again I am not sure, except to say that reason might be able to establish good from bad, but it is revelation that constitutes the source of obligation. Reason can establish that smoking is bad and exercising is good, but without revelation there is no convincing way of making me believe that I am obligated to refrain or not refrain from the commission of performing certain acts. Consider, for instance, meditation, yoga, and prayer. Perhaps reason can establish that it is beneficial to the body (to lower blood pressure, for instance) to meditate or pray. But I am skeptical that reason can obligate me to perform the prayers for my own sake—revelation can instruct me to do so, and if I believe the revelation, then I will oblige. But, as in the case of the rights of God, since my own personal belief is the operative element for the validity of my compliance—since I must believe the revelation for such compliance to be meaningful in God's eyes—the state has no role to play. The state does not represent God, God's approval, or his acceptance, and if the obligation in question involves my own self-interests but no other primary interests are involved, then the state has no capacity to act. If my interests alone are concerned, then I alone can deputize or empower the state to act. The state cannot act as an enforcer on the pretense that the state is protecting God's rights. After all, as in the case of ritual, whether God's rights are fulfilled or not depends not just on my performance but, as importantly, on my intent or will to obey God. If I as an individual refuse to empower the state to act on my behalf in matters that concern only my self-interests, then the state simply does not have jurisdiction or the authority to act.

Within this paradigm, one can imagine difficult or challenging cases. For instance, may the state intervene to prevent me from committing suicide, or from mutilating my body, or from entertaining myself by some extreme sport like diving into Niagara Falls? Some would argue that in the case of suicide, the state should intervene because the value of life is so critical, and when the sacredness of life is concerned, the state cannot afford to be neutral. I believe one can also make the argument that when it comes to suicide, or posing serious danger to oneself, the interests of society will always be implicated because others will always be left with the responsibility of shouldering the burden of the aftermath.

Thus far, I have argued that what one owes God in terms of obligations that fall under the heading of acts of worship and ritual (*'ibadat*)—acts that fall under the jurisdiction of God alone—revelation is the sole venue of access to the divine will. Moreover, when it comes to acts that fall under the category of strict self-interest—acts that have no social ramifications—the existence of an obligation toward the self can only be established by revelation alone as well. As explained, the nature of what is good or bad for the self can fairly easily be established by reason, but the existence of an obligation, in my view, requires revelation. These mixed rights between God and interests of the self, in most cases, fall out of the province or jurisdiction of the state. God's rights here cannot be satisfied unless the individual possesses the intent to abide by God's revelation. This is another way of saying that if I refrain from engaging in conduct that affects me and me alone and I do so because I believe that I am abiding by God's command, then my act of refraining or abstention will discharge my duties toward God. For instance, if after researching the matter I come to the conclusion that God forbids me from getting my body tattooed, assuming that getting a tattoo affects me and me alone, then not getting a tattoo will fulfill my obligation toward God (i.e., God's right will be satisfied). Since my intent to obey, please, or otherwise honor God's commands is a condition for the fulfillment of God's right on this matter, the state has no jurisdiction to intervene.

Critically, in both categories, that of fulfilling a pure right of God (i.e., rituals and worship) and acts that concern the self and do not affect the rights of other people, Shari'ah, in the narrow and strict sense of the word, as in the revealed path of God, plays an essential role because divine guidance is pivotal to forming the requisite sincerity and intent for compliance. As to these categories of interests, it is sensible to investigate God's directives in order to find out exactly how God wants to be remembered and celebrated and how God's grace ought to be pursued—all of this needs an exploration of God's revelation and also the traditions of predecessors who lived closer in time to the period of the Prophet's generation. It is important to recall that divine intent is investigated through the indicators of the divine will in a process that must meet the requirements of due diligence in reading, researching, and analyzing all the available evidence on the divine will. This takes us back to a foundational point; as far as revelation is concerned, the indicators exist in the text of the Qur'an and in the cumulative authorial enterprises that we normally call the hadith and Sunna. It bears emphasis that the Qur'an, Sunna, and cumulative communities of interpretation that recorded their insights and arguments through history cannot and ought not be approached lightly or casually. As I argued in previous books, a conscientious Muslim should exert due diligence and one's best efforts in searching the divine indicators and reach a judgment on the basis of the best available evidence. If a conscientious Muslim does not have the time or training to conduct the research himself or herself, then the reasonable thing is for this Muslim to defer to the advice of a jurist whom he or she trusts and whom this Muslim accepts as qualified and competent.

The remaining issue concerns the third category of acts—those that arise in Ibn Tufayl's inhabited island consisting of obligations that arise from one human being to another because of any direct or indirect interaction. For brevity's sake, I will call this third category social acts. Social acts are not necessarily limited to conduct that is intended to have an impact on other people, but they are acts that affect other living beings by affecting their material and nonmaterial interests. Social acts could have a physical impact in terms of adding to or detracting from someone's material interests or well-being. Classical Muslim jurists labeled social acts that could give rise to injury or that could trigger a duty to compensate as acts of *daman* (responsibility). Here, however, we are dealing with a broader category than tortious conduct or possible breaches of contractual obligations. Social acts include behavior that could affect people aesthetically (people listening to my music), intellectually (listening to my lecture, reading my books, or just conversing with me), erotically (someone dressing in a sexually arousing fashion), or in any other fashion. Ibn Tufayl as well as many other Muslim philosophers would contend that, especially when it comes to social acts, reason and revelation would prescribe the same obligations or rules of goodness. In addition, many contemporary Muslims who believe that modern Islam can do without Shari'ah assume that when it comes to social acts, as those mentioned above, Shari'ah would perform a role that is essentially redundant to reason—in other words, Shari'ah would add nothing beyond what reason would accomplish. Other Muslims contend that even if revelation and reason would not necessarily overlap, revelation is irrelevant because it is outdated or because it was abrogated by the passage of time.[39] Other Muslims fail to distinguish between the objects of the revelation. In other words, they fail to differentiate between revelation directed at the individual and revelation directed at society at large. Consider, for instance, the Qur'anic prohibition on killing: "And do not kill the soul sanctified [by God] except for a right cause,"[40] or the prohibition against the marriage of siblings,[41] or the revelation decreeing particular shares in estate inheritance,[42] or the revelation condemning dealing in usury.[43] Are the laws dictated by revelation addressed to each believer as an individual, or are they addressed to social communities? Put differently, is this genre of revelation addressed to individuals or collectivities? If such laws are addressed to individuals and not to communities or polities, the implications would be quite profound. Among other things, it would mean that revelation is addressed to the conscientious and autonomous individual but not to the norms and mores of society. In this context, society as a whole owes no obligations toward God or godliness, but individual believers would be obligated to follow God's laws. Hence, according to this position, the way revelation would address social acts would be indistinguishable from revelation addressing acts that deal exclusively with self-interest or acts of ritual and worship.

In order to tease out the implications of an approach which considers all revelation a personal matter, it would be helpful to consider a couple of examples. Per this approach, I, as a believer, should refrain from dealing in usury, thus, if I believe a particular transaction to be usurious, I should not engage in it. However, the argument cannot be made at a social level—it would not be hard to argue that God condemns a usurious society. As an individual, if my position is shared by a sufficient number of people, I could enact laws that express my own sense of morals and ethics, but the justification for the legislation would have to be revelation neutral, meaning that the law cannot be justified as a response to God's will or to revelation. Instead, the law can only be justified on neutral public policy grounds—that is, the majority believes this law is good. We can utilize a similar example, but this time we will consider incest. A good Muslim would refrain from incest, bestiality, coprophagia, or perhaps marrying more than four wives, but in each case he would do so as an act of obedience to God if he believes this is God's law. Again, revelation standing alone would not constitute the basis of a social norm or ethic. However, to the extent that a sufficient number of voters would agree with the position of the good Muslim, a law based on public policy, not on God's will, could be enacted to deal with such issues. The consumption and sale of alcohol would provide another good example. A good Muslim would not buy, sell, or drink alcoholic beverages, but unless such a Muslim could persuade others that as a matter of public policy, and not revelation, alcohol should not be consumed or sold, there would be no way for enacting such a public law.

I think it would be exceedingly problematic, if not impossible, to claim that Shari'ah has a neutral stand toward social norms, activities, or projects. It is fairly clear that Shari'ah goes well beyond appealing to the private conscience and does impose normative values on social units. For one thing, the Qur'anic commandment to enjoin the good and resist the evil is addressed to the *umma* (Muslim nation) as a whole. Furthermore, the numerous Qur'anic prescriptions calling on societies to establish justice or conduct all affairs through consultation are imposing collective obligations that go toward the founding of societies that bear witness for God. Shari'ah's concern with social acts is again evident in the central concept of *maqasid al-shari'ah al-kulliyya* (the overarching objects of Shari'ah). According to this doctrine, Shari'ah aims to protect five essential social values—life, lineage, reputation, mind or reason, and property, though many jurists add religion as a sixth value.[44] In other words, a critical component of what makes Shari'ah a path to goodness or godliness is that it is acutely engaged with social values or the norms that from a revelatory perspective ought to prevail in society. Indeed, although as I noted above, not all jurists added religion as one of the central values of Shari'ah, I think there is little doubt that whether specified or not, all Muslim theorists believed that religion is a basic and fundamental value that is at the very foundation of a healthy society. Most jurists further divided the basic values of Shari'ah into two categories: *al-hifz min janib al-wujud wa al-'ijad* (protection through affirmative and positive acts) and *al-hifz min janib al-'adam 'aw al-man'* (protection through prevention of negative or countering acts). Fundamentally, the difference is between serving goodness through affirmative, constructive acts and serving goodness through resistance to wrongfulness. Seen differently, the juristic distinction is between affirmatively establishing a virtuous society and defensively preventing the corruption of society. This duality is repeated in the Qur'anic norm of enjoining good and resisting evil as the primary and fundamental, or what may be called the first-order, obligation.

Returning to the initial question, however, even if Shari'ah demands a virtuous society, do modern Muslims need Shari'ah? Can we argue that logic and reason can provide the basis for all of our social mores and morality and that we do not need Shari'ah for the pursuit of social virtues? I believe that reason and rationality can interrogate social values and decipher whether such values make sense. Reason can even decipher good from its opposite and can establish and defend first principles of ethics such as: treat people as you would like to be treated. But in my view, Shari'ah is a metanarrative of admirable or praiseworthy attributes that acknowledge the good qualities of character necessary for virtuous personhood. Modern Muslims often repeat the dogma that Shari'ah is a way of life. On its face, this statement is true, but not because Shari'ah has a hard-and-fast ruling that applies to every action a person might take. Shari'ah is a way of life because it is a path of salvation and redemption from the moral failures of egoism and idolatry.

Shari'ah is not a path in which believers submit their will, reason, and autonomy to God, and in return, God leads them to the heavenly pastures. It is a path that necessarily begins with human beings becoming the trustees and viceroys of God on earth, and by virtue of this trust, human beings are dignified and honored with the autonomy of choice.[45] The instrument of choice and attribute of our own divinity is rationality—the ability to think, reflect, ponder, and decide. By rationality, I do not mean the philosophical power of reasoning but the ability to acknowledge the attributes of goodness and the obligation to be good. Most importantly, human beings have been honored and dignified by God in being endowed with the ability to grow morally and elevate toward higher states of being. However, this is not a simple mechanical, pedantic process during which a person attains a moment or multiple moments of absolution. According to the Islamic tradition, the possibilities and the potentialities for growth exist not only because of God's compassion and mercy but also through engagements with the divine—the moments of doubt and certitude, trial and error, disappointment and triumph. Through the process of reasoning with the divine, a reciprocated love of God and a state of peace and tranquility is achieved. In other words, through the dialectics of self-engagement, through compliance and rebellion, self-knowledge becomes possible. And the tradition attributed to the Prophet states: "Whoever comes to know oneself, will come to know his Lord."[46] Reasoning with God is a process in which the quest is godliness. This quest uses all the indicators of God, rational and revelatory, to reflect and achieve the balance necessary for a just and good character. But in the same way that God is limitless, possibility and potential for growth with godliness is also without bounds.

How does the quest for godliness inform the discussion on what I described as social acts and the role of Shari'ah in modern polities? I think it is clear that at the individual level, embracing Shari'ah in an effort to grow into godliness is a duty of any person desiring to be a Muslim. But beyond the personal commitment, any community of Muslims has an obligation of unity, cooperation, mutuality, and support. This is powerfully expressed in the Qur'anic exhortation: "And Let there be arising from you a nation inviting to all that is good, enjoining what is right and forbidding what is wrong." Also notice the Qur'anic verse: "And cooperate in righteousness and piety, but do not cooperate in sin and aggression."[47] Further, the Prophet Muhammad said, "Help your brother whether he is an oppressor or is oppressed. . . . You can keep him from committing oppression. That will be your help to him."[48] Not only do these narratives acknowledge the existence of social and communal units that serve necessary normative purposes, but revelation obligates them to do so. In reason-based arguments, one is forced to find a rational justification not just for the construction of social units, such as civil society, but also to overcome the theoretical challenge of explaining why such social units ought to serve a normative moral good such as justice or equality. Secular social theories can provide a rational defense as to why it would be in the best interests of every member of society if individuals are guaranteed basic civic rights. These basic rights could be premised on the promotion of happiness, the potential for intellectual growth, the preservation of human dignity, or something of the sort. But Shari'ah situates the source of obligation for purposeful social growth with revelation. Revelation reminds Muslims that not only individually but collectively they have an obligation to search and promote admirable or praiseworthy attributes that recognize and reinforce the good qualities of character necessary for a virtuous society.

Earlier, I expressed much doubt that not much would remain of Islam without Shari'ah. Shari'ah is an ongoing discourse on how to be a good Muslim within a communal system and a metanarrative on being a good human being within human society. As the history of the Islamic law guilds demonstrates, it is not important that Muslims agree on the same legal determinations or laws. What is important is that they recognize shared common standards of virtue and godliness. Ultimately, the constituent elements of these common standards are a subject for another book, but at a minimum, the ultimate objective is peace, repose, and tranquility (i.e., *salam*). But this salam cannot exist without justice (*qist*), balance and proportionality (*mizan* and *tawazun*), and compassion, love, and care for one another (*tarahum*, *tahabub*, and *takaful*). There is an interconnected symbiotic relationship between these constituent elements and the essential values of Shari'ah (i.e., life, intellect or mind, reputation, lineage or family, and property). The cause and effect here is somewhat elusive, but I believe it is highly doubtful that the constituent elements of a virtuous or godly society are at all possible unless the five values and their necessary derivatives are at least guaranteed and protected.

At this point, I am not talking about Shari'ah as a set of *ahkam* (laws) or adjudications (*qada'*). I am talking about Shari'ah as normative discourse—a discourse about what is good and bad and about what ought or ought not to be. But considering the historical depth, cultural roots, and social participation it becomes a metanarrative about the foundational and defining norms of a people both from a transcendental outlook and from a contextual and contingent perspective. A Shari'ah narrative becomes a living, never-ending discourse about what ought to be eternal and unchanging and what ought to be contingent and evolving. It is a discourse about God but also about who are we and how we as a people could become more godly—more generous, just, compassionate, merciful, balanced, loving—and how we can be filled with peace and extend peace to others. Fundamentally, a Shari'ah oriented society is a society in which there is an institutional commitment to engage God, but not as the political or legal sovereign. The idea of God as the political sovereign is fundamentally flawed. From the early conflict between 'Ali and the Khawarij, who raised the banner that sovereignty belongs to God, and from the time that the earliest generation of Muslims decided that no political leader can be God's caliph or successor and that a caliph is but the people's political deputy, the idea of divine political sovereignty has been thoroughly deconstructed.[49] A Shari'ah-oriented society reasons with God— it consistently visits and revisits the rational and textual indicators to stay on the *sirat al-mustaqim* (straight path) knowing full well that anyone who claims to have an exclusive claim over the *sirat* has by definition deviated from it. As the Qur'an points out, the blessing of the *sirat* comes as an act of grace that can never be taken for granted.[50] Therefore, reasoning with God means endlessly searching and engaging the divine with the hope and belief in God's continued guidance and grace.

It is important to emphasize that the understanding that Shari'ah is inseparable from Islam does not imply that by being Muslim, one is accepting an authoritarian system of government that rules in God's name. Indeed, my argument is that not only do governments not rule in God's name but also that no prescriptive legal rule implemented by the state can pretend to be God's judgment. But a Shari'ah society works toward a foundational commitment and a constitutionalist order in which the basic six values (including freedom of religion) and their derivatives become enshrined as basic inalienable rights. Beyond this, the duty to enjoin the good and resist wrongfulness becomes intimately and intricately connected to the role of Shari'ah as it functions in civil society and through civic institutions. The state can aid, directly or indirectly, promotion of this civic discourse as long as it does not deny any of its citizens their basic political rights. I will address the issue of instrumentalities later, but the essential point is that Shari'ah allows solid roots from the moral trajectory of Muslim societies. Instead of the chaotic crisis of identity, moral displacement, psychological alienation, disaffection, and uprootedness of modern globalized societies, Shari'ah provides an ontological anchor based on the promises of humanity and divinity. Shari'ah is premised on an ontological conviction in virtue as a principle, and on the premise that there are good qualities of character that allow us to distinguish between virtue and the lack of it. The attributes of God acknowledge the characteristics of goodness, but we human beings are the trustees on this earth, and so we, without limitations, possibilities, and potentialities define the epistemologies and deontological implications of these attributes. So, for instance, I know as a Muslim that among God's attributes are mercy, compassion, justice, forgiveness, and so on. Furthermore, reason and revelation impose these attributes as obligations in a variety of circumstances, some of which will require that I reflect on the necessity of balance and proportionality in the application of these attributes. It is the balance and just proportionality that will ultimately allow me to reflect on good character. The perpetual process is to reaffirm goodness but aspire toward godliness. If Shari'ah is understood properly, it will allow us not only to empower ourselves with rational morality but also to continue to be inspired and moved by the promise of divine beauty.

SHARI'AH AND VIRTUE

All experiences with God result in the realization of fundamental and foundational principles, which are premised on the attributes of divine beauty. In short, these are the principles of divinity or the qualities of beauty. Although understanding these principles is subjectively based, various indicators identify these principles as universal attributes or qualities of beauty.[51] For instance, texts, reason, and intuition as well as other possible venues will indicate that justice, mercy, compassion, patience, generosity, and grace are all attributes of beauty and also of divinity. In submitting to God, we seek to fulfill these principles as part of the pursuit of divinity. And in the same way that we seek to convince people of the universality of God, we can also seek to convince people of the universality of these unifying principles of beauty. Efforts at pursuing the principles of beauty that produce determinable results, rules, or laws are simply attempts at realizing the qualities of beauty, but they can never be assumed to have been successful realizations of these qualities. In the same way, every law attempts to fulfill the will of God, but no law can claim to have actually fulfilled it. Critical engagements and critical self-reflection are imperative to constantly question the laws that we do reach while systematically attempting to perfect our realization of beauty and divinity. But, again, we cannot arrogantly claim that we have in fact fulfilled or that we have come to embody the qualities of either beauty or divinity.

Regardless of how often one warns against the risk of empowering the modern state with the claim of divinity, the reality is that whenever the legitimacy base of the institutions of coercion rests even in small part on something transcendental or on a nonearthly logic, the risk of abuse is very real. The same risk exists, however, when the modern state, with all its powers of compulsion, employs a tool of governance, such as law, that is not accountable to its citizens or that is not accessible to criticism and, ultimately, rejection and abrogation by the citizens. As I argue below, despotism and oppression are thoroughly at odds with Islamic ethics and morality. This is exactly why it is critical not to confuse the assertion that divine guidance, or Shari'ah, applies to social acts with the claim that such divine guidance must be coercively enforced by the state. As I argued above, classical Muslim jurists clearly understood the difficulty in empowering the state to enforce the rights of God, and so they raised numerous procedural and evidentiary obstacles to the application of the *hudud* punishments. This, however, does not help us in understanding the relationship between the Shari'ah and the modern state.

On the question of Shari'ah and the modern state, I begin by emphasizing a rather obvious point: Islam is founded on *iman* (faith and conviction). The only legitimate instrument for guidance and method of persuasion is the call for *iman*. What is commonly referred to as free will, or the capacity to make a voluntary decision, is the basis for moral and legal accountability and liability. One cannot be forced to be a Muslim any more than one can be forced to be virtuous because coercion is fundamentally at odds with conviction in the same way that acting in a seemingly virtuous way because one has no choice to do otherwise by definition is not being virtuous. If I pretend to have virtuous moral qualities only because I fear reprisal or punishment, by definition, I am not virtuous. I might act in a fashion that appears virtuous, but coercion denies me the essence of the matter. Nevertheless, most classical jurists made apostasy part of the *hudud* criminal penalties punishable by death as a necessary measure for affirming religion, as a protected Shari'ah value. Again, as in the case of other crimes involving the protected interests of God, classical jurists made the actual enforcement of the punishment difficult. Interestingly, in what I described in my earlier works as the creative linguistic practices of the processes of law, Muslim jurists took a tradition in which the Prophet reportedly protested the killing of an enemy combatant, because only God truly knows what is in the man's heart, and turned it into a doctrinal leverage that a simple affirmation of the testament of faith, with or without sincerity of intent, is sufficient to suspend the application of the hadd.[52] On the mention of the penalty of apostasy, however, I must note that of all the *hudud* crimes, this is the least supported by either rational or revelatory indicators. Even within the epistemic system of its historical context, this *hadd* punishment is very difficult to reconcile with justice as a virtue. Although this would take us too far afield from discussion, it is worth noting that the penalty for apostasy has many shared characteristics with the medieval crimes against the majesty in Roman and other legal systems that were invariably punishable by death. Notably, as the classical jurists tended to do with political crimes in general, they negotiated and altered its form and function so as to mitigate the ability of the state to leverage it against the state's opponents.[53]

Having emphasized the role of conviction in matters of religious faith, does it follow that Islamic law cannot be applied in the modern nation-state because many citizens, even if born Muslim, are atheists or do not believe in the Islamic legal system? As noted earlier, some Muslim reformers have relied precisely on this logic to argue that Islamic law has no place in the modern world except as a private matter of conscience. However, I think the problem turns out to be far more complex. The consent or belief of the citizenry is not always necessary as a precondition to having to obey the law. Think, for instance, of an anarchist—although he might not believe in the legitimacy of the legal system, most would agree that he would still have to obey the law of the land in which he lives. My point simply is that a difference in conviction does not necessarily affect the duty owed to a legal system. The most commonly invoked definition of what constitutes binding legality is that law is the command of the sovereign backed up by the threat of the use of force. Of course, this rather raw positivistic definition of law has been the subject of numerous criticisms and challenges, but I mention it here to focus on the following point. It has often been argued that Islamic law is a convictional system (i.e., it can legitimately apply only to those who believe in it) because the sovereign is God, and if so, by definition, all those who do not recognize this sovereign by the very principle of the matter are outsiders to the process and therefore are not legitimately bound by the laws of such a system. Although this argument does have a considerable amount of emotional appeal, it suffers from some fatal flaws. Part of the problem is in what one means by God's sovereignty and whether God's omnipotence and immutability can be equated with the political concept of sovereignty (*hakimiyya*). But other than the coherence of concept, there are numerous situations where the authority of the lawmaker can be denied and yet the law remains legitimately binding. One of the greatest ironies of contemporary Muslim societies is that they continue to be governed by the transplanted legal systems of their former colonizers. One can hardly point to a legitimate historical moment in which it could be argued that the natives of the former colonies had the choice to consent to the adoption of these alien systems of law. Yet this does not mean that the laws of the colonizers were illegitimate or not binding, either when these laws were first adopted or decades later when they were retained for numerous instrumental reasons.

My point here is not to defend the imposition of so-called religious laws on an unwilling population of doubters or dissidents—quite the opposite. Conviction plays a marginal role in explaining why the law is either legitimate or authoritative when the law belongs to the state and this state has the ability to effectively obtain compliance. The fact that the state's law is binding does not mean that this law is moral, fair, just, or even rational or good. Most importantly, although we hope that laws are just, injustices are perpetuated in the name of working legal systems all the time. There is a material difference between what a modern state claims about its laws and what the law is. The state can claim that its laws are just, moral, or fair, but just because the state describes its laws as such does not mean that in reality they are as they are described. Similarly, a state can claim that its laws are Islamic, Jewish, or Christian, but this means little unless we have an authoritative mechanism that can confirm or deny the state's claims. For example, the legislature in the United States might make it a punishable crime to marry more than one wife, and as a resident in the United States I consider this a valid and binding law. What if the legislature adopted such law and the legislative history clearly showed that the majority of lawmakers believed that polygamy violates Christian ethics; does this alter the nature of my duty to obey the law? Whether such a law would be constitutional or not depends on the constitutional principles on which the legal system is founded. I think most would agree that as long as this remains a valid law, my duty to obey it is the same regardless of my religious faith or convictions.

Consider a different example: What if the legislature in the United States decides to reinstate the prohibition against the consumption of alcoholic beverages? Although the ban only mentions the social cost of crimes committed due to the consumption of alcohol, it is clear from the legislative record that a strong Christian ethic was behind the ban. Again, whether this law is unconstitutional would depend on the constitution or organizing principles of the legal system, but there is little doubt that the law would be binding as long as the state enforced it. Laws that are intended to demean, belittle, degrade, or place a religious, social, or cultural group at a disadvantage, however, even if enforceable, should be challenged as unjust, unfair, or unequal.

Returning to the issue of consent, although it is clear that laws do not require actual or constructive consent before they become binding, the same cannot be said about political systems. All political systems, regardless of how autocratic, claim to speak for a sovereign people; but democratic systems, in principle, have a greater level of credibility and believability. While all governments claim to represent the will and best interests of the governed because of the greater instances of accountability and transparency, democratic systems tend to be far more legitimate. In addition, speaking as a Muslim, I believe that despotism and tyranny are always immoral. Of course, I am not at all impressed by the way that the democratic label is often used to create dichotomous camps of evildoers versus good-doers. But at the same time, for many reasons related to substantive justice and procedural justice, democracy is a morally superior form of governance when compared to any other form of governance. Moreover, the reality of the modern nation-state has created an epistemological awareness of the idea of citizenship and the rights and duties conferred by this citizenship. The first of these epistemological understandings and resulting moral expectations is that of inclusion, or put differently, the expectation of nonexclusion. This does not necessarily guarantee that minorities or unpopular points of view will achieve particular or determinable results, but it does mean that there are objective and reliable rules of inclusion. The rules of inclusion set out transparent, equally access- ible, and independent processes for citizens to express and give effect to their will. Most importantly, it is fair to say that the nations of the world, whether sincere or not, expressed an understanding that all human beings, regardless of citizenship, social or economic status, or beliefs, are entitled to a set of rights due to them by virtue of being human beings. Through their member- ship in the United Nations, the nations of the world have tried to memorialize and document those rights in a series of declarations, conventions, treaties, and institutions. No less important, modern political understandings have confirmed that the construction of democratic systems of governance and civic political orders demand that a set of duties and rights be recognized and that many rights must be held individually, not just against some unspecified and obscure imagined transgressors but specifically against the state and its coercive powers. In other words, there is an understanding that a set of rights must be held equally by all citizens and must be held in order to protect each citizen from violations by the state.

In my view, the Islamic approach to justice can effectively accommodate and bolster the values and norms necessary for the adoption and maintenance of the principles of democracy and civic and human rights. In fact, in a principled ethical approach to the values of Shari'ah, as I argue below, it becomes quickly apparent that one of the primary and most essential objec- tives of the revelation is to contest and challenge the arrogance of power (*al- takabbur wa al-'uluwi fi al-ard*), tyrants (*al-tugha*), the oppressive (*al-jaba- bira al-mutajabbirin*), the unjust (*al-zalimun*), those who destroy and corrupt the earth (*al-mufsidun fi al-ard*), and those who arrogantly pillage and usurp (*wa man yuhlik al-harth wa al-nasl*).[54] Other than the oneness and immut- ability of God, the Qur'an emphasizes justice and mercy as the most persis- tently compelling imperative of divinity. But it is not the existence of materi- al inequality that is the earmark of injustice, but the human tendency toward egoism and the desire for power and control over others. One of the persistent ethical themes of the Qur'an and Sunna is the treatment of empowering of the powerless as a social virtue (*nusrat al-mustad'afin* or *raf' al-qahr 'an al-mustad'afin*). In fact, in my opinion, if one would be interested in developing a comprehensive and systematic theory of Islamic justice, such a theory would have to be constructed around the principle of protecting the least privileged. The Islamic tradition is replete with narratives attributed to the Prophet or one of the companions asserting that the rights recognized by the collectivity must be measured in accordance with the needs of the weakest or least privileged in the community.[55] This approach would ask, if we take the condition of the weakest, most disadvantaged, and least privileged in the community, what set of rights would be necessary to ensure that (1) at least, the five or six values of Shari'ah are adequately and sufficiently guarded and fulfilled and (2) the rights recognized must, at a minimum, protect the necessities and needs of people? However, I would hasten to add that limiting the values protected to five or six is no longer warranted. Again, modern historical experiences have bolstered the emergence of an epistemic awareness of a range of values necessary for the modern cosmopolitan conception of human dignity. For example, human experience and modern consciousness have grown into the awareness that the right to speak freely is as important as, if not more important than, the right to not suffer unfair character assassinations or slander.

At this point, it is worth emphasizing that it is certainly possible to simply copy and transplant one of the bills of rights found in many constitutions around the world, which is what most Muslim countries have done to date. Whether constitutions are seen as a part of the Kelsen's grundnorm, or basic norm, from which the legitimacy of all inferior laws are driven, or whether they are perceived as a component of Hart's rules of recognition[56]—the entrenched customary norms of society on which legality derives its legitimacy—or are construed as preemptory norms of society from which more particularized subnorms are extracted, transplants raise the same set of problems. Transplanted constitutions—typically the donor is a former colonial power and the receiver a former colony of the donor—do not reflect the embedded collective normativities embodied by the sociohistorical experiences of a people. Most often, transplanted constitutions do represent the normative commitments or political accommodations of the intelligentsia that has developed extensive cultural and economic ties to its former colonizers. This does not mean that transplanted constitutions do not work; depending on how one defines the function of legal systems, they serve the purpose of resolving conflicts and affirm the power of the state to rule. But for a constitution to serve the actual functions of constitutionalism (limiting power and the safeguarding of natural and common rights) demands normative commitments that are nothing short of culturally and socially transformative.[57] The Westernized intelligentsia, which often functions as the technocratic class professionally servicing these legal transplants, does not have the intellectual tools, cultural resources, or more importantly, the incentives to root the norms of these legal transplants into the ethos supported by their native cultures.[58] In many ways, the transplants are seen by the Westernized intelligentsia as a shortcut to modern civilizational values by imposing pre-fashioned systems of law that fulfill modern notions, such as the rule of law, judicial impartiality, or due process. But even the most positivist legal theorist would recognize that unless a system of law is to rely on sheer brute force, legitimacy and legality are derived from processes that enjoy deep historical and cultural normative resonance within societies. But to the extent that these transplanted legalities can be said to have anything resembling resonant normative systems, inevitably these systems represent the normative consensus of the elite class of Westernized intelligentsia and not of the people at large. This is akin to saying that in these countries there are grundnorms, rules of recognition, or normative consensus that are effective for the subclass of Westernized intelligentsia but that at the same time have little or no relevance to the rest of the population. Indeed, this is exactly why in many Muslim countries the legal intelligentsia becomes rather paternalistic, domineering, and even imperialistic toward what they see as the reactionary and uncivilized native population.[59] Effectively, the Westernized intelligentsia becomes a loyal patron of and conduit for the value system of the former colonizer and often even replicates the identical supremacist, racist, and arrogantly benevolent attitude of the former colonizers toward the reactionary natives. Of course, the problems raised by legal transplants are but a part of the larger problem of the cultural and social friction and conflicts resulting from the failure to develop an authoritative common set of civic values after colonialism.

At this point, one would have to wonder: So what is the solution? Is the solution, for instance, for Muslim countries desiring to achieve an overlapping consensus over the basic normative values of society to insert a constitutional clause stating that Shari'ah will be a primary source of laws or will be the main source of legislation? For many reasons, I think this would be an unfortunate misstep. The state cannot be given the authority to give meaning to nebulous concepts such as the Shari'ah in the modern age. There is a great deal of difference between a vague mention of Shari'ah in a state's constitution and actually working out what Shari'ah means in a particular context. As argued earlier, Shari'ah should be understood strictly as the equivalent to the virtues of godliness as the higher ideals of society and humanity at large. A constitutional document should affirm and validate these higher ideals as social and political goals, but in all cases, the executive branch—the branch of government that controls and yields the power of coercion and force— should not be empowered to violate the rights of individuals and communities in the name of these ideals. The most natural and rational place for these ideals to be given expression and specificity is the body that represents the consensus and values of the people—in other words, the legislature. When the Qur'an states, for instance, "Do good for God loves those who do good,"[60] it uses the plural command form of *"ya ahsinu,"* or all of you people, do *"ihsan."* This is also the equivalent of a command form to do acts of beauty (or acts of *husn* or *ihsan*). In this, the Qur'an has provided a textual grounding for the rational and natural moral imperative of acting to achieve goodness. As the Muslim philosopher al-Raghib al-Isfahani (d. 502/1108) argued centuries ago, people have a rational moral obligation to live up to the privilege of having inherited the earth. In terms of the duty to do good, this amounts to an obligation to adopt godly virtues (*al-takhalluq bi khalq Al-*

lah).[61] The premodern jurist Ibn al-Qayyim al-Jawziyya (d. 751/1350) noted that the ethics of goodness (*khuluq*) is embodied in acts of justice, wisdom, welfare, and truthfulness.[62]

The Islamic tradition is replete with thinkers who recognized that Shari'ah's call to godliness necessarily included an appeal to natural and common intuitive and rational decency that guides people through most of their social interactions as long as there are conditions conducive for the flourishing of human values. All types of excesses, overindulgence, egoism, and arrogance, on the one hand, and shortages, needs, oppression, and submissiveness, on the other, can encourage human beings away from what is best in them to the abyss within them. But in a virtuous society where there is justice, wisdom, dignity, and truthfulness, the best of what is within humanity will grow and flourish. Many Muslim intellectuals like Ibn al-Qayyim and Ibn al-Khatib (d. 776/1375) believed in the nourishing and nourishments of love—the ability to receive and give love, and the love of God and from God—as the key to the attainment of all virtue.[63] I understand that from the philosophical point of view, there are frequently very significant distinctions and disagreements that often pit one school of thought against another. But for the purposes of legal theory and the construction of constitutional norms for modern societies, there is sufficient commonality between the different approaches to Shari'ah and virtue to allow us to reach some critical resolutions. It is imperative that Muslim countries recognize Shari'ah as a shared historical heritage that endeavors to affirm the unity of humanity in its pursuit of virtues. At the same time, Shari'ah represents a normative commitment to the pursuit of godliness as a social good, but not in any way supporting the idea that a society, nation, group, or people have the right to declare themselves godly and above human accountability and responsibility.

In the Islamic tradition, premodern scholars differentiated between two essential moral spheres—*al-hikma al-ilahiyya* (divine wisdom) and *al-hikma al-insaniyya* (human wisdom). Wisdom in the sphere of the divine is ontological and thoroughly abstract in the sense that it constitutes the knowledge of the true nature of all things. In the human sphere, wisdom is ultimately deontic and practical in that it inquires into the ethical duties and obligations that follow from the nature of things. Although the boundaries of both spheres of wisdom overlap, God's wisdom is founded on certitude while human wisdom is based on probability.[64] The critical point here is that all wisdom and all knowledge of virtue at the metaphysical level is anchored and affirmed in God, but all wisdom in the created physical level unequivocally belongs to human beings. Effectively, this means that our knowledge of right and wrong is the inquiry into godliness; our human efforts effectuating and materializing this knowledge through the pursuit of godliness is thoroughly human. We search godliness assured of God's objective and absolute recognition and support of goodness, but our human efforts remain just that—human. This epistemological structure allows us to integrate Shari'ah in the social and political life of Muslims while guaranteeing that God's immutability and absoluteness is not transgressed on by human beings claiming to have become possessed of and empowered by the consecration of their egos, actions, or speech.[65]

Understanding Shari'ah as a set of natural virtues and adopting it as a normative guide represents an affirmation of moral character and identity of the nation, the continuity of the Islamic heritage and tradition, and a renewed search for common grounds with humanity at large, which shares the responsibility for the well-being and flourishing of the earth as the collective inheritance of humanity.[66] We adopt principles based on divine teachings for the simple reason that we affirm the principle that we need God's grace and we find dignity in submitting to the divine guidance. And also, in principle, we want to affirm the duality of anchoring our aspirations on the eschatology of God's laws and on the collective guidance of accumulations of human wisdom.[67] As W. D. Ross states: "The existing body of moral convictions of the best people is the cumulative product of the moral reflection of many generations, which has developed an extremely delicate power of appreciation of moral distinctions; and this the theorist cannot afford to treat with anything other than the greatest respect. The verdicts of the moral consciousness of the best people are the foundation on which he must build; though he must first compare them with one another and eliminate any contradictions they may contain."[68]

There is an inevitable tension and a necessary balance to be struck between, on the one side, anchoring society in a metaphysical and transcendental ontological purpose that affirms the divine potentiality in human beings and also, at the same time, affirming an authentic sense of identity and historical continuity. But it is due time that Muslim countries realize that there is no choice but to look inward to their own traditions with a critically reflective attitude toward the normatively effective standards that account for internal legitimacy. By internal legitimacy, I mean legitimacy beyond what Hart called the external view of law or the coercive superficial structure of law. In this context, I urge that this reflective attitude be "critical" because while it affirms and empowers the normative potentialities of the citizens, it must also be subversive of power. In other words, the internal resources of the cumulative inherited tradition must be used to empower the people and limit the coercive powers of the state.

I have argued that Shari'ah should be recognized as the foundational natural law of Muslim countries,[69] but this does not mean that Shari'ah should be explicitly mentioned in constitutional documents. In the modern age, there might be significant hermeneutical reasons why Shari'ah, as a term, should not be explicitly set out in a constitutional document. But in all cases, the Shari'ah as a primordial and an all-encompassing metaphysical concept, like that of God, is ultraconstitutional and metaconstitutional and is beyond the formalism of constitutional drafting. However, social and political virtues anchored in Shari'ah, to the extent that these virtues constitute the actual foundations on which duties and rights are recognized, ought to be included in the constitutional text.[70] For example, not all virtues can be translated into a legal principle worthy of inclusion in a constitutional document. Patience, according to most Muslim philosophers, is a Shari'ah-supported virtue, but it is unlikely that it can be transformed into a right. This is very different from the virtue of intellectual growth, which could be translated into a right of freedom of thought, speech, and education. The virtues of justice, dignity, well-being, happiness, and honesty all could bolster a right not to be tortured or subjected to degrading and humiliating treatment. The more a set of virtues seems to correlate in affirming a right or prohibiting a violation of the right, it would stand to reason, the more that such a right is of the highest order of normativity in the pursuit of godliness on earth. Therefore, for example, because of the number of virtues that coalesce to condemn torture and degradation in addition to several textual condemnations against those who harm, torture, or degrade human beings, I would argue that a prohibition of torture is a right of the highest order in the pursuit of godliness. [71]

Other than basing constitutional rights on virtues, I argue below that secondary sources of constitutional law, such as textual refrains or commands or customary practices of traditional Islamic law, can be used as further collaborative evidence of the importance of a right. [72] For instance, the right to life is not only affirmed by an array of coalescing virtues but also by numerous textual commands, and so it is a fair assumption that it must be considered one of the core rights. What I call secondary sources cannot detract from the importance of a right but can only be used to bolster it. Another useful example here is perhaps a right to set inviolable charitable endowments (*awqaf*). Several principles, including the virtue of communal solidarity, fraternity, charity, intellectual and moral development, and many others, support a right to establish *awqaf* that are inviolable and cannot simply be usurped by states in the name of eminent domain or public welfare. The historical legacy and customary practices of many Muslim countries that for centuries respected the integrity and independence of the *awqaf* can only bolster such a right. Moreover, the various textual refrains against usurping money or property that is constructively owned by God because it is dedicated for the benefit of the needy—whether the needy are humans or animals— again strengthens the position of such a right. [73]

The key issue, which cannot be sufficiently emphasized, is that what particular scheme of virtues to be adopted and the set of sacrosanct rights protecting this scheme of virtues from obstruction or interference by the government or other power bodies in society, such as wealthy corporations or landlords that actually yield coercive power, must be constructed on the basis of a genuine consensus that is strong enough to represent the will of the people. But the scheme of virtues and the derivative protective rights can differ from one Muslim country to another. God affirmed virtues of goodness that are imperfectly realizable by people, but each society or each sovereign country has the right to construct the implications of its engagement with the divine. Ultimately, each country will articulate a hierarchy of virtues and rights that is the outcome of its own process of reasoning with God. [74]

There remains a very serious and rather obvious challenge to this argument. How about non-Muslim, or nonbelieving, citizens of the state? Doesn't the idea of rights legitimated on the grounds of virtues analytically derived from Shari'ah violate their rights to being equal citizens of the state? For a first step in developing a response, let's assume that, as some have argued, the Mosaic laws played a critical role in shaping contemporary Western morality or, as even more have argued, that the Judeo-Christian tradition and values are the basis of the moral conceptions that guide Western civilization or are the basis of public civic virtues and values. American presidents are regularly seen attending church services. Crosses and Jewish candlesticks are seen in many public or semipublic areas in the United States and Europe. Many courtrooms in the United States, and especially in postcommunist Europe, display crosses, religious images, or biblical quotes. Countries like Germany have been successfully governed by the Christian Democrats. Moreover, the Vatican is a Catholic sovereign that, in theory, could have citizens that are neither Catholic nor Christian. Although Israel is a secular democracy, its laws of citizenship identify it as a Jewish state, and in Israel, Jewish religious parties compete in elections and are often a part of ruling coalitions. In some areas, such as Jerusalem, there are numerous concessions made for ritualistic Jewish law such as the observance of the Sabbath. In fact, contrary to popular belief, not all secular democratic countries fail to embrace a religious identity.[75] Do such practices deny religious minorities the right to equal citizenship? That the answer is quite challenging is well illustrated by cases ranging from the Islamic scarf cases in France, to the ban against mosques in Bologna, to the ban against minarets in Switzerland, among other examples.[76] The necessary point here is that there is a broad variety of legal secularisms.[77] There is no fixed model of secularism but a range of hermeneutically significant practices of secularism, or what some have called secularity.[78] In most Muslim contexts, I believe that the interiorization and privatization of religion or the exclusion of religion from public spaces is highly problematic. These approaches to secularization construct a false dynamic in which the state controls religion so as to prevent its externalization or manifestation, and in doing so, the state creates a Rousseau-type civil religion.[79] In Muslim countries, this civil religion has often amounted to a state-centered definition of religion that, paradoxically, is exploited by the state to keep any nonconformist or nonorthodox religiosity away from the public sphere. Although many definitions have been proposed, the constitutive elements of legal secularism, in my view, are three: (1) freedom of conscience and belief; (2) equality before the law and nondiscrimination against the right of citizens to practice their religion individually and in congregations; and (3) inability of the state to co-opt religion so as to render its decisions sacred or to immunize its state officials or policies from criticism or accountability. No government can pretend to have exclusive access to the divine will or claim an exclusive relationship with the divine. A state, however, may make reasonable accommodations to facilitate and protect the practice of religion.

Coming back to the question of citizens of a Muslim country who are either not Muslim or not believers, it is fair to say that every constitutional order will by definition express a set of normative commitments that could very well be inconsistent and even irreconcilable with the beliefs of a minority view. So, for instance, assume that the constitution expresses that marriage and family are building blocks of society and thus considers marriage to be a virtue. Alternatively, assume that the constitution recognizes friendship, altruism, or the taking in of orphans as virtues. Now assume that we have a group in society that calls itself the Black Masks who believes marriage is boring, friendship hypocritical, altruism foolish, and taking care of orphans inefficient. Clearly, the Black Masks have a serious tension with the virtues represented in the constitution. This in itself is not a problem as long as their right to believe what they wish to believe is guaranteed, and their rights are guaranteed whether they believe or do not believe in protecting the rights of others. Most certainly, they do have a right to organize, advocate, run for elections, and try to convince other citizens that their view of competing or different virtues not based on Shari'ah is the one worth adopting. As long as they commit no crimes and do not conspire in the commission of crimes, their rights as citizens are protected. The same analysis would apply if members of minority religions wish to form a party to persuade citizenry that Christian or Jewish or Buddhist virtues should be adopted as a superior vision of goodness. I do believe that in principle, in order to avoid conflict that could become uncivil, minorities have a moral obligation to exercise self-restraint and temper their demands so that they could forge a consensus with the majority over a wide range of normative issues. Previously, I made this argument in the context of Muslim minorities living in non-Muslim societies.[80] While contemporary constitutionalism is founded on the principle of protecting the right to individual moral agency and autonomy, a minority does have a moral obligation not just to make reasonable concessions to the demands of the majority but also to acclimate to the collective moral consciousness. Certainly, per its scheme of rights, a constitution must protect the rights of minorities to believe, and practice, and mobilize, and organize in order to be effective in representing their interests and views. There is a civic obligation on the majority not only to protect the rights of the minority but to facilitate civic processes that would help foster understanding and building common grounds, and there is a corollary duty on the minority to exercise self-restraint in making demands so as to avoid the fracturing of the social fabric of the nation-state regardless of how artificial it might be.

ISLAMIC LAW AND REASONABLENESS

Jean-Jacques Rousseau, in his famous book *The Social Contract* (1762), commented: "It would take gods to give men laws."[81] In Rousseau's view, religion is important for civil society because, he believed, reason alone was not capable of motivating people to perform their social duties. Yet Rousseau did not believe in the separation of church and state as much as he believed in the control of the church by the state. He proposed the creation of a civil religion in which the republic came to represent a transcendent goodness and wisdom of sorts. The republican government would be given control of the civil religion as all forms of communitarian, social, and customary laws would fall under the hegemonic control of the civil law of the state. Rousseau's social contract was all encompassing and all inclusive of all social units, convictions, beliefs, and normative orientation, but at the same time, it was also all exclusive toward anyone who resisted the dogma of the new civil faith. Any individual or unit that did not yield to the absolutism of the civil state, civil law, or civil religion was in Rousseau's estimate an outcast and a heretic.[82]

For a number of political reasons, French republicanism became the dominant form of government in much of the third world, and especially in most of the Muslim countries. There were several objective reasons why French republicanism became the system of choice in the precolonized states. Among those reasons is the emphasis on egalitarianism, fraternity, and social equity in the dogmatic symbolism of the French Revolution, the overthrow of the monarchy and destruction of the old French aristocracy—in other words, the defiance of status and privilege—and the widespread belief that a strong executive with sweeping powers is necessary for development. Whatever the merits of these beliefs, the fact is that French republicanism was in clear tension with the native societies it had replaced. Concentrating power in the hands of the executive, including the power to control civil religion and the codification of laws at the expense of communal and customary practices, required the violent uprooting of centuries-old native institutions. Moreover, instead of the practice of legal pluralism, which had marked the tribal and multilinguistic topography of Muslim states, the newly imposed codified system of law demanded the centralization and consolidation of legal theories, causes of action, jurisdictional divisions, and remedies.

The common explanation for the transplantation of the civil law system to a large number of countries around the world usually credits the coherence and accessibility of the Napoleonic Code of law.[83] Although I am sure the ease and facility by which a legal system could be transplanted does play a role, one must wonder about the logic of the colonizer and not just the colonized.[84] Specifically, one wonders to what extent romanticized impressions about Oriental despotism and also the interests of colonizers in streamlining and simplifying their colonized subjects played a role in the exportation of the civil law system to natives.[85] European colonial powers persistently saw indigenous Muslim law as irrational, informal, and unsystematic. The notion of "*qadi* justice" became a virtual archetype for whimsical, personalized, and unreasoned lawmaking fundamentally at odds with the rule of law in civilized societies.[86] Therefore, the eventual replacement of indigenous legal systems became a part of the "white man's burden" and Europe's civilizing mission. But colonial powers sought to secure their economic interests through a system of capitulations and special legal jurisdictions that undermined traditional systems of conflict resolution and adjudication.[87] Western scholars often spoke in somewhat inconsistent terms about Islamic law, describing it simultaneously as irrationally formalistic but also as irrationally arbitrary and unpredictable. However, in all cases, colonial narratives on legality and democracy did not just construct the other, but the self. Just as the paradigm of *qadi* justice was asserted as the antithesis of the rule of law, Western discourses on Oriental despotism and sultanic regimes were constructed as the contrast to the idea of limited government and liberty.[88] All too often it is forgotten that Western cultural icons, such as John Stuart Mill, John Locke, Jean-Jacques Rousseau, and Montesquieu, who played critical roles in constructing the Western self-image, also portrayed the Orient as the exact antithesis. Whether Islam or Muslims—both were portrayed as quintessentially despotic, arbitrary, and unpredictable, which very often amounted to an intellectualized way of expressing the foreignness and alienness of the other.

Perceiving the colonized native as alien and flawed is hardly surprising. But the ascendancy of the West took place in the much larger context of historical transformations that engulfed all of humanity in transitions from false and pretentious universalism to sociologically undeniable globalization to an equally compelling epistemological cosmopolitanism. Practically, this meant that for reasons not directly related to Europe's military victories and supremacy, it became entirely possible for the colonizer to withdraw militarily, and even to give the colonized political autonomy and sovereignty, but to continue defining the epistemological and phenomenological reality of the formerly colonized. More concretely, colonial powers saw the native legal systems as fundamentally unworkable and unreasonable. From the perspective of colonial powers, what made Islamic law unreasonable was that it performed a sociological and anthropological function that often involved negotiating the interests and demands of communal units that did not make sense to the colonizers, often because of their inaccessibility to outsiders. For instance, the syncretic mixture of tribal, folk, or customary laws combined with local Islamic legal doctrines in application as the common law in a large number of provincial jurisdictions was indeed resistant and unaccommodating to the interests of colonial powers since it placed the financial interests of a local nobleman or the chief of a fisherman's guild in a small village in the delta on an equal footing with, if not in an actually privileged position over, the interests of an urban trader doing business with colonial forces. The communal or common-law juridical system as applied on the ground did not just rely on an impersonal and objective application of the law but on recognizing and interacting with the local context and its actors. This necessarily meant that this juridical system worked to serve the interests of the old classes of tradesmen and craftsmen who continued to be part of the traditional alliances of the old regime now defeated and overcome by colonialism. [89]

Western scholars in the service of imperial powers characterized Islamic law as simultaneously unreasonably formalistic but also too arbitrary and discretionary to be dealt with as anything but a primitive system that had either become irrelevant at some point in history or was always an irrelevant abstraction from its very inception. As I mentioned earlier, colonialism bred its own network of native beneficiaries who not only shared extensive converging economic and financial interests with colonialism, but much more importantly, were culturally dependent on the West for their sense of meaning and their understanding of their sociohistorical roles in their own countries. Instead of belonging to the traditional guilds of builders, craftsmen, and jurists, this class of beneficiaries consisted of technocrats, professionals, and intellectuals who not only studied in the West and sent their children to study in missionary or colonial schools but who also were becoming the possessors and arbiters of power in the new emerging world. In the same way that colonizers saw themselves as the bearers of civilization to an irrational and unreasonable people, this new intelligentsia saw itself as the pioneers of development in countries full of reactionaries or fanatics who were incapable of understanding the needs of the new world. After developing an endemic intellectual and cultural dependency on the historical and social narratives of their colonizers, this local Westernized intelligentsia pioneered the flood of legal transplantations in Muslim countries. [90]

It is important to underscore the critical role played by this local intelligentsia that had thoroughly internalized the Western discourses not just about the West but also about their own cultures. Especially when it came to understanding the relationship between law and society and the role of the state as the critical nexus between the two, it is not an exaggeration to say that they saw, and continue to see, their own native cultures largely through Western eyes, especially through the prism of colonial stereotypes. Therefore, in the mind of this intellectual elite, the phenomenon of Oriental despotism and *qadi* justice are not just seen as historical realities but are virtual tropes of self-condemnation and self-exorcisms. The purported existence of such monumental civilizational failures such as Oriental absolutism, closing the doors of *ijtihad*, or the unworkability of Islamic law have become essential foundational mythologies justifying the elites' sense of righteous outrage and moral indignation, and also intellectual superiority vis-à-vis the oblivious and heedless native who does not understand the extent to which the native's own norms and values have become outdated and backward. Having internalized the dominant Western narratives as its own reinforced the intelligentsia's sense of being civilized citizens among primal natives belonging to a dark and unenlightened age.[91] And very much like their former colonizers, this local intelligentsia fell into the continued habit of labeling those who refuse to adopt the colonial narrative as unquestioned truth either as primitive barbarians or as fanatics, extremists, and zealots.[92] Ultimately, this local intelligentsia treats their fellow natives as if they are incapable of rational deliberation as long as these natives refuse to see the intelligentsia as their liberators from the natives' self-imposed backwardness.[93] This is precisely why the postcolonial experience of many former colonies is replete with models of coercively imposed self-development and also autocratically imposed legal modernizations.[94]

Besides the broader class of Westernized intelligentsia, which was quickly becoming the new political elite in their respective Muslim countries, there developed a highly influential technocratic intelligentsia comprising law specialists that spearheaded the importation of European legal codes to Muslim countries. The newly emerged class of Western-style legal specialists had a distinctive understanding of what the role of law in modern societies ought to be. Foundationally, law was seen as an expression of the people's sovereignty and as the natural voice of justice belonging to the people and drawing its legitimacy and authority from the people. The discourse of the new class of legal specialists, however, borrowed a European conception of the law prevalent in the late eighteenth and nineteenth centuries, which maintained that the true spirit or soul of a people is found in its laws and its own specific historical experience.[95] English, French, German, and Dutch legal theorists contended that the law of a people is an intimate, unique, and distinctive expression of their moral spirit, their unique civilizational or national character.[96] But this placed the legal intelligentsia, responsible for wholesale importation of European legal systems, in the rather impossible position where they heralded the state's law as an extension of the sovereignty and spirit of the people but, at the same time, were well aware of the tenuous connection between the transplanted legal systems and their native cultures. The resulting paradox initiated a hallmark incongruence that reverberated through the decades of the twentieth century to practically every issue impacted by questions related to the law, society, and national identity. Particularly after the end of colonialism, the role of this intelligentsia of legal specialists became

not only more prominent but also more paradoxical and explosive. On the
one hand, this intelligentsia was supposed to spearhead and pioneer the new
ideologies of anticolonialism, self-determination, sovereignty, and national
liberation, but on the other hand, this intelligentsia also seemed incapable of
nurturing anything resembling an authentic spirit of legality, even when they
struggled to naturalize the alien souls of their legal systems.[97] For instance,
the Egyptian 'Abd al-Razzaq al-Sanhuri (d. 1391/1971), probably the most
prominent jurist in the Arab world and who played a critical role in promulgating the Egyptian Civil Code of 1949 and in drafting the civil codes of Iraq,
Jordan, Syria, and Libya and the commercial code of Kuwait, was thoroughly
versed in the French, Roman, and civil law traditions. On many jurisprudential questions, Sanhuri opted for the views of his teacher and friend, Edouard
Lambert, a prominent French professor of civil and comparative law and the
dean of the Khedive School of Law in Cairo.[98] Sanhuri tried to infuse imported French laws with an artificial nativity by assimilating Islamic law to
French law. Although Sanhuri claimed that he successfully incorporated Islamic law into the provisions of his civil code, in reality he superimposed the
categories and structure of the civil law onto Islamic law. So, for instance,
just like French law, Islamic law was recast in separate categories of civil,
criminal, and personal law, a distinction between private and public law, and
a distinct law of obligations nearly identical to the concept of *delicto*.[99]
Numerous jurists from Egypt, Jordan, Iraq, Algeria, Kuwait, and many others, typically in the context of pursuing doctoral degrees, would write rather
superficial comparative studies demonstrating the purported similarities between imported national laws and Islamic legal doctrines.[100]

In reality, imported laws, like the influential Sanhuri Code, created the
legal subject as an objective and ideal category, largely unaffected by social
or cultural contexts.[101] The civil and criminal codes that continue to be in
effect in most Muslim countries today were adopted as comprehensive bodies of law that were far more responsive to the inner logic of the legal system
and to the cohesiveness of the jurisprudential theory than to any lived social
realities or cultural contingencies. Whether the average citizen in colonized
countries, such as Egypt or Iraq, saw the law as reasonable or sensible was
entirely irrelevant because the mechanics of the transplanted legal system
had no means of responding to localized variations. Moreover, judges sitting
on the bench were expected to faithfully implement the letter of the law
without any effective means of responding to social demands or social processes. Other than the limited space permitted by law for judicial discretion
in pursuit of equity, judges had no effective means of achieving substantive
justice within their own national social contexts. What this meant was that
the law remained strictly an instrument of the state enjoying absolute and
unmitigated authority and legitimacy, although none of its terminological
usages, standards, legal categories, and definitions or its conceptions of citizenship and nationality were the product of internal or native processes.
Without a robust democratic political process providing oversight and forcing the civil law system to remain responsive to social demands, the imported
legal systems often served as a means to obstructing and defying nativist
cultural and social institutions instead of giving expression to them.[102]

The conception of the legislator in a republican system of government bolstered the formation of the elite class of lawmakers and enhanced an autocratic view of their own roles as legislators. In this role, the lawmakers did not see themselves as representatives of the constituency that brought them to office, nor did they feel that their own legitimacy was thoroughly contingent on the will of the electorate as expressed within the political process. Rather, the lawmaker adopted a far broader role as the self-appointed guardian of the people, empowered to look after the best interests of the state even if he did so in a patriarchal and oligarchic fashion. The intellectual genesis of this view is found in the very idea of civil society in a republican system of government. For example, consider the following quote from Rousseau:

> The task of discovering the best laws, i.e. those that are most salutary for each nation, calls for a mind of the highest order. This mind would have insight into each and every human passion, and yet be affected by none. It would be superhuman and yet understand human nature through and through. It would be willing to concern itself with our happiness, but would seek its own outside us. It would content itself with fame far off in the future; i.e. it would be capable of laboring in one century and reaping its reward in the next. [103]

Rousseau might have sought to construct an inspirational ideal of lawmakers in civil societies in which parliamentarians aspire to fulfill the conditions of the social contract at the heart of the modern nation-state. [104] But in nations emerging from the inherently autocratic experience of colonialism, where the intelligentsia labors under a nonnative epistemological consciousness and where the continuity of the collective and converging historical memory has been severed, the logic expressed by Rousseau has had a very different kind of impact. Law develops incrementally and slowly as it strengthens its durability, authority, and legitimacy by recognizing, protecting, and promoting a matrix of interdependent and reciprocal interests and rights. But having been artificially grafted onto foreign cultures, without any real venues for the vetting of problems and inducing conciliations, contemporary legal systems in the Muslim world did not grow organically per a protracted negotiated dynamic in which the numerous institutional interests, such as the police, army, law guilds, labor unions, and numerous other amalgamations of social, commercial, and trade interests, could develop the fine art of reasonable accommodations and compromises within the context of a constructed sociocultural linguistic practice. In this context, it was inevitable that the judiciary and legal profession would become the guardians of the (imported) code and not of the law as an expression of the will of the people. The guardians of the code, like other institutions built, trained, and supplied by colonial powers such as the military and security forces, become the oligarchic and paternalistic caretakers of the objectified and patronized native. Instead of serving to counsel lawmakers to think of the best interests of the collectivity as they represent the sovereign people, Rousseau's quote aptly describes the elitist and paternalistic attitude of guardians of the legal code and also the military, which is the only other institution in society that possesses a de facto authority and power to force the obscured and absented native to emerge from his supposed backwardness.

All legal systems develop a linguistic practice that in essence is a professional linguistic code that simultaneously not just expresses but invents the categories, conceptions, and standards of law. The linguistic practice of a legal system is a professionalized regimen of symbolisms that define the boundaries of legal legitimacy and the parameters of inclusion and exclusion within a particular legal culture.[105] To help clarify what I mean by the linguistic practices of a legal culture, consider something as simple as standing up when, on the entry of a judge or judges into the courtroom, the court bailiff yells out: "All rise!" This linguistic practice comes with a virtual world of meaning acknowledging the authority and seriousness of the schematics of the judicial process and justice; it symbolizes a tacit affirmation of deference to the court; it objectifies the judge as a representative of the court and, among many other things, implies that those present in the courtroom recognize the judge as an impartial and unbiased adjudicator capable of achieving the possibility of justice. The more a legal system is rooted in its particular sociohistorical context, the more extensive the diffusion is between the linguistic practices of the legal system and the cultures that embrace it and that keep it alive.[106] Of course, this does not mean that the technicalities of the law or the precise linguistic practices of the legal system will be accurately portrayed in popular culture. But in order for the rule of law to become well established in a particular social setting, the authority of the legal system cannot simply rest on the threat of coercion. The legal system must have considerable normative weight, or, in other words, it must enjoy a level of credence as a mechanism for resolving disputes, settling conflicts, and achieving the possibility of justice. In order for members of society to act in accordance with the law, not only must society trust the legal system's fairness or effectiveness, but there must also be a demystification, popularization, and internal validation of the law in popular culture. At the cultural level, critical constitutive elements of the linguistic practices of the legal system are demystified and reduced to archetypal representative concepts that become normatively significant for the social authority of the law. The demystification of these essential constitutive elements is important for breaching some of the distance between legal culture and popular culture and for the creation of a level of social investment in and affinity to the law.[107] Without a level of social ownership, or perhaps what could be called cultural pride toward the law in the popular imagination, the legal system remains immersed in its professionalism and technicalities—indeed, the linguistic legalisms surround the law with barriers of mystification and sanctification. However, unless the rule of law becomes in the public's imagination integral to the rule of the people, the inescapable problem is that although the legal system insists on its mythologies of self-veneration and hallowed ceremonial performances, this does not have any normative resonance at the social and cultural levels. The threat of the use of force by the state does not create the rule of the law. The rule of law is a sense of settled normativity according to which most people, most of the time, consider what they understand to be the law authoritatively binding. This settled normativity could not be born by a simple act of legal draftsmanship or through the technical prowess of an elite group of legalists.[108] It takes a whole culture to uphold the rule of law, and not just a well-orchestrated regiment of punitive threats.

It is this serious deficit in legitimacy and in social effectiveness that drove most of the so-called Islamization initiatives of the 1970s and 1980s. The same autocratic state governments that imported foreign legal systems as elitist enterprises tried to rehabilitate the obvious breaches in their legitimacy by grafting laws of symbolic Islamicity. It is fair to say that by the end of the 1990s, it had become quite obvious that these Islamization legal initiatives were not a success. For one, they were no less elitist than the initiatives that led to the importation of foreign laws. But more importantly, although the idea of Islamicity did possess a considerable symbolic power by appealing to the idea of a lost authenticity, the reality was that these so-called Islamic laws were no more embedded in the cultural practices of Muslim societies than the foreign laws they were supposed to replace or supplement. The so-called Islamic laws, like those implemented in Pakistan, Sudan, and Nigeria, were projected ideological constructs of an imagined Islamicity, but they lacked normative cultural credibility. Indeed, in practically every society in which they were implemented, these Islamized laws were at odds with the normative cultural standards, or, put differently, these laws lacked the critical value of social reasonability.

It is not surprising that the Islamized laws implemented in a broad range of countries clashed with the epistemic consciousness of most modern Muslims. Whether one likes it or not, modern Muslims exist within the epistemic boundaries of an ever-shrinking globalized world and also within the confines of an ever-aggressive cosmopolitan culture. These so-called Islamization initiatives never really had a chance for success because they were implemented as ideological constructs steeped in political symbolism and dogma. Law, including the legal determinations associated with Shari'ah, cannot be the impetus for cultural transformations or social reforms. In fact, the very nature of legal systems is their inherent conservatism and reluctance to be at the forefront of change.[109] This does not mean that law can never initiate change. It does mean that the institution of law does not derive legitimacy from its radical or transformative potential—law derives legitimacy from its predictability, dependability, and conservatism in the vast majority of cases. But if they are to remain relevant and legitimate, the intricate balance that legal systems are forced to negotiate is the need for stability and the appearance of detachment and objectivity against effectuating enough change so as not to be seen as unreasonable and irrelevant. In all cases, those charged with enforcing or implementing a legal system shroud themselves in the protection of legal formalism and objectivity as they negotiate determinations in the name of the law. The true act of real genius comes from the ability of a jurist to employ creative negotiative linguistic practices to effect reasonable change. This means that the reasonableness, or lack thereof, of a legal system cannot be assessed except within the sociological and anthropological lived practice of such a system. Once European legal systems forced Islamic law out of the courtroom and Islamic jurisprudence became an ideological construct, it was perhaps inevitable that Islamic legal determinations would drift into the realm of sociological irrelevance and unreasonableness. As an ideological construct, Islamic law was forced to stand for what legal systems are ill equipped to do, and that is to somehow engage and transform the epistemological consciousness of cultural units. Whether the expectation is for a legal system to stem epistemological transformations taking place in societies and restore a historical consciousness or to produce a new epistemological awareness, such expectations are bound to come into considerable tension with the reality that raw legal commands or orders may obtain compliance but not commitment. As noted earlier, any legal command structure, if it is to obtain compliance through commitment and not just through the threat of violence, ultimately references a larger normative order or grundnorm on which the legitimacy of the legal commands is derived. Having run into a great deal of tension with the lived reality of contemporary Muslims, proponents of these laws found themselves driven to deemphasize the deductive and interpretive nature of such legal commandments and to emphasize these laws as the embodiment of Islamicity. In other words, hoping to overcome unyielding epistemological realities and to give the raw legal commandments power to earn commitment and compliance, proponents sought to endow the raw commandments with metaphysical truth. When laws that are inextricably fused with subjective human interests (for instance, patriarchal laws undermining the worth and dignity of women) are asserted as necessary extensions of metaphysical truth, this leads to a pronounced tension between the epistemological assumptions that spurred these laws into being in the first place and the epistemological realities persisting in society. This tension between rules of law camouflaging as the ultimate metaphysical truth and the societies wrestling with pressing epistemological realities will often become the very platform on which the utterly unreasonable and absurd is produced.

It would be useful at this point to elaborate on what is intended by the notion of reasonableness, or the lack of it. In the common-law system, the standard of reasonableness is employed in a wide variety of contexts in assessing, among other things, duties, approximate causation, breaches, and liability.[110] Reasonableness also plays a significant role in political theory and philosophy.[111] The concept has an unmistakable natural and functional appeal, especially when one is trying to describe what is socially acceptable and desirable as opposed to what is out of the ordinary or repugnant. But at the same time, it would not be intellectually difficult to challenge and deconstruct the very concept of reasonableness as too contingent on situational factors such as class, gender, and race. Although, like most evaluative standards, it tends to work in favor of the privileged and powerful, the fact remains that the concept of reasonableness has a natural appeal because of its affinity to the idea of rationality. Moreover, reasonableness connotes the ideas of moderation and balance, or what is fair and sensible. As such, reasonableness is not an empirical or quantitative standard, but it is an epistemic category that in most cases also translates into a normative value about what ought to be actively and purposefully sought.[112]

As I mentioned earlier, the episteme of reasonableness can be analyzed in terms of three evaluative categories. These three categories are (1) proportionality (*tanasub*) between means and ends; (2) balance (*tawazun*) between all valid interests and roles; and (3) measuredness (*talazum*) in that determinations are tailored to claims so as to preserve reciprocity between agents acting in a social setting. Each of these evaluative categories (*tanasub*, *tawazun*, and *talazum*) by itself is not determinative, but each is a methodological tool that helps ascertain whether a legal judgment, decision, or interpretation is balanced, fair, and relevant. The three evaluative categories help in assessing the ultimate epistemic question of reasonableness. Accordingly, in order to assess the reasonableness of a legal judgment or determination, it would make sense to evaluate the ways that such a determination affects the relationship between the intended ends and the means followed in pursuit of those ends. Moreover, it is necessary to analyze whether similar but competing interests and claims were fairly balanced. Finally, as importantly, it would be most probative to evaluate whether the legal decision fairly apprehended and responded to the legal issue at hand. If the legal decision, for whatever reason, fails to understand or respond to the substantive issue involved and, as a result, overreacts or underreacts—overlegislates or underlegislates, or is simply nonresponsive—this is a further indicator of its unreasonableness.

It is important to make clear that the concept of reasonableness that I reference here is a legal epistemic tool that needs to be differentiated from its conceptual companion, rationality or rationalism. Some might believe that the two concepts perform identical functions, and therefore they might question whether it is necessary to differentiate between reasonableness and rationality at all.[113] Rationality refers to the correct use of reason and to logical thinking. Rational thought produces logical results that are the outcome of precise structural reasoning. Reasonableness is a subjective assessment about the boundaries of rationality in a given context. On any specific issue, rationality will generate divergent results only to the extent that the first (elementary) assumptions made by rational agents could be different; reasonableness is far less determinative, and it is always assessed in terms of the desired or intended objectives. Put differently, rationality is an evaluation or assessment regarding the process of reasoning, but reasonableness is a judgment about the ultimate determination or range of determinations. I think that a couple of illustrations could help clarify my point. In the American legal system, it is very common for defendants convicted of aggravated felony charges to be sentenced to a term of years on each count of the indictment. At times the defendant will end up being sentenced to hundreds of years of imprisonment or will be sentenced to multiple life sentences to be served consecutively (i.e., one life sentence after the other). Unless we plan to imprison a convict's ghost, the idea that a person will serve more than one life sentence is irrational because it is not logical. Nevertheless, a legal decision that imposes several life sentences or a number of death penalties against a convict could be quite reasonable, depending on the functions served by such determinations. The internal legal culture, with its established patterns and practices and its formalized methods of negotiating the complex matrix of interests that are deeply vested in the mechanics of the legal system, in all probability have made this legal fiction the most efficient way to serve the interests of the legal system and of those who participate in it. Examples such as this, of determinations that serve a functional purpose within a legal system and that are reasonable but not necessarily rational or logical, abound in the institutions of law.[114] Similarly, there are many situations where legal institutions will adopt irrebuttable presumptions that do not necessarily accord with logic but that do serve, or once served, a reasonable functional purpose. Take, for instance, the presumptive period of gestation adopted by different schools of thought in Islamic law. In the Hanafi school of law, the maximum period of gestation is two years; the Shafi'i and Hanbali schools say four years; and the Maliki school says five.[115] Furthermore, in the case of a wife whose husband has gone missing, where it is not known if he is alive or dead and when there is no further news of his fate, Islamic legal schools disagree as to when the missing husband may be presumed to be deceased and his wife should be free to remarry. The Hanafi school, the majority of the Shafi'is, and some Hanbalis argued that the relevant period of time is the average life span of a similarly situated male. The wife of a missing husband would be forced to wait until the presumptive average life span of her missing husband has passed, after which the wife assumes the status of a widow and may remarry. Other Shafi'i and Hanbali jurists maintained that the missing husband will be presumed to be alive until reaching his ninetieth birthday, and if no information about the missing husband surfaces by then, the husband is presumed dead, and his wife may remarry. It is reported that Abu Hanifa argued that the appropriate presumptive age for the missing husband should be 120 years, and thus unless the fate of the missing husband is established by preponderance of the evidence, the wife will not be allowed to remarry, while the Maliki school argued that the appropriate presumptive waiting period for the missing husband should be four years.[116]

Legal rules relating to periods of gestation, or the presumptive period of absence before a husband is assumed to be dead, had nothing to do with practical reasoning or logic and very little to do with the physiological realities of pregnancies and life expectancies. Muslim jurists were well aware of the stages of fetus development and of the natural period needed to bring a pregnancy to term, and it is clear from their debates that in a time before the creation of birth certificates, the precise age of people was often subject to social negotiation and mediation. These rulings and debates, however, had everything to do with the legal precedents and mechanics of law established in each legal guild. Especially when these legal positions were first developed, they responded to methodological imperatives within each legal guild as well as to contextual factors relating to the functional objectives of each school of thought. So, for instance, in the case of the gestation debates, the presumptive periods served reasonable functional goals such as providing social identity and welfare to children who would otherwise become orphans. Similarly, on the question of disappeared husbands, the presumptions are not meant to be realistic measurements of the actual life expectancy of men. Again, the reasonableness of these rules are a function of the internal logic and methodological imperatives of each legal school of thought, and also the social functions that triggered the creation of these rules in the first place. In their genesis, these legal debates reflected social concerns about ensuring that the wives of missing men have a continuous source of financial support as well as an undisputed interest in the marital property and custody of the children to a marriage without their claims being contested by the deceased husband's surviving family members. More importantly, when these rules were first formed centuries ago, husbands went missing during trade and military expeditions all the time without there being a dependable way of proving life or death in most cases. Hence, most juristic schools preferred that the wives of missing husbands sue for dissolution of marriage rather than declaring the husband dead and the wife a widow. Legal systems are not always troubled by contradictions and paradoxes, but as a number of theorists have argued, the resolution of paradoxes can be an opportunity for the legal system to grow.[117]

I return to my earlier point about rationality, reasonableness, and law. Very recently, modern critics of Islamic law in Egypt cited the doctrines discussed above regarding periods of gestation as proof that Islamic law is irrational.[118] But it is hardly surprising that the very similar rules including a ten-month gestation period and a presumptive unnaturally long time period before a missing person is presumed dead are found in the common-law system as well as other legal systems.[119] The real challenge is that legal determinations that at one time might have constituted a reasonable accommodation of practical interests could lose their reasonableness with the passage of time. But as long as a legal system remains active, viable, and living, there persists the possibility that the legal system will self-correct and reengage reasonability once again. The problem is that reasonability becomes a real challenge when a legal system is deactivated or disconnected from its social lifeline. If a legal system is no longer energized by a living social practice that challenges it and that forces it to revise and develop, instead of the common jurisprudential phenomenon of lag time, which is the normally slow pace by which a legal system responds to changing social and cultural circumstances, the legal system suffers outright lethargy before becoming frozen in time. If the practitioners of a jurisprudential system, in the name of legal flexibility and responsiveness, ignore methodological discipline and toss aside tradition, they risk the dissolution of the legal system into chaos and anarchy. But no less disastrous is when what some described as the "tenacity of the law" becomes so obstinate and resistant to change that the practitioners of the system assert rules that once represented reasonable accommodations as normatively absolute objectives. But this kind of jurisprudential breakdown and total failure is far more likely when a legal system is fossilized and thus is effectively forced into a persistent state of unreasonableness.

I will use a final example to help illustrate my argument about jurisprudential lethargy and reasonableness, or the lack of it. A few years ago, the chair of the department of hadith studies at Azhar University, Professor 'Izzat 'Atiyya, raised a storm of protest and ridicule when, in response to a question, he stated that if male and female coworkers wished to avoid unlawful seclusion at their place of employment, it is permissible for the female to suckle the male worker so that he may drink her breast milk, and in doing so they become as if siblings prohibited to each other in marriage but allowed to commingle without restriction. 'Atiyya risked treading into the realm of the kinky when he elaborated that the male worker may suckle directly from the woman's breast, lips to nipple, without an intervening instrument such as a baby bottle. The reaction to this opinion was heated—while apologists on behalf of Islamic law insisted that 'Atiyya's opinion was baseless and that he dreamed the whole thing up, other critics cited it as yet another example of

the bizarre results brought about by religious law.[120] It is certainly understandable that some sought to dismiss this *fatwa* (nonbinding legal opinion)
as an unrepresentative oddity while others were tempted to see it as symptomatic of the entire Islamic legal tradition. However, both of these perspectives miss the point. 'Atiyya did not fabricate his *fatwa* from thin air, but at
the same time, the real question is what do *fatawa* that push the limits of
social credibility communicate about the role of Islamic law today?[121] The
genesis of 'Atiyya's *fatwa* is in the law of the so-called suckling siblings—
siblings-in-law not because of a blood relationship but because they were
suckled by the same women. The practice of considering children suckled by
the same woman as if brother and sister and so prohibited to each other in
marriage was pre-Islamic. The social taboo against sexual relations between
suckling siblings was a well-attested custom in Arabia before Islam, but it
was adopted and confirmed by the Qur'an.[122]

The use of wet-nurses was a well-established socioeconomic practice
throughout the Near East, and for a variety of reasons, prohibiting the marriage of suckling siblings became important for the reinforcement of a famil-
ial-like network of relationships. Wet-nurses were from weaker and less
affluent families, but the creation of familial bonds to strengthen the relationship of patronage between families of unequal wealth and status served significant practical purposes. With the development of Islamic jurisprudence,
as was the case with the vast majority of legal issues, early jurists of the
second/ninth century confronted a variety of competing precedents and
trends dealing with what constitutes breast-feeding or a suckling that would
trigger the special familial status. Early precedents, prior to the systematization of Islamic law, represented competing orientations—each orientation
represented by what I previously called an authorial enterprise culminating in
a report attributed to the Prophet, his family, or one of the companions. Each
of the reports represented an early legal initiative—a nascent attempt at intro-
ducing a norm setting legal doctrine that in the great majority of cases was
unsuccessful. Therefore, we find reports (authorial enterprises) that defined
suckling very strictly—any amount of suckling, even for the briefest of times
and for whatever purpose, would trigger the special relationship. Other reports emphasized that only a full and meaningful hunger-satisfying suckling
would be legally effective. Some reports insisted that this law only applies to
children at the age of suckling. So, for instance, if a three-year-old was
breast-fed, this would be legally ineffective. Still other reports asserted that
since establishing exact age is difficult, the law is intended to apply to children but not to adults. However, other reports seemed to negotiate the issue
for entirely different purposes. And so we find that in some reports, suckling
becomes an instrument or tool to overcome restrictions on the private intermingling of men and women in intimate settings. According to these authorial enterprises, Aisha, the Prophet's wife, who when it comes to gender relations is often cast in the role of the subversive mutineer, is reported to have
used the suckling law to overcome the rules of seclusion. In these reports,
after the Prophet's death, when Aisha would want to meet and converse with
a man privately, she would have her niece suckle the man so that he becomes
as if a brother to her. Not surprisingly, other authorial enterprises claimed

that the other wives of the Prophet strongly disagreed with Aisha's purported practice.

Importantly, during the process of systematization and consolidation of Islamic law into the standardized legal guilds, Muslim classical jurists sifted and netted through the competing early authorial enterprises. Through this process, the range of accepted disagreements was considerably narrowed, and some early competing norms, such as Aisha's subversive reports, were marginalized and eventually forgotten. [123] After the period of juristic consolidation, the regularized and accepted legal standards specified that in order for a suckling relationship to be established, the suckling must occur when the child was two years or younger, and the range of accepted disagreements focused on how substantial or extensive the child must have been breast-fed by the milk mother. [124] From this vantage point, there are several points that need to be underscored. As with so many other legal issues, within the first century of Islam several competing doctrinal positions emerged, taking the form of reports constructed by authorial enterprises and attributed to notable figures such as the Prophet or one of his relatives or disciples. In its heyday, Islamic law had the mechanisms and institutions to engage, mediate, and filter through the myriad of inconsistent and at times chaotic reports. After engaging this unsystematic raw material, Muslim jurists generated a range of determinations that were contextually reasonable—they balanced between the legally normative positions, the social impact of these positions, the relationship between the imperatives of law and the social adaptability, and acceptability of these laws. After a legal order becomes more developed, systematic, and institutionalized, it tends to labor under the weight of its own doctrinal commitments and precedents. On the one hand, a law rooted in a social setting will impact societal norms so that the law will help stabilize society, and, in turn, society will allow the law greater stability as the legal system becomes more anchored and also more authoritative. As noted earlier, change never ceases to take place in living legal systems, but the more encumbered a legal system becomes by its own development and sophistication, the greater the level of specialized technical skill required to give effect to the necessary changes in the legal system.

'Atiyya's *fatwa* is a rather stark demonstration of what happens on the unraveling of a legal system. One cannot help but notice that 'Atiyya effectively takes Islamic law back to its preformative period, ignoring the remarkable efforts made by generations of early jurists to standardize legal doctrines and eject outliers and marginal traditions. Suddenly, in the hands of contemporary pundits such as 'Atiyya, Islamic law had regressed hundreds of years back, as long-discredited and marginalized narratives were brought back to life and reasserted in the modern age. In many ways, contemporary Muslims are forced to deal with the raw material—the oral traditions—of Islamic law without the mediating influence of the juristic methods employed within a living institutional context. What enabled Islamic law to persevere for many centuries as a living, authoritative, normative system was that it effectively negotiated the epistemological demands of the times and places in which it existed. Furthermore, through many centuries, functionaries of the Islamic legal system, the *fuqaha'* (jurists), interacted with and thrived in a remarkably rich tapestry of diverse cultures. As is evidenced by numerous topics, such as the history of music and dance, the architecture of sacred spaces, the complex matrix of religious endowments (*awqaf*), or the legal anthropology of commercial instruments, the lived realities of Islamic law were far more complex and multilayered than any of inherited hornbooks of positive law (*ahkam*) would have led one to believe. This is not surprising. All common-law-like legal systems, and perhaps all legal systems, cannot be understood by studying hornbooks, which lay out the proverbial alphabet of the legal order but do not allow much insight into a legal order's vocabulary or sentence structures. Islamic legal studies teach a familiar lesson in the field of comparative law—the law as the command of the sovereign explains little about the functions of law or the rule of a legal order. Far more substantively, law is a commonly accepted standard, a self-enforcing normative obligation, and an authoritative set of commands that earn social deference and respect.[125] The key to a legitimate legal order is persuasion because the threat of the use of force can earn obedience, but it also generates what is known as passive resistance. Fear will compel people to submit to the power of threats, but at the same time that people formally submit and appear to surrender their will, they also creatively invent countless and nearly imperceptible ways to resist and subvert the functions of the law.[126] Legal rules do not need to be consistent with formal or propositional logic, but they need to be rational, in the sense that they need to be seen as reasonable within the epistemological paradigms of their historic place and time. For the law to succeed in setting normative common standards and in earning persuasive deferential authority, the legal system must succeed in convincing its subjects that in most cases it is capable of achieving justness and that in most cases, even if its language and technicalities are not accessible and understandable, its outcomes or determinations are mostly fair.

Earlier in this book, I discussed the controversy surrounding Shaykh Muhammad al-Ghazali's (d. 1416/1996) critique of puritanical Islam. I want to return to this controversy but with a different emphasis. One of al-Ghazali's main points of protest was what he described as the marginalization of the intellect and reason in contemporary Islamic discourses. Al-Ghazali faulted the puritanical movement for deconstructing the rationalism of the juristic method by elevating the literal text over the dictates of reason. Al-Ghazali argued that there are many transmitted texts including oral traditions attributed to the Prophet that cannot possibly be consistent with reason. Al-Ghazali referred to long-established legal maxims that whatever is a rational impossibility cannot be the basis for legal obligations in Islamic law.[127] What al-Ghazali meant here was not just the rationality of the legal determination, but even more foundationally, he argued that Muslim jurists must be able to decide whether a particular hadith or claimed Sunna is authentic or a fabrication by studying the substantive (*matn*) claims of the report and not just the history of its transmission (*isnad*). If the substance of the report is logically impossible or contrary to scientific knowledge, the report must be dismissed as a forgery. Although al-Ghazali was severely criticized for this argument, the reality is that the debate as to what extent reason should be used to interrogate and filter through oral traditions attributed to the Prophet has persisted for centuries. Many of the hadith attributed to the Prophet that bothered al-Ghazali and that gave him much reason to pause were the same exact reports that raised heated debates centuries ago.[128] There is, however, a subtle but critical difference between the modern and premodern Muslim debates. The premodern classical debates were led by jurists who sought to defend the authority and integrity of the legal system against unfettered speculative reasoning, which by the nature of their roles as functionaries of law they saw as too whimsical. For the juristic class, this meant defending the epistemology of law by trying to differentiate it from speculative metaphysics, or ultimate philosophies of truth.

The classical juristic discourses were not so much about whether reason should trump revelation or vice versa but about the appropriate balance to be struck between the spheres of revelation and reason. Contrary to what modern Puritanical-Salafis believe, the debate was rarely about conceding categorical supremacy to reason over revelation or the other way around. Instead, the debate focused on the instrumentalities for evaluating obligation and causality each in its proper sphere of relevance, meaning that the primary preoccupation of this debate was that the miraculous, or what falls outside the realm of physical causation, could not be logically proved or disproved. Therefore, the thrust of many of the arguments made by jurists, as opposed to philosophers, was to prove the rationality of revelation and the possibility of knowledge through it. This did not necessarily mean that reason had no role in assessing the authenticity of revelation or that reason was marginal in the presence of revelation. Contrary to what many contemporary Muslims believe, most classical jurists did not reject reason, but they did argue against philosophical metaphysics.[129]

If one places the discourses of classical jurists within their historically bounded epistemological context, it becomes apparent that they were not opposed to either rationality or reason. Take, for instance, someone such as Abu Hamid al-Ghazali (d. 505/1111)—someone who is frequently vilified by contemporary secularists for his claimed antirationalism.[130] Al-Ghazali clearly thought of reason as no less critical than revelation in discerning the path of righteousness and in establishing normative obligations in a social context. In his *Reviving the Religious Sciences* (*Ihya' 'Ulum al-Din*), al-Ghazali states: "*Al-'aql* (reason or intellect) is the source and fountainhead of knowledge as well as its foundation. Knowledge sprouts from it as the fruit does from a tree, and as light emits from the sun, and as vision extends from eyes. How then could that which is the means of happiness in this world, and in the Hereafter not be most noble or how could it ever be doubted?"[131] In a different work, al-Ghazali makes a case for the twin pillars of revelation and reason. He writes: "For reason is like healthy sight that has no ailments or flaws, and the Qur'an is like the sun that shines abroad. . . . For someone who declines to use reason, being satisfied with just the light of the Qur'an is like someone who stands in the light of the sun with his eyes shut. There is no difference between that person and someone who is blind. For reason together with the Qur'an is 'light upon light.' Someone who has his eyes trained exclusively on only one of these two will remain bound in delusion."[132] The same theme is, again, eloquently affirmed by the same author in a different passage:

The best fields of knowledge are those which combine the methods of revelation and reason, and that integrate reasoned judgment with textual authority. The science of jurisprudence (*usul al-fiqh*) is one such field of knowledge because it relies on sound reason and revelation equally. Its determinations are not derived from reason alone without validation from revelation, and such determinations are not dependent on simple imitation without the critical assessments of reason. Reason and revelation are bound together—one cannot work without the other. [133]

Contemporary Muslims often forget that among the most vilified groups in Islamic history were those given the derogatory label al-Hashawiyya—fideistic Ahl al-Hadith, often portrayed as thuggish boors and dunces. The so-called Hashawiyya rejected reason and considered that the only reliable sources of knowledge and authority are traditions and reports that must be understood in a strict literal sense. So it is not surprising when we find Abu Hamid al-Ghazali asserting that among those who have been a blight and scourge on Islam are those known as the Hashawiyya, who emphasize rigid imitation and the superficial and pedantic because of their ignorance, intellectual incompetence, and lack of rational abilities. [134] As I mentioned earlier, because of the Wahhabis' rigidity and intolerance, on their emergence they were often described as the "Hashawiyya of our time." An apt and powerful description of the Hashawiyya's image throughout Islamic history was provided in the beginning of the twentieth century by Muhammad Zahid al-Kawthari (d. 1371/1951) who described them as closed-minded and ignorant as well as heartless, brutish, and intolerant. They are always hostile to rational scholars, men of science, and philosophers, and they end up persecuting and oppressing their opponents, and wherever they rise to power they destroy all intellectually rigorous books. Furthermore, according to al-Kawthari, they rise to prominence when Muslims are in a state of weakness, and when they do rise, people become revolted by religion and atheism becomes a widespread phenomenon. [135]

In essence, what was so troubling about the Hashawiyya was not their textualism or strict constructionism, although both were contributing factors. What was so bothersome was their unreasonableness; specifically, the way they failed to negotiate between their simplistic textual understandings and the complex social and cultural settings that they encountered. In Islamic history, the Hashawiyya became an archetypal reference to unreasonableness from the emergence of the label, probably in the second century, up to the time it was used to describe the Wahhabis of Arabia. [136] Moreover, as the contemporary scholar Fathi al-Dirini had emphasized, one of the essential characteristics of Islamic jurisprudence is the evaluation of the consequences that follow from laws and acts (*ma'alat al-af'al wa al-ahkam*). [137] Therefore, the imposition of any law without regard to its social, economic, and political consequences is by definition illogical. One of the often-repeated principles of Islamic jurisprudence is that an implicit condition of all rulings is their *ma'quliyya*. *Ma'quliyya* is usually translated as rationality in the sense that the ruling cannot contradict reason. One of the expressions firmly implanted in the linguistic practice of the classical jurisprudence was that the *shart* (condition) of valid rulings is the following: *law 'uridat al-ahkam 'ala al-'uqul al-rajiha la talaqatha bi'l qubul wa al-rujhan* (a condition of valid rulings is that they be accepted and preferred by rational minds).[138] Similarly, among the often-repeated expressions in the linguistic practice of the classical jurisprudential tradition was "Reason and Shari'ah are intertwined twins that cannot be separated" (*al-'aql wa al-shari'a sinwani mutalaziman la yaftariqan*).[139] The gist of these phrases and principles is to say that whatever is illogical or irrational cannot legally stand.[140] The example often given in Islamic jurisprudence is that no one may be heard to claim that plagues are not contagious because all logical evidence and scientific knowledge clearly indicate otherwise.[141] But beyond the questions of scientific reconcilability, there remains the far more complicated issue of the social functionality of the law. As has been long recognized by Islamic jurisprudence, legal facts are distinct and separate from scientific or objective empirical facts. For instance, when the law decides someone's guilt or liability, it is not establishing empirical or scientific facts. Instead, the law determines facts that are recognizable per a set of procedural rules or a preestablished process that defines what is legally relevant and admissible as opposed to the inapposite and inadmissible. There might be very good reasons, policy, moral, and otherwise, for the law not to abide by scientific or empirical data, but in all cases, it would be a mistake to assume that the only type of rationality that matters to a legal system is scientific logic.

Many contemporary Muslim jurists have tried to augment the relevance and responsiveness of Islamic jurisprudence by arguing for paradigm shifts toward what they have described as *fiqh al-waqi'* (practical jurisprudence) or *fiqh al-awlawiyyat* (jurisprudence of priorities).[142] I think that this only bolsters the case for reasonableness as a critical value for the functioning of the Islamic legal system in the contemporary Muslim world. Indeed, when it comes to the discourses on reason and intellect in the context of Islamic law, it is fair to say that in speaking about the role of *'aqlaniyya* (reasonableness) in the production of legal determinations, what they meant is something very close to the idea of reasonableness. Time and again, whether speaking about the customs and practices of societies, or the achievements of *maslaha* (general welfare), or preferring a determination based on equitable consideration instead of simply following the rule of precedent and strict constructionism—in all these cases, Muslim jurists are searching for legal solutions that would reasonably accommodate social realities instead of colliding with them. In fact, I do not think it is an exaggeration to claim that it is reasonableness—or the appearance of being a reasonable, responsive, fair, and relevant system of law—that is the biggest challenge confronting Islamic law today. Without theorizing and establishing reasonableness as a normative value that becomes ingrained in the consciousness of students of Islamic law, the Islamic legal system will continue to risk marginality in the modern age. As I noted earlier, reasonableness is all the more important because Islamic law in the modern nation-state cannot rely on the compulsory powers of the state to obtain compliance but must establish its authority from an internal perspective of the law, where it must rely on persuasion and voluntary deference in order to establish its authority.

One of the more interesting reformers of the early twentieth century, Muhammad bin al-Hasan al-Hajawi al-Tha'alibi (d. 1376/1956), in his study of the history of Islamic jurisprudence, commented that scholars have a habit of "seeking refuge in the powers of the state, or in the zeal of the masses, only when their abilities falter and powers of persuasion wane, and they fear that their deficiencies will become exposed."[143] Al-Tha'alibi's comment was made in the context of his magnum opus evaluating the reasons for intellectual stagnation in the Muslim world—a study in which he complains bitterly about the intellectual dullness and ineptitude of jurists in his age.[144] Like many of the reformers at the dawn of the twentieth century, al-Tha'alibi was a firm believer in the twin pillars of revelation and reason, and although a relentless critic of blind imitation (*taqlid*), he expressed a great deal of confidence and pride in the collective jurisprudential heritage of Islam. Al-Tha'alibi argued that the study and development of the intellectual heritage of the *fiqh* is essential for the survival, preservation, and promotion of Islam itself. However, he goes to considerable length to emphasize that *fiqh* is quintessentially a methodology and process that searches for justice and for the rights and interests of people.[145] In many ways, al-Tha'alibi understood *fiqh* as a kind of natural law in that, in his view, if a rule of *fiqh* leads to injustice, oppression, or harm, it simply cannot be a part of the valid law of God.

I raise al-Tha'alibi's arguments here because they help pinpoint issues that have only become more pressing and urgent in the twenty-first century. Like many of the reformers of his age, al-Tha'alibi conflated Islamic jurisprudence as a repository of methodologies and normative principles aimed at achieving ultimate moral (Shari'ah) goals, and *fiqh* as a set of rulings that might or might not embody the ultimate values of natural law or natural goodness. Al-Tha'alibi and many other jurists at the wake of modernity continued to value the *fiqh* tradition while simultaneously condemning *taqlid* and calling for *ijtihad*.[146] Although this appeared contradictory to the increasingly secularized and Westernized intelligentsia of the twentieth century, jurists such as al-Tha'alibi understood the *fiqh* tradition to be a normative discourse—an intellectual investigation for divine norms sought out and analyzed through the mechanics of textuality and reason. As the very logic of *ijtihad* dictates, the point of *fiqh* is the exertion of due diligence in searching for the profound implications of living through the divine and with the divine. And as the word *fiqh* implies, the *understanding* that is sought after is the pursuit of the full meaning of being God's vicegerents (*khulafa' fi al-ard*) and of bearing witness for God (*shuhada' li'llah*). The purpose of *fiqh* is not just the *ahkam* (positive rules), but more importantly, the objective is to investigate and engage the ethos of living with divinity. This is precisely why numerous jurists from Shihab al-Din al-Qarafi (d. 684/1285), Ibn Qayyim al-Jawziyya (d. 751/1350), and Abu Ishaq al-Shatibi (d. 790/1388) to 'Abd al-Rahman al-Kawakibi (d. 1320/1902), Muhammad bin al-Hasan al-Hajawi al-Tha'alibi, and Muhammad bin Tahir Ibn 'Ashur (d. 1393/1973) argued that the objectives of the processes of *fiqh* are essential ethos as basic as justice, goodness, or the fulfillment of the material interests of people. In effect, being mindful of the principle that God's law exists for the benefit of human beings, and not in any way to augment or add to God, these jurists believed that living with divinity should not, under any circumstances, lead to suffering injustice, deprivation, or degradation. In often-repeated dogma of Islamic jurisprudence, the laws of the divine have not been decreed for their own sake, but all laws are conditioned on the achievement of desired goods, and these goods necessarily consist of the well-being of human beings.[147] Nevertheless, what becomes a moral predicament threatening a complete epistemic collapse is when the engagement with the divine results in harm and suffering instead of the opposite. At this point, the searcher for the divine ethos is forced into a dialectic that could lead to the undermining of the entire *fiqh* enterprise. Either the searcher will cling to pietistic fictions denying people's suffering, or denying their ability to know that they are suffering, or the searcher will acknowledge the failure and rely on her/his rational faculties to reconstitute and reconstruct the way he/she experiences, comprehends, and interprets living with the divine. But this is precisely where the temptation to resort to the compulsory powers of the state is the strongest. The easiest way to avoid having to rise up to the intellectual challenge posed by the contradictions and the imperative of renovation and reconstruction is to seek refuge in the authority of the state. By seeking refuge in the authority of the state, I do not just mean relying on the state to force compliance with rules that could be producing a great deal of suffering and harm. No less devastating is the tendency of the *'ulama* to attempt to rely on their state-defined roles and on their institutional affiliations as functionaries of the state in order to demand authority and deference without having to exert themselves in earning the people's trust or in persuading them. This reality can be observed in numerous places of the Muslim world. The modern-day *'ulama* have become lethargic, indolent, and intellectually ineffective. They habitually surround themselves with layers of apologetics and formulaic responses that very often border on the intellectually inane and farcical. Therefore, *'ulama* from Egypt or Sudan to Saudi Arabia and Iran will often act as if by virtue of their position as state-appointed clergy, that they are entitled to be the custodians of Islam and thus are entitled to deference and obedience. In these and other countries, the *'ulama* have developed a parasitical relationship with the state in which the state institutionalized and bureaucratized their function, and so they are able to demand deference not on the basis of conviction and persuasion but on the basis that they are part of the state apparatus. However, the state-salaried *'ulama* have become intellectually inert, and I dare say slothful, to the point that they seem to be locked in an epistemological lacuna where they attempt to derive legitimacy from a tradition that they no longer represent or from states that are despotic and unrepresentative.

The Maliki jurist Ibn 'Ashur, in an extensive body of work, argued that the basic and most fundamental value of Shari'ah is freedom and that the Islamic message as a whole is a ceaseless rebellion against despotism and tyranny.[148] The problem, however, is that standing up to despotism and injustice is the challenge undertaken by those who stand against, not with, power. I do not mean to take away from the enlightened contributions of Ibn 'Ashur, and in fact, for the most part I agree with him. But I do want to emphasize that the means of promoting the *fiqh* tradition in the contemporary nation-state can only be through voluntary normative compliance. Although the Shari'ah consists of foundational ethical and constitutional norms that can act as organizing principles for society, a democratic state cannot coercively enforce the *fiqh* tradition. By its very nature, the *fiqh* tradition is pluralistic and diverse—it is not a set of determinations but a process of reasoning and wrestling with the implications of divinity in human life. As such, the normativities that arise from the *fiqh* process are dependent on volition and persuasion. The moment *fiqh* is coercively enforced, it loses a critical precondition for its validity, and that is voluntary deference and acceptance. Engaging in the process of reasoning through the divine norms, searching for God's guidance, and honoring the divine law is itself a constant act of supplication and worship. Presenting the results of one's search to others is an act of witnessing and testifying (*shahada*). In rendering this testimony, abiding by an epistemological imperative of reasonableness is practicing al-Kindi's virtue (*fadila*) of moderation (*wasatiyya*). As the one-time Shaykh al-Azhar 'Abd al-Halim Mahmoud (d. 1398/1978) recognized decades ago, al-Kindi's philosophical emphasis on the Aristotelian virtue of moderation is firmly anchored in Qur'anic morality and the Islamic tradition.[149]

Chapter Eleven

Beyond a Reasonable Shari'ah

BEYOND REASONABLENESS: AN ETHICAL APPROACH TO SHARI'AH

Reasonableness is a virtue, but it rests on perhaps an obvious assumption. I assume that when God commands people to pursue ethical values such as justice, mercy, compassion, kindness, or faithfulness that these words have meanings. If they did not have meaning, then God would be speaking frivolously, which is theologically impossible. Furthermore, I assume that God knows that the only way these words will have meaning for us as human beings is through the way we use language—through the tools used in semiotics and hermeneutics. Moreover, I assume that all divine commands regarding doing what is good and beautiful are made with the full expectation and knowledge that the only way we human beings can make sense of semiotic communications is through what we now call epistemology—our knowledge structure and its system. The same Creator who created the intellect also gave that intellect volition and choice. This fact, in and of itself, sets numerous moral boundaries because creation is sacrosanct. So, for example, the Qur'an exclaims: "If your Lord would have willed, all people on earth, without exception, would have believed. So would you compel people to become believers?"[1] In this instant, the text confirms what is accessible to a believer through rational insight, and that is, one cannot undo by human law what was created by God. This belief in human volition is not a libertarian position. A truly libertarian position would necessarily have to accept that the world is perfectly intelligible without an assumption of a creator and law giver, and as a believing Muslim, this I do not concede. But does the fact that there is divine law mean that our rational faculties can only be used hermeneutically in interpreting revelation and nothing else? No, I do not believe that this follows, either. Usually, the argument goes something like this: if one believes in an immutable, omnipotent, and all-powerful God who is the law giver, then it follows that revelation defines what is right or wrong. In other words, there is no inherent right or wrong—something is right because

359

God allowed it or wrong because God forbade it. If so, the argument goes, if God had willed, God could have commanded whatever God pleases—God and God alone could determine what is good or bad, and our sole role as human beings is to submit. As the argument goes, all right and wrong comes from the sheer will of God, and if God so willed, God could have made what is wrong right and also the opposite. God could have ordered us to disbelieve, be unjust, tell lies, and murder, and it would have been fair and good because God said so.[2] But this line of thinking is flawed because it argues the impossible. It is akin to arguing that if God had willed, God could have made us cockroaches, and that because of this possibility (or impossibility), such-and-such follows. The fact is that as human beings we are subject to the laws of humanity that are etched into our very being—these laws are embedded in our cognition and consciousness and are as stable and unwavering as the laws of mathematics or the logic that defines material reality. These are laws of rational elements that allow us to have a shared language about justice, ethics, values, happiness, misery, and beauty.

The divine text repeatedly and persistently refers to ethical concepts and invokes intuition, memory, and rational insight as means to access what is embedded and inherent in and to humanity.[3] Does the fact that the Qur'anic text makes consistent references to ethical concepts as if they have an embedded and inherent meaning help us avoid the debate as to whether natural law preceded divine law or resulted from it? I am not sure. But I do believe that revelation or divine speech has to make sense, and if God spoke in a language that is entirely self-referential, this would create an insurmountable theological problem. If I say to my son, "Be fair to your sister!" that does suppose that I am assuming my son has some understanding of fairness. Now, I might tell my son, "Be fair to your sister, and do not monopolize the computer!" If my son assumes that as long as he shares the computer, he is free to torment his sister as much as he wishes, it would be fair to conclude that my son is either mean-spirited, or an imbecile, or both. Moreover, if on my death my son gives his sister the computer (which by then is quite outdated) and on forging my last testament steals the family estate, I think it would be safe to conclude that my son has not honored my instructions to be fair to his sister. Alas, when I told my son to be fair to his sister and share the computer, I was counting on my son having both common sense and also a moral compass so that he would not subvert the ethical message behind the lesson I sought to impart.

My point is that not only do all linguistic communications assume an epistemological context, but also that specified instructions negotiate meaning within that broader context. So when the Qur'an, for example, invokes ethical and moral terminology, it necessarily assumes a preexisting epistemological context in which it operates and also a moral trajectory that it seeks to engage and negotiate. When the Qur'an sets out specific instructions about a particular situation or issue, these instructions must be analyzed in terms of the moral purpose and trajectory that elicited the instructions in the first place. It is not acceptable or sufficient for one to contend that more specific or particularized instructions narrow and limit broad or general commands and could possibly embody or define them.[4] For example, the Qur'an repeatedly commands Muslims to be just and fair. At the same time, on a specific question involving inheritance, it mandates that female siblings inherit half of what male siblings would inherit. The common approach in Islamic juris-prudence is to maintain that the inheritance rule by definition is just and fair forever, as if the imperative of justice and fairness are forever hinged on this contingency—that is, that women inherit half of what men inherit. New interpretive and explorative possibilities are opened if the inheritance rule is approached as but a part of a Qur'anic normative project and moral trajectory in which the interpreter seeks to analyze and understand the epistemology of justice and fairness in the divine text.

Numerous oral reports in the Islamic tradition describe the very mission of the Prophet Muhammad as part and parcel of an ethical project—a project that builds on and develops people's natural ethical being. This is only bol-stered by the text of the Qur'an, in which God praises Muhammad for his moral rectitude and ethics.[5] There are numerous reports attributed to the Prophet emphasizing the inextricable relationship between ethics and Islam. One such report states: "The most beloved among you to me are those who are of the noblest character."[6] Furthermore, at the very roots of Islamic theology is the demanding and inspiring dogma that Muhammad was sent but as a mercy to humankind.[7] Early Muslim generations, inspired by this envisioned ethical project and challenged by the influx of new Muslims from conquered territories were driven to investigate what eventually became known as *'ilm al-akhlaq* (the science of virtues and ethical obligations). In the second/eighth and third/ninth centuries, as the emerging classes of Mus-lim theologians and jurists wrestled with the implications of divinity, values, and normativity, a very substantial translation movement swept through the nascent Islamic civilization. This translation movement produced numerous studies and commentaries on Greek philosophy, including Aristotle, whom Muslim philosophers fondly labeled "the teacher" (*al-ustadh*).[8] From there on, the discourses on ethics and divinity take four epistemologically bound trajectories, each with a very different social context and very different ob-jectives.

The first of these epistemological trajectories is what Joel Kraemer appro-priately called the humanistic orientation in Islam.[9] As Kraemer explains:

> The overriding objective of the Islamic humanists was to revive the ancient *philosophic* legacy as formative of mind and character. . . . The philosophers considered the ultimate aim of man to be happiness (eudaimonia/sa'ada). Hap-piness, they thought, is achieved through the perfection of virtue, preeminently by the exercise of reason. Attainment of this happiness, or perfection, was said to be something divine. . . . They depicted this attainment, in noetic terms, as the conjoining of man's (particular) intellect with the divine (universal) intel-lect. The end of man was conceived as being his self-realization as a god-like being—we may say his "deification." By rising above the perturbations of sense and the disquiet of the emotions to the serene realm of the intellect and the divine, the philosophical man escapes worldly anxiety (qalaq) and reaches tranquility (sakina).[10]

Most of these ethical approaches were peripatetic and focused on the pursuit of happiness in noetic terms, or through the attainments of the intellect. The peripatetic philosophers were interested in normative obligations that follow

from the knowledge of *haqiqat al-ashya'* (the truth of things) as an intellectual attainment, and not necessarily in positive law. At least for those capable
of attaining intellectual happiness, it was understood that legal commandments and obedience had little to do with the pursuit and fulfillment of
happiness in noetic terms.

The second of the epistemological trajectories in early Islam was that of
the ascetic perennial philosophy of Sufism. Although it is impossible to date
the birth of philosophical Sufism, as an esoteric and transcendental epistemology it is clear that it was among the earliest Islamic creeds. The Muslim
philosopher and scientist Abu Rayhan al-Biruni (d. 440/1048) suggested that
the etymology of the word *Sufi* or *al-Sufiyya* is derived from the Greek *sofia*,
meaning wisdom.[11] Whether Biruni's claim is accurate or not, many of the
Sufi philosophers, such as Ibn 'Ajiba (d. 1224/1809), Abu al-Najib Suhraw-
ardi (d. 563/1168), Ibn 'Arabi (d. 638/1240), Junayd al-Baghdadi (d. 297/
910), Mansur al-Hallaj (d. 309/922), and Harith al-Muhasibi (d. 243/857),
did focus on the question of truth and wisdom. Like the peripatetic philosophers, Sufi philosophers investigated the *haqiqa* (the truth of things), but
they focused on *basira* (perception or insight) as the critical means of attaining real understanding of the truth of things. *Kashf* (unveiling) as a means of
knowing the esoteric and hidden and of returning to a primordial state of
natural and pure intuition (*fitra*) is possible through *ihsan* (the doing of
beautiful deeds) and *lutf* (God's grace). The Sufi philosophical approach to
ethics tended to focus on self-purification as the means to unlocking the
primordial and perennial through the attainment of wisdom and virtue. Only
through self-enlightenment and self-realization does it become possible for
the temporal and illusory to become conjoined with the transcendental and
real.

Both the peripatetic philosophy and the Sufi philosophy appealed to and
engaged an elite strata of society; this segment was literate and cultured
enough to be a part of the world of manuscripts, libraries, seminaries, and
universities. Contemporary readers are often not mindful of the extent to
which literacy, education, and the very practice of reading until a few hundred years ago were a privilege available to a fairly small percentage of
society. I mention this because modern students are often surprised by the
considerable disparity in sophistication and eloquence in works written by
the same exact author on the broad rubric of ethics. The writing style of the
same author will range from the sublimely subtle and nuanced to the perfunctory and didactic, but such works were written for very different audiences
and to serve very different objectives.[12] It would be anachronistic to treat
premodern texts as if they negotiated the same sociocultural roles that they
did in the age of print, leave alone in the age of literary popularism and
electronic print. One of the common themes in premodern Islamic discourses
is the duality of knowledge as a source of enlightenment and also danger. For
the initiated in the arts of reading and reflection, knowledge was a source of
enlightenment, but for so many intellectually modest pretenders, knowledge
was seen as a source of incitement to heretical sectarianism.[13] As is evidenced from the genre of literature on theological creeds and sectarianism
known as *al-farq bayn al-firaq* or *al-milal wa al-nihal*, theological debates
and disputations in early Islam generated a great deal of dissension and

diversity that often bordered on the tumultuous. With the massive eruption of sectarian and creedal conflicts in the first centuries of Islam, the third episte-mological trajectory took firmer hold and spread.[14] The third orientation was scripturalist, or heavily textualist, and popularistic, and it arose as part of the mass accretions in oral traditions attributed to the Prophet, his companions, or successors. This mass-based movement constructed a theatrical archetype of the do-gooder or of the good Muslim reducing this archetype to a model man whose behavior should be ameliorated in every respect. The field known as *al-raqa'iq* or *al-adab* (oral traditions describing the Prophet's personal behavior on matters covering personal hygiene or social manners) was espe-cially susceptible to fantastical fabrications and inventions. Indeed, there are many narratives that openly admit that when it came to this particular field, scholars of hadith and Sunna were not as exacting or critical in weeding out fabrications. The primary reasons for the lowered transmission and authen-ticity standards were that such reports were considered to be of very limited normative legal value. Jurists tended not to place much weight on oral reports describing the Prophet's personal habits, social etiquette, or purely ethical questions that do not have legal relevance. So, for instance, books of juris-prudence did not discuss questions such as backbiting, rudeness, vulgarity, selfishness, envy, rage, greed, gluttony, sloth, or in the alternative, humility, kindness, patience, or generosity, among other possible moral failures or virtues. These sins and virtues have very serious consequences on the well-being of a person's body and soul and are believed to be of great import on a person's fate in the Hereafter, but because they are not ritualistic practices and they do not involve a physical harm that could be addressed by temporal law, they were not dealt with in books of jurisprudence or legal treatises. These virtues and moral failures, however, were discussed at length in the works of the peripatetic philosophers (the first trajectory), the ascetic philos-ophers (the Sufis of the second trajectory), and also in the third trajectory of scripturalist popularists. The first orientation, by the nature of its intellectual rigor, was accessible only to an educated elite, and the second orientation, requiring a long process of apprenticeship and mentorship, was available only to the initiated. But the third trajectory was marshaled by preachers, who communicated ethical teachings through allegorical and often fantastical narratives that captured the attention and imagination of the masses.[15]

The fourth and final trajectory was that represented by the Islamic law and the legal system, which was conspicuously not immersed or often not even engaged with the question of morality and ethics. This lack of engage-ment with *akhlaq* (ethics) in Islamic law was not due to any type of structural defect, and indeed, it is not at all unusual for legal systems not to be guided by a coherent and systematic normative value system of principles and ideals. As noted earlier, legal systems are semiautonomous and self-referen-tial and derive authority from the technical linguistic practices of the institu-tions of law and not from philosophical concepts or vague social standards. By the very nature of the cultures of law, jurists derive authority from the processes and rules of adjudication, shielding themselves as much as possible from the risk of the appearance of individualized or whimsical justice. The mechanics of the process and the highly specialized linguistic practices af-ford the practitioners of a legal system the sense of professionalism, objectivity, and authoritativeness. Put differently, a legal system is far more likely to respond to its own inner logic, such as established processes, settled doctrines, and structural imperatives, than unfettered rules of logic or ethical and moral norms. The Islamic legal tradition did develop doctrinal tools, such as necessity, equity, or public interest, which enabled practitioners to produce legal results that are less draconian or more just and fair. But as would be expected, these tools were utilized sparingly and cautiously because each time a legal system admits the logic of exceptionalism, it risks its own consistency, predictability, and ultimately, legitimacy. The critical point so often missed by so many contemporary researchers of Islamic law is that for a premodern legal system that was not theorized as a normative ideal but that was actually the law of the land for many centuries, one will rarely find clear expositions on normative ethical standards. Even more rare is for researchers to find practitioners within an active legal system freely admitting to giving precedence to rules of morality and ethics over authoritative, well-established legal doctrine. Even when practitioners within a legal system intend to ignore established binding legal doctrine in favor of the call of conscience or in deference to an ethical consideration, truly gifted jurists will go out of their way to camouflage and conceal their concession to moral doctrine and construct a fortress of juridical reasoning and legal language to create the impression that they are not ruling according to the dictates of philosophy or ethics, but law. It is not that functioning legal systems are purposely amoral or disinterested in morality, but the institutional mechanics of law create their own self-propelling and self-sustaining imperatives.

Law and morality are often in a relationship of dialectical praxis; the functions of law tend to gravitate toward conflict resolution, order, and stability, which are objectives often in conflict with the ideal of justice. Morality, however, tends to seek ideals closely associated with justice, which are often disruptive of the status quo, order, and stability. In a living legal system, the process of mutual interrogation and revision and counterrevision that takes place between law and morality helps the institutions of law remain healthy and sustain a reasonable rate of growth and development.

The relationship of Islamic law to morality warrants special attention because of Islamic law's unusual and even unique nature and historical legacy. Islamic law is a hybrid between a religious legal system and a temporal legal system. It aspires to be an expression of the divine will and thus about ultimate questions of right and wrong—good or bad. But, as explained earlier, Islamic law was an actual sociologically functioning legal system with common-law-like characteristics. As such, it incorporated, rationalized, and legitimated many customary norms and practices of nations that for a variety of complex reasons played a critical role in the formation and development of Islamic law. On the one hand, Islamic law is not just about what the state can or cannot punish or compel because breaches and violations are only addressed in the Hereafter. But on the other hand, as discussed earlier, sin, damnation, and salvation are not conditioned or made contingent on the determinations of the legal system or the judgments of duly appointed qadis—the judge's decision is enforced as a matter of law and order, but the law's moral claim to the truth is relative.

Interestingly, this dualistic character of Islamic law is a product of the tension between its normative aspirational status as God's law and its actualized sociological experience as a living legal system that negotiated conflicts and maintained order for centuries. As the positive law of the land, it made perfect sense that Islamic law would not be presumed to embody ethics and morality. Such a presumption would concede to the determinations of the legal absolutism and objectivity that would become impossible to challenge or defy.[16] Furthermore, admitting that the determinations of the legal system have absolute moral claims would have militated against the legal pluralism that has been a consistent feature of the Islamic legal system since its inception. Therefore, while religious and aspirationally moral in its foundation and genesis, at the same time, Islamic law exhibited all the characteristics of a functional positivistic legal system, which meant that precedent, established legal doctrine, and the systematized and anchored processes of law took precedence over philosophical ethics or moral doctrine.[17]

The role and function of Islamic law in the modern age has changed dramatically. In the age of the nation-state, the interpreters of the Shari'ah play a fundamentally different role—they are no longer the maintainers of law and order and functionaries of a living sociologically viable legal system. The jurists of today cannot rely on the authoritative weight yielded by the idea of rule of law because they are no longer the representatives of that principle of law and order. The jurists of Islamic law in the current age ought to be far closer to being theologians and moral philosophers than lawyers. They no longer bear the burden of representing the law of the land, but they do bear the far more onerous and grave burden of being the advocates for the law of God. In other words, they cannot hide behind the functionalities and technicalities of legalism, but they must rise to the challenge of being the voice of conscience reminding people of the primordial, transcendental, and divine. This is nothing short of a complete shift of paradigm and total restructuring of the juristic culture in Islam. This is dictated by the fact that Islamic law in the contemporary democratic state cannot be enforced by the state. By definition, political sovereignty in the nation-state belongs to the citizenry of the state and not to God. The role of the *faqih*, or of the Shari'ah expert, is critical—as the Qur'an describes it,[18] the role of those who study the divine law is to act as teachers and reminders to people of the call of conscience and the indicators (*adilla*) that point to God's will. This necessarily means that the only method available to them is persuasion by appealing to people's minds and hearts. If they fail to convince people to do what is good and right, then they have failed to be persuasive. I believe, however, that the function of those who take on the responsibility of witnessing for God is very different from the role played by those who are practitioners of a legal system. For those who witness on God's behalf, testifying in terms of ethics, virtue, and also the aesthetics of beauty and transcendence is critical. Testifying for God—the very acts of *shahada* and jihad—is fundamentally about witnessing about godliness as opposed to godlessness. If under any set of circumstances a law or set of laws are attributed to God but the concrete results are unjust, unfair, oppressive, or ugly, this cannot be godly, and what is being perpetuated is a state of godlessness and not godliness. At this point, before proceeding with setting out the ethical approach to Shari'ah, I think it is critical that I pause a little to explain the connection between *jahiliyya* (or state of ignorance and darkness) and godlessness and also comment on what godliness means in the context of Shari'ah discourses.

GODLINESS AND GODLESSNESS

A basic tenet of Islamic theology is that God has no wants or needs. Everything that God has revealed through God's angels and prophets is for the well-being and prosperity of the recipients of the revelation. God gave human beings a covenant, which, if they accept, is for their own benefit and, if they reject, is to their own detriment. In Islamic law, this principle is translated into a number of legal maxims that articulate a mandate to remove harm and end suffering. In other words, the law of God mandates a normative obligation, both collective and individual, to act to alleviate harm and suffering. This, in turn, becomes the basis for the often-made argument that anything that causes suffering or misery cannot be a part of the Shari'ah or God's law.

The moral and legal obligation to alleviate or end suffering and hardship help in understanding the importance of well-being and happiness in the Islamic outlook, but the alleviation of suffering and hardship is not the same as the achievement of happiness. Even if the most faithful try their utmost to end hardship, suffering, and misery, this does not amount to the realization of happiness. Although God is self-sufficient and is described as the Giver, contentment or happiness is not realized through simple practice, obedience, or some other formalistic or legalistic dynamic.[19] An effective beginning to understanding the Islamic outlook is to ponder the Prophet Muhammad's refrain: "Whoever succeeds in knowing himself will come to know his Lord."[20] One of the consistent themes in the very large literary corpus dealing with the issue of *sa'ada*, or "happiness," is an inextricable link drawn between knowledge and enlightenment and happiness. The more a believer knows about himself, other people and cultures, and the world, the more such a believer will be capable of understanding the balance (*mizan*), which is necessary for striving for justice with the self and others (*qist*). Indeed, the struggle to learn and to achieve self-knowledge and knowledge of the other is labeled by the Prophet as the highest and most challenging form of jihad. The Qur'an describes those who succeed in understanding the balance and in achieving enlightenment as existing in a true state of happiness.[21] They are in a state of harmony and peace with themselves, creation, and God. This is a state of blissful tranquility, equilibrium, and ultimately peace. In this serene and harmonious state, enlightened believers enjoy a special relationship with God. The Qur'an describes them as people who come to enjoy a complete sense of fulfillment (*rida*); they trust God, and God trusts them; and they love God, and God loves them.[22] The state of enlightenment and happiness that they enjoy pervades every aspect of their being to the point that the Qur'an describes their blissful happiness as manifesting on their joyous and luminous faces, and they tread the earth with their inner light between the palms of their hands, which most scholars agree is a symbolic reference to attainment of the divine grace of wisdom.[23]

The themes of knowledge, enlightenment, balance, peace, and tranquility are central to the Islamic theology of happiness. But if these concepts represent the ideal of happiness, the complete failure of true happiness is literally embodied by the idea of *jahiliyya*. As discussed in chapter 6, *jahiliyya* is a state of godlessness when human beings become consumed by base desires and a loss of moral direction. As the Qur'an asserts, it is not physiological blindness that leads one into darkness and misery, but the blindness of the soul and heart.[24]

As noted earlier, every period of human history has suffered its share of *jahl* and *jahiliyya*.[25] *Jahiliyya* is as entrenched in human history as the social ailments of bigotry, racism, hatred, and oppression. But speaking as a Muslim, I believe in Islam's enduring role of unyielding resistance to the temptations and false pleasures of *jahiliyya*. Islam is the belief in an ideal—the ideal of submission to God and only to God, and freedom from submission to all else, including false idols, the worst of which is the egotistical self. The word "Islam" connotes the dual meanings of submission to God and also the finding of peace in God. To go through the enlightenment of finding peace in God does not mean the annihilation of the self into God. It does mean gaining the wisdom to understand the balance between the self, the other, and God and to exist in harmony with the self, creation, and the Maker. In Shari'ah discourses, God is recognized as having rights (*huquq Allah*), but so do human beings (known as *huquq al-'ibad*).[26] Finding peace in God means comprehending the just balance of rights and struggling to preserve this balance by giving each right its due.[27]

The implications of the theology of submission to God are profound and numerous, and they pervade every aspect of the search for happiness, whether it be at the personal or social levels. If submission to and peace in God are to be meaningful in any real sense, they mandate persistent resistance and rebellion against the personal *jahiliyya* of the iniquitous and uprooted soul and against the social conditions and structures that compel the sufferance of ignorance and hatred. To see with the light of God instead of the fogginess of the ego mandates disciplining the ego with the humility brought about by a searching intellect and an active conscience. The theology of Islam resists the state of *jahiliyya* by calling on human beings to wage a relentless jihad in pursuit of enlightenment and against the oppressiveness of ignorance and against the social and political deformities and illnesses that spread in the absence of justice. The jihad against *jahiliyya* is a constant struggle to bring balance and peace to one's own soul and to pursue balance and peace for one's society and for humanity.[28] In other words, it is a jihad to bring justice within and without—for oneself and for all of humanity. This jihad is a never-ending effort at self-enlightenment as well as the pursuit of enlightenment at the communitarian and social level. The Prophet of Islam described the act of engaging the self, critically and honestly—the confrontation of the self with the self—as the highest form of jihad (*al-jihad al-akbar*, or the greater jihad).[29] It is quite true that it is very hard to gaze long and hard at oneself and see the inequities and faults not as an excuse for nihilistic self-effacement and apathy but as part of an ongoing struggle to cleanse, purify, and grow with divinity or into divinity. Indeed, this is much harder than any armed war one could engage in. Living persistently and patiently to sacrifice the ego for the love of God is much harder than a simple death in the name of God. The sages of Islamic theology have written so much about the perils of leading a life without introspection and self-criticism and of the maladies of a soul that allows fear, anxiety, and insecurity to distract it from the greatest jihad—the jihad against the self.[30] Without introspection and self-judgment, a person grows complacent with his or her ego until all sense of reasonable and just self-perception is gone. And, as noted above, in Islamic theosophy, self-knowledge and knowledge of God are inseparable.

The Qur'an instructs Muslims to discuss and deliberate as a means of confronting and solving problems (known as the obligation of *shura* or consultation), but for these deliberations to be genuine and meaningful, a measure of humility and self-awareness would be necessary.[31] Moreover, one of the central themes of the Qur'an is a heavy emphasis on the normative obligation of enjoining what is good and resisting what is bad or evil (*al-amr bi'l ma'ruf wa al-nahy 'an al-munkar*).[32] In the Qur'anic discourse, the seriousness by which this individual and collective obligation is taken often constitutes the difference between a moral and happy society and a society plagued by injustices and suffering under the weight of moral ignorance. Islamic theological discourses often emphasize that selfishness, egoism, cowardice, ignorance, and apathy are the major reasons why people fail to rise to the challenge of this moral obligation, and in doing so, they end up perpetuating the darkness of *jahiliyya*.[33] Muslim theologians conceived of an interconnected process where reflection and deliberation (*tafakkur wa al-nazar wa'l ta'ammul*) would lead to realizing the importance of goodness, seeking knowledge (*talab al-'ilm*) would lead to comprehending the moral good, and struggling against the ego would enable people actively to engage and pursue goodness.[34] The failure of this dynamic would mean that society would lose its moral anchor and lose itself in the process. Dwelling in this condition of *jahiliyya*, human beings would deny themselves the opportunity to grow from a state of godlessness to godliness.

In the Islamic outlook, a believer is expected to be in a constant state of resistance to the state of *jahl* and the disease of *jahiliyya*. In a sense, in struggling to submit to the Almighty, a Muslim struggles for liberation from and against falling captive to godlessness. Godliness is not just a conviction or belief; it is a practice and a state of being. And this state, which is quintessentially interconnected with beauty—with the attributes of divinity such as love, mercy, justice, tranquility, humility, and peace—is in direct antipathy to *jahiliyya*, which in turn is associated with the ailments suffered in a state of godlessness such as hate, cruelty, inequity, arrogance, anxiety, and fear. In the language of the Qur'an as well as in the teachings of the Prophetic Sunna, godliness is not a status or entitlement; it is a state of being in which a person emanates godliness not just in his or her ethical beliefs and conduct but in the very spirit and aura that emanates from and enfolds such a person.[35] Hence, the Prophet described the truly godly as reaching a stage where it is as if they see with God's eyes and hear with God's ears and feel with God's heart and, as such, become godly human beings (*'ibadun rabbaniyyun*).[36] On the other hand, when human beings embrace their *jahiliyya* and turn away from God's path and grace, they dwell in the misery brought about by their own weaknesses, insecurities, and imbalances. In traditional Islamic theology, the state of embodying godliness is known as *ihsan*—a being beautified by divinity and its goodness.[37] The closer human beings come toward the ideal of godliness or *ihsan*, the more they can experience true happiness. The more they drift away from themselves and descend into and settle for godlessness, the more elusive and misguided their quest for happiness will be. The Qur'an consistently draws a strong connection between those who have forgotten God and those who have forgotten themselves. In the Qur'anic usage, those who have forgotten themselves because of lack of honesty with the self and the failure to wrestle with and discipline the ego and because of their complacency toward their own moral failures are identified as being mired in self-deception and moral alienation.[38] Those who forget themselves are at risk of drifting without the anchoring role and rootedness of God and, therefore, becoming increasingly overcome by fears, anxieties, and sadness.

For believers, faith enables them to reach out for godliness, for the perennial, transcendental, sublime, and beautiful. There is no doubt that throughout human history, religion has been a powerful instigator of change—in fact, religion has possessed the power of truly transformative moments in human history. Not too many forces in history have had the power of religion to inspire, motivate, and inform. Even in the largely secular Western academy, many social theorists have recognized the positive and, in my view, necessary role that religion ought to play in remedying many of the ailments suffered in modernity.[39] Modernity (or post-modernity) has enriched human life with so many advances that brought comfort and safety to our bodies but at the same time infected our souls with the restlessness that comes from the loss of purpose and lack of certitude. Skepticism and deconstructionism liberated the human mind from numerous self-imposed limitations but imprisoned the soul within the confines of empiricism. Modernity uprooted the human soul, but for those who are still able to believe, religion can provide a much-needed anchor. Our faith in the objectivity of the scientific method gave us unprecedented control and mastery over our physical existence, but this has done little to address the fact that we are quintessentially subjective beings and that so many of our challenges are metaphysical in nature.

Overcoming the restlessness and anxieties of the modern age does not mean escaping to religion as an ephemeral and cursory infusion of mindless happiness on a structurally unhappy situation. The point is not to instill a paradigm in which religion could become the opiate of a people, infusing them with dosages of delusional happiness. For me as a Muslim, my faith allows for the pursuit of happiness while at the same time coming to terms with my mortality. I think that for many, religious belief empowers a believer against the greatest oppressor of all, and that is death. Empowerment against the absoluteness and finality of death does not necessarily amount to passivity and resignation, and indeed could inspire the exact opposite. Moreover, the transience of life could tempt one to become concerned solely with self-happiness without regard for the happiness of others. In the Islamic faith, one's fate in the afterlife is in good measure an extension of how one treated others in this earthly life.[40]

I do not doubt that invariably there are believers who use religion as a vehicle for moral banality, apathy, and even nihilism. And I do not doubt that their form of religiously rationalized happiness is more like a hypnotic vegetative state instead of an objective to be deliberately pursued through a dynamic engagement with divinity.[41] Islam, like all systems of faith, can be used to make pain more bearable or to mitigate the harshness of suffering. And indeed, Islamic theology does place a heavy emphasis on patience and perseverance before hardships and on not giving in to despair or despondency (*al-sabr 'ala al-nawa'ib wa al-shada'id*). Resisting hopelessness and enduring through life's trials and tribulations is a moral virtue and a sign of a strong faith. Some Muslims do use the affectations of pious endurance in order to justify moral indifference and apathy, but this is a misuse and corruption of religion and not a necessary consequence of it. This kind of corruption of religious doctrine is most often used not to perpetuate a false notion of pious happiness but to justify the continuation of impious misconduct and to justify the miseries that result therefrom.

For Muslims who have proper understanding of their religion and who are true believers—and by true believers I do not mean those who indulge in the affectations of belief, but those who have felt anchored, inspired, and empowered by their faith—for these believers, happiness can only be attained by resisting the *jahiliyya* within and the *jahiliyya* without. For these Muslims, the engagement with the divine is translated into a dynamic of beauty, peace, balance, mercy, and love, and this dynamic is a vigorous path to empowerment, enlightenment, and happiness. Misusing the doctrine of fate to justify resignation and passivity before oppression or injustice is not the worst kind of corruption of the Islamic faith. Much worse is when Islam itself is used to perpetuate a state of *jahiliyya* in which the religion is usurped and turned into an instrument of hatred, bigotry, prejudice, ignorance, suffering, and ugliness.

The exploitation of Islam to perpetuate values or conditions contrary to godliness is a contradiction in terms and an abomination. As a matter of conviction, to use religion to perpetuate conditions that are theologically associated with godlessness, or the absence of godliness, is offensive. As a Muslim, I believe that the light of God and indeed the light of Islam embody and are embodied by the values of beauty, peace, tranquility, and love. Therefore, when Islam is exploited to justify the opposite conditions, this is akin to the perpetuation of *jahiliyya* in the name of Islam. The illuminations of God cannot coexist with the darkness of *jahiliyya*. To put it in theological terms, God has made it a divine purpose to endow human beings with joy and happiness, and so to exploit God's message to perpetuate misery or suffering is, to say the least, deeply problematic.[42] Similarly, the Qur'an proclaims that God has ordained dignity to all human beings, and so, in principle, the divine cannot be used to justify the perpetuation of indignities or the degradation and humiliation of human beings.[43] As paradoxical as it might be, there can be no denying that all religions have been exploited in ways that are fundamentally at odds with their tenets.

As discussed earlier, the Qur'anic challenge is, in light of the enormous diversity, for human beings to get to know each other. This does not mean inventing an artificial construct of the other and then coming to know that construct. And it also does not mean that regardless of the actions of the other, their ethics and actions must be deemed acceptable and legitimate. While recognizing the legitimacy of a considerable amount of difference, the

Qur'an insists on moral and ethical objective and universal standards encapsulated in the idea of equity and justice. Furthermore, the Qur'an considers particular characteristics such as spying, backbiting, and slander to be inconsistent with the ethical precepts necessary for a just and equitable existence.[44] The acceptance of diversity and pluralism and genuine knowledge of the other is a moral objective in and of itself, but it also serves an important functional purpose. Undertaking such a process enables human beings to discover and learn to differentiate between the universal precepts of morality, on the one hand, and the relative and subjective, on the other.

Claims of ontological or universal truth, whether based on reason or revelation, are not anathema to Islam. Indeed the Qur'an recognizes certain ethical principles as universally applicable and pertinent.[45] The Qur'an states, for instance: "And God does not desire for human beings to suffer injustice."[46] A statement such as this generates layers of meaning, but it is reasonable to conclude that from an Islamic perspective, Muslims are encouraged to search for moral universals that could serve as shared and common goals with humanity at large.[47] This seems to me to be an essential characteristic of a universal religion that is addressed to humanity at large and not to an exclusive cultural, social, or ethnic group. The Qur'an insists that it is the bearer of a message to all humankind and not to a particular tribe or race.[48] Moreover, the Qur'an asserts that the Prophet Muhammad, and in fact the Qur'an itself, was sent to all peoples as a blessing and mercy.[49] The Qur'an also persistently emphasizes the ethical quality of mercy as a core attribute of God and as a fundamental and basic pursuit of Islam.[50] The Qur'an informs human beings that God has decreed and mandated mercy even on himself and therefore is bound to extend it to human beings. In the Qur'anic discourse, mercy and peace are inextricably linked—peace is a divine mercy, and mercy is the bliss of peace. To comprehend and internalize God's mercy is to be in a blissful state of peace.[51] This is at the very essence of the state of divine beautification and of being filled with the goodness of the divine, and having this quality manifest outwardly in everything a person does is known as *ihsan. Ta'aruf* (knowing the other) and *ta'aluf* (amicability between people) is a great gift of divine mercy that leads to the grace of enjoying peace. But knowledge of the other is not possible without the grace of *ihsan*, which calls on people to approach one another not just with mercy and sympathy but with empathy and compassion.

Whether in Saudi Arabia, Afghanistan, Pakistan, or Iran, puritanical movements do tend to generate a considerable amount of social unhappiness and desolation. Not all puritanical movements resort to suicide bombings or political violence. Furthermore, not all puritanical groups believe that Muslims have no sanctity because they are deserving of God's wrath and punishments. However, the modalities of thought in puritanical movements have a consistently demoralizing and dehumanizing effect that persistently undermines the possibilities of social and moral happiness and thus undermines the very purpose of the Islamic faith. I have called these modalities, and the way that they set forth norms that generate repetitive social consequences, the modalities of pietistic affectations and stereotyped determinations.

As discussed earlier, stereotypical determinations are responses that lock Islamicity within a narrow space of interpretive or constructive possibilities.

A stereotyped response is reactive, and to the extent that it affirms a picture of orthodoxy in order to reassert an authoritative image of Islamicity, it is a form of religious affectation. Stereotyped responses assume a narrow view of Islamicity and then seek to reproduce this view as an affirmation of orthodoxy within a specific sense of presupposed determinations. In other words, stereotyped responses are premised on a narrow view of what is truly and authentically Islamic as opposed to what is not, and also on the dogmatic exclusion of alternatives. The Islamic intellectual heritage often contains open possibilities of creative interpretation, and the Shari'ah tradition, in particular, is rich and highly diverse. Stereotyped responses, however, significantly narrow the range of constructive possibilities by restricting potential creative interpretive activity by dogmatically limiting the tools of determination—tools such as text, reason, or customs.

It is much easier, but also dangerous, to deal with life's challenges by identifying the relevant facts not through sociological and cultural experiences but through a religiously motivated imaginary construct. Instead of dealing with the full complexity and richness of life and dealing with challenges on their own terms, it is possible for the religious imaginary to limit what are considered to be the relevant facts in such a way as to avoid having to deal with the challenge in the first place. In this situation, life is not experienced and studied in its full richness and adversity, but the process of living itself is conceptualized in highly stereotyped forms that have little to do with material culture or lived experiences. Consequently, challenges are not dealt with through a dynamic of systematic analysis, and social problems are not treated from within an exhaustive analytical framework. Instead, the stereotyped forms that are used to respond to challenging facts and difficult problems sustain and perpetuate certain fictions of performance or pietistic affectations. In effect, instead of wrestling with contexts and contingencies, practitioners rely on convenient fictions that allow them to avoid confronting the reality existing on the ground, and then they respond to these constructed fictions through stereotypical determinations that affirm and do not challenge these constructed fictions. Stereotyped responses that ignore the nuances of history and life do not just stunt the development of Shari'ah as a field of normative discourse. But they often stunt the development of serious ethical evaluations, the social development of standards of reasonableness, and the cultivation of shared human and humane values. This occurs because practitioners fall into the habit of avoiding the pain of wrestling with uncomfortable facts, and as they escape to ready-made dogma, this acts to dull the intellect and hamper the continual development of a critical sense of moral responsibility.

As discussed in earlier chapters, since the 1970s there has been an enormous growth of movements that emphasize symbolic performances such as forms of attire, facial hair, smells and perfumes, specific expressions, and phraseology as a representation of genuine Islamicity.[52] Of course, symbolic performances of religiosity are not problematic. What does become problematic is when these performances become a form of pietistic affectation that compensates for or conceals social tensions and frustrations. While stereotyped responses to complex and contingent social realities lead to a great deal of social frustrations and failures, pietistic affectations only help in further ignoring and concealing the existence of suffering.

SHARI'AH AND SEEKING GODLINESS

It seems to me that those who aspire to witness on God's behalf and to remind people of their obligation to live their lives according to God's supreme laws must approach God's commandments, given within the parameters of a time and place, as steps taken in the context of prevalent epistemological orientations toward the fulfillment of godliness. The approach suggested here would understand God's commandments as representing moral and transcendental trajectories that would fulfill the purposes of Shari'ah and bring the world closer to godliness. This, however, requires three critical steps: (1) the interpreter of God's commandments and God's higher law must understand the epistemological paradigms that God's commandments had to negotiate at the time of revelation; (2) the interpreter must study and make every effort to understand the epistemological positioning of the same problems and issues raised by the commandment but in its contemporary context and circumstance; and most critically, (3) the interpreter must seek to understand the moral and ethical objectives and trajectories set in motion and direction by the commandment. Essentially, the person who takes on himself/herself the responsibility of searching the divine will must go to the inescapable additional step of investigating the intent and objectives of the legislator. Of course, this is not a new concept or approach. As noted earlier, many Muslim jurists have advocated approaches focused on the objectives of Shari'ah (*maqasid al-shari'ah*), but these approaches have tended to emphasize exceptions or suspensions of the law in order to promote the well-being and welfare of people. The *maqasid al-shari'ah* field, as demonstrated by the work of Abu Ishaq al-Shatibi (d. 790/1388), focused on overcoming the inflexibility and rigidity created by the accumulation of legal determinations and precedents by emphasizing the need to achieve a greater degree of legal responsiveness to social demands and also legal equity.[53]

The approach I suggest here is epistemological in that it tries to understand the logic of godliness—the moral objectives behind the semiotics of the text and the ethical trajectories recognized and affirmed by the divine text. The process of genuinely living with Shari'ah mandates that we reason with God in that we reason with God's speech. When God speaks, by virtue of God's mercy, compassion, and love, God educates and illuminates through an unending, perpetual, and ongoing process of exemplars, demonstrations, and anecdotes.[54] As such, the entire experience of the Prophet in Mecca and Medina is but a moral lesson and an education in divine grace. Indeed every commandment is instructional in that, if taken in its proper appropriate epistemological context, it is demonstrative of how to migrate from an existential godlessness (*jahiliyya*) to godliness (*uluhiyya*). For the sake of convenience, I will call the heuristic method focusing on engaging texts as a part of the edifying process of learning the normative moral and ethical potentialities and trajectories of godliness the "instructional approach." I seek to explore and investigate the instructional approach in a series of examples taken on a number of topics and a wide range of issues. As I noted earlier, puritans construct the meaning of the divine text by reading Qur'anic verses in isolation, as if the meaning of the verses were transparent and as if God's speech and will are fully contained in the specific words or sentences being read. In fact, however, it is impossible to analyze Qur'anic verses except in light of the overall moral thrust of the Qur'anic message. Very often it is impossible to understand the moral thrust or ethical trajectory of the Qur'an unless we analyze the historical circumstances and epistemological parameters in which specific Qur'anic ethical norms were negotiated. To understand the thrust and trajectories of the Qur'an, we need to understand the starting point of the text and what types of dynamics it undertook in light of the specific contexts with which it had to deal.[55] To illustrate the instructional approach, I will review several examples of ethically purposeful readings, shedding light on the way such a reading would affect the production of law. The first set of examples will deal with inter-Muslim relations. The second set of examples will deal with the interaction of Muslims with non-Muslims. In discussing these examples, I will attempt to differentiate between the qualities that can be said to be a part of the moral objectives of the Qur'an—objectives that help establish the universal qualities of beauty—and the positive legal commandments that do not enjoy the same level of sanctity or immutability because they played a functional role at a certain point in time, but the more critical role and immutable roles were anecdotal and morally instructive. The point of these examples is to demonstrate the moral trajectories of the Qur'an and the importance of understanding these trajectories to the pursuit of beauty and godliness in Islam.[56]

There is a Qur'anic revelation often cited by literalists as clear proof of the imperative to follow God's law without succumbing to the vagaries of human whim. The revelation instructs the Prophet to follow God's law and not to permit the whims and vagaries of people to lead him astray from the divine path. In fact, the Qur'an informs the Prophet that if he obeys the whims of human beings and judges according to their biases and preferences instead of God's law, the heavens and earth will be corrupted and strife will overtake the earth.[57] Puritanical thinkers cite this verse as decisive proof in support of the claim that not only is God's law determinable, but the injunctions of Islamic law must be enforced by the state. According to the way that Puritanical-Salafis have chosen to read it, this Qur'anic injunction clearly condemns any reliance on human subjectivities and commands Muslims to rely exclusively on injunctions derived from divine texts. By condemning reliance on human subjectivities, the Qur'an indicates that not only is God's will determinable, but the only legitimate frame of reference is the objective rules of law, and Muslims are under an obligation to implement God's positive commandments to all aspects of life. Furthermore, this is cited as one of the main justifications for asserting God's sovereignty on the earth and for declaring all human legislation illegitimate.

The literalist approach adopted by Puritanical-Salafis, however, fails to deal with a more basic question, and that is: When the Qur'an commands the Prophet to enforce God's law and not to defer to human whim, to which laws is the Qur'an referring? In addition, why does the failure to enforce God's law lead to the corruption of the earth? If the Qur'an is referring to the details and specifics of the positive commandments of Islamic law—for instance, the rules of ablutions, or the Islamic law of marriage and divorce—why would neglecting such laws lead to the corruption of the earth? In this context, to get a sense of the range of epistemological possibilities, and the place of this command in the totality of the Qur'anic discourse, it is very useful to examine the narrated reports surrounding this revelation. In the genre of literature known as the occasions of revelation (*asbab al-nuzul*), we find narratives that significantly reorient the epistemological possibilities of this verse.[58] It was reported that several prominent non-Muslim leaders of a community in Medina had a long-standing business dispute with a neighboring community. Another version of the same report claims that the community in question and its leaders were Jewish. The leaders requested that the Prophet, as the ruler of Medina, resolve the dispute between them and their neighbors. However, the leaders suggested to the Prophet that if he would adjudge the case in their favor and against their opponents, they would be willing to convert to Islam in return. The community leaders also advised the Prophet that because of their prominent position in their community, if they converted, many people would follow them. In effect, in return for the conversion of a sizeable number of people—at a time when Muslims were under siege by Mecca and in dire need of new converts joining their ranks—the Prophet was asked to settle a commercial dispute in a way that would serve his political interests while helping out the would-be converts. The Prophet refused the offer because if he was going to arbitrate or adjudge a dispute between two parties, he was going to do so according to the principles of justice and not by unfairly favoring the group that would be willing to convert to Islam. The Qur'anic verse was revealed addressing this context, in essence affirming a basic principle of justice and fairness and rejecting political or even religious opportunism.[59] These narratives are evidence of negotiated epistemological possibilities. But at the very least, it is clear that the Qur'an is exhorting people to follow moral principles such as justice, truthfulness, or compassion, which the Qur'anic text persistently emphasizes. So, in other words, the Qur'an is stressing the moral qualities of goodness (*ihsan*) that are at the essence of godliness. The occasion of revelation narrative is emblematic of a consistent Qur'anic theme: standing by moral principle regardless of the material advantages or personal costs. An example of this Qur'anic discourse is found in the following verse: "Oh you who believe, be persistent and stand firm in justice, bearing witness for God, even if it be against yourselves or your parents or your close ones. Whether rich or poor, God is their sustainer. Refrain from following your whims and desires lest you fail to be just, for if you fail to uphold justice, God is fully aware of what you do."[60]

The reported dialectic about the refusal of the Prophet to achieve political gains at the cost of corrupting the principle of justice is essentially a heuristic device affirming a point repeatedly made in the Qur'an. If people drift to a state of godlessness—a state in which there is an absence of God's law—corruption and strife will spread unabated. The law that is referred to in this revelation is the law of ethics and morality, and not necessarily the rules of legal technicalities. It is critical that the Qur'an equates the adherence to moral principle with the path of God because in the pursuit of moral principle is the pursuit of beauty and divinity. This is exactly why the Qur'an informs the Prophet that if he follows the whims of people, the heavens and earth will become corrupted. The whims referenced here are not necessarily the subjectivities of human beings, because the subjective emotions of persons could be consistent with moral principles, but functional opportunism, the lack of principle, and the denial of basic and universal (godly) moral laws that bind all human beings. Contrary to what Puritanical-Salafis have often claimed, this revelation does not invalidate the legitimacy of human legislation; what it does mandate is that human legislation be consistent with the laws of morality and ethics.

Godliness, and indeed Shari'ah itself, cannot be contained or encapsulated within a set of determinable rules. But standing on a solid foundation of sanctified normativities it becomes possible to engage divinity in all its illimitable magnanimity and reason with God. In my view, the archetypal image of a person reasoning with God is powerfully portrayed in the Qur'an in the story of Joseph's father. When grappling with the great tragedies that have befallen him, Joseph's father, Jacob, supplicates: "I only complain of my sorrows and agony to God."[61] One is the closest to God when one is beset with tragedies, pain, and suffering.[62] Very much like the archetype portrayed by Joseph's father, at times of great tribulations a believer enters into an intuitive, imperceptible, and nearly subconscious dialogue with God. Whether one is seeking consolation, validation, justification, or explanation, the engagement with God is nearly an innate, unaffected, and instinctual process of reasoning with the divine. In suffering, a believer, expressly or not, speaks with God in an attempt to make sense of his/her pain and in contemplation of his/her existence and God's presence and role. From a theological perspective, one is never closer to God than when one is a victim of injustice (*zulm*) or oppression (*istid'af*).[63] Closer here means not just that the heavens are especially attentive and empathetic toward those who suffer unjustly, but as argued earlier, the very moral thrust of Islamic ethics is geared toward empowering the disempowered and rebelling against oppressors (*al-tugha*).[64] However, there is an unmistakable tension between the very nature of legal thinking, which is often wedded to the structures of power that maintain order, stability, and predictability, and critical subversive thinking, which seeks to interrogate and deconstruct power.[65] Hence, it is rather unremarkable that the Islamic legal system, as a system of positive rules and as the law of the land for centuries, like all legal systems, often maintained and protected the privileged status of the powerful. This, however, is in great tension with Shari'ah as a normative moral and ethical system. In other words, while the role of ethical and theological thinking mandates that we question the inherited systems of privilege and power, the inherited interpretive traditions of Islamic jurisprudence preserved and perpetuated the very enterprise of law, which by its nature tended to favor the power structure that created it in the first place.

One of the most important theological works written in the modern era is *The Reconstruction of Religious Thought in Islam* by Muhammad Iqbal (d. 1357/1938).[66] Iqbal perceptively realized that any account of an Islamic beingness must begin with the metaphysics of selfhood and personhood in relation to an active and engaged God constantly creating in a perpetual movement toward growth. As Iqbal argued, the Islamic message must be premised on the metaphysics of constant motion and activeness. The Qur'anic message is but a sustained and incessant demonstration of the dynamic of action in partnership with a fully engaged and involved God. A state of stagnation, inertia, or lethargy is antithetical to the Qur'anic message. It is not just that the physical world is in constant motion and is in perpetual evolution, but human epistemology and its realizations and comprehensions of godliness, beauty, and virtue is in perpetual movement as well. And understanding the Qur'anic message, especially when it comes to the empowerment of the habitually subjugated, is in motion toward an ethical trajectory and purpose.

In the Qur'anic discourse, archetypes of the habitually disempowered include groups such as the orphaned, the destitute, the marginalized and alienated, and the enslaved, and in my view, it also includes women. With groups that have been habitually at a weaker position or in need of added protection, there is normative goodness or virtue in applying special scrutiny to the moral objectives and purposes of the Qur'an. Quite simply, failing to protect those most in need of protection or the failure to alleviate persistent and repeated suffering is antithetical to godliness. The persistent deprivation of a category of people threatens to make all those who tolerated their suffering immoral. To paraphrase a lesson attributed to the Prophet, one should treat the weakest in society as if they are the most influential until their rights are restored to them, and deal with the most powerful in society as if they have no power until they are forced to give the weak their rights.[67] This tradition, like so many others, is similar to a parable (*mithal*) that is intended to teach, not a rule or literal law but a normative moral attitude and a demand on the conscience. The point of the parable: the weaker party in any given situation ought to be empowered and supported so that the moral balance (*mizan*) may be restored. The moral imbalance here is the epistemic injustice in the ways that the narratives, the history, and the exasperations of the powerful are emphasized, amplified, and most of all believed, while the voice of the weak is obfuscated, muffled, and doubted.

One of the systematic and definitely most persistent epistemic injustices has been the place of women in patriarchal societies. Applying the instructional approach to this issue, I believe, will allow us to begin to lift the veil on the path to godliness despite the many obfuscations, dissimulations, and obstructions that traditional patriarchy has thrown in the way. Historically, Muslims have tended to read the Qur'anic revelation on matters relating to women as enunciating a set of positive commands that form the basis for determinable legal rules. Therefore, as far as women are concerned, the Qur'anic verses on marriage, divorce, inheritance, testimony, and many other topics have served as the basis for specific legal rules that mirror the instructions set out in a particular verse. So, for instance, if a particular verse provides that a sister should inherit from her father half of what a brother inherits, there would be a rule of Islamic law that codifies the instruction set forth in verse. But what has been woefully missing is an attempt to examine the ethical norms and moral objectives that guide the Qur'anic discourse on women and then to try to shape the law in such a fashion that these norms and objectives are pursued. If one systematically examines the dynamics of the Qur'anic discourse on women, what becomes apparent is that the specific rules set out in the Qur'an are always intended to prevent or mitigate an abusive situation that actually existed at the time of revelation. The primary mode of the Qur'anic discourse, when it provides for specific legislation relating to women, was to respond to an ongoing abusive situation. It is clear that the Qur'anic revelation on women addresses particular problems that arose in a specific context, but it is equally clear that there are ethical and moral objectives that the Qur'an unfailingly pursues. In many ways, ethical and moral objectives being the same, the Qur'an does not explicate unwavering rules that are applicable to women; rather, the Qur'an illustrates an ethical methodology on how to deal with situations that were abusive to women. For instance, regarding the inheritance of women, which, according to the Qur'an in various circumstances, is half of what men inherit, we have a variety of reports that provide a context to the revelation on the matter. According to the sources, in pre-Islamic Arabia, the only class of individuals qualified to share in the inheritance were people who fought in battles. Since normally women did not fight in battles, in most situations, women were excluded from inheritances. At the Islamic city-state in Medina, although some women did participate in battles, the men of the city insisted that they should not inherit because women are not expected to fight. In other words, the men argued in effect that if women go to battle, they do so as volunteers, and so the pre-Islamic rule should not be amended to allow these Muslim fighting women a share of the inheritance. Women in Medina, however, complained to the Prophet that although they may not share in battle, they contributed in material and crucial ways to the well-being of the city-state in Medina, and therefore they saw no reason for being excluded from inheritance. The Prophet was unable to give the women a response and asked them to wait until he received revelation on the matter. Shortly after, the Prophet reported that he received revelation giving women a share of the inheritance that often is half of the share received by men.[68] Not surprisingly, men protested. They argued that it was unfair that most women did not take part in battle and yet women, depending on their lineage, were entitled to a share equal to that of men or, more often, half of that received by men. In response, a Qur'anic revelation addressing men and women instructed: "Do not covet what God has favored some of you with over others. For men is a share in accordance with what they earned and for women is a share in accordance with what they earned. And ask God for His favors for God is all knowing."[69] Interestingly enough, a variant report reflecting a competing historical dynamic claims that this verse, instructing men and women not to covet the favors God has bestowed on the other, was revealed in response to women's protests—not protests by men. According to this report, a group of women went to the Prophet protesting that women inherit half of what men inherit, and the testimony of women in some legal cases counts as half of the testimony of men, and yet a good deed done by a woman is valued as equal to a man's good deed. They asked why the inequality and variance between the rights of women on earth and the rights of women with God? According to some reports, in response to this incident, the Qur'anic verses were revealed, in effect telling each gender to be satisfied with their status on this earth.[70] I already alluded to the fact that both versions, the one with men protesting and the other with women protesting, reflect competing dynamics in early Islamic history. But I do not think it is necessary to resolve which of these versions is true or false—it is possible that both incidents took place— that after women were given a share in the inheritance, some men and some women continued to be dissatisfied. It is worth noting, however, that the women who reportedly protested had a good point. In the Hereafter, women enjoy equality in accountability, responsibility, and reward before God, but on earth they do not enjoy equal rights. In Islamic thought, there has been a tendency to read the verse quoted above essentially as a tool for conservative legitimation—preserving the status quo particularly as it relates to women. However, if the verse is read structurally instead of literally, it acquires a meaning that is far more consistent with the Qur'anic moral message.

It is important to notice that the verse advises people not begrudge each other the favors that God has bestowed *in accordance with what they have earned*. The verse even goes on to leave open the possibility that one may earn more of God's favors by praying to God for such favors. Far from implying that there is a stable and static condition in which men and women have a set of unchanging predetermined rights, the verse indicates that there is a fluid dynamic and evolving situation in which men and women earn rights in accordance with what they have earned, and in which, instead of envy and working to undermine each other, people supplicate to God for further rights—further favors. Whatever rights or favors are enjoyed are not bestowed as a matter of status but are earned by a dual engagement with the mundane and the divine—by work and prayer. The same dynamic is found, for instance, in another verse that has often been cited to legitimate inequality between men and women. There are two main alternative ways to translate this verse. The verse could be read to say: "Men are the guardians of women in accordance with the favors God has bestowed upon some over others, and in accordance with the wealth they spend to provide for the others." The verse could also be read to say: "Men are the supporters of women in accordance with the favors God has bestowed upon some over others, and in accordance with the wealth they spend to provide for the others."[71] The variant readings depend on the way that the word *qawwamun* is understood and interpreted—the word could mean guardians, masters, supporters, or servants. Either way, the important point is that the verse does not define the relationship of men to women in an absolute and noncontingent fashion. Rather, the verse explicitly states that whatever the status—whether as guardians or supporters—it is a status contingent on the actions of human beings (i.e., "in accordance with wealth they spend to provide for the others") and the action of the divine (i.e., by the favors the divine has bestowed on one over the other).

The word used in the Qur'an for God's favor is *fadl*, and this word and its variant forms were used repeatedly throughout the Qur'an to connote a physical or spiritual blessing or preference granted by God either as a reward for good deeds or as an act of grace. If one analyzes the well over fifty times that the Qur'an uses the word *fadl*, the clear and ascertainable fact is that both the reward and grace of God are accessible to all seekers. Consistently, the Qur'an calls on the believers to struggle and strive and seek the reward and grace of God. Once it is realized that God's reward and grace are accessible to all and are contingent on the efforts of human beings and God's blessing, this materially affects the way we approach the verses cited above. Rather tellingly, as further demonstrated below, many of the rights women achieved in early Islam were in response to demands made by women in Medina. A basic set of moral rights were offered to women without there being a social demand for such rights. For instance, the Qur'an strictly forbade the morally offensive practice in pre-Islamic Arabia in which poor families murdered their young daughters and offered their soul to the gods, believing that engaging in this sacrificial practice, the gods would send them boys to replace the girls. However, financial and property rights, as well as some social rights, were often conceded by the Qur'an after women mobilized into a demand group. This is consistent with the Qur'an's principle of accessibility of reward and grace.

As I explained earlier, Shari'ah, contrary to *fiqh*, is the divine potential fulfilled in the divine reality—Shari'ah is the ideal, immutable, and eternal laws of goodness, justice, beauty, and ultimately, divinity as conceived in God's mind. And, as noted, *fiqh* is the human effort to reach the ideal. In the case of the relationship between women and men, what is the divine ideal— what is the moral eternal law of Shari'ah? The Qur'an itself answers this question by emphasizing that in the eyes of God, there is no distinction between gender, races, or classes. In God's eyes, women are equal to men because they are rewarded and punished exactly in equal measure to men, and they have equal access to God's grace and beneficence. If Shari'ah seeks to protect women from exploitative situations and from situations in which they are treated inequitably, and if the divine ideal, the quality of beauty, is that women be treated equally, this should be the charge and task of *fiqh*. *Fiqh* should, through the systematic tools of jurisprudence, seek to the extent possible to make the earthly reality as close as possible to the divine reality. While envy and hatefulness are decried as immoral, this does not mean that the laws dealing with women should be static and unchanging. The Qur'anic discourse on coveting what is in the hands of others deals with the motive for change, not the fact of change. Put differently, if the reason for change is to achieve the moral objectives of Shari'ah, that is legitimate and necessary. Furthermore, if change achieves a more authentic proportionality between duties and rights, it would be consistent with the moral trajectory of the Qur'an. Moreover, if change is sought because there is a social need and rising demand for change, again, that would be consistent with Qur'anic methodology. However, if change is sought by begrudging people their achievements and regardless of the proportionality between rights and needs, and if change is sought not in furtherance of the moral objectives of Shari'ah, then such change might be illegitimate. Part of the reason for its illegitimacy is that if it is not justified by social needs and demands, and if it is not guided by an effort to fulfill the moral objectives of Shari'ah, then such change could produce a situation that is unjust and destabilizing and that ultimately does more harm than good.

The clear meaning of what I am arguing here is that provided that social dynamics mandate equality for women—for instance, women carry a financial responsibility equal to men—it is more consistent with Shari'ah to allow women an equal share to men in inheritance. This change and new right could be justified by women's struggle to obtain God's grace, which in this case is the right to inherit equal to men; by the fact that the social status of women has changed where there is proportionality between their duties and rights; and by the pursuit to have earthly law approximate to the extent possible the divine truth, which is strict equality between men and women. At this point, the pertinent question is: If the Qur'an sought to empower women by setting in motion a process according to which women gained greater rights, and according to which this process should increasingly approximate the divine truth of equality, why the process at all? Why didn't the Qur'an simply grant women full equal rights instead of granting incomplete rights? For instance, if God had willed brothers and sisters to inherit equal shares—if that is the ideal of beauty, and if that is the divine truth—why give sisters the right to inherit only half?

I think that the answer has to be that while it was imperative to set the process toward moral beauty in motion, it is not necessarily the case that implementing the moral ideal at the time of the Prophet would have been just or equitable. For instance, in Arab society at that time, a sister would be under the care of her father, uncles, brothers, and sons. There was a social welfare network that created legally and socially enforceable expectations so that, for example, a woman without means could resort to this network to compel her uncle to take care of her. This network has all but vanished in the modern age. Considering the historical context, allowing women to inherit any share at the time of the Prophet was genuinely radical. But there is another dynamic that relates to the idea of striving to acquire God's grace. It is perhaps unusual to think of social and political rights as part of God's grace that should be acquired by hard work and struggle. But I think that once the basic moral principle is affirmed—once God identifies a particular category of beauty as valid for human pursuit—how much of that category is to be fulfilled depends on matters other than God's simple dictates. One way of conceptualizing it is that there are basic moral principles: for instance, slaves ought to be freed; women should be able to inherit; criminals should be punished; the poor should be treated with compassion and mercy; and if attacked, one should be allowed to defend oneself. These rights are foundational. How much or to what extent we achieve those basic rights can be called derivative or contingent. Foundational rights are established as basic and primary. Derivative or contingent rights are born out of social demands and needs and serve to promote and further foundational rights. Although based on subjective human experiences, derivative or contingent rights under the right set of circumstances become necessary for the maintenance and greater fulfillment of foundational rights. Being subjectively based—that is, based on the social and political experiences of people—the demand for such rights increases, and the implementation of these rights becomes more equitable as the conditions for the fulfillment of the derivative or contingent rights become more welcoming. This process is incremental and gradual and is directly proportional to the rising demands for these rights. As noted before, if subjectively based rights are widely claimed, there must be an effort to claim these rights as objective and universal. If a derivative or contingent right is consistently asserted as objective and universal, it might reach the status of becoming a foundational right. To reiterate, foundational rights identified in the Qur'an are not incremental or evolving—contingent or derivative rights evolve as they move from the realm of the subjectively based to the objective and universal, and thus, they, in turn, become foundational. Why all of this? Because attempting to treat foundational rights as the same as contingent or derivative rights would necessitate the application of a substantial amount of social coercion, and the Qur'an prohibits coercion in matters of religion.[72] Forcing people to abide by derivative or contingent rights when the structural setting of society is not able to accommodate such a change is likely to lead to a substantial amount of injustice—which would be contrary to the condition of beauty. Furthermore, the Qur'an consistently emphasizes that God does not change a people unless they first change themselves.[73] Put simply, the Qur'an sets out moral goals and ethical trajectories, but if people want to advance on the road of morality and beauty, they must change themselves first and struggle toward acquiring God's blessings and grace.

In my view, the Qur'an pushes people toward particular moral goals by limiting abusive situations. But the prevalent logic of the Qur'an is that people ought to strive and struggle to obtain God's blessings. God's blessings are not limited to rewards in the Hereafter, but they include social progress, more rights and entitlements to human beings, and a fuller expression of beauty in the social institutions and laws that govern people. Although God's blessings are not normally thought of in this way, the reality is that the Qur'an consistently speaks about socially advantageous conditions, such as peace, tranquility and safety, a secure homeland, adequate shelter, financial success, thriving commerce, and lack of oppression, as blessings from God that are contingent on the efforts of human beings. Importantly, however, the enjoyment of socially advantageous conditions cannot be based on coercive dynamics. In fact, coercive dynamics are often portrayed in the Qur'an as leading to oppression and to the corruption of the earth. The Qur'an teaches that calling to the path of the Lord should be done with wisdom and a beautiful demeanor and that one should reason with people in a gracious fashion. "For your Lord knows who strays from the path, and God knows those who are rightly guided."[74] It is contrary to the prerequisites of goodness to coerce people to be good or beautiful. Rather, there is no alternative to seeking what might be called an overlapping consensus according to which, through advocacy and persuasion, Muslims are convinced to move closer to conditions of goodness and beauty by pursuing the moral and ethical lessons taught by God.

Reading Islamic texts, especially the Qur'an, in order to derive moral and ethical lessons, requires a major epistemological shift in understanding the way that God affirms a moral and ethical principle and then illustrates the lesson by responding to and treating abusive situations. Especially among modern Muslims, the Qur'anic methodology in dealing with what it calls situations of *istid'af* (oppression by rendering the other weak and dependent) has been a largely neglected field of study. In fact, one way of understanding Qur'anic moral and ethical trajectories and also understanding the dynamics of the Qur'an in dealing with the establishment of foundational rights as well as derivative and contingent rights is by analyzing the Qur'anic efforts to put an end to situations of *istid'af* within the historical context of early Islam. Put simply, *istid'af* is the existence of social conditions that made certain groups or classes of people weak and dependent in relation to others. Because of this relationship of *istid'af*, the ideal of submission to God is rendered more difficult due to the fact that people in this condition find themselves vulnerable to the demands and whimsies of others. In effect, the weak and dependent are rendered submissive to other human beings, and because of this, their submission to God is compromised by their powerlessness before other human beings. Interestingly, the idea of *istid'af* is not purely physical or material but also has a psychological component. The *mustad'afun* (the victims of *istid'af*) are not just materially weak and dependent but are also seen as such by their oppressors. In other words, whatever the material conditions that make such a people objectively weak and dependent, they are also seen as subservient and inferior and are treated with a distinct sense of arrogance on the part of those who have power over them. Significantly, if those who find themselves in a condition of *istid'af* fail to take action to change their condition, the Qur'an holds them blameworthy by describing them as unjust to themselves.[75] If people meekly accept *istid'af* and do not actively attempt to challenge their condition and alter it, they are suborning injustice by allowing it to exist. Two points follow from the Qur'anic discourse on *istid'af*. First, Qur'anic reforms were often intended to end conditions of *istid'af* and to break the moral arrogance that pervaded these relationships. This meant that the reforms introduced by the Qur'an were proportional with the need to put an end to conditions of *istid'af* and to alter prevalent attitudes of moral arrogance that existed within the Qur'anic context. But this also means that under a different set of circumstances, further reforms might be needed to deal with different forms of *istid'af* prevalent at a particular time and that further measures might needed to challenge new forms of moral arrogance. Second, the connection between *istid'af* and moral arrogance is yet another reason that the Qur'an expects people to strive toward attaining more rights consistent with the foundational rights recognized by God. Furthermore, if people help themselves and God reciprocates their efforts by putting an end to a situation of *istid'af*, they have walked in God's path, and they also have earned God's blessings. The victims of *istid'af* need to become empowered not just materially but emotionally and psychologically as well, and by articulating and pursuing their ethical demands, they need to challenge and deconstruct socially ingrained moral arrogance. Perhaps most importantly, Muslims have not yet explored the full implications of the notion that by accepting oppressive situations, acquiescing in relationships of weakness and dependency, and failing to demand justice in the sense of a proportional and reciprocal relationship between rights and duties, they are deviating from the divine path and committing a sin toward themselves. If Muslim women, for instance, internalize this idea, the effect would be nothing short of revolutionary.

To make the discussion more concrete, I will give a few illustrative examples of the Qur'anic treatment of abuse and situations of *istid'af*, and I will explore the moral and ethical implications of these treatments. In pre-Islamic Arabia, one of the prevailing abusive practices considered a wife as part of the inheritable legacy of the deceased. Accordingly, typically, a brother would inherit his deceased brother's wife, but he did not inherit the wife as property. Rather, the brother would have an option to marry the wife if he so desired, and the wife would not be free to marry again until the brother had decided whether or not to exercise his option. The resulting practice was that brothers having the option would refuse to release the wife unless she paid him a sum of money for her freedom, or if the wife received a marriage proposal, the brother would usurp the dowry in return for granting the wife a release. Of course, this practice created a class of oppressed and highly dependent women, and the Qur'an strictly prohibited the taking of women as heritage. In addition, more generally, the Qur'an forbade the tyrannizing of women in order to usurp their money and laid out a broad principle that when men live with women, the basis for their cohabitation must be kindness and equanimity.[76] Another widespread social practice with a detrimental effect on women involved the taking of the dowry. Normally in marriage, the groom would pay the bride a dowry, the amount of which she was supposed to decide on with input from her family. Fathers, however, got into the habit of taking dowries to themselves without consulting with their daughters. This created a strong potential for abuse because fathers had an incentive to marry their daughters off to the person paying the highest dowry. Furthermore, this practice undermined the very purpose for dowries in Islam, which were supposed to provide women with some form of financial security. In re-sponse, the Qur'an ordered men to refrain from usurping women's dowries and went further by advising men that it is immoral to covet money they have given women (*'an tib nafs*) and that it is also immoral to connive to take back money that was given to women in good will.[77] Not surprisingly, considering the practices of the age, the idea that there is a distinction between the property of fathers and husbands on the one hand and daughters and wives on the other was nothing short of shocking. Nevertheless, the distinction was necessary to address actual abuses confronting the early Muslim community.

Divorce presented a whole separate set of problems. Among pervasive practices, on divorcing women, men would seek to take back whatever mon-ey or property they gave their wives during the course of the marriage. In addition, quite often on divorce, men would make alimony payments or other forms of support conditional. If, for whatever reason, men became displeased with the demeanor or conduct of their divorced wives, they, at will, would refuse to make any postmarriage payments. The Qur'an emphasized that it is a serious sin to take money given to wives during the course of a marriage, and it could be done only under a limited and restricted set of conditions.[78] As to alimony, the Qur'an asserted: "And for divorced women make fair provision—this is a duty upon the God-fearing and pious."[79] In other words, the Qur'an removed the element of discretion from the hands of men and correlated between obedience to God, piety, submission to God, and the removal of the condition of *istid'af* in which these women found themselves. What was problematic in these situations were the oppressive and dependent conditions in which certain women found themselves, but in addressing the particular social problem in question, the Qur'an also affirmed moral and ethical principles that have a broad application.

Another social practice that posed serious moral challenges and that elic-ited a strong Qur'anic response related to repeated marriages and divorces done in an abusive way. In pre-Islamic Arabia, a man enjoyed the exclusive right to divorce his wife with or without cause, and after the divorce, a woman was compelled to go through something known as the *'idda* (a specific waiting period before she could marry again), during which a husband could remarry his divorcée without a new contract or dowry. Many men started using these privileges as a way to torment women—as a way of spite, a man would divorce his wife, wait until a day or two before the *'idda* period was about to expire, and then remarry his wife again, only to divorce her again immediately so that a new waiting period would begin. This would be done repeatedly and over and over without any limit. This was used as a way of keeping a woman hanging—such a woman would neither be married nor divorced, and as long as the husband kept taking his divorcée back shortly before the end of the waiting period, the wife would remain in an impossible situation, never being able to remarry as long as her husband kept exercising his option during the waiting period. In one version of this same practice, husbands would add insult to injury by proclaiming one or two days before the end of the waiting period, "*La'ibt*" (I was just playing, jesting, or fooling around). Several women complained to the Prophet about these practices and asked for a solution, and the Prophet asked them to wait until he received revelation on the matter. The Qur'anic response to these practices was manifold, and as is typical of Qur'anic methodology, the Qur'an limited the potential for abuse without fundamentally changing the existing social structure. Condemning those who divorce and remarry women out of a desire to torment and harass them, the Qur'an exclaimed that either a husband should live with his wife in kindness and honor or divorce her also in kindness and honor, but in all situations, those who hold on to their wives in order to torment or harass them have committed a great sin and they have become among those who are unjust toward themselves.[80] In addition, while not eradicating the practice of *'idda*, the Qur'an limited the process to two times. A husband and wife may divorce and return to each other during the waiting period, but only two times. If there is a third divorce, they cannot remarry during the waiting period.[81] As to those who insulted their wives by telling them they were just jesting, the Qur'an describes such behavior as sinful and responds by saying: "Do not mock the words and decrees of your Lord."[82] It is interesting that mocking a divorced wife is equated in the Qur'anic discourse with the sin of mocking the words, decrees, and will of the Lord. It is as if this demeaning way of dealing with divorced women is considered directly offensive to God.

There are many other examples that could be cited demonstrating the same basic Qur'anic dynamic. For instance, the evidence indicates that the abuses of the very widespread practice of polygamy were restricted, but not terminated, by restricting the number of wives to four and by affirming that monogamy is the basis and polygamy ought to be treated as the exception. In addition, the legitimacy of polygamy was hinged on what may be called control factors. The Qur'an clearly states that marriage to more than one wife is conditional on the existence of a fear that one will not be equitable toward orphaned children. The Qur'an states: "If you fear that you cannot be equitable to orphaned children, then marry women who are lawful to you, two, three, or four." The Qur'an goes on to say that the wives must be treated fairly and equitably, and if people fear that they cannot be just, then they should limit themselves to one wife.[83] Elsewhere, the Qur'an pronounces an ominous warning to husbands—it informs them that they will not be able to be fair and equitable even if they try hard to be so. It also warns husbands not to intentionally or unintentionally neglect a wife until she becomes as if left suspended or hanging (*mu'allaqa*).[84] Furthermore, the Qur'an warns of the danger of people fooling themselves by allowing their whims to lead them away from justice. The Qur'an articulates the general principle: "O' you believers, be custodians of justice and bear witness for God even if it be against yourselves, your parents, or your relatives. . . . So do not follow your whims lest you swerve away from justice, and if you prevaricate and turn away from justice, know that God is cognizant of all that you do."[85]

As a text, the Qur'an demands a conscientious and morally active reader—a reader who does not stop where the text concludes but who seeks to understand the ethical path the text is setting out and then proceeds to travel along that path. Many Muslims read the passages discussed above, and the primary conclusion that they derive is that a woman should own her dowry, that couples can be married and divorced three times, that a divorcée is entitled to support payments for a set period of time, and that inheritance rights of women are such-and-such. But I think this is only the starting point of the process, not the end of it. I do not believe that the Qur'anic potential is fulfilled by morally inert and apathetic readers who wait to receive the rules and regulations that they rush to enforce without much reflection on or comprehension of the ethical processes that the Qur'an was setting in motion. This necessarily means that the human agent, who is God's viceroy and who is charged with the duty to avoid corrupting the earth, who is charged with the duty of bearing witness on God's behalf, establishing justice on earth and achieving submission to God by approximating divinity through the pursuit of beauty—it necessarily means that such an agent carries a heavy burden of walking in the path of divinity. The very idea of walking in the path of divinity implies a process of growth and discovery and implies that the engagement with the divine is not a static or mechanical process where people simply receive technical commands and implement them. The Qur'an refers to the burden that God's viceroys shoulder as the trust (*amana*). In a powerful symbolic discourse, the Qur'an demonstrates the seriousness and heaviness of this trust by stating that God offered the trust in the heavens, earth, and mountains, but all refrained from bearing it, and in fact, because of its onerous nature, all became frightened by it. But human beings accepted the divine trust, for human beings are often foolhardy and arrogant.[86] The point of this anecdote is to emphasize both the potential and risk. Everything, including the mountains, could not shoulder the trust because, although big and enormous in size, they have no capacity for rational and moral reflection and growth. Their status, characteristics, and qualities are predetermined and set, and their reactions are humble but instinctive. They are safe and risk averse, and they are obedient to God and submissive, but they also cannot tread in the path of divinity and grow in that path. As the Qur'an emphasizes, willingly or not, all creation is submissive to God, and all creation knows and accepts its station.[87] In other words, whatever potentialities these creations possess, they have been fulfilled from the moment of inception. Human beings, although possessing enormous potential, have as their pitfall their ego that inclines them toward arrogance and foolishness.

The Qur'an emphasizes a similar point in another anecdotal narrative relating to the moment of creation. God created Adam and Eve and destined them to inherit the earth. The angels who, unlike human beings, do not possess volition and free will inquired of God as to the wisdom behind giving the earth to creatures who could cause great corruption and spill much blood and, in doing so, disobey God. The angels, on the other hand, sanctify God and intone his litanies. God responded to the angels' puzzlement by reminding them that he knows what they do not know. Importantly, however, God revealed the virtue of human beings by demonstrating the human capacity for comprehension, thought, and rationality, and after doing so, God ordered the angels to prostrate themselves before Adam out of respect and in recognition of the divine potential that humans represent.[88] The prostration of the angels before Adam also represented the enormity of the honor and burden of the trust placed in human beings.

If the trust shouldered consisted simply of the capacity to understand specific laws and then enforce them, this would have hardly required the magnanimous capacities that God had endowed human beings with. It would not have been the kind of trust that the Heavens, earth, and mountains shirked and became frightened by. Importantly, passages of the Qur'an that address specific problems and that articulate particular solutions must be read with full awareness of the trust placed in human beings, in general, and Muslims, more specifically. Such passages served to assist and illustrate methods and ways according to which the obligations of the trust could be discharged. The specific resolutions reached by the Qur'an in response to particular historical problems did not articulate the full nature and scope of the trust and did not exhaustively inform Muslims as to the measures they need to take to fully satisfy the burdens of this trust. Such passages point and direct toward a course—they do not define a destination.

As I mentioned earlier, one of the central duties of a Muslim as an individual and Muslims in general, as a nation, is to enjoin the good and forbid the evil. In the language of the Qur'an, Muslims are to call for the *ma'ruf* and enjoin against the *munkar*. Both of these terms imply a sense of consensus—*ma'ruf* is what is known to be good, and *munkar* is what is known to be wrong. In a sense, the Qur'an itself engages in the same process that it advocates—it enjoins the good and forbids what is wrong by engaging the morality that already exists among people and then by propelling people toward the betterment of their moral consciousness. The Qur'an engages the overlapping consensus that already exists, critiques it, and then seeks to create a new overlapping consensus, and this is exactly the process that Muslims must undertake if they are to carry the burden of the trust placed in them. By doing so, they are able to witness for God against themselves and over others, but what they cannot do is to stand arrogant and aloof, judging people. Addressing Muslims, the Qur'an reminds them that to God belongs the East and West, and that whatever direction they face therein is the glory and truth of God. Within this context, the Qur'an describes the true nature of what Muslims are supposed to stand for—God has made Muslims a people right in the middle so that they will bear witness over humanity, and so that the Prophet will bear witness over Muslims. [89] Maybe these verses more than any others remind Muslims of a truth that the Puritanical-Salafis and others have long forgotten. The word used by the Qur'an to describe the position of Muslims is *wasata*, which could mean temperate, moderate, or in the middle of things. To occupy this position of moderation and balance necessarily means that one does not look at other human beings from a point of arrogant supremacy and epistemological self-sufficiency. Rather, Muslims are charged with being right in the midst of humanity—learning, interacting, and teaching. To occupy this position, however, Muslims have to be intimately connected with all moral progress and epistemological growth, learning from it and, in turn, influencing it. As the Qur'an emphasizes, the imperative confronting Muslims is to understand the moral and ethical and epistemological overlapping consensus that exists in this globalized world, critique it, and improve on it—grow with it, and seek to establish a new epistemological, moral, and ethical realization. Along this path and process, the Qur'an provides moral and ethical directives as well as epistemological illustrations.

Given the implications of what I am arguing here, it might very well be that the rules of inheritance, marriage and divorce, or criminal law would have to be materially changed. But I think that the import of this argument is that instead of sanctifying rules, we sanctify the path of God. By learning from the Qur'anic methodology of reform and giving it full effect, we move from the realm of serving the *ahkam* (positive rules) to a more authentic realization of Shari'ah. Most importantly, in putting substance before form, this methodology would more faithfully carry the burden of the trust by struggling to come closer to divinity. To return to the analogy of classical music, it is not that we neglect or ignore the form—far from it. We carefully study the existing forms but then proceed to compose new symphonies that represent greater accomplishments in beauty.

One can write a fairly thick volume of text analyzing the Qur'anic reforms and Qur'anic methodology in pursuing these reforms. In the premodern age, some of this work was accomplished under the rubric of abrogation (*naskh*), and, as noted earlier, there is serious work done on the objectives of Shari'ah (*maqasid al-shari'ah*). Much of this premodern literature will be of great use in the contemporary age if studied through a critical and analytic methodology. But even these fields cannot replace the urgent need to analyze the relationship between the Qur'anic discourses that articulate broad moral and ethical principles, and the many examples in which the Qur'an engaged and reformed a living problem. I have discussed specific closely related examples to demonstrate the point, but there are many others. In order to demonstrate the rather broad range of the examples of Qur'anic reforms, I will close this section by describing an illustration of a very different kind and with a different point than the ones discussed above. The examples discussed so far have all related to the unpleasant and sad circumstances of oppression and dependency, but the next example conveys a sense of empowerment and dignity through loyalty and love.

A man by the name of Ma'qal bin Yassar had a sister whom he married to a man from the Ansar of Medina, referred to as Laka' in some reports. The sister and her husband loved each other, and their marriage was going well. Things, however, started going sour between the two spouses until it got to a point that the husband divorced his wife. During the waiting period there was no reconciliation, and after the prescribed three months, the husband and wife became permanently divorced. If they wished to remarry, they would need a new contract and dowry. Eventually, the ex-husband and ex-wife started missing each other, and they wanted to remarry. Ma'qal, however, would not hear of it. He berated Laka' and accused him of being ungrateful and without honor. He said, in effect, "Laka', I honored you by marrying my sister to you, and you disrespected her by divorcing her! I will never agree to the two of you marrying again!" Despite his sister's fervent urgings and the repeated efforts of Laka', Ma'qal would not change his mind. But according to the reports, God knew how much they loved each other and needed each other, and God knew of their repeated supplications to him to make Ma'qal change his mind. Around this time, the following revelation was recited for the first time by the Prophet: "If there be among you women who are divorced, and they have completed the fixed term of waiting (three months), do not prevent them from marrying (again) whom they choose, if the man and woman agree with each other honorably. This is wise advice to those who believe in God and the Last Day. This is more proper and pure for God knows and you do not know."[90] On hearing this revelation, Ma'qal realized that he had no right to stop his sister from marrying whom she loves, even if his bruised ego told him otherwise. Ma'qal confessed his error by telling his sister: "I heard my God, and now I must obey." And he promptly agreed to the marriage.[91]

Stories of vindicated lovers are a prototype in Islamic literature that expressed the dreams, aspirations, and longings of the early Muslim community. For instance, a very similar story is reported about Jabir bin 'Abd Allah and his cousin, and in this narrative as well, the Qur'an vindicates the committed lovers, who are forced apart by someone whose pride and ego stands in the way of love. Significantly, this person's pride and ego not only obstruct the path of the lovers but also the path of God. In essence, this person, who prevents the union of the committed lovers, fails to understand that as far as God is concerned, it is not his pride, dignity, or honor that is relevant, but the will, honor, dignity, and autonomy of the lovers, and especially the autonomy and dignity of the woman who finds herself forced into a position of *istid'af*. Notably, for instance, the Qur'an explicitly refers to and vindicates the will and choice of the woman in question because she is the one who suffers the burden of social institutions and practices that coerce her into a dependent position. If one reflects on the Qur'anic treatment and dynamic motion toward empowerment and reform, I think it becomes clear that greater autonomy and dignity for women is the Islamic moral trajectory and the divine path of beauty.

Chapter Twelve

The Caliphate of Humanity

ON CURSING THE DEVIL AND OTHER MEMORIES

During the long, exhausting hours of studying Islamic law, I would sit cross-legged on the floor with a book in my lap and papers or notebook on a small table before me. I struggled to comprehend and memorize so much of the intellectual product of the interpretive communities of the past. It often felt like I was standing at the shore trying to drink the waters of a raging storm—a storm of terms, definitions, ideas, concepts, categories, approaches, distinctions, and differentiations. What I was dealing with was a formidable intellectual heritage of numerous interpretive communities that could either drown or empower a person to persevere through any storm. This formidable tradition, depending on whether the person who handles it is spiritually and intellectually weak or strong, either could turn a person into a corpse decaying under the accumulations of minutiae and rotting in a grave of ineptitude and redundancies or could empower a person to stand straight and high on top of a tower of ideas. This tradition could make a person hide from the world in a closed tomb, or it could supply a person with a virtual life source of inspiration and thought. It all depends not only on the quality of the student, but also on the quality of the teacher. I would find myself drawn to teachers who tormented us with the quality of their questions, rather than those who assured us with the authoritativeness of their responses. We were a large number of students, all hearing the same lectures and reading the same materials. Although we read the same exact texts and dealt with the same teachers after the licenses were issued, the wildly divergent attitudes of students never ceased to amaze me. Some of us felt burdened by the license—now people will come to you for answers about God's law, and the torturous feeling of "What do I know?" refused to go away. Other students armed themselves with the license as if it were rocket fuel and flew off, volunteering their learned speculations on everything they wanted to believe they knew. Some of us felt that the material we studied qualified us to ask the right questions, and some thought that this same material provided all the right answers to any type of question. But I always noticed that the second group, the know-it-alls, came increasingly in vogue as Puritanical-Salafism spread, and as sociopolitical anxieties increased, these folks enjoyed more respect and greater authoritativeness. Annoyed and bothered, I and some of my friends went to the nearly empty stationery store in 'Abasiyya, Cairo, owned by one of our teachers, Shaykh Jarudi. Although a stationery store, the place was packed with books, none of them for sale, for between the occasional sale here and there, the shaykh spent his days reading books with yellowish pages, underlining about half of what he read in pencil and writing comments in the margins in small but perfectly legible handwriting. Before each class, which most of the time was held in his store, a group of us would arrive early so that we could rummage through the books and read the Shaykh's spirited comments in the margins. To this very day, I still remember some of the surprising comments written in these margins, which at times seemed so unrelated to the texts the Shaykh was reading that not one of us dared to ask him about them. In one of those comments, for instance, he wrote something to the effect of: "An unbeliever who is sincere about his lack of belief will always be victorious over a Muslim who is insincere about his faith." I had not heard this statement before, but it struck me as sensible. Whoever is most sincere about his beliefs will end up winning the heart of the world, but, alas, I never verified this understanding with the shaykh.[1]

We waited until the shaykh was done with one of his customers, and after wishing him the Islamic greeting of peace, one of us, who was also the oldest of the group, started to explain the reason for our unexpected visit. When frustrated, our friend was in the habit of cursing the devil, and after heaping profound curses on Satan for all his evil, speaking on our behalf he proceeded to whine about the fact that after strenuous studies, we felt that we had only become qualified to ask more questions. But betraying our preoccupation with our bruised collective ego, he complained bitterly that our classmates, belonging to the second group, who did not perform as well as we did, were rising in social status and were becoming authoritative representatives of the divine will—people went to them with their questions, asked them to lead prayers, and on special religious occasions, more people made sure to convey their respects, and according to our friend, people were even starting to court them to marry their daughters. This last point we had not previously discussed, and the claim came as a bit of a surprise to the rest of us. The shaykh was visibly pleased with our visit—other than his books, he lived for his students. He was now retired after teaching for decades in one of the Azhar Seminary–affiliated schools. Unlike many of his colleagues, however, he had never been to the Gulf countries on sabbatical or any type of leave— he had never tasted the sweetness of oil money, and so he remained poor. It was said, however, that his brother who worked in Saudi Arabia was the one who bought the stationery store for him. The shaykh's first piece of advice was: "Do not curse the devil! Instead of cursing the devil, mention the name of God." This caught us by surprise, and it only emphasized our collective sense of ignorance. Seeing that we were a bit confused, the shaykh explained: "It is reported that this is what the Prophet, peace and blessings be upon him, taught. There are people who prefer to curse the devil, and there are people who prefer to mention God's name. Which of the two would you rather be? The question is which kind of Muslim do you want to be?"

Our friend who had spoken earlier apparently could not resist the temptation to engage the shaykh—he said: "I recall that after the Battle of Uhud, when Muslims suffered a military setback, reportedly, the Prophet in anger cursed some of the unbelievers who fought against the Muslims, and, as we studied, God corrected the Prophet, reminding him that he is but a messenger who is to convey God's message and nothing else. God in the Qur'an responded by saying: 'You have no say in the matter; it is up to God to pardon them or punish them for they have been unjust. To God belongs all that is in the heavens and earth. God may pardon whom God pleases and punish whom God pleases. And God is most forgiving and merciful.'[2] But Shaykh, surely cursing men who fought against the Prophet is entirely different from cursing the devil! Those men God reserves the right to forgive or punish, but the devil is most certainly excluded from God's grace, so why can't I curse him?"

The rest of us looked at each other uncomfortably; we were not as preoccupied with the right to curse the devil, but the shaykh had a different point to make. "The issue is not cursing the devil," the shaykh responded, "The issue is how do you serve God? It is a frame of mind—confronted by the darkness of evil do you curse the darkness or do you remember the light? Cursing is an act of destruction but to mention God's name is to build and construct. My sons, remember what you love, not what you hate."

He looked at our faces as if to read the effect, but I am sure that he could see that we were anxious about the issue that precipitated this visit in the first place. It was not long before the shaykh continued with a hint of reprimand in his tone: "As to this momentary lapse in humility, ask yourself, what do you offer people? People come to you, and you teach them questions—they go to others, they teach them answers. Who do you think they will go to? But that is the wrong question—the right question is: Which way, which path is more consistent with submission to God? When you deal with people, you could either say that 'I know' or you could say 'I don't know'—when you approach God, you could say 'God, I approach you and I know' or you could approach God and say 'God, I approach you and I don't know'—which of these two is more consistent with submission before God?"

The meeting with the shaykh went on for several hours, and after a long discussion it became clear that the shaykh's point was that a student of Shari'ah must always seek to remain a student. Once a student starts coveting becoming a teacher and a source of authority, the integrity of the process becomes compromised. If we wished to maintain our integrity, the shaykh gave us a choice: either speak on God's behalf—claim to represent the divine will—and say very little, or speak on your own behalf—claim to express your own opinions—and say all you want.

What the shaykh said has remained with me for many years—the challenge, however, was far more serious than our petty egos and concerns. In the modern age, the challenge was not limited to which of us mattered, but whether any of us mattered at all. We were living in an age that had grown increasingly unaccommodating to God and that left an ever-decreasing space for religion in general. People went to the Puritanical-Salafis and their like to ask them practical questions so that they could get practical responses. People went to them for definite answers. But what my friends and I did not realize back then was that the Puritanical-Salafis and their like were useful in the modern age because they offered people a religion that worked well with their thoroughly secularized lives. By offering concrete, determinable, and specific responses to people's religious questions, the Puritanical-Salafis and others supplied people with a neatly and tightly packaged religion that occupied a limited sphere of space and time. People could unwrap the package, consume the product, and move on with living their lives, unburdened by religion. The Puritanical-Salafis and others offered a religion that does not demand much from the intellect and conscience—it could be literally performed within a limited frame of reference without impinging on the full complexities of life and without affecting every aspect of consciousness. This is the reason that one notices that modern-day life is often compartmentalized and segmented into the religious and the areligious or nonreligious. This is also why one often observes what appears like a severe gap between piety and morality and also the shocking inconsistency between the solemn and tranquil beauty of religious ritual and the extreme ugliness committed by purportedly religious people. People could go to the mosque on Friday for an hour and be with God, but on Saturday, their conduct and frame of reference could have little or nothing to do with God. By making Islam so tangible, concrete, and determinable, Puritanical-Salafis made it far more possible to compartmentalize and segment it in a neat and clean fashion and make it largely irrelevant and marginal to how Muslims conduct public life. Therefore, as long as Islam can be limited to what is performed as a matter of ritual, we do not have to confront more abstract and open-ended questions, for instance, about the nature of mercy, justice, or beauty. For instance, in this context, the technical and mechanical act of covering (the hijab) has replaced the far more subtle and nuanced process of practicing modesty. Furthermore, in this framework, it becomes possible to perform the ritual of hijab and then proceed with the rest of life with an essentially areligious or nonreligious frame of reference. If, on the other hand, women believe that no ritual is sufficient to discharge their obligations toward God and believe that Islam is a total moral and intellectual engagement that permeates every aspect of life, it becomes difficult to relegate religion to any particular ritual, no matter how central it may be. Ultimately, in the Puritanical-Salafi paradigm, it becomes possible for Islam to control people's bodies while their conscience, heart, and intellect are abandoned to something or someone else. In this paradigm, it becomes possible for Islam to lay claim to the whole world, but at the same time remain entirely marginal in it. Even more, it becomes possible for Muslims to follow Islam but not submit to God.

By pursuing open-ended questions and by insisting that Islam is an open-ended moral, intellectual, and physical engagement, our approach invaded the space dominated by secular paradigms in the modern age. If submission to God was going to be the basis of how Muslims related to ethics, morality, aesthetics, and beauty, then religion could not occupy a neatly defined space in life. Religion, as a basic frame of reference, would be relevant to public as well as private life; to politics, economics, society, family, and individuality; to work, leisure, and death; to science, philosophy, and art; and to the physical as well as the metaphysical. Religion is as essential and relevant as the human conscience to whatever goes into forming the convictions of the human intellect. The reason for this is straightforward enough: for a believing Muslim, whatever the endeavor or undertaking, as a matter of conscience and conviction, this Muslim must strive to bring existence as close as possible to a state of divinity. This would necessarily mean that in a pluralist society people would be free to advocate comprehensive views of the good life, even if such views are based on religion, in an attempt to convince their fellow citizens that their view is desirable and wise. A Muslim, for instance, could formulate a comprehensive view of the good life based on a variety of elements, including submitting to a sovereign and engaged God, bearing the burden of viceroyship, and witnessing for God. But by tolerating other competing comprehensive views, they would find points of overlapping consensus with others and agree to pursue the collective good on matters of overlapping consensus with those others. The advantage of this approach is that it is clearly premised on the notion that submission to God does not imply and cannot be equated with domination or control over others. In fact, in my view, it is exactly because we dominate or control no other that we are truly able to submit to God. However, by articulating and vigilantly pursuing a comprehensive view of the good life and seeking to broaden the space of overlapping consensus with others, the Islamic duties of enjoining the good, bearing witness, and being the middle nation are discharged. Admittedly, this is a new framework and a way of thinking that might be unfamiliar to many Muslims, but I think that if seriously considered, it becomes rather self-evident. Note, for example, that by playing an active role in persuading others and being persuaded by others, in uncovering the universal standards that are common to all people, and by being in the heart and core of human engagements and struggling to shift the center of discourse to a greater fulfillment of beauty and divinity, Muslims can play an active role in the fulfillment of the duties of the covenant. Muslims can pursue *ta'aruf* (knowing the other and dynamic social intercourse) on the basis of mercy and compassion, prevent the corruption of the earth, establish the ideal of peace and tranquility, and actively enjoin the good and advocate against the evil. In doing so, literally speaking, Muslims become a genuinely middle nation in the sense that they are in the very center of any emerging overlapping consensus, and they become true witnesses to the interactions of humanity. The more successful Muslims are in discharging their duties and in persuading others of the imperative of beauty and the more effective their role in producing and defining the universal overlapping consensus, the more successful they are in achieving submission to God.

The difficulty with this approach is that it is challenging and not very satisfying to the ego. It requires Muslims to engage in an international dynamic that makes many demands on Muslims. If Muslims are going to be persuasive to others, this mandates that they take the world around them very seriously. The framework advocated here does not produce any easy and immediate results; it does not rely on the comforts of affectation, and it has little use for pretentious slogans that allow Muslims to feel that they are in control and even superior to the world. In reality, it renders them increasingly marginal and irrelevant. Not only would Muslims need to dynamically and confidently engage the thought and beliefs of others, but they would also need to critically engage and reflect on their own traditions. In order for the ideas of Islam to be relevant, Muslim thought needs to become accessible and accountable to others. In this framework, Islam would not be like an exclusive private club, where Muslims simply speak to each other and persuade each other of what they already believe. Rather, taking seriously the notion of a universal message addressed to humanity at large, Muslims must struggle with the challenging process of rendering their claims about good and evil, beauty and ugliness, right and wrong comprehensible and therefore accessible as well as accountable to others. This will necessarily mean a greater reliance on the rational and intuitive and what is ultimately communicable. This, however, does not mean that Muslims ought to limit their belief system to what is scientific or to what is empirically or philosophically verifiable. Rather, Muslims must be able to communicate their convictions and strive to make them persuasive. This will mean a greater reliance on what is rational, communicable, and conciliatory. Muslims would have to struggle with rendering what is adopted as a matter of intuition, faith, or in deference to text persuasive to others on grounds that are relevant or relatable to others.

It is important to emphasize that in this framework, the religious and secular would have to deal with each other in an effort to reach overlapping consensus without either orientation assuming an air of superiority toward the other. There would have to be equal and mutual tolerance in religious and secular discourses, and both would have an equal claim over the public sphere. In the same way that I believe that it is unfair and unjust to exclude religiously based comprehensive views of the good life from participation in the public sphere, I also think that it would be equally unfair and unjust to exclude secular comprehensive views of the good life from the public sphere. Both the religious and secular should have access to advocate their views of the good life in public forums, and neither has the right to exclude the other. In addition, the goal is not to have one of these approaches ultimately dominate the other or to become subservient to the other. The point is to find points of overlap and consensus and through discourse and interaction increase the depth and width of that valuable moral space.

It is of crucial significance to underscore two points at this juncture. Nothing that I have said thus far is intended to imply that every doctrine or rule in a religious system should be accessible and accountable to others. In the case of Islam, what falls in the category of what should be rendered accessible and accountable to others are matters that are appropriate for enjoining the good and forbidding the evil and matters on which Muslims have a duty to bear witness. This largely covers matters of social and political ethics and morality. The point is to make God's message more relevant and to contribute actively to the pursuit of goodness on this earth, not to deconstruct or unravel religious beliefs and doctrines. Moreover, the point is to find areas of overlap and commonality among human beings, not to deconstruct or destroy diversity and difference in human existence. All systems of belief, including secular systems, have their symbolisms and rituals that are essentially self-referential and not susceptible to rational scrutiny. The real question is the extent or amount of dogma within a system—in limited and

small amounts it might provide a necessary anchor and play a useful sociological role in strengthening the fabric of belief systems. But in large dosages, dogma is lethal—it produces paralysis, stagnation, and mental deficiencies. Furthermore, nothing I have said is intended to undermine the importance of ritual in religious life. Ritual, as long as it not forced on others, often
acts to structure the relationship of a human being with God. It is entirely
plausible that a religious person would believe that ritual is mandated by
God. Again, however, the issue is how much of life's space is covered by the
formalism and structuralism of ritual and whether ritual, as performance,
comes to subvert and replace the conscience and intellect. As noted earlier,
from an Islamic perspective, the issue is balance and moderation or reasonableness. The Prophet in repeated teachings emphasized that even worship
must be performed in moderation, and the Qur'an focuses on the idea of the
balance and reasonable measure as of essence to sustaining human life. As a
matter of faith and conviction, I believe that a Muslim who does away altogether with ritual is as imbalanced as someone who does away altogether
with the intellect. For me, the performance of rituals symbolizes my recognition of the very principle of submission to God and also represents my
personal acknowledgment of my fundamental commitment to God and my
need for and dependence on God's grace and providence. Defining these acts
of symbolic significance and identifying the basic language through which I
communicate with God are not discoverable or known by rational criteria.
They are invented and scripted by God. This is why, for instance, classical
Muslim jurists used to say that in matters of worship and ritual, the rule is
imitation (*al-ittiba'*), and in matters pertaining to human interaction and
interhuman dealings, the rule is innovation (*al-ibtida'*). Depending on how
we define what falls in the first category and what falls in the second, this
maxim makes a lot of sense.[3] As a Muslim, praying, fasting, paying alms,
pilgrimage, and other core rituals that define the skeletal structure of Islam
are as crucial to my religious faith as justice, beauty, mercy, compassion, and
peace, which can be described as Islam's flesh and brain. To me, someone
who ignores the skeleton is as lost as someone who does away with the rest.
The problem I am focusing on is that all too often, there are Muslims who
believe that the skeletal structure represents the full engagement of the faith,
and this I think is a grossly misguided view.

The challenge for all religious people is to define the place and contribution of religion in an age that seems to deal with religion as having no useful
function other than to serve as the occasional tranquilizer or sedative. The
challenge is to defy and alter the mental attitude that relegates religion to a
mindless "feel-good" dynamic, as if in the contemporary age religion has
become another forum for entertainment and self-indulgence. In my view, in
the age of postmodernism, there is a clear tendency in secular societies to
deal with God as if a personal pet whose sole job it is to love his companion
unequivocally and unconditionally, but, ironically, human beings do not feel
duty bound to reciprocate. Although God is expected to love a person regardless of what he or she does, God is not loved regardless of what he does. Like
a personal pet, God is expected to fit into our lives without being too imposing or demanding—without disrupting the basic pace and rhythm of our
lives—he owes us attention and concern, and we reciprocate only to the

extent that it is not too disruptive of the way we construct our lives and define our preferences. We expect God to sympathize and know us, as we heedlessly and egotistically define ourselves, but we do not bother with knowing God in the way that God chooses to define and describe himself. The odd posture of the secular age is that it sanctions a basic inequality in the relationship between human beings and the divine, and in this relationship God is effectively dealt with as the subservient party.

In my view, the Islamic theology of submission to God is fundamentally at odds with the self-idolatry of the secular age. The problem, however, is that there is a real absence of alternative models. The idolatry of the secular age came partly as a reaction to a different form of idolatry—the idolatry of religious intolerance and despotism. The secular experience has been that when God is taken more seriously—when God is treated as the master of the earth, and when submission becomes physical as well as metaphysical—a different type of self-idolatry is borne—instead of God becoming as if an ego-stroking pet, God becomes as if an ego-inflating rubber stamp validating the usurpation of the powers of divinity and depositing them in the hands of an institution or a group of people who rule and oppress in God's name. Modern Muslims will often point to the golden age of the four Rightly-Guided Caliphs as proof that the Western experience with theocracy is false and that it is possible for a polity to submit to the divine will without being despotic. Therefore, modern Muslims will often argue that secularism is anchored in the Western experience but that it is irrelevant to the Muslim context—Muslims, it is often claimed, never had a problem between church and state, hence secularism is a false paradigm as far as Muslims are concerned. The fact, however, is that while the dynamics between the church and state that took place in the West were indeed different from the historical experience of Muslims, at the same time, references to a presumed golden age in which the tension between political power and religion was eradicated is not possible without a grossly oversimplified and essentialistic reading of early Islamic history. Nevertheless, regardless of how one reads the Islamic historical experience, the problem today is to present a model that navigates a middle course between the despotic experience of theocracy and the godless experience of secularism. The most effective response in the modern age is to offer a successful model in which it is possible to submit to God while promoting human liberty, in which God's sovereignty does not impinge on the sovereign will of human beings, and in which honoring God's rights does not mean the deprecation of the rights of human beings. In my view, in the modern secular age, this is both a challenge and opportunity to Muslims. The opportunity is for Muslims to provide a positive demonstrative example of the affirmative and inclusive role that Islam could play in producing a way of life that is equally respectful toward God as it is toward human beings.

This, however, is not possible without assuming a particular moral attitude toward our position in the world. Part of this attitude was captured by my shaykh's comment regarding cursing the devil. The attitude is one in which Muslims become a positive force in the world, actively supporting the presence of God, instead of being a negative force complaining and griping about the presence of evil; to contribute something divine to human existence instead of to curse and hate the failures of human beings; and, ultimately, to recall what one loves, not what one hates. The most important part of this attitude, whether in dealing with Muslims or non-Muslims, is to seek to submit to God but seek to dominate no other. Beyond tolerance, the ethics that are needed at this stage are not simply to put up with and indulge the existence of the other but to discover ways to include others in a collective enterprise for the common good of all human beings. At a minimum, this collective enterprise should include all believers, whether Muslim or non-Muslim, but ideally, even the believers and unbelievers should be able to find what is common to both of them and should be able to pursue shared or reconcilable visions of beauty.

Finding a basis for this participatory model in Judaism and Christianity is the burden and duty of the theologians and thinkers of these traditions. Muslims, however, are under an obligation to care for their own tradition and to rethink and reconstruct it so that it can achieve its moral potential. For the balance of this section, I will investigate the moral and ethical thrust of the Islamic tradition on dealing with the non-Muslim other, and I will point to areas that would need rethinking and restructuring in order to facilitate the process of reaching this moral potential.

One of the pressing problems that Muslims confront and that often functions to derail many reform efforts is the image of Islam in the modern world. There is no doubt that the image of Islam as the religion of the sword and blood is to a large extent a product of prejudice and ignorance, but Muslims cannot ignore the impact that Puritanical-Salafis and other extremists have had on what Islam has come to represent to many people around the world. Without doubt, part of the challenge of reclaiming Islam has become that of reclaiming the reputation and image of the religion. But the needed changes in the modern age are not cosmetic—the modern legacy of defensiveness, reactiveness, militant thinking, and extremism has made the required changes pressing and substantial. What is needed today is a paradigm shift, but not a shift away from Islam, or toward diluting Islam as a set of traditions, convictions, and institutions, but a shift back toward the ethical foundations of the Islamic religion. In many ways, what is needed is to take Islamic ideas about dealing with the other far more seriously—seriously enough to figure out the points of tension within the Islamic tradition and strive to resolve them. Methodologically, the basic framework of working out the moral trajectories of the Qur'an and struggling to realize them is necessary to this context as well. One of the most pressing challenges in this subject is not to be distracted or discouraged by the ugliness of the Islam haters from achieving what is true and necessary for the realization of the path of beauty. This must necessarily include not being satisfied with condemning what we do not like but moving beyond that and toward contributing a positive moral vision in the world in which we live.

Whatever the details of the Islamic model that could be offered in the postmodern age, it is important to realize that one of its core processes must be to build on the centrality of the ethic of noncoercion in Islam. The Qur'an is straightforward enough about this—it clearly informs the Prophet that his role is to remind people of God's message and that he, as God's messenger, was not sent to control or dominate human beings. His most basic and quintessential function is to remind, teach, and advocate. Addressing the Prophet, the Qur'an states: "Remind them for you are but a reminder; you are not a warden over them."[4] Moreover, many of the historical reports surrounding Qur'anic revelation emphasize that belief and conviction cannot be coerced. For example, it was reported that at the time of the Prophet, a Muslim man called Husayn bin Salim bin 'Awf had two daughters who were Christian. This fellow seems to have tried to persuade his daughters to become Muslim, but they were persistent in their refusal. Fed up, the father went to the Prophet and asked for permission to compel his daughters to convert to Islam, but the Prophet resolutely refused. Shortly thereafter, the Qur'anic revelation arrived, declaring that truth and falsity are clear and distinct, and whoever wishes to believe may do so, and whoever refuses to believe may do so— there can be no coercion in religion.[5] "There is no compulsion in matters of faith," the Qur'an proclaimed.[6]

This doctrinal insistence on coercion (*ikrah*) not being a proper way of bringing people to God within its historical context more than fourteen hundred years ago was unusual. Voluntarism and deference to personal autonomy, as an ethical position, has had a troubled and tumultuous record in human history. Until fairly recently, autonomy and sovereignty was thought to reside in the person of a king, church, father, or head of a tribe or clan. Therefore, historically, the conversion of the sovereign king to a particular faith, like the conversion of Constantine to Christianity, effectively meant that his subjects became converted to the same faith, regardless of their personal convictions, and that the sovereign king was thought to have a right to compel his subjects to adopt whatever faith he chose.[7] Furthermore, although for more than twelve hundred years Islamic jurisprudence prohibited the use of duress in obtaining criminal convictions or confessions, such methods were considered lawful in most legal systems of the time, including Roman law, canon law, Jewish law, and Anglo-Saxon law. Again, it was a fairly recent development that duress was seen as unethical and unreliable by most non-Muslim legal systems.[8] For instance, what was known as the practice of judicial torture as practiced in different Western countries was not abolished until the eighteenth century. Although judicial torture has had a checkered history in Islamic law, as far as the doctrines of law were concerned, it has been condemned as unlawful conduct since the ninth century.[9]

In many ways, the Islamic principle of noncoercion was ahead of its time, and being a product of their historical contexts, premodern Muslims were not always able to live up to this ideal. I think it is fairly clear that during the military expansion of Islam, every time there were forced conversions this represented a failure to live up to the Qur'anic ideal. I think that it also ought to be admitted that the Islamic law of apostasy, which punishes conversions out of the faith by death, is a major failure and even a betrayal of the Qur'anic teachings. It is possible to engage in a long and complicated evidentiary debate about the basis of the law of apostasy and to prove that at the time of the Prophet, several people converted back to their original faith after converting to Islam without the Prophet punishing them for apostasy. In this context, it is also possible to refute the claims made that the original position of religious liberty was abrogated by later legislation. Although there is a time and place for such technical and specialized juristic debates, the point here is more basic. As emphasized above, in a structural reading of the

Qur'an, it becomes apparent that there are core ethical prescriptions, and the technicalities of the law, whatever they may be, must further these ethical prescriptions, not obstruct them. In my view, Muslims must have the moral courage to recognize situations in which the ethics and moral principles of the Qur'an were derailed or continue to be derailed by either the technical doctrines of law or the historical practice of Muslims belonging to any generation.

Because various aspects of Qur'anic ethics and morality were ahead of their time, earlier generations of Muslims did not even come close to realizing their moral potential. Significantly, the normative categories and paradigms of the modern age offer Muslims a much better chance than ever before to start the process of pursuing the normative potential inherent in these Qur'anic teachings. I will deal with the issue of war later, but it is worth noting, for instance, the moral potential of the incident referred to above. Even as to those who waged war against the Prophet, oppressed him and his followers, and forced them out of their homes in Mecca, the Qur'anic revelation still confirmed that the committed injustices do not give Muslims a right to seek domination over others. Muslims may have to wage war in response to aggression, but in encountering evil, Muslims must be steadfast in upholding moral principle over any functional considerations. In the Qur'anic example discussed above, the Qur'an is keen on warning Muslims against allowing the circumstances of rancor and hostility from penetrating and corrupting their hearts and dismantling their moral fabric. This is why the Qur'an advises Muslims to refrain even from cursing their enemies—not only do Muslims not have the right or power to decide who becomes the recipient of God's grace or damnation, but the injustice committed by others should not be allowed to alter the attitude of Muslims toward their moral obligations. This point is emphasized time and again in the Qur'an—for instance, it states: "O' you who believe, stand up as witnesses for God in justice, and do not let your hatred of a people lead you away from justice. Be just! This is closest to piety and be mindful of God in all you do for God is aware of all you do."[10] It is of particular significance that the Qur'anic prohibition against cursing the enemy was affirmed after Muslims had suffered a military defeat in the Battle of Uhud. Perhaps it is exactly when the collective Muslim ego had suffered a severe blow that it became particularly imperative for Muslims to be extra vigilant in upholding the moral principle. In fact, the Qur'an is rather specific on this point. It instructs Muslims in the following way: "And do not let your anger at those who barred you from the Holy Mosque [in Mecca] lead you to commit aggression. Help one another in goodness and piety and do not assist each other in committing sin and aggression, and be mindful of God for God is severe in retribution."[11]

I must confess, with a bit of frustration, that I do not know how the Qur'an could have instructed Muslims more clearly that their morality should not be reactive and that their ethical commitments should not be defined in anger. Despite these Qur'anic instructions, in the modern age, the most often cited justification for committing unethical behavior such as taking hostages or murdering civilians is that there is no other way to respond to the overwhelming power and injustices perpetuated by the enemies of Muslims. Yet the Qur'an makes it clear that it is not acceptable for a Muslim to define his moral position in reaction to the injustice of others. In my view, if the idea of submission to God is taken seriously, it might be necessary to be martyred standing by principle rather than live after having compromised all principles. The way a Muslim deals with others ought to be guided by ethical principles and not simply by functional and opportunistic considerations.

Added to the principle of noncoercion are several other Qur'anic prescriptions that elaborate on the methodology of dealing with non-Muslims and inviting people to Islam. First, the Qur'an repeatedly emphasizes that God does not like aggression and does not love aggressors, and it warns Muslims that they must critically reflect on the way they deal with others so that they do not find that they have unwittingly fallen in the position of the unjust.[12] The Qur'an clearly recognizes the law of retribution and acknowledges that at times it might be necessary to act in a punitive fashion. For instance, the Qur'an reaffirms the pre-Islamic rule that recognized certain months during the year as sanctified and prohibited acts of violence during these months. However, Muslim opponents violated the sanctity of the months by attacking Muslims, and the Qur'an allowed Muslims to defend themselves by responding in kind. In a long passage, the Qur'an instructs Muslims not to fight in sanctified places or during the sanctified months unless they are attacked first. If attacked, Muslims can respond in kind, but if the enemy desists, Muslims must refrain from further acts of violence. In this context, the Qur'an states: "So if you are transgressed against, deal with them as you have been dealt with and fear God, and know that God is with those who are pious."[13] Some contemporary Muslims have taken this Qur'anic passage to mean that the morality of Muslims can appropriately be defined by their opponents. This means, according to the simple rationale of reciprocity, that the immoral conduct of opponents justifies the immoral conduct of Muslims because Muslims have a right to respond in kind. A fair reading of the Qur'an, however, would clearly refute this logic. The Qur'an is referring to the right of self-defense—particularly, to a situation in which the failure to respond effectively would constitute Muslims "casting themselves onto ruin" by failing to protect themselves.[14] But as shown below, sanctioning a right to self-defense does not mean the abolition of all ethical standards in responding to aggression. In all cases, what one may call the ethics of survival or necessity in Islam does not represent an ideal normative condition. Such ethics become relevant under exceptional circumstance, but they do not identify the moral goals that Muslims ought to strive and struggle to achieve.

"Good and evil are not equal (in status) to each other," the Qur'an states. "Repel evil with goodness and then you will find that your erstwhile enemy has become like an affectionate close companion. This will not be attained except by those who forbear, and by those who have been greatly blessed (by wisdom). And if the Devil incites you to evil, seek refuge in God for God hears all and know all."[15] In the Qur'anic discourse, this is the higher moral existence—the way of those endowed with forbearance, fortitude, and wisdom. Beyond self-defense, they provide a moral example of leadership by higher acts of virtue. But the Qur'an emphasizes that the pursuit of virtue is not an exceptional condition—it is self-defense that can be described as warranted by exceptional circumstance. The pursuit of the path of virtue is what is supposed to engage a Muslim on a regular basis. According to the

Qur'an, the moral norm is advocacy and persuasion—the norm is for Muslims to expend effort in pursuit of virtue and to engage others in an ethically upright fashion. For instance, the Qur'an instructs Muslims in the following fashion: "Cultivate forgiveness, enjoin goodness, and turn away from the ignorant."[16] This means that Muslims ought to cultivate and nurture an attitude of tolerance and forgiveness and not seek confrontations with those who do not understand the moral worth of either value. Elsewhere, the Qur'an asserts: "Call to the path of your Lord with wisdom and kind advice, and discourse with them in kindness and patience, for your Lord surely knows who has strayed from the path and also knows the rightly-guided."[17] The same theme is emphasized in what might be called the salam verses—salam is the same term from which the word Islam is derived, which means peace, tranquility, repose, or serenity. In the salam verses, the Qur'an stresses that in dealing with their interlocutors, Muslims should seek to remind them of their moral obligations toward God, but if the interlocutors stubbornly reject the truth, Muslims turn away while wishing their opponents salam. In this dynamic, Muslims should act to assure their interlocutors that their disagreements are not personal and that Muslims do not bear a grudge or enmity toward their opponents. Even as the interlocutors refuse the message and turn away, the Qur'an instructs Muslims that the only appropriate response to this rejection is to wish their interlocutors the bliss of peace.[18] Moreover, the Qur'an explicitly commands Muslims not to use foul language or curse their opponents, even if these opponents initiate the verbal abuse. Significantly, the Qur'an justifies this prohibition by explaining that attempting to reciprocate verbal abuse leads to a dynamic that is essentially uncontrollable and that is bound to result in much ugliness.[19]

Oddly enough, despite this clear Qur'anic text, the Puritanical-Salafis have managed to prohibit Muslims from greeting non-Muslims with the greeting of Islam: peace be upon you (*al-salamu 'alaykum*). Again, there are various technical evidentiary arguments that get into details such as whether it is appropriate to initiate the greeting of peace with non-Muslims or whether a Muslim should only return the greeting if non-Muslims initiate it. But these technical debates completely miss the point of the Qur'anic discourse. The Qur'an is not talking about ritualistic expressions of well wishes that are proclaimed as a polite way of ignoring and avoiding the other. The Qur'an associates the prayer of peace with forgiveness and mercy—it counsels Muslims to forgive and say peace, or it instructs Muslims to say peace and then explain that God has decreed mercy on God's self.[20] Both forgiveness and merciful treatment of the other are necessary for the coexistence with others in a state of peace. In order to cultivate this condition of peacefulness, then, forgiveness, mercy, and importantly, dealing with others in wisdom has to be actively promoted. As the Qur'an succinctly puts it, "Work with one another in promoting goodness and piety, and do not conspire to commit offenses and aggression, and fear God for God is severe in punishment."[21]

In essence, what the Qur'an constructs is an ideal—an ideal in which there is a dynamic discourse, in which opponents wish each other peace, in which forgiveness and mercy is cultivated, and in which there is an active movement seeking wisdom. At the most basic level, there would be a society in which people enjoy the right to self-defense and also do not commit aggression. But this is not an ideal prototype. Although people can enjoy a right to self-defense and aspire for a policy of nonaggression, nevertheless such a people could still fail to construct an order that enjoys genuine peace. According to the Qur'an, for a state of peace to exist, there needs to be an order that actively cultivates forgiveness and mercy. The most intriguing and perhaps challenging Qur'anic instruction is that pertaining to discoursing in wisdom and kindness. There is no reason to assume that the Qur'an is setting out a methodology of dealing that only applies to Muslim and non-Muslim interaction. The same standards apply to the inter-Muslim context that would apply to discourses between Muslims and non-Muslims. But these ideas are more workable and more susceptible to being authentically pursued in a civilized and nonviolent world. I do not think it is an exaggeration to say that human beings today are in a better position to pursue collective policies of self-defense, nonaggression, forgiveness, mercy, and wisdom than they were a thousand years ago. But it is also true that this places an exceptional burden on Muslims of the contemporary age. According to the Qur'an, they must set a moral example for humanity as to how to live cultivating and pursuing these virtues. But these virtues cannot be pursued in isolation; they must be rendered accessible and accountable to others. For instance, if Muslims produce completely idiosyncratic definitions of nonaggression, forgiveness, mercy, or wisdom that are incomprehensible to others, it would be difficult to imagine how Muslims would be able to cultivate a life with others that would be based on these virtues. By definition, if these virtues are going to define the way Muslims will interact with others, these virtues must be capable of being shared with others. The particular burden placed on Muslims is that they must take a leading role in thinking about what can be considered wisdom today. Before Muslims are able to invite people to the way of God through wisdom (*hikma*), first they must cultivate and nurture wisdom within themselves. The same dynamic can be said about mercy and forgiveness. In many ways, the same spirit that ignited the love of knowledge and the pursuit of humanistic sciences in the Muslim heart during the height of the Muslim civilization must be reignited today. However, if I am correct in arguing that the Qur'an sets moral objectives and trajectories to be vigilantly pursued by Muslims in fulfillment of their covenant with God, then there is no reason to assume that the golden age of Islam has passed. It would seem that the contemporary age, with the ideals enshrined in the United Nations Charter, has already gone some distance in achieving the Islamic ideal. Furthermore, through several humanitarian law conventions, the international community has pursued the ideal of mercy and perhaps wisdom. These humanitarian achievements are a strong starting point, but what remains missing is an active, dynamic, and leading Muslim role. In my view, the leading role that Muslims could and ought to play is to analytically and critically engage the achievements of humanity and further it. It is true that humanity has made progress in furthering the standards of humaneness, but many problems remain. The current international system is replete with inequities and structural injustices that fall far short of the very ideals that inspired the system's existence in the first place.

Thus far, I have discussed the Islamic ethic of noncoercion and the principle of nonaggression, but I would like to comment more specifically on the ethics of diversity in Islam. This is of material significance to any potential for collective pursuits with non-Muslims and for the possibility of reaching points of overlapping consensus between Muslims and the rest of the world.

ON THE ETHICS OF DIVERSITY

The Qur'an not only accepts but even expects the reality of difference and diversity within human society: "O humankind, God has created you from male and female and made you into diverse nations and tribes so that you may come to know each other. Verily, the most honored of you in the sight of God is he who is the most righteous."[22] Elsewhere, the Qur'an asserts that diversity is part of the divine intent and purpose in creation: "If thy Lord had willed, He would have made humankind into a single nation, but they will not cease to be diverse. . . . And, for this God created them [humankind]."[23] The classical commentators on the Qur'an did not fully explore the implications of this sanctioning of diversity or the role of peaceful conflict resolution in perpetuating the type of social interaction that would result in people "knowing each other." Nor does the Qur'an provide specific rules or instructions about how "diverse nations and tribes" are to acquire such knowledge. Although it is fair to say that the Islamic civilization was pluralistic and unusually tolerant of various social and religious denominations, the existence of diversity as a primary purpose of creation, as suggested by the verse above, remained underdeveloped in Islamic theology. It is reasonable to assume, however, that the Qur'anic command to know one another, at a minimum, ought to mean that people are not to destroy each other. As noted earlier, if coupled with the imperative of mercy and empathy, the duty of knowledge becomes a powerful bond drawing people together. Diversity in the human condition is not an ailment or a weakness of creation. Diversity is part of the remarkable richness of the divine—the infinite capacity of the divine to create. But even more, diversity is a sign of the moral beauty that God teaches. The Qur'an emphasizes time and again that if God had willed, he would have created people all the same and all of humanity would have believed as well. The fact that God has not willed it is an indication of the beauty of the virtue of tolerance—a virtue that God himself practices, apparently without limit because of the unbounded nature of human free will. At the most basic level, it is incomprehensible that human beings would seek to undo what God has willfully done except through persuasion—except by respecting the same free will that God has honored and respected.

Other than a general endorsement of human diversity, the Qur'an also accepts the more specific notion of a plurality of religious beliefs and laws. Although the Qur'an clearly claims that Islam is the divine truth and demands belief in Muhammad as the final messenger in a long line of Abrahamic prophets, it does not completely exclude the possibility that there might be other paths to salvation. The Qur'an insists on God's unfettered discretion to accept in His mercy whomever He wishes. In fact, the Qur'an expresses indignation at those who attempt to limit or apportion God's mercy according to their wills or desires. First, the Qur'an asserts that the Prophet was sent but as a mercy to humanity.[24] And second, only God decides who shall receive the divine mercy either on this earth or in the Hereafter, and it is considered a great act of transgression for a human being to attempt to speculate as to who will deserve and who will not.[25]

Beyond the fact that in principle anyone might be entitled to God's mercy, and that this is simply a topic not appropriate for human speculation, the Qur'an goes on to give what it describes as good tidings to some people who are not necessarily Muslim. In a passage, the Qur'an states: "God has made for each nation a way and method that they follow. So they should not contend with you in this matter. Call to your Lord for you are surely on the right path. If they argue with you, tell them: God knows all that we do, and God will judge between you on the Final Day as to what you disagreed upon."[26] In this verse, the Qur'an intimates that one of the reasons that God has created this remarkable diversity is so that people will not fight with each other. This has profound implications that Muslims have not even started to explore. Effectively, the Qur'an is saying that God has made many different pathways for people, and therefore it is not appropriate that some would try to deny the Prophet his pathway—it is not right that some would try to dominate the Prophet and extinguish his path to God. As noted earlier, the Qur'an, however, acknowledges reciprocity as a basic premise of justice. Therefore, if people ought to leave Muslims alone to pursue their path, this implies that each path holder should respect the choice of the other. If so, Muslims would have the same obligation—if they should be left to pursue their path, they should let others do the same.

In a similar passage, the Qur'an provides a different emphasis on the theme. It states: "For each nation We have ordained a way and path so that they will mention the name of God for the blessings He has given them. Your God is a single God so submit to God and give good tidings to those who bow down before God."[27] This verse implies that as different as the pathways may be, they may still be directed toward God. Interestingly, the Qur'an acknowledges that those who worship God deserve to receive good tidings, and that the core issue regardless of the path, is submission to God. The Qur'an does clearly, on repeated occasions, affirm Islam as the true and authentic religion. However, as long as certain other criteria—criteria known only to God—are fulfilled, there always remains the possibility of being the beneficiary of God's merciful grace.

In a rather remarkable set of passages that, again, have not been adequately theorized by Muslim theologians, the Qur'an recognizes the legitimate multiplicity of religious convictions and laws. In one such passage, for example, the Qur'an asserts: "To each of you God has prescribed a Law and a Way. If God would have willed, He would have made you a single people. But God's purpose is to test you in what he has given each of you, so strive in the pursuit of virtue, and know that you will all return to God [in the Hereafter], and He will resolve all the matters in which you disagree."[28] Emphasizing the same reconciliatory point, addressing itself to Muslims, the Qur'an states: "Do not argue with the People of the Book unless in a kind and fair way, apart for those who have been oppressive towards you. Tell them that we believe in what has been sent down to us and we believe in what has been sent down to you. Our God and your God is one and to Him we submit."[29] The Qur'an goes on to state: "Those who believe, those who follow Jewish scriptures, the Christians, the Sabians, and any who believe in God and the Final Day, and do good, all shall have their reward with their Lord and they will not come to fear or grief."[30]

In Qur'anic usage, "People of the Book" refers to the followers of the Abrahamic faith, mostly Christians and Jews. It is a tenet of faith in Islam that Muhammad is the final prophet in a long line of Abrahamic prophets all conveying the same basic message to humanity. Therefore, a Muslim must necessarily believe in Abraham, Moses, Jesus, and many others as prophets of the same and one God—all bearing the same essential message of submission to God. Therefore, for example, the Qur'an proclaims the following testament of faith: "The Prophet believes in what has been revealed to him by his Lord. And so do the faithful believe in the same. Each one believes in God and His angels, His Books and the prophets and We make no distinction between the prophets. They all say, 'We hear and obey, and we seek your forgiveness O Lord, for to you we shall journey in the end.'"[31] The same idea is made even more explicit in the following Qur'anic revelation addressed to Muslims: "Say, we believe in God, and in what has been revealed to us, and in what had been sent down to Abraham and Ishmael and Isaac and Jacob and their offspring, and what has been revealed to Moses and Jesus and to all other prophets by their Lord. We make no distinction between them, and we submit to Him and obey."[32] However, according to Muslim theology, while some of the Abrahamic prophets were sent to a particular tribe or nation, Muhammad carried the final and perfected divine message to humanity. In addition, Muslims believe that aspects or parts of the earlier messages sent by God were altered, deformed, corrupted, or otherwise derailed from their initial purpose, and Islam was sent to reclaim and restore the original message to its pristine form. The easiest example of this is the concept of Trinity in Christianity. Muslims do not believe that Jesus made any claims to being divine or that he taught the doctrine of Trinity. Therefore, in Muslim belief, Jesus was another Abrahamic prophet, just like Moses, preaching the same message of submission to God. In Qur'anic discourses, Jesus is claimed as a Muslim prophet, in the sense that his message to humanity was in its core the same as that of Muhammad. According to the Qur'an, the Torah and Ingil (New Testament) are divine books revealed by the same God who authored the Qur'an. However, Muslims believe that various historical forces interceded, leading to a process in which parts of these divine texts became corrupted by human revisions, alterations, and omissions. Nevertheless, the Qur'an insists on the essential unity of all the Abrahamic messages; the moral and spiritual path they set out is in a fundamental way of a similar nature. Therefore, for instance, the Qur'an asserts: "God has laid down for you the same way of life and belief that He had set out to Noah, and that We have enjoined for you, and that We had bequeathed to Abraham, Moses, and Jesus so that you will establish the faith, and not divide amongst yourself."[33]

Doing justice to the subject of Islam and its theological relationship to other Abrahamic religions would require a separate book. For our purposes, however, it is important to emphasize that although the Qur'an claims that the earlier versions of the Abrahamic religions have been superseded by the latest and final version, which is Islam, the Qur'an does not exclude the possibility that the former pathways could lead to salvation. As discussed, this depends on God's mercy and discretion. The other significant point is that apart from the issue of salvation, diversity and the duty to come to know one another plays a dynamic role on this earth that is not necessarily connected to the dynamics of the Hereafter. This is intimately connected to the obligation of humility and connected to the need for human beings to know their place. Whether a human being might be entitled to salvation in the Hereafter is separate and apart from the obligations and rights that such a human being enjoys on this earth. In the conciliatory verses quoted above, it is worth noting that Muslims are instructed to emphasize and concentrate on the commonalities with others, not the differences. For instance, the Qur'an instructs Muslims to remind their interlocutors that they all worship the same God—that although they have different pathways to God, their aim and objective is still the same. This emphasis on commonalities represents a moral choice that is consistent with respecting diversity and with coming to know one another. Importantly, this way of dealing with the other does not dilute the distinctiveness of the Islamic message, and it is a separate matter from how God decides to deal with people in the Hereafter.

Various Prophetic precedents in Islamic history emphasize that regardless of the consequences in the Hereafter, human beings are entitled to honor and respect on this earth. For instance, it is reported that the funeral procession of a Jewish woman was passing in Medina when the Prophet was sitting with some of his companions. On seeing the procession, the Prophet stood up out of respect. Some of the Prophet's companions, thinking that perhaps there was some misunderstanding, told the Prophet that the deceased was Jewish. The Prophet responded: "Yes, but isn't she a soul?"[34] In a report communicating the same basic message, on hearing that Najashi, the king of Ethiopia, had died, the Prophet performed ritual prayer on his soul with several of his companions. Najashi, a Christian, had helped early Muslims and granted them sanctuary at a time when they suffered severe oppression at the hands of the non-Muslim Meccans. Nevertheless, several of the companions inquired of the Prophet, how could Muslims pray over the soul of a Christian? In response, the following Qur'anic revelation was transmitted by the Prophet: "Among the People of the Book, there are those who believe in God. They believe in what has been revealed to you, and also in what has been revealed to them. They bow in humility before God, and they do not trade for paltry gain God's messages. Verily, those have their reward with God for God is swift in reckoning."[35] The Qur'an repeats this point on many occasions and circumstances, stressing that in dealing with others, Muslims cannot preclude the possibility that they may be entitled to salvation. This goes to addressing the basic attitude that Muslims ought to hold toward others. Muslims are simply not privy to how God will decide to deal with Muslims or non-Muslims, and therefore, Muslims ought to deal with others on this earth in terms of the potentiality for beauty and goodness that God has deposited into every human being.

One of the most pivotal Qur'anic discourses deals with what might be called the diversity of laws that are applied by different nations and people. In repeated contexts, the Qur'an not only accepts that different peoples are to be governed by different laws, but it goes beyond that by emphasizing that the laws appropriate for one group of people ought not be binding on others.

Although these Qur'anic injunctions are a part of what inspired an enormous jurisprudential diversity within the Islamic civilization, the ethical and political implications of this Qur'anic discourse have not been adequately explored by Muslims. I will let the text of the Qur'an speak for itself by reproducing a long quote on this point. The reader will observe that the Qur'an is addressing a complex historical dynamic that needs to be investigated and theorized. But there is no way to convey a sense of this complexity without quoting the text itself. As part of a long chapter titled "The Feast," addressing itself to the Prophet, the Qur'an states:

> But why should they make you a judge (between them) when the Torah is in their midst and it contains the Law of God?
>
> We sent down the Torah containing guidance and light, and in accordance with (the Torah) the prophets who were obedient (to God) gave instructions to the Jews, as did the rabbis and priests, for they were the custodians and witnesses of God's writ. So, therefore, do not fear men, fear Me, and barter not My messages away for a paltry gain. Those who do not judge by God's revelations are indeed unbelievers.
>
> After that We sent Jesus, son of Mary, confirming the Torah, which had been (sent down) before him, and We gave him the Gospel containing guidance and light, as an affirmation of what We revealed in the Torah, and as a guidance and warning for those who are pious.
>
> Let the people of the Gospel judge by what God has revealed in it. And those who do not judge in accordance with what God has revealed are transgressors.
>
> And to you We have revealed the Book containing the truth, confirming the earlier revelations, and preserving them. So judge between them (Muslims) by what God has revealed to you, and do not ignore the truth that has been revealed to you by following people's whims. To each of you We have given a law and a way of life. If God would have desired He could surely have made you into a single people—professing one faith (and following one law). But He wished to try and test you by that which He has given each of you. So excel in good deeds. To Him will you all return in the end, when He will resolve that upon which you disagreed. [36]

It is clear from this discourse, for reasons not adequately explored by Muslims, that the Qur'an embraces the idea of multiplicity and pluralism of laws and that any unity between Muslims and others should not include an attempt to eradicate or abolish differences. While the Qur'an does emphasize that the spirit, which unites at least the followers of the Abrahamic message, at its core and essence is the same; it is a part of the divine objective that people remain different in some significant and important ways. From that perspective, any universalism that would ignore all differences and impose a unitary and single law to human beings would be challenged by the text of the Qur'an. At the same time, however, the Qur'an does not endorse unmitigated moral relativism. Some truths are generalizable and applicable to all, while others, at least as far as life on this earth is concerned, are specific to a particular people and creed. Analyzing the various Qur'anic discourses on the relationship between Muslims and non-Muslims, it is quite clear that

what unites all human beings under particular universals are moral principles, while laws pertaining to religious rituals and rites and organizational
laws relating to the administration of justice are expected or even encouraged
to be different. This creates a considerable amount of space for collective
human pursuits—whatever human beings can cooperate on in order to bring
the earth closer to divinity is considered as a form of submission to God or as
a prostration before God and is therefore Islamically and morally desirable.
While clearly there is a certain moral affinity and spiritual closeness between
Muslims and the followers of the Abrahamic tradition, nothing in the Qur'an
precludes cooperation with all others in order to create an earth that is morally more pleasing to God. The fact that some do not believe in God or that
some might pursue moral goodness while they, in their hearts, do not accept
any notion of divinity is something that must be left to God in the Hereafter.
In the same fashion that God could have willed all people to be Muslim, God
could have also willed all to be believers in Him. Therefore, as far as life on
earth is concerned, there is no basis for excluding unbelievers from a cooperative venture that seeks goodness.

On the acceptability of cooperative ventures, Puritanical-Salafis often refer to Qur'anic verses that address the issue of *wala'* (seeking an alliance
with non-Muslims) in an attempt to prove that Islam forbids any friendship,
leave alone any active cooperation, between Muslims and non-Muslims.
Interestingly, the same chapters in the Qur'an that speak about the basic unity
of all Abrahamic religions or that command respect for difference and diversity will also contain passages that instruct Muslims not to ally themselves
with non-Muslims. Some Orientalists have gone as far as claiming that the
two types of passages are fundamentally inconsistent and irreconcilable.
However, if we read the text with moral and historical guidance, we can see
the different passages as part of a complex and layered discourse about
reciprocity and its implications in the historical situation in Muhammad's
Medina. In part, the chapter exhorts Muslims to support the newly established Muslim community in Medina. But its point is not to issue a blanket
condemnation against Jews and Christians (who "shall have their reward
with their Lord"[37]). Instead, it accepts the distinctiveness of the Jewish and
Christian communities and their laws while also insisting that in the case of
conflict, Muslims should not ally themselves against their fellow Muslims.
At the background of every single Qur'anic revelation warning Muslims not
to ally themselves with non-Muslims is a historical context in which it was
necessary to choose sides. But even then the Qur'an addresses itself to situations in which during active hostilities between Muslims and non-Muslims, a
Muslim party is commanded to refrain from giving active support to non-
Muslims against Muslims—the operative word here being "against." The
Qur'an was revealed in a context in which the nascent Muslim community
struggled against a well-established network of alliances between the various
Arab tribes, and the Qur'an played an active role in trying to persuade various segments of society to abolish their tribal alliances and transfer them to
the Muslim community. Importantly, however, the Qur'anic verses address a
situation where conflicts already exist and in which the facts on the ground
already require the participants to choose sides. The Qur'an, however, does

not mandate that Muslims create these polarized and conflict-filled situations in the first place.

THE CALIPHATE OF HUMANKIND: ASCENDING TO AN ETHEREAL HUMANITY

Is it really coherent to speak of a collective enterprise for goodness in which Muslims and non-Muslims, believers and nonbelievers, and developed and underdeveloped can all take part in for the benefit of humanity? With all the gross inequalities and inequities, with all the double standards and exploitation, and with all the bigotry and hatred that fills our so-called cosmopolitan projects, the answer would militate toward the disheartening. Sometimes the horrors of what human beings do to each other and to themselves makes one wonder why God created beings capable of perpetuating such ugliness. Indeed, at times, one feels confounded at a God that allowed the kind of free will that enables people to feel the urges they feel, covet what they covet, and desire what they desire. What is so profound about free will and determination when so many use it to abuse themselves and others? So many times, when I work with exploited and trafficked women and children, read bigoted or racist tracts disgorging a pile of virulent hate and malice against a people, or deal with the victims of torture and abuse even in the so-called civilized nations of the world, I feel like throwing my hands up in the air, finding some isolated cottage in a remote land, and living the rest of my life as a bitter curmudgeon grouch. Most certainly, I am very tempted to expend all my energy cursing the devil rather than praising God!

Yet this is hardly a unique, original, or novel issue. After all, it is not just rancorous human beings who raised this issue with God, but according to the Qur'an, the issue was first raised in the heavens by angels when they questioned God: Why create such beings capable of committing evil and of causing so much corruption? This is the Qur'anic passage: "When your God told the angels, 'I am placing a successor (*khalifa*) on earth,' they said, 'You will give the earth to beings who will cause corruption, and bloodshed, when we celebrate Your praise and proclaim Your holiness?' God said, 'I know what you do not!'"[38] What follows after this parable is one of the most intriguing and perhaps enigmatic passages of the Qur'an. How does God demonstrate that God knows what the angels do not? Here is the passage that follows: "He then taught Adam all the names (*asma'*) then he showed them (the things named) to the angels, and said, 'Tell me the names of these things if you are correct (about your doubts)!' They (angels) said, 'May You be glorified! We have knowledge only of what You have taught us. You are the All Knowing and Wise.' Then God said, 'Adam, tell them the names (of things)!' And when Adam told them the names (of things), God said: 'Did I not tell you that I know the secrets (*ghayb*) of the Heavens and earth, and I know what you reveal and what you try to conceal!'"[39] If anything, this parable begs the question: What are the "names of things" (*asma'*) that Adam learned and the learning of which was sufficiently compelling to persuade the angels that God "knows what they do not know," and that the creation of beings who are capable of shedding blood, and causing corruption is apparently worthwhile?

Not only does this parable of learning and knowledge quiet down the angels, but the parable is followed by another describing a magnanimous moment elevating and dignifying humanity and, at the same time, forever earning the ire and hostility of the symbol of evil, Iblis (Satan). God commands the angels and jinn to prostrate before the new being created to become God's viceroy and to inherit the earth. While God celebrates the event as the moment when human beings (children of Adam) were honored and dignified, Iblis protests on supremacist grounds. According to the Qur'an, Iblis refuses to prostrate before this human creature because, after all, the inheritors of earth are created from mud, while Iblis was created from something more ethereal like fire.[40]

It is worth noting that according to the Qur'anic discourse, angels are aware of the human ability to corrupt God's earth and shed blood before Satan even enters the picture. In other words, although Satan will do his share of mischief, human beings are quite capable of perpetuating their share of evil quite on their own. In the Qur'anic narrative, human beings were destined to inherit the earth as God's viceroys (as caliphs) before Adam and Eve's indulgences at the infamous tree.[41] Significantly, all of humanity is made God's caliphs (*khulafa' li'llah*) on earth, and human beings are equipped with an ability that promises something so compelling, impressive, and meaningful that if one is able to overcome his own pride and prejudice, just like the prostrating angels, one would be very content with sharing in honoring and celebrating this most special creature capable of learning "the names of things." Of course, there is a very old tradition found in Gnosticism, Jewish mysticism, Christian gnosis, and many other esoteric traditions that associated the true names of things with knowledge of their real nature. Knowing the true names of things not only revealed their surreptitious and innate nature, but one gained real power over everything named. So did God demonstrate Adam's ability to tap into the true knowledge by understanding the esoteric and hidden meaning of things? Troubled by the gnostic overtones of this argument, many Muslim scholars rejected the esoteric approach and insisted that the unique gift that God gave Adam was the creative intellect, or the power of reason (*'aql*), which is the locus of all responsibility and accountability.[42] However, I think it would be misguided to assume that human beings were honored simply by virtue of having reason or for reason's own sake. The idolatries of reason are more than capable of committing their own share of miseries. Reason and rational faculties are honored for the moral good they can contribute—for the ability to become God's caliphs and pursue godliness.

Human beings are honored and celebrated because they are godlike, capable of doing godlike things.[43] Many narratives in the Islamic tradition emphasize that God created humans in beauty and that this is sufficient to obligate human beings to act beautifully—to make their external beauty, as bearers of God image, reflective of their inner beauty.[44] In another Qur'anic parable, God is said to have offered the trust (*al-amana*) to all of creation, but ultimately it was shouldered only by human beings. The Qur'an then somberly notes that bearing this trust is such an onerous and arduous task.[45] I believe that this weighty trust for which human beings were honored and dignified is the marvel of divinity itself. Human beings are but nuances of the divine—inexhaustible anecdotes of divinity capable of creating such immeasurable acts of true beauty.[46] As human beings invent and create beauty, they move toward the majestic caliphate of godliness. When human beings no longer seek or create beauty, forget their bonds to the ethereal and sublime, and slump into indolence and despair, human beings drift further away from godliness into its antithesis. God is the light of the heavens and earth—light upon light![47] In every act of beauty—in every nuance that commemorates the truth of our divine nature and memorializes the caliphate of humanity in the world, we move closer to the divine light. But in remaining static—in existing without beautification or in false beautification, or in subsisting without service born out of love, mercy, and compassion—that is, without the attributes and nuances of divinity—we no longer move toward the light and in fact drift from the possibility of godliness to the darkness of godlessness.[48]

I return to my teacher's advice: there is no point to cursing the devil instead of remembering God! There is no point to cursing the darkness instead of moving toward the light. We human beings do not perpetuate evil because of the diabolical craftiness of the devil—all we need to do is to forget our trust and our caliphate—we act ungodly by failing to do good, and before long the darkness sets in. Hannah Arendt's famous remark about the banality of evil is certainly true, but the question is: What precedes this thoroughly compromised state? What gets human beings to a point where they no longer see a higher version of themselves—something other than being a mere keg in a stale and mundane virtual mill of dehumanization? The human soul sours when its own self-perceptions and existential consciousness drift into a staleness and prosaicness of being. It moves through a series of corporal attainments impervious to its own ethereal truth, forgetful of the transcendent and obstinately defiant in recognizing the equal divinity of all. In other words, it no longer believes in its own beauty and goodness or the beauty and goodness of others.

So is there hope? Does it make any sense to even dream that the world can ascend to an ethereal humanity—a joint and cooperative just caliphate to treat every human being on earth, regardless of creed, race, gender, class, or any other distinction, as divine beings? Of course one does not need to believe in the divine to be treated as divine. Is it insane to dream of a world in which we are in harmony with each other, and in harmony with the heavens and earth and all that is in between? Of course, I do realize that this is so far fetched that it will strike so many as naïve.

The best way to close this book is to recall a memory with Shaykh Jarudi, who was a walking, breathing proof of God and a parable of God's majesty. I was always a dreamy boy asking naïve questions in silly ways and of the mysteries that would bother me to no end is how people could inflict such pain and agony on each other. How could so many people become so oblivious to the suffering of others—how could people go on with their lives untroubled when they know that the children of their neighbors are rotting in political prisons, tortured, raped, and killed? How could we drive by street children every day as we know that they are tormented, abused, and often murdered without conscience? How could so many people live with themselves when they know the abysmal conditions and the suffering that children who serve in the private homes of the wealthy are forced to endure?

Shaykh Jarudi could see I was working myself into a rambling tirade; he quieted me down by asking: "Son, what are you looking for? A reason for the cruelty, or a cure?" I wondered loudly, "Well, is there a cure?"

In response, Shaykh Jarudi simply recited a verse, "If only people would have learned humility when suffering came to them from Us (God)! No, their hearts only became harder, and (when their hearts had hardened) the devil made their foul misdeeds appear even more alluring to them."[49]

In our self-idolatry, we become so oblivious—absorbed in arrogance, we forget others, forget God, and forget ourselves.

I muttered as if to myself: "We forget God until God allows us to drift in forgetfulness!"[50] Then I raised my voice and recited, "God reveals the signs so you might understand! But your hearts become as hard as rock, or even harder!"[51] And despondently, I started to walk toward the door, but I must have looked defeated because I heard Shaykh Jarudi: "Why don't you complete it? Complete the verse!"

I looked at him, but before I could respond, he proceeded to complete the Qur'anic passage himself: "For there are rocks that are porous through which streams flow, and there are rocks that split open and from which water pours out, and there are some rocks that crumble down in awe of God. And God does not fail to observe what you do."[52]

I stared at the *shaykh*, looking stupefied or perhaps stunned—I am not sure which! He commented rather matter-of-factly: "Son, even at our hardest—even when our hearts become as hard as rock, good—like the water—still comes, and even among the most obstinately arrogant, at a single unexpected moment, we fall to our knees in love! If water can come through the hardest of rocks, you think that God cannot come through the most forgetful of souls and the hardest of hearts?"

Concluding the Journey

RECLAIMING THE PATH TO THE SELF IN GOD AND TO GOD IN THE SELF

The functional practices or competing discourses that a religion might have inspired do not define the future of a faith. Every religion and even ideological orientation inevitably inspires a wide variety of often competing and conflicting efforts all claiming to be an authentic fulfillment of this religion or ideology. If one looks at the history of the Christian Church and its relationship to music, for example, it is nothing short of remarkable to observe how the same basic theological doctrines inspired some of the most virulic and hateful statements against rhythms and melodies as demoniac and satanic inventions intended to corrupt the most devout souls and at the same time inspired some of the most magnanimous and sublime musical compositions that ever existed. Perhaps this is the nature of all strong systems of belief and conviction. As such, they are a powerful force, and being a powerful force, they have the ability to thrust people toward the abyss or carry them to unprecedented heights. Fearing extremes, it is possible to dilute and compromise belief systems until their force is spent and weakened, and the risk they pose and the potential they offer is nullified. In many ways, this is what secularism, by privatizing religion, is able to do. But by removing the force of religion from the public arena, secularism opens itself to other types of extremist onslaughts, such as socialist nationalism or vulgar capitalism, that leave their own share of damaging effects on humanity. Those who are fond of speaking of the evils of religion are well advised to remember the competing ugliness of secular systems such as fascism and communism. I do not think, however, that conceding space for religion in the public space necessarily means that human beings are doomed to suffer the megalomania of pretenders who claim to rule in God's behalf nor the pretense of applying a set of objective rulings that claim to embody the divine will.

I think that the universal challenge and obligation that confronts all believers is to harness and direct the powerful force of religion toward the pursuit of goodness and beauty in life. As a Muslim, I have attempted to discharge this obligation as far as the Islamic religion is concerned. The Islamic religion, like all ideological orientations and all systems of thought and belief, is represented by many competing orientations. The truth of the matter is that the institutions of slavery, the exclusion of Chinese nationals, or the internment of Japanese nationals are as much of the American histori-cal experience as the lofty ideas of freedom of expression or liberty and justice for all. Regardless of what the American creed was in the eighteenth century, or 1930s, or 1940s, what this creed represents today depends entire-ly on the active will of those who represent the American creed. The American creed could stand for the best that humanity has to offer or the worst, and this depends on what parts of a tradition are emphasized, co-opted, reinvented, and promoted. The same can be said of Christianity and Judaism, and most certainly, the same can be said of Islam.

I have emphasized elements within the Islamic tradition that could inspire a movement toward beauty, goodness, and ultimately divinity. As a Muslim, I believe that those elements are not marginal to the Islamic tradition but are at the heart and core of that religion. As a Muslim, I believe that these elements are the true spirit of Islam. But the reality is that the impact of such elements entirely depends on how modern Muslims choose to understand, develop, and assert them. Perhaps it is painfully obvious that regardless of how rich, humanistic, and moral the Islamic tradition is in fact, this tradition will be of very limited usefulness if it is not believed and acted on by Muslims today. But herein is the true travesty of modern Islam and the agony of every Muslim intellectual: the prevailing social, economic, and political circumstances are not conducive or supportive to the realization of visions of beauty. Muslim realities are stark and ugly, often plagued by poverty, despot-ism, and underdevelopment. We Muslims are the children of a lost civiliza-tion—left as if orphans in modernity. If we analyze the Muslim condition according to entirely objective empirical and scientific criteria, this would inevitably lead us to despair. Moral achievement and beauty often grow in the midst of economic and political leisure when human beings have the luxury of time and peace of mind to dream, hope, and aspire. A people who are too busy surviving most often are never afforded the opportunity to do anything but survive.

This all might be depressingly true, but I think that here is where the magical power of faith comes in. Muslims are commanded to apply them-selves and struggle, while leaving the results to God. The trust was offered to the mountains, but it is human beings who carried this trust because the human will is more formidable than mountains. I think that long before certain secular philosophies invented the idea of the supreme human, relig-ions constructed the idea of the divine human being. In Islam, this human being can do wonders through the humility of submission instead of the arrogance and delusion of supremacy. This is so because there is a magical element in Islamic belief, and perhaps it exists in all religious belief as well. In summary, this belief is that when the physical burdens and challenges appear most overwhelming and oppressive, one ought to turn to the meta-physical for aid and assistance. In Islam, this hope is not a form of blind and irrational dependence on the metaphysical—as the Qur'an makes clear, God does not cause a people to change unless they first attempt to change themselves. Hence, regardless of how dim and dark the Muslim objective reality appears, to fail to attempt to alter this reality means reneging on the covenant Muslims have with God. Furthermore, there is an express promise in this relationship: if Muslims seek to change themselves and work hard to achieve that goal, God will help them change. This conviction and belief, which defies empirical verification, is part of the force and power of religion—against all odds, through willpower, perseverance, and patience, and by God's aid and assistance, much can change, and the once-crumbling Islamic civilization could be resuscitated to something resembling a civilizational renaissance.

In the twelfth and thirteenth centuries, from the midst of the Dark Ages in Europe and the extreme ugliness of the Crusades, Europe commenced a period of major transformation. The trauma and despair of this age sparked a powerful reaction generating an intellectual movement that was oriented toward God but that was also powerfully humanistic. The extreme forms of ugliness that endured during the European Dark Ages ignited an aesthetic movement that pursued beauty in its various forms but that was vigilantly led by the prevailing theme of *Deus vult* (Latin: God wills it) or for the glory of God. Hence, the same period that brought about the tragedy of the Crusades also gave birth to thinkers such as Abelard, John of Salisbury, Bernard of Clairvaux, Roger Bacon, Duns Scotus, St. Francis of Assisi, St. Dominic, and Thomas Aquinas. Significantly, the contact with the Muslim East greatly intensified during this era and played a major role in the birth of Christian humanism and the Renaissance, which ultimately brought Europe out of its Dark Ages. The transmission of knowledge from the lands of Islam to Europe and the Christianizing of this knowledge so that it was rendered indigenous and therefore acceptable played a key role in the rebirth of the West.[1] For instance, although the etymology of the word *troubadour*, describing the people of Occitania in the south of France—a people who contributed a great deal to European culture, including the ethics of courtly love—goes back to the verb *taraba* (to sing) in Arabic, premodern and modern European scholars continued to deny this historical linkage to Muslims. Nevertheless, the etymology of the word is yet another indication of the pervasive influence of Muslim art, literature, philosophy, and science on medieval Spain, France, and Italy.[2] But the significant point is not the Western debt to Islam—borrowing and transplanting is at the heart and core of any civilizational process.[3] The point is that even in the darkest points in history, rebirth and regeneration remains possible. Whether the Europeans borrowed this wisdom from Muslims or not, Europeans learned that to serve the glory of God necessarily means manifesting the beauty of God on this earth and that dishonoring God's creation is an offense against divinity. As importantly, the Europeans also learned that in order to serve God, it is necessary to gain a distance away from divinity. To pretend that the temporal and divine could be one and the same does not lead to the elevation of either and in fact deprecates both.

For many Muslims, citing the European example is fraught with risks. Many Muslims assume that the historical processes that took place in the West are inevitable—that the Renaissance not eventually but inevitably led to stark securalism and that Thomas Aquinas or Martin Luther inevitably led to Nietzsche or Sartre. I think this is an inaccurate essentialism, and it constitutes a misreading of European history, especially of critical junctures in this history such as the French Revolution and its aftermath. But even more fundamentally, to this point, there is no serious body of comparative scholarship that attempts to analyze the similarities and linkages between the thought of Christian reformers such as Thomas Aquinas (d. 1274) and Martin Luther (d. 1546) and Islamic thought contemporaneous to them. In my opinion, however, the similarities between certain aspects of the theological thought of Aquinas and Luther and several of the most influential Muslim theologians are striking and remarkable. In many ways, the theological thought that informed and fed into the European Renaissance and Reformation was already firmly established in Islamic civilization. In fact, the irony is that the tragedy and trauma of the Crusades and the reconquest of Andalusia had very different effects in Europe than in Islam. In Europe, the exposure to the East and the horrors of the Crusades sparked a movement toward rationalism and humanism. In the East, the trauma and tragedy of Crusades and the Reconquista were experienced in a very different way. Being the invaded, as opposed to the invader, these wars fed into a protracted process of increasing conservatism, less openness to rationalism, and a drift away from humanism. In Europe and the Muslim world, the same historical events sparked converse movements heading in opposite directions.

Much could be learned from studying history and its movement, but history does not dictate inevitabilities. Analyzing historical dynamics can yield a considerable amount of wisdom in dealing with the future, but staying frozen in the moment and immobile, clinging to static rules and regulations for security while refusing to change because of anxiety and fear about what the future may bring, is most unwise. In periods of intense fluctuation and insecurity, clinging to a system of rules for security and stability is sociologically understandable. The problem, however, is that history is relentless in its progress, and the high cost of this false sense of security is marginalization and irrelevancy to a constantly moving and developing world. Clinging to a set of inaccessible and unaccountable rules and pretending that they are the soul and heart of Islam does create the false impression of being in control of Heaven, but meanwhile, the command of the earth slips away. More fundamentally, the moderation and balance that Islam is supposed to represent puts human beings firmly in command of the earth—which is the object of their delegation and inheritance—while their hearts and eyes are fixed on heaven. It is on this earth that Muslims prove their worthiness of God's covenant, and it is on this earth that Muslims are supposed to manifest their ability to produce beauty.

The turmoil that Muslims have witnessed since the puritan movement exploded on the scene serves as a reminder that success and failure is enjoyed and suffered by human beings. It is by Islam's impact on humanity that its influence will be measured. This is exactly why numerous Prophetic reports emphasize that the personal salvation of a Muslim is hinged on his or her ability to do good by other human beings. Innumerable traditions stress time and again that if a Muslim hopes to attain God's favor, he or she must treat people with the level of kindness, compassion, and mercy that he or she hopes people will afford to him or her. In addition, this is also why in Shariʻah it is often emphasized that a person can supplicate to God a thousand times a day, but this will avail him or her nothing if he or she is unjust toward other human beings. According to Shariʻah, if a person usurps the rights of another, his or her repentance is ineffective unless he or she performs full restitution for the wrong committed and restores the balance of justice to its rightful place.[4]

Doing good and living in pursuit of goodness (*ihsan*) is such a dominant theme in the Qur'an that, to my mind, it takes a level of obstinacy or moral vapidity for a believer (in the Qur'an), at a minimum, not to be challenged by it.[5] In the Qur'anic usage, to do acts of *ihsan* is to perform beautiful deeds or acts of grace and beauty. It is as if *ihsan* is at the very logic of creation, as natural as the rules of symmetry that define not just balance and beauty but reality. *Ihsan* is not just kindness or generosity; it is life giving and life sustaining. "Do good as God has been good to you,"[6] the Qur'an exhorts. Does this narrative reveal an ontological truth about what we are? Good in nature because God is good? Not necessarily—the Qur'an reminds us of what we could be. The Qur'anic narrative is a reminder that we were created in an act of goodness and beauty and that invoking and reigniting this realization could draw us back to this transcendental and primordial reality. It took so much goodness, beauty, and grace for any of us to be that destruction of being is a disruption and breakdown of the dynamic of existence. This is why the Qur'an emphasizes that whoever murders a soul murders humankind, and whoever saves a soul saves humankind.[7] This fundamental dynamic is again emphasized in repeated Qur'anic imperative declarations: "Do beautiful deeds (*ihsanu*), for God loves those who do."[8] Moreover, the elements of this dynamic are made more apparent in the Qur'anic declaration: "God's mercy abides closely by those who do beautiful deeds (*muhsinin*)."[9] Here, the Qur'an emphasizes what is grounded in our very being—when human beings pursue the sublime and majestic, they affirm God's grace—they affirm that they are the bearers of divinity.[10]

Acting in goodness and beauty—indeed, being good and beautiful—is so elemental to human being-ness that the Qur'an often indicates that its message will be lost on those whose hearts have become hard and cruel.[11] In the Qur'anic discourse, those who are pious and who pursue goodness are the people most receptive to the guidance and mercy of the Holy Book. So the Qur'an declares: "These are the verses of the judicious scripture, guidance and mercy for those who do beautiful deeds (*muhsinin*), who maintain their prayers, give alms (to the needy), and are certain of the Hereafter; those are the ones who follow the Lord's rightful guidance, and it is they who will prosper."[12] The nurturing of conscientiousness toward the pursuit of beautiful deeds readies the heart and makes it especially receptive to the guidance that elicits God's merciful grace and elevates a human being to his/her divine potential. On the other hand, without this perseverance in nurturing that sense of beautiful goodness, it is possible that the Qur'an will become like seeds planted in foul soil. What goes into the soil is beautiful, but this beauty is stillborn and deformed, unable to do justice to the goodness it received.

In the final analysis, I do believe that human beings have an intuitive sense of ugliness and beauty, and unless Islam is associated with beauty in the minds and hearts of people, its universal message will be frustrated. According to the Qur'an, the Islamic message is intended as a mercy for all humanity, and according to the Qur'an, Muslims have been created as a nation in the middle—it is a nation that should be anchored in the midst and heart of humanity bearing witness on God's behalf. The laws of basic rituals are supposed to provide a solid foundation and firm backbone anchoring Muslims on their feet as they meet the burden of their covenant with God. But from that point of anchor, Muslims should gain the power to leap and thrust forward in the moral and ethical direction God has given to them. The serious danger is that if Muslims fail to understand the nature of the legacy with which they have been entrusted, the cumulative accretion of laws will become a heavy burden weighing them down until they sink in place. Islam is a message of mercy, compassion, and justice to humanity, and submission to the God of this message can only mean that the followers of this faith must use all available means, whether of intellect or spirit, in the pursuit of these values. There is no escaping the fact that the primary and essential law of God is the path that leads to the exploration and realization of these moral goals. The further Muslims walk along that path, the more beauty they will achieve, and the closer they will come to divinity. What also seems to be an equally inescapable conclusion is that those Muslims who have forgotten that the way to humanity passes through God and that the way to God passes through humanity, at least for now, have lost the path to God and lost the path to beauty.

Notes

AUTHOR'S NOTE

1. On mainstream Islam, moderation, and extremism, see Khaled Abou El Fadl, *The Great Theft: Wrestling Islam from the Extremists* (New York: HarperOne, 2005).

PREFACE

1. Qur'an 4:135; 5:8. See note below on the subject.

2. The Khawarij are known throughout Islamic history for their uncompromising zeal and even fanaticism. Their origin stems from the struggle for power that ensued between 'Ali (the fourth rightly guided caliph, and the Prophet's cousin and son-in-law) and Mu'awiya following the assassination of the third rightly guided caliph, 'Uthman. When 'Ali agreed to Mu'awiya's proposal to submit their disagreement over who should hold power to arbitration, a group of soldiers from 'Ali's camp vehemently disagreed with his decision to submit to arbitration. They withdrew from him, insisting that "judgment belongs to God alone." They proceeded to rebel against whatever authority they found to be illegitimate. On modern groups that have ideological roots with the Khawarij, see Said Amir Arjomand, "Unity and Diversity in Islamic Fundamentalism," in *Fundamentalisms Comprehended*, ed. Martin E. Marty and Scott R. Appleby (Chicago: University of Chicago Press, 1995), 179–98; Jeffrey T. Kenney, *Muslim Rebels: Kharijites and the Politics of Extremism in Egypt* (Oxford: Oxford University Press, 2006); Hussam S. Timani, *Modern Intellectual Readings of the Kharijites* (New York: Peter Lang, 2008), esp. 99–114; Umar 'Abdallah Kamil, *Al-Mutatarrifun: al-Khawarij al-Judud* (Cairo: Maktaba al-Turath al-Islami, 1998). On the Khawarij generally, see Elie Adib Salem, *Political Theory and Institutions of the Khawarij* (Baltimore, MD: Johns Hopkins University Press, 1956); G. Levi Della Vida, "Kharidjites," in *Encyclopaedia of Islam*, 2nd ed., ed. P. Bearman et al., *Brill Online*, http://referenceworks.brillonline.com/entries/encyclopaedia-of-islam-2/kharidjites-COM_0497.

3. See Jerome Taylor, "Mecca for the Rich: Islam's Holiest Site 'Turning into Vegas,'" *Independent*, September 24, 2011, http://www.independent.co.uk/news/world/middle-east/mecca-for-the-rich-islams-holiest-site-turning-into-vegas-2360114.html; "Mecca versus Las Vegas," *Economist*, June 24, 2010, http://www.economist.com/node/16438996; Irfan Al-Alawi, "Turning Mecca into Las Vegas: Saudi Wahhabis Continue Assault on Islamic Heritage," *Gatestone Institute*, December 12, 2012, http://www.gatestoneinstitute.org/3496/mecca-islamic-heritage; Oliver Wainwright, "Mecca's Mega Architecture Casts Shadow over Hajj," *Guardian*, October 23, 2012, http://www.theguardian.com/artanddesign/2012/oct/23/mecca-architecture-hajj1.

4. See Khaled Abou El Fadl, *The Great Theft: Wrestling Islam from the Extremists* (New York: HarperOne, 2005), esp. 16–25.

5. Thucydides, *Peloponnesian War*, trans. Richard Crawley (London: J.M. Dent, 1903), 3:38.

6. For instance, see Ergun Mehmet Caner and Emir Fethi Caner, *Unveiling Islam: An Insider's Look at Muslim Life and Beliefs* (Grand Rapids, MI: Kregel, 2002); Hal Lindsey, *The Everlasting Hatred: The Roots of Jihad* (Murrieta, CA: Oracle House, 2002); David Earle Johnson, *Conspiracy in Mecca: What You Need to Know about the Islamic Threat* (Cape Canaveral, FL: David Johnson, 2002); Bat Ye'or, *Islam and Dhimmitude: Where Civilizations Collide* (Madison, NJ: Fairleigh Dickinson University Press, 2002); Bat Ye'or, *Eurabia: The Euro-Arab Axis* (Madison, NJ: Fairleigh Dickinson University Press, 2005); Robert Spencer, *Islam Unveiled: Disturbing Questions about the World's Fastest-Growing Faith* (San Francisco: Encounter, 2002); Robert Spencer, *Onward Muslim Soldiers: How Jihad Still Threatens America and the West* (Washington, DC: Regnery, 2003); Robert Spencer, *The Politically Incorrect Guide to Islam (And the Crusades)* (Washington, DC: Regnery, 2005); Robert Spencer, *The Truth about Muhammad: Founder of the World's Most Intolerant Religion* (Washington, DC: Regnery, 2006); Robert Spencer, *Stealth Jihad: How Radical Islam Is Subverting America without Guns or Bombs* (Washington, DC: Regnery, 2008); Mark Gabriel, *Islam and Terrorism: What the Quran Really Teaches about Christianity, Violence and the Goals of the Islamic Jihad* (Lake Mary, FL: Charisma House, 2002); Mark Gabriel, *Islam and the Jews: The Unfinished Battle* (Lake Mary, FL: Charisma House, 2003); Daniel Pipes, *Militant Islam Reaches America* (New York: Norton, 2003); Patton Howell, *The Terrorist Mind in Islam and Iraq* (Dallas, TX: Saybrook, 2003); R. C. Sproul and Abdul Saleeb, *The Dark Side of Islam* (Wheaton, IL: Crossway, 2003); Christopher Catherwood, *Christians, Muslims, and Islamic Rage: What Is Going On and Why It Happened* (Grand Rapids, MI: Zondervan, 2003); William Wagner, *How Islam Plans to Change the World* (Grand Rapids, MI: Kregel, 2004); David Horowitz, *Unholy Alliance: Radical Islam and the American Left* (Washington, DC: Regnery, 2004); Walid Shoebat, *Why I Left Jihad: The Root of Terrorism and the Rise of Islam* (Newtown, PA: Top Executive Media, 2005); Walid Shoebat and Joel Richardson, *God's War on Terror: Islam, Prophecy and the Bible* (Newtown, PA: Top Executive Media, 2008); Joel Richardson, *The Islamic Antichrist: The Shocking Truth about the Real Nature of the Beast* (Los Angeles: WND, 2009); Paul Sperry, *Infiltration: How Muslim Spies and Subversives Have Penetrated Washington* (Nashville, TN: Nelson Current, 2005); Paul L. Williams, *The Day of Islam: The Annihilation of America and the Western World* (Amherst, NY: Prometheus, 2005); Walid Phares, *Future Jihad: Terrorist Strategies against America* (New York: Palgrave MacMillan, 2005); Walid Phares, *The War of Ideas: Jihadism against Democracy* (New York: Palgrave MacMillan, 2007); Walid Phares, *The Coming Revolution: Struggle for Freedom in the Middle East* (New York: Threshold Editions, 2010); Brigitte Gabriel, *Because They Hate: A Survivor of Islamic Terror Warns America* (New York: St. Martin's, 2006); Brigitte Gabriel, *They Must Be Stopped: Why We Must Defeat Radical Islam and How We Can Do It* (New York: St. Martin's, 2008); Bruce Bawer, *While Europe Slept: How Radical Islam Is Destroying the West from Within* (New York: Doubleday, 2006); P. David Gaubatz and Paul Sperry, *Muslim Mafia: Inside the Secret Underworld That's Conspiring to Islamize America* (Los Angeles, CA: WND, 2009); Andrew McCarthy, *The Grand Jihad: How Islam and the Left Sabotage America* (New York: Encounter, 2010); Rebecca Bynum, *Allah Is Dead: Why Islam Is Not a Religion* (Nashville: New English Review, 2011); Ander G. Bostom, *Sharia versus Freedom: The Legacy of Islamic Totalitarianism* (Amherst, NY: Prometheus, 2012); Geert Wilders, *Marked for Death: Islam's War against the West and Me* (Washington, DC: Regnery, 2012).

7. See Irshad Manji, *The Trouble with Islam Today: A Muslim's Call for Reform in Her Faith* (New York: St. Martin's, 2003); Irshad Manji, *Allah, Liberty and Love: The Courage to Reconcile Faith and Freedom* (New York: Free Press, 2012); Nonie Darwish, *Now They Call Me Infidel: Why I Renounced Jihad for America, Israel, and the War on Terror* (New York: Sentinel, 2006); Nonie Darwish, *Cruel and Usual Punishment: The Terrifying Global Implications of Islamic Law* (Nashville: Thomas Nelson, 2008); Ayaan Hirsi Ali, *Infidel* (New York: Free Press, 2007); Wafa Sultan, *A God Who Hates: The Courageous Woman Who Inflamed the Muslim World Speaks Out against the Evils of Islam* (New York: St. Martin's, 2009).

8. Wajahat Ali et al., *Fear, Inc.: The Roots of the Islamophobia Network in America* (Center for American Progress, 2011); Nathan Lean, *The Islamophobia Industry: How the Right Manufactures Fear of Muslims* (London: Pluto, 2012); Stephen Sheehi, *Islamophobia: The Ideological Campaign against Muslims* (Atlanta, GA: Clarity, 2011); Carl W. Ernst, *Islamophobia in America: The Anatomy of Intolerance* (New York: Palgrave Macmillan, 2013).

9. See, for example, Martha C. Nussbaum, *The New Religious Intolerance: Overcoming the Politics of Fear in an Anxious Age* (Cambridge, MA: Harvard University Press, 2012); Matti Bunzl, *Anti-Semitism and Islamophobia: Hatreds Old and New in Europe* (Chicago: Prickly Paradigm, 2007); Peter Gottschalk and Gabriel Greenberg, *Islamophobia: Making Muslims the Enemy* (Lanham, MD: Rowman & Littlefield, 2007).

10. For example, the French President François Mitterrand advised President Clinton that Bosnia "did not belong" in what British officials called a "restoration of Christian Europe." Taylor Branch, *The Clinton Tapes: Conversations with a President, 1993–2001* (New York: Simon & Schuster, 2009), 10. See also Esther Kaplan, *With God on Their Side: George W. Bush and the Christian Right* (New York: New Press, 2004), 12–23; Bruce Holsinger, *Neomedievalism, Neoconservatism, and the War on Terror* (Chicago: Prickly Paradigm, 2007). Finally, for a collection of essays on this phenomenon, see Emran Qureshi and Michael Sells, eds., *The New Crusades: Constructing the Muslim Enemy* (New York: Columbia University Press, 2003). No less alarming is the rise of far-right political parties throughout Europe with thinly veiled if not outright agendas of intolerance against Muslims, as the recent success of Geert Wilders at the polls indicates. See Ian Traynor, "Big Gains for Far-Right Leader Geert Wilders as Dutch Go to the Polls," *Guardian*, March 3, 2010, http://www.guardian.co.uk/world/2010/mar/03/geert-wilders-dutch-polls; Bruno Waterfield, "Geert Wilders on Course to Be Next Dutch Prime Minister," *Telegraph*, March 4, 2010, http://www.telegraph.co.uk/news/worldnews/europe/netherlands/7369693/Wilders-on-course-to-be-next-Dutch-prime-minister.html; Stephen Castle and Steven Erlanger, "Dutch Voters Split, and Right Surges," *New York Times*, June 10, 2010, http://www.nytimes.com/2010/06/11/world/europe/11dutch.html?pagewanted=all&_r=0.

11. The clash of civilizations paradigm was first expounded by Samuel P. Huntington in "The Clash of Civilizations?," *Foreign Affairs* 72, no. 3 (1996): 22–49; Samuel P. Huntington, *The Clash of Civilizations and the Remaking of World Order* (New York: Touchstone, 1996).

12. See Edward Said, *Orientalism* (New York: Vintage, 1994), esp. 49–73, 315–21; Bryan S. Turner, *Orientalism, Postmodernism and Globalism* (London: Routledge, 1994), esp. 3–114; A. L. Macfie, *Orientalism* (London: Pearson Education, 2002); Ahmad Gunny, *Perceptions of Islam in European Writings* (Leicester, UK: Islamic Foundation, 2004). See also Khaled Abou El Fadl, "Islamic Law and Ambivalent Scholarship," review of *Comparative Perspectives on Islamic Law and Society* (Oxford: Oxford University Press, 2000), by Lawrence Rosen, *Michigan Law Review* 100, no. 6 (May 2002): 1421–43.

13. This belief is textually attested by the Qur'an. Qur'an 4:135 states, "Uphold justice and bear witness to God," while Qur'an 5:8 reverses this and states, "be steadfast in your devotion to God and bear witness for justice." It is no coincidence that being steadfast for God and justice are equated and that bearing witness for God and justice are also equated.

14. On the Israeli apartheid regime, see Virginia Tilley, *Beyond Occupation: Apartheid, Colonialism and International Law in the Occupied Palestinian Territories* (London: Pluto, 2012); Roane Carey, ed., *The New Intifada: Resisting Israel's Apartheid* (London: Verso, 2001); Amneh Daoud Badran, *Zionist Israel and Apartheid South Africa: Civil Society and Peace Building in Ethnic-National States* (New York: Routledge, 2010); Uri Davis, *Apartheid Israel: Possibilities for the Struggle Within* (London: Zed, 2003), esp. 82–144; Hussein Abu Hussein and Fiona McKay, *Access Denied: Palestinian Land Rights in Israel* (London: Zed, 2003); Daryl Glaser, "Zionism and Apartheid: A Moral Comparison," *Ethnic and Racial Studies* 26, no. 3 (2003): 403–21.

15. On the illegality of drone warfare, see Noam Chomsky and Andre Vltchek, *On Western Terrorism: From Hiroshima to Drone Warfare* (London: Pluto, 2013); Neta C. Crawford, *Accountability for Killing: Moral Responsibility for Collateral Damage in America's Post-9/11 Wars* (Oxford: Oxford University Press, 2013); Joseph Pugliese, *State Violence and the Execution of Law: Biopolitical Caesurae of Torture, Black Sites, Drones* (New York: Routledge, 2013), 184–220; Melina Sterio, "The United States' Use of Drones in the War on Terror: The (Il)legality of Targeted Killings under International Law," *Case Western Reserve Journal of International Law* 45, no. 1–2 (Fall 2012): 197–214; Richard Falk, "The Menace of Present and Future Drone Warfare," *Global Research*, February 15, 2012, http://www.globalresearch.ca/the-menace-of-present-and-future-drone-warfare/29296; Sikander Ahmed Shah, "War on Terrorism: Self Defense, Operation Enduring Freedom, and the Legality of U.S. Drone Attacks in Pakistan," *Washington University Global Studies Law Review* 9, no. 77 (2010): 79–129.

16. On the destruction of holy sites in Mecca and Medina, see "Saudi Arabia to Raze Prophet Mohammed's Tomb to Build Larger Mosque," *World Observer*, January 13, 2014, http://worldobserveronline.com/2014/01/13/saudi-arabia-raze-prophet-mohammeds-tomb-build-larger-mosque/; "Islamic Heritage Lost as Makkah Modernizes," *Center for Islamic Pluralism*, January 7, 2009, http://www.islamicpluralism.org/764/islamic-heritage-lost-as-makkah-modernises; Jerome Taylor, "Medina: Saudis Take a Bulldozer to Islam's History," *Independent*, October 26, 2012, http://www.independent.co.uk/news/world/middle-east/medina-saudis-take-a-bulldozer-to-islams-history-8228795.html; Ifan Ahmed, "The Destruction of the Holy Sites in Mecca and Medina," *Islamica Magazine*, no. 15, http://islamica-magazine.com/?p=424; Oliver Wainwright, "As Hajj Begins, the Destruction of Mecca's Heritage Continues," *Guardian*, October 14, 2013, http://www.theguardian.com/artanddesign/2013/oct/14/as-the-hajj-begins-the-destruction-of-meccas-heritage-continues.

AN INTRODUCTION TO SHARI'AH

1. The concept of Qadi justice was expounded by Max Weber in *Economy and Society*, ed. Guenther Roth and Claus Wittich (Berkeley: University of California Press, 1978), 3:976–80; first published in 1922.

2. Subhi Mahmassani, *Falsafat al-Tashri' fi al-Islam: The Philosophy of Jurisprudence in Islam*, trans. Farhat Ziadeh (Leiden: Brill, 1961), 168; Mohammad Hashim Kamali, *Principles of Islamic Jurisprudence* (Cambridge: Islamic Texts Society, 1991), 197; Wael B. Hallaq, *A History of Islamic Legal Theories: An Introduction to Sunni Usul al-Fiqh* (Cambridge: Cambridge University Press, 1997), 83–84.

3. Mahmassani, *Falsafat al-Tashri'*, 172–75; Kamali, *Principles of Islamic Jurisprudence*, 253–57.

4. Mahmassani, *Falsafat al-Tashri'*, 172–75; Muhammad Abu Zahra, *Usul al-Fiqh* (Cairo: Dar al-Fikr al-'Arabi, 1958), 291; Mustafa Zayd, *Al-Maslaha fi al-Tashri' al-Islami wa Najm al-Din al-Tufi*, 2nd ed. (Cairo: Dar al-Fikr al-'Arabi, 1964), 22; Y. Hamid al-'Alim, *Al-Maqasid al-'Ammah li al-Shari'a al-Islamiyya* (Herndon, VA: International Institute of Islamic Thought, 1991), 80; Muhammad bin 'Ali bin Muhammad al-Shawkani, *Talab al-'Ilm wa Tabaqat al-Muta'allimin: Adab al-Talab wa Muntaha al-'Arab* (Cairo: Dar al-Arqam, 1981), 145–51.

5. A more historical translation for text would be *matn* or *khitab*.

6. Joseph Schacht, *An Introduction to Islamic Law* (Oxford: Oxford University Press, 1983), 37–48. See also Patricia Crone and Martin Hinds, *God's Caliph: Religious Authority in the First Centuries of Islam* (Cambridge: Cambridge University Press, 1986), 43–57; Norman Calder, *Studies in Early Muslim Jurisprudence* (Oxford: Clarendon, 1993), 198–222.

7. Schacht, *Introduction*, 45–48. See also Noel J. Coulson, *A History of Islamic Law* (Edinburgh, UK: Edinburgh University Press, 1995), 53–61, who considered al-Shafi'i to have been the "master architect" of Islamic jurisprudence. For a refutation of this view, see Wael B. Hallaq, *Shari'a: Theory, Practice, Transformations* (Cambridge: Cambridge University Press, 2009), 30–35; Wael B. Hallaq, "Was al-Shafi'i the Master Architect of Islamic Jurisprudence?," *International Journal of Middle East Studies* 25 (1993): 587–605; Yasin Dutton, *The Origins of Islamic Law: The Qur'an, the Muwatta, and Madinan 'Amal* (Surrey, UK: Curzon, 1999), 4–5.

8. In some cases throughout, years are given first in the Islamic calendar year (AH, "anno Hegirae") and next in the Gregorian calendar year (AD, "anno Domini").

9. Mahmassani, *Falsafat al-Tashri'*, 59; Abu al-'Aynayn Badran, *Usul al-Fiqh* (Cairo: Dar al-Ma'arif, 1965), 322; Subhi al-Salih, *Ma'alim al-Shari'a al-Islamiyya* (Beirut: Dar al-'Ilm li-al-Malayin, 1975), 46; Kamali, *Principles of Islamic Jurisprudence*, 285.

10. Mahmassani, *Falsafat al-Tashri'*, 200–202; Muhammad al-Zarqa, *Sharh al-Qawa'id al-Fiqhiyya*, 4th ed. (Damascus: Dar al-Qalam, 1996), 227–29; C. R. Tyser, trans., *The Mejelle: Being an English Translation of Majallah-el-Ahkam-Adliya and a Complete Code on Islamic Civil Law* (Lahore: Punjab Educational Press, 1967), 8.

11. Abu al-Ma'ali 'Abd al-Malik bin 'Abd Allah bin Yusuf al-Juwayni, *Kitab al-Ijtihad min Kitab al-Talkhis* (Damascus: Dar al-Qalam, 1987), 50–51.

12. In jurisprudential sources, this field is known as *'ilm al-tarjih*, or *'ilm al-ta'arud wa al-tarjih*, or *'ilm al-ta'dil wa al-tarjih*—the field of conflict and preponderance or the field of balance and preponderance.

13. Bernard G. Weiss, *The Search for God's Law: Islamic Jurisprudence in the Writings of Sayf al-Din al-Amidi* (Salt Lake City: University of Utah Press, 1992), 734–38.

14. I memorized this statement during my youth, but I have not been able to locate it in a source. However, I found the quote cited in Ahmad Z. Hammad, *Islamic Law: Understanding Juristic Difference* (Oak Brook, IL: American Trust, 1992), 44, but the author does not indicate that it belongs to Abu Hanifa. This statement has also been attributed to al-Shafi'i. Another version of this report states that Abu Hanifa is reported to have said: "We know [that] this [position] is one opinion, and it is the best we can arrive at. [If] someone arrives at a different view, then he adopts what he believes [is best] and we adopt what we believe [is best]." See Abu Muhammad 'Ali bin Ahmad bin Sa'id bin Hazm, *Kitab al-Fasl fi al-Milal wa al-Nihal* (Cairo: al-Matba'a al-Adabiyya, 1317/1899), 2:46; Subhi Mahmassani, *Falsafat al-Tashri' fi al-Islam: Muqaddima fi Dirasat al-Shari'a al-Islamiyya 'ala Daw' Madhahibuha al-Mukhtali-fa wa Daw' al-Qawanin al-Haditha* (Beirut: Dar al-'Ilm lil-Malayin, 1961), 42.

15. Jalal al-Din 'Abd al-Rahman bin al-Suyuti, *Ikhtilaf al-Madhahib*, ed. 'Abd al-Qayyum Muhammad Shafi' al-Bastawi (Cairo: Dar al-I'tisam, 1404/1983), 22–23; Dutton, *Origins of Islamic Law*, 29; Crone and Hinds, *God's Caliph*, 86–87.

16. Al-Suyuti, *Ikhtilaf al-Madhahib*, 22–23; Dutton, *Origins of Islamic Law*, 29; Crone and Hinds, *God's Caliph*, 86–87. Incidentally, there is a disagreement over whether the Caliph in question was al-Mansur (d. 158/775) or Harun al-Rashid (d. 193/809).

17. Al-Juwayni, *Kitab al-Ijtihad*, 61.

18. Sayf al-Din Abu al-Hasan 'Ali bin Abi 'Ali bin Muhammad al-Amidi, *Al-Ihkam fi Usul al-Ahkam*, ed. 'Abd al-Razzaq 'Afifi, 2nd ed. (Beirut: al-Maktab al-Islami, 1402/1981), 4:183; Jamal al-Din Abi Muhammad 'Abd al-Rahim bin al-Hasan al-Asnawi, *al-Tamhid fi Takhrij al-Furu' 'ala al-Usul*, 3rd ed. (Beirut: Mu'assasat al-Risalah, 1984), 531–34; Muhammad bin al-Hasan al-Badakhshi, *Sharh al-Badakhshi Manahij al-'Uqul ma' Sharh al-Asnawi Nihayat al-Sul* (Beirut: Dar al-Kutub al-'Ilmiyya, 1984), 3:275–81; Abu Hamid Muhammad bin Muhammad al-Ghazali, *al-Mustasfa min 'Ilm al-Usul*, ed. Ibrahim Muhammad Ramadan (Beirut: Dar al-Arqam, n.d.), 2:375–78; al-Juwayni, *Kitab al-Ijtihad*, 41; Abu al-Thana' Mahmud bin Zayd al-Lamishi, *Kitab fi Usul al-Fiqh*, ed. 'Abd al-Majid Turki (Beirut: Dar al-Gharb al-Islami, 1995), 202–3; Shihab al-Din Abu al-'Abbas Ahmad bin Idris al-Qarafi, *Sharh Tanqih al-Fusul fi Ikhtisar al-Mahsul fi al-Usul*, ed. Taha 'Abd al-Rauf Sa'd (Beirut: Dar al-Fikr, 1973), 440; Fakhr al-Din al-Razi, *al-Mahsul fi 'Ilm Usul al-Fiqh*, ed. Taha Jabir Fayyad al-'Alwani, 3rd ed. (Beirut: Mu'assasat al-Risala, 1997), 6:34–35, 6:43–50; Zaki al-Din Sha'ban, *Usul al-Fiqh al-Islami* (Cairo: Matba'at Dar al-Ta'lif, 1965), 418–19; Badran, *Usul al-Fiqh*, 474.

19. The Arabic is "*kull mujtahid musib*" and "*li kulli mujtahid nasib*." I will discuss these traditions in greater detail later.

20. Muhammad Amin Ibn 'Abadin, "Nashr al-'urf fi bina' ba'd al-Ahkam 'ala al-'urf," in *Majmu'a Rasa'il Ibn 'Abadin* (Beirut: Dar Ihya' al-Turath al-'Arabi, 1970), 112–63; Abu Zahra, *Usul al-Fiqh*, 217–19; Muhammad Khalid Masud, *Islamic Legal Philosophy: A Study of Abu Ishaq al-Shatibi's Life and Thought* (New Delhi: International Islamic, 1989), 226, 293–99.

21. Muhammad Sa'id Ramadan Buti, *Dawabit al-Maslaha fi al-Shari'a al-Islamiyya*, 6th ed. (Beirut: Mu'assassat al-Risala, 1992), 207–16, 285–357; 'Allal al-Fasi, *Maqasid al-Shari'a al-Islamiyya wa Makarimuha*, 5th ed. (Beirut: Dar al-Gharb al-Islami, 1993), 137–40; Mahmassani, *Falsafat al-Tashri'*, 172–75; John Makdisi, "Legal Logic and Equity in Islamic Law," *American Journal of Comparative Law* 33 (1985): 63–92; Kamali, *Principles of Islamic Jurisprudence*, 167–68; Hallaq, *Islamic Legal Theories*, 107–13; Dutton, *Origins of Islamic Law*, 34.

22. Mahmassani, *Falsafat al-Tashri'*, 172–75; Kamali, *Principles of Islamic Jurisprudence*, 253–57.

23. For instance, Najm al-Din al-Tufi (d. 716/1316) was widely criticized by his fellow jurists when he suggested that public interest could be an independent and sufficient source of law even with the existence of text that is on point on a particular issue. Zayd, *Al-Maslaha fi al-Tashri' al-Islami wa Najm al-Din al-Tufi*, 65–172; al-Buti, *Dawabit al-Maslaha*, 178–89; Masud, *Islamic Legal Philosophy*, 165, 174–75; Hallaq, *Islamic Legal Theories*, 208; Ihsan Abdul Baghby, "Utility in Classical Islamic Law: The Concept of 'Maslahah' in 'Usul al-Fiqh'" (PhD diss., University of Michigan, 1986), 166–70.

24. This division is not at all unusual. Jewish law tended to divide commandments into negative and positive and divided duties into duties to God and duties to men; see Harry Austryn Wolfson, *Philo: Foundations of Religious Philosophy in Judaism, Christianity and Islam* (Cambridge: Harvard University Press, 1948), 2:200.

1. GENESIS: NEGOTIATING THE MUSLIM AND THE ISLAMIC

1. "*Ya Rabb*" is an expression meaning "Oh, Lord" or "Oh, God." I clarify the meaning of jihad at several points in the book.

2. Qur'an, chapter 10, verse 69—hereinafter Qur'an 10:69.

3. *Allah* is the Arabic word for God. Christian Arabs use the same word to refer to God.

4. Kuwaiti law guaranteed Kuwaiti citizens at least a 51 percent interest in any business, regardless of their contribution in capital or labor. Since the only way a foreigner could do business in Kuwait was by finding a Kuwaiti partner, Kuwaitis often contributed neither capital nor labor and simply collected at least 51 percent of the profits on a regular basis. A non-Kuwaiti who was unhappy with this situation had no choice but to either leave the country or replace one Kuwaiti partner with another.

5. For example, see Qur'an 9:39, 11:57, and 47:38. I will develop this theme later.

6. For Napoleon's invasion of Cairo, including his bombardment of the Azhar Mosque, see, for instance, Paul Strathern, *Napoleon in Egypt* (New York: Bantam, 2008), 245–48; J. Christopher Herold, *Bonaparte in Egypt* (Barnsley, UK: Pen & Sword Military, 2005), 192–200. Also see Roger Owen, *Lord Cromer: Victorian Imperialist, Edwardian Proconsul* (New York: Oxford University Press, 2005).

7. For Lawrence, the division of the Ottoman Empire, and the Sykes-Picot Agreement, see David Fromkin, *A Peace to End All Peace: The Fall of the Ottoman Empire and the Creation of*

the Modern Middle East (New York: Henry Holt, 2009), 188–99; 309–25; James Barr, *A Line in the Sand: The Anglo-French Struggle for the Middle East, 1914–1948* (New York: Norton, 2012), 3–55.

8. A good many books have been written on these subjects. For Western interference in the Middle East, see Aftab A. Malik, *Shattered Illusions: Analyzing the War on Terrorism* (Bristol, UK: Amal Press, 2002); Michael R. Fischbach, *Records of Dispossession: Palestinian Refugee Property and the Arab-Israeli Conflict* (New York: Columbia University Press, 2003); Jeremy Salt, *The Unmaking of the Middle East: A History of Western Disorder in Arab Lands* (Berkeley: University of California Press, 2008).

9. See Noam Chomsky, *Middle East Illusions* (Lanham, MD: Rowman and Littlefield, 2003); Jeremy Brecher, Jill Cutler, and Brendan Smith, eds., *In the Name of Democracy: American War Crimes in Iraq and Beyond* (New York: Metropolitan, 2005); Robert Fisk, *The Great War for Civilization: The Conquest of the Middle East* (New York: Knopf, 2005); Rashid Khalidi, *The Iron Cage: The Story of the Palestinian Struggle for Statehood* (Boston: Beacon, 2006); Rashid Khalidi, *Sowing Crisis: The Cold War and American Dominance in the Middle East* (Boston: Beacon, 2009); Sonali Kolhatkar and James Ingalls, *Bleeding Afghanistan: Washington, Warlords, and the Propaganda of Silence* (New York: Seven Stories, 2006); Assaf Kfoury, ed., *Inside Lebanon: Journey to a Shattered Land with Noam and Carol Chomsky* (Monthly Review, 2007); Neve Gordon, *Israel's Occupation* (Berkeley: University of California Press, 2008); Norman G. Finkelstein, *'This Time We Went Too Far': Truth and Consequences of the Gaza Invasion* (New York: OR, 2010)); Norman G. Finkelstein, *Knowing Too Much: Why the American Jewish Romance with Israel Is Coming to an End* (New York: OR, 2012).

10. For example, see Daniel Pipes, "[Moderate] Voices of Islam," *New York Post*, September 23, 2003, reposted at *Middle East Forum*, http://www.danielpipes.org/1255/moderate-voices-of-islam. Also, see Daniel Pipes, "Radical Islam vs. Civilization," *FrontPageMagazine.com*, February 1, 2007, reposted at *Middle East Forum*, http://www.danielpipes.org/4254/radical-islam-vs-civilization; Daniel Pipes, "Is Tariq Ramadan Lying [about Magdi Allam]," *FrontPageMagazine.com*, March 5, 2007, reposted at *Middle East Forum*, http://www.danielpipes.org/4325/is-tariq-ramadan-lying-about-magdi-allam; Daniel Pipes, "Tariq Ramadan, Magdi Allam, and Me—Updates," *Middle East Forum*, March 25, 2013, http://www.danielpipes.org/blog/2007/03/tariq-ramadan-magdi-allam-and-me-updates; Imran Firasat, "Imran Firasat: I Am Going to Be Killed Soon," *Jihad Watch*, May 24, 2013, http://www.jihadwatch.org/2013/05/imran-firasat-i-am-going-to-be-killed-soon.html.

11. There are many examples of these hypocritical works. For instance, see Daniel Pipes, *Militant Islam Reaches America* (New York: Norton, 2002); Robert Spencer, *Onward Muslim Soldiers: How Jihad Still Threatens America and the West* (Washington, DC: Regenery, 2003); Robert Spencer, *Stealth Jihad: How Radical Islam Is Subverting America without Guns or Bombs* (Washington, DC: Regnery, 2008); Robert Spencer, *Religion of Peace? Why Christianity Is and Islam Isn't* (Washington, DC: Regnery, 2007); Robert Spencer, *Not Peace but a Sword: The Great Chasm between Christianity and Islam* (San Diego, CA: Catholic Answers Press, 2013).

12. Qur'an 5:2.

13. Qur'an 4:135; 58:22.

14. Qur'an 4:105–112. All translations of the Qur'an throughout the book from the original Arabic are mine.

15. See Abu Hasan 'Ali ibn Ahmad al-Wahidi, *Asbab Nuzul al-Qur'an* (Beirut: Dar al-Kutub al-'Ilmiyya, 2001), 124; Muhammad ibn Jarir al-Tabari, *Tafsir al-Tabari: Jami' al-Bayan 'an Ta'wil Ay al-Qur'an*, ed. Mahmoud Muhammad Shakir (Cairo: Maktabat Ibn Taymiyya, n.d.), 9:175–99; Abu al-Hasan 'Ali ibn Muhammad al-Mawardi, *Al-Nukatu wa al-'Uyun: Tafsir al-Mawardi*, ed. al-Sayyid bin 'Abd al-Maqsud bin 'Abd al-Rahim (Beirut: Dar al-Kutub al-'Ilmiyya, n.d.), 1:527–28; Fakhr al-Din al-Razi, *al-Tafsir al-Kabir Aw Mafatih al-Ghayb* (Beirut: Dar al-Kutub al-'Ilmiyya, 1990), vol. 6, pt. 11:26–31.

16. See Jalal al-Din 'Abd al-Rahman bin Abi Bakr al-Suyuti, *Asbab al-Nuzul* (Cairo: Dar al-Tahrir lil-Tiba'a wa-al-Nashr, AH 1383), 2:63–65; al-Tabari, *Tafsir al-Tabari: Jami' al-Bayan 'an Ta'wil Ay al-Qur'an*, 9:199–201; Muhammad bin Isma'il al-Bukhari, *Sahih Bukhari* (Damascus: Dar Ibn Kathir, 2002), 1798.

17. See Khaled Abou El Fadl, *And God Knows the Soldiers: The Authoritative and Authoritarian in Islamic Discourses* (Lanham, MD: University Press of America, 2001), 91; Khaled Abou El Fadl, *Speaking in God's Name: Islamic Law, Authority, and Women* (Oxford: Oneworld, 2001), 32, 56, 265.

18. See Khaled Abou El Fadl, *The Place of Tolerance in Islam*, ed. Joshua Cohen and Ian Lague (Boston: Beacon, 2002), 17–18.

19. For instance, see Qur'an 2:105; 3:74; 35:2; 38:9; 43:32.

20. Qur'an 4:123–24. Also, see 2:111.

21. Not happy with leaving the story with this inconclusive finale, some commentators argued that when the Qur'an referred to "the believers who do good deeds," the Qur'an meant

to refer to Muslims. See al-Suyuti, *Asbab al-Nuzul*, 2:65; al-Wahidi, *Asbab Nuzul al-Qur'an*, 184; al-Mawardi, *Al-Nukatu wa al-'Uyun: Tafsir al-Mawardi*, 1:530–31; al-Tabari, *Tafsir al-Tabari: Jami' al-Bayan 'an Ta'wil Ay al-Qur'an*, 9:227–29; al-Razi, *Al-Tafsir al-Kabir Aw Mafatih al-Ghayb*, vol. 6, pt. 11:44.

22. Qur'an 21:107; 46:12.

23. Al-'Allamat 'Abd al-Hayy al-Husani, *Tahdhib al-Akhlaq* (Leicester, UK: Islamic Academy, 2003), 153; 'Izz al-Din Bulayq, *Minhaj al-Salihin min Ahadith wa Sunnat Khatim al-Anbiya wa al-Mursalin* (Beirut: Dar al-Fath, 1978), 197. In one report, in response to a man who asks the Prophet about Islam, the Prophet responds, "Good character" ("*Husn al-khuluq*"). Abi Bakr Ahmad bin Husayn al-Bayhaqi, *al-Jami' li-Shu'ab al-Iman* (Riyadh: Maktabat al-Rushd al-Nashir wa al-Tawzi', 2003), 10:375.

24. See Qur'an 10:85; 60:5.

25. al-Mawardi, *Al-Nukatu wa al-'Uyun: Tafsir al-Mawardi*, 5:517; al-Tabari, *Jami' al-Bayan Ta'wil Ay al-Qur'an*, 23:319–20; al-Razi, *Al-Tafsir al-Kabir Aw Mafatih al-Ghayb*, vol. 15, pt. 29:262–63.

26. See Abu Dawud Sulayman ibn al-Ash'ath al-Azdi al-Sijistrani, *Sunan Abi Dawud* (Beirut: Al-Maktaba al-'Asriyya, n.d.), 4:211–12.

27. For instance, see Qur'an 3:144; 3:176–77; 47:32.

28. Imam al-Nawawi, *Riyad al-Salihin*, ed. Muhammad Mahmoud 'Abd al-'Aziz and 'Ali Muhammad 'Ali (Cairo: Dar al-Hadith, 1994), 516; Ahmad bin 'Ali bin Hajar al-'Asqalani, *Fath al-Bari bi-Sharh Sahih al-Bukhari* (Beirut: Dar al-Ma'rifa, 1963), 13:333.

29. For the Qur'anic parable about the angels prostrating before humans, see Qur'an 2:30–33. I use the word *parable* here to mean a story communicated for demonstrative reasons. Whether the story is historical—in other words, whether the story actually occurred in some physical sense—is a question I do not reach.

30. This tradition is attributed to the Prophet. See 'Abd Allah ibn 'Umar Abu Zayd al-Dabusi, *Taqwim al-Adilla fi Usul al-Fiqh* (Beirut: Dar al-Kutub al-'Ilmiyya, 2001), 2:452; Jalal al-Din 'Abd al-Rahman bin Abi Bakr al-Suyuti (d. 911/1505), "*Al-Qawl al-ashbah fi hadith man 'arafa nafsahu faqad 'arafa rabbahu*," Daiber Collection, GAL II 148 nr. 72, Tokyo University. Also, see Ibn 'Arabi, *Divine Governance of the Human Kingdom: At-Tadbirat al-ilahiyyah fi islah al-mamlakat al-insaniyyah*, trans. Tosun Bayrak al-Jerrahi al-Halveti (Louisville, KY: Fons Vitae, 1997), 231–54.

2. AWAKENING: REASONABLENESS AND ISLAM

1. In the contemporary age, the term *Usuliyya* is often used to refer to Islamic fundamentalism. This should be differentiated from the Usulis I am referring to here. The roots of the Usulis, as students of Islamic jurisprudence, go back many centuries in Islamic history and are to be differentiated from the fundamentalists of the modern age.

2. See Qur'an 62:5.

3. Ibn Taymiyya said, "*Ma akthar ma yashtabih al-jubn wa al-fashal bi al-wara' idh kulun minhuma kaffun wa imsak.*" See Ahmad bin 'Abd al-Halim bin Taymiyya, *Al-Siyasa al-Shar'iyya fi Islah al-Ra'iyya* (Beirut: Dar al-Kutub al-'Ilmiyya, 2000), 87–88.

4. Abu Bakr Ahmad bin Husayn al-Bayhaqi, *Al-Sunan al-Kubra*, ed. Muhammad 'Abd al-Qadir 'Ata (Beirut: Dar al-Kutub al-'Ilmiyya, 2003), 10:213–14.

5. Abu Bakr Ahmad bin Husayn al-Bayhaqi, *Al-Jami' li-Shu'ab al-Iman* (Riyadh: Maktabat al-Rushd al-Nashir wa al-Tawzi', 2003), 10:375 (Islam is good ethical character); 'Abd al-Hayy al-Hasani, *Tahdhib al-Akhlaq*, 153; 'Izz al-Din Bulayq, *Minhaj al-Salihin min Ahadith wa Sunnat Khatim al-Anbiya wa al-Mursalin* (Beirut: Dar al-Fath, 1978), 197 (the most faithful are those who have the most ethical character or most ethical conduct).

6. Qur'an 6:162.

7. This is enshrined in the Prophet's famous statement: '*Innama bu'ithtu li 'utammima makarim al-akhlaq* (I was sent to perfect the ethical character of human beings). Malik ibn Anas, *Muwatta* (Cairo: Mustafa al-Babi al-Halabi, 1985), 904–5. See also 'Abd Allah bin Muhammad bin Abi al-Dunya, *Makarim al-Akhlaq* (Cairo: Maktabat al-Qur'an, 1990), 21.

8. See Jalal al-Din 'Abd al-Rahman bin Abi Bakr al-Suyuti, *Asbab al-Nuzul* (Cairo: Dar al-Tahrir lil-Tiba'a wa-al-Nashr, AH 1383), 2:62.

9. For the tradition about good moral character being the means of following the Prophet, see Muhammad bin 'Ali bin al-Husayn bin Babawayh al-Qummi, '*Uyun Akhbar al-Rida*, ed. Mahdi al-Husayn al-Lajavardi (Qum: Chapkhana Dar al-'Ilm, 1377/1970), 2:50. For traditions about how those most beloved to the Prophet and those highest in God's grace in the afterlife are those with the highest ethical character, see 'Izz al-Din Bulayq, *Minhaj al-Salihin*, 198–99; 'Abd al-Hayy al-Hasani, *Tahdhib al-Akhlaq*, 153.

10. The accusation that "Islam spread by the sword" has become part of the often-repeated jargon of Islamophobes. However, this claim qualifies as propaganda rather than a historical assertion that can be taken seriously. While it is undeniable that in early Islam, there were excesses committed during the spread of the religion, this is a far cry from the sweeping, generalized claim that the religion spread by the sword. The extremely rapid dissemination of the Islamic faith was due to a variety of complex factors, including economic, commercial, and urbanization dynamics as well as cultural transplantations in addition to the moral energy of the new faith. On this complicated topic, see Fred McGraw Donner, *The Early Islamic Conquests* (Princeton, NJ: Princeton University Press, 1981); T. W. Arnold, *The Preaching of Islam: A History of the Propagation of the Muslim Faith* (London: Adam, 2002); Jonathan P. Berkey, *The Formation of Islam: Religion and Society in the Near East, 600–1800* (Cambridge: Cambridge University Press, 2003); Maurice Lombard, *The Golden Age of Islam* (Princeton, NJ: Markus Wiener, 2004).

11. Abu Bakr Muhammad bin Ahmad bin Sahl Shams al-Din Sarakhsi, *Al-Mabsut* (Beirut: Dar al-Ma'rifa, 1986), 10: 92.

12. Qur'an 2:272. Also see Qur'an 32:13.

13. See al-Suyuti, *Asbab al-Nuzul*, 1:35.

14. This is consistent with and perhaps derived from the Qur'anic verse: "We have dignified human beings" (*wa laqad karamana bani adam*). See Qur'an 17:70.

15. See Khaled Abou El Fadl, *And God Knows the Soldiers: The Authoritative and Authoritarian in Islamic Discourses* (Lanham, MD: University Press of America, 2001), 57.

16. See al-Suyuti, *Asbab al-Nuzul*, 1:48; Abu Hasan 'Ali ibn Ahmad al-Wahidi, *Asbab Nuzul al-Qur'an* (Beirut: Dar al-Kutub al-'Ilmiyya, 2001), 144. Later generations of Muslims claimed that the reason for the Prophet performing funeral prayers for Najashi was that he secretly converted from Christianity to Islam before his death.

17. See Qur'an 3:128 and, commenting on this verse, see al-Suyuti, *Asbab al-Nuzul*, 1:42.

18. In other writings, I have described this participatory approach as the search for beauty in Islam. See Khaled Abou El Fadl, *The Search for Beauty in Islam: A Conference of the Books* (Lanham, MD: Rowman and Littlefield, 2006), xiii–xiv, 84–86, 245–47, 344–53; Abou El Fadl, "The Culture of Ugliness in Modern Islam and Reengaging Morality," *UCLA Journal of Islamic and Near Eastern Law* 2, no. 1 (Fall/Winter 2002–2003): 33–97. I will return to this issue later in the book, but for a good discussion on the relation between beauty, love, and ethical investigations in Islamic thought, see Ahmad Sayyid Ahmad al-Musayyar, *Al-Hubb wa al-Jamal fi al-Islam* (Cairo: Dar al-Ma'arif, 2006), 155–57.

19. Qur'an 3:75.

20. See Qur'an 2:256; also, commenting on this verse, see al-Suyuti, *Asbab al-Nuzul*, 1:34; al-Wahidi, *Asbab Nuzul al-Qur'an*, 86.

21. Sarakhsi, *al-Mabsut*, 10:129.

22. Kamal al-Din Muhammad bin 'Abd al-Wahid al-Siwasi Ibn al-Humam, *Sharh Fath al-Qadir*, ed. 'Abd al-Razzaq Ghalib al-Mahdi (Beirut: Dar al-Kutub al-'Ilmiyya, 1995), 6:102.

23. See al-Suyuti, *Asbab al-Nuzul*, 3:144; 'Abd Allah Isma'il 'Ammar, *Al-Musannaf al-Hadith fi Asbab al-Nuzul* (Gaza, Palestine: Dar Ahaya' al-Kutub al-'Arabiyya, 1999), 325.

24. 'Abd al-Rahman Badawi, *Madhahib al-Islamiyin* (Beirut: Dar al-'Ilm lil-Malayin, 1996), 667–69.

25. See al-Suyuti, *Asbab al-Nuzul*, 2:73.

26. See al-Suyuti, *Asbab al-Nuzul*, 2:80–81.

27. For a good study on Islamic ethics and their social and political function, see Ahmad 'Ali Khidr, *Makarim al-Akhlaq fi Du' al-Qur'an wa Sunna* (Cairo: Dar al-Ma'arif, 2008).

28. Imam Muhammad Ibn Khalifa al-Washtani al-Ubbi, "Ikmal Ikmal al-Mu'allim," in *Sahih Muslim*, Imam Muslim Ibn al-Hajjaj al-Qushayri al-Nayshaburi (Beirut: Dar al-Kutub al-'Ilmiyya, 1994), 6:534.

29. Muhammad Ibn Ya'qub Kulayni, *Usul min al-Kafi* (Tehran: al-Matba' al-Islamiyya, 1962), 3:164, 4:458–61; Ibn Taymiyya, *Al-Siyasa al-Shar'iyya fi Islah al-Ra'iyya*, 115–18.

30. I have argued that many reports attributed to the Prophet are the product of an authorial enterprise that took place over the span of several historical developments. See Abou El Fadl, *Speaking in God's Name: Islamic Law, Authority and Women* (Oxford: Oneworld, 2001), 86–95, 98–115, 213–18, 232–47.

31. Ibid., 180–85.

32. In my book *The Authoritative and the Authoritarian in Islamic Discourses: A Contemporary Case Study* (Alexandria, VA: Saadawi, 2001), I took a single incident involving the issuance of a *fatwa* prohibiting Muslims from saluting or standing up out of respect for the American flag and analyzed its basis and implications. This single incident and the resulting *fatwa* took a short book to analyze.

33. The most systematic and comprehensive treatment of the subject is Salim bin 'Ali al-Thaqafi, *Ahkam al-Ghina' wa al-Ma'azif* (Cairo: Dar al-Bayan, 1996). In my view, the author presents a very compelling case proving the permissibility of music in Islamic law.

34. Makram Muhammad Ahmad, "Hadith fi al-'Amq ma' Shaykh al-Azhar," *Al-Ahram al-Yawmi*, July 10, 2010, http://digital.ahram.org.eg/articles.aspx?Serial=187680&eid=786.

35. The Wahhabis relied on traditions attributed to the Prophet instructing Muslims not to sing the text of the Qur'an. However, the meaning of these traditions depends on what was considered singing at the time of the Prophet.

36. The three mosques mentioned in the text are regulated by the Egyptian Ministry of Religious Affairs. The ministry, however, denied that it was responsible for these segregation policies. Meeting with the Shaykh of Azhar and the Mufti of Egypt did not yield results. It was suggested to me, however, by an official at Azhar who does not wish to be identified that the source of the segregation policies was the Ministry of Interior, which in turn adopted these policies in response to Saudi pressure.

37. Muhammad Rizq, *Hadha Huwa al-Walid Bin Talal* (Cairo: Dar Ibda', 2007); 'Ali Yusuf 'Ali, *Fatawa Marfuda* (al-Muhandisin: Majmu'at Ajyal li-Khidmat al-Taswiq wa al-Nashr wa al-Intaj al-Thaqafi, 2008); Sami Zubaida, *Islam, the People and the State: Political Ideas and Movements in the Middle East*, 3rd ed. (New York: I. B. Tauris, 2009).

38. For a demonstrative example, see 'Ali, *Fatawa Marfuda*. See also Khaled Abou El Fadl, "The Orphans of Modernity and the Clash of Civilisations," *Global Dialogue* 4, no.2 (Spring 2002): 1–16; Abou El Fadl, *And God Knows the Soldiers*, 4–13, 101–5, 108–20; Abou El Fadl, *Speaking in God's Name*, 9–18, 172–77; Khaled Abou El Fadl, *The Great Theft : Wrestling Islam from the Extremists* (New York: HarperOne, 2005), 35–38, 162–79; Khaled Abou El Fadl, *The Place of Tolerance in Islam*, ed. Joshua Cohen and Ian Lague (Boston: Beacon, 2002), 6–7; Khaled Abou El Fadl, *Islam and the Challenge of Democracy*, ed. Joshua Cohen and Deborah Chasman (Princeton, NJ: Princeton University Press, 2004), 122–28.

39. For example, see 'Ali, *Fatawa Marfuda*; Fu'ad Matar, *Alf Fatwa . . . wa Fatwa! Muslimun fi Mahabb Fawda al-Fatawa: Azhariyya, Sunniyya, Wahhabiyya, Shi'iyya, Khumayniyya* (Beirut: al-Dar al-'Arabiyya li-al-'Ulum, 2009). See also Gary R. Bunt, *Virtually Islamic: Computer-Mediated Communication and Cyber Islamic Environments* (Cardiff, Wales: University of Wales Press, 2000); Gary R. Bunt, *Islam in the Digital Age: E-Jihad, Online Fatwas and Cyber Islamic Environments* (Sterling, VA: Pluto, 2003); Mohammed el-Nawawy and Sahar Khamis, *Islam Dot Com: Contemporary Islamic Discourses in Cyberspace* (New York: Palgrave Macmillan, 2009); Mohamed Chawki, "Islam in the Digital Age: Counselling and Fatwas at the Click of a Mouse," *Journal of International Commercial Law and Technology* 5, no.4 (2010): 165–80; Yasmin Moll, "Islamic Televangelism: Religion, Media and Visuality in Contemporary Egypt," *Arab Media & Society*, no. 10 (Spring 2010), available at http://www.arabmediasociety.com/articles/downloads/20100407165913_Mollpdf.pdf.

40. Ahmad Kamal Abu al-Majd, *Hiwar la Muwajaha* (Cairo: Dar al-Shuruq, 1988); Muhammad al-Ghazali, *Al-Sunna al-Nabawiyya Bayn Ahl al-Fiqh wa Ahl al-Hadith* (Cairo: Dar al-Shuruq, 1989).

41. Ibn Taymiyya, *Minhaj al-Sunna al-Nabawiyya fi Naqd Kalam al-Shi'a wa al-Qadariya* (Beirut: Dar al-Kutub al-'Ilmiyya, n.d.), 2:248; Muhammad bin Isma'il al-Bukhari, *Sahih Bukhari* (Damascus: Dar Ibn Kathir, 2002), 921.

42. 'Ali, *Fatawa Marfuda*, 38–39; "Breastfeeding Fatwa Causes Stir," *BBC News*, May 22, 2007, http://news.bbc.co.uk/2/hi/6681511.stm; Abraham Rabinovich, "Fatwa Promotes Adult Breastfeeding," *Australian*, May 28, 2007, http://www.theaustralian.com.au/news/world/fatwa-promotes-adult-breastfeeding/story-e6frg6so-1111113622471; Raymond Ibrahim, "Islam's 'Public Enemy #1,'" *National Review*, March 25, 2008, http://www.nationalreview.com/articles/223965/islams-public-enemy-1/raymond-ibrahim; "Breastfeeding Fatwa Sheikh Back at Egypt's Azhar," *Al Arabiya News*, May, 18, 2009, http://www.alarabiya.net/articles/2009/05/18/73140.html.

43. Abou El Fadl, *Speaking in God's Name*, 273.

44. "Bride Shot Dead on Wedding Night," *Arab News*, March 6, 2002, http://www.arabnews.com/node/218954; "Court Rejects Onaizah Girl's Divorce Plea," *Arab News*, December 22, 2008, http://www.arabnews.com/node/319198; Mail Foreign Service, "Saudi Court Tells Girl Aged EIGHT She Cannot Divorce Husband Who is 50 Years Her Senior," *Daily Mail*, December 22, 2008, http://www.dailymail.co.uk/news/article-1099447/Saudi-court-tells-girl-aged-EIGHT-divorce-husband-50-years-senior.html; Laura Bashraheel, "Court Annuls Onaizah Girl's Marriage with 58-Year-Old," *Arab News*, May 4, 2009, http://www.arabnews.com/node/323774; Caryle Murphy, "Child Marriage Reignites Debate in Saudi Arabia," *National*, October 11, 2010, http://www.thenational.ae/news/world/middle-east/child-marriage-reignites-debate-in-saudi-arabia.

45. See "Bosnians Get Qur'an in Their Own Language," *Arab News*, March 16, 1994, available at LexisNexis Academic, http://www.lexisnexis.com/hottopics/lnacademic/?.

46. On the critical importance of the quality of education, see Fazlur Rahman, *Islam and Modernity: Transformation of an Intellectual Tradition* (Chicago: University of Chicago Press, 1984).

47. Abou El Fadl, "The Culture of Ugliness."

48. Dan Diner, *Lost in the Sacred: Why the Muslim World Stood Still*, trans. Steven Rendall (Princeton, NJ: Princeton University Press, 2009), 163. Also see Khaled Abou El Fadl, "Islamic Law and Ambivalent Scholarship," review of *Comparative Perspectives on Islamic Law and Society* (Oxford: Oxford University Press, 2000), by Lawrence Rosen, *Michigan Law Review* 100, no. 6 (Spring 2002): 1424, 1440–43.

49. Diner, *Lost in the Sacred*, 160–61.

50. A very good recent example of how paying attention to the legal details leads to very different and much deeper understandings of Islamic law, see Ahmad Atif Ahmad, *Islam, Modernity, Violence, and Everyday Life* (New York: Palgrave Macmillan, 2009), esp. 1–42.

51. Often referred to as *ma yakun 'ala al-'a 'amma* or *al-'ilm al-'adi*. See Muhammad Baqir ibn Muhammad Akmal Bahbahani, *Al-Fawa'id al-Ha'iriyya* (Qum, Iran: Majma' al-Fikr al-Islami, 1415/1995), 129–30. Also see Mohammad Fadel, "The True, the Good and the Reasonable: The Theological and Ethical Roots of Public Reason in Islamic Law," *Canadian Journal of Law and Jurisprudence* 21, no. 1 (January 2008): 38–40, 55–56, 96–100. Exploring the Islamic tradition through the Rawlsian lens of an overlapping consensus, Fadel argues that Islamic political institutions, necessarily grounded in public reason and not revelation, require a theological and ethical freedom of enquiry. Such ethical and theological prerequisites are, though not inevitable, consistent and, practically speaking, desirable with a liberal democracy comprising multiple social and even religious interests. Fadel also cites instances in which substantive law was employed by premodern jurists as endeavors toward the development of a normative pluralism.

52. The idea of reasonableness is also well represented in the Islamic juristic discourses on majority decisions or common standards in law; see Ermin Sinanovic, "The Majority Principle in Islamic Legal and Political Thought," *Islam and Christian-Muslim Relations* 15, no. 2 (April 2004): 237–56.

53. On the distinction between rationality and reasonableness, see W. M.Sibley, "The Rational versus the Reasonable," *Philadelphia Review* 62 (October 1953): 554–60.

54. It should be noted that John Rawls, *Political Liberalism* (New York: Columbia University Press, 2005), 48–54 differentiates between rationalism and reasonableness. He develops the definition of reasonableness in the public space as a means for achieving an overlapping consensus over varying and possibly competing visions of a rational good life. As I argue later, this is not necessarily the conception of reasonableness that I share.

55. "Saudi Arabia: Rape Victim Punished for Speaking Out: Court Doubles Sentence for Victim, Bans Her Lawyer from the Case," *Human Rights Watch*, November 15, 2007, http://www.hrw.org/news/2007/11/15/saudi-arabia-rape-victim-punished-speaking-out. Also see Rasheed Abou-Alsamh, "Ruling Jolts Even Saudis: 200 Lashes for Rape Victim," *New York Times*, November 16, 2007, http://www.nytimes.com/2007/11/16/world/middleeast/16saudi.html?_r=0; "Saudi Defends Rape Victim Verdict," *Al Jazeera*, November 25, 2007, http://www.aljazeera.com/news/middleeast/2007/11/2008525135429470542.html; Rasheed Abou-Alsamh, "Saudi Rape Case Spurs Calls for Reform," *New York Times*, December 1, 2007, http://www.nytimes.com/2007/12/01/world/01saudi.html.

56. Scott MacLeod, "A Saudi Hero: Abdul Rahman al-Lahem," *Middle East Blog*, Time, November 16, 2007, http://web.archive.org/web/20080225181416/http://time-blog.com/middle_east/2007/11/a_saudi_hero_abdul_rahman_alla.html?; Faiza Saleh Ambah, "Saudi Lawyer Takes on Religious Court System," *Washington Post*, December 23, 2007, http://www.washingtonpost.com/wp-dyn/content/article/2006/12/22/AR2006122201579.html.

57. "MAS Freedom Condemns Saudi Miscarriage of Justice in Gang Rape Sentencing," *Muslim American Society's Freedom Newsletter* (MAS Freedom Newsletter), November 20, 2007, http://web.archive.org/web/20071227211818/http://www.masnet.org/takeaction.asp?id=4570; Aishah Schwartz, "MAS Freedom Welcomes Saudi King's Pardon of 'Qatif Girl' but Reiterates the Need for Change," *MAS Freedom Newsletter*, December 17, 2007; Allegra Stratton, "Saudi King Pardons Gang Rape Victim," *Guardian*, December 17, 2007, http://www.theguardian.com/world/2007/dec/17/saudiarabia.allegrastratton; Ebtihal Mubarak, "Abdullah Pardons 'Qatif Girl,'" *Arab News*, December 18, 2007, http://www.arabnews.com/node/306849; Editorial, "The Saudi Pardon," *International Herald Tribune*, December 22, 2007, available at LexisNexis Academic, http://www.lexisnexis.com/hottopics/lnacademic/?.

58. For the 1979 Pakistani law, see *Offence of Zina (Enforcement of Hudood) Ordinance, 1979* [Pakistan], Ordinance No. VII of 1979, February 10, 1979, available at http://www.unhcr.org/refworld/docid/4db999952.html. However, the law has been amended. See Immigration and Refugee Board of Canada, *Pakistan: The Protection of Women (Criminal Laws Amendment) Act, 2006 and Its Implementation*, November 30, 2011, PAK103864.E, available at http:/www.refworld.org/docid/5072d3242.html; Amnesty International, "Pakistan's Rape Laws Amended," February 13, 2007, http://www.amnesty.org.au/svaw/comments/2257/. Also see Shahnaz Khan, *Zina, Transnational Feminism, and the Moral Regulation of Pakistani Women* (Vancouver: University of British Columbia Press, 2006); "Anger over Afghan Girl's Flogging," *Al Jazeera*, September 25, 2012, http://www.aljazeera.com/video/asia/2012/09/201292513949172636.html; Human Rights Watch, *"I Had to Run Away": The Imprisonment*

of Women and Girls for 'Moral Crimes' in Afghanistan (New York: Human Rights Watch, 2012), 64–71.

59. 'Abd al-Qadir 'Awda, *Al-Tashri' al-Jina'i al-Islami: Muqaranan bi-al-Qanun al-Wad'i* (Beirut: Mu'assasat al-Risala, 1977), 1:690–708; Muhammad Rawwas al- Qal'ahji, *Al-Maw-su'a al-Fiqhiyya* (Beirut: Dar al-Nafa'is, 2000), 1:514–20.

60. Reportedly, the Prophet said that no convict may receive more than ten thrashings unless *hudud* crimes are involved. For various reasons, however, most jurists rejected this report and disagreed whether the maximum number of lashes on any crime is thirty-nine or a hundred or a number in between. 'Abd al-Qadir 'Awda, *Al-Tashri' al-Jina'i*, 1:688–90; also see Muhammad bin 'Ali al-Shawkani, *Nayl al-Awtar min Asrar Muntaqa al-Akhbar* (Beirut: Dar Ibn Hazm, 2000), 1503–4. Some jurists, such as Ibn Hazm, argued that *ta'zir* is applicable only to specifically enumerated crimes and warned against the state being able to criminalize whatever conduct it wished. See Ibn Hazm al-Zahiri, *al-Muhalla fi Sharh al-Muhalla bil Hijaj wa al-Athar* (Riyadh: Bayt al-Afkar al-Dawliyya, n.d.), 2214–16. Other jurists argued that *ta'zir* is possible only as to legal obligations already firmly established in law, but *ta'zir* cannot be justified on broad or general public interest or policy grounds. See Ahmad Fathi al-Bahnasi, *Al-'Uquba fi al-Fiqh al-Islami* (Cairo: Dar al-Shuruq, 1980), 29–30, 133–34.

61. See, al-Bahnasi, *Al-'Uquba*, 30.

62. The discursive and contingent nature of the jurisprudential investigations on the subject of *ta'zir* is richly represented in many classical legal sources. For instance, see Shams al-Din Muhammad bin Muflih al-Maqdisi, *Kitab al-Furu'* (Amman: Bayt al-Afkar al-Dawliyya, 2005), 1535–41.

63. See "Human Rights in Saudi Arabia: A Deafening Silence," *Human Rights Watch*, December 19, 2001, http://www.hrw.org/legacy/backgrounder/mena/saudi/saudi.pdf; "Saudi Arabia: Flogging Used to Silence Protestors," *Human Rights Watch*, January 17, 2005, http://www.hrw.org/news/2005/01/16/saudi-arabia-flogging-used-silence-protesters; "Saudi Arabia: Men 'Behaving Like Women' Face Flogging," *Human Rights Watch*, April 7, 2005, http://www.hrw.org/news/2005/04/06/saudi-arabia-men-behaving-women-face-flogging; "Memorandum to the Government of Saudi Arabia on Human Rights Priorities in the Kingdom," *Human Rights Watch*, February, 7, 2006, http://www.hrw.org/legacy/english/docs/2006/02/07/saudia12622_txt.htm; "Men Get 7000 Lashes for Sodomy," *Herald Sun*, October 4, 2007, http://www.news.com.au/heraldsun/story/0,21985,22532620-23109,00.html; "Saudi Court Upholds 'Sex Boast' Convictions," *BBC Online*, February 9, 2010, http://news.bbc.co.uk/2/hi/middle_east/8506874.stm.

64. Reem Leila, "Public Backlash: The Harsh Sentencing of Two Egyptian Doctors for Allegedly Being the Cause of a Saudi Princess's Addiction to Painkillers Has Caused an Outcry," *Al-Ahram Weekly*, no. 921, November 6–12 2008, http://weekly.ahram.org.eg/2008/921/eg11.htm; Reem Leila, "Employment Ban," *Al-Ahram Weekly*, no. 923, November 20–26, 2008, http://weekly.ahram.org.eg/2008/923/eg4.htm; Associated Press, "Egyptians Protest Doctor's 1,500-Lash Sentence in Saudi Arabia, *Fox News*, November 11, 2008, http://www.foxnews.com/story/2008/11/11/egyptians-protest-doctor-1500-lash-sentence-in-saudi-arabia/. See also Human Rights Watch, "Precarious Justice: Arbitrary Detention and Unfair Trials in the Deficient Criminal Justice System of Saudi Arabia," *Human Rights Watch* 20, no. 3 (E) (March 2008), available at http://www.hrw.org/sites/default/files/reports/saudijustice0308_1.pdf.

65. Ann Elizabeth Mayer, *Islam and Human Rights: Tradition and Politics*, 4th ed. (Boulder, CO: Westview, 2007), 198; Human Rights Watch, "Precarious Justice: Arbitrary Detention and Unfair Trials in the Deficient Criminal Justice System of Saudi Arabia"; Human Rights Watch, "Human Rights Watch Memorandum to the Government of Saudi Arabia on Human Rights Priorities in the Kingdom"; Amnesty International, "Saudi Arabia: Torture: Culture of Brutality," AI Index MDE 23/10/00, June 1, 2000, http://www.amnesty.org/en/library/info/MDE23/010/2000.

66. For instance, see Azzam Tamimi, "Islam, Democracy, and Compatibility," *New Nation*, January 8, 2005, available at http://web.archive.org/web/20080114203332/http://nation.ittefaq.com/artman/exec/view.cgi/26/15265. For Tamimi's critique of my views in *Islam and the Challenge of Democracy*, see Azzam Tamimi, "Liberalism, Democracy, and Islam: Looking for the Odd Man Out," *Daily Star*, July 24, 2004, http://www.dailystar.com.lb/Culture/The-Review/Jul/24/Liberalism-Democracy-and-Islam-looking-for-the-odd-man-out.ashx#axzz2axP1Mp4o. Also see Khaled Abou El Fadl, *The Place for Tolerance in Islam*, ed. Joshua Cohen and Ian Lague (Boston: Beacon, 2002); Abou El Fadl, *Islam and the Challenge of Democracy*. On some television shows that aired in Egypt I was even accused of being an apologist for the West.

67. Advocates of this kind of argument often claim that Islam is the last frontier not yet controlled by Western hegemony; for instance, see Simon Murden, *Islam, the Middle East and the New Global Hegemony* (Boulder, CO: Lynne Rienner, 2002), 1–16.

68. See Bernard Lewis, "The Roots of Muslim Rage: Why So Many Muslims Deeply Resent the West, and Why Their Bitterness Will Not Easily Be Mollified," *Atlantic Monthly*,

September 1990, http://www.theatlantic.com/magazine/archive/1990/09/the-roots-of-muslim-rage/304643/?single_page=true; Bernard Lewis, *What Went Wrong? The Clash between Islam and Modernity in the Middle East* (New York: Oxford University Press, 2002); Christopher Catherwood, *Christians, Muslims, and Islamic Rage: What Is Going On and Why It Happened* (Grand Rapids, MI: Zondervan, 2003); Daniel Pipes, *Militant Islam Reaches America* (New York: Norton, 2003); Robin Wright, *Rock the Casbah: Rage and Rebellion across the Islamic World* (New York: Simon & Schuster, 2011); Brigitte Gabriel, *Because They Hate: A Survivor of Islamic Terror Warns America* (New York: St. Martin's, 2006).

69. For example, see Gerard Delanty, *Inventing Europe* (London: MacMillan, 1995), 23–25; Anthony Pagden, "Europe: Conceptualizing a Continent," in *The Idea of Europe: From Antiquity to the European Union*, ed. Anthony Pagden (Washington, DC: Woodrow Wilson Center Press; Cambridge: Cambridge University Press, 2002), 33–54; Paul Collins, *The Birth of the West: Rome, Germany, France, and the Creation of Europe in the Tenth Century* (New York: Public Affairs, 2013), 103–10.

70. See George Makdisi, *The Rise of Humanism in Classical Islam and the Christian West: With Special Reference to Scholasticism* (Edinburgh: Edinburgh University Press, 1990); Dimitri Gutas, *Greek Thought, Arabic Culture: The Graeco-Arabic Translation Movement in Baghdad and Early 'Abbasid Society* (London: Routledge, 1998); George Saliba, *Islamic Science and the Making of the European Renaissance* (Cambridge, MA: MIT Press, 2007); Jonathan Lyons, *House of Wisdom: How the Arabs Transformed Western Civilization* (New York: Bloomsbury, 2009).

71. Jawhari Tantawi, *Nahdat al-Ummah wa Hawatuha* (Cairo: Mustafa Babi al-Halabi, 1934), 166–67.

3. CRISIS: MAKING SENSE OF SHARI'AH TODAY

1. Ahmad Atif Ahmad, *The Fatigue of the Shari'a* (New York: Palgrave Macmillan, 2012), 11–20.

2. Here I mean not just that whatever is contrary to human reason cannot stand, but the various principles that mandate that interpretations of the divine law serve the welfare of human beings and avoid harsh or unbearable results. For example, see 'Abd Allah ibn 'Umar Abu Zayd al-Dabusi, *Ta'sis al-Nazr* (Beirut: Dar Ibn Zaydun, n.d.); al-Dabusi, *Taqwim al-Adilla fi Usul al-Fiqh* (Beirut: Dar al-Kutub al-'Ilmiyya, 2001); Ibn Rushd, *Manahij al-Adilla fi 'Aqa'id al-Milla* (Cairo: Maktabat al-Anjlu al-Misriyya, 1955); Mustafa Sabri, *Mawqaf al-'Aql wa al-'Ilm wa al-'Alam* (Cairo: Dar al-Aqaf al-'Arabiyya, 2006); Ibn Taymiyya, *Dar' Ta'arud al-'Aql wa al-Naql aw Mawafaqa Sahih al-Manqul li-Sarih al-Ma'qul*, 11 vol. (n.p.: Dar al-Kanuz al-'Adabiyya, n.d.); 'Abd Allah 'Arawi, *Mafhum al-'Aql: Maqala fi al-Mufaraqat* (Beirut: Dar al-Markaz al-Thaqafi al-'Arabi, 1997); Muhammad al-Jawad Mughniyya, *al-Islam wa al-'Aql* (Beirut: Dar al-Jawad, 1991); Khaled Abou El Fadl, *Speaking in God's Name: Islamic Law, Authority and Women* (Oxford: Oneworld, 2001), 33–36; Yossef Rapoport, "Ibn Taymiyya's Radical Legal Thought: Rationalism, Pluralism and the Primacy of Intention," in *Ibn Taymiyya and His Times*, ed. Yossef Rapoport and Shahab Ahmed (Oxford: Oxford University Press, 2010), 193–209.

3. In a book that hardly received the attention it rightly deserves, Steven Fish demonstrates that Muslims are *not* particularly inclined toward the idea of mixing religion and politics. See M. Steven Fish, *Are Muslims Distinctive? A Look at the Evidence* (New York: Oxford University Press, 2011), 63–64.

4. See Abou El Fadl, *Speaking in God's Name*; Khaled Abou El Fadl, *And God Knows the Soldiers: The Authoritative and Authoritarian in Islamic Discourses* (Lanham, MD: University Press of America, 2001); Khaled Abou El Fadl, *The Great Theft: Wrestling Islam from the Extremists* (New York: HarperOne, 2005).

5. On the British invasion and the dismantling of Shari'ah law and replacing it with a positivist legal system, see Samera Esmeir, *Juridical Humanity: A Colonial History* (Stanford, CA: Stanford University Press, 2012), 21–65.

6. See Noel Coulson, *A History of Islamic Law* (Edinburgh: Edinburgh University Press, 1964), 182–217; J. N. D. Anderson, *Islamic Law in the Modern World* (New York: New York University, 1959); Muneer Goolam Fareed, *Legal Reform in the Muslim World: The Anatomy of a Scholarly Dispute in the 19th and the Early 20th Centuries on the Usage of Ijtihad as a Legal Tool* (San Francisco: Austin & Winfield, 1996), 4–5.

7. The Saudi Grand Mufti Shaykh 'Abd al-'Aziz al-Shaykh spoke out against the protests, saying that they were orchestrated by the "enemies of Islam." See "Saudi Top Cleric Blasts Arab, Egypt Protests-Paper," *Reuters Africa*, February 5, 2011, http://af.reuters.com/article/

egyptNews/idAFLDE71403F20110205. Furthermore, Shaykh al-Rajhi, a Saudi jurist, issued a *fatwa* condemning the protests. This *fatwa* was widely circulated and was available in February 2011 at http://www.dd-sunnah.net/forum/showthread.php?t=98063. However, it has since been taken down. Also see "Hi'a Kibar al-'Ulama' fi al-Sa'udiyya Tuharram al-Muzaharat fi al-Bilad wa Tuhadhir min al-Irtibatat al-Fikriyya wa al-Hizbiyya al-Munharifa," *Asharq al-Awsat,* March 7, 2011, http://www.aawsat.com/details.asp?section=4&issueno=11787&article= 611299#.UgB_KVMpdaF; "Mufti al-Sa'udiyya—Yukaffar—al-Thawra al-Misriya—wa Ya'tabarha—Fitnah wa Kharab," *Asharq al-Awsat,* March 7, 2011, http://www.aawsat.com/ details.asp?section=4&issueno=11787&article=611299#.UgSkI1MpdaG; "Fatawa al-Muzaha-rat," *Asharq al-Awsat,* March 12, 2011, http://www.aawsat.com/leader.asp?section=3&article= 612175&issueno=11792#.UgCAbFMpdaF; "Saudi Arabia's Halal and Haram Revolutions," *Arabia Today,* May 6, 2011, http://arabia2day.com/featured/saudi-arabias-halal-and-haram-revolutions/.

8. The imam also claimed that Abu Hanifa, the founder of the Hanafi school of legal thought, did the same by marrying on the same day his wife died. I have not been able to verify this alleged incident in the sources.

9. Hafiz al-Din, *Manaqib Abi Hanifa* (Beirut: Dar al-Kitab al-'Arabi, 1981), 2:351.

10. Jamal al-Din Abu al-Faraj 'Abd al-Rahman bin 'Ali bin Muhammad Ibn al-Jawzi, *Al-Shifa' fi Mawa'iz al-Muluk,* ed. Fu'ad 'Abd al-Mun'im Ahmad (Alexandria: Dar al-Da'wa, n.d.), 57.

11. Khamis bin Sa'id al-Rustaqi, *Manhaj al-Talibin wa Balagh al-Raghibin* (Oman: Wizarat al-Turath al-Qawmi wa al-Thaqafi, n.d.), 8:21, 26.

12. Bob Woodward, *Bush at War* (New York: Simon & Schuster, 2002), 260.

13. Fariba Amini, "We Shall Never Forget: Interview with Abdol-Karim Lahiji," *Ira-nian.com,* December 5, 2003, http://www.iranian.com/FaribaAmini/2003/December/Lahiji/index.html.

14. See United Nations Development Programme, *The Arab Human Development Report 2003: Building a Knowledge Society* (New York: United Nations Publications, 2003), 3–4, 6, 55, 67, available at http://hdr.undp.org/en/reports/regional/arabstates/name,3204,en.html.

15. For more case studies and an analysis of the evidentiary basis of these examples, see Abou El Fadl, *Speaking in God's Name,* 272–96.

16. On *tarjih* in Islamic jurisprudence, see Wael Hallaq, *Authority, Continuity, and Change in Islamic Law* (Cambridge: Cambridge University Press, 2001), 127–32; Bernard G. Weiss, *The Search for God's Law: Islamic Jurisprudence in the Writings of Sayf al-Din al-Amidi* (Salt Lake City: University of Utah Press, 1992), 734–38; Mohammad Hashim Kamali, *Shari'ah Law: An Introduction* (Oxford: OneWorld, 2008), 110–11; Wali Allah al-Dihlawi, *Al-Insaf fi bayan Sabab al-Ikhtilaf fi al-Ahkam al-Fiqhiyya* (Cairo: Al-Matba'a al-Salafiyya wa-Maktaba-tuha, 1965); 'Abd al-Majid Muhammad Ismail Susawah, *Manjah al-Tawfiq wa-al-Tarjih bayn Mukhtalif al-Hadith: Wa-Atharuhu fi al-Fiqh al-Islami* (Cairo: Dar al-Tawzi' wa-al-Nashr al-Islamiyya, 1992).

17. On Muslim minorities and their relationship to the host non-Muslim society, see Khaled Abou El Fadl, "Islamic Law and Muslim Minorities: The Juristic Discourse on Muslim Minor-ities from the Second/Eighth to the Eleventh/Seventeenth Centuries," *Journal of Islamic Law and Society* 1, no. 2 (1994): 141–87.

18. On Muslim minorities, see Khaled Abou El Fadl, "Legal Debates on Muslim Minorities: Between Rejection and Accommodation," *Journal of Religious Ethics* 22, no. 1 (1994): 127–62; Khaled Abou El Fadl, "Muslim Minorities and Self-Restraint in Liberal Democra-cies," *Loyola Law Review* 29, no. 4 (1996): 1525–42; Abou El Fadl, "Islamic Law and Muslim Minorities"; Khaled Abou El Fadl, "Muslims and Accessible Jurisprudence in Liberal Democ-racies," *Fordham Law Review* 66, no. 4 (1998): 1227–31; Khaled Abou El Fadl, "Striking the Balance: Islamic Legal Discourses on Muslim Minorities," in *Muslims on the Americanization Path,* ed. Yvonne Yazbeck Haddad and John L. Esposito (New York: Oxford University Press, 2000), 47–64.

19. See Abou El Fadl, *And God Knows the Soldiers,* 11–19.

20. Christopher H. Schmitt and Joshua Kurlantzick, "When Charity Goes Awry; Islamic Groups Say They May Lose Control of Money They Send Overseas," *U.S. News and World Report ,* October 21, 2001; Judith Miller, "A Nation Challenged: The Money Trail; U.S. Raids Continue, Prompting Protests," *New York Times ,* March 22, 2002, http://www.nytimes.com/ 2002/03/22/us/a-nation-challenged-the-money-trail-us-raids-continue-prompting-protests.html; Mary Jacoby and Graham Bring, "Saudi Form of Islam Wars with Moderates," *St. Petersburg Times ,* March 11, 2003, http://www.sptimes.com/2003/03/11/Worldandnation/Saudi_form of_Islam_w.shtml; Jerry Markon, "Muslim Anger Burns over Lingering Probe of Charities," *Washington Post ,* October 11, 2006, http://www.washingtonpost.com/wp-dyn/content/article/ 2006/10/10/AR2006101001234.html; "U.S. Probe Makes Islamic Group Drop University Of-fer," *China Post ,* January 7, 2008, http://www.chinapost.com.tw/international/2008/01/07/ 138021/U.S.-probe.htm.

21. See generally "Publications," *Al Furqan Islamic Heritage Foundation*, http://www.al-furqan.com.

22. See generally "Research and Publications," *Institute of Ismaili Studies*, http://www.iis.ac.uk/.

23. See "Zaytuna College," http://www.zaytunacollege.org/; Scott Korb, *Light without Fire: The Making of America's First Muslim College* (Boston: Beacon, 2013).

24. On this subject, see George Makdisi, *The Rise of Colleges in Islam: Institutions of Learning in Islam and the West* (Edinburgh: Edinburgh University Press, 1981).

25. Muhammad Amin Ibn 'Umar Ibn 'Abidin, *Al-'Uqud al-Durriyya fi Tanqih al-Fatawa al-Hamidiyya: fi al-Fiqh al-Hanafi* (Beirut: Dar al-Kutub al-'Ilmiyya), 1:72.

26. See Afaf Lutfi Al-Sayyid Marsot, *Egypt in the Reign of Muhammad Ali* (Cambridge: Cambridge University Press, 1984), 66–67, 143; Khaled Fahmy, *Mehmed Ali* (Oxford: One-World, 2009), 42–44; Khaled Fahmy, *All the Pasha's Men: Mehmed Ali, His Army and the Making of Modern Egypt* (Cambridge: Cambridge University Press, 1997), 9–13.

4. REPOSE: THE ISLAMIC BETWEEN HARMONY AND DISSONANCE

1. Those who prohibit clapping base their argument on the fact that non-Muslims before Islam used to worship around the Ka'ba in Mecca by whistling and clapping. From this, they conclude that clapping is un-Islamic. I guess that following this logic, Muslims should never whistle either.

2. For example, see Abdul Hamid Abu Sulayman, *Islamization of Knowledge: General Principles and Work Plan* (Herndon, VA: International Institute of Islamic Thought, 1989); Abdul Hamid Abu Sulayman, *Islamization: Reforming Contemporary Knowledge* (Herndon, VA: International Institute of Islamic Thought, 1994); 'Imad al-Din Khalil, *Islamization of Knowledge: A Methodology* (Herndon, VA: International Institute of Islamic Thought, 1991); Abdel Wahab M. Elmessiri, ed., *Bias: Epistemological Bias in the Physical and Social Sciences* (Herndon, VA: International Institute of Islamic Thought, 2006).

3. On the persecution of Muslim charities and organizations in the United States, see Ibrahim Warde, *The Price of Fear: The Truth behind the Financial War on Terror* (Berkeley: University of California Press, 2007), 74–75, 95–105, 127–50; Jeanne K. Giraldo and Harold A. Tinkunas, eds., *Terrorism Financing and State Reponses: A Comparative Perspective* (Stanford, CA: Stanford University Press, 2007), 25, 285–90; Mark Sidel, *Regulation of the Voluntary Sector: Freedom and Security in an Age of Uncertainty* (Abingdon, Oxon: Routledge, 2010), 14–34; Elaine Cassel, *The War on Civil Liberties: How Bush and Ashcroft Dismantled the Bill of Rights* (Chicago, IL: Chicago Review, 2004), 87–109; Maurice R. Greenberg, William F. Wechsler, and Lee S. Wolosky, eds., *Terrorist Financing: Report of an Independent Task Force* (New York: Council on Foreign Relations, 2002), 12–14; Jonathan Benthall, "An Unholy Tangle: Biom versus the Holy Land Foundation," *UCLA Journal of Islamic and Near Eastern Law* 10, no. 1 (2010): 1–10; Nina J. Crimm, "Reframing the Issue and Cultivating U.S.-Based Muslim Humanitarian Relief Organizations," *UCLA Journal of Islamic and Near Eastern Law* 10, no. 1 (2010): 11–34; Sally Howell, "(Re)Bounding Islamic Charitable Giving in the Terror Decade," *UCLA Journal of Islamic and Near Eastern Law* 10, no. 1 (2010): 35–64; Erica Caple James, "Governing Gifts: Law, Risk, and the 'War on Terror,'" *UCLA Journal of Islamic and Near Eastern Law* 10, no. 1 (2010): 65–84; Ramzi Kassem, "From Altruists to Outlaws: The Criminalization of Traveling Islamic Volunteers," *UCLA Journal of Islamic and Near Eastern Law* 10, no. 1 (2010): 85–98; Khalid Mustafa Medani, "Informal Networks, Economic Livelihoods and the Politics of Social Welfare: Understanding the Political and Humanitarian Consequences of the War on Terrorist Finance," *UCLA Journal of Islamic and Near Eastern Law* 10, no. 1 (2010): 99–137.

4. Khaled Abou El Fadl, *The Search for Beauty in Islam: A Conference of the Books* (Lanham, MD: Rowman & Littlefield , 2006), 319–26.

5. Muhammad ibn Khalaf Ibn al-Marzubaan, *The Book of the Superiority of Dogs over Many of Those Who Wear Clothes*, ed. and trans. G. R. Smith and Muhammad Abdul Halim (Warminster, UK: Aris and Phillips, 1978).

6. For the humanistic orientation in Islam, see Joel Kraemer, *Humanism in the Renaissance of Islam: The Cultural Revival during the Buyid Age* (Leiden: Brill, 1992).

7. Khaled Abou El Fadl, "Dogs in Islam," in *Encyclopedia of Religion and Nature*, ed. Bron Taylor et al. (New York: Continuum International, 2004).

8. George Makdisi, *The Rise of Colleges: Institutions of Learning in Islam and the West* (Edinburgh: Edinburgh University Press, 1981), 96–98. See also Mehdi Khan Nakosteen, *His-*

tory of Islamic Origins of Western Education, A.D. 800–1350 (Boulder: University of Colorado Press, 1964).

9. On taqlid, see N. J. Coulson, *A History of Islamic Law* (Edinburgh: Edinburgh University Press, 1964), 182–201. See Muhammad ʿAli al-Shawkani, *Al-Qawl al-Mufid fi Adillat al-Ijtihad wa al-Taqlid*, ed. Abu Musʿab al-Badri (Cairo: Dar al-Kitab al-Misri, 1991); Abu al-Nasr Hasan Khan al-Qanuji, *Al-Qawl al-Sadid fi Adillat al-Ijtihad wa al-Taqlid*, ed. Abu ʿAbd al-Rahman Miʿshasha (Beirut: Dar Ibn Hazm, 2000). For a 1935 critique of this orientation and an attempt to reclaim the importance of honoring and, at times, deferring to the interpretations of the past, see Yusuf bin Ahmad al-Dijawi, "Jawaz al-taqlid wa al-radd ʿala mann yuharrima-hu," *Nur al-Islam* (a.k.a. *Majallat al-Azhar*; *Azhar University Journal*) 10, no. 5 (1935): 669–79.

10. On the varieties of Islamist movements, see Mohammed Ayoub, *The Many Faces of Political Islam: Religion and Politics in the Muslim World* (Ann Arbor: University of Michigan Press, 2008), esp. 152–69.

11. Khaled Abou El Fadl, "The Orphans of Modernity and the Clash of Civilisations," *Global Dialogue* 4, no.2 (Spring 2002): 1–16.

12. Javier Martinez-Torron and W. Cole Durham Jr., *Religion and the Secular State: Interim National Reports Issued for the Occasion of the XVIIIth International Congress of Comparative Law* (Provo, UT: International Center for Law and Religious Studies, 2010); Elizabeth Shakman Hurd, *The Politics of Secularism in International Relations* (Princeton, NJ: Princeton University Press, 2008), 127–33; Linell E. Cady and Elizabeth Shakman Hurd, eds., *Comparative Secularisms in a Global Age* (New York: Palgrave Macmillan, 2010), 217–28.

13. See Charles Taylor, *A Secular Age* (Cambridge, MA: Belknap, 2007).

14. The Saudi *fatwa* can no longer be retrieved from the web; however, for accusations of heresy against Mohammad Arkoun, see "Saudi Doctorate Encourages the Murder of Arab Intellectuals," *Middle East Media Research Institute*, January 12, 2006, http://www.memri.org/report/en/print1579.htm; Muhammad Mahmoud, "Mohammad Arkoun Obituary," *Guardian*, October 19, 2010, http://www.theguardian.com/world/2010/oct/19/mohammed-arkoun-obituary; Giancarlo Bosetti, "Mohammad Arkoun, the 'Demystification' of the Qurʾan," *Reset-Doc*, July 11, 2011, http://www.resetdoc.org/story/00000021664. For an analysis of Arkoun's thought and its reception in the Muslim world, see Carool Kersten, *Cosmopolitans and Heretics: New Muslim Intellectuals and the Study of Islam* (London: Hurst, 2011), 177–237.

15. See Mohammad Arkoun, *Rethinking Islam : Common Questions, Uncommon Answers*, ed. and trans. Robert D. Lee (Boulder: Westview, 1994); Mohammad Arkoun, *The Unthought in Contemporary Islamic Thought* (London: Saqi, 2002).

16. Khaled Abou El Fadl, "Islamic Law and Ambivalent Scholarship," review of *The Justice of Islam: Comparative Perspectives on Islamic Law and Society*, by Lawrence Rosen, *Michigan Law Review* 100, no. 6 (May 2002): 1421–43.

17. Max Weber, *The Protestant Ethic and the Spirit of Capitalism*, trans. Talcott Parsons (London: George Allen & Unwin, 1930); E. Digby Baltzell, *Puritan Boston and Quaker Philadelphia: Two Protestant Ethics and the Spirit of Class Authority and Leadership* (New York: Free Press, 1979); Michael Novak, *The Catholic Ethic and the Spirit of Capitalism* (New York: Free Press, 1993); Russell Kirk, *The Roots of American Order* (Wilmington, DE: ISI, 2003); Thomas E. Woods, *How the Catholic Church Built Western Civilization* (Washington, DC: Regnery, 2005); Rodney Stark, *The Victory of Reason: How Christianity Led to Freedom, Capitalism, and Western Success* (New York: Random House, 2005); Robert Royal, *The God That Did Not Fail: How Religion Built and Sustains the West* (New York: Encounter, 2006); Hugh Heclo, *Christianity and American Democracy* (Cambridge, MA: Harvard University Press, 2007); Hans Joas and Klaus Wiegandt, eds., *The Cultural Values of Europe*, trans. Alex Skinner (Liverpool: Liverpool University Press, 2008); Samuel P. Huntington, *Who Are We?: The Challenges to America's National Identity* (New York: Simon & Schuster, 2004), 171–77, 365; Niall Ferguson, *Civilization: The West and the Rest* (New York: Penguin, 2011), 259.

5. FAULTY PARADIGMS IN CONSTRUCTING THE ISLAMIC

1. See Elizabeth F. Thompson, *Justice Interrupted: The Struggle for Constitutional Government in the Middle East* (Cambridge, MA: Harvard University Press, 2013). For post-WWI uprisings throughout the Middle East and Persia, see Nader Sohrabi, *Revolution and Constitutionalism in the Ottoman Empire and Iran* (Cambridge: Cambridge University Press, 2011); David Fromkin, *A Peace to End All Peace: The Fall of the Ottoman Empire and the Creation of the Modern Middle East* (New York: Henry Holt, 2009), 415–62; M. W. Daly, ed., *The Cambridge History of Egypt (Volume Two): Modern Egypt from 1517 to the End of the*

Twentieth Century (New York: Cambridge University Press, 2008), 242–51; T. G. Fraser, *The Makers of the Modern Middle East* (London: Haus, 2011), 195–244 (esp. 202–10 [Egypt; Iraq]); Arthur Goldschmidt, Amy J. Johnson, and Barak A. Salmoni, eds., *Re-Envisioning Egypt: 1919–1952* (Cairo: American University in Cairo Press, 2005); Abbas Kadhim, *Reclaiming Iraq: The 1920 Revolution and the Founding of the Modern State* (Austin: University of Texas Press, 2012); Amirhassan Boozari, *Shi'i Jurisprudence and Constitution: Revolution in Iran* (New York: Palgrave Macmillan, 2011), 45–98; Janet Afary, *The Iranian Constitutional Revolution, 1906–1911: Grassroots Democracy, Social Democracy, and the Origins of Feminism* (New York: Columbia University Press, 1996).

2. For instance, the US actor and documentary filmmaker Sean Stone recently converted to Islam following a visit to Iran; see "Sean Stone, Oliver Stone's Son, Converts to Islam during Iran Visit," *Huffington Post*, February 14, 2012, http://www.huffingtonpost.com/2012/02/14/sean-stone-oliver-stone-son-convert-islam-iran_n_1276389.html. In 2010, Lauren Booth, Tony Blair's sister-in-law, also converted to Islam following a visit to the country; see Helen Carter, "Tony Blair's Sister-in-Law Converts to Islam," *Guardian*, October 24, 2010, http://www.guardian.co.uk/politics/2010/oct/24/lauren-booth-converts-to-islam. After witnessing firsthand the bloodshed in the Algerian war for independence in 1961 and gaining a deep appreciation for Islamic art, the German diplomat Murad Hofmann converted to Islam; see Roya Shokatfard, "The Journey of a German Ambassador to Islam," *Brunei Times*, February 26, 2010, http://www.bt.com.bn/files/digital/Islamia/Issue87/SP26Feb.12.pdf; Siham Al Najami, "Hofmann Named Islamic Personality of the Year," *Gulf News*, September 2, 2009, http://gulfnews.com/news/gulf/uae/general/hofmann-named-islamic-personality-of-the-year-1.537874.

3. Masoud Popalzai, "Extremists Poison Schoolgirls' Water, Afghan Officials Say," *CNN*, April 17, 2012, http://www.cnn.com/2012/04/17/world/afghanistan-girls-poisoned/index.html?hpt=hp_t3; Mohammad Hamid, "Afghan Schoolgirls Poisoned in Anti-Education Attack," *Reuters International*, April 17, 2012, http://in.reuters.com/article/2012/04/17/afghanistan-women-idINDEE83G0CI20120417; "Afghan Schoolgirls Poisoned by Drinking Water," *Radio Free Europe: Radio Liberty*, April 17, 2012, http://www.rferl.org/content/afghan_schoolgirls_poisoned/24551409.html; Ivana Kvesic, "150 Afghan Girls Poisoned in Attack against Female Education," *Christian Post*, April 18, 2012, http://www.christianpost.com/news/150-afghan-girls-poisoned-in-attack-against-female-education-73427/; "Afghan Schoolgirls 'Poisoned by Taliban,'" *Al Jazeera*, May 24, 2012, http://www.aljazeera.com/news/asia/2012/05/201252451931671453.html; Rahiem Faiez and Heidi Vogt, "Taliban Poisoned School Girls, Say Afghan Officials," *Huffington Post*, June 6, 2012, http://www.huffingtonpost.com/2012/06/06/taliban-poison-school-girls-afghanistan_n_1573325.html; Quentin Sommerville, "Afghans Fear Mysterious School 'Poisonings,'" *BBC News Magazine*, July 4, 2012, http://www.bbc.co.uk/news/magazine-18118818.

4. "Egyptian Ferry Sinks in Red Sea," *BBC News*, February 3, 2006, http://news.bbc.co.uk/2/hi/middle_east/4676916.stm; AP/Reuters, "Most of 1,400 on Egypt Ferry Feared Lost," *China Daily*, February 4, 2006, http://www.chinadaily.com.cn/english/doc/2006-02/04/content_517042.htm.

5. For instance, between 1,000 and 3,000 people died when a ship sank in China; see "China Ship Deaths May Exceed 1,100," *New York Times*, December 5, 1948; "China's Spate of Mishaps," *Times of India*, December 7, 1948. In 1954, over 1,000 passengers died on a ferry wrecked by a typhoon in Toya Maru, Japan; see Lindesay Parrott, "Toll Passes 1,000 in Ferry Sinking," *New York Times*, September 28, 1954; "380 Still Missing in Ferry Disaster," *Washington Post and Times Herald*, October 5, 1954. In 1987, over 4,000 passengers died aboard a ferry in the Philippines; see "Toll in Philippine Ferry Disaster Now Tabulated at 4,000." *Los Angeles Times*, February 13, 1988, http://articles.latimes.com/1988-02-13/news/mn-10721_1_ferry-disaster; Joey A. Gabieta, "Doña Paz Victims Waiting for Justice 25 Years After," *Philippine Daily Inquirer*, December 20, 2012, http://newsinfo.inquirer.net/327123/dona-paz-victims-waiting-for-justice-25-years-after. In 2002, a Senegalese government-owned ferry capsized, killing over 1,800 passengers onboard; see "Hundreds Are Missing after Senegal Ferry Capsizes in Fierce Winds," *New York Times*, September 28, 2002, http://www.nytimes.com/2002/09/28/world/hundreds-are-missing-after-senegal-ferry-capsizes-in-fierce-winds.html; "Senegal Raises the Death Toll in September's Ferry Disaster," *New York Times*, February 4, 2003, http://www.nytimes.com/2003/02/04/world/senegal-raises-the-death-toll-in-september-s-ferry-disaster.html.

6. David Kirkpatrick, "Court in Egypt Says Rights of Women Were Violated," *New York Times*, December 27, 2011, http://www.nytimes.com/2011/12/28/world/africa/egyptian-court-says-virginity-tests-violated-womens-rights.html; "Egypt: Military Impunity for Violence against Women," *Human Rights Watch*, April 7, 2012, http://www.hrw.org/news/2012/04/07/egypt-military-impunity-violence-against-women; "Egypt Clears 'Virginity Test' Military Doctor," *Al Jazeera English*, March 11, 2012, http://www.aljazeera.com/news/middleeast/2012/03/2012311104319262937.html; Mai Shams El-Din, "Admin Court to Rehear Samira Ibrahim's Case," *Daily News Egypt*, March 20, 2012, http://www.dailynewsegypt.com/2012/03/20/admin-court-to-hear-samira-ibrahims-case/.

7. Khaled Fahmy, "Women, Medicine, and Power in Nineteenth-Century Egypt," in *Remaking Women: Feminism and Modernity in the Middle East*, ed. Lila Abu-Lughod (Princeton, NJ: Princeton University Press, 1998), 42–46; Khaled Fahmy," Women, Revolution, and Army," *Egypt Independent*, September 1, 2012, http://www.egyptindependent.com/opinion/women-revolution-and-army.

8. Ahmad ibn 'Ali ibn Hajar al-'Asqalani, *Bulugh al-Maram min Adillat al-Ahkam*, ed. Salman ibn Fahd 'Awdah (Riyadh: Maktabat al-Rushd Nashirun, 2005), 540; Imam al-Nawawi, *Riyad al-Salihin*, ed. Muhammad Mahmoud 'Abd al-'Aziz and 'Ali Muhammad 'Ali (Cairo: Dar al-Hadith, 1994), 90–91.

9. On the modern origins of the *mutawwa'un* and their often violent practices, see Michael Cook, "The Expansion of the First Saudi State: The Case of *Washm*," in *Essays in Honor of Bernard Lewis: The Islamic World From Classical to Modern Times*, ed. C. E. Bosworth et al. (Princeton, NJ: Princeton University Press, 1989), 672–75; Michael Cook, "On the Origins of Wahhabism," *Journal of the Royal Asiatic Society* 3, no. 2 (1992): 191–202; Ameen Fares Rihani, *The Maker of Modern Arabia* (New York: Greenwood, 1983), 203. William Gifford Palgrave, *Personal Narrative of Year's Journey through Central and Eastern Arabia* (London: Gregg, 1883), 243–50, 316–18, reports that during the reign of King Faysal bin Turki (r. 1249–1254/1834–1838 and 1259–1282/1843–1865), in response to a cholera outbreak, twenty-two so-called zealots were selected to combat vice in Mecca and elsewhere. Apparently, this was beginning of the system of the *mutawwa'un*.

10. This incident was reported in Saudi newspapers such as the *Saudi Gazette* and *Al-Iqtisadiyya*, but as of 2013 both newspapers have removed the story from their websites. In rarely voiced criticism against the religious police, both papers demanded investigations and prosecutions of those responsible. The day after the event, Crown Prince 'Abdullah announced that the government would investigate and punish those responsible. Three days after the event, the Saudi government ordered all newspapers to desist from publishing anything about the tragedy, and to date, no one has been prosecuted or fired for the deaths of the girls. The tragedy was reported in the media extensively in the West but received very limited coverage in the Muslim world. On the tragedy, its causes, and aftermath, see Eleanor Doumato, "Saudi Sex-Segregation Can Be Fatal," *Providence Journal*, March 31, 2002, http://www.projo.com/opinion/contributors/content/projo_20020331_ctdou31.1032e23f.html; Tarek Al-Issawi, "Saudi Schoolgirls' Fire Death Decried," *Washington Times*, March 18, 2002, available at http://www.washingtontimes.com/news/2002/mar/18/20020318-041124-5594r/; Mona Eltahawy, "They Died for Lack of a Head Scarf," *Washington Post*, March 19, 2002, A21. Also available at: https://www.library.cornell.edu/colldev/mideast/mutawsc.htm; "Saudi Police 'Stopped' Fire Rescue," *BBC News*, March 15, 2002, http://news.bbc.co.uk/2/hi/middle_east/1874471.stm; "Naif Denies Commission Men Prevented Rescuers," *Arab News*, March 18, 2002, http://web.archive.org/web/20120418223557/http://archive.arabnews.com/?page=1&section=0&article=13582&d=18&m=3&y=2002&pix=kingdom.jpg&category=Kingdom.

11. As of 2013, the *fatwa* has been removed from the Internet. See Ali Al-Ahmed, "Author of Saudi Curriculums Advocates Slavery," *Arabia News*, November 7, 2003, available at http://web.archive.org/web/20120524043027/http://www.arabianews.org/english/article.cfm?qid=132&sid=2. See also Brian Whitaker, "Saudi Textbooks 'Demonise West,'" *Guardian*, July 14, 2004, http://www.theguardian.com/world/2004/jul/14/saudiarabia.schoolsworldwide.

12. Joy Raphael, *Slaves of Saudis: Terrorisation of Foreign Workers* (Juhu, Mumbai: Turtle, 2013); "Saudi Arabia: Domestic Worker Brutalized; Protections for Domestic Workers, Systemic Reform Urgently Needed," *Human Rights Watch*, September 2, 2010, http://www.hrw.org/news/2010/09/02/saudi-arabia-domestic-worker-brutalized; Human Rights Watch, *"As If I Am Not Human": Abuses against Domestic Workers in Saudi Arabia* (New York: Human Rights Watch, 2008), available at http://www.hrw.org/reports/2008/07/07/if-i-am-not-human.

13. The expression "vulgarization of Islam" was inspired by an essay written by Robert Scott Appleby, "The Quandary of Leadership," in *The Place of Tolerance in Islam*, ed. Joshua Cohen and Ian Lague (Boston: Beacon, 2002), 85–92.

14. Quoted in A. A. Vasiliev, *History of the Byzantine Empire* (Madison, WI: University of Wisconsin Press, 1952), 1:216. During that time a large number of Christians adopted the Arabic language without adopting Islam and became known as the *mozarabs* (the Arabized). See also Richard Hitchcock, *Mozarabs in Medieval and Early Modern Spain: Identities and Influences* (Aldershot: Ashgate, 2008); John V. Tolan, *Saracens: Islam in the Medieval European Imagination* (New York: Columbia University Press, 2002), 85–86, 97; Richard Fletcher, *The Cross and the Crescent: Christianity and Islam from Muhammad to the Reformation* (New York: Viking, 2003), 44–49; Maria Rosa Menocal, *The Ornament of the World: How Muslims, Jews, and Christians Created a Culture of Tolerance in Medieval Spain* (Boston: Little, Brown, 2002), 66–70, 78; Thomas E. Burman, *Religious Polemic and the Intellectual History of the Mozarabs, c. 1050–1200* (Leiden: Brill, 1994), 13–32.

15. It is rather telling that the overwhelming majority of Muslim classical jurists were ethnically not Arabs, but they composed their works of jurisprudence in Arabic. Although most Muslim jurists descended from non-Arab ethnicities such as those in Central and South Asia

and North Africa, the vast majority of Islamic law was composed in Arabic. Through the dynamic transformative power of Arabic language in the premodern period, these jurists became Arabized.

16. For excellent studies on the historical misconceptions about Islam prevalent in Europe, see Franco Cardini, *Europe and Islam* (Oxford: Blackwell, 2001); Albert Hourani, *Islam in European Thought* (Cambridge: Cambridge University Press, 1991); Maxime Rodinson, *Europe and the Mystique of Islam* (London: Tauris, 1987); Thierry Hentsch, *L'Orient Imaginaire: La Vision Politique Occidentale de l'Est Mediterraneen* (Paris: Ed. Minuit, 1988); R. W. Southern, *Western Views of Islam in the Middle Ages* (Cambridge, MA: Harvard University Press, 1962). The most comprehensive work on the subject, however, remains: Norman Daniel, *Islam and the West: The Making of an Image* (Oxford: OneWorld Press, 1960, reprinted 2000). Also, see Norman Daniel, *The Arabs and Medieval Europe* (London: Longman, 1975). For a particularly useful and sophisticated collection of studies on the topic, see John Victor Tolan, *Medieval Christian Perceptions of Islam* (London: Routledge, 2000). Hugh Goddard, *A History of Christian-Muslim Relations* (London: New Amsterdam, 2001), provides an informative overview of mutual misperceptions between Muslims and Christians during the medieval period and the growth of Western academic studies on Islam in the nineteenth and twentieth centuries CE.

17. On binary instincts, their impact, and challenge, see Rush W. Dozier, *Why We Hate: Understanding, Curbing, and Eliminating Hate in Ourselves and Our World* (New York: McGraw-Hill, 2002), 39–48. On how binary views contribute to the "social death" and dehumanization of the other and ultimately to the production of cruelty, see James Waller, *Becoming Evil: How Ordinary People Commit Genocide and Mass Killings* (Oxford: Oxford University Press, 2002), 236–57. See also Neil J. Kressel, *Mass Hate: The Global Rise of Genocide and Terror* (Boulder, CO: Westview, 2002).

18. This is evidenced, for instance, by the influence of Muslim thought on Maimonides, the intellectual movement known as the Averroists in medieval Europe, and the teaching of the medical treatises of Ibn al-Haytham and Ibn Sina in European universities. See Montgomery Watt, *The Influence of Islam on Medieval Europe* (Edinburgh: Edinburgh University Press, 1972). Also see Goddard, *Christian-Muslim Relations*, 101–2; Nancy G. Siraisi, *Avicenna in Renaissance Italy: The Canon and Medical Teaching in Italian Universities after 1500* (Princeton, NJ: Princeton University Press, 1987).

19. Tragic events such as the Salman Rushdie incident, the treatment of women by the Taliban, and the 9/11 terrorist attacks against the United States have fed an extensive amount of vulgar anti-Islamic propaganda. For a partial list of Islamophobic works that were published after 9/11, see Anthony J. Dennis, *The Rise of the Islamic Empire and the Threat to the West* (New York: Wyndham Hall, 2001); Marvin Yakos, *Jesus vs. Jihad* (New York: Creation House, 2001); George Grant, *The Blood of the Moon: Understanding the Historic Struggle between Islam and Western Civilization*, rev. ed. (New York: Thomas Nelson, 2001); John F. MacArthur, *Terrorism, Jihad, and the Bible* (New York: W, 2001); Steven Emerson, *American Jihad: The Terrorists among Us* (New York: Simon & Schuster, 2002); Daniel Pipes, *Militant Islam Reaches America* (New York: Norton, 2002); Dan Benjamin, *The Age of Sacred Terror: Radical Islam's War against America* (New York: Random House, 2002); Ergun Caner and Emir Caner, *Unveiling Islam: An Insider's Look at Muslim Life and Beliefs* (Grand Rapids, MI: Kregel, 2002); Mark A. Gabriel, *Islam and Terrorism: What the Quran Really Teaches about Christianity, Violence, and the Goals of the Islamic Jihad* (New York: Charisma House, 2002); S. F. Fleming, *Islam and New Global Realities: The Roots of Islamic Fundamentalism* (Surprise, AZ: Selah, 2002); David Earle Johnson, *Conspiracy in Mecca: What You Need to Know about the Islamic Threat* (New York: David Johnson, 2002); Lester Sumrall, *Jihad—The Holy War: Time Bomb in the Middle East* (New York: Sumrall, 2002); David Friedman, *Sudden Terror: Exposing Militant Islam's War against the United States and Israel* (Clarksville, MD: Messianic Jewish Publishers, 2002); Hal Lindsey, *The Everlasting Hatred: The Roots of Jihad* (Murrieta, CA: Oracle House, 2002); Morgan Norval, *The Fifteen Century War: Islam's Violent Heritage* (San Luis Obispo, CA: McKenna, 2002); John F. Murphy Jr., *The Sword of Islam: Muslim Extremism from the Arab Conquests to the Attack on America* (New York: Prometheus, 2002); Larry Spargimino, *Religion of Peace or Refuge for Terror?* (New York: Hearthstone, 2002); Adam Parfrey, ed., *Extreme Islam: Anti-American Propaganda of Muslim Fundamentalism* (New York: Feral House, 2002); Robert Spencer, *Islam Unveiled: Disturbing Questions about the World's Fastest Growing Faith* (New York: Encounter, 2002); Robert Spencer, *Onward Muslim Soldiers: How Jihad Still Threatens America and the West* (Washington, DC: Regnery, 2003); Robert Spencer, *The Truth about Muhammad: Founder of the World's Most Intolerant Religion* (Washington, DC: Regnery, 2006); Bruce Bawer, *While Europe Slept: How Radical Islam Is Destroying the West from Within* (New York: Broadway, 2006); Nonie Darwish, *Now They Call Me Infidel: Why I Renounced Jihad for America, Israel, and the War on Terror* (New York: Sentinel, 2006); Nonie Darwish, *Cruel and Usual Punishment: The Terrifying Global Implications of Islamic Law* (Nashville: Thomas Nelson, 2008); Wafa Sultan, *A God Who Hates: The Courageous Woman Who Inflamed the Muslim World*

Speaks Out against the Evils of Islam (New York: St. Martin's, 2009); Ayaan Hirsi Ali, *Nomad: From Islam to America (A Personal Journey through the Clash of Civilizations)* (New York: Free Press, 2010); Geert Wilders, *Marked for Death: Islam's War against the West and Me* (Washington, DC: Regnery, 2012). For blatantly anti-Islamic and, by all measures, Islam-hating works that were published pre-9/11 but that have found new popularity in current times, see Anis A. Shorrosh, *Islam Revealed: A Christian Arab's View of Islam* (New York: Thomas Nelson, 1988); Robert A. Morey, *The Islamic Invasion: Confronting the World's Fastest Growing Religion* (New York: Harvest House, 1992); Norman L. Geisler and Abdul Saleeb, *Answering Islam: The Crescent in Light of the Cross* (New York: Dimensions, 1994); Ibn Warraq, *Why I Am Not a Muslim* (New York: Prometheus, 1995); Victor Mordecai, *Is Fanatic Islam a Global Threat?* (Taylor, SC: printed by author, 1997); Paul Fregosi, *Jihad in the West: Muslim Conquests from the 7th to the 21st Centuries* (New York: Prometheus, 1998).

20. The term *Islamist* is vague; it could apply to al-Qaeda-type religious extremists and fanatics or to Muslim activists who hope to establish a democratic state that respects and honors the ethics and morals of Islam as well as human rights and civil liberties. I think that the common factor to all Islamists is that they believe that Islam in one form or another ought to provide guidance to people in the public as well as the private sphere. Furthermore, Islamists utilize Muslim texts, traditions, or ethics and morals as basic normative frames of reference that help distinguish between what is acceptable and unacceptable in life. Besides advocating that Islamic texts and values ought to constitute an authoritative frame of reference in the private and public contexts, Islamists do not agree on a specific political system or social structure as the authentically Islamic form.

21. If one considers the total of Daniel Pipes's attitudes toward Islamists as expressed in his own writings and statements, it becomes clear that he believes that Islamism is the moral equivalent of fascism, totalitarianism, and generally, something evil. For an example of Pipes accusing me of being an Islamist, see Daniel Pipes, "Conference of the Books: The Search for Beauty in Islam (Book Review)," *Middle East Quarterly*, Summer 2002, accessed August 1, 2012, http://www.danielpipes.org/483/conference-of-the-books-the-search-for-beauty-in-islam. For Pipes's views on Islamism and its connection to fascism, totalitarianism, and Nazism, see Daniel Pipes, "Where the Nazi 'Big Lie' Endures," *New York Sun*, May 1, 2007, http://www.danielpipes.org/4472/where-the-nazi-big-lie-endures; Daniel Pipes, review of *Nazi Propaganda for the Arab World*, by Jeffrey Herf, *Commentary* (April 2010), available at www.danielpipes.org/8257/nazi-propaganda-for-the-arab-world; Daniel Pipes, "Islamism's Unity in Tunisia," *National Review Online*, October 30, 2012, available at http://danielpipes.org/12103/islamism-unity. See also "CAIR: Daniel Pipes Compares 'Islamic People' to 'Nazis'; White House Asked to Drop Nomination of 'Islamophobe,'" *PR Newswire*, July 27, 2003, http://www.thefreelibrary.com/CAIR%3A+Daniel+Pipes+Compares+%27Islamic+People%27+to+%27Nazis%27%3B+White+House...-a0105932105, and Pipes's subsequent article where he states that he was misquoted and had said, "Islamists" instead of "Islamic people," "CAIR's Dirty Tricks against Me," *FrontPageMagazine.com*, September 7, 2007, available at http://www.danielpipes.org/4886/cairs-dirty-tricks-against-me.

22. See Richard Land, "President Bush, Faith Convictions, and Media Cynicism: Christians and Muslims Do Not Worship the 'Same God,'" *Beliefnet*, http://www.beliefnet.com/News/Politics/2003/12/President-Bush-Faith-Convictions-And-Media-Cynicism.aspx?p=1. Also see Dan Eggen, "Ashcroft Invokes Religion in U.S. War on Terrorism," *Washington Post*, February 20, 2002, A2, also available at http://www.commondreams.org/headlines.shtml?/headlines02/0220-03.htm. Speaking about Islam in an interview with syndicated columnist and radio commentator Cal Thomas, Ashcroft said: "Islam is a religion in which God requires you to send your son to die for him. Christianity is a faith in which God sends his son to die for you." Ashcroft contends that this quote does not reflect what he thought he said.

23. Basil Mathews, *Young Islam on Trek* (New York: Friendship, 1926), 126.

24. Winston S. Churchill, *The River War* (London: Longmans, Green, 1899), 2:248–50.

25. Bernard Lewis, "The Roots of Muslim Rage: Why So Many Muslims Deeply Resent the West, and Why Their Bitterness Will Not Easily Be Mollified." *Atlantic Monthly*, September 1990; Bernard Lewis, *What Went Wrong? The Clash between Islam and Modernity in the Middle East* (New York: Oxford University Press, 2002).

26. Samuel P. Huntington, "The Clash of Civilizations?" *Foreign Affairs* 72, no. 3 (Summer 1993): 22–49; Samuel P. Huntington, *The Clash of Civilizations and the Remaking of World Order* (New York: Simon & Schuster, 1996).

27. For books by neoconservative intellectuals and politicians that draw on or adopt the clash of civilizations thesis, see Condoleezza Rice, *No Higher Honor: A Memoir of My Years in Washington* (New York: Crown, 2011), 329–32; Alvin J. Schmidt, *The Great Divide: The Failure of Islam and the Triumph of the West* (Boston: Regina Orthodox, 2004); Tony Blankely, *The West's Last Chance: Will We Win the Clash of Civilizations?* (Washington, DC: Regnery, 2006); Mark Steyn, *America Alone: The End of the World as We Know It* (Washington, DC: Regnery, 2006). For books that describe and analyze the connection between neoconservative ideology and Samuel Huntington's work and the clash of civilizations thesis, see Jeremy

Salt, *The Unmaking of the Middle East: A History of Western Disorder in Arab Lands* (Berkeley: University of California Press, 2008), 18–21; John Trumpbour, "The Clash of Civilizations: Samuel P. Huntington, Bernard Lewis, and the Remaking of the Post–Cold War Order," in *The New Crusades: Constructing the Muslim Enemy*, ed. Emran Qureshi and Michael A. Sells (New York: Columbia University Press, 2003), 88–130; Arshin Adib-Moghaddam, *A Metahistory of the Clash of Civilizations: Us and Them beyond Orientalism* (New York: Columbia University Press, 2011).

28. Interestingly, Samuel Huntington used the expression "false universalisms" in arguing that the Western belief in universality of their values is both immoral and dangerous. See Huntington, *Clash of Civilizations*, 310.

29. For the relativism argument in the international human rights field and a critique of this position, see Ann Mayer, *Islam and Human Rights: Tradition and Politics*, 5th ed. (Boulder, CO: Westview, 2013), 8–17. Also see Khaled Abou El Fadl, "Soul Searching and the Spirit of Shariʻa," *Washington University Global Studies Law Review* 1, no. 1–2 (Winter/Summer 2002): 553–72.

30. For instance, see Lawrence Rosen, *The Justice of Islam: Comparative Perspectives on Islamic Law and Society* (Oxford: Oxford University Press, 2000). Rosen argues that Arabs and Muslims have no sense of set reality, and their only realities are highly negotiated and contingent. Rosen advises that in attempting to resolve the Arab-Israeli conflict and making peace, Westerners must understand the Arab particular sense of justice. According to Rosen, Arabs can only seek to make peace "against [a] tangled, ambivalent, refractory, and transcendent feeling of justice . . . which shapes their expectations and hopes." Ibid., 175. On the condescending attitude of some Western scholars in dealing with the issue of universal human rights, see Mayer, *Islam and Human Rights*, 6–13.

31. For the debate on the issue of the clash of civilizations, see Huntington, *Clash of Civilizations*; Colin Chapman, *Islam and the West: Conflict, Co-Existence or Conversion?* (Carlisle, UK: Paternoster, 1998); John Esposito, *The Islamic Threat: Myth or Reality?*, rev. ed. (Oxford: Oxford University Press, 1995); John Esposito and Zafar Ishaq Ansari, eds., *Muslims and the West: Encounter and Dialogue* (Islamabad: Islamic Research Institute, 2001); Fred Halliday, *Islam and the Myth of Confrontation* (London: Tauris, 1995); Shireen T. Hunter, *The Future of Islam and the West: Clash of Civilizations or Peaceful Coexistence?* (West Post, CT: Praeger, 1998); Karim H. Karim, *The Islamic Peril: Media and Global Violence* (Montreal: Black Rose, 2000); Jorgen S. Nielsen, ed., *The Christian-Muslim Frontier: Chaos, Clash or Dialogue?* (London: Tauris, 1998); Dieter Senghaas, *The Clash within Civilizations: Coming to Terms with Cultural Conflicts* (London: Routledge, 1998); Victor Segesvary, *Dialogue of Civilizations: An Introduction to Civilizational Analysis* (Lanham, MD: University Press of America, 2000); Victor Segesvary, *Inter-Civilizational Relations and the Destiny of the West: Dialogue or Confrontation* (Lanham, MD: University Press of America, 2000).

32. Lawrence E. Harrison and Samuel Huntington, eds., *Culture Matters: How Values Shape Human Progress* (New York: Basic, 2000).

33. See Jack Goody, *Islam in Europe* (Cambridge, UK: Polity, 2004), 10–109. Also see Maria Rosa Menocal, *The Arabic Role in Medieval Literary History: A Forgotten Heritage* (Philadelphia: University of Pennsylvania Press, 2004).

34. There are many works that document the extensive influence of Islamic culture and thought on Europe. For instance, see Stanwood Cobb, *Islamic Contributions to Civilization* (Washington, DC: Avalon, 1963); Rom Landau, *The Arab Heritage of Western Civilization* (New York: Arab Information Center, 1962); Ellen Seiden, "The Muslim Impact on Medieval Europe," *Renaissance Magazine* 7:3, no. 27 (2002): 38–42; W. Montgomery Watt, *The Influence of Islam on Medieval Europe* (Edinburgh: Edinburgh University Press, 1972). Two particularly impressive works are George Makdisi, *The Rise of Humanism in Classical Islam and the Christian West* (Edinburgh: Edinburgh University Press, 1990); Mourad Wahba and Mona Abousenna, eds., *Averroes and the Enlightenment* (New York: Prometheus, 1996). Also see Gerhard Endress and Jan A. Aertsen, eds., *Averroes and the Aristotelian Tradition: Sources, Constitutions, and Reception of the Philosophy of Ibn Rushd 1126–1219* (Leiden: Brill, 1999). Even when preserving the Greek philosophical tradition, Muslim scholars did not act as mere transmitters but substantially developed and built on Greek philosophy. In a fascinating text which demonstrates the level of penetration that Islamic thought achieved in Europe, Thomas Aquinas, in an attempt to refute Ibn Rushd (Averroes), whom he labels as a "perverter of Peripatetic philosophy," and Ibn Sina (Avicenna), ends up quoting Hamid al-Ghazali in support of his arguments against Ibn Rushd's. Both al-Ghazali and Ibn Rushd were medieval Muslim philosophers and jurists. See Thomas Aquinas, *On the Unity of the Intellect against the Averroists*, trans. Beatrice Zedler (Milwaukee, WI: Marquette University Press, 1968), 46–47. On Aquinas and Muslim thought, see Goddard, *A History of Christian-Muslim Relations*, 102–3; also see Majid Fakhry, *Averroes, Aquinas and the Rediscovery of Aristotle in Western Europe* (Washington, DC: Georgetown Center for Muslim-Christian Understanding, 1997). For a collection of articles that demonstrate cross-intellectual influences, see John Inglis, *Medieval Philosophy and the Classical Tradition: In Islam, Judaism, and Christianity* (Richmond, UK:

Curzon, 2002). For an awe-inspiring example of the contributions of medieval Muslim scholars to Greek philosophy, see Kwame Gyekye, *Arabic Logic: Ibn al-Tayyib's Commentary on Porphyry's Eisagoge* (Albany: State University of New York Press, 1979). On the pervasive influence of Islamic philosophy, especially of the *Mu'tazili* school of thought, on the Jewish philosophical tradition, see Harry Austryn Wolfson, *Repercussions of the Kalam in Jewish Philosophy* (Cambridge, MA: Harvard University Press, 1979), esp. 175–233.

35. Monica M. Gaudiosi, "Influence of the Islamic Law of Waqf on the Development of the Trust in England: The Case of Merton College," *University of Pennsylvania Law Review* 136, no. 4 (1988): 1232; John Makdisi, "The Islamic Origins of the Common Law," *North Carolina Law Review* 77, no. 5 (1999): 1635–1739; George Makdisi, "The Guilds of Law in Medieval Legal History: An Inquiry into the Origins of the Inns of Court," *Cleveland State Law Review* 34, no. 1 (1985).

36. Although Muslims articulated a coherent and theoretical framework of the social contract, it could also be shown that Greek philosophy influenced and played a large role in this development. Muhammad ibn 'Abd al-Malik ibn Tufayl, *Hayy Ibn Yaqzan*, ed. Jamil Saliba (Damascus: Maktabat Jami'at Dimashq, 1962); English trans. in Ibn Tufayl, *Ibn Tufayl's Hayy Ibn Yaqzan: A Philosophical Tale*, trans. Lenn Evan Goodman (Chicago, IL: University of Chicago Press, 2009); Abu Nasr al-Farabi, "The Attainment of Happiness," in *AlFarabi's Philosophy of Plato and Aristotle*, ed. and trans. Muhsin Mahdi (New York: Free Press of Glencoe, 1962), esp. 22–25; Abu Nasr al-Farabi, *On the Perfect State : Abu Nasr al-Farabi's Mabadi' Ara' Ahl al-Madina al-Fadila*, trans. Richard Walzer (Oxford: Clarendon, 1985); Majid Fakhry, *Al-Farabi, Founder of Islamic Neoplatonism: His Life, Works, and Influence* (Oxford: OneWorld, 2002), 101–17; Muhsin S. Mahdi, *Alfarabi and the Foundation of Islamic Political Philosophy* (Chicago, IL: University of Chicago Press, 2001), esp. 140–44.

37. Fakhry, *Rediscovery of Aristotle*; Majid Fakhry, *Averroes (Ibn Rushd): His Life, Works and Influence* (Oxford: OneWorld, 2001), esp. 129–39; Endress and Aertsen, *Averroes and the Aristotelian Tradition*; Wahba and Abousenna, *Averroes and the Enlightenment*; Charles Burnett, "Arabic into Latin: The reception of Arabic Philosophy into Western Europe," in *The Cambridge Companion to Arabic Philosophy*, ed. Peter Adamson and Richard C. Taylor (Cambridge: Cambridge University Press, 2005), 370–404; Dag Nikolaus Hasse, "The Attraction of Averroism in the Renaissance: Vernia, Achillini, Prassicio," in *Philosophy, Science, and Exegesis in Greek, Arabic, and Latin Commentaries*, ed. P. Adamson, H. Baltussen, and M. W. F. Stone (London: Institute of Classical Studies, 2005), 2:131–47; Ruth Glasner, "Levi Ben Gershom and the Study of Ibn Rushd in the Fourteenth Century," *Jewish Quarterly Review* 86, no. 1–2 (July–October, 1995): 51–90; Steven Harvey, "Arabic into Hebrew: The Hebrew Translation Movement and the Influence of Averroes upon Medieval Jewish Thought," in *The Cambridge Companion to Medieval Jewish Philosophy*, ed. Daniel H. Frank and Oliver Leaman (Cambridge: Cambridge University Press, 2003), 258–80.

38. For an analysis of this process of projection and construction of an image of Islamic law, see Khaled Abou El Fadl, "Islamic Law and Ambivalent Scholarship," *Michigan Law Review* 100, no. 6 (2002): 1421–43.

39. For a detailed study on the role of authorial enterprise, communities of interpretation, and Islamic law, see Khaled Abou El Fadl, *Speaking in God's Name: Authority, Islamic Law, and Women* (Oxford: OneWorld, 2001).

40. For example, see Dennis, *The Rise of the Islamic Empire*; Grant, *The Blood of the Moon*. On the essentializing of Islam in Western scholarship and its prejudicial effects, see Edward Said, "Impossible Histories: Why the Many Islams Cannot Be Simplified," *Harper's Magazine* (July 2002): 69–74.

41. In my view, this is the gist of Huntington's argument about the wrongfulness of believing in universal Western values; Huntington, *Clash of Civilizations*, 308–12. This is also Lawrence Rosen's argument in his *The Justice of Islam*, 153–75, where he contends that what Westerners would consider despotic and oppressive is entirely acceptable for Muslims because of their own conceptions of justice and reality. See my critique of this book in Abou El Fadl, "Islamic Law and Ambivalent Scholarship." Also, see Mayer, *Islam and Human Rights*, 7–13; Abou El Fadl, "Soul Searching and the Spirit of Shari'a," 553–72.

42. The event was sponsored by the Global Policy Exchange and held in Washington, DC on October 29, 2002. The dialogue was supposed to be published as a book, but these plans never materialized.

43. On the doctrine of necessity (*darura*), see Subhi Mahmassani, *The Philosophy of Jurisprudence in Islam*, trans. Farhat Ziadeh (Leiden: Brill, 1961), 152–59; Mohammad Hashim Kamali, *Principles of Islamic Jurisprudence* (Cambridge: Islamic Texts Society, 1991), 267–81. See, on the subject, Abou El Fadl, *Speaking in God's Name*, 196–97; Khaled Abou El Fadl, "Constitutionalism and the Islamic Sunni Legacy," *UCLA Journal of Islamic and Near Eastern Law* 1, no. 1 (Fall/Winter, 2001–02): 86–92.

44. Qur'an 33:59.

45. Not even the puritanical Saudi religious police believe that men are commanded to cover the hair on their head. The custom of Saudi men, including the religious police, however, is to wear a piece of cloth that covers a part of their heads.

46. Qur'an 5:32.

47. For the details of the case, see Clarisa Bencomo, *Flawed Justice: The Execution of 'Abd al-Karim Mara'i al-Naqshabandi*, a report of Human Rights Watch/Middle East Division (New York: Human Rights Watch, 1997); Geoff Simons, *Saudi Arabia: The Shape of Client Feudalism* (London: St. Martin's, 1998), 48. For other wide-scale human rights abuses committed in Saudi Arabia in the name of Islam, see ibid., 3–68.

48. Qur'an 13:11.

49. In Arabic this is known as: *al-amr bi'l ma'ruf wa al-nahy 'an al-munkar*. For a study on the duty to enjoin the good and forbid the evil in the Islamic tradition, see Michael Cook, *Commanding Right and Forbidding Wrong in Islamic Thought* (Cambridge: Cambridge University Press, 2000).

50. For a very helpful discussion of these terms, see Toshihiko Izutsu, *Ethico-Religious Concepts in the Qur'an* (Kuala Lumpur: Islamic Book Trust, 2004), 248–52.

51. On *qist*, see Izutsu, *Ethico-Religious Concepts in the Qur'an*, 243–45.

52. See Khayr al-Din al-Tunisi, *Aqwam al-Masalik fi Ma'rifat Ahwal al-Mamalik: al-Muqaddima wa Taqariz al-Mu'asirin* (Tunis: al-Dar al-Tunisiyya lil-Nashr, 1972); for an English translation, see Khayr al-Din al-Tunisi, *The Surest Path to Knowledge concerning the Condition of Countries*, trans. L. Carl Brown (Cambridge, MA: Harvard University Press, 1967); 'Abd al-Rahman al-Kawakibi, *Taba'i' al-Istibdad wa Masari' al-Isti'bad*, 2nd ed. (Beirut: Dar al-Qur'an al-Karim, 1973); Boozari, *Shi'i Jurisprudence and Constitution*.

53. For Shaykh al-Azhar's speech shortly after the overthrow of Mubarak, see "Al Azhar Grand Sheikh Calls for a Speedy Transition to Democracy," *Islamopedia*, February 16, 2011, http://www.islamopediaonline.org/news/al-azhar-grand-sheikh-calls-speedy-transition-democracy; for the full speech in Arabic, see "Bayan wa Mu'amar Sahafi li-Shaykh al-Azhar Ahmad al-Tayyib al-Safwa al-Islamiyya, Address," *YouTube.com*, February 16, 2011, http://www.youtube.com/watch?v=MIjgBCQ28yM. For the Azhar statement issued in June 2011, which has come to be known as the Al-Azhar Document, see *Wathiqat al-Azhar bisha'n Mustaqbil Misr*, June 20, 2011, http://www.sis.gov.eg/Ar/Templates/Articles/tmpArticles. aspx?ArtID=48572; English translation available at http://www.sis.gov.eg/En/Templates/Articles/tmpArticles.aspx?ArtID=56424. Also see Khaled Abou El Fadl, "The Language of the Age: Shari'a and Natural Justice in the Egyptian Revolution," *Harvard International Law Journal* 52 (April 2011): 311–21; Khaled Abou El Fadl, "Conceptualizing Shari'a in the Modern State," *Villanova Law Review* 56, no. 5 (2012): 803–18.

54. Khaled Abou El Fadl, *Rebellion and Violence in Islamic Law* (Cambridge: Cambridge University Press, 2001), 256–58, 296, 303, 312.

55. Khaled Abou El Fadl, "Law of Duress in Islamic Law and Common Law: A Comparative Study," *Arab Law Quarterly* 6, no. 2 (1991): 121.

56. Khaled Abou El Fadl, "The Death Penalty, Mercy and Islam: A Call for Retrospection," in *A Call for Reckoning: Religion and the Death Penalty*, ed. Erik C. Owens et al. (Grand Rapids, MI: Eerdmans, 2004), 73–108.

57. Burhan al-Din Ibrahim bin Muhammad al-Ramini ibn Muflih al-Dimashqi, *Al-Mubdi' fi Sharh al-Muqni'* (Beirut: al-Maktab al-Islami, 1980), 9:168; Muhammad ibn 'Ali al-Shawkani, *Nayl al-Awtar Sharh Muntaqa al-Akhbar* (Cairo: Dar al-Hadith, n.d.), 7:168; Abu Ja'far Muhammad bin Jarir al-Tabari, *Jami' Bayan fi Tafsir al-Qur'an* (Beirut: Dar al-Ma'rifa, 1989), 25:82.

58. On this case, see Simons, *Saudi Arabia*, 38.

59. On the Islamic law of rebellion, which the Saudi government cited in justification of the death sentence, see Abou El Fadl, *Rebellion and Violence in Islamic Law*.

60. Al-Shawkani, *Nayl al-Awtar*, 7:168.

61. Simons, *Saudi Arabia*, 10–11.

62. "Qaradawi Says Bahrain's Revolution Sectarian," *Al Arabiya News*, March 19, 2011, http://www.alarabiya.net/articles/2011/03/19/142205.html; Salah Hemeid, "Sectarian Slants: Can Deep-Rooted Sectarianism Succeed in Thwarting the Region's Democracy Revolutions," *Al-Ahram Weekly*, March 24–30, 2011, http://weekly.ahram.org.eg/2011/1040/re801.htm; for the Bahraini response to al-Qaradawi, see "Bahraini Response to al-Qaradawi's Sectarian Accusation," *Jadaliyya*, March 20, 2011, http://www.jadaliyya.com/pages/index/968/bahraini-response-to-al-qaradawis-sectarian-accusa.

63. See Human Rights Watch, *The Ismailis of Najran: Second-Class Saudi Citizens* (New York: Human Rights Watch, 2008), available at http://www.hrw.org/reports/2008/09/22/ismailis-najran.

64. Qur'an 9:39; 11:57; 47:38.

65. Qur'an 9:67; 59:19.

66. Qur'an 3:104, 110.

67. Qur'an 9:67; 59:19.

68. Qur'an 17:16.
69. Qur'an 43:54.
70. Taqi al-Din Ahmad Ibn Taymiyya, *Majmu'a al-Fatawa*, ed. Muhammad bin 'Abd al-Rahman (Riyadh: Wizarat al-Shu'un al-Islamiyya wa al-Awqaf wa al-Da'wa wa al-Irshad, 1995), 35:20.
71. Qur'an 6:129.
72. See Waller, *Becoming Evil*, 202–29; Erich Fromm, *The Heart of Man: Its Genius for Good and Evil* (New York: Harper and Row, 1964), 19–21.
73. Even under the most conservative and draconian reading of classical Islamic law, possession of offending books is insufficient to support a death sentence, if any crime at all. Moreover, coerced confessions of being a sorcerer are inadmissible.
74. For a detailed study on the role of authorial enterprise, communities of interpretation, and Islamic law, see Abou El Fadl, *Speaking in God's Name*.
75. Qur'an 2:143; 3:110.
76. Qur'an 4:135; 5:8.

6. BEYOND ISLAMOPHOBIA

1. Sayyid Qutb in his *Ma'alim fi al-Tariq* relied on the same idea of *jahiliyya* but for different purposes. Qutb used it to create a dichotomy between Islamic and non-Islamic societies. For Qutb, if Muslims turn away from the path of Islam, they are not part of the *jahiliyya* and are no longer Muslim. See Sayyid Qutb, *Ma'alim fi al-Tariq* (Cairo: Dar al-Shuruq, 1991); for an English translation, see Sayyid Qutb, *Milestones* (New Delhi: Islamic Book Service, 2011). For an overview of Qutb's theories on governance, see Sayed Khatab, *The Political Thought of Sayyid Qutb: The Theory of Jahiliyyah* (London: Routledge, 2006); Sayed Khatab and Gary D. Bouma, *Democracy in Islam* (New York: Routledge, 2007), 72–92. Also see "Sayyid Kutb," in *Encyclopedia of Islam*, 2nd ed., ed. P. Bearman et al., Brill Online, 2013.
2. See Amirhassan Boozari, *Shi'i Jurisprudence and Constitution: Revolution in Iran* (New York: Palgrave Macmillan, 2011), 45–152; Homa Katouzian, *Musaddiq and the Struggle for Power in Iran* (London: Tauris, 1999).
3. See Wajahat Ali et al., "Fear, Inc.: The Roots of the Islamophobia Network in America," *Center for American Progress*, August 26, 2011, http://www.americanprogress.org/issues/religion/report/2011/08/26/10165/fear-inc/; Nathan C. Lean, *The Islamophobia Industry: How the Right Manufactures Fear of Muslims* (New York: Pluto, 2012); Robert Steinback, "Jihad against Islam," *Southern Poverty Law Center*, Summer 2011, http://www.splcenter.org/get-informed/intelligence-report/browse-all-issues/2011/summer/jihad-against-islam. For profiles of leading Islamophobes, see the Muslim Public Affairs Council's report, "Not Qualified: Exposing the Deception behind America's Top 25 Pseudo Experts on Islam," *Muslim Public Affairs Council*, September 11, 2012, http://www.mpac.org/publications/policy-papers/not-qualified-exposing-pseudo-experts-on-islam.php.
4. Qur'an 13:17.
5. Qur'an 49:9–13.
6. Qur'an 11:118.
7. A. R. Fausset, *A Critical and Expository Commentary on the Book of Judges* (London: James Nisbet, 1885), 26; Anthony Smith, *Chosen Peoples* (New York: Oxford University Press, 2003), 142.
8. Philip Jenkins, *Laying Down the Sword: Why We Can't Ignore the Bible's Violent Verses* (New York: HarperOne, 2011), 149; Elliott Horowitz, *Reckless Rites: Purim and the Legacy of Jewish Violence* (Princeton, NJ: Princeton University Press, 2006), 129–34.
9. Linda Paterson, *The World of the Troubadours* (Cambridge: Cambridge University Press, 1998), 161. Also see Olivia Remie Constable, *Housing the Stranger in the Mediterranean World: Lodging, Trade, and Travel* (Cambridge: Cambridge University Press, 2004), esp. 328–30; Kathryn L. Reyerson, *The Art of the Deal: Intermediaries of Trade in Medieval Montpellier* (Leiden: Brill, 2002), 21–24; Julie Anne Taylor, *Muslims in Medieval Italy: The Colony at Lucera* (Lanham, MD: Lexington, 2005), 49, 179; David Abulafia, "Monarchs and Minorities in the Christian Western Mediterranean around 1300: Lucera and Its Analogues," in *Mediterranean Encounters, Economic, Religious, Political, 1100–1550* (Aldershot, UK: Ashgate, 2000), 234–63.
10. Addressing a specific context, the Qur'an states that under the particular circumstances, the jizya was a preferred alternative to forced conversion, enslavement, or execution. Qur'an 9:29.
11. John V. Tolan, *Saracens: Islam in the Medieval European Imagination* (New York: Columbia University Press, 2002), 84.

12. Tolan, *Saracens*, 191–92.

13. Pope Leo XIII, "Encyclical of Pope Leo XIII on the Nature of Human Liberty," *Vatican: The Holy See*, http://www.vatican.va/holy_father/leo_xiii/encyclicals/documents/hf_l-xiii_enc_20061888_libertas_en.html; Paul E. Sigmund, *Natural Law in Political Thought* (Lanham, MD: University Press of America, 1971), 188.

14. Bernard Lewis, *What Went Wrong? Western Impact and Middle Eastern Response* (Oxford: Oxford University Press, 2002).

15. For a critique of Lewis's book, see Edward Said, "Impossible Histories: Why the Many Islams Cannot Be Simplified," *Harper's Magazine* (July 2002), 69.

16. See Khaled Abou El Fadl, *The Great Theft: Wrestling Islam from the Extremists* (New York: HarperOne, 2005).

17. See George Eliot, *Daniel Deronda* (New York: Harper & Brothers, 1876), 123. Also, see a study on George Eliot's moral development in relation to her novels by Gertrude Himmelfarb, *The Jewish Odyssey of George Eliot* (New York: Encounter, 2009).

18. Martha C. Nussbaum, *The New Religious Intolerance: Overcoming the Politics of Fear in an Anxious Age* (Cambridge, MA: Belknap), 169.

19. See Robert Spencer, ed., *The Myth of Islamic Tolerance: How Islamic Law Treats Non-Muslims* (Amherst, NY: Prometheus, 2005); Robert Spencer, *Islam Unveiled: Disturbing Questions about the World's Fastest-Growing Faith* (San Francisco: Encounter, 2002); Robert Spencer, *The Truth about Muhammad: Founder of the World's Most Intolerant Religion* (Washington, DC: Regnery, 2006); Ergun Mehmet Caner and Emir Fethi Caner, *Unveiling Islam: An Insider's Look at Muslim Life and Beliefs* (Grand Rapids, MI: Kregel, 2002); David Earle Johnson, *Conspiracy in Mecca: What You Need to Know about the Islamic Threat* (Cape Canaveral, FL: David Johnson Books, 2002); Hal Lindsey, *The Everlasting Hatred: The Roots of Jihad* (Murrieta, CA: Oracle House, 2002); Peter Hammond, *Slavery, Terrorism, and Islam: The Historical Roots and Contemporary Threat* (Cape Town, South Africa: Christian Liberty, 2005); Brigitte Gabriel, *Because They Hate: A Survivor of Islamic Terror Warns America* (New York: St. Martin's, 2006); Wafa Sultan, *A God Who Hates: The Courageous Woman Who Inflamed the Muslim World Speaks Out against the Evils of Islam* (New York: St. Martin's, 2009), esp. 1–10.

20. Cinnamon Stillwell and Eric Golub, "UCLA's Professor of Fantasy," *American Thinker*, December 24, 2010, http://www.americanthinker.com/2010/12/uclas_professor_of_fantasy.html; Judith Greblya, "Pushing 'Islamophobia' at UCLA," *Front Page Mag*, May 5, 2011, http://frontpagemag.com/2011/judith-greblya/pushing-%E2%80%98islamophobia%E2%80%99-at-ucla/; Jamie Glazov, "Islamism at UCLA Law School," *American Thinker*, January 7, 2012, http://www.americanthinker.com/2012/01/islamism_at_ucla_law_school.html.

21. Jenkins, *Laying Down the Sword*, 248.

22. John Shelby Spong, *The Sins of Scripture: Exposing the Bible's Texts of Hate to Reveal the God of Love* (San Francisco: HarperSanFrancisco, 2005); Evan Fales, "Satanic Verses: Moral Chaos in Holy Writ," in *Divine Evil? The Moral Character of the God of Abraham*, ed. Michael Bergmann et al. (New York: Oxford University Press, 2011), 93–108; Robert Eisen, *The Peace and Violence of Judaism: From the Bible to Modern Zionism* (New York: Oxford University Press, 2011), 17–64, 145–77; Hector Avalos, *Fighting Words: The Origins of Religious Violence* (Amherst, NY: Prometheus, 2005); Timothy K. Beal, "The White Supremacist Bible and the Phineas Priesthood," in *Sanctified Aggression: Legacies of Biblical and Post-biblical Vocabularies of Violence*, ed. Jonneke Bekkenkamp and Yvonne Sherwood (New York: T & T Clark, 2003), 120–31; Alastair G. Hunter, "(De)nominating Amalek: Racist Stereotyping in the Bible and the Justification of Discrimination," in *Sanctified Aggression: Legacies of Biblical and Post-biblical Vocabularies of Violence*, ed. Jonneke Bekkenkamp and Yvonne Sherwood (New York: T & T Clark, 2003), 92–108; Eric A. Seibert, *The Violence of Scripture: Overcoming the Old Testament's Troubling Legacy* (Minneapolis, MN: Fortress, 2012), 15–26; Malachie Munyaneza, "Genocide in the Name of 'Salvation': The Combined Contribution of Biblical Translation/Interpretation and Indigenous Myth to the 1994 Rwandan Genocide," in *Sanctified Aggression: Legacies of Biblical and Post-biblical Vocabularies of Violence*, ed. Jonneke Bekkenkamp and Yvonne Sherwood (New York: T & T Clark, 2003), 60–75, esp. 65–71, 73–74; Steven Leonard Jacobs et al., eds., *Confronting Genocide: Judaism, Christianity, Islam* (Lanham, MD: Lexington, 2009); Edward W. Said, "Michael Walzer's 'Exodus and Revolution': A Canaanite Reading," *Grand Street* 5, no. 2 (1986): 91–93; Thomas Sizgorich, *Violence and Belief in Late Antiquity: Militant Devotion in Christianity and Islam* (Philadelphia: University of Pennsylvania Press, 2009); Beth Berkowitz, *Execution and Invention: Death Penalty Discourse in Early Rabbinic and Christian Cultures* (New York: Oxford University Press, 2006).

23. Nussbaum, *The New Religious Intolerance*, 163–64.

24. For instance, see Qur'an 2:113; 3:55; 5:48; 6:164; 10:93; and many other references. For commentary on Qur'an 5:48, see Abu Hasan 'Ali bin Muhammad bin Habib al-Mawardi, *Al-Nukatu wa al-'Uyun Tafsir al-Mawardi* (Beirut: Dar al-Kutub al-'Ilmiyya, n.d.), 2:44–45;

Muhammad ibn Jarir al-Tabari, *Tafsir al-Tabari: Jami' al-Bayan 'an Ta'wil Ay al-Qur'an*, ed. Mahmoud Muhammad Shakir (Cairo: Maktabat Ibn Taymiyya, n.d.), 10:383–85. This is a common theme in many types of Islamic literature, including *usul al-fiqh* and philosophy. See Abu Hamid al-Ghazali, *Al-Mustafsa min 'Ilm al-Usul*, ed. Ibrahim Muhammad Ramadan (Beirut: Dar al-Arqam, 1997), 2:375–78; Fakhr al-Din al-Razi, *Al-Mahsul fi 'Ilm Usul al-Fiqh*, 3rd ed., ed. Taha Jabir Fayyad al-'Alwani (Beirut: Mu'assasat al-Risala, 1997), 6:34–35, 43–50; Zaki al-Din Sha'ban, *Usul al-Fiqh al-Islami* (Cairo: Matba'at Dar al-Ta'lif, 1965), 418–19.

25. See Khaled Abou El Fadl, *Speaking in God's Name: Authority, Islamic Law, and Women* (Oxford: OneWorld, 2001), 145–51.

26. Deuteronomy 25:2. For the discourse on corporal punishment and flogging in the Babylonian Talmud, see B. Makkoth 13a–24a, in *Hebrew-English Edition of the Babylonian Talmud*, trans. Dayan H. M. Lazarus (London: Soncino, 1987).

27. The classic work on this is George Ryley Scott, *The History of Corporal Punishment: A Survey of Flagellation in Its Historical, Anthropological, and Sociological Aspects* (London: T. Werner Laurie, 1938). Also see Raymond L. Gard, *The End of the Rod: A History of the Abolition of Corporal Punishments in the Courts of England and Wales* (Boca Raton, FL: Brown Walker, 2009); R. G. Van Yelyr, *The Whip and the Rod: An Account of Corporal Punishment Among All Nations and for All Purposes* (London: G. Swan, 1941).

28. The quote above is slightly modified from Matthew Bacon, *A New Abridgement of the Law*, 5th ed. (London: A. Strahan, 1798), 1:475.

29. Maeve E. Doggett. *Marriage, Wife-Beating and the Law in Victorian England* (Columbia: University of South Carolina Press, 1993), 1–33, 100–148, esp. 142–43.

30. Alan W. Clarke, *Rendition to Torture* (New Brunswick, NJ: Rutgers University Press, 2012), 135–58; Michael Mandel, *How America Gets Away with Murder: Illegal Wars, Collateral Damage and Crimes against Humanity* (London: Pluto, 2004), 3–56; Elaine C. Hagopian, ed., *Civil Rights in Peril: The Targeting of Arabs and Muslims* (Chicago and London: Haymarket and Pluto, 2004); Tzvetan Todorov, *The Fear of Barbarians*, trans. Andrew Brown (Chicago: University of Chicago Press, 2010), 106–10, 200–212; Jeremy Salt, *The Unmaking of the Middle East: A History of Western Disorder in Arab Lands* (Berkeley and Los Angeles: University of California Press, 2008), 329–39; Patrick Tyler, *A World of Trouble: The White House and the Middle East—from the Cold War to the War on Terror* (New York: Farrar, Straus and Giroux, 2009), 540, 547; Jeremy Brecher, Jill Cutler, and Brendan Smith, eds., *In The Name of Democracy: American War Crimes in Iraq and Beyond* (New York: Metropolitan, 2005); Irum Shiekh, *Detained without Cause: Muslims' Stories of Detention and Deportation in America after 9/11* (New York: Palgrave Macmillan, 2011); Arundhati Roy, "War Is Peace," in *September 11 and the U.S. War: Beyond the Curtain of Smoke*, ed. Roger Burbach and Ben Clarke (San Francisco: City Lights and Freedom Voices, 2002), 101–10; Marjorie Cohn, ed., *The United States and Torture: Interrogation, Incarceration, and Abuse* (New York: New York University Press, 2011); Tara McKelvey, *Monstering: Inside America's Policy of Secret Interrogations and Torture in the Terror War* (New York: Carroll & Graf, 2007); Jennifer K. Harbury, *Truth, Torture, and the American Way: The History and Consequences of U.S. Involvement in Torture* (Boston: Beacon, 2005), 183–84; Alfred W. McCoy, *A Question of Torture: CIA Interrogation, from the Cold War to the War on Terror* (New York: Metropolitan, 2006), 151–87.

31. Nussbaum, *The New Religious Intolerance*.

32. Norman Housley, *Contesting the Crusades* (Malden, MA: Blackwell, 2006), 37; Rodney Stark, *God's Battalions: The Case for the Crusades* (New York: HarperOne, 2009), 2–3; Matthew Carr, *Blood and Faith: The Purging of Muslim Spain* (New York: New Press, 2009), 183–201; Nasir Khan, *Perceptions of Islam in the Christendoms: A Historical Survey* (Oslo: Solum Forlag, 2006), 210–26, 233–48; John V. Tolan, ed., *Medieval Christian Perspectives of Islam* (New York: Routledge, 2000); Minou Reeves, *Muhammad in Europe: A Thousand Years of Western Myth-Making* (Lebanon: New York University Press, 2003); W. Montgomery Watt, *The Influence of Islam on Medieval Europe* (Edinburgh: University of Edinburgh Press, 2001), 49–57, 72–84.

33. David Abulafia, "Ethnic Variety and Its Implications: Frederick II's Relations with Jews and Muslims," in *Mediterranean Encounters, Economic, Religious, Political, 1100–1550*, 213–24; David R. Blanks and Michael Frassetto, eds., *Western Views of Islam in Medieval and Early Modern Europe: Perception of Other* (New York: Palgrave Macmillan, 1999); Carr, *Blood and Faith*, 25–39; Dominique Iogna-Prat, *Order and Exclusion: Cluny and Christendom Face Heresy, Judaism, and Islam (1000–1150)*, trans. Graham Robert Edwards (Ithaca, NY: Cornell University Press, 2002), 275–357; John Edwards, *The Spain of the Catholic Monarchs: 1474–1520* (Oxford: Blackwell, 2000), 234, 238–40; Haim Beinart, *The Expulsion of the Jews from Spain*, trans. Jeffrey M. Green (Oxford: Littman Library of Jewish Civilization, 2002), 10–11; Nasir Khan, *Perceptions of Islam in the Christendoms: A Historical Survey* (Oslo: Solum Forlag, 2006), 210, 228–33, 251–52; Debra Higgs, *Saracens, Demons, and Jews* (Princeton, NJ: Princeton University Press, 2003), 221–28; Norman Zacour, *Jews and Saracens*

in the Consilia of Oldradus de Ponte (Toronto: Pontifical Institute of Medieval Studies, 1990), 16–19. For the demonization of Saracens/Muslims in particular, see Tolan, *Saracens*, 50–55.

34. On the complex relationship between freedom of expression and religious bigotry, see Paul M. Taylor, *Freedom of Religion: UN and European Human Law and Practice* (Cambridge: Cambridge University Press, 2005), 7–114; Ivan Hare and James Weinstein, eds., *Extreme Speech and Democracy* (Oxford: Oxford University Press, 2009), 289–356, 430–44; Jeroen Temperman, *State-Religion Relationships and Human Rights Law: Towards a Right to Religiously Neutral Governance* (Leiden: Brill, 2010), 203–74; Toger Seidenfaden, "Hard Secularism as Intolerant Civil Religion: Denmark and the Cartoon Case," in *Civil Religion, Human Rights and International Relations: Connecting People across Cultures and Traditions*, ed. Helle Porsdam (Northampton, MA: Edward Elgar, 2012), 178–91; Carolyn Evans, "Religion and Freedom of Expression," in *Religion and Human Rights*, ed. John Witte Jr. and M. Christian Green (Oxford: Oxford University Press, 2012), 188–203; Katharine Gelber and Adrienne Stone, eds., *Hate Speech and Freedom of Speech in Australia* (Sydney: Federation Press, 2007), 145–93; Jytte Klausen, *The Cartoons That Shook the World* (New Haven, CT: Yale University Press, 2009), 13–14, 32, 148.

35. For torture instances immediately after 9/11 (2001–2004), see Jeremy Waldron, *Torture, Terror, and Trade-Offs: Philosophy for the White House* (New York: Oxford University Press, 2010), 217–22. Also, see calls for a host of measures against Muslims, including increased profiling, increased surveillance, the monitoring of universities and publications, contacting local officials, and supporting the campaigns in the Middle East by Brigitte Gabriel, *Because They Hate: A Survivor of Islamic Terror Warns America* (New York: St. Martin's, 2006), 223–34; Brigitte Gabriel, *They Must Be Stopped: Why We Must Defeat Radical Islam and How We Can Do It* (New York: St. Martin's Griffin, 2010), 224–38. For media campaigns against and public perceptions of Islam in the United States, see Evelyn Alsultany, *Arabs and Muslims in the Media: Race and Representation after 9/11* (New York: New York University Press, 2012), 132–33.

36. See Khaled Abou El Fadl, "Fascism Triumphant?," *Political Theology* 10, no. 4 (2009): 577–81. According to Wilders, "'Islam is not a religion; it is an evil ideology and while there are moderate Muslims . . . there is no moderate Islam.' Because he is such a firm believer in human rights and personal freedoms, he wants to make the persecution of Muslims in Europe legal, and because he is a firm believer in freedom of speech, he wants to ban the Quran." Abou El Fadl, "Fascism Triumphant?," 578. For a sketch of Wilders's ideas, see "Netherlands Islam Freedom: Profile of Geert Wilders," *BBC News*, June 23, 2011, http://www.bbc.co.uk/news/world-europe-11443211.

37. Anders Behring Breivik's manifesto titled *2083: A European Declaration of Independence* heavily cites Robert Spencer and other American Islamophobes. See Ali, "Fear, Inc.," 1–2, 42, 44–45, 49, 87, 90, 94–95, 101.

38. For the victimization of the Serbs at the hands of the Islamic jihadists and the United States, see Yosseff Bodansky, *Offensive in the Balkans: The Potential for a Wider War as a Result of Foreign Intervention in Bosnia-Herzegovina* (London: International Media, 1995). For Islamic terrorism and takeover of Bosnia, see Bodansky, *Some Call It Peace: Waiting for War in the Balkans* (London: International Media, 1996). For the Islamic conspiracy to take over the world, see Bodansky, *Target America: Terrorism in the U.S. Today* (New York: S.P.I., 1993).

39. See Taylor Branch, *The Clinton Tapes: Wrestling History with the President* (New York: Simon & Schuster, 2009), 9–10. As Branch relates about his session with the president, "Clinton said U.S. allies in Europe blocked proposals to adjust or remove the embargo. . . . [P]rivately, said the president, key allies objected that an independent Bosnia would be "unnatural" as the only Muslim nation in Europe. He said they favored the embargo precisely because it locked in Bosnia's disadvantage. . . . [Clinton] said President François Mitterrand of France had been especially blunt in saying that Bosnia did not belong, and that British officials also spoke of a painful but realistic restoration of Christian Europe."

40. Islamophobic discourses have contributed to atrocities in Burma, Thailand, Southern Philippines, Kashmir, Kujurat India, and Chechnya. See H. John Poole, *Tactics of the Crescent Moon: Militant Muslim Combat Methods* (Emerald Isle, NC: Posterity Press, 2004); Andrew Selth, *Burma's Muslims: Terrorists or Terrorised? Canberra Papers on Strategy and Defense* (Canberra: Strategic and Defence Studies Centre, Australian National University, 2003), esp. 8–11. For a recent report on the sectarian violence in Burma (and the Islamophobic discourse that both initiated and came out of it), see "'The Government Could Have Stopped This': Sectarian Violence and Ensuing Abuses in Burma's Arakan State," *Human Rights Watch*, August 1, 2012, http://www.hrw.org/reports/2012/07/31/government-could-have-stopped. For a personal account that seeks to expose the "truth" about Islam and its destruction of Europe and policy recommendations for defeating Islamofascism, see Geert Wilders, *Marked for Death: Islam's War against the West and Me* (Washington, DC: Regnery, 2012), 203–17. Also see Samuel P. Huntington, *The Clash of Civilizations and the Remaking of World Order* (New York: Simon & Schuster, 2011), 246–65; Luca Mavelli, *Europe's Encounter with Islam: The*

Secular and the Postsecular (New York, Routledge, 2012), 62–87, 108–15; Selda Dagistanli and Kiran Grewal, "Perverse Muslim Masculinities in Contemporary Orientalist Discourse: The Vagaries of Muslim Immigration in the West," in *Global Islamophobia: Muslims and Moral Panic in the West*, ed. George Morgan and Scott Poynting (Surrey: Ashgate, 2012), 119–42, 133–37; Tzvetan Todorov, *The Fear of Barbarians*, trans. Andrew Brown (Chicago: University of Chicago Press, 2010), 86–106.

7. GOD THE UNIVERSAL

1. John Renard, "Al-Jihad al-Akbar: Notes on a Theme in Islamic Spirituality," *Muslim World* 78, no. 3–4 (1988): 225–42.

2. For a very interesting study, see Charlos Upton, *The Science of the Greater Jihad: Essays in Principial Psychology* (San Rafael, CA: Sophia Perennis, 2011); Maher Jarrar, "The Martyrdom of Passionate Lovers: Holy War as a Sacred Wedding," in *Jihad and Martyrdom*, ed. David Cook (London: Routledge, 2010), 2:95–111, originally published in *Myths, Historical Archetypes and Symbolic Figures in Arabic Literature: Towards a New Hermeneutic Approach, Proceedings of the International Symposium in Beirut, June 25th–June 30th, 1996*, ed. Angelica Neuwirth et al. (Beirut; Stuttgart: Franz Steiner, 1999), 87–107.

3. 'Ali 'Abd Allah al-Qusaymi, *Al-Thawra al-Wahhabiyya* (Cairo: Al-Matba'a al-Rahmaniyya, 1936), 1.

4. Albert Hourani, *Arabic Thought in the Liberal Age* (London: Oxford University Press, 1970). Also, for this transformative period, see Albert Hourani, *A History of the Arab Peoples* (New York: MJF Books, 1991), 333–49.

5. Louis Alexandre Olivier de Corancez, *Histoire des Wahabis depuis leur origine jusqu'a la fin de 1809* (Paris: Chez Crapart,1810); republished as *History of the Wahabis from Their Origin until the End of 1809*, trans. Eric Tabet (Reading, UK: Garnet, 1995); republished as *al-Wahhabiyun: Tarikh ma Ahmalihu al-Tarikh* (*The Wahhabis: A History of What History Ignored*) (Beirut: Riad El-Rayyes, 2003), 68. Charles Didier, a nineteenth-century French Orientalist, compared Muhammad bin 'Abd al-Wahhab to the Christian reformers John Calvin, John Huss, Martin Luther, and Savonarola. See Charles Didier, *Sojourn with the Grand Sharif of Makkah*, trans. Richard Boulind (Cambridge: Oleander Press, 1985), 94; for an Arabic translation, see Charles Didier, *Rihla ila al-Hijaz fi al-Nusf al-Thani min al-Qarn al-Tasi' 'Ashr al-Miladi*, trans. Muhammad Khayr al-Biqa'i (Riyadh: Dar al-Faysal al-Thaqafiyya al-Sa'udiyya, 2002), 235–36. Similarly, Joseph Von Hammer-Purgstall in 1835 described Ibn 'Abd al-Wahhab as the John Calvin of the Islamic world in his well-known history of the Ottoman Empire. See Joseph Freiherr Von Hammer-Purgstall, *Histoire de L'Empire Ottoman depuis son origine jusqu'a nos jours*, trans. J. J. Hellert (Paris: Bellizard, Barthes, Dufour & Lowell, 1835), 15:189.

6. Hafiz Wahba, "Wahhabism in Arabia: Past and Present," *Journal of the Royal Society for Asian Affairs* 16, no. 4 (1929): 458–67. Interestingly, the pro-Wahhabi apologist 'Ali 'Abd Allah al-Qusaymi is keenly aware of the favorable descriptions of Western Orientalists and implies that some Muslim intellectuals who have taken up the Wahhabi cause have done so after reading Western sources but are otherwise ill informed about Wahhabi thought. See al-Qusaymi, *Al-Thawra al-Wahhabiyya*, 2–3.

7. Corancez, *History of the Wahabis*, 192–95; John Lewis Burckhardt, *Notes on the Bedouins and Wahabys* (Reading, UK: Garnet, 1992), 2:99–106; for an Arabic translation, see John Lewis Burckhardt, *Mulahazat Haula al-Badu al-Wahhabiyyin*, trans. Muhammad al-Asyuti (Beirut: Dar Suyahan, 1995), 149, 202–11.

8. Corancez, *History of the Wahabis*, 178.

9. For examples of such accusations, see the essay critiquing my work by Abid Ullah Jan, "Text and Context," in Khaled Abou El Fadl, *The Place of Tolerance in Islam*, ed. Joshua Cohen and Ian Lague (Boston: Beacon, 2002), 51–55. Also see Khaled Abou El Fadl et al., *Islam and the Challenge of Democracy*, ed. Joshua Cohen and Deborah Chasman (Princeton, NJ: Princeton University Press, 2004); Leti Volpp, "The Citizen and the Terrorist," in *September 11 in History: A Watershed Moment?*, ed. Mary Duziak (Durham, NC: Duke University Press, 2003), 147–62.

10. On this subject, see Khaled Abou El Fadl, *And God Knows the Soldiers: The Authoritative and Authoritarian in Islamic Discourses* (Lanham, MD: University Press of America, 2001), 138–56.

11. For instance, see the valuable studies on the usage of ethical terms in the Qur'an: Toshihiko Izutsu, *The Structure of Ethical Terms in the Quran* (Chicago: ABC International Group, 2000); Toshihiko Izutsu, *Ethico-Religious Concepts in the Quran* (Montreal: McGill-Queen's University Press, 2002).

12. Qur'an 3:108.
13. On this subject, see George F. Hourani, *Reason and Tradition in Islamic Ethics* (Cambridge: Cambridge University Press, 1985).
14. See my essays in Abou El Fadl, *The Place of Tolerance in Islam*, 14–23.
15. Qur'an 38:87.
16. Qur'an 7:52; 7:203; 17:82; 21:107.
17. Qur'an 12:111.
18. For instance, Qur'an 6:54; 27:77; 29:51; 45:20.
19. See Daryush Shayegan, *Cultural Schizophrenia: Islamic Societies Confronting the West*, trans. John Howe (London: Saqi, 1989). Also see Louay M. Safi, *The Challenge of Modernity: The Quest for Authenticity in the Arab World* (Lanham, MD: University Press of America, 1994), esp.153–93; Malise Ruthven, *A Fury for God: The Islamist Attack on America* (London: Granta, 2002), 134–68.
20. See Wael Hallaq, "Was the Gate of Ijtihad Closed," *International Journal of Middle East Studies* 16 (1984): 3–41; Wael Hallaq, "*Ifta*' and *Ijtihad* in Sunni Legal Theory: A Developmental Account," in *Islamic Legal Interpretation: Muftis and Their Fatwas*, ed. Muhammad Khalid Masud, B. Messick, and D. S. Powers (Cambridge: Harvard University Press, 1996), 33–43, 336–37; Wael Hallaq, "Murder in Cordoba: *Ijtihad, Ifta*' and the Evolution of Substantive Law in Medieval Islam," *Acta Orientalia* 55 (1994): 55–83; Wael Hallaq, "From *Fatwas* to *Furu*': Growth and Change in Islamic Substantive Law," *Islamic Law and Society* 1, no. 1 (1994): 29–65; Wael Hallaq, *A History of Islamic Legal Theories: An Introduction to Sunni Usul al-Fiqh* (Cambridge: Cambridge University Press, 1999); Wael Hallaq, *Authority, Continuity and Change in Islamic Law* (Cambridge: Cambridge University Press, 2001); see also David Powers, *Law, Society, and Culture in the Maghrib, 1300–1500* (Cambridge: Cambridge University Press, 2002).
21. The classic studies on Orientalism and its effects remain those of Edward Said, *Orientalism* (New York: Random House, 1979), and Edward Said, *Culture and Imperialism* (New York: Vintage, 1994). For informative surveys of Orientalism and its practices, see Bryan S. Turner, *Orientalism, Postmodernism and Globalism* (London: Routledge, 1994), 3–114; Asaf Hussain, Robert Olson, and Jamil Qureshi, eds., *Orientalism, Islam, and Islamists* (Brattleboro, VT: Amana, 1984); and A. L. Macfie, *Orientalism* (London: Pearson Education, 2002).
22. Khaled Abou El Fadl, "Islamic Law and Muslim Minorities: The Juristic Discourse on Muslim Minorities from the Second/Eighth to the Eleventh/Seventeenth Centuries," *Islamic Law and Society* 1, no. 2 (1994): 141–87; Khaled Abou El Fadl, "The Unbounded Law of God and Territorial Boundaries," in *States, Nations, and Borders: The Ethics of Making Boundaries*, ed. Allen Buchanan and Margaret Moore (Cambridge: Cambridge University Press, 2003), 214–27; Khaled Abou El Fadl, "Between Functionalism and Morality: The Juristic Debates on the Conduct of War," in *Islamic Ethics of Life: Abortion, War, and Euthanasia*, ed. Jonathan E. Brockopp (Columbia, SC: University of South Carolina Press, 2003), 103–28.
23. See Khaled Abou El Fadl, *Rebellion and Violence in Islamic Law* (Cambridge: Cambridge University Press, 2001), 321–33.
24. For examples of scholars whose perception and understanding of Islamic law reflect all the Orientalist paradigms, including closing the doors of *ijtihad*, the abode of Islam versus the abode of war, the death of reason with the extinction of the *Mu'tazila*, and many others, see Mohamed Charfi, *Islam and Liberty: The Historical Misunderstanding*, trans. Patrick Camiller (London: Zed, 2005); first published as *Islam et Liberté* (Paris: Albin Michel, 1998); Abdullahi Ahmed An-Na'im, *Islam and the Secular State: Negotiating the Future of Shari'a* (Cambridge, MA: Harvard University Press, 2008), 129–30.
25. See Khaled Abou El Fadl, *And God Knows the Soldiers*, 121–38; Khaled Abou El Fadl, *Speaking in God's Name: Islamic Law, Authority and Women* (Oxford: OneWorld, 2001), 98, 108, 152–53, esp. 232–47.
26. On the epistemology of Islamic law, see Wael Hallaq, *Authority, Continuity and Change*; Hallaq, *A History of Islamic Legal Theories*.
27. Allan Christelow, *Muslim Law Courts and the French Colonial State in Algeria* (Princeton, NJ: Princeton University Press, 1985); J. N. D. Anderson, "Modern Trends in Islam: Legal Reform and Modernisation in the Middle East," *International and Comparative Law Quarterly* 20 (1971): 1–21, reprinted in *Islamic Law and Legal Theory*, ed. Ian Edge (New York: New York University Press, 1996), 547–67; William L. Cleveland, *A History of the Modern Middle East* (Boulder, CO: Westview, 2004), 61–98; Jasper Yeates Brinton, *The Mixed Courts of Egypt*, rev. ed. (New Haven, CT: Yale University Press, 1968); Ruth Mitchell, "Family Law in Algeria before and after the 1404/1984 Family Code," in *Islamic Law: Theory and Practice*, ed. R. Gleave and E. Kermeli (London: Tauris, 1997), 194–204, esp.194–96. Of course, at times, colonial powers took over the implementation of Islamic law, as in the case of the Anglo-Muhammadan law experience in India. See Syed Ameer Ali, *Muhammadan Law* (New Delhi: Kitab Bhavan, 1986), 1–4; Joseph Schacht, *An Introduction to Islamic Law* (London: Oxford University Press, 1964; reprint, Oxford: Clarendon, 1993), 94–97; N. J. Coulson, *A History of Islamic Law* (Edinburgh: Edinburgh University Press, 1964), 164–72. On the impact

of colonialism on the institutions of Islamic law in India, see Radhika Singha, *A Despotism of Law: Crime & Justice in Early Colonial India* (Delhi: Oxford University Press, 1998), 52–53, 60–70, 294–96, 300.

28. See, J. N. D. Anderson, *Islamic Law in the Modern World* (New York: New York University Press, 1959); J. N. D. Anderson, *Law Reform in the Muslim World* (London: Athlone, 1976); Wael Hallaq, *A History of Islamic Legal Theories*, 207–11. On the adoption of secularized law and the emergence of Western legal professionals in Egypt, see Farhat J. Ziadeh, *Lawyers, The Rule of Law, and Liberalism in Modern Egypt* (Stanford, CA: Hoover Institution, 1968), 3–61.

29. Qur'an 5:48.

30. Ahmad bin 'Ali bin Hajar al-'Asqalani, *Fath al-Bari bi-Sharh Sahih al-Bukhari* (Beirut: Dar al-Fikr, 1963), 14:308; Muhammad bin 'Ali al-Shawkani, *Nayl al-Awtar min Ahadith Sayyid al-Ahyar: Sharh Muntaqa al-Akhbar* (Beirut: Dar al-Kutub al-'Ilmiyya, 1985), 7:168. On the legal discourse on the presumption of innocence, see 'Ali Ahmad al-Nadhwi, *Al-Qawa'id al-Fiqhiyya*, 3rd ed. (Damascus: Dar al-Qalam, 1994), 400–401.

31. Qur'an 5:32.

32. Qur'an 2:105; 3:74; 35:2; 38:9; 39:38; 40:7; 43:32.

33. Qur'an 5:6; 7:2; 22:78; 33:38.

8. WHAT *REALLY* WENT WRONG

1. For several studies on Islamic ethical philosophy, see Amyn B. Sajoo, *Muslim Ethics: Emerging Vistas* (London: Tauris, 2004); Majid Fakhry, *Ethical Theories in Islam* (Leiden: Brill, 1991); Ayman Shihadeh, *The Teleological Ethics of Fakhr al-Din al-Razi* (Leiden: Brill, 2006); George H. Hourani, *Reason and Tradition in Islamic Ethics* (Cambridge: Cambridge University Press, 1985).

2. Khaled Abou El Fadl, "Islam and the Theology of Power Islam," *Middle East Report* 221 (Winter 2001): 28–33.

3. On the hegemony of the United States and the West and Muslim reaction, see Simon W. Murden, *Islam, the Middle East and the New Global Hegemony* (Boulder, CO: Lynne Rienner, 2002), esp. 43–128. Also see Gilbert Achcar, *The Clash of Barbarisms: Sept. 11 and the Making of the New World Disorders* (New York: Monthly Review, 2003), 73–81.

4. For a study on Muslims, the West, and the prevalence of siege mentalities, see Graham E. Fuller and Ian O. Lesser, *A Sense of Siege: The Geopolitics of Islam and the West* (Boulder, CO: Westview, 1995).

5. See Human Rights Watch, *"As If I Am Not Human": Abuses against Asian Domestic Workers in Saudi Arabia* (New York: Human Rights Watch, 2008), available at http://www. hrw.org/sites/default/files/reports/saudiarabia0708_1.pdf; Human Rights Watch, *Slow Reform: Protection of Migrant Domestic Workers in Asia and the Middle East* (New York: Human Rights Watch, 2010), available at http://www.hrw.org/sites/default/files/reports/ wrd0410webwcover_0.pdf; Human Rights Watch, "Bad Dreams: Exploitation and Abuse of Migrant Workers in Saudi Arabia," *Human Rights Watch* 16, no. 5 (July 2004), http://www. hrw.org/sites/default/files/reports/saudi0704.pdf.

6. For an example of politicized *fatawa* on child marriages in Saudi Arabia, see John R. Badley, *Behind the Veil of Vice: The Business and Culture of Sex in the Middle East* (New York: Palgrave Macmillan, 2010), 144.

7. For a systematic analysis of this issue, see Khaled Abou El Fadl, *Speaking in God's Name: Islamic Law, Authority and Women* (Oxford: OneWorld, 2003), 170–249.

8. See Muhammad bin 'Abd al-Wahhab, *Mu'allafat al-Shaykh al-Imam Muhammad bin 'Abd al-Wahhab: Qism al-Hadith* (Riyadh: Jami'at al-Imam Muhammad bin Sa'ud al-Islamiyya, n.d.), pt. 4, 141–51.

9. See Susan A. Spectorsky, *Women in Classical Islamic Law: A Survey of the Sources* (Leiden: Brill, 2010); Asma Sayeed, *Women and the Transmission of Religious Knowledge in Islam* (Cambridge: Cambridge University Press, 2013).

10. For a critical and similarly grim assessment by a Muslim on the state of intellectual thought in the Islamic world, see Tariq Ramadan, *Islam, the West and the Challenges of Modernity*, trans. Said Amghar (Markefield, UK: Islamic Foundation, 2001), 286–90. For an insightful analysis on the role of apologetics in modern Islam, see Wilfred Cantwell Smith, *Islam in Modern History* (Princeton, NJ: Princeton University Press, 1977). Also see Ali Allawi, *Crisis of the Islamic Civilization* (New Haven, CT: Yale University Press, 2009).

11. Roxanne L. Euben, *Enemy in the Mirror: Islamic Fundamentalism and the Limits of Modern Rationalism* (Princeton, NJ: Princeton University Press, 1999), argues somewhat per-

suasively that Islamic fundamentalism is a form of critique or protest against rationalist modernism.

12. Afaf Lutfi al-Sayyid Marsot, "The Ulama of Cairo in the Eighteenth and Nineteenth Century," in *Scholars, Saints, and Sufis*, ed. Nikki Keddi (Berkeley: University of California Press, 1972), 149–65, 162–63.

13. For an example of this in Muhammad 'Ali's (r. 1805–1848) Egypt, see Afaf Lutfi al-Sayyid Marsot, *Women and Men in Late Eighteenth-Century Egypt* (Austin: University of Texas Press, 1995), 136, 141–42.

14. See Yusuf bin Ahmad al-Dijawi, "Al-hukm 'ala al-muslimin bi'l kufr," *Nur al-Islam* (a.k.a. *Majallat al-Azhar; Azhar University Journal*) 1, no. 4 (1933): 173–74. On the limited intellectual abilities of Ibn 'Abd al-Wahhab, see Aziz al-Azmeh, *Muhammad bin 'Abd al-Wahhab* (Beirut: Riad El Rayyes, 2000).

15. See Arnold Toynbee, *Civilization on Trial* (Oxford: Oxford University Press, 1948), 184–212; Arnold Toynbee, *The World and the West* (Oxford: Oxford University Press, 1953), 18–33.

16. Qur'an 12:18; 12:83; 15:85; 33:28; 33:49; 70:5; 73:10.

17. Khaled Abou El Fadl, *The Great Theft: Wrestling Islam from the Extremists* (New York: HarperOne, 2005); for the Arabic translation, see Abou El Fadl, *Al-Sirqah al-Kubra*, trans. Ali Ahmed Abdullah (Cairo: Maktabat Madbouli, 2008).

18. The puritan obsession with excluding women from public life was already the subject of my book *Speaking in God's Name*. But as further evidence of this pervasive phenomenon, one should read the three-volume work written on the merits and importance of secluding women in Islam; see Muhammad Ahmad al-Muqaddim, *'Awdat al-Hijab* (Riyadh: Dar Tayba, 1996).

19. See Salih Al-Fawzaan, *Rulings Pertaining to Muslim Women*, trans. Burhan Loqueman (Houston: Dar-us-Salam, 2002).

20. Al-Sadiq 'Abd al-Rahman al-Ghiryani, *Fatawa min Hayat al-Mar'a al-Muslima* (Beirut: Dar al-Rayyan, 2001), 47, 59–60, 62, 63, 77, 82–83, 86–87, 111–12, 116–17, 122, 130, 137–38, 146, 149.

21. On the importance of custom in Islamic law, see Ayman Shabana, *Custom in Islamic Law and Legal Theory: The Development of the Concepts of 'Urf and 'Adah in the Islamic Legal Tradition* (New York: Palgrave Macmillan, 2012).

22. For this story, see "Imam Rapped for Wife-Beating Book," *BBC News*, January 14, 2004, http://news.bbc.co.uk/2/hi/europe/3396597.stm.

23. Khaled Abou El Fadl, *The Search for Beauty in Islam: A Conference of the Books* (Lanham, MD: University Press of America, 2001), 107–13, 114–22.

24. See Abdul Karim Zaydan, *Mufassal fi Ahkam al-Mar'a wa Bayt al-Muslim* (Beirut: Ressalah, 1994), 4:173–76; Shaykh Mustafa Adawi, *Jami' Ahkam al-Nisa'* (Cairo: Ibn Affan and Ibn Qayyim, 1999), 3:417–20; Muhammad Bultaji, *Fi Ahkam al-Usra: Dirasa Muqarana: al-Zawaj wa al-Furqa* (Cairo: Dar al-Taqwa, 2001), 337–43; Muhammad 'Ali Mahjub, *al-Usra wa Ahkamha fi al-Shari'a al-Islamiyya* (Shams: College of Law, 1973), 302–8; Muhammad Sidiq Hasan Khan, *Husn al-Uswa bi-ma Thabuta min Allah wa-Rasulihi fi al-Niswa* (Beirut: Mu'assasat al-Risala, 1976), 161–67; Abu Bakr al-Jaza'iri, *Kitab al-Mar'a al-Muslima* (Beirut: Dar al-Kutub al-'Ilmiyya, 1987), 108; Abdul-Aziz al-Musnad, ed., Jamal al-Din Zarabozo, trans., *Islamic Fatawa Regarding Women* (Riyadh: Darussalam, 1996); Qamaruddin Khan, *Status of Women in Islam* (Lahore: Islamic Book Foundation, 1988).

25. Laleh Bakhtiar, trans., *The Sublime Qur'an* (Chicago: Islamicworld.com; distributed by Kazi Publications, 2007), 94. Qur'an 4:34 in Bakhtiar's translation reads: "So the ones (f) who are in accord with morality *are* the ones (f) who are morally obligated, the ones (f) who guard the unseen of what God has kept safe. But those (f) whose resistance you fear, then admonish them (f) and abandon them (f) in their sleeping place then go away from them (f)."

26. On the issue of the Qur'an and wife beating, see Abou El Fadl, *The Search for Beauty in Islam*, 167–89.

27. Examples of these types of works include: Mona El-Tahawy, "Why Do They Hate Us?" *Foreign Policy* (May/June 2012), http://www.foreignpolicy.com/articles/2012/04/23/why_do_they_hate_us; Bernard Lewis, "The Roots of Muslim Rage," *The Atlantic* (September 1990), http://www.theatlantic.com/magazine/archive/1990/09/the-roots-of-muslim-rage/304643/; Robin Wright, *Sacred Rage: The Wrath of Militant Islam* (New York: Touchstone, 1985); Ayaan Hirsi Ali, "Muslim Rage and the Last Gasp of Islamic Hate," *Newsweek Magazine* (September 2012), http://www.thedailybeast.com/newsweek/2012/09/16/ayaan-hirsi-ali-on-the-islamists-final-stand.htm.

28. Kamal al-Din Muhammad bin 'Abd al-Wahid al-Siwasi ibn al-Humam, *Sharh Fath al-Qadir*, ed. 'Abd al-Razzaq Ghalib al-Mahdi (Beirut: Dar al-Kutub al-'Ilmiyya, 1995), 6:97.

29. See Abou El Fadl, *Speaking in God's Name*, 210–64, 272–98.

30. 'Ali 'Abd Allah al-Qusaymi, *Al-Thawra al-Wahhabiyya* (Cairo: al-Matba'a al-Rahmaniyya, 1936), 131. It is worthy to note that the author of this passionate defense of Wahhabism, al-Qusaymi, later on in life not only lost faith in Wahhabism but became an outright atheist. See Jurgen Wasella, *'Abd Allah al-Qusaymi: al-Tamarrud 'ala al-Salafiyya*, trans. Mahmoud

Kabibu (Beirut: Jadawel, 2011). For a response to al-Qusaymi's attack on Islam, see Muhammad 'Abd al-Razzaq Hamza, *Al-Shawahid wa al-Nusus min Kitab al-Aghlal 'ala ma fihi min Zaygh wa Kufr wa Dalal bi-A'qil* (Cairo: n.p., 1378/1958).

31. On the inherent conservatism of the Wahhabi movement and its rejection of all things based on reason, philosophy, and all foreign ideas, see Nabil Muhammad Rashwan, *Al-Islam al-Sa'udi: Dur al-Sa'udiyyin fi Ifsad Din al-Muslimin* (Cairo: Madbouli al-Saghir, 1994), 24–27.

32. On the *Mihna*, see Walter M. Patton, *Ahmed Ibn Hanbal and the Mihna: A Biography of the Imam Including an Account of the Mohammedan Inquisition Called the Mihna* (Leiden: Brill, 1897); Muhammad Qasim Zaman, *Religion and Politics under the Early Abbasids: The Emergence of the Proto-Sunni Elite* (Leiden: Brill, 1997); Patricia Crone and Martin Hinds, *God's Caliph: Religious Authority in the First Centuries of Islam* (Cambridge: Cambridge University Press, 1986), 92–97; Michael Cooperson, *Classical Arabic Biography: The Heirs of the Prophet in the Age of al-Ma'mun* (Cambridge: Cambridge Univeristy Press, 2000), 33–40, 107–53; John Nawas, "A Reexamination of Three Current Explanations for al-Ma'mun's Introduction of the Mihna," *International Journal of Middle East Studies* 26 (1994): 615–29.

33. For the classical Orientalist narrative on al-Ghazali supposedly causing the decline of philosophy in Islam, see Solomon Munk, *Melanges de la Philosophie Juive et Arabe* (Paris: Alophe Franck, 1859), 382; Ernest Renan, *Averroes et L'averroisme: Essai Historique* (Paris: Librairie Auguste Durand, 1852), 22–24, 133–36; Ignaz Goldziher, "Die und die Judische Philosophie des Mittelalters," in *Allgemeine Geschichte der Philosophie*, 2nd ed., ed. Wilhelm Wundt (Berlin: B. G. Teubner, 1913), 301–37; Montgomery Watt, *Islamic Philosophy and Theology* (Edinburgh: Edinburgh University Press, 1985), esp. 89–92. For a critique of this Orientalist narrative, see George Saliba, *Islamic Science and the Making of the European Renaissance* (Cambridge, MA: MIT Press, 2007); Dimitri Gutas, "The Study of Arabic Philosophy in the Twentieth Century: An Essay on the Historiography of Arabic Philosophy," *British Journal of Middle Eastern Studies* 29, no. 1 (May 2002): 5–25.

34. One of the best examples of this were the papers presented at the Ash'ari conference held at al-Azhar University May 8–11, 2010. A large number of prominent scholars presented, and without exception nearly all scholars tried to force Ash'ari theology to be identical with Ahl al-Hadith. Some of these papers included: Salman Tahir al-Husayni al-Nadwa, "Al-Imam Abu al-Hassan al-Ash'ari: Ra'id al-Minhaj al-Wasat fi al-Madhahib al-Kalamiyya"; Muhammad al-Tahir al-Misawi, "Al-Imam Abu al-Hassan al-Ash'ari Imam Ahl al-Sunna wa al-Jama'a: nahwa Wasatiyya Islamiyya Tawajaha al-Ghulu wa al-Tatarruf"; Sharif Hatim bin 'Arif al-Awni, "Al-Yaqini wa al-Thani min al-Akhbar, Sijal bayn al-Imam Abu al-Hassan al-Ash'ari wa al-Muhadithin."

35. Muhammad Hasanayn Makhluf, *Bulugh al-Suwul fi madkhl 'Ilm al-Usul* (Cairo: Mustafa al-Babi al-Halabi, 1966), 164–65.

36. As early as 1808, Louis Olivier de Corancez commented on the influence of the Wahhabis due to their control of Mecca and Medina. He attested that pilgrims from Damascus made sure that they complied with all Wahhabi instructions just so that they would not be molested or harassed by Wahhabis, and because of the politics of *hajj*, this would give the Wahhabi creed incredible influence in the Muslim world. He further comments that if the Wahhabis managed to make Syria and Egypt subject to their creed, it was inevitable that Wahhabism would spread all over the Muslim world; see Louis Olivier de Corancez, *Al-Wahhabiyun: Tarikh ma Ahmalihu al-Tarikh* (*The Wahhabis: A History of What History Ignored*) (Beirut: Riad El Rayyes, 2003), 177, 193–94. Also see 'Abd Allah bin Hasan bin Fadl al-Sharif al-Husayni, *Sudq al-Khabr fi Khawarij al-Qarn al-Thani 'Ashr* (Paris: Byblion, 2008), 159; Muhammad Kamil Dahir, *Al-Da'wa al-Wahhabiyya wa Atharuha fi al-Fikr al-Islami al-Hadith* (Beirut: Dar al-Islam, 1993), 199–200.

37. Ahmad Amin, *Fajr al-Islam: Yabhathu 'an al-Haya al-'Aqliyya fi Sadr al-Islam ila Akhir al-Dawla al-Ummawiyya* (Tunis: Dar al-Ma'arif, 2005), 2:197–203; A'isha 'Abd al-Rahman, *Tarajum Nisa' Bayt al-Nubuwa* (Cairo: Dar al-Kitab, 2003), 773–828.

38. Ibn 'Afaliq (d. 1163/1750), a Hanbali jurist, severely criticized the Wahhabis for refusing to recognize the differences of juristic opinion. He testified that Ibn 'Abd al-Wahhab was arrogant, convinced of his own righteousness, and dismissive toward any opinion that disagreed with his; see Ibn 'Afaliq, "Risala Ibn 'Afaliq al-Mashkuk fiha (manuscript no. 2157)," in *Al-Radd 'ala al-Wahhabiyya: Nusus al-Sharq al-Islami*, ed. Hamadi al-Radisi and Asma' Nawira (Beirut: Dar al-Tali'a, 2012), 85–107. Ibn 'Abd al-Wahhab was exiled from the Najd in 1744. George Rentz, "The Wahhabis," in *Religion in the Middle East: Three Religions in Concord and Conflict*, ed. A. J. Arberry (Cambridge: Cambridge University Press, 1969), 2:272.

39. 'Abd al-Rahman bin 'Abd al-Wahhab, "Bayan al-Mahajja: al-Risala al-Thalitha 'Ashra," in *Majmu'at al-Tawhid*, collected by Hamad bin 'Atiq al-Najdi (Damascus: al-Maktab al-Islami, 1962), 494–95. For a Wahabi defense of the idea that Wahhabism was necessary because Muslims had ceased to be true Muslims, see Sulayman bin Sahman, *Kitab al-Daya' al-*

Sharq fi Radd Shibhat al-Maziq al-Mariq, 2nd ed. (Riyadh: Ri'asa Idara al-Buhuth al-Isla-miyya wa al-Ifta', 1954), 8–9.

40. For an example of a list containing acts the commission of which would make a Muslim an infidel, see 'Abd al-Wahhab, "Bayan al-Najah wa al-Fakak min Muwalat al-Murtaddin wa Ahl al-Shirk: al-Risala al-Thaniya 'Ashra," in *Majmu'at al-Tawhid*, 413–16.

41. Muhammad bin 'Abd al-Wahhab, "Kashf al-Shubuhat: al-Risalah al-Thalitha," in *Majmu'at al-Tawhid*, 106; 'Abd al-Rahman bin Muhammad bin 'Abd al-Wahhab, "Bayan al-Mahajja fi al-Radd 'ala al-Lujja: al-Risala al-Thalitha 'Ashra," in *Majmu'at al-Tawhid*, 459, 534.

42. See Muhammad bin 'Abd al-Wahhab, *Mu'allafat al-Shaykh al-Imam Muhammad bin 'Abd al-Wahhab: Qism al-'Aqidah wa al-Adab al-Islamiyya*, pt. 1, 13–14. It is reported that around 1726, Ibn 'Abd al-Wahhab's teachings caused a considerable controversy in Basra and that Ibn 'Abd al-Wahhab would mention hadith that no one had heard of and interpret the Qur'an in ways that no one had known before. See Hussayn Khulf al-Shaikh Khaza'i, *Hayya al-Shaykh Muhammad bin 'Abd al-Wahhab* (Beirut: Dar al-Kutub, n.d.), 61–62. Georg August Wallin, an Orientalist scholar and traveller in the mid-1800s who took the name 'Abd al-Wali, commented on the books of Ibn 'Abd al-Wahhab and noted that his works contained nothing new but that they were merely books that primarily were concerned with Qur'anic verses and traditions of the Prophet. See Georg August Wallin, *Suwar min Shamali Jazira al-'Arab fi Muntasif al-Qarn al-Tasi' 'ashr*, trans. Samir Salim Shibli and Yusuf Ibrahim Yirankib (Beirut: Awraq Lubnaniyya, 1971), 108.

43. See Abu 'Ubayda Mashhur bin Hasan al-Salman, *Kutub Hadhdhar minha al-'Ulama'* (Riyadh: Dar Ibn Hazm, 1995). The author also includes all the books that criticized the Wahhabis or the founder of their movement; see 1:250–87. For a work by a Wahhabi author attacking all rationalist orientations within Islam, see al-Amin al-Sadiq al-Amin, *Mawqif al-Madrasa al-'Aqliyya min al-Sunna al-Nabawiyya* (Riyadh: Maktabat al-Rushd, 1998), vols. 1–2.

44. On the destruction of historical sites by the Wahhabis, see Yusuf al-Hajiri, *Al-Baqi': Qissat Tadmir Al Sa'ud lil-Athar al-Islamiyya fi al-Hijaz* (Beirut: Mu'assasat al-Baqi' li-Ihya al-Turath, 1990); 'Umr 'Abd Allah Kamil, *La Dhara'i: Li-Hadam Athar al-Nubuwa* (al-Qahira: Dar al-Mustafa, 2003); 'Amr 'Abd al-Qadir al-Maghribi, *Al-Athar al-Nabawiyya: allati Hadamaha al-Hukm al-Sa'udi fi al-Madina al-Munawara* (n.p.,n.d.); Sami Qasim Amin al-Miliji, *Al-Wahhabiyya* (Cairo: Maktabat Madbouli, 2006), 44–48.

45. On the incident, see Muhammad 'Awad al-Khatib, *Safahat min Tarikh al-Jazira al-'Arabiyya al-Hadith* (Cairo: Dar al-Mi'raj, 1995), 189; 'Awad al-Khatib, *Al-Wahhabiyya: Fikran wa Mumarsa* (Beirut: Dar al-Mi'raj, 2000), 189. For a diary of a Russian soldier who travelled through Arabia in 1898–1899 and reported on the libraries in Mecca before the burning of them by the Wahhabis, see Efim Rezvan, *Al-Hajj Qabl mi'a sina: al-Sira' al-Dawli 'ala al-Jazira al-'Arabiyya wa al-'Alam al-Islami* (Beirut: Dar al-Taqrib, 1999), 174. On the Wahhabis burning a large number of books of fiqh, *tafsir*, and hadith commentaries that they deemed to be unorthodox, see Sulayman bin Sahman, *Kitab al-Daya' al-Sharq fi Radd Shibhat al-Maziq al-Mariq*, 28.

46. Muhammad bin 'Abd al-Wahhab, "Al-Risala al-Ula," in *Majmu'at al-Tawhid*, 37–39, 50–52; Ibn 'Abd al-Wahhab, "Kashf al-Shubuhat: al-Risala al-Thalitha," in *Majmu'at al-Tawhid*, 100–3, 114; Ibn 'Abd al-Wahhab, "Asbab Najat al-Sul min al-Sayf al-Maslul: al-Risala Thamina," in *Majmu'at al-Tawhid* , 205; Ibn 'Abd al-Wahhab, "Bayan al-Najah wa al-Fakak: al-Risala al-Thaniya 'Ashra," in *Majmu'at al-Tawhid*, 401.

47. Ahmad bin Zayni Dahlan, *al-Dawla al-'Uthmaniyya min al-Kitab al-Futuhat al-Isla-miyya ba'd mudi al-Futuhat al-Nabawiya* (Istanbul: Hakikat Kitabevi, 1986), 2:230–33; Hirsi Muhammad Hiloleh, *Al-Salafiyya al-Wahhabiyya bayn Mu'ayyidiha wa Muntaqidiha* (Malaysia: Borneo Printers and Trading, 1996), 140–49; Mahmud Shukri al-Alusi, *Tarikh Najd* (Cairo: Maktabat Madbouli, n.d.), 50–53; Husayn Ibn Ghannam, *Tarikh Najd al-Musamma Rawdat al-Afkar al-Afham* (Cairo: n.p., 1949), vol. 1.

48. See Abu Uthman Amr b. Bahr al-Jahiz, *The Epistle on Singing Girls*, trans. A. F. L. Beeston (Warminster, Eng.: Aris and Phillips, 1980); Ibn Hazm, *The Ring of the Dove*, trans. A. J. Arberry (London: Luzac Oriental, 1994).

49. Taqi al-Din Abu al-'Abbas 'Abd al-Halim, "'Ubudiyya: al-Risala al-Rabi'a 'Ashra," in *Majmu'at al-Tawhid*, 569. Julius Euting, a nineteenth-century German traveller in Arabia, commented that the Wahhabis considered smiling or showing happiness at all as un-Islamic and also that they banned music. See Euting, *Rihla Dakhul al-Jazira al-'Arabiyya*, trans. Sa'id Fayis (Riyadh: Dara al-Malik 'Abd al-'Aziz, 1999), 31.

50. See 'Abd al-Rahman bin Muhammad bin 'Abd al-Wahhab, "Bayan al-Mahajja: al-Risala al-Thalitha 'Ashra," in *Majmu'at al-Tawhid*, 436–42, 465–67, 480–81.

51. Muhammad bin 'Abd al-Wahhab, "Awthaq al-'Ura: al-Risala al-Sadisa," in *Majmu'at al-Tawhid*, 171.

52. See Muhammad bin 'Abd al-Wahhab, "al-Risala al-Ula," in *Majmu'at al-Tawhid*, 30–31, 68; Ibn 'Abd al-Wahhab, "Bayan al-Najah wa al-Fakak: al-Risala al-Thaniya 'Ashra," in *Majmu'at al-Tawhid*, 394, 400, 421–23, 433.

53. J. J. Lorimar, *Tarikh al-Bilad al-Sa'udiyya fi Dalil al-Khalij*, trans. Muhammad bin Sulayman al-Khadiri (Riyadh: Maktabat al-Malik 'Abd al-'Aziz, 2001), 29. Louis Olivier de Corancez, *The History of the Wahhabis from Their Origin until the End of 1809*, trans. Eric Tabet (London: Garnet, 1995), 101–3; Corancez, *Al-Wahhabiyyun: Tarikh ma Ahmalihu al-Tarikh*, 66; John Lewis Burckhardt, *Notes on the Bedouins and Wahabys* (London: Elibron Classics, 2005), 1:104. Corancez noted that Ibn 'Abd al-Wahhab viewed himself as an instrument of God's wrath on Muslims who had become deviant and heretical in his eyes. See Corancez, *Al-Wahhabiyyun: Tarikh ma Ahmalihu al-Tarikh*, 19–20. Burckhardt wrote that the Wahhabis assumed all Turks to be apostates, even if they tried to convince them otherwise, and that while the Wahhabis were kind to Christians and Jews, they were brutal to Muslims, and he was unable to find one incident in which the Wahhabis showed mercy to a Muslim who was an Egyptian, Syrian, or Turk. John Lewis Burckhardt, *Mulahazat Haula al-Badu al-Wahhabiyyin*, trans. Muhammad al-Asyuti (Beirut: Dar Suyahan, 1995), 1:236–37. 'Awad al-Khatib noted that scholars of Wahhabism, as early as the 1800s, met and decided that the Ottomans were *kufar* and could be killed on sight, but the English were "People of the Book" and thus were protected; see 'Awad al-Khatib, *Safahat min Tarikh al-Jazira al-'Arabiyya al-Hadith*, 213.

54. See Sayyid Qutb, *Ma'alim fi al-Tariq* (Cairo: Dar al-Shuruq, 1982); for an English translation, see Qutb, *Milestones on the Road* (Plainfield, IL: American Trust Publications, 1991); Ahmad S. Mousalli, *Radical Islamic Fundamentalism: The Ideological and Political Discourse of Sayyid Qutb* (Syracuse, NY: Syracuse University Press, 1993).

55. Muhammad bin 'Abd al-Wahhab, "Bayan al-Najah wa al-Fakak: al-Risala al-Thaniya 'Ashra," in *Majmu'at al-Tawhid*, 358–68, 375, 412.

56. Alphonse de Lamartine (d. 1285/1869), a French writer and politician, noted that Britain subsidized and supported the Wahhabi rebellions as early as 1813. See Lamartine, *Narrative of the Residence of Fatalla Sayeghir: Among the Wandering Arabs of the Great Desert* (Philadelphia, PA: Carey, Lea & Blanchard, 1836), 130.

57. See Muhammad bin 'Abd al-Wahhab, "al-Risala al-Ula," in *Majmu'at al-Tawhid*, 36, 70–72; 'Abd al-Wahhab, "Kashf al-Shubuhat: al-Risala al-Thalitha," in *Majmu'at al-Tawhid*, 117–18; 'Abd al-Wahhab, "Bayan al-Najah wa al-Fakak: al-Risala al-Thaniya 'Ashra," in *Majmu'at al-Tawhid*, 403–9.

58. On the Abu Bakr precedent, see Khaled Abou El Fadl, *Rebellion and Violence in Islamic Law* (Cambridge: Cambridge University Press, 2000).

59. Muhammad bin 'Abd al-Wahhab, "Al-Risala al-Ula," in *Majmu'at al-Tawhid*, 34–35; 'Abd al-Wahhab, "Kashf al-Shubuhat: al-Risala al-Thalitha," in *Majmu'at al-Tawhid*, 104; also see 'Abd al-Wahhab, "Bayan al-Najah wa al-Fakak: al-Risala al-Thaniya 'Ashra," in *Majmu'at al-Tawhid*, 356–57.

60. Muhammad bin 'Abd al-Wahhab, "Al-Risala al-Thaniya," in *Majmu'at al-Tawhid*, 4–6; 'Abd al-Wahhab, "Asbab Najat al-Sul: al-Risala Thamina," in *Majmu'at al-Tawhid*, 208–12; 'Abd al-Wahhab, "Bayan al-Najah wa al-Fakak: al-Risala al-Thaniya 'Ashra," in *Majmu'at al-Tawhid*, 382–83; 'Abd al-Rahman bin 'Abd al-Wahhab, "Bayan al-Mahajja: al-Risala al-Thalitha 'Ashra," in *Majmu'at al-Tawhid*, 453.

61. See the treatise written by Muhammad bin 'Abd al-Wahhab's son, who was a devout follower of his father: 'Abd al-Rahman bin 'Abd al-Wahhab, "Bayan al-Mahajja: al-Risala al-Thalitha 'Ashra," in *Majmu'at al-Tawhid*, 466–93. Interestingly, in response to the controversial views of Ibn 'Abd al Wahhab and his son, some Najdi jurists attempted to argue that in reality the Wahhabis only considered the Shi'a and their sympathizers to be heretics but did not condemn orthodox Sunnis as apostates, see Sulayman bin Sahman bin Muslih bin Hamdan bin Misfir al Faza'i al-Khath'ami, *Kashf al-Awham wa al-Iltibas 'an tishbihi ba'd al-Aghbiya'* (unpublished manuscript at King Saud University), esp. 110.

62. For a treatise that notes the acrimony between 'Abd al-Wahhab and his father and brother and their hostility to 'Abd al-Wahhab's religious views, see Sabagha Allah Haidiri al-Baghdadi, "'Unwan al-Majd fi Bayan Ahwal Baghdad wa al-Basra wa Najd," in *al-Radd 'ala al-Wahhabiyya: Nusus al-Sharq al-Islami*, 157–66.

63. Sulayman bin 'Abd al-Wahhab, *Kitab al-Sawa'iq al-Ilahiyya* (Cairo: Maktabat al-Qahira, 2007), 60–61, 120. Ibn Humaydi reports the tragic stories of some jurists who were assassinated by the followers of Ibn 'Abd al-Wahhab; see Muhammad bin 'Abd Allah bin Humaydi al-Najdi, *Al-Suhub al-Wabila 'ala Dara'ih al-Hanabila* (Beirut: Maktabat al-Imam Ahmad, 1989), 276–80, 402, 405; Ali Bey Abbasi, *Travels of Ali Bey in Morocco, Tripoli, Cyprus, Egypt, Arabia, Syria, and Turkey between the Years of 1803 and 1807* (Reading, Eng.: Garnet, 1993), 2:129. Some critics of Ibn 'Abd al-Wahhab believed that he wished to declare himself a prophet and bring about a new faith; however, he was not able to do so, so instead he claimed himself to be a reformer. See Sulayman bin Sahman, *Kitab al-Daya' al-Sharq fi Radd Shibhat al-Maziq al-Mariq*, 26. Interestingly, the only other source which makes this claim is a diary of the British intelligence operative Oliver Hempher in which Hempher claims that Ibn 'Abd al-

Wahhab wanted to declare himself a prophet, but Hempher advised against this and instead told him to reform Islam. This was in order to subvert the power of the Ottomans. See M. Siddik Gumus, *Confessions of a British Spy and British Emnity against Islam* (Istanbul: Hakikatevi Publications, 2001).

64. Sulayman bin 'Abd al-Wahhab, *Al-Sawa'iq al-Ilahiyya*, 9, 34–35. On Muhammad bin 'Abd al-Wahhab's education, see Michael Cook, "On the Origins of Wahhabism," *Journal of the Royal Asiatic Society* 3, no. 2 (July 1992): 191–202. In a *risala* attributed to Muhammad bin 'Abd al-Wahhab, he recognized that there was tension between the living tradition of Muslims of his time and what he took to be the literal and clear meaning of textual sources. He argued that jurists who do not agree with him or his detractors who gave credence to the social customs of people were wrong, while he gave his fidelity to only the texts of the Qur'an and Sunna; see Husayn Ibn Ghannam, *Tarikh Najd al-Musamma Rawdat al-Afkar wa al-Afham*, 2:93–108. A treatise written by 'Abd Allah al-Baghdadi al-Suwaydi in 1798 asserted that the Wahhabis issued legal opinions without much regard to the juristic tradition of Islam and referred to hadith alone without considering the interpretive tradition. He identified the Wahhabis as the extremist movement of the Khawarij of early Islam; see al-Suwaidi, "Al-Mishkat al-Madiyy'a Radd 'ala al-Wahhabiyya," in *Al-Radd 'ala al-Wahhabiyya: Nusus al-Sharq al-Islami*, 21–83. In another contemporaneous treatise Ibn 'Afaliq accused Ibn 'Abd al-Wahhab of ignorance. He asserted that his intolerance was due to his lack of training in the Islamic tradition. He focused his criticism on the practice of *takfir* and the amount of insolence and lack of respect that the Wahhabis showed toward other Muslims as an unprecedented corruption of the faith; see Ibn 'Afaliq, "Risala Ibn 'Afaliq (manuscript no. 2158)," in *Al-Radd 'ala al-Wahhabiyya: Nusus al-Sharq al-Islami*, 109–33.

65. Muqbil bin 'Abd al-'Aziz al-Dhakir al-Najdi, "Al-'Uqud al-Dariyya fi Tarikh al-Bilad al-Najdiyya," in *Khizanat al-Tawarikh al-Najdiyya*, ed. 'Abd Allah ibn 'Abd al-Rahman ibn Salih al-Bassam (Beirut: n.p., 1999), 7:108. On the Wahhabi rejection of rationalism and the Islamic interpretive tradition, see Hassin bin 'Ali al-Saqqaf, *Al-Salafiyya al-Wahhabiyya: Afkarha al-Asasiyya wa Judhurha al-Tarikhiyya* (Beirut: Dar al-Mizan, 2005), 77–86; Sulayman bin Sahman, *Kitab al-Diya' al-Shariq fi Radd Shubahat al-Maziq al-Mariq*, 140. Al-Basri (d. 1250/1834) mentions that the Wahhabis were ignorant and intolerant and committed not only errors in interpreting the Qur'an and hadith but also grammatical and spelling errors. See 'Uthman bin Muhammad bin Ahmad bin Sind al-Basri, "Matla' al-Saud bi-Akhbar al-Wali Dawud," in *Khizanat al-Tawarikh al-Najdiyya*, 6:292–93.

66. There is a *risala* that Ibn 'Abd al-Wahhab reportedly authored in which he defended himself against the attacks by those who thought he was not a trained jurist. He acknowledged the accusation of his detractors who emphasized his lack of training and lack of qualifications for *ijtihad* and responds by diluting the requirements and qualifications for the practice; see Husayn Ibn Ghannam, *Tarikh Najd al-Musamma Rawdat al-Afkar wa al-Afham*, 2:9–25.

67. Ibn Humaydi, *al-Suhub al-Wabila*, 275.

68. Sulayman bin 'Abd al-Wahhab, *Al-Sawa'iq al-Ilahiyya*, 21, 25, 30–32, 38.

69. Sulayman bin 'Abd al-Wahhab, *Al-Sawa'iq al-Ilahiyya*, 16, 72. Ibn Humaydi, who was an admirer of Ibn Taymiyya as well, makes the same claim about Ibn 'Abd al-Wahhab; see Ibn Humaydi, *Al-Suhub al-Wabila*, 275.

70. For an account contemporaneous with the Wahhabi movement, which states that the most controversial aspect of Wahhabi theology is its practice of *takfir*, see al-Khath'ami, *Kashf al-Awham wa al-Iltibas 'an tishbihi ba'd al-Aghbiya'*. Also see Ahmad al-Katib, *Al-Fikr al-Siyasi al-Wahhabi* (Cairo: Maktabat Madbouli, 2008), 47–65; 'Awad al-Khatib, *Safahat min Tarikh al-Jazira al-'Arabiyya al-Hadith*, 130; Sami Qasim Amin al-Miliji, *Al-Wahhabiyya* (Cairo: Maktabat Madbouli, 2006), 26; al-Saqqaf, *Al-Salafiyya al-Wahhabiyya*, 71–76; al-Sayyid Muhammad al-'Assala (d. 1937), *Risala fi Radd Madhhab al-Wahhabiyya*, ed. al-Shaykh Nu'man al-Nassari (n.p., 1999), 110–14, 174; Mujah al-Ta'i, *Al-Wahhabiyyun: Khawarij am Sunna?* (Beirut: Dar al-Mizan, 2005), 171–74; Sulayman bin Sahman, *Kitab al-Diya' al-Shariq fi Radd Shubahat al-Maziq al-Mariq*, 27, 33–35; Malik bin Shaykh Dawud, *Al-Haqa'iq al-Islamiyya fi al-Radd 'ala al-Maza'm al-Wahhabiyya* (Istanbul: Hakikat Kitabevi, 1986), 6–14; al-Khath'ami, *Kashf al-Awham wa al-Iltibas 'an tishbihi ba'd al-Aghbiya'*. For a large collection of refutations and protestations against Wahhabism written in the nineteenth century by jurists in North Africa, see Hamadi al-Radisi and Asma' Nawira, eds., *Al-Radd al-Wahhabiyya fi al-Qarn al-Tasi' 'ashr* (Beirut: Dar al-Tali'a, 2008). For further evidence, see the manuscript written in 1887 by Dawud bin Sulayman al-Baghdadi al-Naqshabandi al-Khalidi titled "Ashadd al-Jihad fi Ibtal da'wa al-Ijtihad," in *al-Radd 'ala al-Wahhabiyya: Nusus al-Sharq al-Islami*, 167–71, which claims that the Wahhabis think they are the only ones who are qualified to use *ijtihad* and act as the only Muslims in history who have managed to understand the true Islam while everyone else is a heretic and that this is the basis for which they have waged jihad against fellow Muslims and made it legal.

71. In Arabic: "*Wa taj'alun mizan kufr al-nass mukhalafatakum wa mizan al-Islam muwafaqatakum.*" Sulayman bin 'Abd al-Wahhab, *Al-Sawa'iq al-Ilahiyya*, 54; also see 14, 42.

72. Hamadi al-Radisi and Asma' Nawira, eds., *Al-Radd 'ala al-Wahhabiyya: Nusus al-Sharq al-Islami*, 192.

73. Sulayman bin 'Abd al-Wahhab, *Al-Sawa'iq al-Ilahiyya*, 48–49.

74. Sulayman bin 'Abd al-Wahhab, *Al-Sawa'iq al-Ilahiyya*, 121–42.

75. Reportedly, a debate took place between 'Abd al-Wahhab and other authorities concerning his view that those who do not agree with him may be killed as infidels. The source notes that this was such a shocking view at the time and was considered *bida' min 'Abd al-Wahhab* (the innovation of 'Abd al-Wahhab); see Anonymous, "Luma' al-Shihab fi Sirat Muhammad bin 'Abd al-Wahhab," in Aziz al-Azmeh, *Muhammad bin 'Abd al-Wahhab*, 119.

76. Sulayman bin 'Abd al-Wahhab, *Al-Sawa'iq al-Ilahiyya*, 17–19, 62–64, 70–71, 74–75, 80–82, 92, 100–102, 110–12. For Rashid Rida's view on the merit of the first three centuries of Islam, see Muhammad Rashid Rida, *Majallat al-Manar* (Mansura, Egypt: Dar al-Wafa', 1327), v. 28:502–4. (Hereinafter Rida, *Al-Manar*).

77. For a source emphasizing that the Wahhabis theologically belonged to the culture of the underdeveloped region of Najd, see al-Sayyid Muhsin al-Amin, *Tajdid Kashf al-Irtiyab fi Atba' Muhammad bin 'Abd al-Wahhab* (Qum: Manshurat Maktabat al-Haramayn, 1952), 12–13; R. Bayly Winder, *Saudi Arabia in the Nineteenth Century* (New York: St. Martin's, 1965), 75–78; John Keane, *Six Months in the Hijaz: Journeys to Makkah and Madinah 1877–1878* (Manchester: Barzan, 2006), 184.

78. Ali Bey Abbasi (d. 1818) stated that if the Wahhabis "persist in maintaining the rigour prescribed by their reformer, it will be almost impossible for them to make the nations who have some principles of civilization adopt their doctrine. . . . Their history would in that case be insignificant to the rest of the world." See Abbasi, *Travels of Ali Bey*, 2:128. 'Abd al-Wahhab's teachings were highly controversial in his time, and many scholars objected to his teaching. 'Abd al-Wahhab bin Ahmad Barr kat al-Shaf'i al-Azhari al-Tandatawi, a Hijazi jurist, wrote a refutation of the Wahhabis in 1743 condemning them for their whimsical legal inductions in that they based their opinions on the Qur'an and Sunna while ignoring the interpretive tradition and juristic methodologies and also criticized them for their extremism and intolerant actions; see al-Tandatawi, "Kitab Rad'a al-Dilala wa Qam'a al-Jihala," in *Al-Radd 'ala al-Wahhabiyya: Nusus al-Sharq al-Islami*, 143–49. For a treatise that was written in 1817, which refers to the Wahhabis and 'Abd al-Wahhab as a *mu'tada* (heretical innovator) and to Wahhabism as *bida'*, see Anonymous, "Luma' al-Shihab fi Sirat Muhammad bin 'Abd al-Wahhab," in *Al-Radd 'ala al-Wahhabiyya: Nusus al-Sharq al-Islami*, 150–56. Further, see Muhammad Bashir al-Sahsawani, *Kitab Siyanat al-Insan 'an Waswasa al-Shaykh Dahlan* (Cairo: n.p., 1351/1932), 434–56; Ja'far al-Subhani, *Al-Wahhabiyya fi al-Mizan* (Qom, Iran: Mussasat al-Nashr al-Islami), 36–52, which notes that the theological and legal tendencies of Wahhabism are not representative of mainstream Islam. Also see Dawud bin al-Sayyid Sulayman (d. 1881), *Al-Mihna al-Wahhabiyya fi Radd al-Wahhabiyya* (Istanbul: Hakikat Kitabevi, 1986); Ahmad bin Zayni Dahlan, *Hadha Khulasat al-Kalam fi Bayan Umara' al-Haram* (Cairo: Maktabat al-Kuliyat al-Azhariyya, 1977), 228–29; Dahlan, *Al-Dawla al-'Uthmaniyya*, 2:229.

79. Ahmad Dallal has already established the relative marginality of Wahhabi extremist thought in the eighteenth and nineteenth centuries. Dallal has also shown that the thought of Salafi revivalists such as Muhammad al-Shawkani (d. 1250/1834) and al-Jalal al-San'ani (d. 1225/1810) were quite dissimilar to Wahhabi thinking and far more influential at that time. See Ahmad Dallal, "The Origins and Objectives of Islamic Revivalist Thought, 1750–1850," *Journal of the American Oriental Society* 113, no. 3 (1993): 341–59. John Lewis Burckhardt (d. 1817), a Swiss traveller and Orientalist scholar, noted that all the provinces of the Ottoman Empire agreed in condemning the Wahhabis and, in fact, compared the Wahhabis to the old Crusade invaders and called for the leaders to save them from the Wahhabis; see Burckhardt, *Mulahazat Haula al-Badu al-Wahhabiyyin*, 1:250.

80. For a contemporaneous account of Muhammad 'Ali's campaign by an Italian traveller and conscript who joined the campaign against the Wahhabis, see Giovanni Finati, *Narrative of the Life and Adventures of Giovanni Finati, Native of Ferrara; Who, under the Assumed Name of Mahomet, Made the Campaigns against the Wahabees for the Recovery of Mecca and Medina*, ed. William John Bankes (Murray, 1830), 1:240–96. On Muhammad 'Ali's liberation of the Hijaz and the reasons for Muhammad 'Ali's aid to the Hijazis, see 'Abd al-Rahim 'Abd al-Rahman 'Abd al-Rahim, *Min Watha'iq Tarikh Shibr al-Jazira al-'Arabiyya fi al-'Asr al-Hadith* (Doha, Qatar: Dar al-Mutanabi al-Nashr wa al-Tawazli', 1982), 34–36, 309–10. For a remarkable manuscript, written by Ahmad bin Al-Dayaf in 1814, which celebrated the overthrow of the Wahhabis in Mecca by Egyptian forces, see the letter from Ahmad bin al-Dayaf in *Ithaf Ahl al-Raman bi-Akhbar Muluk Tunis* (Tunis: Kitabat al-Dawla al-Shu'un al-Thaqafiyya, 1963), 2–16. This letter reportedly was sent to the Wahhabi governor of Mecca but was not responded to. The author ends his letter by thanking God for the fall of Wahhabism and the end of this fanatic plight in the Muslim world. This is an important manuscript documenting that as early as 1814 the Wahhabi movement was viewed as a theological outlier.

81. D. Van der Meulen, *The Wells of Ibn Sa'ud* (London: Kegan Paul International, 2000), 35–36.

82. For historical surveys on these and subsequent events, see Muhsin al-Amin, *Tajdid Kashf al-Irtiyab*, 17–21; Dahlan, *Al-Dawla al-'Uthmaniyya*, 2:234; Van der Meulen, *The Wells of Ibn Sa'ud*, 33–34; Geoff Simons, *Saudi Arabia: The Shape of Client Feudalism* (London: St. Martin's, 1998), 151–73; Rasul Muhammad Rasul, *Al-Wahhabiyyun wa al-'Iraq: 'Aqidat al-Shayukh wa Sayuf al-Muharibin* (Beirut: Riad El-Rayyes, 2005), 34–59; Lorimar, *Tarikh al-Bilad al-Sa'udiyya fi Dalil al-Khalij*, 52; Dhakir al-Najdi, "al-'Uqud al-Dariyya fi Tarikh al-Bilad al-Najdiyya," in *Khizanat al-Tawarikh al-Najdiyya*, 7:144–45. Ali Bey Abbasi describes the massacre of Karbala and states that the Wahhabis "put to the sword all the men and male children of every age. Whilst they executed this horrible butchery, a Wehhabite doctor cried from the top of a tower, "'Kill, strangle all the infidels who give companions to God.' Abdelaaziz seized upon the treasures of the temple, which he destroyed, and pillaged and burnt the city, which was converted into a desert." See Abbasi, *Travels of Ali Bey*, 2:134; Joseph Kostiner, *The Making of Saudi Arabia 1916–1936: From Chieftaincy to Monarchical State* (Oxford: Oxford University Press, 1993), 62–70, 100–117; Joseph A. Kechichian, *Succession in Saudi Arabia* (New York: Palgrave, 2001), 161–68; Richard Harlakenden Sanger, *The Arabian Peninsula* (Freeport, NY: Books for Libraries, 1954), 27–35. For a description of the Wahhabi massacres in Hadhramaut, Yemen, in 1809, see Sala'a al-Bakra, *Fi Fanawub al-Jazira al-'Arabiyya* (Cairo: Mustafa al-Babi al-Halabi, 1949), 140–41. For a description of the massacres in Hasa' in 1210/1795 and in the Hijaz in 1225/1810, see Hamad bin Muhammad bin Nasir bin La'bun (d. 1275/1858), "Tarikh Ibn La'bun," in *Khizanat al-Tawarikh al-Najdiyya*, 1:205, 236.

83. For a Western account noting that the Wahhabi movement was viewed as heretical by many of the *fuqaha'* in Mecca and that Muslims have an obligation to wage jihad against them, see Alois Musil, *Al Sa'ud: Dirasa fi Tarikh al-Dawla al-Sa'udiyya*, trans. Sayyid bin Fayyiz al-Sa'id (Riyadh: Dar al-'Arabiyya al-Musu'at, 2003), 67.

84. Muhsin al-Amin, *Tajdid Kashf al-Irtiyab*, 17–30; Sharif al-Husayni, *Sudq al-Khabr fi Khawarij al-Qarn al-Thani 'Ashr*, 129; 'Abd al-Wahhab bin Muhammad bin Hamidan bin Turki (d. mid-1200s/1800s), "Tarikh Najd," in *Khizanat al-Tawarikh al-Najdiyya*, 4:165.

85. Sharif al-Husayni, *Sudq al-Khabr fi Khawarij al-Qarn al-Thani 'Ashr*, 142–43; Lorimar, *Tarikh al-Bilad al-Sa'udiyya fi Dalil al-Khalij*, 65; Ibrahim bin Salih bin Ibrahim bin 'Aysa (d. 1343/1924), "Tarikh Ibn 'Aysa," in *Khizanat al-Tawarikh al-Najdiyya*, 2:89, 117; Muhammad bin 'Abd Allah bin Muhammad bin 'Amr al-Fakhiri, "Tarikh al-Fakhiri," in *Khizanat al-Tawarikh al-Najdiyya*, 3:116–19; Ibrahim bin Muhammad bin Salim bin Dwayan (d. 1353/1934), "Tarikh Ibn Dwayan," in *Khizanat al-Tawarikh al-Najdiyya*, 3:182–83; 'Abd Allah bin Muhammad bin 'Abd al-'Aziz bin Muhammad al-Bassam (d. 1346/1927), "Tarikh 'Abd Allah al-Muhammad al-Bassam," in *Khizanat al-Tawarikh al-Najdiyya*, 5:50; Dhakir al-Najdi, "Al-'Uqud al-Dariyya fi Tarikh al-Bilad al-Najdiyya," in *Khizanat al-Tawarikh al-Najdiyya*, 7:155–56; 'Abd Allah bin Muhammad Ghazi, "Izada al-Anam bi-Tarikh balad Allah al-Haram," in *Khizanat al-Tawarikh al-Najdiyya*, 10:329–31; C. Snouck Hugronje, *Safahat min Tarikh Makka al-Mukarrama*, trans. 'Ali 'Awda al-Shayukh (Riyadh: Darat al-Malik 'Abd al-'Aziz, 1999), 1:261, 269–70; Sulayman bin Sahman, *Kitab al-Diya' al-Shariq fi Radd Shubahat al-Maziq al-Mariq*, 41–42; Abbasi, *Travels of Ali Bey*, 2:136. On the invasion of Hijaz by the Wahhabis in the early nineteenth century, the siege of Medina, the massacres committed in Mecca, and the disruption of *hajj*, see Turki, "Tarikh Najd," in *Khizanat al-Tawarikh al-Najdiyya*, 4:170–74, 180.

86. When the Wahhabis conquered Mecca, they destroyed any building that was higher than the Ka'ba, and the Wahhabis destroyed and looted the tombs of the Prophet, his family, and companions. The irony is that the Ka'ba is probably the smallest building in all of Mecca today. See Sharif al-Husayni, *Sudq al-Khabr fi Khawarij al-Qarn al-Thani 'Ashr*, 130–31, 141.

87. Sharif al-Husayni, *Sudq al-Khabr fi Khawarij al-Qarn al-Thani 'Ashr*, 131–32; Muhsin al-Amin, *Tajdid Kashf al-Irtiyab*, 47–56; al-Shaykh Ja'far al-Sajistani, *Al-Wahabiyya fi al-Mizan* (Qum: Mu'assasat al-Nashr al-Islami, n.d.), 49; Muhammad al-'Assala, *Risala fi Radd Madhhab al-Wahhabiyya*, 135; Burckhardt, *Mulahazat Haula al-Badu al-Wahhabiyyin*, 1:247. Eldon Rutter, *The Holy Cities of Arabia* (London: Putnam, 1928), vi, reports on the 1925 Egyptian *fatwa* advising Muslims not to go to *hajj* that year because of the Wahhabi occupation of Mecca. Also see Khayr al-Din al-Zirikli, *Shibh al-Jazira fi 'Ahd al-Malik 'Abd al-'Aziz* (Beirut: Dar al-'Ilm lil-Malayin, 1985), 1:666–67; Dhakir al-Najdi, "Al-'Uqud al-Dariyya fi Tarikh al-Bilad al-Najdiyya," in *Khizanat al-Tawarikh al-Najdiyya*, 155–56.

88. Muhammad Amin Ibn 'Abidin, *Hashiyat Radd al-Muhtar* (Cairo: Mustafa al-Babi, 1966), 6:413; Ahmad al-Sawi, *Hashiyat al-'Allama al-Sawi 'ala Tafsir al-Jalalayn* (Beirut: Dar Ihya' al-Turath al-'Arabi, n.d.), 3:307–8. Also see Dallal, "The Origins and Objectives of Islamic Revivalist Thought, 1750–1850," 341–59. The same accusation of being the Khawarij of modern Islam is made in Sulayman bin 'Abd al-Wahhab, *Al-Sawa'iq al-Ilahiyya*, 10, 28, 50–51; Yusuf bin Ahmad al-Dijawi, "Tawhid al-Uluhiyya wa Tawhid al-Rububiyya," *Nur al-Islam* 1, no.4 (1933): 320, 329; Muhsin al-Amin, *Tajdid Kashf al-Irtiyab*, 112–17; Sharif al-Husayni, *Sudq al-Khabr fi Khawarij al-Qarn al-Thani 'Ashr*, 160–67; Sulayman bin Sahman, *Kitab al-Diya' al-Shariq fi Radd Shubahat al-Maziq al-Mariq*, 34. For the same arguments from a scholar from Mali, see Malik bin al-Shaykh Dawud, *Al-Haqa'iq al-Islamiyya fi al-Radd*

'ala Maza'im al-Wahhabiyya, 13–14, 42–45. For a response from a Tunisi offering many of the same criticisms, see Ibn Abi al-Dawaf, *Ithaf Ahl al-Zamam bi Akhbar Muluk Tunis wa Ahd al-Aman*, 12–15. Also see Mawlana Shah Fadl Rasul, *Sayf al-Jabar al-Maslul 'ala al-Ada' al-Abrar* (Istanbul: Yayinidir, n.d.). Muhammad Ashiq Rahman al-Qadari, *Suyuf Allah al-Ajilla* (Istanbul: Yayinidir, n.d.) reproduces a purported confrontation and debate that took place between the author and the chief Wahhabi judge in Arabia.

89. Sind al-Basri, "Matla' al-Sa'ud bi-Akhbar al-Wali Dawud," in *Khizanat al-Tawarikh al-Najdiyya*, 6:296; 'Umar Qadib Muhammad Mu'ayn, *Al-Bawaraq al-Muhamadiyya li-rajm al-Shayatin al-Najdiyya* (India: Matba' Sawil, 1249/1848). On the resistance of Arabian tribes and the unpopularity of the nascent Najdi movement in the 1870s, see 'Abd al-Fatah Hassan Abu 'Alayh, *Tarikh al-Dawla al-Sa'udiyya al-Thaniyya* (Riyadh: Dar al-Marikh, 1985), 225–27. Charles Didier, a nineteenth-century French Orientalist, thought that the Wahhabis were defeated due to their unpopularity in the Hijaz. See Charles Didier, *Rihla ila al-Hijaz fi al-Nusf al-Thani min al-Qarn al-Tasi' 'Ashr al-Miladi*, trans. Muhammad Khayr al-Biqa'i (Riyadh: Dar al-Faysal al-Thaqafiyya al-Sa'udiyya, 2002), 243, 260. On the origins of Al Saud as a little-known tribe prior, and for a sympathetic portrayal of Wahhabism from a marginal movement in Najd to a movement dominant throughout the Muslim world, see Qasim bin Khulfa al-Ruways, *Rushdi Malhas min Nablis ila al-Riyad* (Beirut: Jadawel, 2011), 375–80.

90. One of the most important original sources written by a member of the Ashraf of Mecca to be printed recently is Sharif al-Husayni, *Sudq al-Khabr fi Khawarij al-Qarn al-Thani 'Ashr*. The author methodically documents the numerous atrocities committed by the Wahhabis. But he emphasizes that the most compelling evidence of the Wahhabis' errors is that they espouse doctrines that are fundamentally at odds with the consensus of Muslims through the cumulative centuries. The author stresses that the Wahhabis are a marginal heretical group that has managed to survive because of the exceptional historical circumstances gripping the region. Two recently published compilations of historically significant texts written in the nineteenth century responding to Wahhabism are Hamadi al-Radisi and Asma' Nuwira, eds., *Al-Radd 'ala Al-Wahhabiyya: Nusus al-Sharq al-Islami* (Beirut: Dar al-Tali'a, 2012; and Hamadi al-Radisi and Asma' Nuwira, eds., *Al-Radd 'ala al-Wahhabiyya fi al-Qarn al-Tasi' 'Ashar: Nusus al-Gharb al-Islami* (Beirut: Dar al-Tali'a, 2008). Both these collections contain excerpts from what are now difficult-to-locate printed texts reacting to the Wahhabi threat.

91. Van der Meulen, *The Wells of Ibn Sa'ud*, 65–68; Kostiner, *The Making of Saudi Arabia*, 117–40.

92. For a source which documents the close ties between British intelligence and diplomats with Al Saud's family and other political leaders within the Wahhabi movement through the 1800s and 1900s, see 'Awad al-Khatib, *Al-Wahhabiyya: Fikran wa Mumarasa*, 211–36. Also see Zirikli, *Shibh al-Jazira fi 'Ahd al-Malik 'Abd al-'Aziz*, 1:302; Ahmad al-Katib, *Al-Fikr al-Siyasi al-Wahhabi*, 107–13; Winder, *Saudi Arabia in the Nineteenth Century*, 81–83, 257–59. For a treaty between the British and Wahhabi amir in 1866 in which the amir promises not to attack Muslim tribes with British protection, see C. U. Aitchison, *Treaties and Engagements Relating to Arabia and the Persian Gulf* (Trowbridge, UK: Redwood Burn, 1987), 206. On the relationship between the British and Ibn Saud in the early twentieth century, see Amin al-Rihani, *Tarikh Najd wa Mulhaqatih* (Beirut: Dar al-Rihani, 1972), 229–33; Muhsin al-Amin, *Tajdid Kashf al-Irtiyab*, 47–50; Lorimar, *Tarikh al-Bilad al-Sa'udiyya fi Dalil al-Khalij*, 530; Murshad bin 'Abd al-'Aziz bin Sulayman al-Najdi, *Al-Kawashif al-Jaliyya fi Kufr al-Dawla al-Sa'udiyya* (Riyadh: Dar al-Qusaym, 1994), 17–18. Reportedly, Ibn Saud would claim to his supporters that the gold he received from the British was not a salary but a *jizya* (poll tax) paid to him by the infidels. See Muhammad 'Ali Sa'id, *Britanya wa Ibn Sa'ud* (Tehran: Munazzamat al-I'lam al-Islami, 1987), 27–28; Nasir al-Falah, *Qiyam al-'Arsh al-Sa'udi: Dirasa Tarikhiyya li'l 'Ilaqat al-Sa'udiyya al-Britanniyya* (London: al-Safa li'l Nashr, n.d.), 88–91; al-Zirikli, *Shibh al-Jazira*, 1:287–88.

93. Simons, *Saudi Arabia*, 152–59; Kostiner, *The Making of Saudi Arabia*, 119; Van der Meulen, *The Wells of Ibn Sa'ud*, 62–113. For a list of the historical monuments and sites destroyed by the Wahhabis and Al Saud, see Sa'id al-Samarra'i, *Al Sa'ud wa Athar al-Islam* (London: Mu'assasat al-Fajr, 1993), 21–48.

94. See, on these events and others, Michael Cook, *Commanding Right and Forbidding Wrong in Islamic Thought* (New York: Cambridge University Press, 2000), 180–91; Van der Meulen, *The Wells of Ibn Sa'ud*, 104–13.

95. Munir al-'Ajlani, *Tarikh al-Bilad al-'Arabiyya al-Sa'udiyya: al-Juz' al-Thalath* (n.p., n.d.), 57; "Luma' al-Shihab fi Sirat Muhammad bin 'Abd al-Wahhab," in *Al-Radd al-Wahhabiyya: Nusus al-Sharq al-Islami*, 150–56; Abu 'Alayh, *Tarikh al-Dawla al-Sa'udiyya al-Thaniyya*, 268–69; Didier, *Rihla ila al-Hijaz fi al-Nusf al-Thani min al-Qarn al-Tasi' 'Ashr al-Miladi*, 247–48; Lamartine, *Narrative of the Residence of Fatalla Sayeghir*, 99; Abbasi, *Travels of Ali Bey*, 2:143; Winder, *Saudi Arabia in the Nineteenth Century*, 86–87; Ahmad al-Siba'i, *Tarikh Makka: Dirasat fi al-Siyasa wa al-'Ilm wa al-Ijtima' wa al-'Umran*, 4th ed. (Mecca: Dar Makka, 1979), 498. This source also notes that the Wahhabis were the first to

order that only a single short Hanbali text, *Kashf al-Shubuhat*, be taught as the authentic orthodox text at the main mosque in Mecca.

96. 'Ali al-Wardi, *Qisat al-Ashraf wa Ibn Sa'ud* (London: Ibn Warraq, 2010), 239 also mentions the diplomatic incident involving the arrest of two Indian Muslims who were arrested and imprisoned for visiting the now demolished gravesite of Khadija, the Prophet's wife.

97. Amin al-Rihani notes that the punishment given to this woman shocked Muslims; see *Tarikh Najd wa Mulhaqatih*, 39. Also see Dhakir al-Najdi, "Al-'Uqud al-Dariyya fi Tarikh al-Bilad al-Najdiyya," in *Khizanat al-Tawarikh al-Najdiyya*, 7:109. Muhsin al-Amin, who was the Shafi'i Mufti of Mecca, criticized the Wahhabis for their unjust punishments and misapplications of *hudud* to the crime of theft and also the misapplication of the punishment of stoning for a woman accused of adultery, which was unprecedented in the history of the Hijaz. He also provides a large account on the numerous ways in which the Wahhabis' application of *hudud* violated Islamic procedures and principles. See Muhsin al-Amin, *Tajdid Kashf al-Irtiyab*, 58–60, 90–111.

98. Ibn Ghannam, *Tarikh Najd al-Musamma Rawdat al-Afkar wa al-Afham*, 2:2 and al-Qusaymi, *Al-Thawra al-Wahhabiyya*, 13, 128 criticize Muslims who were horrified by this incident and other applications of the *hudud* punishments by the Wahhabis as having become corrupt and lax. Amin al-Rihani, a historian sympathetic to the Wahhabis, mentions the stoning incident without apologetics; see Rihani, *Tarikh Najd wa Mulhaqatih*, 39. Also see Nestor Sander, *Ibn Saud: King by Conquest* (Vista, CA: Selwa, 2009), 67; Charles Allen, *God's Terrorists: The Wahhabi Cult and Hidden Roots of Modern Jihad* (London: Little, Brown, 2006), 51; Alexei Vassiliev, *The History of Saudi Arabia* (London: Saqi, 1998), 81. Natana DeLong-Bas, a modern-day Wahhabi apologist, mentions this incident. By copying Ibn Bishr's account, titled *Unwan al-Majd fi Tarikh Najd*, 4 vols. (Riyadh: Matba'at Darat al-Malik 'Abd al-'Aziz, 1982), DeLong emphasizes Ibn 'Abd al-Wahhab's reluctance to apply the hudud and claims that Ibn 'Abd al-Wahhab tried in every way to give the woman an opportunity to recant her confession. See DeLong, *Wahhabi Islam: From Revival and Reform to Global Jihad* (Oxford: Oxford University Press, 2004), 128–30. There are numerous problems with this book, but chief among them is that DeLong attempts to cast Ibn 'Abd al-Wahhab in the role of a reformist, a progressive, and even a feminist thinker. She does so by relying on the Saudi collection of works titled *Mu'allafat al-Shaykh al-Imam Ibn 'Abd al-Wahhab*. This is a twelve-volume collection, which is loosely attributed to Ibn 'Abd al-Wahhab. Among this collection are two volumes of Hanbali *fiqh* (jurisprudence). The two volumes include several works that could have plausibly been authored by Ibn 'Abd al-Wahhab but also include a large number of jurisprudential chapters of Hanbali fiqh of unknown authorship and are not at all likely authored by Ibn 'Abd al-Wahhab. DeLong goes through various legal discourses on marriage and divorce in an effort to prove the progressive thinking of Ibn 'Abd al-Wahhab. However, there is a fundamental and irreconcilable problem with DeLong's approach. As the Saudi editors of this collection themselves point out, there is no evidence that Ibn 'Abd al-Wahhab is the actual author of this work of jurisprudence. Indeed, no biographical or historical source attributes this work of Hanbali jurisprudence to Ibn 'Abd al-Wahhab. Equally troubling, DeLong believes these to be progressive and unprecedented legal determinations. If DeLong had bothered to compare this text to other Hanbali works, she would have realized that these determinations are typical Hanbali positions on a number of juridical issues that predate Ibn 'Abd al-Wahhab by hundreds of years. It is far more likely that the book of jurisprudence that the author erroneously attributes to Muhammad bin 'Abd al-Wahhab was actually written by his father or his brother, Sulayman, who were both Hanbali jurists. All of the works that are decisively attributed to Ibn 'Abd al-Wahhab are short and rather superficial on theology or simply a collection of Qur'anic verses and hadith. The text that DeLong relies on could not have been authored by Muhammad bin 'Abd al-Wahhab, and even if it was, all the positions contained within this book are traditional Hanbali jurisprudential positions. For Wahhabi apologists who include a chapter of Muhammad bin 'Abd al-Wahhab's works and do not include the collection just discussed, see 'Abd Allah Salih al-'Uthmaymin, *Muhammad bin 'Abd al-Wahhab: The Man and His Works* (London: Tauris, 2009), 76–109; Ibn Ghannam, *Tarikh Najd al-Musamma Rawdat al-Afkar*, 1:85; Jalal Abualrun, *Muhammad Ibn Abdul Wahab*, ed. Alaa Mencke (Orlando, FL: Madinah, 2003), 470–72; 'Abd Allah bin Sa'd al-Ruwayshid, *Al-Imam al-Shaikh Muhammad bin 'Abd al-Wahhab fi al-Tarikh* (Cairo: Rabt al-Adib al-Harb, n.d.), 2:233–34.

99. See Rida, *Al-Manar*, v. 27:463–68. See "Luma' al-Shihab fi Sirat Muhammad bin 'Abd al-Wahhab," in Aziz Al-Azmeh, *Muhammad bin 'Abd al-Wahhab*, 119–20, where Wahhabism is described as a bid'a and fitna. On the *mahmal* incident and Egyptian reaction, see al-Zirikli, *Shibh al-Jazira*, 1:663–68; Harry St. J. B. Philby, *Sa'udi Arabia* (Beirut: Librairie du Liban, 1955), 299; Munir al-'Ajlani, *Tarikh al-Bilad al-'Arabiyya al-Sa'udiyya: al-Juz' al-Thalath*, 60.

100. For a scholar who argues that Wahhabism was considered an extremist, fanatic, and nonrepresentative Islam at its inception and only spread effectively in the Muslim world in the 1970s, see Shaykh Dawud, *Al-Haqa'iq al-Islamiyya*, 6–14.

101. On conquering the Hijaz in 1924, the Wahhabis executed a number of very prominent jurists, including former Mufti of Mecca Shaykh 'Abd Allah al-Zawawi. See Sharif al-Husayni, *Sudq al-Khabr fi Khawarij al-Qarn al-Thani 'Ashr*, 147; Ahmad al-Katib, *Al-Fikr al-Siyasi al-Wahhabi*, 65–104. John Philby, *Arabian Days* (London: R. Hale, 1948), 242 notes, "The one thing [Ibn Saud] wanted to avoid at all costs was a conflict with Britain and other European Powers." And because of his fear of upsetting Europeans, Ibn Saud's stringent command to his commanders in Mecca was not to commit atrocities in the holy city.

102. On the special status and particular identity of the Hijaz, see Mai Yamani, *Cradle of Islam: The Hijaz and the Quest for Identity in Saud Arabia* (London: Tauris, 2009), 1–19; 'Abd al-Rahim, *Min Watha'iq Tarikh Shibr al-Jazira al-'Arabiyya fi al-'Asr al-Hadith*, 22–26. On the historical tension between the Ashraf of the Hijaz and Najdis, see Asmar al-Saba'ai, *Tarikh al-Makka*, 624–26.

103. For a study on the role the British played in forming Saudi Arabia, see John C. Wilkinson, *Arabia's Frontiers: The Story of Britain's Boundary Drawing in the Desert* (London: Tauris, 1991).

104. Such promises were supposed to be captured by the Hussein-McMahon Correspondence of 1915–16.

105. Amin Sa'id, *Asrar al-Thawra al-'Arabiyya al-Kubra* (Beirut: Dar al-Katib al-'Arabi, n.d.), 358–59; Salah al-Din al-Mukhtar, *Tarikh al-Sa'udiyya* (Beirut: Dar Maktabat al-Hayya, n.d.), 2:268–69.

106. David Howarth, *The Desert King: The Life of Ibn Saud* (London: Collins, 1964), 141 correctly notes that the purported telegrams of support were reported by a journal loyal to Faisal, and so the accuracy of the claim of wide Muslim support for the Caliphate of Sharif Husayn cannot be verified. On the popularity of the Ashraf of Mecca, see Hugronje, *Safahat min Tarikh Makka al-Mukarrama*, 1:305.

107. In a rather telling correspondence between Winston Churchill and Chaim Weizman, Churchill said of Ibn Saud, "He would never give any undertaking or take any secret or open action with any Moslem or (other) foreign government which might damage British interests or affect his relations with his Majesty's Government." Churchill further stated that he "would like to see Ibn Saud made Lord of the Middle East—the boss of the bosses." See Jerald L. Thompson, *H. St. John Philby, Ibn Saud and Palestine* (Amsterdam: Fredonia, 2002), 84, 98. In another document, Churchill praised Ibn Saud for his numerous services to the British Empire. See Himada Imam, *Dur al-Usra al-Sa'udiyya fi Iqama al-Dawla al-Isra'iliyya* (Cairo: Maktab Madbouli al-Saghir, 1997), 124. Also, see 'Ali al-Wardi, *Qisat al-Ashraf wa Ibn Sa'ud*, 212–13. On the deterioration of British relations with Sharif Husayn and the turn toward Ibn Saud, see Wahim Talib Muhammad, *Tarikh al-Hijaz al-Siyasi 1916–1925* (Beirut: al-Dar al-'Arabiya lil-Mawsu'at, 2007), 190–94. On the conflict between King Saud and the Sharif of Mecca, see Randall Baker, *Mamluka al-Hijaz: al-Sira' bayn al-Sharif Husayn wa al-Sa'ud*, trans. Sadiq 'Abd Ali al-Rakabi (Amman, Jordan: al-Ahliyya, 2004). On Ibn Saud's loyalty to the British during the First World War and his refusal to help the Ottomans, see Musil, *Al-Sa'ud: Dirasa fi Tarikh al-Dawla al-Sa'udiyya*, 100–1.

108. 'Ali al-Wardi, *Qisat al-Ashraf wa Ibn Sa'ud*, 251.

109. During the First World War, Ibn Saud communicated to Britain that he was on the British side against the Ottomans and assured them of his support. See 'Awad al-Khatib, *Safahat min Tarikh al-Jazira al-'Arabiyya al-Hadith*, 229. Interestingly, Dawud bin Sulayman al-Iraqi (d. 1881) accused the Wahhabis of being supported and aided by British colonial forces in order to weaken the Ottoman Islamic Caliphate. From Baghdad he wrote a book in which he accused the Wahhabis of being instigated and supported by British colonialism. See Abdullah bin 'Abd al-Rahman Ababtin, *Ta'sis al-Taqdis* (Cairo: 1344/1925), 307–8.

110. Philby, *Arabian Days*, 157, 170.

111. For a discussion on the relationship between the Najd and Hijaz, the influence of the British on the Najd/Hijaz issue, and the decisive role of British politics, see Mustafa al-Nahhas Jabr, *Siyasat Baritaniya Tujaha Najd wa al-Hijaz: 1914–1919* (Cairo: Dar al-Hidaya, n.d.).

112. Rutter, *The Holy Cities of Arabia*, 79 claimed that "in their hearts all the town-dwellers and most of the Hijazi Bedouins hated the Wahhabis." Also see Philby, *Arabian Days*, 258.

113. Madawi Al-Rasheed, *A History of Saudi Arabia* (Cambridge: Cambridge University Press, 2010), 43.

114. 'Ali al-Wardi, *Qisat al Ashraf wa Ibn Sa'ud*, 196; Sharif al-Husayni, *Sudq al-Khabr fi Khawarij al-Qarn al-Thani 'Ashr*, 132–33; Philby, *Arabian Days*, 178; Turki, "*Tarikh Najd*," in *Khizanat al-Tawarikh al-Najdiyya*, 4:158–59. For example, when Saud entered a town called al-Husayn many of the inhabitants fled out of fear and became refugees in Basra. See Dwayan, "Tarikh Ibn Dwayan," in *Khizanat al-Tawarikh al-Najdiyya*, 3:183–84.

115. Eldon Rutter, a witness to the events, described the fear that gripped the Hijazis and their distress at the desecrations committed by the Wahhabis against many sacred objects and sites. Rutter reports that Wahhabi fanaticism at times reached the point of refusing to repeat the supplication uttered by Muslims on hearing the Prophet mentioned: "Peace and blessings be upon him." Rutter also recounts an incident in which a scuffle broke out because a Wahhabi

contended that his stick is more useful than the Prophet because the Prophet is dead and can profit him nothing. See Rutter, *The Holy Cities of Arabia*, 270–75. On the shocked response of the Muslim world to the Wahhabi takeover of the Hijaz, see Madiha Ahmad Darwish, *Tarikh al-Dawla al-Sa'udiyya: Hata al-Rabi' al-Awil min al-Qarn al-'Ishrin* (Cairo: Dar al-Shuruq, 2008), 123–33.

116. Philby, *Arabian Days*, 242; Ja'far al-Subhani, *Al-Wahhabiyya fi al-Mizan*, 32–34. For a letter from Ibn Saud to the Hijazis apologizing for the massacres committed by his forces in Taif and assuring the Hijazis that he had no plans to usurp the Hijaz, see Ghazi, *"Ifada al-Anam bi-Tarikh Balad Allah al-Haram,"* in *Khizanat al-Tawarikh al-Najdiyya*, 10:168–69.

117. Madawi Al-Rasheed, *A History of Saudi Arabia*, 39, 62; Sa'ud Ibn Hadhlul, *Tarikh Muluk Al Sa'ud* (Riyadh: Matabi al-Riyad, 1961), 174–75.

118. Ahmad al-Katib, *Al-Fikr al-Siyasi al-Wahhabi*, 141–42. On the formation of the National Hijaz Party (Hizb al-Watani al-Hijazi) and its efforts at maintaining Hijazi independence before and after the invasion of Ibn Saud, see Ahmad al-Siba'i, *Tarikh Makka*, 634–58. On several of the proclamations and publications of the National Hijaz Party in Jedda, see Ghazi, "Ifada al-Anam bi-Tarikh Balad Allah al-Haram," in *Khizanat al-Tawarikh al-Najdiyya*, 10:112–20. For a copy of a telegram from the government of Najd assuring the National Hijaz Party that Najd had no designs to control the Hijaz and that after the removal of the Sharif the fate of Hijaz would be placed in the hands of the Muslim world, see reproduced telegram in ibid., 10:121. For a copy of a telegram from the Association of the Khilafa in India seeking assurance from Ibn Saud that the Najdis would not occupy the Hijaz, see ibid., 10:121–22. For a telegram from the Indian delegation, which called for Hijazi self-determination and insisted that the fate of the Hijaz should not be left in the hands of Ibn Saud, see ibid., 10:228–29.

119. Yusuf Kamal Hanana, *Kitab al-Masala al-Hijaziyya* (Baghdad: Matba'at al-Iraq, 1926), 6, 19–20, 30–31, 63–72. Ibn Saud had opportunistically exploited the idea of the right of Hijaz to self-determination to help consolidate his power over the region. When Sharif Husayn offered a peace settlement on the condition that the Najdi forces withdraw from the Hijaz, Ibn Saud's response was that Sharif Hussayn's family had for long maintained a dynasty in the Hijaz and it was due time that the Hijaz determine its own sovereign fate. See Rihani, *Tarikh Najd wa Mulhaqatih*, 352.

120. On Britain's role in facilitating the Hijaz conference, see Mahmoud, *Tarikh al-Hijaz al-Siyasi*, 430–35; Madiha Ahmad Darwish, *Tarikh al-Dawla al-Sa'udiyya: Hata al-Rabi' al-Awil min al-Qarn al-'Ishrin*, 135–57. For a copy of the speech given by Ibn Saud at the Islamic conference, see Himada Imam, *Dur al-Usra al-Sa'udiyya fi Iqama al-Dawla al-Isra'iliyya*, 145–47. On the conference called by Ibn Saud after the fall of the Hijaz, including a record of the proceedings and demands made by various Muslim parties, see Ghazi, *"Ifada al-Anam bi-Tarikh Balad Allah al-Haram,"* in *Khizanat al-Tawarikh al-Najdiyya*, 10:264–96, 311–25.

121. For Ibn Saud's proclamation affirming the subjugation of the Hijaz under his authority, including specific legislation taking the Hijazi's ability to have any form of self-government, such as appointing only Wahhabi preachers in all Hijazi mosques and banning any schools of thought that were not consistent with Wahhabi ideology, see Ghazi, *"Ifada al-Anam bi-Tarikh Balad Allah al-Haram,"* in *Khizanat al-Tawarikh al-Najdiyya*, 10:338–39.

122. For a detailed report on the conference, see Hanana, *Kitab al-Masala al Hijaziyya*, 6–10; 18–31; John Philby, *Arabian Jubilee* (New York: John Day, 1953), 84–86; Philby, *Sa'udi Arabia*, 301–2; Sander, *Ibn Saud: King by Conquest*; Michael Darlow and Barbara Bray, *Ibn Saud: The Desert Warrior Who Created the Kingdom of Saudi Arabia* (New York: Skyhorse, 2010), 317; Kostiner, *The Making of Saudi Arabia 1916–1936*, 100–117.

123. For a copy of Shaykh al-Zawahri's speech, see Himada Imam, *Dur al-Usra al-Sa'udiyya fi Iqama al-Dawla al-Isra'iliyya*, 148–51. This work contains a series of valuable and important original documents in the appendix.

124. For the international declarations of Saudi sovereignty over the Hijaz, see Ghazi, "Ifada al-Anam bi-Tarikh Balad Allah al-Haram," in *Khizanat al-Tawarikh al-Najdiyya*, 10:299–302.

125. 'Ali al-Wardi, *Qisat al-Ashraf wa Ibn Sa'ud*, 321–27; al-Zirikli, *Shibh al-Jazira*, 1:660–63; Rihani, *Tarikh Najd wa Mulhaqatih*, 427–30; Hanana, *al-Masala al-Hijaziyya*, 10–27; Sander, *Ibn Saud: King by Conquest*, 72–74; Darlow and Bray, *Ibn Saud*, 317, 325. On Zawahri's speech at the conference, also see al-Samarra'i, *Al Sa'ud wa Athar al-Islam*, 67–77.

126. For a review of Wahhabi atrocities committed against Muslims in Arabia, see 'Awad al-Khatib, *Al-Wahhabiyya: Fikran wa Mumarasa*, 170–205. Also see al-Samarra'i, *Al Sa'ud wa Athar al-Islam*.

127. Aziz Al-Azmeh, *Muhammad bin 'Abd al-Wahhab*, 10–14.

128. Hanana, *Al-Masala al-Hijaziyya*, 8–9.

129. C. U. Aitchison, *Al-Sa'udia wa al-Imarat al-'Arabiyya wa Oman fi al-Watha'iq al-Britaniyya*, trans. 'Abd al-Wahhab al-Qasab (Beirut: al-Dar al-'Arabiyya al-Mawsu'at, 2007), 15.

130. I read in several sources that Ibn Saud considered the British to be his friends and refused to betray them or deal with their opponents even when it could have been to his advantage. Philby writes extensively about how loyal Ibn Saud is to the British and how he was

at times disappointed that the British government did not reciprocate! See Philby, *Sa'udi Arabia*, 335–38. Ibn Saud's ties with the British track back to the early 1900s. Various documents in the Ottoman and British archives indicate that the Ottomans were aware of Ibn Saud's connections with the British as early as 1907. Amin al-Rihani (d. 1940) notes that Ibn Saud felt isolated in the Muslim world and that his only friends were the British. See Amin al-Rihani, *Muluk al-'Arab: Rihlat fi al-Bilad al-'Arabiyya Muzayyana bi-Rusum wa Khara'it wa Fihrist A'lam* (Beirut: Dar al-Jayl, 1987), 810. A memorandum compiled by G. Laithwaite of the India Office on the relations between Ibn Saud and the Wahhabis with the British government states that the British government promised Ibn Saud that in return for his cooperation and "eviction of the Turks from Basra" the British would recognize him as an independent ruler of Najd and Hass, and that Ibn Saud assured the British that he would be allied with the British against his fellow Muslim Turks in the wake of the First World War; see G. Laithwaite, comp., "Historical Memorandum on the Relations of the Wahabi Amirs and Ibn Saud with Eastern Arabia and the British Government, 1800–1934," in *The Expansion of Wahhabi Power in Arabia, 1798–1932: The British Documentary Records*, ed. A. L. P. Burdett (Cambridge: Cambridge University Press, 2013), 1:42–43. Well before the First World War, Ibn Saud and the king of Kuwait, al-Mubarak, had built a connection to secure British patronage and had rejected Ottoman authority. 'Abd al-'Aziz Sulayman Nuwar, *Al-Jazira al-'Arabiyya fi al-Watha'iq al-Britaniyya* (Cairo: 'Ayn lil-Dirasat wa al-Buhuth al-Insaniyya wa al-'Ijtama'iyya, 2001), 22, 63, 65–70, 113–16. In the anticolonial Iraqi rebellion against the British, Ibn Saud refused to support the Iraqis. See N. Bray, *Mughamirat li-Jimn fi al-'Iraq wa al-Jazira al-'Arabiyya: 1908–1920*, trans. Salim Baha al-Takriti (Baghdad: Dar Wasit, 1990), 193–201; Rihani, *Muluk al-'Arab*, 820; Zirikli, *Shibh al-Jazira fi 'Ahd al-Malik 'Abd al-'Aziz*, 1:660.

131. For an eyewitness description of this ceremony, see Gerald De Gaury, *Arabia Phoenix: An Account of a Visit to Ibn Saud, Chieftain of the Austere Wahhabis and Powerful Arabian King* (London: Harrap, 1946), 67–71. Also see Hamid Algar, *Wahhabism: A Critical Essay* (Oneonta, NY: Islamic Publications International, 2002), 39; De Gaury's obituary in "LT. Colonel G. S. H. R. V. De Gaury, MC," *Asian Affairs* 15, no. 2 (1984): 257. Photography at this ceremony was not permitted; however, the assistant consul, Captain de Gaury, made a drawing of the ceremony. For this drawing, see the photo insert in Charles Allen, *God's Terrorists*, after p. 224.

132. On the theological foundations of the Ikhwan rebellion and the role of the British, see Madawi Al-Rasheed, *A History of Saudi Arabia*, 59–68.

133. For a contemporaneous account of the devastation of tombs and domes in Mecca, see Rutter, *The Holy Cities of Arabia*, 551–52; Burckhardt, *Mulahazat Haula al-Badu al-Wahhabiyyin*, 1:244; Lorimar, *Tarikh al-Bilad al-Sa'udiyya fi Dalil al-Khalij*, 61; Abbasi, *Travels of Ali Bey*, 2:135, 159; Muhsin al-Amin, *Tajdid Kashf al-Irtiyab*, 36–37; Turki, "Tarikh Najd," in *Khizanat al-Tawarikh al-Najdiyya*, 4:169; Hugronje, *Safahat min Tarikh Makka al-Mukarrama*, 1:266; Didier, *Rihla ila al-Hijaz fi al-Nusf al-Thani min al-Qarn al-Tasi' 'Ashr al-Miladi*, 249.

134. For example, in 2012 the Saudi government barred over one thousand women from performing *hajj* because of absence of *mahram* (male guardianship). See "Saudi Deports Nigerian Women Pilgrims 'without *Mahram*,'" *Middle East Online*, Sept. 27, 2012, http://www. middle-east-online.com/english/?id+54593; Alex Thurston, "To Hajj without an Escort," *Revealer*, Oct. 16, 2012, http://therevealer.org/archives/14039. Similarly, in 2010 the Saudi government banned Moroccan women "of a certain age" from performing the *umra* (lesser *hajj*) because, according to the Saudi government, they might engage in illegal prostitution while there. See Nesrine Malik, "Saudi Ban on Moroccan Women Is a Stereotype Too Far," *Guardian*, Aug. 29, 2010, http://www.guardian.co.uk/commentisfree/2010/aug/29/saudi-arabia-ban-moroccan-women-stereotype; Stephanie Plasse, "Rage over Saudi Ban on Mecca Pilgrimage for Moroccan Women," *Afrik-News*, Sept. 13, 2010, http://www.afrik-news.com/article18235.html.

135. Muhammad al-Ghazali, *Al-Sunna al-Nabawiyya bayn Ahl al-Fiqh wa Ahl al-Hadith* (Cairo: Dar al-Shuruq, 1989).

136. Aziz al-Azmeh, *Muhammad bin 'Abd al-Wahhab*, 12. For an example of the extent to which Ibn Saud's public persona as a pan-Islamist and a pan-Arabist differed from his actual private policies, see the correspondence between Ibn Saud and Amin Rihani. Rihani is constantly assured that Ibn Saud is a defender of Arab and Islamic causes against British colonialism, while Ibn Saud's policies at the time reflected a very close alliance to the British government and British interests. Rihani grew progressively desperate as he tried to solicit Ibn Saud to act against British interests and increasingly was put off, given nonresponses; see Al Saud, King 'Abd al-'Aziz, Amin al-Rihani, *Al-Malik 'Abd al-'Aziz, Al-Sa'ud wa Amin al-Rihani: al-Risa'il al-Mutabadala* (Beirut: Dar Amwaj, 2001); Rihani, *Muluk al-'Arab*, 838–46.

137. Mahmud Shukri al-Alusi, *Tarikh Najd* (Cairo: Maktabat Madbouli, n.d.); al-Ruwayshid, *Al-Imam al-Shaykh Muhammad bin 'Abd al-Wahhab fi al-Tarikh*, vol.1; Ahmad Ra'if, *Al-Dawla al-Sa'udiyya: Fajr al-Takwin wa Afaq al-Islam* (Cairo: al-Zahra' lil-'Alam al-'Arabi, Qism al-Nashr, 1995), 456, 466.

138. al-Qusaymi, *Al-Thawra al-Wahhabiyya*, 72–73. For a critique of the attempts at portraying Wahhabism as akin to rationalism and enlightenment, see Rashwan, *Al-Islam al-Sa'udi*, 1–13.

139. For an example of the phenomenon of Wahhabi apologists citing Orientalist scholars in praise of Wahhabism to bolster their prestige, see al-Ruwayshid, *Al-Imam al-Shaykh Muhammad bin 'Abd al-Wahhab*, 2:413–22; Muhammad Mustafa Abu Hakima, *Mahadarat fi Tarikh Sharq al-Jazira al-'Arabiyya fi al-'Asur al-Haditha*, 126–27. Hafiz Wahba himself wrote extensively about his role as an ambassador for Ibn Saud and on his apologetics on behalf of Wahhabism. See Hafiz Wahba, *Arabian Days* (London: Barker, 1964); Hafiz Wahba, "Wahhabism in Arabia: Past and Present," *Journal of the Royal Central Asian Society* 16 (1929): 458–67. On Wahba's influence on Saudi foreign policies, see Sabri Falih al-Hamdi, *Al-Mustasharun al-'Arab wa al-Siyasa al-Kharijiyya al-Sa'udiyya khilala Hukm al-Malik 'Abd al-'Aziz bin Sa'ud (1915–1953)* (London: Dar al-Hikma, 2011), 69–117. On Hafiz Wahba and his centrality as an ambassador to the West, see Philby, *Sa'udi Arabia*, 295; David Commins, *The Wahhabi Mission and Saudi Arabia* (London: Tauris, 2008), 96.

140. Musil, *Al Sa'ud: Dirasa fi Tarikh al-Dawla al-Sa'udiyya*, 56–57; Alexei Vassiliev, *The History of Saudi Arabia*, 75; Edwar Juan, *Misr fi al-Qarn al-Tasi' 'Ashr*, trans. Muhammad Mas'ud (Cairo: n.p., 1921), 441; Hugronje, *Safahat min Tarikh Makka al-Mukarrama*, 1:254. Charles Didier compared Ibn 'Abd al-Wahhab to John Calvin, Martin Luther, John Huss, and Savonarola. See Didier, *Rihla ila al-Hijaz fi al-Nusf al-Thani min al-Qarn al-Tasi' 'Ashr al-Miladi*, 235–36; Didier, *Sojourn with the Grand Sharif of Makkah*, trans. Richard Boulind (Cambridge: Oleander, 1985), 94.

141. Andrew Crichton, *The History of Arabia, Ancient and Modern* (New York: Harper and Brothers, 1834), 2:256. However, not all Orientalists portrayed Wahhabism as the true Islam but rather saw it as an unpopular and fanatic new sect. See Carsten Niebuhr, *Travels through Arabia, and Other Countries in the East*, trans. Robert Heron (Edinburgh: n.p., 1792), 2:131–33; Efim Rezvan, *Al-Hajj al-Qabl mi'a sina: al-Sira' al-Dawli 'ala al-Jazira al-'Arabiyya wa al-'Alam al-Islami*, 112. William Palgrave recognized that Wahhabis were the minority, were fanatic, and committed brutal atrocities against other Muslims; however, he was dismissive of this because he thought Wahhabism represented the true spirit of Islam. See Palgrave, *Narrative of a Year's Journey through Central and Eastern Arabia (1862–1863)*, 3rd ed. (London: Macmillan, 1866), 1:120; 2:14–15. On the widespread perception by Muslims that Wahhabism was effectively a new religion, see Sulayman bin Sahman, *Kitab al-Daya' al-Sharq fi Radd Shibhat al-Maziq al-Mariq*, 35–36.

142. Crichton, *The History of Arabia, Ancient and Modern*, 2:305.

143. Burckhardt, *Notes on the Bedouins and Wahabys*, 2:108.

144. Burckhardt, *Notes on the Bedouins and Wahabys*, 2:112; Crichton, *The History of Saudi Arabia, Ancient and Modern*, 2:255 conveys the same idea, stating: "The religion and government of this sect (Wahhabism) may be very briefly defined as a Mohammedan Puritanism joined to a Bedouin phylarchy in which the great chief is both the political and religious leader of the nation." Also see Didier, *Rihla ila al-Hijaz fi al-Nusf al-Thani min al-Qarn al-Tasi' 'Ashr al-Miladi*, 234–38.

145. Corancez, *The History of the Wahhabis from Their Origin until the End of 1809*, 5. Also see Corancez, *Al-Wahhabiyyun: Tarikh ma Ahmalihu al-Tarikh*, 13–36, 68. The French philosopher Rousseau similarly understood Wahhabism as the pure form of the primitive faith of the Qur'an, but somewhat paradoxically and inconsistently, he acknowledged the widespread belief among Muslims that the Wahhabis were viewed as akin to the extremist movement of the Qaramita (the extremist Shi'a movement that sacked Mecca in 930 CE). See Jean Baptise Louis Jacques Rousseau, *Description Du Pachalik De Bagdad: Suivie D'une Notice Historique Sur Les Wahabis, Et De Quelques Autres Pi?? Ces Relatives?? L'Histoire Et?? La Litt?? Rature De L'Orient* (Paris: Chez Treauttel et Wurtz, 1809), 125–29.

146. Palgrave, *Narrative of a Year's Journey through Central and Eastern Arabia (1862–63)*, 2:83.

147. For a source which documents that Ibn Saud, in return for British protection, began giving oil concessions to the British as early as 1923, see Aitchison, *Al-Sa'udia wa al-Imarat al-'Arabiyya wa Oman fi al-Watha'iq al-Britaniyya*, 17. On Ibn Saud's financial concessions to the British in the Hijaz, see Zirikli, *Shibh al-Jazira*, 1:660.

148. Abu 'Alayh, *Tarikh al-Dawla al-Sa'udiyya al-Thaniyya*, 129–49; Muhammad 'Ali Sa'id, *Britanya wa Ibn Sa'ud*, 26–32; Himada Imam, *Dur al-Usra al-Sa'udiyya fi Iqama al-Dawla al-Isra'iliyya*, 113–17; Qasim bin Khulfa al-Ruways, *Rushdi Malhas min Nablis ila al-Riyad* (Beirut: Jadawel, 2011), 410–13. For an interesting study on John Philby demonstrating the pivotal role he played in the foundation of the Saudi state and furthering commercial and political bonds between Al Saud and Western companies, see Khayri Hammad, *'Abd Allah Filbi: Qita'a min Tarikh al-'Arab al-Hadith* (Beirut: Dar al-Kutub).

149. On Philby's conversion, see Elizabeth Monroe, *Philby of Arabia* (London: Faber and Faber, 1973), 170–71. It is clear that Philby's conversion to Islam was an extension of his perception that Islam is a primitive religion for the Arabs—that it was an Arab thing. His

conversion was a cultural conversion due to his cultural curiosity about the Arabs, and he converted as a way of attaining greater access to what he viewed as the inside dynamics of the indigenous culture of Arabia.

150. Quoted in Allen, *God's Terrorists*, 244. For a *fatwa* by the Wahhabis stating that all Shi'a are apostates and can be killed on sight, see Sharif al-Husayni, *Sudq al-Khabr fi Khawarij al-Qarn al-Thani 'Ashr*, 150.

151. Philby, *Arabian Days*, 278–79.

152. Philby, *Arabian Days*, 279. Apparently, Philby is unaware that the Ten Commandments are a basic and fundamental part of the so-called code of Islam. Interestingly, Philby is under the common Orientalist misimpression that Islam has a code of sorts. Islamic law is not a code but a complex jurisprudential methodology.

153. Allen, *God's Terrorists*, 257. On the roles of the *mutawwa'un* and the Ikhwan in reducing populations to obedience and submission, see Madawi Al-Rasheed, *A History of Saudi Arabia*, 48–64.

154. Rutter, *The Holy Cities of Arabia*, 342–43.

155. See Allen, *God's Terrorists*, 246. On Britain's interest in keeping the Arab and Muslim world divided, see Mutlaq al-Balawi, *Al-Wujud al-'Uthmani fi Shamal al-Jazira al-'Arabiyya* (Beirut: Jadawel, 2011), 287–88.

156. Van der Meulen, *The Wells of Ibn Saud*, 68.

157. Many Arab intellectuals took what Orientalists said about Wahhabism and the Islamic tradition at face value. For example, see Muhammad Mustafa Abu Hakima, *Mahadarat fi Tarikh Sharq al-Jazira al-'Arabiyya fi al-'Asur al-Haditha* (n.p.: Ma'had al-Buhuth wa al-Dirasat al-'Arabiyya, 1967).

158. See Natana DeLong Bas, *Wahhabi Islam: From Revival and Reform to Global Jihad* (Oxford: Oxford Univeristy Press, 2004); John L. Esposito and John O. Voll, *Makers of Contemporary Islam* (Oxford: Oxford University Press, 2001); John O. Voll, "Muhammad Hayya al-Sindi and Muhammad ibn 'Abd al-Wahhab: An Analysis of an Intellectual Group in Eighteenth-Century Madina," *Bulletin of the School of Oriental and African Studies* 38, no. 1 (1975): 32–39.

159. For examples of Wahhabi apologists citing Orientalist scholars, see al-Ruwayshid, *Al-Imam al-Shaykh Muhammad bin 'Abd al-Wahhab*, 2:413–22; Muhammad bin 'Abdullah al-Sikakir, *Imam Muhammad bin 'Abd al-Wahhab* (Riyadh: Maktabat al-Malik 'Abd al-'Aziz al-A'amah, 1419/1998), 289–93; Muhammad Kamil Dahir, *Al-Da'wa al-Wahhabiyya wa Atharuha fi al-Fikr al-Islami al-Hadith*, 235–46.

160. For an apologetic defense of Wahhabi atrocities against Muslims in order to cleanse Islam from all innovations, see Muhammad Bashir al-Sahsawani, *Kitab Siyanat al-Insan 'an Waswasa al-Shaykh Dahlan*, 424–523.

161. On the connection of Wahhabism to Arab nationalism, see George Rentz, "The Wahhabis," in *Religion in the Middle East*, 2:270–84.

162. Shortly after the pilgrimage season in 2012, a controversy broke out about the Saudi government's new plans to demolish more historical sites. Millions of Muslims around the world demand an end to the destruction of the Islamic cultural heritage sites by Saudi Arabia. See All India Ulema and Mashaikh Board, "Indian Muslims March in Protest against Saudi Wahhabi Cultural Vandalism," *Center for Islamic Pluralism*, January 14, 2013, http://www.islamicpluralism.org/2174/indian-muslims-march-in-protest-against-saudi. Also see Tim Hume and Sayma Ayish, "Mecca Redevelopment Sparks Heritage Concerns," *Center for Islamic Pluralism*, February 7, 2013, http://www.islamicpluralism.org/2188/mecca-redevelopment-sparks-heritage-concerns. For another example of the destruction of cultural heritage by puritanical groups, but this time in Mali, see Luke Harding, "Timbuktu Mayor: Mali Rebels Torched Library of Historic Manuscripts," *Guardian*, January 28, 2013, http://www.theguardian.com/world/2013/jan/28/mali-timbuktu-library-ancient-manuscripts.

163. On this process and the use of *talfiq* and *maslaha* in modern Islam, see Noel J. Coulson, *A History of Islamic Law* (Edinburgh: University of Edinburgh Press, 1964), 197–217. Also see Rida, *Al-Manar* 17:372–84.

164. Rashid Rida's main work was a monthly journal, titled *Majallat al-Manar*, which he issued from 1315/1897 to 1354/1935. Rida wrote most of the articles of the journal himself. Eventually, the issues of the journal were collected and published in a multivolume work. Below I cite the *Dar al-Wafa'* edition of the multivolume work, which contains all the issues of the *Manar* save the Qur'anic commentary, which was published separately. Other than his articles in *al-Manar*, Rida published several apologetic works defending Wahhabism. It is clear from these works that he was responding to a large number of jurists who were critical of Wahhabi ideas. See Rashid Rida, *Al-Rafida wa al-Wahhabiyya*, ed. 'Abd al-Rahman bin 'Abd al-Jabbar al-Furaywa'i (Cairo: Maktaba al-Nafidha, 2007).

165. For Rida's defense of his relationship with King 'Abd al-'Aziz, see Rida, *Al-Manar* 27:548–55. For his defense of his support of the Wahhabis, see 29:531–38, 604–7. On Rashid Rida and the Wahhabi movement, see Muhammad bin Abdullah al-Salman, *Rashid Rida wa Da'wa: al-Shaykh Muhammad bin 'Abd al-Wahhab* (Kuwait: Maktabat al-Mu'alla, 1988). On

the Azhari opposition to the Wahhabis in the 1930s, see Jurgen Wasella, *'Abd Allah al-Qusaymi: al-Tamarrud 'ala al-Salafiyya*, 39–40, 43–46.

166. See Rida, *Al-Manar* 31:745–50; Jurgen Wasella, *'Abd Allah al-Qusaymi: al-Tamarrud 'ala al-Salafiyya*, 55–56.

167. Rida chronicled his disagreements with a number of jurists from al-Azhar and chronicled the attempts made to bring a reconciliation to their disagreements, which included the contentious issue of the merit, or lack thereof, of the Wahhabis; see Rida, *Al-Manar* 32:673–704. However, it is clear that the rift between Rida, on the one hand, and al-Dijawi and several other Azhari jurists, on the other, continued until 1933, the last year in which the *Manar* journal was published; see vol. 33:34–41, 118–19, 373–82, 682–83.

168. Rida, *Al-Manar* 12:389–96; 16:776; 24:584–92.

169. Rida, *Al-Manar* 12:371–87, 525–28; 19–20:342–52; 29:40–51. For an analysis of the modernist debates regarding the authenticity of traditions, especially in the thought of Rashid Rida and his teacher, Muhammad 'Abduh, see G. H. A. Juynboll, *The Authenticity of the Tradition Literature: Discussions in Modern Egypt* (Leiden: Brill, 1969), 15–32.

170. On philosophy, see Rida, *Al-Manar* 5:727–70. For his condemnation of political despotism and advocacy of democratic government, see Rida, *Al-Manar* 4:809–13; 7:899–912; 23:751; 27:357–59. For an article written on the same subject by Jamal al-din al-Afghani, see *Al-Manar* 3:577–82, 602–7.

171. Although supportive of the juristic class and their tradition, Rida was also critical of overly conservative jurists who resisted the reformation of Islamic law; see Rida, *Al-Manar* 1:462–66, 696–704, 822–26; 4:401–11, 441–48. This issue was one of the causes for the rift between him and the Azhar seminary in the early 1930s; see Rida, *Al-Manar* 33:33–49, 113–20, 130–33, 290–304. However, Rida was also concerned about the turmoil and divisiveness that could result from too rigid of an adherence to the established schools of thought in jurisprudence; see vol. 14:775–81; 28:423–32.

172. On Rida and his views regarding Salafism and Hanbalism, see Rida, *Al-Manar* 8:614–20, 649–55; 29:185–96. Also see the excerpt on Ibn Taymiyya, vol. 24:473–78.

173. For his criticism of Sufi orders but his opposition to *takfir*, see Rida, *Al-Manar* 1:404–16, 447–54, 598–601, 722–30; 2:401–6, 449–54, 481–88, 545–52; 3:617–23; 4:318–20; 6:12–20, 41–62, 109–15, 184–95, 255–59, 286–93, 369–73, 406–12; 11:504–27, 911–17; 23:345–60; 27:556–68. On Shi'ism and worshipping at gravesites, see 28:350–67, 429–49, 516–33, 593–601, 684–92, 776–81.

174. See Rida, *Al-Manar* 3:635–40, 676–83, 715–25, 796–804; 4:51–60, 161–70, 205–17, 280–97, 521–29, 692–702, 852–66; 5:522–45, 570–78; 6:500–506, 539–44, 594–98, 696–99, 766–70, 768–71, 820–22, 853–56, 939–43; 7:121–33, 222–25, 253–58, 409–12, 449–53, 491–95; 12:615–21; 13:105–8, 529–38, 569–71, 665–80, 779–82; 14:137–38, 510–15, 743–50; 17:501–3. On closing the doors of *ijtihad*, see 7:374–80; 15:183–87. For an excerpt by Jamal al-Din al-Qasimi opposing the practice of *takfir* and criticizing the *Ahl al-Hadith* for attacking innovative jurists, see 15:857–74, 912–20; also see the excerpt in 17:41–53.

175. Rida, apologetically, defended the Wahhabis despite their insistence on *takfir*, destruction of Islamic monuments, attacking pilgrims to Mecca, and killing of innocents; see Rida, *Al-Manar* 21:226–49, 281–84; 26:200–205, 320, 454–77; 29:162–80; 33:544–47. Rida argued that even if the Wahhabis committed some excesses, their opponent, the Hashmite Sharif Hussayn, did much worse; see 26:462–63. Rida critically noted that some of his contemporaries praise Muhammad 'Ali, Egypt's ruler, for defeating the Wahhabis; see Rida, *Al-Manar*, 5:183. Rida strongly defended the Wahhabis over the Egyptian mahmal incident in 1926; see Rida, *Al-Manar* 27:463–68. Also see his *fatwa* in favor of the Wahhabi Ibn Saud and against King Hussayn bin 'Ali, who seized control of Mecca in 1916, 24:593–618; 25:713–18. On the refusal of King Husayn to accept the Egyptian medical mission to Mecca, see 24:625–29. Muhsin al-Amin vehemently criticized Rida for ignoring and denying the atrocities committed by the Wahhabis; see *Tajdid Kashf al-Irtiyab*, 50–51.

176. Rida, *Al-Manar* 12:818–32, 913–32; 14:849–53; 16:773–76; 19–20:129–69, 278–88, 433–43; 25:540–60, 604–21, 761–79. Rather tellingly, in 1928, Rida finally acknowledged that some Salafis and Wahhabis had nothing but disdain toward jurists like himself; see 29:618. This was indicative of the contradictions between his theology and nationalism—contradictions that Rida did not seem willingly to confront openly.

177. For instance, Rida urged Muslims to support the Turkish Kemalists against the British colonialists; see Rida, *Al-Manar* 23:713–720. But when it became that clear Kemal Ataturk was pro-Western and anti-Islamic, Rida wrote opposing him; see 25:273–92; 27:356.

178. For a *fatwa* on whether King 'Abd al-'Aziz may declare a national holiday on the occasion of his becoming king of Arabia, see Rida, *Al-Manar* 30:521–23.

179. Rida argued that one of the reasons that he supported the Wahhabis was because the Bedouins of Arabia and the Ottomans had become areligious in many of their practices and cared little for what Islamic law had to say about anything. In contrast, the Wahhabis were religiously committed and, in principle, put Islamic law before social customs or politics. See Rida, *Al-Manar* 21:226–49. While Rida probably did believe this to be true, the vast majority

of his writings focused on nationalistic considerations such as anticolonialism and pro-Arab nationalism.

180. On public interest (*maslaha*) and Islamic law in Rida's thought, see Rida, *Al-Manar* 9:721–70.

181. On the difference between Salafism and Wahhabism and the co-optation of Salafism by Wahhabis, see Ahmad Mahmoud Sabhi, *Hal Y'ad al-Madhhab al-Wahhabi Salafyan?* (Alexandria: Dar al-Wafa', 2004); al-Saqqaf, *Al-Salafiyya al-Wahhabiyya*, 87–88.

182. My two books *And God Knows the Soldiers: The Authoritative and Authoritarian in Islamic Discourses* (Lanham, MD: University Press of America, 2001) and *Speaking in God's Name* are primarily concerned with this phenomenon.

183. John O. Voll, "Fundamentalism in the Sunni Arab World: Egypt and the Sudan," in *Fundamentalisms Observed*, ed. Martin E. Marty and R. Scott Appleby (Chicago: University of Chicago Press, 1991), 345–402; Mumtaz Ahmad, "Islamic Fundamentalism in South Asia: The Jamaat-i-Islami and the Tablighi Jamaat," in *Fundamentalisms Observed*, ed. Martin E. Marty and R. Scott Appleby (Chicago: University of Chicago Press, 1991), 457–530; Abdel Azim Ramadan, "Fundamentalist Influence in Egypt: The Strategies of the Muslim Brotherhood and the Takfir Groups," in *Fundamentalisms and the State: Remaking Polities, Economies, and Militance*, ed. Martin E. Marty and R. Scott Appleby (Chicago: University of Chicago Press, 1993), 152–83; Said Amir Arjomand, "Unity and Diversity in Islamic Fundamentalism," in *Fundamentalisms Comprehended*, ed. Martin E. Marty and R. Scott Appleby (Chicago: University of Chicago Press, 1995); Valerie J. Hoffman, "Muslim Fundamentalists: Psychosocial Profiles," in *Fundamentalisms Comprehended*, ed. Martin E. Marty and R. Scott Appleby (Chicago: University of Chicago Press, 1995). It is rather remarkable that in all the volumes of the Fundamentalism Project, not one article is on Wahhabism. Also see Oliver Roy, *The Failure of Political Islam*, 3rd ed., trans. Carol Volk (London: Tauris, 2007).

184. For an example of one of the very few voices who dared to challenge Wahhabism in the 1980s, see Haj Malik Ibn Shaykh Dawud, *Al-Haqa'iq al-Islamiyya fi al-Radd 'ala al-maza'm al-Wahhabiyya* (Istanbul: Hakikat Kitabevi, 1986).

185. For examples of such works, see Muhammad Fathy Osman, *Al-Salafiyya fi al-Mujtama'at al-Mu'asira* (*Salafis in Modern Societies*) (Kuwait: Dar al-Qalam, 1981). The author equates the Wahhabis with the Salafis and also engages in lengthy and unequivocal praise of Ibn 'Abd al-Wahhab and his movement; see esp. 31–87. Interestingly, the author was a professor in Saudi Arabia when he wrote the book. Another unabashed defense of the Wahhabi movement by a liberal scholar is Muhammad Jalal Kishk, *Al-Sa'udiyyun wa al-Hall al-Islami* (*The Saudis and the Islamic Solution*) (West Hanover, MA: Halliday Lithograph, 1981). This book, however, is a bit more balanced than Osman's work. Interestingly, Kishk became the recipient of the influential King Faysal award. For a sympathetic analysis of these modern intellectuals that defended Wahhabism, see Ghada Osman, *A Journey in Islamic Thought: The Life of Fathi Osman* (London: Tauris, 2011).

186. Muhammad al-Bahy, a professor of Islamic philosophy at al-Azhar, wrote a book about Islamic movements in history, which contained a short chapter about the Wahhabi movement. In this chapter he criticized the Wahhabis for being unrooted in the Islamic tradition and for causing a great deal of disunity among Muslims. A student of al-Bahi, Muhammad Khalil Haras, accused his teacher of ignorance and praised the Wahhabis in a book sponsored by the Saudi government; see Muhammad Khalil Haras, *Al-Haraka al-Wahhabiyya* (Beirut: Dar al-Katib al-'Arabi, 1978).

187. Muhammad al-Ghazali, *Al-Sunna al-Nabawiyya Bayn Ahl al-Fiqh wa Ahl al-Hadith* (Cairo: Dar al-Shuruq, 1989).

188. On Ahl al-Hadith, see Abou El Fadl, *Speaking in God's Name*, 114; Abou El Fadl, *And God Knows the Soldiers*, 48, 78.

189. Al-Muwaffaq bin Ahmad al-Makki, *Manaqib Abi Hanifa* (Beirut: Dar al-Kitab al-'Arabi, 1981), 1:350.

190. The following is a partial list of books attacking Muhammad al-Ghazali: Muhammad Jalal Kishk, *Al-Shaykh al-Ghazali bayn al-Naqd al-'Atib wa al-Madh al-Shamit* (Cairo: Maktabat al-Turath Islami, 1990); Ashraf bin Ibn al-Maqsud bin 'Abd al-Rahim, *Jinayat al-Shaykh al-Ghazali 'ala al-Hadith wa Ahlihi* (al-Isma'iliyya, Egypt: Maktabat al-Bukhari, 1989); Jamal Sultan, *Azmat al-Hiwar al-Dini: Naqd Kitab al-Sunna al-Nabawiyya bayn Ahl al-Fiqh wa Ahl al-Hadith* (Cairo: Dar al-Safa, 1990); Salman bin Fahd 'Awda, *Fi Hiwar Hadi' ma'a Muhammad al-Ghazali* (Riyadh: n.p., 1989); Rabi' bin Hadi Madkhali, *Kashf Mawqif al-Ghazali min al-Sunna wa Ahliha wa Naqd Ba'd Ara'ihi* (Cairo: Maktabat al-Sunna, AH 1410); Muhammad Salamah Jabr, *Al-Radd al-Qawim 'ala man Janab al-Haqq al-Mubin* (Kuwait: Maktabat al-Sahwa al-Islamiyya, 1992), esp. 100–108. Also see Abu 'Ubayda, *Kutub Hadhdhar minha al-'Ulama'*, 1:214–28, 327–29. At the time of the controversy, the influential Egyptian jurist Yusuf al-Qaradawi remained conspicuously silent, but a few years after al-Ghazali died, he wrote two books: one about al-Ghazali's life and the other about the controversy. In both books, he defended al-Ghazali's piety and knowledge, but he stopped short of criticizing the Wahhabis; see Yusuf al-Qaradawi, *Al-Imam al-Ghazali bayn Madihih wa Naqidih* (Beirut:

Mu'assasat al-Risala, 1994); al-Qaradawi, *Al-Shaykh al-Ghazali kama 'Araftuh: Rihlat Nisf Qarn* (Cairo: Dar al-Shuruq, 1994).

191. For a Sufi response to many of the doctrines of Wahhabism, see Muhammad Hisham al-Kabbani, *Encyclopedia of Islamic Doctrine* (Mountain View, CA: As-Sunna Foundation of America, 1998), 7 vols. For a response to Wahhabism by a Shi'i scholar who does not cite Shi'i sources and cites only Sunni sources, see Najm al-Din al-Tabasi, *Al-Wahhabiyya Da'awi wa Rudud* (n.p.: Matba'at al-Hadi, AH 1420).

192. This period has been described by some scholars as the liberal age of modern Islam; see Albert Hourani, *Arabic Thought in the Liberal Age: 1798–1939* (Cambridge: Cambridge University Press, 1983); Leonard Binder, *Islamic Liberalism: A Critique of Development Ideologies* (Chicago: University of Chicago Press, 1988). For excerpts from the works of Muslim liberals, see Charles Kurzman (ed.), *Liberal Islam: A Sourcebook* (Oxford: Oxford University Press, 1998). On the vigorous Muslim debates regarding the authenticity of the traditions attributed to the Prophet in the first half of the twentieth century, see Juynboll, *The Authenticity of the Tradition Literature*, 10–46. Also see Huseyn Hilmi Isik, *The Religion Reformers in Islam*, 3rd ed. (Istanbul: Wakf Ikhlas, 1978).

193. See Jamal Banna, *Nahwa Fiqh Jadid* (Cairo: Dar al-Fikr al-Islami, 1996); Jamal Banna, *Hal Yumkin Tatbiq al-Shari'a* (Cairo: Dar al-Fikr al-Islami, 2005); Muhammad Shahrur, *Nahwa Usul Jadida lil-Fiqh al-Islami* (Damascus: al-Ahali lil-Tiba'a wa al-Nashr al-Tawzi', 2000); Muhammad Sa'id al-'Ashmawi, *Usul al-Shari'a* (Cairo: Maktabat Madbouli, 1983).

194. My own book *The Great Theft* was translated into Arabic and sold well across the Middle East.

195. In my past works, I analyzed the process by which Puritans formulated authoritarian interpretive constructs that idiosyncratically limited Islam to whatever they deemed to be an authentic expression of Islamicity. These authoritarian interpretive processes ultimately greatly impoverished and also corrupted the Islamic tradition. See Abou El Fadl, *And God Knows the Soldiers*; Abou El Fadl, *Speaking in God's Name*.

196. Daniel W. Brown, *Rethinking Tradition in Modern Islamic Thought* (Cambridge: Cambridge University Press, 1996); Leonard Binder, *Islamic Liberalism: A Critique of Development Ideologies* (Chicago: University of Chicago Press, 1988); Charles Kurzman, ed., *Liberal Islam: A Sourcebook* (Oxford: Oxford University Press, 1998); Robert D. Lee, *Overcoming Tradition and Modernity: The Search for Islamic Authenticity* (Boulder, CO: Westview, 1997).

9. GOD, SHARI'AH, AND BEAUTY

1. For instance, see "Egypt Mob Attack Kills Four Shia Muslims Near Cairo," *BBC News*, June 24, 2013, http://www.bbc.co.uk/news/world-middle-east-23026865.

2. On temptation to join the perceived superior culture by converting, see John V. Tolan, *Saracens: Islam in the Medieval European Imagination* (New York: Columbia University Press, 2002), 85–86, 97.

3. For a powerful example on the effect of intellectual culture and the pervasiveness of the Muslim intellectual tradition in the medieval world, see George Makdisi, *The Rise of Colleges: Institutions of Learning in Islam and the West* (Edinburgh: Edinburgh University Press, 1982); Umberto Eco, *The Name of the Rose* (San Diego: Harcourt Brace, 1983).

4. Abi Bakr Ahmad bin Husayn al-Bayhaqi, *Al-Jami' li-Shu'ab al-Iman* (Riyadh: Maktabat al-Rushd, 2003), 8:257.

5. For instance, see the discussion on this tradition in Ibn Qayyim al-Jawziyya, *Fawa'id al-Fara'id* (Beirut: Dar al-Fikr, 1988), 181–86.

6. See Khaled Abou El Fadl, "Constitutionalism and Islamic Sunni Legacy," *UCLA Journal of Islamic and Near Eastern Law* 1, no. 1 (Fall/Winter 2001–2002): 94–96; Muhammad 'Imara, *Al-Islam wa Falsafat al-Hukm* (Beirut: al-Mu'assasa al-'Arabiyya li-al-Dirasat wa al-Nashr, 1977), 76–125. Also see the masterful study by the nineteenth-century Syrian jurist on power and the evils of despotism, 'Abd al-Rahman al-Kawakibi, *Taba'i' al-Istibdad wa Masari' al-Isti'bad*, 2nd ed. (Beirut: Dar al-Qur'an al-Karim, 1973).

7. On the relationship between psychological insecurities and cruelty, see Roy F. Baumeister, Brad J. Bushman, and W. Keith Campbell, "Self-Esteem, Narcissism, and Aggression: Does Violence Result from Low Self-Esteem or from Threatened Egotism?" *Current Directions in Psychological Science* 9, no. 1 (February 2000): 26–29; Roy F. Baumeister, Laura Smart, and Joseph M. Boden, "Relation of Threatened Egotism to Violence and Aggression: The Dark Side of High Self-Esteem," *Psychological Review* 103, no. 1 (January 1996): 5–33.

8. Masoud Popalzai, "Official: 160 Girls Poisoned at Afghan School," *CNN*, May 29, 2012, http:www.cnn.com/2012/05/29/world/asia/Afghanistan-girls-poisoned. Another example of this brutality is the recent attack on a school in Nigeria by the militant group Boko Haram

(meaning "Western education is forbidden"). See Adamu Adamu and Michelle Faul, "Nigeria: Islamic Militants Attack School, Killing 30," *Huffington Post*, July 6, 2013, http://www.huffingtonpost/2013/07/06/nigeria-school_n_3554393.html. It should also be noted that Boko Haram receives funding from various groups in the Middle East and United Kingdom, including backing from wealthy Saudi businessmen and the Islamic World Society with its headquarters in Saudi Arabia. See Kimeng Hilton Ndukong, "Nigeria: Boko Haram's Funding Sources Uncovered," *AllAfrica*, February 14, 2012, http://allafrica.com/stories/201202141514.html. On the issue of female genital mutilation (FGM), see Irfan Al-Alawi, "FGM Debate Continues in Muslim Lands," *Center for Islamic Pluralism*, July 18, 2013, http://www.islamicpluralism.org/2261/fgm-debate-continues-in-muslim-lands.

9. In praetorian states, an autocratic elite—usually a military junta—rules by perpetuating a state of social paralysis and dysfunction involving the use of bureaucratic governance and the perpetuation of divisions and polarizations in society. The classic work on praetorian states remains Amos Perlmutter, *Political Roles and Military Rulers* (London: Frank Cass, 1981). Also see Amos Perlmutter, *Egypt the Praetorian State* (New Brunswick, NJ: Transaction, 1974); Amos Perlmutter, *The Military and Politics in Modern Times: On Professionals, Praetorians, and Revolutionary Soldiers* (New Haven, CT: Yale University Press, 1977).

10. On the relationship between authoritarianism, prejudice, and cruelty, see Bob Altemeyer, *The Authoritarian Specter* (Cambridge: Cambridge University Press, 1996).

11. See Albert Bandura, "Moral Disengagement in the Perpetration of Inhumanities," *Personality and Social Psychology Review* 3 (1999): 193–209; Craig Haney, "Violence and the Capital Jury: Mechanisms of Moral Disengagement and the Impulse to Condemn to Death," *Stanford Law Review* 49 (1997): 1447–86; Albert Bandura, Bill Underwood, and Michael E. Fromson, "Disinhibition of Aggression through Diffusion of Responsibility and Dehumanization of Victims," *Journal of Research in Personality* 9, no. 4 (1975): 253–69; James E. Waller, *Becoming Evil: How Ordinary People Commit Genocide and Mass Killing* (Oxford: Oxford University Press, 2002), 185–90. For an analysis and case studies of the process that constructs and justifies cruelty, see John Conroy, *Unspeakable Acts, Ordinary People: The Dynamics of Torture* (New York: Knopf, 2000); Fred Katz, *Ordinary People and Extraordinary Evil: A Report on the Beguilings of Evil* (Albany: State University of New York Press, 1993).

12. On the role of disparaging language in degrading, oppressing, and even destroying a people, see Haig A. Bosmajian, *The Language of Oppression* (Lanham, MD: University Press of America, 1983), 29–33.

13. On the concept of social death and its role in promoting acts of cruelty, see the studies: Orlando Patterson, *Slavery and Social Death: A Comparative Death* (Cambridge, MA: Harvard University Press, 1990); Marion A. Kaplan, *Between Dignity and Despair: Jewish Life in Nazi Germany* (Oxford: Oxford University Press, 1998). The social psychologist James Waller notes: "The social death of victims may come after the extraordinary evil, or may lead to it" (Waller, *Becoming Evil*, 237). But even if the social death comes after the atrocity, as precedent, it sets the ground for further atrocities either against the previously targeted group or other groups. In their very long book, Theodor Adorno, Else Frenkel-Brunswik, Daniel Levinson, and Nevitt Stanford, *The Authoritarian Personality* (New York: Harper and Row, 1950) demonstrated that prejudice and hate can be easily transferred from one group to another.

14. On the Puritanical-Salafi orientation and its use of language that is demeaning to women, see Khaled Abou El Fadl, *Speaking in God's Name: Islamic Law, Authority and Women* (Oxford: OneWorld, 2001), 210–49.

15. See James E. Waller, "Ordinary People, Extraordinary Evil: Understanding the Institutional Frameworks of Evildoing," *Proteus* 12 (1995): 12–16.

16. See Ervin Staub, *The Roots of Evil: The Origins of Genocide and Other Group Violence* (Cambridge: Cambridge University Press, 1989), 16–18; Ervin Staub, "The Roots of Evil: Social Conditions, Culture, Personality, and Basic Human Needs," *Personality and Social Psychology Review* 3 (1999): 179–92.

17. On the construction and impact of the culture of cruelty, see Roy F. Baumeister, *Evil: Inside Human Cruelty and Violence* (New York: Freeman, 1997); Katz, *Ordinary People and Extraordinary Evil*; Staub, *The Roots of Evil*; Waller, *Becoming Evil*. On the construction of a culture of cruelty in Iraq, see Kanan Makiyya, *Cruelty and Silence: War, Tyranny, Uprising and the Arab World* (New York: Norton, 1994).

18. On the importance of the balance between good and evil in preserving the moral autonomy of human beings, see Erich Fromm, *The Heart of Man: Its Genius for Good and Evil* (New York: Harper and Row, 1964), 149–50. On the Qur'an and balance as a moral value, see Fazlur Rahman, *Major Themes of the Qur'an* (Minneapolis, MN: Bibliotheca Islamica, 1980), 28–36.

10. SHARI'AH AS REASONING WITH GOD

1. Some of these critics included: Tariq al-Bishri, Salah Sultan, Ahmad al-Rawi, Muhammad bin Mukhtar Shanqiti, Taha Jabir al-Alwani, and 'Ali Jum'a. For al-Azhar's response and others, see "Ara' Jama' min al-'Ulama' Da'wa Tariq Ramadan li-Ta'liq al-Hudud," *Multaqan*, August 6, 2005, http://www.ikhwan.net/forum/showthread.php?2810.

2. See Tariq Ramadan, "Response to the Official Statement of the Al-Azhar Legal Research Commission on the Call for a Moratorium Published on March 30th, 2005," *Tariq Ramadan*, http://www.tariqramadan.com/spip.php?article308.

3. "Saudi Arabia: News of Paralysis Sentence 'Outrageous,'" *Amnesty International*, April 2, 2013, http://www.amnesty.org/en/news/saudi-arabia-news-paralysis-sensence-outragious-2013-04-02.

4. Intisar A. Rabb, "Islamic Legal Maxims as Substantive Canons of Construction: Hudud-Avoidance in Cases of Doubt," *Islamic Law and Society* 17 (2010): 63–125.

5. 'Abd Allah 'Ali al-Qusaymi, *Al-Thawra al-Wahhabiyya* (Cairo: al-Matba'a al-Rahmaniyya, 1936), 13, 128.

6. See Jeremy Waldron, "How to Argue for a Universal Claim," *Columbia Human Rights Law Review* 30 (1998–1999): 308, 312; for a concise description of cosmopolitanism, see Jeremy Waldron, "What Is Cosmopolitan?," *Journal of Political Philosophy* 8, no. 2 (2000): 227–43; Jeremy Waldron, "Minority Cultures and the Cosmopolitan Alternative," *University of Michigan. Journal of Law Reform* 25 (1992): 751–93. Also see H. Patrick Glenn, *The Cosmopolitan State* (Oxford: Oxford University Press, 2013).

7. On the three systems of law and government, see Muhsin Mahdi, *Ibn Khaldun's Philosophy of History: A Study in the Philosophic Foundation of the Science of Culture* (Chicago, IL: University of Chicago Press, 1964), 196, 237–51, 261–63.

8. 'Ali Ibn Muhammad al-Mawardi, *Ahkam al-Sultaniyya wa al-Wilayat al-Diniyya* (Cairo: Dar al-Fikr, 1983); Khaled Abou El Fadl, "The Centrality of Shari'ah to Government and Constitutionalism in Islam," in *Constitutionalism in Islamic Countries: Between Upheaval and Continuity*, ed. Rainer Grote and Tillman Roder (Oxford: Oxford University Press, 2011); Khaled Abou El Fadl, "Constitutionalism and the Islamic Sunni Legacy," *UCLA Journal of Islamic and Near Eastern Law* 1 (2002): 67–101.

9. Ibn Qayyim al-Jawziyya, *I'lam al-Muwaqqi'in 'an Rabb al-'Alamin*, ed. 'Abd al-Rahman al-Wakil (Cairo: Maktabat Ibn Taymiyya, n.d.), 3:5–6.

10. Sachiko Murata and William C. Chittick, *The Vision of Islam* (New York: Paragon House, 1994), 141–64; Toshihiko Izutsu, *Ethico-Religious Concepts in the Qur'an* (Montreal and Kingston: McGill-Queen's University Press, 2002), 221–26.

11. See *Wathiqat al-Azhar bisha'n Mustaqbil Misr*, June 6, 2011, available at http://www.sis.gov.eg/Ar/Templates/Articles/tmpArticles.aspx?ArtID=48572; English translation available at http://www.sis.gov.eg/En/Templates/Articles/tmpArticles.aspx?ArtID=56424.

12. *Hadd* (pl. *hudud*) means boundary, borderline, or limit.

13. Rabb, "Islamic Legal Maxims as Substantive Canons."

14. Qur'an 4:97.

15. For example, see Juan J. Linz, *Totalitarian and Authoritarian Regimes* (Boulder, CO: Lynne Rienner, 2000); Hannah Arendt, *The Origins of Totalitarianism* (New York: Schocken, 1951); Giorgio Agamben, *Homo Sacer: Sovereign Power and Bare Life* (Stanford, CA: Stanford University Press, 1998); Giorgio Agamben, *State of Exception* (Chicago, IL: University of Chicago Press, 2005); Roger Griffin, *Modernism and Fascism* (New York: Palgrave Macmillan, 2010); Barrington Moore Jr., *Social Origins of Dictatorship and Democracy* (Harmondsworth: Penguin, 1967).

16. Ahmad Atif Ahmad, *The Fatigue of Shari'a* (New York: Palgrave Macmillan, 2012).

17. For the view that Shari'ah should be excluded from public discourses, see Abdullahi Ahmed An-Naim, *Islam and the Secular State: Negotiating the Future of Shari'a* (Cambridge, MA: Harvard University Press, 2010); An-Na'im, "Towards an Islamic Society, not an Islamic State," in *Islam and English Law: Rights, Responsibilities and the Place of Shari'a*, ed. Robin Griffith-Jones (Cambridge: Cambridge University Press, 2013), 238–44. Also see my response to these views in Khaled Abou El Fadl, "Violence, Personal Commitment and Democracy," in *Islam and English Law: Rights, Responsibilities and the Place of Shari'a*, ed. Robin Griffith-Jones (Cambridge: Cambridge University Press, 2013), 256–71.

18. Qur'an 3:104, 110, 114; 4:114; 7:157; 9:71, 112; 22:41; 31:17.

19. Qur'an 2:213; 3:79, 81; 4:58, 105; 5:44–45, 47, 49; 6:114; 8:46; 24:51.

20. The classical Islamic philosophical tradition contains extensive discourses on the nature of obligations (*taklif*) and also the nature of things (*mahiyyat al-ashya'*), but in jurisprudential discourses this debate took a different form. See Ayman Shihadeh, *The Teological Ethics of Fakhr al-Din al-Razi* (Leiden: Brill Academic, 2006); Jasser Auda, *Maqasid al-Shariah as Philosophy of Islamic Law: A Systems Approach* (Herndon, VA: International Institute of

Islamic Thought, 2008); Muhammad Khalid Masud, *Shatibi's Philosophy of Islamic Law* (Islamabad: Islamic Research Institute, 1995); Kevin Reinhart, *Before Revelation: The Boundaries of Muslim Moral Thought* (Albany: State University of New York Press, 1995).

21. I am simplifying this sophisticated doctrine in order to make a point. Muslim jurists engaged in lengthy attempts to differentiate between the two concepts of Shari'ah and *fiqh*. See Subhi Mahmassani, *Falsafat al-Tashri' fi al-Islam*, 3rd ed. (Beirut: Dar al-'Ilm li al Malayin, 1961), 21–24, 199–200; Bernard G. Weiss, *The Spirit of Islamic Law* (Athens: University of Georgia Press, 1998), 119–21; Muhammad Abu Zahra, *Usul al-Fiqh* (Cairo: Dar al-Fikr al-'Arabi, n.d.), 291; Mustafa Zayd, *Al-Maslahah fi al-Tashri' al-Islami wa Najm al-Din al-Tufi*, 2nd ed. (Cairo: Dar al-Fikr al-'Arabi, 1964), 22; Yusuf Hamid al-'Alim, *Al-Maqasid al-'Amma li al-Shari'a al-Islamiyya* (Herndon, VA: International Institute of Islamic Thought, 1991), 80; Muhammad bin 'Ali bin Muhammad al-Shawkani, *Talab al-'Ilm wa Tabaqat al-Muta'allimin: Adab al-Talib wa Muntaha al-'Arab* (n.p.: Dar al-Arqam, 1981), 145–51.

22. The Arabic is *"kull mujtahid musib"* and *"li kulli mujtahid nasib."* See Abu al-Husayn Muhhamad bin 'Ali bin al-Tayyib al Basri, *Al-Mu'tamad fi Usul al-Fiqh* (Beirut: Dar al-Kutub al-'Ilmiyya, 1983), 2:370–72; 'Ala' al-Din 'Abd al-'Aziz bin Ahmadi al-Bukhari, *Kashf al-Asrar'an Usul Fakhr al-Islam al-Bazdawi*, 3rd ed., ed. Muhammad al-Mu'tasim bi Allah al-Baghdadi (Beirut: Dar al-Kitab al-'Arabi, 1997), 4:30–55; Abu Hamid Muhammad bin Muhammad al-Ghazali, *Al-Mustasfa min 'Ilm al-Usul*, ed. Ibrahim Muhammad Ramadan (Beirut: Dar al-Arqam, n.d.), 2:363–67; Abu al-Ma'ali 'Abd al-Malik bin 'Abd Allah bin Yusuf al-Juwayni, *Kitab al-Ijtihad min Kitab al-Talkhis* (Damascus: Dar al-Qalam, 1987), 26–32; Abu Muhammad 'Ali bin Ahmad bin Sa'id Ibin Hazm, *Al-Ihkam fi Usul al-Ahkam* (Cairo: Dar al-Hadith, 1984), 5:68–81, 8:589–92; Muhammad bin Ahmad bin 'Abd al-'Aziz bin 'Ali al-Fatuhi Ibn al-Najjar, *Sharh al-Kawkab al-Munir al-Musamma Mukhtasar al-Tahrir wa al-Mukhtabar al-Mubtakar Sharh al-Mukhtasar fi Usul al-Fiqh*, ed. Muhammad al-Zuhayli and Nazir Hammad (Riyadh: Maktabat al-'Ubaykan, 1993), 4:488–92; Abu Bakr Ahmad bin 'Ali bin Thabit al-Khatib al-Baghdadi, *Kitab al-Faqih wa al-Mutafaqqih wa Usul al-Fiqh* (Cairo: Zakariyya 'Ali Yusuf, 1977), 245–50; Abu al-Thana' Mahmud bin Zayd al-Lamishi, *Kitab fi Usul al-Fiqh*, ed. 'Abd al-Majid Turki (Beirut: Dar al-Gharb al-Islami, 1995), 201–2; Shihab al-Din Abu al-'Abbas Ahmad bin Idris al-Qarafi, *Sharh Tanqih al-Fusul fi Ikhtisar al-Mahsul fi al-Usul*, ed. Taha 'Abd al-Rauf Sa'd (Beirut: Dar al-Fikr, 1973), 438–41; Fakhr al-Din al-Razi Muhammad bin 'Umar bin al-Husayn, *Al-Mahsul fi 'Ilm Usul al-Fiqh*, 3rd ed., ed. Taha Jabir Fayyad al-'Alwani (Beirut: Mu'assasat al-Risala, 1997), 6:29–36; Muhammad bin 'Ali bin Muhammad al-Shawkani, *Irshad al-Fuhul ila Tahqiq al-Haqq min 'Ilm al-Usul* (Beirut: Dar al-Kutub al-'Ilmiyyah, n.d.), 383–89; Abu Ishaq Ibrahim bin 'Ali bin Yusuf al-Fayruzabadi al-Shirazi, *Sharh al-Lum'ah*, ed. 'Abd al-Majid Turki (Beirut: Dar al-Gharb al-Islami, 1988), 2:1043–71; al-Shirazi, *Al-Tabsira fi Usul al-Fiqh*, ed. Muhammad Hasan Haytu (Damascus: Dar al-Fikr, 1980), 496–508. In this context, Muslim jurists also debated a report attributed to the Prophet in which he says, "Whoever performs *ijtihad* and is correct will be rewarded twice and whoever is wrong will be rewarded once. See Jalal al-Din 'Abd al-Rahman bin Abi Bakr al-Suyuti, *Ikhtilaf al-Madhahib*, ed. 'Abd al-Qayyum Muhammad Shafi' al-Bastawi (Cairo: Dar al-I'tisam, AH 1404), 38; Ibn Hazm, *Al-Ihkam*, 5:73–74, 8:591; al-Suyuti, *Al-Nubadh fi Usul al-Fiqh al-Zahiri*, ed. Muhammad Subhi Hasan Hallaq (Beirut: Dar Ibn Hazm, 1993), 119–20; Abu al-Hasan 'Ali bin 'Umar Ibn al-Qassar, *Al-Muqaddima fi al-Usul*, ed. Muhammad bin al-Husayn al-Sulaymani (Beirut: Dar al-Gharb al-Islami, 1996), 114–15; Mahfuz bin Ahmad bin al-Hasan Abu al-Khattab al Kaluzani, *Al-Tamhid fi Usul al-Fiqh*, ed. Muhammad bin 'Ali bin Ibrahim (Mecca: Markaz al-Bahth al-'Ilmi wa Ihya' al-Turath al-Islami, 1985), 4:317–18; al-Qarafi, *Sharh*, 440; Abu 'Abd Allah Muhammad bin Idris al-Shafi'i, *Al-Risala*, ed. Ahmad Muhammad Shakir (n.p.: Dar al-Fikr, n.d.), 494; al-Shirazi, *Al-Tabsira*, 499; Muhammad bin 'Abd al-Hamid al-Asmandi, *Badhl al-Nazar fi al-Usul*, ed. Muhammad Zaki 'Abd al-Barr (Cairo: Maktabat Dar al-Turath, 1992), 702–3.

23. For discussions of the two schools, see al-Bukhari, *Kashf*, 4:18; Abu Hamid al-Ghazali, *Al-Mankhul min Ta'liqat al-Usul* (Damascus: Dar al-Fikr, 1980), 455; al-Ghazali, *Al-Mustasfa*, 2:550–51; al-Razi, *Al-Mahsul fi 'Ilm Usul al-Fiqh*, 2:500–508; al-Qarafi, *Sharh*, 438; Wahba al-Zuhayli, *Al-Wasit fi Usul al-Fiqh al-Islami*, 2nd ed. (Beirut: Dar al-Fikr, 1969), 638–55; 'Ali Hasab Allah, *Usul al-Tashri' al-Islami*, 3rd ed. (Cairo: Dar al-Ma'arif, 1964), 82–83; Badran Abu al-'Aynayn Badran, *Usul al-Fiqh* (Cairo: Dar al-Ma'arif, 1965), 474.

24. Al-Juwayni, *Kitab al-Ijtihad*, 50–51.

25. Al-Juwayni, *Kitab al-Ijtihad*, 61.

26. Sayf al-Din Abu al-Hasan 'Ali bin Abi 'Ali bin Muhammad al-Amidi, *Al-Ihkam fi Usul al-Ahkam*, 2nd ed., ed. 'Abd al-Razzaq 'Afifi (Beirut: al-Maktab al-Islami, AH 1402), 4:183; Jamal al-Din Abi Muhammad 'Abd al-Rahim bin al-Hasan al-Asnawi, *Al-Tamhid fi Takhrij al-Furu' 'ala al-Usul*, 3rd ed. (Beirut: Mu'assasat al-Risala, 1984), 531–34; Muhammad bin al-Hasan al-Badakhshi, *Sharh al-Badakhshi Manahij al-'Uqul ma' Sharh al-Asnawi Nihayat al-Sul* (Beirut: Dar al-Kutub al-'Ilmiyya, 1984), 3:275–81; al-Ghazali, *Al-Mustasfa*, 2:375–78; al-Juwayni, *Kitab al-Ijtihad*, 41; Abu al-Thana' Mahmud bin Zayd al-Lamishi, *Kitab fi Usul al-Fiqh*, ed. 'Abd al-Majid Turki (Beirut: Dar al-Gharb al-Islami, 1995), 202–3; al-Qarafi, *Sharh*,

440; Fakhr al-Din al-Razi, *Al-Mahsul*, 6:34–35, 43–50; Zaki al-Din Sha'ban, *Usul al-Fiqh al-Islami* (Egypt: Matba'at Dar al-Ta'lif, 1965), 418–19; Badran, *Usul al-Fiqh*, 474; al-Zuhayli, *al-Wasit*, 643.

27. See Robert Kane, *Through the Moral Maze: Searching for Absolute Values in a Pluralistic World* (New York: Paragon House, 1994).

28. For instance, see William Gifford Palgrave, *Narrative of a Year's Journey through Central and Eastern Arabia: (1862–63)*, 3rd ed. (London: Macmillan, 1866), 1:409, 2:11; Louis Alexandre Olivier de Corancez, *The History of the Wahabis from Their Origin until the End of 1809*, trans. Eric Tabet (Reading, UK: Garnet, 1995), 5; Carsten Niebuhr, *Travels through Arabia, and Other Countries in the East*, trans. Robert Heron (Dublin: Gilbert, Moore, Archer, and Jones, 1792), 2:134; Ali Bey Abbasi, *Travels of Ali Bey in Morocco, Tripoli, Cyprus, Egypt, Arabia, Syria, and Turkey between the Years 1803 and 1807* (Reading, UK: Garnet, 1993), 2:131. It is likely, however, that these travellers misunderstood Wahhabi teachings because of the Wahhabi hostility to folkloric traditions that sanctified the Prophet Muhammad.

29. Hans-Georg Gadamer, *Truth and Method*, 3rd ed. (London: Continuum, 2004), 282–83.

30. Eric J. Hobsbawm and Terence Ranger, eds., *The Invention of Tradition* (Cambridge: Cambridge University Press, 1983).

31. See Jourj Tarabishi, *Min Islam al-Qur'an ila Islam al-Hadith: al-Nash'a al-Musta'nafa* (Beirut: Dar al-Saqi, 2010).

32. Khaled Abou El Fadl, *Speaking in God's Name: Islamic Law, Authority and Women* (Oxford: OneWorld, 2001), esp. 98–133.

33. Abu Zayd 'Abd al-Rahman bin Muhammad Ibn Khaldun, *Al-Muqaddima* (Beirut: Dar Ihya' al-Turath, n.d.), 9–10.

34. For instance, see al-Hakim Abi Sa'd al-Muhassin bin Muhammad bin Karama al-Jishumi al-Bayhaqi, *Risalat Iblis ila Ikhwanihi al-Manahis*, ed. Hossein Modarressi (Beirut: Dar al-Muntakhab al-'Arabi, 1995), 51–60.

35. Taqi al-Din Ibn Taymiyya, *Dar' Ta'arud al-'Aql wa al-Naql*, ed. Muhammad Rasad Salim (Cairo: Matba'at Dar al-Kutub, 1971); Muhammad ibn 'Abd al-Malik ibn Tufayl, *Hayy Ibn Yaqzan*, ed. Jamil Saliba (Damascus: Maktabat Jami'at Dimashq, 1962); English trans. in Ibn Tufayl, *Ibn Tufayl's Hayy Ibn Yaqzan: A Philosophical Tale*, trans. Lenn Evan Goodman (Chicago, IL: University of Chicago Press, 2009); Muhammad bin Ahmad Ibn Rushd, *Kitab Fasl al-Maqal*, ed. George F. Hourani (Leiden: Brill, 1959); English trans. in Ibn Rushd, *On the Harmony of Religions and Philosophy: A Translation with Introduction and Notes of Ibn Rushd's Kitab Fasl al-Maqal*, trans. George F. Hourani (London: Luzac, 1961).

36. For studies on Ibn Tufayl's philosophy, see generally Zafar Ahmad Siddiqi, *Philosophy of Ibn Tufayl* (Aligarh: Aligarh Muslim University, 1965); Sami S. Hawi, *Islamic Naturalism and Mysticism: A Philosophic Study of Ibn Tufayl's Hayy bin Yaqsan* (Leiden: Brill, 1974); Lawrence I. Conrad, *The World of Ibn Tufayl: Interdisciplinary Perspectives of Hayy Ibn Yaqzan* (Leiden: Brill, 1996); Samar Attar, *The Vital Roots of European Enlightenment: Ibn Tufayl's Influence on Modern Western Thought* (Lanham, MD: Lexington, 2007); Salman H. Bashier, *The Story of Islamic Philosophy: Ibn Tufayl, Ibn al-'Arabi, and Others on the Limit between Naturalism and Traditionalism* (Albany: State University of New York Press, 2011).

37. Abu Bakr Muhammad bin 'Abd Allah bin al-'Arabi, *Ahkam al-Qur'an*, ed. 'Ali Muhammad al-Bajawi (Cairo: Dar al-Ma'rifa, n.d.), 2:603.

38. Khaled Abou El Fadl, "Law of Duress in Islamic Law and Common Law: A Comparative Study," *Islamic Studies* 30, no. 3 (1991): 305–50.

39. For instance, see an-Naim, *Islam and the Secular State: Negotiating the Future of Shari'a*.

40. Qur'an 6:151.

41. Qur'an 4:23.

42. Qur'an 4:11.

43. Qur'an 2:276–80.

44. See Samih Abd al-Wahhab al-Jundi, *Ahamiyyat al-Maqasid fi al-Shari'a al-Islamiyya* (Beirut: al-Risala, 2013), 171–270. Also see Abu Ishaq al-Shatibi, *al-Muwfaqat fi Usul al-Shari'a*, ed. 'Abd Allah Daraz (Beirut: Dar al-Ma'rifa, 1975), 4:23; al-Shatibi, *The Reconciliation of the Fundamentals of Islamic Law*, trans. Imran Ahsan Khan Nyazee (Reading, UK: Garnet, 2011), 1:6; Muhammad al-Tahir Ibn Ashur, *Ibn Ashur: Treatise on Maqasid al-Shari'ah*, trans. Mohamed El-Tahir El-Mesawi (London: International Institute of Islamic Thought, 2006), 117–21; Jasser Auda, *Maqasid Al-Shariah as Philosophy of Islamic Law: A Systems Approach* (London: International Institute of Islamic Thought, 2008), 24; Mohammad Hashim Kamali, *Principles of Islamic Jurisprudence*, 3rd ed. (Cambridge: Islamic Texts Society, 2005); Kamali, *Shari'ah Law: An Introduction* (Oxford: OneWorld, 2008), 123–40; Ahmad al-Raysuni, *Imam Al-Shatibi's Theory of the Higher Objectives and Intents of Islamic Law* (London: International Institute of Islamic Thought, 2005), 317–23.

45. Qur'an 7:69, 74; 27:62. Also see Fazlur Rahman, *Major Themes of the Qur'an* (Chicago, IL: University of Chicago Press, 1980), 54–60.

46. See 'Abd Allah ibn 'Umar Abu Zayd al-Dabusi, *Taqwim al-Adilla fi Usul al-Fiqh* (Beirut: Dar al-Kutub al-'Ilmiyya, 2001), 2:452; Jalal al-Din 'Abd al-Rahman bin Abi Bakr al-Suyuti (d. 1505), *"Al-Qawl al-ashbah fi hadith man 'arafa nafsahu faqad 'arafa rabbahu,"* Daiber Collection, GAL II 148 nr. 72, Tokyo University. Also see Ibn 'Arabi, *Divine Governance of the Human Kingdom: At-Tadbirat al-ilahiyyah fi islah al-mamlakat al-insaniyyah*, trans. Tosun Bayrak al-Jerrahi al-Halveti (Louisville, KY: Fons Vitae, 1997), 231–54.

47. Qur'an 3:104; 5:2.

48. Imam al-Nawawi, *Riyad al-Salihin*, ed. Muhammad Mahmoud 'Abd al-'Aziz and 'Ali Muhammad 'Ali (Cairo: Dar al-Hadith, 1994), 103.

49. See Khaled Abou El Fadl, *Rebellion and Violence in Islamic Law* (Cambridge: Cambridge University Press, 2001), esp. 34–37, 124–30, 133–41, 271–73.

50. Qur'an 1:6–7; 2:142–43; 3:101; 20:133–35; 23:73–74; 37:118–28. On the concept of "the straight path," see Rahman, *Major Themes of the Qur'an*, 3–20, 60.

51. Immanuel Kant, *Observations on the Feeling of the Beautiful and Sublime*, trans. John T. Goldthwait (Berkeley: University of California Press, 1960); Stephen David Ross, *The Gift of Beauty: The Good as Art* (Albany: State University of New York Press, 1996); Gregory Wolfe, *Beauty Will Save the World: Recovering the Human in an Ideological Age* (Wilmington, DE: ISI, 2011); Howard Gardner, *Truth, Beauty, and Goodness Reframed: Educating for the Virtues in the Twenty-First Century* (New York: Basic, 2011); George Dardess and Peggy Rosenthal, *Reclaiming Beauty for the Good of the World: Muslim and Christian Creativity as Moral Power* (Louisville, KY: Fons Vitae, 2010); Roger Scruton, *Beauty* (Oxford: Oxford University Press, 2009); Michael Boylan, *The Good, the True and the Beautiful* (New York: Continuum International, 2008); A. C. Grayling, *The Heart of Things* (London: Orion, 2006); Ian Stewart, *Why Beauty Is Truth: A History of Symmetry* (New York: Basic, 2007); George Santayana, *The Sense of Beauty: Being the Outline of Aesthetic Theory* (New York: Dover, 1955); John Griffin, *On the Origin of Beauty: Ecophilosophy in the Light of Traditional Wisdom* (Bloomington, IN: World Wisdom, 2011); Richard Viladesau, *Theological Aesthetics: God in Imagination, Beauty, and Art* (New York: Oxford University Press, 1999); Johann Gottfried Herder, ed., *Selected Writings on Aesthetics* (Princeton, NJ: Princeton University Press, 2006); Anthony O'Hear, ed., *Philosophy, the Good, the True and the Beautiful* (Cambridge: Cambridge University Press, 2000).

52. The report states that during a battle, just before a combatant was about to be struck down, he yelled that he had decided to become a Muslim. The Muslim fighter, believing that his enemy only said this because he had lost the sword fight and wished to escape death, went ahead and dispatched his enemy. Reportedly, when the Prophet heard of this, he disapproved. Even after being assured that the enemy only pretended to be Muslim to save his life, the Prophet said, "Did you open his heart to know what was in it?" Abu Dawud Sulayman ibn al-Ash'ath al-Sijistrani, *Sunan Abi Dawud*, ed. Shu'ayb Ama'ut and Muhammad Kamil Qarah Balili (Beirut: Dar al-Risala al-'Alamiyya, 2009), 4:278–79. On the refutation of the legitimacy of the law of apostasy, see Mohamed S. El-Awa, *Punishment in Islamic Law* (Indianapolis, IN: American Trust Publications, 1982), 49–56, 61–64; Ahmad Subhi Mansour, *Penalty of Apostasy: A Historical and Fundamental Study* (Toronto: International Publishing and Distributing, 1998); Mansour, "The False Penalty of Apostasy," *Ahl AlQuran: International Quranic Center*, http://www.ahl-alquran.com/English/show_article.php?main_id=3776.

53. See Khaled Abou El Fadl, "Political Crimes in Islamic Jurisprudence and Western Legal History," *U.C. Davis Journal of International Law & Policy* 4, no. 1 (Winter 1998): 2–28; Abou El Fadl, *Rebellion and Violence in Islamic Law*, 324–25.

54. Qur'an 2:205; 7:146; 18:24; 29:39.

55. See Hasan Hanafi, *Min al-'Aqida ila al-Thawra* (Cairo: Maktabat Madbouli, 1988); Muhammad 'Imara, *Al-Islam wa al-Thawra* (Beirut: al-Mu'assasa al-'Arabiyya lil-Dirasat wa al-Nashr, 1972); 'Abd al-Rahman Sharqawi, *'Ali, Imam al-Muttaqin* (Cairo: Maktaba Gharib, 1985). Also see 'Abd al-Salam Tunji, *Mu'assasat al-'adala fi al-Shari'a al-Islamiyya* (Tripoli, Libya: Kulliyat al-Da'wa al-Islamiyya, 1993); Muhammad bin Mahdi al-Hussayni al-Shirazi, *Al-'Adala al-Islamiyya* (n.p.: n.p., 1959); Muhammad Qutb, *Jahiliyya al-Qarn al-'Ishrin* (Cairo: Dar al-Shuruq, 1980).

56. On the rule of recognition, see H. L. A. Hart, *The Concept of Law*, 3rd ed. (Oxford: Oxford University Press, 2012), esp. 100–123.

57. For the notion that legal transplants work well enough, see Alan Watson, *Legal Transplants: An Approach to Comparative Law*, 2nd ed. (Athens: University of Georgia Press, 1993). See Walter F. Murphy, *Constitutional Democracy: Creating and Maintaining a Just Political Order* (Baltimore, MD: Johns Hopkins University Press, 2007).

58. For examples of people who tried to create a link between native ethos and the norms of the legal transplants by writing on the similarities between French law and Shari'ah law, see 'Abd al-Razzaq Ahmad Sanhuri, *Masadir al-Haqq fi al-Fiqh al-Islami, Dirasa Muqarana bi-al-Fiqh al-Gharbi* (Cairo: Jami'at al-Duwal al-'Arabiyya, Ma'had al-Buhuth wa al-Dirasat al-'Arabiyya, 1968); 'Abd al-Qadir al-'Awda, *Al-Tashri' al-Jina'i al-Islami bi-al-Qanun al-Wad'i* (Cairo: Maktabat Dar al-'Uruba, 1963); Subhi Mahmassani, *Falsafat al-Tashri' fi al-Islam:*

Muqaddima fi Dirasat al-Shari'a al-Islamiyya 'ala Daw' Madhahibuha al-Mukhtalifa wa-Daw' al-Qawanin al-Haditha (Beirut: Dar al-'Ilm lil-Malayin, 1961). For a study which expresses the fakeness of the efforts to reconcile Shari'ah and French law, see Oussama Arabi, "Intention and Method in Sanhuri's Fiqh Cause as Ulterior Motive," *Islamic Law and Society* 4, no. 2 (1997): 200–23.

59. Antony Anghie, "Imperialism, Sovereignty and the Making of International Law," vol. 37 of *Cambridge Studies in International and Comparative Law* (Cambridge: Cambridge University Press, 2007); Upendra Baxi, "'The State's Emissary': The Place of Law in Subaltern Studies," in *Subaltern Studies: Writings on South Asian History and Society*, vol. 7, eds. Partha Chatterjee and Gyanendra Pandey (New York: Oxford University Press, 1994), 247; Nathan J. Brown, "Law and Imperialism: Egypt in Comparative Perspective" *Law & Society Review* 29 (1995): 103; B. S. Chimni, "Capitalism, Imperialism, and International Law in the Twenty-First Century," *Oregon Review of International Law* 14 (2012): 17; Boaventura de Sousa Santos and César A. Rodríguez-Garavito, "Law, Politics, and the Subaltern in Counter-hegemonic Globalization," in *Law and Globalization from Below: Towards a Cosmopolitan Legality* (Cambridge: Cambridge University Press, 2005), 1–26; Thomas M. Franck, *Fairness in International Law* (New York: Oxford University Press, 1995); Turan Kayaoğlu, *Legal Imperialism: Sovereignty and Extraterritoriality in Japan, the Ottoman Empire, and China* (Cambridge: Cambridge University Press, 2010); Dianne Otto, "Rethinking the 'Universality' of Human Rights Law," *Columbia Human Rights Law Review* 29 (1997): 1–46; Gyan Prakash, "Subaltern Studies as Postcolonial Criticism," *American Historical Review* 99, no. 5 (1994): 1475; Gerry Simpson, "Is International Law Really Fair," *Michigan Journal of International Law* 17 (1996): 615; Gayatri Chakravorty Spivak, "Can the Subaltern Speak?," in *Marxism and the Interpretation of Culture*, ed. Cary Nelson and Lawrence Grossberg (Urbana: University of Illinois Press, 1988), 271.

60. Qur'an 2:195; 3:134.

61. Al-Husayn bin Mufaddal al-Raghib al-Isfahani, *Al-Dhari'a ila Makarim al-Shari'a*, ed. Taha 'Abd al-Ra'uf Sa'd (Cairo: Maktabat al-Kulliyat al-Azhariyya, 1973), 59. On godliness and virtue, see 'Abd al-Halim Mahmoud, *Al-Tafkir al-Falsafi fi al-Islam* (Cairo: Dar al-Ma'arif, 1989), 229.

62. Mustafa Hilmi, *Al-Akhlaq Bayn al-Falasifa wa Hukama' al-Islam* (Cairo: Dar al-Thaqafa al-'Arabiyya, 1986), 198.

63. 'Abd al-'Aziz bin 'Abd Allah, *Al-Falsafa wa al-Akhlaq 'inda Ibn al-Khatib* (Beirut: Dar al-Gharb al-Islami, n.d.), 46–51.

64. Al-Isfahani, *Al-Dhari'a ila Makarim al-Shari'a*, 41; Hilmi, *Al-Akhlaq Bayn al-Falasifa wa Hukama' al-Islam*, 174.

65. On Ibn Rushd and knowledge, see Oliver Leaman, *The Biographical Encyclopedia of Islamic Philosophy* (London: Bloomsbury, 2006), 1:115.

66. On the promising relationship of virtue ethics theory to natural law theory, see Christopher Martin, "The Relativity of Goodness: A Prolegomenon to a Rapprochement between Virtue Ethics and Natural Law Theory," in *Contemporary Perspectives on Natural Law*, ed. Ana Marta Gonzalez (Surrey, UK: Ashgate, 2008), 187–209. On virtue and natural goodness, see Philippa Foot, *Natural Goodness* (Oxford: Oxford University Press, 2001), 81–82; Robert Merrihew Adams, *A Theory of Virtue: Excellence in Being for the Good* (Oxford: Clarendon, 2006); Julia Annas, *Intelligent Virtue* (Oxford: Oxford University Press, 2011).

67. See the interesting discussion in Richard J. Mouw, *The God Who Commands: A Study in Divine Command Ethics* (Notre Dame, IN: Notre Dame University Press, 1990), 6–42. Also see C. Stephen Evans, *God & Moral Obligation* (Oxford: Oxford University Press, 2013); Angus Ritchie, *From Morality to Metaphysics: The Theistic Implications of Our Ethical Commitments* (Oxford: Oxford University Press, 2012); Kieran Setiya, *Knowing Right from Wrong* (Oxford: Oxford University Press, 2012); Mark C. Murphy, *God & Moral Law: On the Theistic Explanation of Morality* (Oxford: Oxford University Press, 2011).

68. W. D. Ross, *The Right and Good* (Oxford: Clarendon, 1930), 40–41.

69. On theories of the good, natural law, and rights, see Francis Oakley, *Natural Law, Laws of Nature, Natural Rights: Continuity and Discontinuity in the History of Ideas* (New York: Continuum International, 2005), 87–109. On the possibility of knowledge and transcendence and the relation of moral good and law to God, see Owen Anderson, *The Natural Moral Law: The Good after Modernity* (Cambridge: Cambridge University Press, 2012), 1–28, 263–88.

70. Many Muslim philosophers defined virtues so as to include ultimate values such as the intellect and all that nourishes and enriches it: knowledge and its pursuit; modesty and its enrichment through piety; bravery and its perfection through jihad; and justice perfected by fairness. The exact elements of virtue were a debated matter in both Greek and Muslim philosophies. For instance, there were debates as to the place of virtues, such as patience, moderation, abstinence, fraternity, generosity, truthfulness and honesty, happiness, friendship, or marriage. Debates also included whether properly understood virtues could really be subsumed under a limited number of mega- or overarching virtues. See Hilmi, *Al-Akhlaq Bayn al-Falasifa wa Hukama' al-Islam*, 190, 200; As'ad al-Sahmarani, *Al-Akhlaq fi al-Islam wa al-Falsafa al-*

Qadima, 99–140. Also see Oliver Leaman, ed., *Friendship East and West: Philosophical Perspectives* on the virtue of friendship and companionship.

71. For a very useful overview of virtue jurisprudence, see Robert George, "The Central Tradition: Its Value and Limits," in *Making Men Moral: Civil Liberties and Public Morality* (Oxford: Oxford University Press, 1993), 24–47. Also see Liezl Van Zyl, "Virtue Ethics and Right Action," in *The Cambridge Companion to Virtue Ethics*, ed. Daniel Russell (Cambridge: Cambridge University Press, 2013), 172–94.

72. On secondary systems of law, which are not customary but constitutive and normative, see Andrei Marmor, *Positive Law and Objective Value* (Oxford: Oxford University Press, 2001), 1–48.

73. This approach combines the methodologies of *al-istinbat al-fiqhi* and *al-istidlal al-'aqli*—an approach well represented by jurists such as Ibn al-Sa'ati (d. ca. 619/1222) and al-Bazdawi (d. 480/1087). See Muhammad 'Abd al-Latif Subki, *Tarikh al-Tashri' al-Islami*, ed. Muhammad 'Ali Sayis et al. (Damascus: Dar al-'Asma', 2006), 260–62.

74. The critical importance of local customs and practices in Shari'ah determinations is well supported in the Islamic tradition. See 'Ali Hasab Allah, *Usul al-Tashri' al-Islami*, 262–63. Also see Ayman Shabana, *Custom in Islamic Law and Legal Theory: The Development of the Concepts of 'Urf and 'Adah in the Islamic Legal Tradition* (New York: Palgrave MacMillan, 2010).

75. Javier Martinez-Torron and W. Cole Durham Jr., eds., *Religion and the Secular State: National Reports* (Provo, UT: International Center for Law and Religion Studies, Brigham Young Unversity Press, 2010), 405, 553, 630. On secularism in Israel, see Asher Cohen and Bernard Susser, eds., *Israel and the Politics of Jewish Identity: The Secular-Religious Impasse* (Baltimore, MD: Johns Hopkins University Press, 2000); Yaacov Yadgar, *Secularism and Religion in Jewish-Israeli Politics: Traditionists and Modernity* (Florence, KY: Routledge, 2010). On secularism in Germany, Poland, and Greece, see Gerhard Robbers, *Religion and Law in Germany* (London: Kluwer Law International, 2010); Esther Peperkamp and Magorzat Rajtar, eds., *Religion and the Secular in Eastern Germany: 1945 to Present* (Boston: Brill, 2010); Brian Porter-Szucs, *Faith and Fatherland: Catholicism, Modernity, and Poland* (Oxford: Oxford University Press, 2011); William Safran, ed., *The Secular and the Sacred: Nation, Religion, and Politics* (London: Frank Cass, 2005), esp. 130–46, 147–60.

76. Jean Bauberot, "The Evolution of Secularism in France: Between Two Civil Religions," trans. Pavitra Puri, in *Comparative Secularisms in a Global Age*, ed. Linell E. Cady and Elizabeth Shankman Hurd (New York: Palgrave Macmillan, 2010); Jocelyne Cesari, *When Islam and Democracy Meet: Muslims in Europe and in the United States* (New York: Palgrave Macmillan, 2004); Sarah Hackett, *Foreigners, Minorities and Integration: The Muslim Immigration Experience in Britain and Germany* (Manchester: Manchester University Press, 2013); Yvonne Hasbeck Haddad, *Not Quite American? The Shaping of Arab and Muslim Identity in the United States* (Waco: Baylor University Press, 2004); Jonathan Laurence, *The Emancipation of Europe's Muslims: The State's Role in Minority Integration* (Princeton, NJ: Princeton University Press, 2012); Maleiha Malik, ed., *Anti-Muslim Prejudice: Past and Present* (New York: Taylor & Francis, 2010); Sean Oliver-Dee, *Muslim Minorities and Citizenship: Authority, Islamic Communities and Shari'a Law* (New York: Tauris, 2012).

77. Winnifred Fallers Sullivan, "Varieties of Legal Secularism," in *Comparative Secularisms in a Global Age*, ed. Linell E. Cady and Elizabeth Shakman Hurd (New York: Palgrave Macmillan, 2010), 107–20. Also see Rajeev Bhargava, ed., *Secularism and Its Critics* (New Delhi: Oxford University Press, 1998); Jose Casanova, *Public Religions in the Modern World* (Chicago, IL: University of Chicago Press, 1994).

78. William Connolly, "Europe: A Minor Tradition," in *Powers of the Modern Secular*, ed. David Scott and Charles Hirschkind (Stanford, CA: Stanford University Press, 2006), 75–92; Veit Bader, *Secularism or Democracy? Associational Governance of Religious Diversity* (Amsterdam: Amsterdam University Press, 2007).

79. Jean-Jacques Rousseau, *On the Social Contract*, ed. Drew Silver (New York: Dover, 2003), Book IV.

80. Khaled Abou El Fadl, "Muslim Minorities and Self-Restraint in Liberal Democracies," *Loyola Law Review* 29, no. 4 (1996): 1525–42.

81. Rousseau, *On the Social Contract*, 25.

82. Robert N. Bellah, "Rousseau on Society and the Individual," in *The Social Contract and the First and Second Discourses*, ed. Susan Dunn (New Haven, CT: Yale University Press, 2002), 282; Victor Gourevitch, "The Religious Thought," in *The Cambridge Companion to Rousseau*, ed. Parick Riley (Cambridge: Cambridge University Press, 2001), 193–246; Yolande Jansen, "*Laicite*, or the Politics of Republican Secularism" in *Political Theologies: Public Religions in a Post-Secular World* (New York: Fordham University Press, 2006), 452–93; Talal Asad, "Trying to Understand French Secularism," in *Political Theologies: Public Religions in a Post-Secular World* (New York: Fordham University Press, 2006), 494–526.

83. See Watson, *Legal Transplants: An Approach to Comparative Law*; Alan Watson, "Comparative Law and Legal Change," *Cambridge Law Journal* 37, no. 2 (November 1978): 313–36.

84. There is often an unjustified assumption that the colonized voluntarily decided to adopt the civil law system.

85. On Oriental despotism, see Montesquieu, *Persian Letters*, trans. Margaret Mauldon (Oxford: Oxford University Press, 2008), esp. 174–76; Montesquieu, *The Spirit of Laws*, ed. David Wallace Carrithers (Berkeley: University of California Press, 1977), esp. 322–25; Joan-Pae Rubies, "Oriental Despotism and European Orientalism: Botero to Montesquieu," *Journal of Early Modern History* 9, no. 1–2: 109–80. See Robert Launay, "Montesquieu: The Specter of Despotism and the Origins of Comparative Law," in *Rethinking the Masters of Comparative Law*, ed. Annlese Riles (Oxford: Hart, 2001), 22–39. In *The Spirit of the Laws*, Montesquieu argued that there are three forms of government: republican, monarchical, and despotic; Montesquieu, *The Spirit of Laws*, 10. Throughout his work, Montesquieu equates despotic forms of government with Oriental nations, especially Muslims. Interestingly, more than five centuries earlier, Muslim scholars contended that there are three forms of government: (1) the *Khilafa*, which is founded on the existence of a political contract, deputyship, and the rule of Shari'ah law; (2) monarchical, where the sovereign is the prince but there is a limited application of the rule of law; and (3) tyrannical, where the making and application of law is entirely whimsical. At that time, Muslim scholars used to cite the *Faranj* (Franks), by which they meant Christian Europeans, as the example par excellence of the third category. Such scholars argued that while the Islamic ideal is the first category, most Muslim dynasties failed to meet the ideal and fell somewhere in the second category. See Abu al-Faraj al-Baghdadi Ibn al-Jawzi, *Al-Shifa' fi Mawa'iz al-Muluk wa al-Khulafa'*, ed. Fu'ad Ahmad (Alexandria: Dar al-Da'wa, 1985), 56–57; Muhammad 'Imara, *Al-Islam wa Falsafat al-Hukm* (Beirut: n.p., 1979), 54–55; Muhammad Sharaf and Ali Abd al-Mu'ti, *al-Fikr al-Siyasi fi al-Islam* (Alexandria: Dar al-Jami'at al-Misriyya, 1978), 300.

86. Toby E. Huff and Wolfgang Schluchter, eds., *Max Weber and Islam* (New Brunswick, NJ: Transaction, 1999); Bryan S. Turner, *Weber and Islam* (London: Routledge, 1974), 107–21; Richard W. Bulliet, *The Case for Islamo-Christian Civilization* (New York: Columbia University Press, 2004), 64–67; Muhammad Khalid Masud, Rudolph Peters, and David S. Powers, "Qadis and Their Courts: An Historical Survey," in *Dispensing Justice in Islam: Qadis and Their Judgements* (Leiden: Brill, 2006), 1–44.

87. See John Strawson, "Islamic Law and English Texts," in *Laws of the Postcolonial*, ed. Eve Darian Smith and Peter Fitzpatrick (Ann Arbor: University of Michigan Press, 1999), 109–26; Aziz Al-Azmeh, "Islamic Legal Theory and the Appropriation of Reality," in *Islamic Law: Social and Historical Contexts*, ed. Aziz Al-Azmeh (New York: Routledge, 1988), 250–65; James Le Sueur, "France's Instruction in Colonial and Anticolonial Minds before and after Algerian Independence," in *The French Colonial Mind, Volume 1: Mental Maps of Empire and Colonial Encounters*, ed. Martin Thomas (Lincoln: University of Nebraska Press, 2012), 194–214; Todd Shepard, "Thinking between Metropole and Colony," in *The French Colonial Mind, Volume 1*, 298–318; Teemu Ruskola, *Legal Orientalism: China, the United States and Modern Law* (Cambridge, MA: Harvard University Press, 2013), 135; W. J. Mommsen and J. A. De Moor, eds., *European Expansion and Law: The Encounter of European and Indegenous Law in the 19th and 20th Century Africa and Asia* (Oxford: Berg, 1992), see especially Esin Orucu, "The Impact of European Law on the Ottoman Empire and Turkey," 39–58; Lauren Benton, *Law and Colonial Cultures: Legal Regimes in World History, 1400–1900* (Cambridge: Cambridge University Press, 2001); Karen Barkey, "Aspects of Legal Pluralism in the Ottoman Empire," in *Legal Pluralism and Empires, 1500–1850*, ed. Lauren Benton and Richard J. Ross (New York: New York University Press, 2013), 83–108; Jane Burbank and Frederick Cooper, "Rules of Law, Politics of Empire," in *Legal Pluralism and Empires, 1500–1850*, ed. Lauren Benton and Richard J. Ross (New York: New York University Press, 2013), 275–94; Robin Bidwell, *Morocco under Colonial Rule: French Administration of Tribal Areas 1912–1956* (London: Routledge, 1973) 307–27.

88. Edward Said, *Orientalism* (New York: Vintage, 1978), 201–54; Bryan S. Turner, *Orientalism, Post-Modernism & Globalism* (London: Routledge, 1994), 36–50; Saree Makdisi, *Romantic Imperialism: Universal Empire and the Culture of Modernity* (Cambridge: Cambridge University Press, 1998); Michael Curtis, *Orientalism and Islam: European Thinkers on Oriental Despotism in the Middle East and India* (Cambridge: Cambridge University Press, 2009), 31–37; Alain Grosrichard, *The Sultan's Court: European Fantasies of the East*, trans. L Heron (London: Verso, 1998).

89. Walter Dostal and Wolfgang Kraus, eds., *Shattering Tradition: Custom, Law and the Individual in the Muslim Mediterranean* (London: Tauris, 2005); Reem Meshal, *Sharia and the Making of the Modern Egyptian: Islamic Law and Custom in the Courts of Ottoman Cairo* (Cairo: American University in Cairo Press, 2014).

90. For an overview of secularization and codification in the Muslim legal systems, see Sami Zubaida, *Law and Power in the Islamic World* (London: Tauris, 2003), 121–53; Esin

Orucu, "The Impact of European Law on the Ottoman Empire and Turkey," in *European Expansion and Law: The Encounter of the European and Indigenous Law in 19th- and 20th-Century Africa and Asia*, ed. W. J. Mommsen and J. A. Moor (London: Bloomsbury Academic, 1992), 57; Samera Esmeir, *Juridical Humanity: A Colonial History* (Stanford, CA: Stanford University Press, 2012), 65–69; Walter Dostal and Wolfgang Kraus, eds., *Shattering Tradition: Custom, Law and the Individual in the Muslim Mediterranean* (Islamic Mediterranean Series, Pt. 1) (London: Tauris, 2005); Avi Rubin, *Ottoman Nizamiye Courts: Law and Modernity* (New York: Palgrave MacMillan, 2011), 133–51.

91. This is why politicians and social activists often called nativists or traditionalists "*dhala-miyyun*," meaning people of the darkness or dark ages. One should also note that labels such as political Islam (*al-Islam al-Siyasi*), fundamentalism (*usuliyya*), jihadist Islam (*al-Islam al-jihadi*), and many others, such as the Arab Spring (*al-rabi' al-Arabi*), are terms and categories invented and rationalized in the West and were exported to Muslims in the Muslim world. The Westernized intelligentsia plays this endemic role in seeing themselves through the eyes of the other.

92. Arnold Toynbee argued that anyone who resists the tides of Westernization should be labeled a zealot. See Arnold J. Toynbee, *A Study of History: Abridgement of Volumes I–VI*, ed. D. C. Somervell (New York: Oxford University Press, 1946).

93. See Khaled Abou El Fadl, "The Collapse of Legitimacy: How Egypt's Secular Intelligentsia Betrayed the Revolution," *ABC Religion and Ethics*, July 11, 2013, http://www.abc.net.au/religion/articles/2013/07/11/3800817.htm.

94. For instance, see Touraj Atabaki and Erik J. Zurcher, *Men of Order: Authoritarian Modernization under Attaturk and Reza Shah* (London: Tauris, 2004); Touraj Atabaki, *The State and the Subaltern: Modernization, Society and the State in Turkey and Iran* (London: Tauris, 2007).

95. For instance, Montesquieu states: "Laws should be so appropriate to the people for whom they are made that is very unlikely that the laws of one nation can suit another." *The Spirit of Laws*, ed. Anne Cohler, Basia Miller, and Harold Stone (Cambridge: Cambridge University Press, 1989), 8. Interestingly, Montesquieu was criticized by intellectuals in France for being too tolerant toward Islam and too critical of Christianity. Introduction by Thomas Nugent to *The Spirit of Laws*, trans. Thomas Nugent (Whitefish, MT: Kessinger), 7–8.

96. For a general history, see Nathan Rotenstreich, "Volksgeist," in *Dictionary of the History of Ideas*, ed. Philip P. Wiener, vol. IV (New York: Scribner's, 1973), 490–96. Also see Johann Herder, *Outlines of a Philosophy of the History of Man*, trans. T. Churchill (London: Luke Hansard, 1880); Giambattista Vico, *The New Science*, trans. Thomas Goddard Bergin and Max Harold Fisch (Ithaca, NY: Cornell University Press, 1948); Friedrich von Savigny, *Systems des heutigen römischen Rects* (Berlin: Veit, 1840), 14; K. Zweigert and H. Kotz, *An Introduction to Comparative Law* (Oxford: Oxford University Press, 1977), 144–45; Benedicte Fauvarque-Cosson, "Development of Comparative Law in France," in *The Oxford Handbook of Comparative Law*, ed. Mathias Reimann and Reinhard Zimmerman (Oxford: Oxford University Press, 2008), 35–36; Reinhard Zimmermann, "Savigny's Legacy: Legal History, Comparative Law, and the Emergence of a European Legal Science," *Law Quarterly Review* 112 (1996): 576–605; William Ewald, "Comparative Jurisprudence (II): The Logic of Legal Transplants," *American Journal of Comparative Law* 43, no. 4 (1995): 489–510.

97. For a fascinating comparative study of two law schools, the first established to train Western-style lawyers willing to serve the interests of the colonizer and to import foreign laws, and the second a nationalist law school established by Zionist lawyers that sought to establish an organic relationship between the law and its national community and that cautioned against excessive importation of British laws, see Assaf Likhovski, "Colonialism, Nationalism, and Legal Education: The Case of Mandatory Palestine," in *The History of Law in a Multi-Cultural Society, Israel 1917–1967*, ed. Ron Harris, Alexandre Kedar, Pnina Lahav, and Assaf Likhovski (Surrey, UK: Ashgate, 2002), 75–93. For a study of the failure of law as a project in the Sudan after the postcolonial elites espoused three conflicting legal systems, the common law, the civil law, and Islamic law, see Mark Fathi Massoud, "Lawyers and the Disintegration of the Legal Complex in Sudan," in *Fates of Political Liberalism in the British Post-Colony: The Politics of the Legal Complex*, ed. Terence C. Halliday, Lucien Karpik, and Malcolm Feeley (Cambridge: Cambridge University Press, 2012), 193–217. On the significance of organic legal traditions in the creation of epistemic communities, see H. Patrick Glenn, *Legal Traditions of the World* (Oxford: Oxford University Press, 2000), 1–53.

98. Lambert was an advocate of sociological jurisprudence, according to which the study of law is approached in terms of its actual workings in society rather than its content or form. But it would be a mistake to confuse the school of thought followed by Lambert and the sociological jurisprudence of the school of American realism that was advocated by Roscoe Pound, Justice Holmes, and Llewellyn. Lambert's school of thought had a forerunner in the thought of Montesquieu and is best represented by the thought of Heck and his "Jurisprudence of Interests." Most significantly, Lambert incorporated elements of evolutionary jurisprudence per which he believed that there are universally valid and ideal principles of law appropriate for all

societies. Such ideals can be adopted by any and all societies because each society develops its own particularities and mechanics of law. Lambert thought to overcome local and native jurisprudential traditions through a movement of codifications that embraced laws of universal validity but could accommodate social variations at the practical and micro levels. Therefore, David Kennedy writes the following about Lambert's approach: "In retrospect, many of Lambert's proposals seem contradictory and idiosyncratic. For later scholars, the codes which emerged from anti-formalist enthusiasm in the 1920s would seem as out of touch with social reality as the national legal traditions Lambert sought to overcome through codification." David Kennedy, "The Methods and the Politics," in *Comparative Legal Studies: Traditions and Transitions*, ed. Pierre Legrand and Roderick Munday (Cambridge: Cambridge University Press, 2003), 378.

99. Enid Hill, "Islamic Law as a Source For the Development of a Comparative Jurisprudence: Theory and Practice in the Life and Work of Sanhuri," in *Islamic Law: Social and Historical Contexts*, ed. Aziz al-Azmeh (London: Routledge, 1988), 146–97; Amr Shalakany, "Between Identity and Redistribution: Sanhuri, Genealogy, and the Will to Islamise," *Islamic Law and Society* 8, no. 2 (2001): 201–44; Amr Shalakany, "Sanhuri, and the Historical Origins of Comparative Law in the Arab World (or How Sometimes Losing Your *Asalah* Can Be Good for You?)," in *Rethinking the Masters of Comparative Law*, ed. Annelise Riles (Oxford: Hart, 2001), 152–189; Guy Bechor, *The Sanhuri Code, and the Emergence of Modern Arab Civil Law (1932 to 1949)* (Leiden: Brill, 2008).

100. A prime example of this is al-'Awda, *Al-Tashri' al-Jina'i al-Islami bi-al-Qanun al-Wad'i*, and Muhammad Ahmad Shihata Husayn, *Al-Qanun: Dirasa Muqarana bi-al-Shari'a al-Islamiyya* (Alexandria: al-Maktab al-Jami' al-Hadith, 2009).

101. See Bechor, *The Sanhuri Code, and the Emergence of Modern Arab Civil Law*; Nabil Saleh, "Civil Codes of Arab Countries: The Sanhuri Codes," *Arab Law Quarterly* 8, no. 2 (1993): 161–67. Also see Chibli Mallat, "Arab Countries, Islamic Law," in *The Oxford International Encyclopedia of Legal History*, ed. Stanley N. Katz (Oxford: Oxford University Press, 2009), 1:204–6.

102. This is precisely why most Arab countries, as opposed to Israel, for instance, have not found a way of forging their own culturally unique means of balancing between the modern nation-state and traditional religious social institutions. See the interesting study by Muhammad Fadel, "Judicial Institutions, the Legitimacy of Islamic State Law and Democratic Transition in Egypt: Can a Shift toward a Common Law Model of Adjudication Improve the Prospects of a Successful Democratic Transition?," *International Journal of Constitutional Law* 11, no. 3 (2013): 646–65.

103. Rousseau, *The Social Contract*, 41.

104. Mouw, *The God Who Commands*, 187.

105. On the challenges of defining legal culture, see David Nelken, "Defining and Using the Concept of Legal Culture," in *Comparative Law: A Handbook*, ed. Esin Orucu and David Nelken (Oxford: Hart, 2007), 109–32.

106. For instance, consider the extent to which expressions or conceptions such as "beyond reasonable doubt," "cruel and unusual," "best interests of the child," "jury of my peers," "clear and present danger," or "due process of law" have become a seamless part of the living cultural fabric of the United States. See Michael Asimow and Shannon Mader, *Law and Popular Culture* (New York: Peter Lang International Academic, 2004); Kitty Calavita, *Invitation to Law and Society: An Introduction to the Study of Real Law* (Chicago, IL: University of Chicago Press, 2010), 10–49; Oscar Chase, *Law, Culture, and Ritual: Disputing Systems in Cross-Cultural Contexts* (New York: New York University Press, 2007); Nelken, "Defining and Using the Concept of Legal Culture." For an insightful study on the mutual dynamics between law and social practices, see Martha J. McNamara, *From Tavern to Courthouse: Architecture and Ritual in American Law, 1658–1860* (Baltimore, MD: Johns Hopkins University Press, 2004).

107. Tom Bingham, *The Rule of Law* (London: Penguin, 2010), 37–47. For a review of the theoretical debates, see Brian Z. Tamanaha, *On the Rule of Law: History, Politics, Theory* (Cambridge: Cambridge University Press, 2004), 102–12. For an excellent exposition on colonialism and exploitation of the doctrine of the rule of law, see Ugo Mattei and Laura Nader, *Plunder: When the Rule of Law Is Illegal* (Malden, MA: Blackwell, 2008), esp. 202–10; also, for a collection of essays on how authoritarian systems abuse the principle of rule of law, see Tom Ginsburg and Tamir Moustafa, eds., *Rule by Law: The Politics of Courts in Authoritarian Regimes* (Cambridge: Cambridge University Press, 2008).

108. For instance, short of Sanhuri himself, the single most influential legalist on the Egyptian Civil Code of 1949 was the French comparativist Edouard Lambert. In 1906, Lambert was the dean of the first law school dedicated to the teaching of the civil law system in Cairo. In 1908 Lambert played a critical role in sponsoring the most talented Egyptian law graduates to study French law (at the Egyptian government's expense) at the Seminar of Oriental Jurisprudence at the University of Lyon. The students who studied in France at the beginning of the

twentieth century played a decisive role in importing French civil law to most of the Arab world.

109. On the conservatism of legal systems, see Alan Watson, *Sources of Law, Legal Change and Ambiguity* (Philadelphia: University of Pennsylvania Press, 1984), 111; Alan Watson, *Failures of the Legal Imagination* (Philadelphia: University of Pennsylvania Press, 1988), 35–39. Some have described this inherent conservatism as "tenacity of law." As Bernard Grossfeld notes, this innate conservatism is simply the law's tendency to favor tradition. As he states: "On the positive side, tradition helps to preserve cultural identity, to temper the excesses of the latest fashion, to curb the most powerful interests of the day, and to maintain continuity and stability. Tradition is a democracy where predecessors have a vote. To this extent law is an expression of cultural experience, of an understanding exceeding that of a single generation." Bernard Grossfeld, *The Strength and Weakness of Comparative Law*, trans. Tony Weir (Oxford: Oxford University Press, 1990), 44.

110. Robert Alexy, "The Reasonableness of Law," in *Reasonableness and the Law*, ed. Giorgio Bongiovanni, Giovanni Sartor, and Chiara Valentini (London: Springer, 2009), 5–15; Rick Kennedy, *A History of Reasonableness: Testimony and Authority in the Art of Thinking* (Rochester, NY: University of Rochester Press, 2004); Riccardo Dottori, ed., *Reason and Reasonableness* (Munster: Lit Verlag, 2005); Charles W. Bacon and Franklyn S. Morse, *The Reasonableness of the Law: The Adaptability of Legal Sanction to the Needs of Society* (Washington, DC: Beard, 1924).

111. Philip Petit, "Law, Liberty, and Reason," in *Reasonableness and the Law*, 109–27; John Rawls, *Political Liberalism* (New York: Columbia University Press, 2005), 48–54 differentiates between rationalism and reasonableness and develops the definition of reasonableness in the public space as a means for achieving an overlapping consensus over varying and possibly competing visions of a rational good life. Also see Shaun Young, *Reasonableness in Liberal Political Philosophy* (New York: Routledge, 2008).

112. See Giorgio Bongiovanni and Chiara Valentini, "Reciprocity, Balancing, and Proportionality: Rawls and Habermas on Moral and Political Reasonableness," in *Reasonableness and the Law*, 81–106.

113. For instance, in the summer of 2011, I was lecturing at the Azhar College of Islamic Jurisprudence (*Kulliyyat Usul al-Din*) at Cairo on the dialectics of rationality and reasonableness in the Islamic legal tradition. After the lecture, I met with Ahmad al-Tayyib, the rector (*shaykh*) of Azhar, who seemed completely unimpressed with the distinction between rationality and reasonableness. The rector insisted that rationality has a time-honored place in Islamic jurisprudence, but reasonableness is a superfluous idea.

114. Khaled Abou El Fadl and Alan Watson, "Fox Hunting, Pheasant Shooting and Comparative Law," *American Journal of Comparative Law* 48 (2000): 1–37.

115. Muhammad Jawad Mughniyya, *Al-Fiqh 'ala al-Madhahib al-Khamsa* (Beirut: Dar al-Jawad, 1985), 360–66.

116. If the wife of an absentee husband whose whereabouts is unknown wants to have the marriage dissolved, she can plead harm in a court, and if she proves harm from the absence of the husband, she can be granted a divorce. See Mughniyya, *Al-Fiqh 'ala al-Madhhib al-Khamsa*, 437–39.

117. See Oren Perez and Gunther Teubner, eds., *Paradoxes and Inconsistencies in the Law* (Portland, OR: Hart, 2006), especially Fatima Kastner, "The Paradoxes of Justice: The Ultimate Difference between a Philosophical and a Sociological Observation of Law," 167–80.

118. This was the subject of many discussions on a number of Egyptian television stations in 2012 and 2013. The show host, Basim Yusuf, made it the topic of jeering and sarcasm as a way of making the point that Islamic law is not capable of being rational.

119. For instance, see Matthew Bacon, *A New Abridgement of the Law*, 7th ed. (London: A. Strahan, 1832), 756; John H. Mathews, *A Treatise on the Doctrine of Presumption and Presumptive Evidence* (London: Joseph Butterworth and Son, Law Booksellers, 1827), 24. For a more recent example, California Family Code section 7540 states that "the child of a wife cohabiting with her husband, who is not impotent or sterile, is conclusively presumed to be a child of the marriage." Section 7541(a) allows the presumption to be rebutted by blood tests under sections 7550 and 7557 if action is brought within two years of the child's birth. The list of parties who can rebut the presumption does not include the genetic father of the child if the genetic father does not have any independent presumed status. For a further discussion, see Anthony Miller, "Baseline, Bright-Line, Best Interests: A Pragmatic Approach for California to Provide Certainty in Determining Parentage," in *McGeorge Law Review* 34 (2003): 637; Jeanne Louise Carriere, "The Rights of the Living Dead: Absent Persons in the Civil Law," in *Louisiana Law Review* 50 (1990): 901, 904–5.

120. See 'Ali Yusuf 'Ali, *Fatawa Marfuda* (al-Muhandisin: Majmu'at Ajyal li-Khidmat al-Taswiq wa al-Nashr wa al-Intaj al-Thaqafi, 2008), 38–39; "Breastfeeding Fatwa Causes Stir," *BBC News*, May 22, 2007, http://news.bbc.co.uk/2/hi/middle_east/6681511.stm; Abraham Rabinovich, "Fatwa Promotes Adult Breastfeeding," *The Australian*, May 28, 2007, http://www.theaustralian.com.au/news/world/*fatwa*-promotes-adult-breastfeeding/story-e6frg6so-

1111113622471; Raymond Ibrahim, "Islam's 'Public Enemy # 1'," *National Review*, March 25, 2008, http://www.nationalreview.com/articles/223965/islams-public-enemy-1/raymond-ibrahim; "Breastfeeding Fatwa Sheikh Back at Egypt's Azhar," *Al Arabiya News*, May, 18, 2009, http://www.alarabiya.net/articles/2009/05/18/73140.html.

121. By all measures, 'Atiyya is a puritanical theologian who imagines himself a jurist. 'Atiyya was following in the footsteps of Nasir al-Albani (d. 1999), another puritanical Wahhabi scholar, who contended that it is permissible for an adult male to drink the breast milk of a women so that they may become prohibited to one another even if the male suckles directly from the woman's breast.

122. Qur'an 4:23. Also see Fakhr al-Din Muhammad ibn 'Umar Razi, *Tafsir al-Fakhr al-Razi: al-Mushahhar bi-al-Tafsir al-Kabir wa Mafatih al-Ghayb* (Beirut: Dar al-Fikr, 1981), 10:30–35.

123. For instance, Ibn 'Abd al-Barr (a Maliki author of *al-Tamhid*) argued that in the early days of Islamic law there were some who believed an adult male could drink the breast milk of any nursing woman and become prohibited in marriage to her as a result. He, however, says that this opinion has been discredited and forgotten centuries ago.

124. Abi Ishaq al-Shirazi, *Al-Muhadhdhab fi Fiqh al-Imam al-Shafi'i*, ed. Muhammad al-Zuhayli (Damascus: Dar al-Qalam, 1996), 4:583–84.

125. This distinction between law as the command of the sovereign, backed up by the threat of the use of force, and law as common normative standards is the same as Hart's doctrine of external views of the law as opposed to internal views of the law. Hart, *The Concept of Law*, 57, 82.

126. See James C. Scott, *Weapons of the Weak: Everyday Forms of Peasant Resistance* (New Haven, CT: Yale University Press, 1987).

127. Among modern jurists, Muhammad al-Ghazali was not alone in rejecting reports (hadith) on the basis of their substantive irrationality or illogicalness. See Shafiq bin 'Abd bin 'Abd Allah Shuqayyir, *Mawqif al-Madrasa al-'Aqliyya al-Haditha min al-Hadith al-Nabawi al-Sharif* (Beirut: al-Maktab al-Islami, 1998), 277–357; Riwa' Mahmud, *Mushkilat al-Nass wa al-'Aql* (Beirut: Dar al-Kutub al-'Ilmiyya, 2006), 252–63. Also see the discussion in Samih 'Abd al-Wahhab al-Jundi, *Ahmiyyat al-Maqasid fi al-Shari'a al-Islamiyya*, 135–47.

128. Abu Muhammad 'Abd Allah ibn Qutayba (d. 276/889), *Ta'wil Mukhtalaf al-Hadith*, ed. Muhammad Muhyi al-Din al-Asfar (Beirut, 1999) 334–39, 458–59 reports on ongoing debates in his age on the irrationality of hadith prescribing eating with the left hand, the hadith alleging that flies carry disease on one wing and the antidote on the other, and many others. Ibn Qutayba, who is considered by many contemporary commentators to have been a hadith apologist, was not defending the actual authenticity of the oral reports attributed to the Prophet but defending the integrity of the interpretive process. Ibn Qutayba repeatedly makes the point that hadith that is illogical or irrational cannot be authentic. However, he differentiates between empirical indisputable facts and philosophical assumptions, which cannot be considered as proof of physical facts. Jurj Tarabishi's discussion on Ibn Qutayba is an unfortunate example of the application of historical anachronisms. The author completely ignores the functionalities of the text and the way it thought to negotiate issues effectuating change without forcing unnecessary conflicts with established precedent. Tarabishi, however, in a style full of haughty hubris, mocks, jeers, and ridicules what he sees as the rational contradictions of Ibn Qutayba's work. See Jourj Tarabishi, *Min Islam al-Qur'an ila Islam al-Hadith: al-Nash'a al-Musta'nafa* (Beirut: Dar al-Saqi, 2010), 391–416.

129. For a deeply flawed argument that the belief in miraculous events is the cause of intellectual stagnation in Islam, see Jourj Tarabishi, *Al-Mu'jiza: aw Sibat al-'Aql fi al-Islam* (Beirut: Dar al-Saqi, n.d.). See Wael Hallaq, trans., *Ibn Taymiyya against the Greek Logicians* (Oxford: Oxford University Press, 1993). Reportedly, Ibn Taymiyya was atypical in that he rejected both reason and philosophical metaphysics. However, reading his multivolume work on Shari'ah and reason shows that he sharply separated matters of theological dogma from social laws. He rejected rational inquiry in all matters of religious dogma, which led him to endorse anthropomorphism, but he employed practical reasoning in a wide range of legal issues.

130. For instance, see Jourj Tarabishi, *Min Islam al-Qur'an ila Islam al-Hadith*, 577–81.

131. Abu Hamid al-Ghazali, "Book of Knowledge," in *Ihya' Ulum Al Din*, trans. Nabih Amin Faris (New Delhi: Islamic Book Service), 213.

132. English translation in Dennis Morgan Davis Jr., "Al-Ghazali on Divine Essence: A Translation from *Iqtisad fi al-I'tiqad*" (PhD diss., University of Utah, 2005), 73.

133. This was quoted by Fathi Dirini, *Dirasat wa Buhuth fi al-Fikr al-Islami al-Mu'asir* (Damascus: Dar Qutayba, 1988), 32–34 (translation mine). For a thorough examination of Ghazali's nuanced arguments about reason, causality, and revelation, see Frank Griffel, *Al-Ghazali's Philosophical Theology* (Oxford: Oxford University Press, 2009), 111–22, 147–73.

134. Abu Hamid al-Ghazali, *Iqtisad fi al-I'tiqad*, ed. I. A. Cubukcu and H. Atay (Ankara: n.p., 1962), 1; Davis, "Al-Ghazali on Divine Essence," 72.

135. Muhammad Zahid al-Kawthari, introduction to *Tabyyin Kadhib al-Muftari fima Nusiba ila al-Imam Abi Hasan al-Ash'ari*, by 'Ali ibn al-Hasan Ibn 'Asakir (Cairo: Matb'a al-Tawfiq, n.d.), 18. Kawthari lived and wrote in a critical period when he witnessed the fall of the Hijaz to the Wahhabis. He was born in1878 and died in 1951. He studied and taught in Istanbul, but escaping Ataturk's repression, he fled to Egypt in 1922.

136. The term always meant those who are closed-minded and pedantic, but it is not clear when it first entered into usage. According to Ibn 'Asakir, *Tabyyin Kadhib al-Muftari*, 11, it was first used when Hasan al-Basri (d. 110/728) banished a group of students in his class to sit at the margins because of their intellectual dullness and thick-headedness, and so they became known as the people of marginality. Hashawiyya was used after that in a derogatory manner to refer to Hanbali Ahl al-Hadith scholars known for their conservatism and rigidity.

137. Dirini, *Dirasat wa Buhuth*, 15–17, 37, 55. Also see Fathi al-Dirini, *Al-Manahij al-Usuliyya fi al-Ijtihad bi'l Ra'y fi al-Tashri' al-Islami* (Beirut: Mu'assasat al-Risala, 1997), 25.

138. See Dirini, *Dirasat wa Buhuth*, 32–34.

139. Discussed in Dirini, *Dirasat wa Buhuth*, 32.

140. See Subki, *Tarikh al-Tashri' al-Islami*, 213. On 'aql and Shari'ah, see Muhammad al-Jawad Mughniyya, *Al-Islam wa al-'Aql* (Beirut: Dar al-Jawad, 1991); Ibn Taymiyya, *Dar' Ta'arud al-'Aql wa al-Naql aw Mawafaqa Sahih al-Manqul li-Sarih al-Ma'qul*, 11 vol. (n.p.: Dar al-Kanuz al-Adabiyya, n.d.); Mustafa Sabri, *Mawqif al-'aql wa al-'ilm wa al-'alam min Rabb al-'alamin wa 'abadihu al-Mursalin* (Dar al-Afaq, 2006); al-Sadiq bin 'Abd al-Rahman al-Ghiryani, *Al-Hukm al-Shar'i Bayn al-Naql wa al-'Aql* (Beirut: Dar Ibn Hazm, 2006); Riwa' Mahmud, *Mushkila al-Nass wa al-'aql*; Ibn Rushd, *Manahij al-Adilla fi 'Aqa'id al-Milla* (Cairo: Maktabat al-Anjlu al-Misriyya, 1955), 233–38; Averroes, *Faith and Reason in Islam: Averroes' Exposition of Religious Arguments*, trans. Ibrahim Najar (Oxford: Oneworld, 2001).

141. Dirini, *Dirasat wa Buhuth*, 32–33. The reason this example is often given is because there is a report attributed to the Prophet that states: "There are no infections or bad omens (*la 'adwa wa la tira*)." Ibn Qutaybah claims that this hadith was meant to condemn the belief in bad omens and that bad omens or curses could be infectious; see Ibn Qutayba, *Ta'wil Mukhtalaf al-Hadith*, 169.

142. Fawzi Bilthabit, *Fiqh Maqasid al-Shari'a fi Tanzil al-Ahkam aw Fiqh al-Ijtihad al-Tanzili* (Damascus: Mu'assasit al-Risala, 2011), 125–28; Samih 'Abd al-Wahhab al-Jundi, *Ahammiyyat al-Maqasid fi al-Shari'a al-Islamiyya* (Beirut: Mu'assasat al-Risala, 2013), 105–8. Also see Yusuf Qaradawi, *Fi Fiqh al-Awlawiyyat: Dirasa Jadida fi Daw' al-Qur'an wa al-Sunna* (Cairo: Maktaba Wahba, 1995).

143. Muhammad bin al-Hasan al-Hajawi al-Tha'alibi al-Fasi, *Al-Fikr al-Sami fi Tarikh al-Fiqh al-Islami* (Beirut: Dar al-Kutub al-'Ilmiyya, 1995), 2:14. It is noteworthy that the author made this argument in the context of discussing the *mihna* (inquisition) imposed by the Caliph of al-Ma'mun in 833 CE in an attempt to centralize the authority of the state over religion. The author, however, argues that the involvement of the state in the inquisition or the counterinquisition only polarized and corrupted the discourse and that the rationalists and traditionalists would have negotiated the middle course if the state had not become involved in favoring one or the other of the parties.

144. Ibid., 2:490–91.

145. Ibid., 1:68–72.

146. Jurists such as Muhammad 'Abduh (d. 1323/1905), Muhammad Rashid Rida (d. 1354/1935), 'Abdul Hamid bin Badis, (d. 1359/1940), Muhammad al-Shawkani (d. 1250/1834), and Ibn 'Ashur (d. 1393/1973).

147. For surveys of this dogma, see al-Dirini, *Dirasat wa Buhuth*, 13–15; Tha'alibi, *Al-Fikr al-Sami*, 1:70–71; al-Sadiq bin 'Abd al-Rahman al-Ghiryani, *al-Hukm al-Shar'i Bayn al-Naql wa al-'Aql* (Beirut: Dar Ibn Hazm, 2006), 247–72; al-Shaykh 'Ali Hubb Allah, *Dirasat fi Falsafat Usul al-fiqh wa al-Shari'a wa Nazariyyat al-Maqasid* (Beirut: Dar al-Hadi, 2005), 138–55; Abu al-Fadl 'Abd al-Salam bin Muhammad bin 'Abd al-Karim, *Al-Tajdid wa Mujaddidun fi Usul al-Fiqh* (Cairo: al-Maktaba al-Islamiyya, 2007), 490–513.

148. Jamal al-Din Darawil, *Mas'alat al-Huriyya fi Mudawwanat al-Shaykh Muhammad al-Tahir bin 'Ashur* (Beirut: Dar al-Hadi, 2006), 172–78; Ibn 'Ashur, *Usul al-Nizam al-Ijtima'i* (Tunisia: n.p., 1979), 126; Ibn 'Ashur, *Tafsir al-Tahrir wa al-Tanwir* (Tunisia: n.p., 1984), 30:321; Ibn 'Ashur, *Maqasid al-Shari'a al-Islamiyya* (Tunisia: n.p., 1978), 131–34.

149. 'Abd al-Halim Mahmud, *Al-Tafkir al-Falsafi fi al-Islam* (Cairo: Dar al-Ma'arif, 1984), 229–34.

11. BEYOND A REASONABLE SHARI'AH

1. Qur'an 10:99.

2. See Abu Muhammad 'Ali bin Ahmad bin Sa'id Ibn Hazm, *Al-Ihkam fi Usul al-Ahkam* (Cairo: Dar al-Hadith, 1984), 1:19–20, 52–57; 3:272, 478; 4:377.

3. For example, see Toshihiko Izutsu, *Ethico-Religious Concepts in the Qur'an* (Montreal: McGill-Queen's University Press, 2002).

4. In classical juristic theory, the *mutlaq* (the general) is restricted and specified by the *muqayyad* (the restricted). See Muhammad Hashim Kamali, *Principles of Islamic Jurisprudence* (Cambridge: Islamic Texts Society, 1991), 113–16; Bernard G. Weiss, *The Search for God's Law: Islamic Jurisprudence in the Writings of Sayf Al-Din Al-Amidi* (Salt Lake City: University of Utah Press, 2010), 385–89.

5. Qur'an 68:4. There is also a famous saying of the Prophet which states: "I was sent to perfect the ethical character of human beings." See Malik bin Anas, *Muwatta* (Cairo: Mustafa al-Babi al-Halabi, 1985), 904–5; 'Abd Allah ibn Muhammad ibn Abi al-Dunya, *Makarim al-Akhlaq* (Cairo: Maktabat al-Qur'an, 1990), 21.

6. The report's terminology is *"ahsanukum akhlaqa,"* more literally meaning "of the highest or most beautiful ethical character." In a hadith, the Prophet is reported to have said: "I have been sent to perfect the nobility of character." Another report states: "The best of deeds after faith in God (*iman*) is benevolent love towards people." See Tayeb Chourief, *Spiritual Teachings of the Prophet: Hadith with Commentaries by Saints and Sages of Islam*, ed. Fatima Jane Casewit, trans. Edin Q. Lohja (Louisville, KY: Fons Vitae, 2011), 1–2, 10. For many Prophetic reports on the centrality of ethics, see Abu Hamid al-Ghazali, *Ihya' 'Ulum al-Din* (Cairo: Mustafa Babi al-Halabi, 1952), 3:48–51.

7. Qur'an 21:107. On the treatment of ethics in the Qur'an and early Sunna, see Mariam al-Attar, *Islamic Ethics: Divine Command Theory in Arabo-Islamic Thought* (New York: Routledge, 2010), 11–25. Syed Ameer Ali did a very good job in collecting and analyzing some of the authorial enterprises of oral traditions attributed to the Prophet on the question of the central ethics of early Islam; see Syed Ameer Ali, *The Ethics of Islam* (Calcutta: Thacker Spink, 1893), 1–51.

8. See Dimitri Gutas, *Greek Thought, Arabic Culture: The Graeco-Arabic Translation Movement in Baghdad and Early 'Abbasid Society (2nd–4th/5th–10th c.)* (London: Routledge, 1998); Mariam al-Attar, *Islamic Ethics: Divine Command Theory in Arabo-Islamic Thought*, 1–10; As'ad al-Sahmarani, *Al-Akhlaq fi al-Islam wa al-Falsafa al-Qadima* (Beirut: Dar al-Nafa'is, 2007), 64–96.

9. See Joel Kraemer, *Humanism in the Renaissance of Islam: The Cultural Revival during the Buyid Age* (Leiden: Brill, 1992); George Makdisi, *The Rise of Humanism in Classical Islam and the Christian West: With a Special Reference to Scholasticism* (Edinburgh: Edinburgh University Press, 1990); Lenn E. Goodman, *Islamic Humanism* (Oxford: Oxford University Press, 2003).

10. Kraemer, *Humanism in the Renaissance of Islam*, 6, 19.

11. See Titus Burckhardt, *Introduction to Sufi Doctrine* (Bloomington, IN: World Wisdom, 2008), 3, 9.

12. Compare, for instance, Hamid Al-Ghazali's *Mustasfa fi Usul al-Fiqh* and his *Ihya' 'Ulum al-Din*.

13. See Ibn Rushd, *Manahij al-Adilla fi 'Aqa'id al-Milla* (Cairo: Maktabat al-Anjlu al-Misriyya, 1955).

14. Muhammad bin al-Hasan al-Hajawi al-Tha'alibi al-Fasi, *Al-Fikr al-Sami fi Tarikh al-Fiqh al-Islami* (Beirut: Dar al-Kutub al-'Ilmiyya, 1995), 2:12–13 discusses political turmoil caused by competing ethnic conflicts in the early Islamic empire. The emergence of the Ahl al-Hadith movement and the emergence of the schools of *fiqh* provided a critical stabilizing factor in establishing an orthodoxy that provided a powerful distraction from the heated ethnic political conflicts that were taking place at the time.

15. For the claim that hadith scholars were more accepting of fabrications when it came to the *raqa'iq* (matters dealing with outward piety), see Muhammad al-Khudari, *Tarikh al-Tashri' al-Islami* (Beirut: Dar al-Kutub al-'Ilmiyya, 1985), 91–92; Muhammad 'Abd al-Latif Subki, *Tarikh al-Tashri' al-Islami* , ed. Muhammad 'Ali Sayis et al. (Damascus: Dar al-'Asma', 2006), 205.

16. On the relativity of power and the legality of rebellion, see Khaled Abou El Fadl, *Rebellion and Violence in Islamic Law* (Cambridge: Cambridge University Press, 2001), esp. 16–18, 24–28, 264–284.

17. However, I should mention that Fathi Dirini, *Dirasat wa Buhuth fi al-Fikr al-Islami al-Mu'asir* (Damascus: Dar Qutayba, 1988), 36 argues that ethics did have a dialectical role with law throughout the development of Islamic law. For instance, the author gives the example of Malikis who believed that the use of one's property was a private matter and did not need to take into account how it affects the neighbor's property. However, he argues later that because of ethical reasons, both Malikis and Hanafis decided that the use of private property must always be contingent on not harming the neighboring property.

18. See Qur'an 9:122.

19. See, for example, Qur'an 22:37; 64:16.

20. Jalal al-Din Suyuti (d. 1505), "*Al-Qawl al-ashbah fi hadith man arafa nafsahu faqad arafa rabbahu*," Daiber Collection, GAL II 148 nr. 72, Tokyo University. See Ibn 'Arabi, *Divine Governance of the Human Kingdom: At-Tadbirat al-ilahiyyah fi islah al-mamlakat al-insaniyyah*, trans. Tosun Bayrak al-Jerrahi al-Halveti (Louisville, KY: Fons Vitae, 1997), 231–54; Sachiko Murata and William C. Chittick, *The Vision of Islam* (New York: Paragon House, 1994), 216–21.

21. See Muhammad Ibn Abi Bakr Ibn Qaiyim al-Jawziyya, *Miftah Dar al-Sa'ada wa Man-sur Wilayat al-'Ilm wa al-Irada*, ed. Mahmud Hasan Rabi' (Alexandria: Maktabat Hamidu, AH 1399); Abu al-'Abbas Ibn al-'Arif, *Miftah al-Sa'ada wa Tahqiq Tariq al-Sa'ada* (Beirut: Dar al-Gharb al-Islami, 1993); Lex Hixon, *The Heart of the Qur'an: An Introduction to Islamic Spirituality*, 2nd ed. (Wheaton, IL: Quest, 2003), 66–67, 163.

22. See Qur'an 13:28; 5:119; 9:100; 58:22; 98:8.

23. See Qur'an 57:12; 66:8; 24:40.

24. Qur'an 22:46.

25. See Muhammad Qutb, *Jahiliyat al-Qarn al-'Ishrin* (Beirut: Dar al-Shuruq, 1995). This influential book describes what Qutb calls the jahiliyya of the twentieth century.

26. Khaled Abou El Fadl, "The Islamic Legal Tradition," in *The Cambridge Companion to Comparative Law*, ed. Mauro Bussani and Ugo Mattei (Cambridge: Cambridge University Press 2012), 295–312; Khaled Abou El Fadl, *Speaking in God's Name: Islamic Law, Authority and Women* (Oxford: OneWorld, 2001), 13, 47, 301.

27. The Prophet is reported to have said: "*I'tu kulla dhi haqqin haqqahu*" (give each posses-sor of rights his due rights). See Ahmad bin Shu'ayb Nasa'i, *Sunan an-Nasa'i* (Beirut: Dar Ibn Hazm, 1999), 350; Abu 'Abd Allah Muhammad bin Isma'il Bukhari, *Jam' Jawami' al-Ahadith wa al-Asanid wa Maknaz al-Sihah wa al-Sunan wa al-Masanid* (Vaduz, Liechtenstein: Jami'yat al-Maknaz al-Islami, 2000), 1:369.

28. Mustafa Hilmi, *Al-Akhlaq bayn al-Falasifa wa Hukama' al-Islam* (Cairo: Dar al-Thaqa-fa al-Arabiyya, 1986), 206–9.

29. John Renard, "Al-Jihad al-Akbar: Notes on a Theme in Islamic Spirituality," *Muslim World* 78, no. 3–4 (October 1988): 225–42.

30. See Bukhari, *Sahih al-Bukhari* (Beirut: Sharikat Dar al-Arqam bin Abi Arqam, n.d.), 1382. For a very interesting study on the greater jihad, see Charles Upton, *The Science of the Greater Jihad: Essays in Principial Psychology* (San Rafael, CA: Sophia Perennis, 2011); Maher Jarrar, "The Martyrdom of Passionate Lovers: Holy War as a Sacred Wedding," in *Jihad and Martyrdom*, ed. David Cook (Oxnard, CA: Routledge, 2010), 2:95–111.

31. For verses pertaining to consultation, see Qur'an 3:159; 42:38. See Fazlur Rahman, *Major Themes of the Quran*, 2nd ed. (Chicago: University of Chicago Press, 2009), 37–64.

32. For verses on enjoining the good and forbidding what is bad or evil, see Qur'an 3:104, 110; 7:157, 199; 9:71.

33. For a comprehensive study on the original sources on enjoining the good and forbidding the evil, see Michael Cook, *Commanding Right and Forbidding Wrong in Islamic Thought* (New York: Cambridge University Press, 2001).

34. This literature is so vast, deep, and numerous that it defies citation, but for a good introduction to some of these concepts see Murata and Chittick, *The Vision of Islam*, 267–88; Rahman, *Major Themes of the Quran*, 17–20, 33–34; Hixon, *The Heart of the Qur'an*, 185, 202–3.

35. Hilmi, *Al-Akhlaq bayn al-Falasifa wa Hukama' al-Islam*, 172–73.

36. Qur'an 3:79; 5:44. See Abu 'Abdullah al-Harith Ibn Asad al-Muhasibi, *Risala al-Mus-tarshidin* (Cairo: Dar al-Salam, 2000), 245–48; al-Sayyid 'Abd Allah al-Shubbar, *Al-Akhlaq* (Beirut: 1991), 301–3.

37. Murata and Chittick, *The Vision of Islam*, 151–64.

38. See Qur'an 58:19; 59:19; Ahmad 'Abd al-Rahman Ibrahim, *Al-Fada'il al-Khalqiyya fi al-Islam* (Cairo: Dar al-Wafa', 1989), 251–66; Rahman, *Major Themes of the Quran*, 24–26; Hixon, *The Heart of the Qur'an*, 190–91.

39. See, for example, Charles Taylor, "A Catholic Modernity?," in *A Catholic Modernity? Charles Taylor's Marianist Award Lecture*, ed. James L. Heft (New York: Oxford University Press, 1999), 13–38; Cornel West, "Prophetic Religion and the Future of Capitalist Civiliza-tion," in *The Power of Religion in the Public Sphere*, ed. Eduardo Mendieta and Jonathan Vanantwerpen (New York: Columbia University Press, 2011), 92–100; Jürgen Habermas, "'The Political': The Rational Meaning of a Questionable Inheritance of Political Theology," in *The Power of Religion in the Public Sphere*, 26–27; Christopher Lane, *The Age of Doubt* (New Haven, CT: Yale University Press, 2011); William Egginton, *In Defense of Religious Modera-tion* (New York: Columbia University Press, 2011); Howard Wettstein, *The Significance of Religious Experience* (Oxford: Oxford University Press, 2012).

40. See Murata and Chittick, *The Vision of Islam*, 267–317; Rahman, *Major Themes of the Qur'an*, 106–20.

41. For a historical refutation on the thesis of political quietism, see Abou El Fadl, *Rebellion and Violence in Islamic Law*. There are many Western scholars who consistently portray

Muslims as fatalistic and politically quietist and then usually go on to fault these purported characteristics for what has been described as Oriental despotism. But like so many of the arguments of Orientalism, accusing Islam of being the source of pacifism and quietism is culturally prejudiced and politically driven. It is a gross oversimplification to claim that Islamic theology is fatalistic or that it espouses ethical indeterminacy.

42. For the argument that the whole purpose of religion is the attainment of happiness in this life and the Hereafter, see Hilmi, *Al-Akhlaq bayn al-Falasifa wa Hukama' al-Islam*, 190–92.

43. Qur'an 17:70.

44. See Qur'an 4:112; 49:12.

45. On this subject, see George F. Hourani, *Reason and Tradition in Islamic Ethics* (Cambridge: Cambridge University Press, 1985).

46. Qur'an 3:108.

47. See my essays in Khaled Abou El Fadl, Joshua Cohen, and Ian Lague, eds., *The Place of Tolerance in Islam* (Boston: Beacon, 2002), 3–26, 93–112.

48. Qur'an 38:87.

49. Qur'an 7:52, 203; 17:82; 21:107.

50. Qur'an 12:111.

51. For instance, see Qur'an 6:54; 27:77; 29:51; 45:20.

52. See Khaled Abou El Fadl, *The Great Theft: Wrestling Islam from the Extremists* (New York: HarperOne, 2005), 85–110.

53. So, for example, even the groundbreaking work of Ibn Ashur remained locked in the paradigms of demonstrating the historical flexibility of Islamic law or advocating the importance of yielding to public social interests, or to exceptions based on necessity. See Muhammad al-Tahir Ibn 'Ashur, *Maqasid al-Shari'a al-Islamiyya* (Alexandria: Alexandria Bibliotheca, 2011). Nevertheless, Ibn 'Ashur's work remains groundbreaking because he convincingly demonstrates the extent to which many laws sought to be divine were in reality based on social conventions and contextual contingencies.

54. Qur'an 13:17; 14:25, 45; 24:35; 29:43; 59:21.

55. Jorge J. E. Gracia, *How Can We Know What God Means? The Interpretation of Revelation* (New York: Palgrave, 2001), 161–89, argues that hermeneutical interpretation of divine text only makes sense in a theological context. Gracia aptly demonstrates the analytical challenges in claiming to decipher what God means and the importance of interpretation within a theological community. In my view, a theological community could plausibly include a community of theological moral objectivism.

56. On moral trajectories in Islam and the prohibition of slavery, see Fazlur Rahman, *Major Themes of Qur'an*, 47–48.

57. Qur'an 5:49; 23:71.

58. Some contemporary scholars have argued that *asbab al-nuzul* traditions are particularly problematic and of suspect authority. However, the flaw in this argument is that it imposes a false dichotomy between the *asbab al-nuzul* traditions and the rest of hadith literature. Other than the fact that premodern Muslim scholars started extracting traditions from hadith literature that relate to the occasions of revelation, in terms of historical issues raised, the *asbab al-nuzul* traditions raised the same exact issues of historicity, or lack there of, that are raised in the hadith genre in general. See Bassam al-Jamal, *Asbab al-Nuzul: 'Ilman min 'Ulum al-Qur'an* (Beirut: al-Markaz al-Thaqafi al-'Arabi, 2005). The irony is that many of the scholars who have argued that the hadith literature is largely fabricated and invented have relied on the *asbab al-nuzul* tradition to impeach the historicity of the hadith literature. For instance, George Tarabishi, in his book *Min Islam al-Qur'an ila Islam al-Hadith*, relies extensively on *asbab al-nuzul* literature in attempting to prove that the hadith were not an original part of the religion of Islam and that the Prophet Muhammad was not seen as a religious leader or teacher but rather simply as a transmitter of the Qur'an. Tarabishi, however, does not seem to notice the inconsistency in attempting to prove the unhistoricity of hadith by relying on *asbab al-nuzul*—essentially hadith. He relies on *asbab al-nuzul* to prove that Muhammad was not intended to have any legislative authority or power and then uses this point to deconstruct the inauthentic nature of hadith, which recognizes the Prophet's legislative role. See Jourj Tarabishi, *Min Islam al-Qur'an ila Islam al-Hadith: al-Nash'a al-Musta'nafa* (Beirut: Dar al-Saqi, 2010), 7–85.

59. Jalal al-Din 'Abd al-Rahman bin Abi Bakr al-Suyuti, *Asbab al-Nuzul* (Cairo: Dar al-Tahrir lil-Tiba'a wa-al-Nashr, AH 1383), 2:73. Also see Muhammad ibn Jarir al-Tabari, *Tafsir al-Tabari: Jami' al-Bayan 'an Ta'wil Ay al-Qur'an*, ed. Mahmoud Muhammad Shakir (Cairo: Maktabat Ibn Taymiyya, n.d.), 10:392–94; Abu 'Abd Allah Muhammad bin Abi Bakr al-Qurtubi, *Al-Jami' li-Ahkam al-Qur'an* (Beirut: al-Risala, 2006), 8:40–43.

60. Qur'an 4:135. Qur'an 5:8 states, "O' you who believe, be steadfast in your devotion to God, and bear witness justly. Do not allow your hatred towards others lead you astray from justice. Adhere to justice for that is closer to piety, and be ever mindful of God for God is always aware of all that you do." Another verse and incident illustrating a similar moral point involves revelation 80:1. The Prophet was meeting with the notables of Mecca when he was approached by a poor and blind man (reportedly named Ibn Umm Maktum) with inquiries

about Islam. Eager to persuade the unbelieving noblemen, the Prophet turned away from the poor blind man. Thereupon, chapter 80 was revealed, reproaching the Prophet for favoring the noblemen over a lowly member of society. See Samira al-Zayid, *Al-Jami' fi al-Sira al-Nabaw-iyya* (n.p., n.d.), 1:449–50.

61. Qur'an 12:86. Of course, a chapter of the Qur'an titled *al-mujadala* is named after an incident in which a woman improperly divorced from her husband entreated and complained to God her plight. The chapter begins: "God has heard the words of the woman who argued with you (Muhammad) about her husband, and complained to God (about her plight)," 58:1.

62. So, for instance, a report attributed to the Prophet explains that God's love is with every sad heart. See Tayeb Chourief, *Spiritual Teachings of the Prophet*, 186–87.

63. Muhammad Bakr Isma'il, *Wasaya al-Rasul wa Atharuha fi Taqwim al-Fard wa Islah al-Mujtama'* (Cairo: Dar al-Manar, 1999), 1:433–37.

64. On liberation theology in Islam, see Hamid Dabashi, *Islamic Liberation Theology: Resisting the Empire* (New York: Routledge, 2008); Farid Esack, *Qur'an, Liberation & Pluralism: An Islamic Perspective of Interreligious Solidarity against Oppression* (Oxford: One-World, 1997); Sherman Jackson, *Islam and the Problem of Black Suffering* (New York: Oxford University Press, 2009).

65. See Jose Medina, *The Epistemology of Resistance: Gender and Racial Oppression, Epistemic Injustice, and Resistant Imaginations* (Oxford: Oxford University Press, 2012); Miranda Fricker, *Epistemic Injustice: Power and the Ethics of Knowing* (Oxford: Oxford University Press, 2009).

66. Muhammad Iqbal, *The Reconstruction of Religious Thought in Islam* (London: Oxford University Press, 1934).

67. 'Abd al-Malik bin Hisham bin Ayyub al-Hamiri, *Al-Sira al-Nabawiyya* (Mecca: Maktaba al-Matbu'at al-Islamiyya, 1375/1955), 2:660.

68. See al-Suyuti, *Asbab al-Nuzul*, 2:51. Also, see Abu al-Hasan 'Ali ibn Muhammad al-Mawardi, *Al-Nukatu wa al-'Uyun: Tafsir al-Mawardi*, ed. al-Sayyid bin 'Abd al-Maqsud bin 'Abd al-Rahim (Beirut: Dar al-Kutub al-'Ilmiyya, n.d.), 1:476–78; al-Tabari, *Tafsir al-Tabari*, 8:260–69; al-Qurtubi, *Al-Jami' li-Ahkam al-Qur'an*, 6:267–73.

69. Qur'an 4:32.

70. See al-Suyuti, *Asbab al-Nuzul*, 2:51.

71. Qur'an 4:34.

72. Qur'an 2:256.

73. Qur'an 13:11; 8:53; 12:11.

74. Qur'an 16:125.

75. See Qur'an 4:97–98.

76. Qur'an 4:19. For the occasion of this revelation, see al-Suyuti, *Asbab al-Nuzul*, 2:49–50.

77. See al-Suyuti, *Asbab al-Nuzul*, 1:48.

78. Qur'an 2:229. Also see al-Suyuti, *Asbab al-Nuzul*, 1:32.

79. Qur'an 2:241. Also see al-Suyuti, *Asbab al-Nuzul*, 1:34; al-Mawardi, *Al-Nukatu wa al-'Uyun: Tafsir al-Mawardi*, 1:311; al-Tabari, *Tafsir al-Tabari*, 5:262–64; al-Qurtubi, *Al-Jami' li-Ahkam al-Qur'an*, 4:207–8.

80. Qur'an 2:231. Also see al-Suyuti, *Asbab*, 1:31–33; al-Mawardi, *Al-Nukatu wa al-'Uyun: Tafsir al-Mawardi*, 1:296–97; al-Qurtubi, *Jami' li-Ahkam al-Qur'an*, 4:99–102; al-Tabari, *Tafsir al-Tabari*, 5:8–16.

81. Qur'an 2:229. Also see al-Suyuti, *Asbab*, 1:31–33; al-Mawardi, *Al-Nukatu wa al-'Uyun: Tafsir al-Mawardi*, 1:293–95; al-Qurtubi, *Jami' li-Ahkam al-Qur'an*, 4:54–72; al-Tabari, *Tafsir al-Tabari*, 4:558–63.

82. Qur'an 2:231. Also, see ibid.

83. Qur'an 4:3.

84. Qur'an 4:129.

85. Qur'an 4:135.

86. Qur'an 33:72.

87. Qur'an 13:15; 22:18; 7:206.

88. Qur'an 2:30–34.

89. Qur'an 2:115, 142–43.

90. Qur'an 2:232.

91. See al-Suyuti, *Asbab al-Nuzul*, 1:33.

12. THE CALIPHATE OF HUMANITY

1. This and other narratives of the same genre often emphasize the ineffectiveness of piety or rituals if they fail to elevate a person's ethics and moral character. For examples of such

narratives, see Abu Hamid al-Ghazali, *Ihya' 'Ulum al-Din* (Cairo: Mustafa Babi al-Halabi, 1952), 3:51.

2. Qur'an 3:128–29. The report my friend referred to is mentioned in 'Abd al-Rahman bin Abi Bakr al-Suyuti, *Asbab al-Nuzul* (Cairo: Dar al-Tahrir lil-Tiba'a wa-al-Nashr, AH 1383), 1:42–43. Also see Qur'an 88:21–22.

3. This is quite similar to the division between the laws that follow from "duties owed to God" and "duties owed to people" and the implications of each. The division is common to Jewish law, Mosaic law, Noachian laws, and Islamic law. The same division is a consistent theme in the thought of the Jewish Greek philosopher Philo, Maimonides, and Thomas Aquinas, as well as numerous Muslim philosophers, including Ibn Rushd, Ibn Baja, and Ibn Aqil. See Harry Austryn Wolfson, *Philo: Foundations of Religious Philosophy in Judaism, Christianity, and Islam* (Cambridge: Harvard University Press, 1948), 2:187–200, 310–14.

4. Qur'an 88:21–22.

5. al-Suyuti, *Asbab al-Nuzul*, 1:34.

6. Qur'an 2:256; 10:99; 18:29.

7. See Ramsay MacMullen, *Christianizing the Roman Empire A.D. 100–400* (New Haven, CT: Yale University Press, 1984). On conversion to Christianity by coercion, see 86–101.

8. See Khaled Abou El Fadl, "Law of Duress in Islamic Law and Common Law: A Comparative Study," *Arab Law Quarterly* 6, no. 2 (1991): 121.

9. On condemnation of torture in Islamic law, see Fakhr al-Din 'Uthman bin 'Ali al-Zayla'i, *Tabyyin al-Haqa'iq: Sharh Kanz al-Daqa'iq* (Medina: Dar al-Kitab al-Islamiyya, n.d.), 3:240; Shaykh Nizam et al., eds., *Al-Fatawa al-Hindiyya* [a.k.a. *al-'Alamjiriyya*] (Beirut: Dar al-Ihya' al-Turath al-'Arabi, 1986), 6:430.

10. Qur'an 5:8.

11. Qur'an 5:2.

12. For instance, Qur'an 2:190; 5:87; 7:55.

13. Qur'an 2:192–93.

14. Qur'an 2:195.

15. Qur'an 41:34–36.

16. Qur'an 7:199.

17. Qur'an 16:125.

18. For instance, Qur'an 25:63; 28:55; 43:89.

19. Qur'an 6:108.

20. Qur'an 6:54; 43:89; 36:58.

21. Qur'an 5:2.

22. Qur'an 49:13.

23. Qur'an 11:118–19.

24. Qur'an 21:107.

25. Qur'an 2:105; 3:74; 35:2; 38:9; 39:38; 43:32.

26. Qur'an 22:67–68.

27. Qur'an 22:34.

28. Qur'an 5:49.

29. Qur'an 29:46.

30. Qur'an 5:69; 2:62.

31. Qur'an 2:285.

32. Qur'an 3:84.

33. Qur'an 42:13.

34. Khaled Abou El Fadl, *And God Knows the Soldiers: The Authoritative and Authoritarian in Islamic Discourses* (Lanham, MD: University Press of America, 2001), 57.

35. Qur'an 3:199. Also, see al-Suyuti, *Asbab al-Nuzul*, 1:48.

36. Qur'an 5:43–48.

37. Qur'an 5:69; 2:62.

38. Qur'an 2:30–31.

39. Qur'an 2:32–33.

40. Qur'an 7:12–13. Reportedly, Adam and Eve were created from the soil of the earth—the word *Adam* comes from *adim al-ard* (surface of the earth). See Franz Rosenthal, trans., *The History of Al-Tabari: General Introduction and from the Creation to the Flood* (New York: State University of New York Press, 1989), 259.

41. The Qur'an does make reference to Satan ending Adam and Eve's time in Eden (*Janna*). In Islamic theology, it is believed that Adam and Eve would inherit the earth but their so-to-speak honeymoon came to an end when they succumbed to the temptations of Satan and were ejected from the Garden of Eden. Importantly, Adam and Eve's sin was not generalizable to their progeny and descendants, and in all cases, God absolved Adam and Eve of their sin of disobedience before they left Eden. See Brannon M. Wheeler, *Introduction to the Qur'an: Stories of the Prophets* (New York: Continuum, 2001); Al-Imam ibn Kathir, *Stories of the Prophets* (Riyadh: Maktaba Dar us-Salam, 2003); Torsten Lofstedt, "The Creation and Fall of

Adam: A Comparison of the Qur'anic and Biblical Accounts," *Swedish Missiological Themes* 93, no. 4 (2005): 455.

42. Other sources like Ibn Kathir (d. 774/1373) claimed that God taught Adam and Eve how to plant seeds, farm, utilize fire, and other skills needed for survival. For both premodern and modern tafsirs on Qur'an 2:30–39, see Isma'il bin 'Umar Ibn Kathir, *Tafsir al-Qur'an al-'Azim* (Riyadh: Dar Tiba, 1997), 1:217–40; Abu al-Hasan 'Ali ibn Muhammad al-Mawardi, *Al-Nukatu wa al-'Uyun: Tafsir al-Mawardi*, ed. al-Sayyid bin 'Abd al-Maqsud bin 'Abd al-Rahim (Beirut: Dar al-Kutub al-'Ilmiyya, n.d.), 1:93–109; Abu 'Abd Allah Muhammad bin Abi Bakr al-Qurtubi, *Al-Jami' li-Ahkam al-Qur'an* (Beirut: al-Risala, 2006), 1:391–490; Fakhr al-Din Muhammad ibn 'Umar al-Razi, *Tafsir al-Fakhr al-Razi: al-Mushahhar bi-al-Tafsir al-Kabir wa Mafatih al-Ghayb* (Beirut: Dar al-Fikr, 1981), 2:174–258; Muhammad 'Abduh, "Tafsir al-Qur'an," in *Al-A'mal al-Kamila lil-Imam al-Shaykh Muhammad 'Abduh*, ed. Muhammad 'Imara (Cairo: Dar al-Shuruq, 1993), 4:125–49; Muhammad al-Tahir Ibn 'Ashur, *Tafsir al-Tahrir wa al-Tanwir* (Tunis: Dar al-Tunisiyya, 1984), 1:406–46.

43. According to the hadith tradition, Adam was reportedly created in God's image. For a discussion of the topic, see Christopher Melchert, "God Created Adam in His Image," *Journal of Qur'anic Studies* 13 (2011): 113–24, although I have serious reservations about the author's arguments.

44. See Abu Hamid al-Ghazali, *Ihya' 'Ulum al-Din*, 3:54.

45. Qur'an 33:72.

46. See the commentary on the reported narrative stating: "God is beautiful and loves beauty!" Tayeb Chourief, *Spiritual Teachings of the Prophet: Hadith with Commentaries by Saints and Sages of Islam*, ed. Fatima Jane Casewit, trans. Edin Q. Lohja (Louisville, KY: Fons Vitae, 2011), 188–89.

47. Qur'an 24:35.

48. Abu Hamid al-Ghazali, *Ihya' 'Ulum al-Din*, 3:54 argues that the perfection of ethics elevates one toward the example of the Prophet and toward godliness. The lack of ethics draws one closer to darkness and the demonic.

49. Qur'an 6:43.

50. At the time, I was thinking of Qur'an 59:19.

51. Qur'an 2:74.

52. Ibid.

CONCLUDING THE JOURNEY

1. Jack Goody, *Islam in Europe* (Cambridge: Polity, 2004), 13, 56–68.

2. Maria Rosa Menocal, *The Arabic Role in Medieval Literary History: A Forgotten Heritage* (Philadelphia: University of Pennsylvania Press, 2004), esp. ix–xii; Linda Paterson, *The World of the Troubadours* (Cambridge: Cambridge University Press, 1998), 180, 187–88.

3. On covering up the Western debt to Islam and transforming Muslims into the archetypal enemy, see Gil Anidjar, *The Jew, the Arab: A History of the Enemy* (Stanford, CA: Stanford University Press, 2003), 3–39.

4. Abu Muhammad Mahmud bin Ahmad al-'Ayini, *Al-Binaya fi Sharh al-Hidaya* (Beirut: Dar al-Fikr, 1990), 6:482; Imam Muhammad Ibn Khalifa al-Washtani al-Ubbi, "Ikmal Ikmal al-Mu'allim," in *Sahih Muslim*, ed. Imam Muslim Ibn al-Hajjaj al-Qushayri al-Nayshaburi (Beirut: Dar al-Kutub al-'Ilmiyya, 1994), 6:534.

5. Toshihiko Izutsu, *Ethico-Religious Concepts in the Qur'an* (Montreal and Kingston: McGill-Queen's University Press, 2002), 221–26.

6. Qur'an 28:77.

7. Qur'an 5:32.

8. Qur'an 2:195; 5:93.

9. Qur'an 7:56.

10. A number of inherited narratives in the Islamic tradition emphasize that God created human beings in beautiful physical form and that they are under an obligation to beautify their moral character; see Abu Hamid al-Ghazali, *Ihya' 'Ulum al-Din* (Cairo: Mustafa Babi al-Halabi, 1952), 3:49.

11. For example, see Qur'an 39:22; 6:43.

12. Qur'an 31:3.

Index

Manufactured by Amazon.ca
Bolton, ON

36364831R00321